THE PRACTICAL GUIDE TO FISHING

Georges Cortay
Pascal Durantel
Patrick Maître
Maurice Sainton

KÖNEMANN

Original title: ***Encyclopédie pratique de la pêche***
ISBN of the original edition: 2-7098-0652-5
ISBN of the German edition: 3-8331-1301-4

Design and production: ATP Chamalières – France
Concept: Hervé Chaumeton
Editing: Valérie Blanchout, Muriel Bresson, Stéphanie Castaing
Editorial assistance: Laurence Borot, Carole Ferrari, Claire Riol
Layout and typesetting: Vincent Allier, Stéphane Josse, Nathalie Mathonnat, Isabelle Véret
Illustrations: Christophe Courtier, Philip Loup, Vincent Moulinot
Graphic assistance: Myriam Bach, Serge Dupuy, Anne Guillemain, Jacques Theillard
Corrections: Valérie Sper

Acknowledgements:
Jean-Paul Goutte-Quillet, Alain Masseret,
Marc et Martin Arnoud

English translation and adaptation:
Chanterelle Translations (Josephine Bacon, Dermot Byrne, Christophe Géronimi, Kirstie Hart,
Jacques Redon, Christopher Scully)

Managing Editor: Bettina Kaufmann
Project Coordination: Nadja Bremse

Printed in Slovakia

ISBN 3-8331-1455-X

10 9 8 7 6 5 4 3 2 1
X IX VIII VII VI V IV III II I

FOREWORD

The growing popularity of angling is surely partly attributable to the development of "green" tourism and the opening up of the waterways, which has been a priority for several years. The sheer size of the phenomenon is best expressed in a few facts and figures: three million people pay for fishing rights in England and Wales alone every year and, because more and more anglers are moving away from public fishing areas toward private lakes and streams, the real number of anglers in the United Kingdom (difficult to estimate because a rod licence is not required in Scotland) is more likely to be six million. In the United States where fishing is even less regulated, the number of dedicated anglers is at least twelve million and to them must be added those who enjoy sport fishing only on vacation. That all adds up to an enormous potential market! Thanks to extensive media coverage, angling is no longer a simple pastime, it has become a whole way of life. "Saint Peter's disciples" therefore expect more and have created a whole new approach to fishing.

Angling is no longer a calm and simple pleasure, in which a lonely fisherman (or woman) sits by the gentle waters of a lake in the early hours of the morning. With modern technological advances in equipment, angling has become a science which makes use of state-of-the-art technology. When crossing dangerous canyons, angling takes on the true meaning of the word "sport." Above all, there is a whole new attitude and angling is now seen as a means of protecting and even restoring aquatic ecosystems and fish populations.

In this book, four well-known angling writers have attempted to meet the new requirements of the fishing enthusiast. Techniques and tackle are described in great detail, and the articles, which are richly illustrated with detailed diagrams, have taken the very latest advances into account. The authors also attempt to warn of the various dangers facing the aquatic ecosystems, and in particular those faced by salmon, king of the rivers but also a victim of the sometimes poor quality of the environment. That said, the authors haven't forgotten the admirable work of all of the other contributors who had only one aim when creating this book – to pass the sum total of their knowledge down to future generations.

Contents

JE FAIS DES TOUCHES
AVEC
Sensas
L'AMORCE DES AS!
TEIGNES DORÉES

TROUT AND CHAR

THE TACKLE

No single fishing technique is adequate for angling for trout and char (or charr). Their habitat is too diverse, their diet too eclectic, and their behavior too capricious. Brown trout lurk below the banks of a fast-flowing stream, rainbow trout leap at the base of rocky crevice in a mountain lake, or arctic trout swim 133 ft (40 m) down in the murky depths of the glacial waters of a mountain stream. Each encounter with a member of the salmonidae family is a special case, both in terms of the technique required to get it to bite and the way of making the most of the tackle used for each technique.

A classic small telescopic rod with guide rings for trotting or minnow fishing. ▷

Natural bait fishing in all its forms (trotting, float fishing, spinning, etc.) is the "all-rounder" technique from March through September – as long as it is adapted to conditions! ▽

FISHING A POSITION

Fishing a position is one of the most reliable techniques for picking out trout and char. It also happens to be one of the most popular methods of fishing for those new to the salmonidae in general. Furthermore, for both trout and char, at least 90 percent of natural bait consists of larvae, worms, or insects. But don't be fooled: despite its apparent simplicity, fishing a position using livebait or deadbait can require as much skill as the more "noble" techniques such as fly-fishing or ultra-light fishing.

TROTTING AND TROTTING TACKLE

This technique is best practiced early in the fishing season. It involves using a very simple line to present a bait wherever trout may be present: downstream of rocks which stick up out of the water, on the inside of narrow bends in the river or just below the banks. The worm or maggot should also be dragged or trotted along the bottom of gravel-covered beds and the sand at the edge of banks. Every spot should be investigated. A bite is recognizable by a series of little jerks on the line, which makes the rod-tip jump and shakes the arm. Trotting can be summarized as mastering the drift of the line and presentation of the bait, whatever the type and flow of water you're fishing, while knowing how to recognize the faintest bite when you feel it. Trotting is the

mother of all techniques for anglers, representing the epitome of the angler's art. It requires sensitivity and a great knowledge of your fish and the places they inhabit.

• Rods

Rods should be (20 to 27 ft (6 to 8 m)) long so you can keep your distance without scaring wary fish away. The rod should also be as light as possible (carbon fiber for preference) because of the sustained effort required to maneuver it correctly. The tip section should be extremely sensitive, so as to transfer a trout's slightest sniff at the hook without giving any resistance to the bait, which would make the fish drop it immediately. Rods with guide-rings mean you can use a reel or line-holder, but these models often have too stiff a tip. Rather, hold a length of line between your fingers so you can immediately give it some slack at the slightest touch or stop while the line is drifting.

• Rods with an internal line

Many rivers and streams are, to say the least, tricky to negotiate. The banks may be choked with thickets of bramble and dog-rose, and overhung with canopies of alder and hazel. With a large trotting-rod, you're bound to get all tangled up! By using a shorter rod, you'll have greater freedom of movement, but getting close to trout will be hard, if not impossible. The internal line rod can help solve all these problems. It is about 13 ft (4 m) long, with a line holder or semi-automatic fly reel that requires a short backing line, so you can explore the most inhospitable banks without worrying about snagging your line, since it is held inside the rod. Don't cut corners on quality, especially in terms of the number of internal guide-rings, of which there should be at least 30 for perfect line movement. Don't forget to take your "lancet" with you – you'll need it to pass the line through the rod!

• Line for pole-fishing

This is simplicity itself. You need 14-18/100 mainline, the length of which will vary depending upon the type of river being fished.

Shotting is a very important factor in making sure that the line moves perfectly, and depends on the depth and strength of the current. Use large grouped shot for deep water or strong currents, light and well-separated shot for shallows or slower water. In practice, between these two extremes, you need to vary the line for each attempt. "Soft" weights are perfect for ledgering because you can move them and

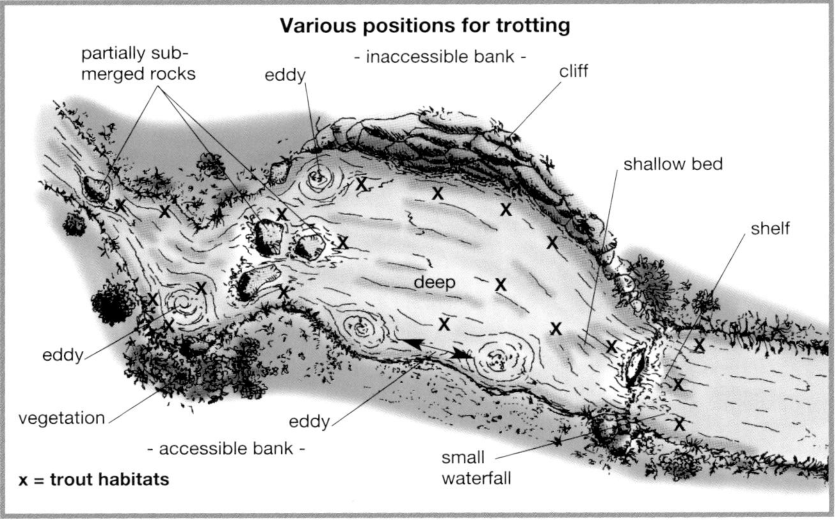

△ *The ledgering technique involves moving from downstream to upstream, along one bank after another, while ensuring that the angler's movements and catches do not disturb any other fish.*

△ *High-quality closed-face spinning reel reduces serious tangles and means you can instantly reel your line in.*

even remove them without damaging the line, depending on whether conditions require you to lighten, spread out, or regroup the shot. The hook length should be thin (14-10/100), even for slightly cloudy water, because, regardless of visual considerations, the most important thing is a totally natural presentation of the bait. Finally, don't forget your choice of hook is important. It should be strong, but made of thin iron, with a relatively short shank and, if possible, reversed. The hook size, which depends upon the size of the bait, should normally be a no. 8 through a no. 12.

FLOATING LINE FISHING AND EQUIPMENT

As soon as you start fishing in rivers that are more than 25 to 35 feet (8–10 m) wide, in

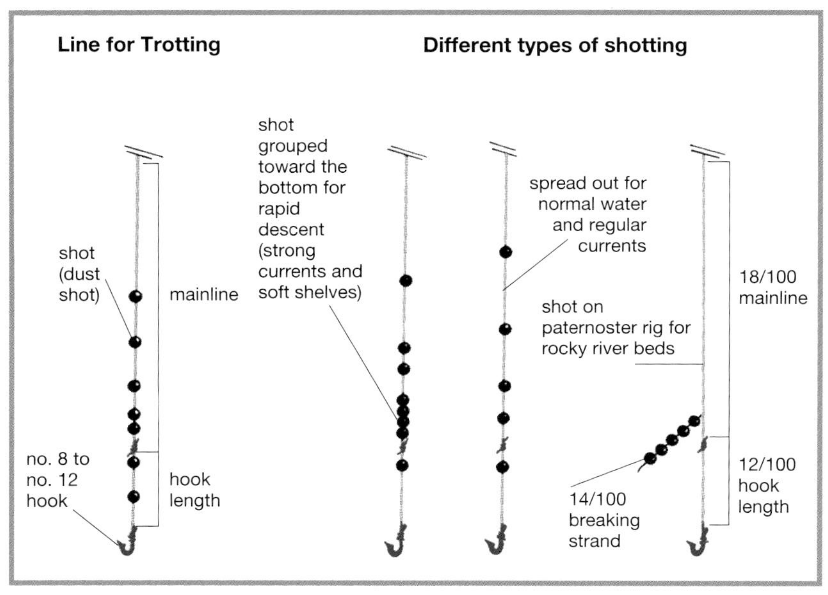

△13 ft (3.9 m) fixed-reel rod, light reel, line in the hand. Bait fishing is becoming a more skilled technique as trout become wiser!

lakes, or simply when the fish have become unapproachable because the water is too low and too clear, trotting becomes unsuitable. Float-fishing is far more suitable in these conditions, and gives a newcomer to bait-fishing more places to explore. The angling technique involves exploring the areas which traditional trotting cannot reach, which are usually the less intensively fished parts. Alongside wooded banks, let your line drift under branches which overhang the water. Move your line across all eddies which are more than 33 feet (10 m) from the bank or beneath steep embankments where fish are rarely disturbed. Later in the season, and especially in heavily-fished areas, trout will stay further and further out in mid-stream – and ledgering with a floating line will become an important method of fishing.

Two types of knot for a spade-end hook.

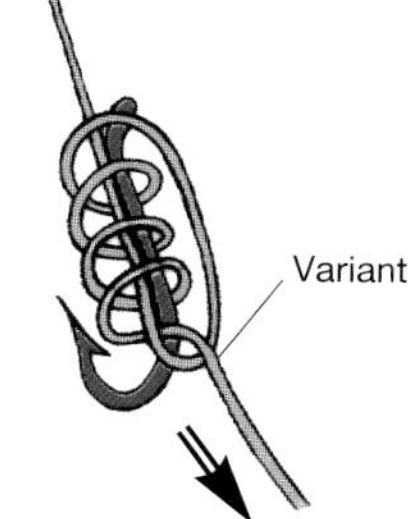

△ *Make a loop with the end part of the hook length, tied along the hook's shank. Make six to eight turns, trapping the hook and loop, then place the free end through the loop and pull tightly.*

USE LINES WHICH SINK QUICKLY

Quick-sinking lines used by English anglers are particularly useful for bait fishing. These special lines, which are available in diameters covering all our needs here, drop quite quickly underwater and save the need for a few shot. Moreover, to fish without any sinker in low water, they are great for accurately positioning hookbait in the smallest of streams.

AN INDICATOR ON THE LINE

Old-time anglers used to tie a piece of wool or burlap to their line so they could keep track of its position and control the speed and height of the bait. Copy your elders by using the same material for bobbins, the little polystyrene balls in fluorescent colors which are placed on the line like floats. A strand of fluorescent nylon, which can slide on the line, even if it is a little less visible, is even more useful because it offers no resistance to a bite.

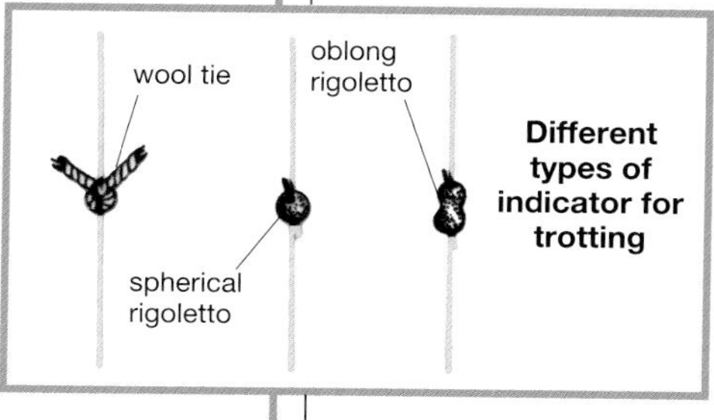

Different types of indicator for trotting

a line and indicator

• Rods

Rods with handles or telescopic rods should be at least 13–17 feet (4–5 m) long so you can to some extent submit the line to the action of the current and avoid the rig drifting too far with potentially disastrous consequences. Several guide-rings are a good idea, as they will help prevent the wet line from sticking to the rod.

• The reel

Attach a strong fixed-spool reel to your rod. The reel should function perfectly, i.e. the line should pay out evenly, and the clutch should be of the smooth-action, progressive type. The line should be an evenly wound 14/100 to 18/100 nylon line.

• The line

A floating line is very simple to set up. All you do is place a float on the mainline, then add a 12 through 16 inch (30 to 40 cm) hook length with a diameter of 10/100 to 14/100, and

Different spots for a Floating Line

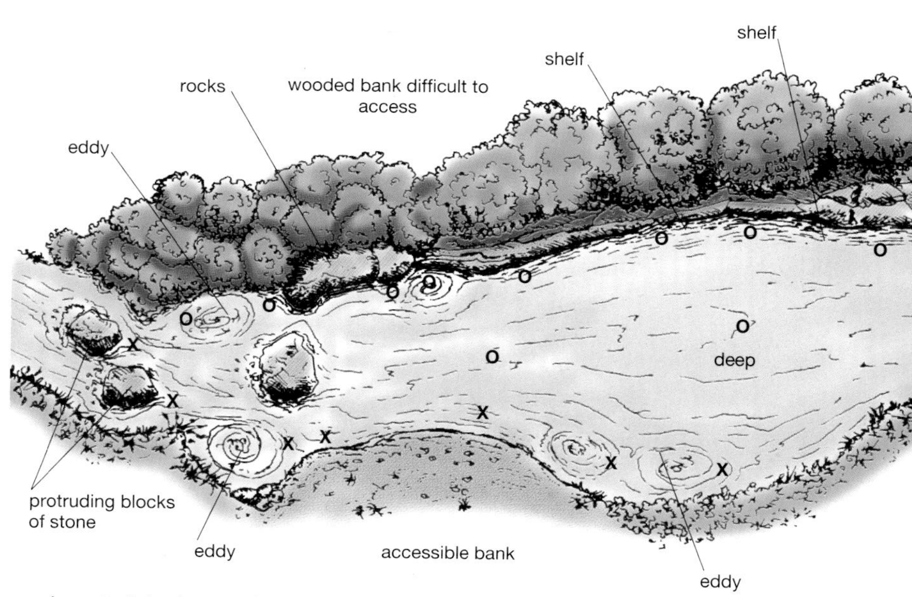

x = places to fish when trotting or float fishing
o = places which can only be fished with a float

△ *Fishing technique obviously supposes initial exploration of the opposite bank, progressing downstream-upstream if possible in small sections.*

finally a sinker. Choose the shape (spherical or conical) and size of your float to match the weight it has to bear and the force of the current and any eddies. It is essential to carry several different sizes of float with you so you can adapt your line to suit any situation.
Small round, cylindrical, or pear-shaped floats come in different sizes, so you can change them when the strength of the current or weight of the shot require it. To avoid fiddling endlessly with your line, think about slitting the floats sideways to the center with a craft-knife so you can change from one to the other in a matter of seconds. As for trotting, the use of soft shot is very useful for quickly changing the arrangement of the shot without damaging the line. In deep rivers, opt for a line with a sliding float, which will make casting easier while allowing you to accurately regulate the depth of fishing.

ROD AND REEL FISHING

Rod and reel fishing shows just how "sporting" angling can be. It is an itinerant and very active technique which is occasionally frowned upon by lure fishermen, but it is far from the mechanical and repetitive technique that they claim. It involves hitting the water without worry with the first available lure.
Some rod and reel specialists, or "swashbucklers" as they are sometimes known, work their rod like artists, casting a lure weighing a few grams 50 feet (15 m), just a few inches away from a lurking brown trout!

LURES FOR ROD AND REEL FISHING

Lure manufacturers have hundreds of models on the market, each one supposedly more efficient than the other, and choosing the right one might seem like something of a lottery. To simplify the choice, you should approach lures by "family". Do not choose a lure for its esthetic appeal or decoration. It is the fish, not you, which needs to be

Stop-knot for sliding float

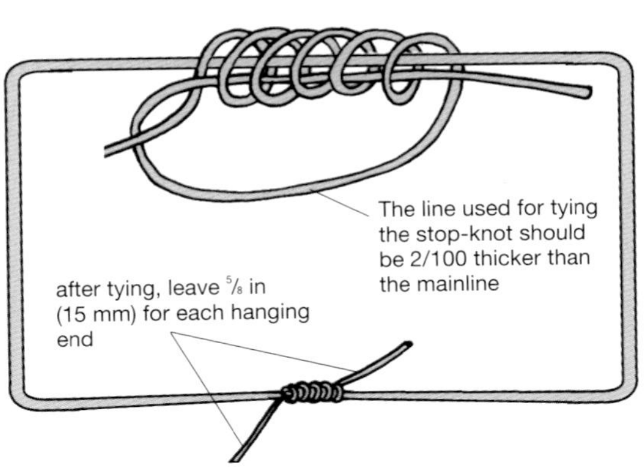

The Fixed Floating Line

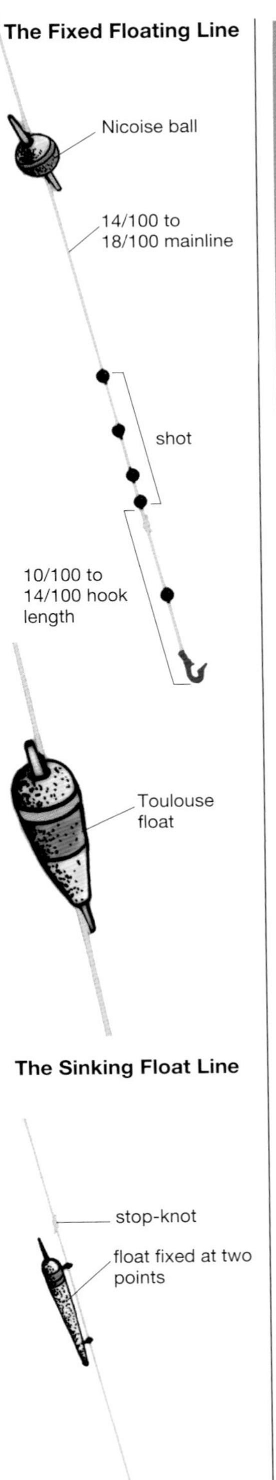

The Sinking Float Line

Adapting Your Float

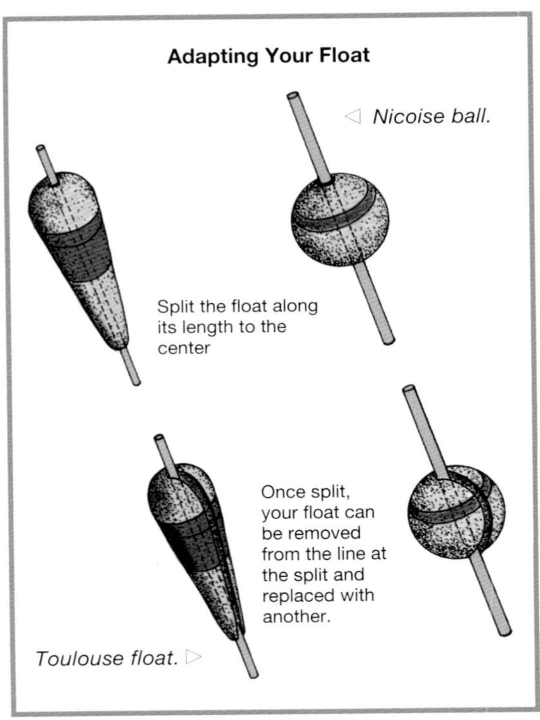

NEVER BE WITHOUT A BUBBLE-FLOAT

Often used as an ordinary float, although that is not putting it to its best use, the bubble-float consists of a little hollow plastic ball weighted with an amount of water. How can you present a live insect 65 through 100 ft (20 through 30 m) from the bank without a bubble-float? Without this clever device, how else could you send a rig through clear, shallow water, when very wary fish don't let you get within 50 or 100 feet (15 or 20 m) of them? Bubble-floats are so light and small, you can slip a few of them into one of your pockets and this will often get you out of a tricky situation. On a river, cast the bubble-float upstream of the fish so as to avoid a noisy splash as it hits the water, which would scare the fish away. On lakes, where the fish are constantly moving, anticipate their movements by casting in front of them.

16/100 to 18/100 mainline

Bubble-float with insect

16/100 to 18/100 mainline

Bubble-float with lure

◁ *A small Irish brown trout caught with an ultra-light rig.*

attracted! Concentrate instead on its weight and size and the type of signal it gives off underwater. The size and weight of the lure (which are often interdependent) are a factor of the type of water being fished, its depth, and the strength of the current. It would be as useless to attack a mountain river with an ultralight (2g) spoon as to use a lure four times that weight in a narrow, little trout brook!

• Trout spinners

The good old spinner, the most reliable and brilliant of all lures, is still in use after decades of good and loyal service. The spinner consists basically of a more-or-less oval blade which turns freely on a usually shotted axis terminating in a treble hook, or sometimes in a single hook so as not to mutilate young trout. The spinner, which looks like no living creature on earth (it would be

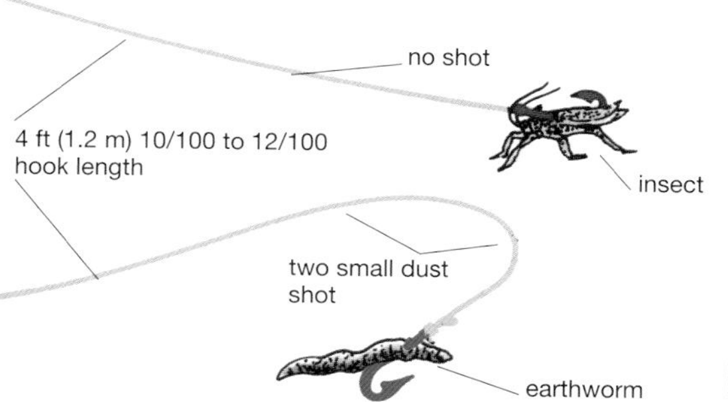

Coarse fishing rig for wide river

stop-knot

float with one attachment

14/100 to 16/100 mainline

shot

approx 12 in (30 cm) 10/100 to 12/100 hook length

HOORAY FOR SPINNING!

In the same way as float-fishing is better than trotting as soon as you work in larger rivers, spinning brilliantly replaces the simple floating-line rig in very particular circumstances, for example, when fishing in a very deep and calm pool, fishing a very long swim 65 through 100 feet (20 through 30 m) from the bank on a large river, and especially on lakes. A flexible 13 through 14 foot (3.9 through 4.2 m) carbon fiber rod with a 14/100 to 16/100 line on a reel is perfect. For spinning, use wagglers, tapered floats that are slightly bulbous at the base with a single attachment. You should use short hooklengths (around 12 inches (30 cm)) with 10/100 to 12/100 line to avoid the line getting snagged or tangled when casting. This technique gives you high-quality presentation at a distance of several dozen feet and extreme sensitivity for recognizing a bite.

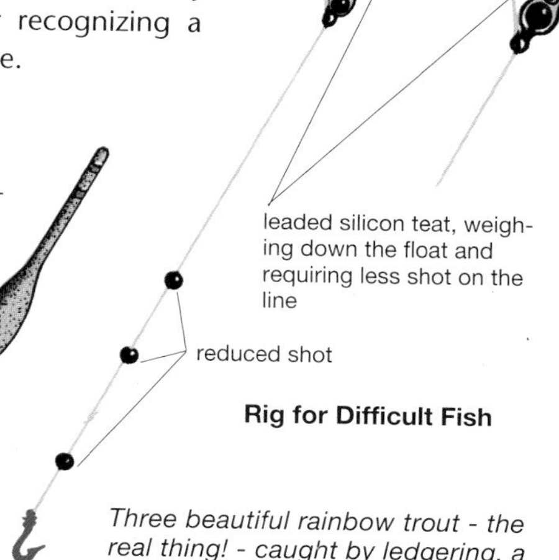

Three beautiful rainbow trout - the real thing! - caught by ledgering, a great technique in certain circumstances. ▽

astonishing if the eagle-eyed trout mistook a spinner for a small fish!), attracts fish by vibrating in the water while its shiny metal flashes underwater. The spinner is more of an intruder than a prey for the trout, an uninvited guest which is there to irritate and disturbs the trout, often forcing it to lunge in anger and bite the irritant ...

The first thing to look for in a good spinner is the way the blade rotates on its axis. Avoid any spinner which does not rotate at the slightest touch. How else can you efficiently explore awkward spots where the spinner only has a few inches of water in which to seduce a fish when the lure is hardly inclined to leave its hiding place?

In the same way, do not use spinners which stop rotating if the line moves too slowly. You need the spinner to turn constantly so you can fish the very bottom of hollows and pools in rivers and deep lakes. Choose the size and particularly the weight of lure to match the size of the swim being fished. A 2–8 g range should cover most situations.

For very deep waters, you may need to add additional shot to the head of the spinner so it can reach the bottom. Spinners come in all sorts of colors and designs, and it is totally up to you which ones you choose. Just go for the spinners that work for you.

In practice, there is very little difference between a dark, silvery, or gold-colored model and one covered with splashes of color, painted with an enormous eye, or wearing an alluring skirt to conceal the hook.

Trout and char do not have much time to attack a lure, especially if they live in running water. It is the vibrating signal, together with great precision on the part of the angler, which makes the fish respond, rather than an excess of artistic decorations!

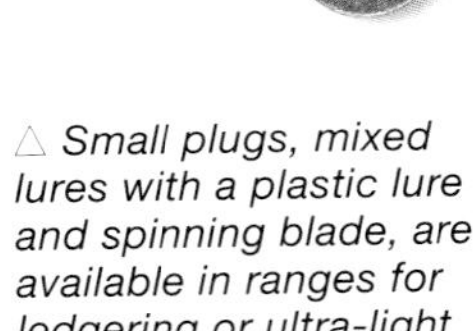

△ *Small plugs, mixed lures with a plastic lure and spinning blade, are available in ranges for ledgering or ultra-light rod-and-reel fishing.*

• Spoons

Rarely used by trout and char fishermen (and they're wrong!), spoons are generally to be found in a bankside angler's tackle box. Available in sizes from 1¹/₄ to 2³/₄ in (3 to 7 cm), with weights of 4–12 g, spoons which are curved enough to work well on the water are extremely efficient.

To make the most of the spoon's intrinsic qualities, use small jerking movements, pulling in with small stops and starts, thus creating a random gliding motion.

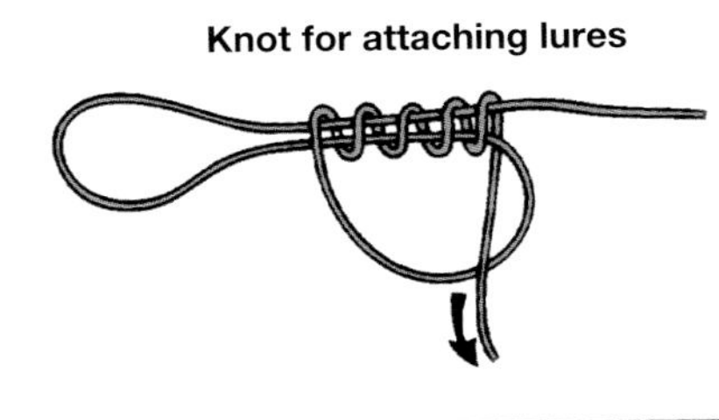

On a lake, fluorescent spoons in bright yellow and orange can prove deadly to trout and char in depths of 27 through 40 feet (8–12 m).

• Plugs

Plugs are cleverly shaped and colored to resemble small fish, insects, and even harvest mice. They are effective because of the vibrations they give off under water. For years, a famous Finnish manufacturer has made beautifully finished plugs which are real gems and at the same time are renowned for triggering hugely aggressive reactions in fish. They are around 1¹/₄ through 2³/₄ inches (3 through 7 cm) in size painted in gold, silver, and other colors to resemble minnow, small trout, and other livebait, all of which are very effective. Plugs drop through the water and start working more slowly than a spinner. They are generally intended for medium and large rivers and lakes, where they work best. Small floating plugs, which you let drift downstream – especially into foliage where it is impossible to cast – and which you can then pull up the bank current, will ensure you catch more than one trout! Occasionally, the vibrations of a plug so stimulate the urge to hunt that a trout will bite savagely at a plug or lure when it has just ignored a perfectly good piece of livebait right under its nose!

• Flexible Lures

These are generally used for coarse fishing for other carnivorous fish, but some flexible lures can be used for char and trout angling. These fish imitations, which are ingeniously articulated with a succession of body parts and available in many different colors and sizes, are suitable for tracking most types of salmonid, and have proved even more alluring than tadpoles and other types of flagellate. The weights of shotted heads or rigs for these lures are adapted for all fishing situations.

Knot for attaching a spinner

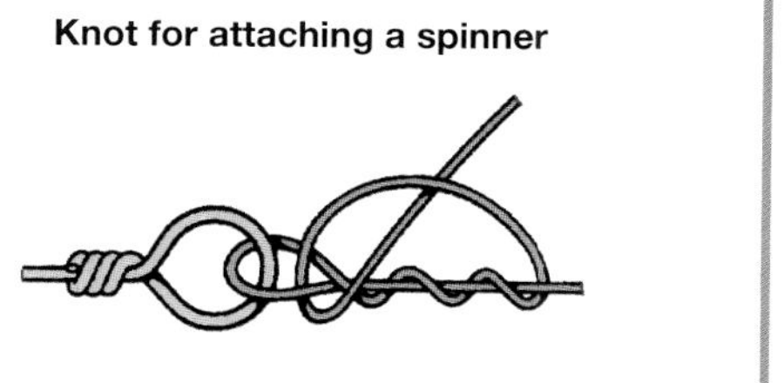

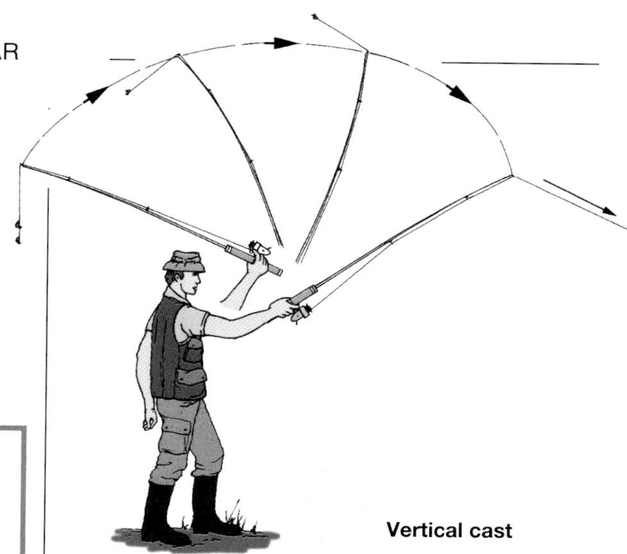

Vertical cast

THE DEVON

Born out of an angling tradition in fast-flowing rivers, the devon – which is rarely used nowadays – is a top-quality lure. This method is often criticized for twisting lines until they become unusable. This can be compensated for if you take the precaution of fixing a swivel between the line and the lure and if you use a mixture of devons that turn left and turn right, between which you can switch during a fishing session. Unfortunately, devons are quite difficult to get hold of in the stores and by mail order, so for home handymen, here is the advice of a fishing guide for salmon and trout from Ireland. Get hold of some brass tractor tyre valves and cut them into 1¼–2½ inch (3–6 cm) sections, depending upon your requirements. Grind down the ends to make an oval shape, then make two cuts with a saw at the top, each at a 45° angle forming an x-shape (so that the device will rotate on the line). Cut two paddles of exactly the same size out of copper or brass, and solder them onto the two saw cuts. Slip some piano wire through the devon to link your treble hook at one end to the swivel at the other, and in this way the line will not become tangled or twisted.

Tractor tyre air valve.

Grind the ends to obtain this sort of shape.

Make two cuts with a saw, in opposite directions, about 1 cm from the front end of the devon.

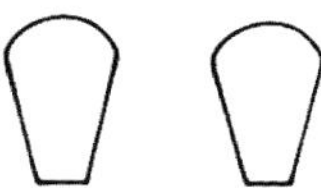

Cut two paddles from a sheet of copper.

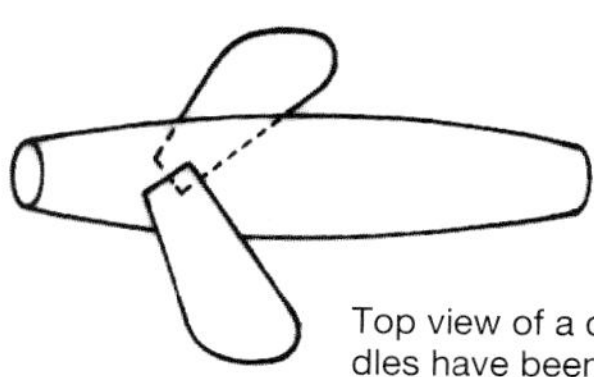

Top view of a devon, once the paddles have been soldered into place.

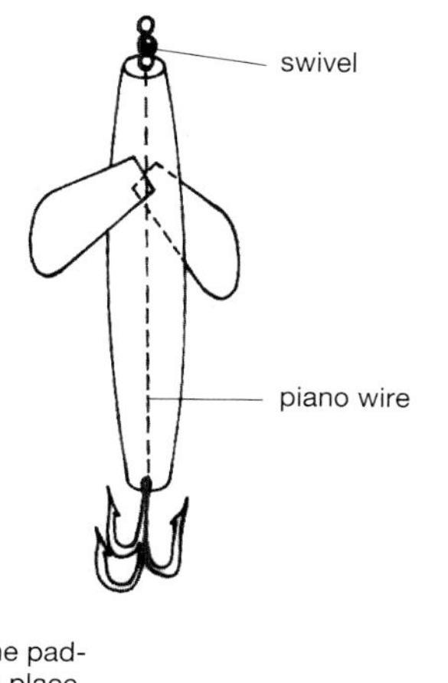

LIGHTWEIGHT ROD-AND-REEL TACKLE

Lightweight rod-and-reel fishing, which requires you to have an excellent knowledge of your river, is a combination of approach, observation, precision, and physical exertion. You have to "read" the swim so as to discover each potential habitat. Cast your lure just below banks where the current allows the fish to rest quietly, against all obstacles breaking the strength of the current (rocks, submerged roots, tree-trunks carried downstream by rivers in spate, etc.). Have a shot at underarm casting, at the water level, so you can slide your lure under overhanging branches. Don't neglect areas away from the regular current or flow, especially water 5 to 10 feet (1.5 to 3 m) deep where the bottom consists of sand or gravel, and concentrate all your efforts on trying to play your lure effectively, training it near to the bottom, exploring every foot of the river.

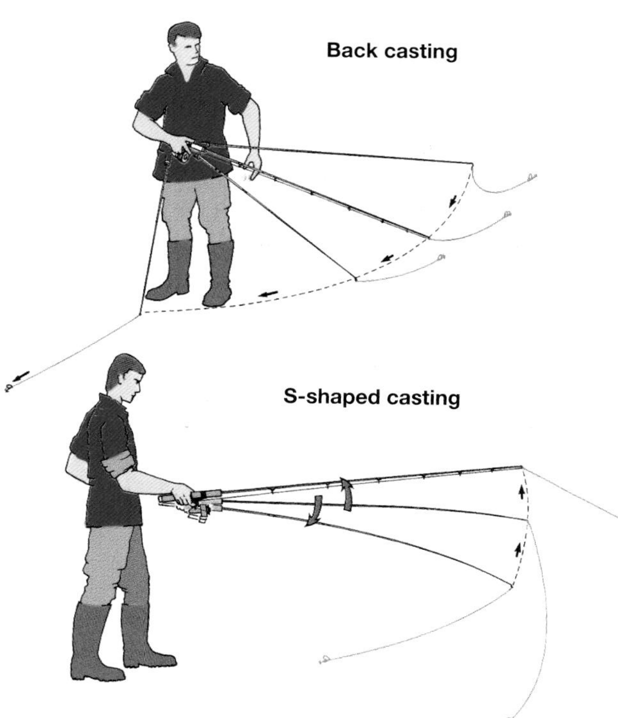

Back casting

S-shaped casting

• Rods

Rod manufacturers offer a whole range of rods designed for lightweight rod-and-reel fishing and ledgering. However, by no means all of them are good enough for the job. In practice, a good casting rod should be 6 to 8 feet (1.8 to 2.5 m) in length, depending on where you intend to fish. It's a difficult choice, because although a shorter rod gives you more freedom of movement to fish more difficult spots, it won't have the "muscle" to deal with the really big fish, especially when they're being helped along by a strong current. The opposite problem pertains to a large rod. Wherever possible, then, use a rod of around 7–8 feet (2.2–2.5 m) which will give you more precise casting, easier lure presentation and better maneuvering of a sturdy trout. For good rod technique, choose a moderately flexible tip section for precise casting, which is still strong enough to control a catch when it happens. Alloys and carbon are perfect for this twofold requirement. The rod has to be strong enough to cast 2–10 g lures correctly.

• The reel

A "lightweight" fixed-spool reel should usually meet the two main requirements. It should be in excellent working order and be of the right weight. Every time you fish, the bale-arm, which is opened and closed hundreds of times, is put under enormous strain. The slightest fault in this device will reduce efficiency and ruin your sport. It is also very important to go for a reel heavy enough to perfectly balance the rod you are using; that way, you will optimize precision and reduce effort. Finally, don't forget to load the spool correctly. Incorrect winding of the line on the spool is a common error, since beginner anglers fail to appreciate the importance of correct winding, and how crucial it is for when the line is played out to its full extent. The last few turns of the line on the reel should sit to the site of the spool so the line can be played out without any problem.

• Check the knot regularly

We have all had it happen to us. Just because the fish are biting regularly, you forget to check the knot and you lose your tackle. With every snag, strike, or catch, remember that the knot strands get weaker, rapidly reducing the initial strength of the line by as much as 50 percent. Re-tie your lure knot from time to time – you'll be glad you did!

This brown trout has just been caught under a waterfall, using lightweight rod-and-reel and ultra-light technique. ▷

How to load a reel correctly

Line away from the edge of the spool. ▽

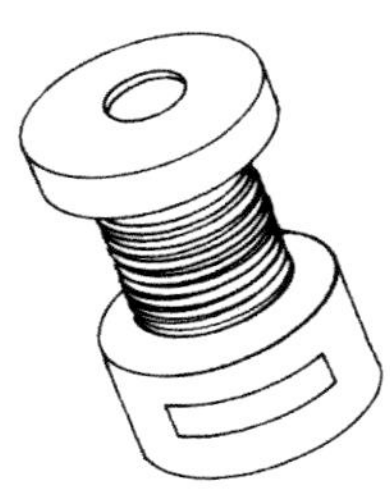

Wrong way
The spool isn't full enough and the line feeds out incorrectly: loss of distance and precision.

Line goes over the edge of the spool. ▽

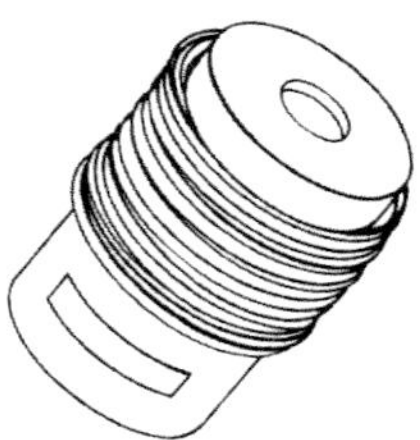

Wrong way
The spool is too full and prone to tangling.

Line flush with the edge of the spool. ▽

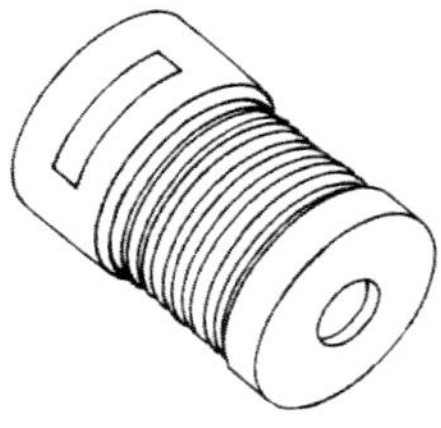

Right way
The line just touches the edge of the spool, giving the best casts without tangling the line.

Never choose a flimsy reel – robustness, good line feeding and clutch precision are essential. ▷

Ultra-light Rod-and-reel and Equipment

Ultra-light rod-and-reel fishing is a technique used by trout "hunters". In principle, it's very similar to light rod-and-reel, but uses much more sensitive equipment, a very thin line and extremely small lures, weighing no more than 2 g. This technique is best employed in tumbling streams and brooks of fast-flowing water where casting with standard equipment may be very difficult or even impossible. Ultra-light angling is a wonderful technique for exploring very delicate habitats or enticing highly "educated" fish on most rivers, even larger ones.

Tangling, Swivel, and Untangling

A revolving lure like a spoon or spinner is very susceptible to tangling your line, often causing huge tangles when casting which are impossible to unravel. A swivel, a metal clip fastener which revolves, should help solve this problem, but the line will still tangle a little. To untangle it, stand at the head of a long pool, open your bale-arm and let the whole line out until it is taut, then reel in again. If you have an extra spool for your reel, wind your used line around it. It will be rewound the other way, in perfect condition. Finally, change your line regularly so you can get the best out of it.

Casting under branches and in the middle of densely wooded water or imitating grasshoppers in tiny streams will give surprising results.

• Rods

Given the small size of the swim, the amount of trees and branches surrounding fishing positions and the tiny lures, ultra-light rods are usually quite short, not more than 4–5 feet (1.2–1.7 m) long. Of course, if you are able to use a longer rod, you will have greater precision, better lure presentation, and a more comfortable battle when large fish happen to bite. As the rod is so short, strong materials such as carbon or kevlar are the best.

• Reels

An open-face spinning reel which is small and fairly light but which works like clockwork is essential for balancing this kind of tackle which has been stripped down to the bare essentials. Use a 12/100 or 14/100 line, going up to 16/100 if you really need to tame the fish, or alternatively use 10/100 if you are trying to deceive wary fish. You will also need to have impeccable line technique in order to play with an intrepid brown trout on such a thin line! Given the small amount of line required for ultra-light fishing (where you are often casting no further than 27 through 33 feet (8 or 10 m)), use a 20/100 backing line followed by around 133 feet (40 m) of thinner line.

△ Two rods designed specifically for ultra-light lure angling.

• Lures

Any lure is suitable for light rod-and-reel fishing, as long as you use the smallest models which are best for this technique. Spinners which imitate flies and grasshoppers, and plugs or streamers with flowing strands of shiny plastic or sparkling tinsel, which imitate young fish will also work well. As ultra-light fishing is designed mainly to catch trout or char, both of which have limited hunting areas, make the most of the element of surprise and the short space of time which the fish have for analyzing the intruders which you are flashing before their eyes. Let your imagination run wild!

The Jonte, in France, is a river with extremely clear waters, and is ideal for ultra-light fishing, as long as the angler is careful. ▽

Minnow deadbait and tackle

Deadbaits have gained in popularity in recent years, even in countries where live bait coarse and game fishing are permitted. The protests of animal rights enthusiasts have had some effect, and the element of cruelty of passing a hook through a living creature is eliminated. There is also the fact that a dead bait is much more convenient to store than a live one, especially now that refrigeration is always an option. There are even parts of Europe where using live fish as bait is illegal, so check the rules before fishing in unfamiliar territory. The problem is always of how to present deadbait to a potential catch in a realistic manner.

Fishing with minnow deadbait is a technique which combines bait-fishing and lightweight rod-and-reel fishing and as such is a force to be reckoned with. The angler offers a natural bait to the fish while employing line techniques which are fairly similar to those used for lure-fishing. The idea is to present a small fish, leaded at the head and armed with one or two hooks, in the sort of habitats it might naturally frequent. In practice, by pulling in your deadbait with irregular jerks, known as "wobbling", you are giving the trout the chance to bite what looks like a wounded fry. Remember that, like most predators, trout nearly always take the easy option. When given the choice between a wounded fish and one that is in perfect health, the trout will always attack the wounded one.

All deadbait should be kept deep-frozen until required. They should be individually wrapped in freezer-safe plastic wrap. This prevents the bait sticking together and tearing or distorting when removed from the freezer. Only defrost as many fish as you will need for a day's angling.

◁ Maneuvered deadbait, very effective for trout fishing, uses adapted rigs. The simplest are often the best.

A small and lightweight but very robust and reliable reel: ideal for fishing trout with rod and reel! ▷

△ Anglers fishing on high plateaux frequently use a coarse rod and line which is stiff enough for minnow fishing. This is simple but very effective rod fishing. The rig includes a simple 4 ft (1 m) strand of nylon and the tackle for it.

Deadbait minnow fishing is a trolling technique that is ill-suited to toting bulky equipment around. Leave your bait-box, with an aerator, in your vehicle or, better still, use a basket-type bait-container which you can submerge by a bank. Take care to hide it from the prying eyes of a dishonest fellow-angler! Fix a vacuum flask with a large stopper to your belt and fill it with around 20 minnows. Your constant movement will oxygenate the water in the flask and keep the bait in perfect condition.

Deadbait rods

Use a fairly rigid rod for deadbait minnow fishing – carbon or composite fiber rods are best – so you can manipulate the dead fish precisely and strike immediately there is a bite. A light rod will allow you to move it around without tiring your arms too much, especially during long sessions. Rods of 8 to 9 feet (2.4 to 2.8 m) in length are generally versatile enough, but some require a few modifications. Where there are thickets of waterside vegetation, use a fairly stiff, short rod. On small rivers and streams with little or no surrounding vegetation, a 13 through 15 foot (4 to 4.5 m) rod will allow you to trot the minnow in one place without having to get too near to possible habitats.

• Deadbait rigs

Even though fishing with deadbait is a trolling technique which requires the minimum of tackle, rigs such as drifting and deadbait snap-tackle rigs can be used. A deadbait rig is mounted by piercing both lips of the minnow with one hook of an end treble. This is attached to a length of line terminating in another treble and another length of line, finishing with a swivel for attaching it to the reel line. Winding this rig around a large, light, bobbin will make it easy to carry.

• Reels

A light casting reel with a 20–24/100 nylon line is perfect for deadbait fishing with minnows.

FLY-FISHING

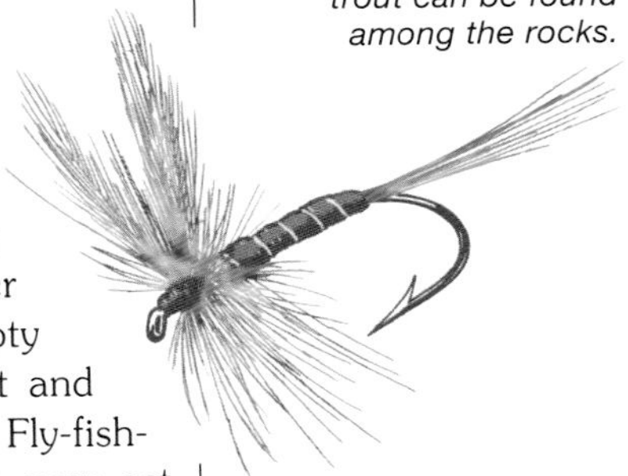

Fly-fishing is an exciting sporting technique which is luckily no longer viewed as a demonstration of empty gestures using overpriced equipment and the prerogative of a privileged elite. Fly-fishing nowadays is based on a whole new set of values which associate this particular technique with an increased understanding of the watery ecosystems and the problems faced by members of the salmonidae family.

△ *Fly fishing on the Sioule, a French river where beautiful trout can be found among the rocks.*

△ *Although it is a constant bone of contention, the choice of artificial fly should not monopolize all the angler's attention.*

◁ *You do not need much tackle for fly-fishing, since freedom of movement is all-important.*

Modern rods made of high-performance materials such as carbon, boron, or kevlar come in sizes of 6 to 10 foot and cover all possible situations. ▷

The snobbery surrounding fly-fishing has all but disappeared (and anyway, country fishermen have been practicing it for several hundred years!) and it has become a wonderful way of observing the water and an ecologically sound combination of fishing and communing with nature.

DRY-FLY-FISHING AND TACKLE

This technique is designed for trout and char feeding at the surface and is used in areas where insects hatch on the water. On stretches of slow current in perfectly clear waters, it is difficult to lure a trout because it can easily see and watch the artificial fly before biting. However, dry-fly-fishing in fast-flowing water is a wonderful technique, based on elements of surprise, rhythm, and approach rather than perfect presentation of the bait.

• Fly-fishing rods

Light modern fly rods are made of composite materials such as carbon, boron, or kevlar and are marvels of precision. They are also very lightweight and are not particularly expensive,

except for a few famous brands. Depending on the angler's physique and temperament, the technique used and the fishing conditions, there is a choice between a whole range of different types. The standard length for a fly fishing rod is 8½ feet. On a river lined with trees, a 6 through 7 foot rod makes fishing a lot easier. But on large and easily-accessible rivers, you will be able to cast much further with a 10-footer. On smaller rivers with fast-flowing currents, a long rod, even for shorter casts, is very useful and prevents the line being dragged too far away downstream.

• Fly-fishing reels

To cover all situations, use a manual reel which perfectly balances the weight of the rod and contains around 100 feet (30 m) of silk and

△ *The manual reel, simple and never out of order, is ideal for lightweight tackle, giving the best possible balance with your rod.*

about the same length of reserve line (backing). With an automatic reel, you can reel in your silk more quickly, but these are generally quite heavy and not always reliable. A semi-automatic is a good compromise since it is lighter and has an ergonomic quick-reel handle, but these reels can be quite expensive.

• Fly-fishing lines

Use a double-thread floating synthetic silk line for casting the negligible weight of the line tip and fly. Choose your silk depending on the strength of your rod and the type of fish you are after (ranging between no. 2 and no. 5).

– Line Tip

Your line tip should be at least as long as your rod, with line of a decreasing diameter from the

△ *The manual reel is simple and never breaks down so it is ideal for lightweight tackle, giving the best balance with the rod.*

Tying the line to the backing line

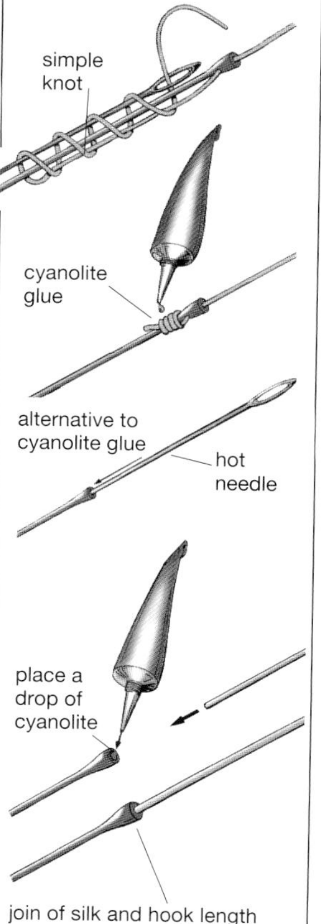

join with the silk to the fly attachment. It can be made industrially in a single tapered line or made by attaching lengths of nylon line in different sections. The tip of the "rat's tail" can be anything from 6/100 to 14/100, depending on the size of the fly, the sort of terrain, the behavior of the fish – and the angler's skill.

– Backing, or reserve line

A 100 feet (30 m) length of silk used should in principle be more than enough for bringing in a trout or char. However, you should be prepared for the possibility of a big fish escaping down a long swim and taking all of your line with it. Take the precaution therefore of loading 100–170 feet (30 –50 m) of nylon or Dacron, then attaching your silk, and this will protect you from any such disasters. Furthermore, the reserve line will pad out the reel and means that you can reel in your silk faster with larger turns and thus prevent the line from jamming.

• Dry flies

A fly-fisherman's choice of fly has always been subject to endless and passionate disputes between two schools of thought – those who extol specificity in fly-fishing on the one hand

Setting up a Drop for Fly-Fishing

The drop consists of five lengths of nylon of smaller diameters from the tip section down ▽

1.7 ft (0.5 m) in 30/100
2.3 ft (0.7 m) in 40/100
1.7 ft (0.5 m) in 26/100
2 ft (0.6 m) in 14/100
tip
1.7 ft (0.5 m) in 20/100

and those who prefer the "one-size-fits-all" type of fly. In actual fact, you should choose your fly somewhere between these two extremes, between the scientific approach involving differentiating between males and females of the species and a radical simplification of the problem by using a "fantasy fly". However, without getting too wrapped up in the details, you do need to have some understanding of the main insect families and the major preferences of the fish you are after. It is not the exact imitation of a real insect that is important. A fly also needs to be the right size and shape, it needs to be the sort of insect the fish would be likely to find alive at that particular time of year (don't try a mayfly when it is time for crane flies (daddy longlegs), and it needs to float well and be correctly presented.

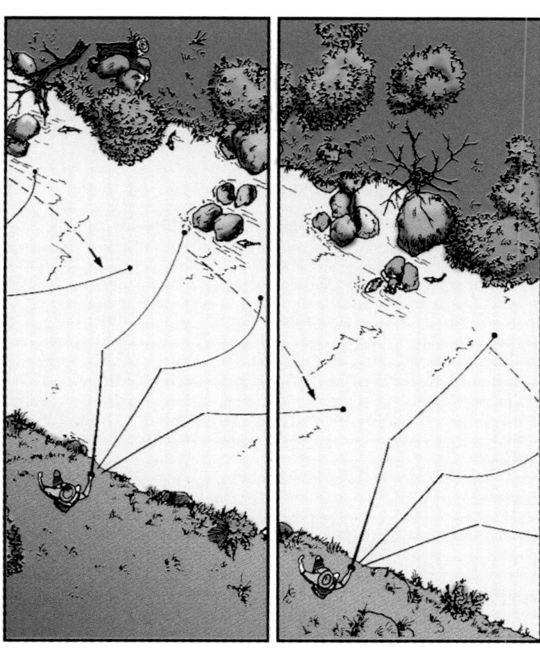

Wet fly arc drift

Types of silk

The first letters show the type of silk: DT = Double Thread, WF = Weight Forward, L = Level.
Silks are numbered from 1 to 12 to indicate weight and diameter. The choice should depend on the type of rod used. The letters after the number indicate the type of silk: F = Floating, S = Sinking, F/S = Sinking Tip and I = Intermediate.
For example, a DT 5 F is a double-threaded no. 5 floating silk.

A handsome bunch of arctic char fished on the Noatak in Alaska.

Wet-Fly-Fishing and tackle

For every fish that feeds on the surface, there are at least ten which feed below it. However, wet-fly-fishing is not as popular with most fly fishermen, despite its great effectiveness as a technique. Some argue, rightly or wrongly, that wet fly-fishing is a far less elegant and beautiful sport than dry-fly-fishing. Wet-fly-fishing is normally practiced downstream. The fly is required to drift in arcs or circles in search of all potential habitats. The main difficulty lies in identifying possible bites, which must be responded to immediately. Line control therefore should be fairly firm, neither slack nor taut. Because the fish are so quick to reject an artificial fly, an honest angler will admit to probably recognizing only one bite out of every two.

The fundamental difference between wet and dry flies is the different methods of tying, and the material. Wet flies are made of softer, absorbent materials to enable them to sink quickly, and some are even weighted to speed up the sinking process. The wet fly may represent not only flies, but other prey such as water-spiders, crawfish, snails, bugs, and even fish fry.

• The wet-fly rod

Use an 8½ to 10 foot rod with quivertip action which can withstand violent strikes without slowing them down by being too flexible.

• The wet-fly reel

As long as the clutch system is accurate enough, a manual or a semi-automatic reel are both fine.

◁ *The more game fishing you do, the more indispensable you will find the landing net. This racket-type which uses elasticated loose netting is the best compromise.*

• The wet-fly line

Use a floating line to fish the top few inches near the surface, or a sinking-tip line for fishing at deeper levels. Use a no. 4 to no. 6 silk depending on the strength of your rod. The line tip, which should be the same length as the rod, should have a point with a diameter of more than 12/100 or 14/100 to withstand the strike and to be able to handle a fish which will nearly always be aided by the current; remember that you are fishing downstream.

The wicker fishing basket, an inseparable partner for the trout angler. ▽

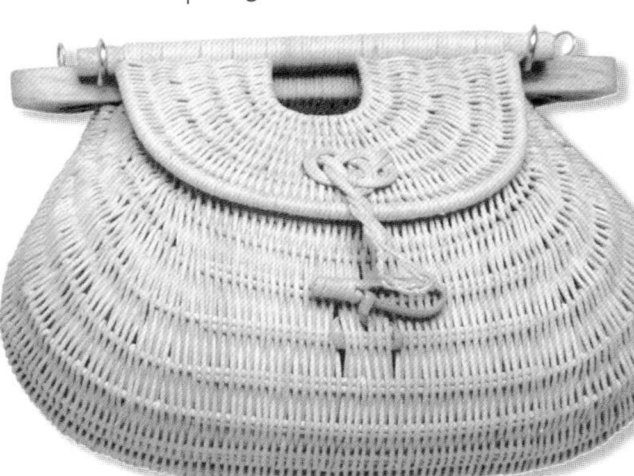

• Wet Flies

Wet flies are far less elaborate than their dry equivalents and are usually adorned with hackles, fibers which give them a good hold in the water and help them to sink. It is sensible to fish using two different flies on the line, thus offering two options at the same time. The best fly will be attached to the end of the line, while the "jumping" fly will be paternostered higher up the line, so you can fly fish on the surface and to some depth underwater at one and the same time.

The Return of Materials from a Bygone Age

Some esthetes and fly-fishing purists swear by natural materials, handcrafted by skilled artisans. Although not as light as carbon, split bamboo rods can be quivertip or semi-quivertip and have an incredibly sensitivity and a finish which is close to perfection. Natural silks give an extremely delicate cast and are excellent for wet fly-fishing, as long as you grease the last few feet of the line. They are gaining in popularity but remain expensive objects of desire.

Leaded nymphs

Wrap the hook in leaden wire before making the nymph itself. ▽

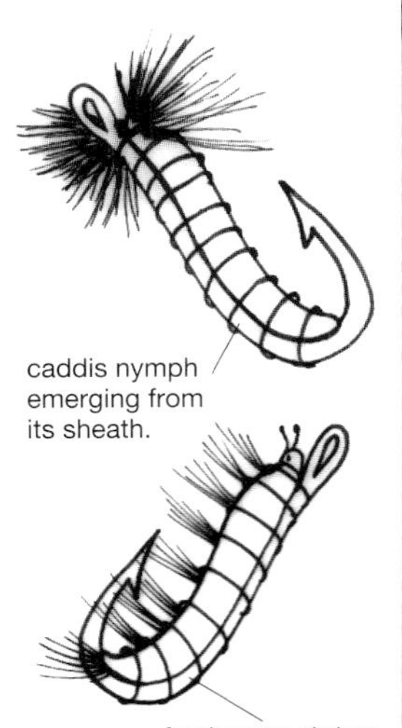

Nymph Fishing and Equipment

Fishing with artificial nymphs was slow in gaining acceptance but it is now popular with fishermen for both trout and char, especially in still waters. It involves presenting larvae at different stages of growth either close to the bottom or on the film just below the surface. The tackle is the same as for dry fly-fishing. The technique requires careful observation and a very cautious approach, as fishing at a close distance to the catch is often the most successful. Nymph fishing for fish which eat nymphs just before they hatch is a great technique for clear, shallow water, but requires a keen eye and a steady hand, as the angler has to be able to spot the fish going for the nymph and strike immediately.

• Nymphs

Many nymphs are simplicity itself. They are small, with an exaggerated thorax, thin, elongated abdomen, and perhaps a few strands of plumage representing wing-cases and legs. Leaded nymphs which imitate different types of bottom-dwelling animal life, are used for fishing at the river bed.

Conversely, nymphs which are reproductions of emerging insects or insects without an alar sac which are heading toward the surface are for fishing near to the surface, on sight, or upstream of signs of surface-feeding.

Although plenty of nymphs are available from tackle stores and by mail order, it is fun to make them yourself, using suitable materials, such as woolen thread, sewing silks, game-bird feathers, rabbit fur, and tinsel. Like flies, nymphs do not need to be entomologically correct specimens in order to do the trick. However, they should all be of the same basic type, with a body consisting of tail, abdomen, thorax, wingcase, and legs.

THE CATCH

BROWN TROUT

*Shimmering silhouette, nose pointing into the current, golden or brown flanks with ruby red flashes, always alert, disappearing at the slightest sign of danger at breakneck speed ... The brown trout (*Salmo trutta*) is a bank-running sylph-like creature.*

The little speckled queen of the river. ▽

A FISH WHICH HAS ALWAYS FASCINATED MAN

The brown trout is one of the oldest fish in our rivers, and the salmonidae family has developed very little since its primitive form which goes back 50 million years! No other fish has been so frequently mentioned in literature. Nearly two thousand years ago, Aelius described the first form of artificial fly-fishing in great detail, and much of the information is still relevant today. Our ancestors attempted to catch the trout by all imaginable means, and that passion remains the ultimate expression of the art of angling. Modern-day anglers are only perpetuating that ancient sport, albeit with the aid of undreamed-of technological advances but certainly with the same excitement and enthusiasm!

THE MOST DYNAMIC OF SPECIES

Brown trout are found almost everywhere. They live all over Europe, from Spain in the west to Scandinavia in the north, via the United Kingdom, Austria, Poland, Slovenia, and even Greece. Trout are also found in the United States, in New England and in the Rocky Mountains, in north in Africa (especially in the Atlas Mountains of Morocco), South Africa, Nepal and Afghanistan. In France, when men respect their environment, trout can be found across the land, from the swollen rivers of the Atlantic coast to the Pyrenees mountain streams, from the tiny streams in the center of France to the large rivers in the east, not forgetting the Alpine lakes. The trout lives at altitudes of up to 6,600 feet (2,000 m) above sea level in all sorts of habitats and is undoubtedly the most lively species of freshwater game fish in the world.

The char or charr is a closely related species, and in the United States, some species of char, particularly the American lake char (*Salvelinus namaycush*) are called trout. Furthermore, the rainbow trout is actually an

American native, introduced into Europe, some would say unwisely (see box on page 30). Trout, char, and whitefish are all related and are all important sport fish in the U.S.

GLORIOUS COLORS

Although it can be found in lakes and slow-moving rivers, the brown trout is the jewel of fast-flowing rivers and streams. It is perfectly adapted for swimming in turbulent and forceful currents. The slender and sleek body has strong fins for setting off in a flash and achieving impressive speeds over short distances. The skeleton is powerful and supple and gives this intrepid fish the ability to perform acrobatic about-turns in very small spaces and leap large waterfalls. These athletic qualities make trout-watching a very educational experience. The trout uses all its skill to make use of powerful currents staying in the flow without the slightest effort or it may plant itself on the bottom or behind a rock. It attacks with great speed and has the keenest sense of vision, taste, and smell, which keep it always on the alert.

The trout typically has a black stripe running along the spine, yellow or golden flanks adorned with red and/or black spots, often surrounded with white, and usually a pale underside. The scales are very small and numerous. There are 110 through 120 along the lateral line. The large rounded head is fairly flat underneath and it has a typical carnivore's mouth, with the corners just below and behind the level of the eyes. The eyes are fairly large and mostly black in color, with just a circle of golden yellow iris round the pupil. The operculum often has a large black spot level with the eye.

AN ADVENTUROUS FISH

Trout are great opportunists and quickly adapt to the most unusual of environments. They know how to make the most of all of the resources of a river or lake.

THE TROUT OF A THOUSAND FACES

The body of the trout can come in all sorts of colors and hues. Only the characteristic red or black spots (sometimes both) are a constant feature. The trout's coloring is beautiful and serves as a wonderful camouflage, and the colors exactly match those of its habitat. There are light brown trout covered in small spots in limpid, shallow brooks with sandy, clear bottoms, brown and yellow marbled trout near river beds of dark shingle and clear sand, gold and green trout near aquatic plants, and black trout in the almost permanent darkness of gorges or streams running through the bottom of wooded ravines. There are lake trout with blue spines and very pale flanks with nearly no spots at all which swim on the surface and constantly pursue the small fish that swim there. In certain types of trout, the lower lobe of the caudal and anal fins has an orange or sometimes pearly white fringe. The adipose fin is sometimes colored a brilliant scarlet. The colorways are infinite and, in waters into which few young fish have been introduced, it is easy to recognize a "true" trout which has adapted to its surroundings simply by its look and the color of its flanks.

Streams on high plateaux are ideal for trotting, especially at the beginning of the season. Because of the lack of cover, however, approach the banks discreetly. ▽

Differences Between Trout and Parr

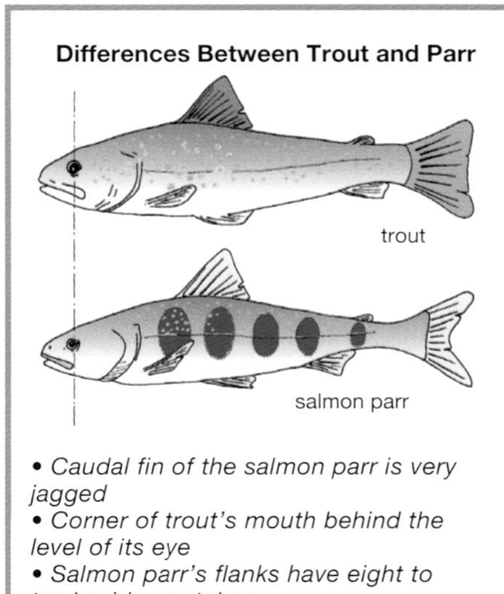

- *Caudal fin of the salmon parr is very jagged*
- *Corner of trout's mouth behind the level of its eye*
- *Salmon parr's flanks have eight to twelve blue patches*

Trout are very territorial fish, and dwell in a particular habitat, depending on the season and the water conditions of the moment. In shallow and slower currents, trout will explore all the food-bearing channels, on the outside of eddies caused by waterfalls or whitewater created by rocks obstructing the river bed, the deep crevices of hollow banks, near wooded banks, and in water which flows through aquatic vegetation. During periods of high water (heavy rains, thawing, and runoffs from upstream dams), trout take refuge from the strong current of a river in spate, sticking to banks and tight river bends so they can easily maintain their position and make the most of any interesting new food.

Bottom-dwelling animals and insects constitute 80 percent of a trout's usual diet. For a large part of the year, water fleas and the larvae of trichoptera, ephemera, and others make up most of its daily food intake. During good weather, usually from May to September, the large amount of hatching insects encourages trout to remain close to the surface, where their almost bulimic feeding frenzies can be easily seen! Hatching does, however, take place all year round, though not so intensely, and in shallow water, it is perfectly possible to see trout feeding in the middle of winter! On top of insects whose development cycle is aquatic, there are also diptera, spiders, different small beetles and all crickets and grasshoppers which fall into the water and cannot escape and which are particularly appreciated by the brown trout. Finally, don't forget that larger trout are great lovers of minnows. Our little ogre will hide close to a bank, hidden by a sunken branch, rocky crevice or bank of weeds, only to leap upon the small fish like a torpedo. From time to time, a bullhead or small trout can be just as tasty. In large Alpine barrage lakes where trout live alongside a large cyprinid population, trout tend to hunt shoals of bleak, a hearty diet which often produces enormous trout of 10 lb 1/2 oz – 18 lb (5–8 kg) and sometimes more!

A Bed of Gravel for Spawning

Brown trout reach sexual maturity at 3 years. From November onwards (October in mountainous regions), trout migrate short distances, from a few dozen yards to a mile or so (1 or 2 km), in order to find more suitable areas for reproduction. These are usually shallow gravel beds (often less than 3.3 feet (1 m) deep), oxygenated by a regular and fairly constant current. The type of bed is very important for the reproduction

The Trout's Low Reproduction Rate

The longer the incubation period of eggs, the fewer the chances of success. The brown trout is one of the most glaring examples of this problem. For the two months (on average) between fertilization and hatching, the eggs are exposed to all sorts of dangers. Floodwaters can churn up the river bed and carry the eggs far away downstream. When dams are emptied, mud covers and suffocates virtually everything which lives on the bottom of the waterways downstream. Small power stations also produce erratic water flow. Then, after hatching, the young fish are prey to large larvae or dippers, those birds which so nimbly walk on water. When they get slightly larger, the young trout move to gravel beds near to the banks, and that's when herons and kingfishers take an interest in them. In waters where perch and chub prevail, there are further and greater losses. Indeed, larger trout themselves will happily eat their own spawn. Out of a clutch of 1000 to 1500 eggs, only five trout will reach sexual maturity at three years of age.

◁ *Irish waters, so far spared from pollution, are well-populated with brown trout. Here is one which has been caught with a well-presented little sedge.*

process and should consist of small and medium-sized gravel, the ideal granulometry being between $^{1}/_{2}$ to $1^{1}/_{4}$ inches (10 to 30 mm). It is not unusual to see dozens of trout gathered in the four hundred or so square feet (100 m^2) of the spawning ground of a well-populated river. Reproduction peaks in December, although if there is a cold snap in November or January this may well become the peak mating period. Away from silt or plant debris, the female trout creates a groove in the gravel known as a redd by thrashing her fins, especially the caudal fin. The female produces between 1,500 and 2,000 eggs per kilogram (2¼ lb) of bodyweight, which she lays over the redd. Her eggs are instantly fertilized by the male, who hovers close by during the procedure. The two fish then cover the eggs with gravel by flapping their fins. Oxygenated by the current which runs constantly through the gravel bed, the eggs will incubate for a long time, at 410 degree-days or 50 to 80 days depending on the water temperature, which can be between 41 and 50°F (5 and 10°C). Once they hatch, the fry live in the gravel and live off their vitelline vesicle reserves. By the time these are used up, the fish will have reached a size of $^{3}/_{4}$–1 in (2–2.5 cm) in length and can feed off plankton. It can take two years for the young trout to reach a size of 8 in (20 cm), although of course, this varies greatly depending on the habitat. A brown trout living in granite rapids in a mountain stream can often reach 11 inches (28 cm) by the time it is five years old. In a large limestone river, it could be 16 in (40 cm), and weigh nearly 1 kg at the same age. And in a dammed lake full of whitefish to feast upon, the same trout could grow up to 26 in (65 cm) and weigh nearly 6 lb 8 oz (3 kg) in the same amount of time.

Is the brown trout really under threat?

Brown trout suffer as a result of the state of our waterways. Many are affected by the building of new dams which block their swims, whether they are small dams or large hydro-electric projects. These dams slow down the water which runs downstream, cause occasional and considerable changes in the current (up to 66 cu ft (20 m^3) a second) and do not respect reserved flow during the summer months. The flow is consequently too strong or too weak for the fish. This distresses their metabolism, disrupts reproduction, and depletes bottom-living life forms which are the brown trout's main source of food. If strong water flow makes spawning difficult, weak flow makes it even more dangerous, because slower water becomes warmer, oxygen levels are reduced, and the river bed becomes sealed off or calcified, killing off bottom-living fauna and making spawning almost impossible.

Similarly, the realignment and straightening of the banks of certain waterways, both natural and man-made, has turned them into aquatic freeways devoid of hiding places or even the slightest variation in the current for many miles.

At the other extreme, many European and American rivers are in an alarming state of neglect. Their banks are so overgrown that they have become impassable, and their beds are cluttered with dead branches and vegetation, which rapidly leads to silting up. Kayaks, canoes, and whitewater rafts have invaded our rivers, plundering the spawning areas and disturbing the trout's peaceful existence.

The only improvements to waterways have come from anglers, not water sports enthusiasts, and even that is woefully inadequate. To conclude this rather pessimistic survey, we urge anglers to limit their catch of trout. The maximum catch permitted in France for instance, is ten per day per angler (twenty on rivers in some places where trout are still very prolific) but even that is still too much! The minimum size of catch permitted is 8 inches (20 cm) (7 inches (18 cm) in some areas) meaning that it remains legal in France and some other countries to catch immature trout which have not yet reproduced and helped propagate the species.

How can the brown trout be helped to proliferate?

• Communication with the waterways authorities and the angling associations

Each angling society and association should attempt to work together with those bodies which are responsible for waterways, and the hydroelectric

A remarkably well-kept river. The French river Jonte in the Cévennes, which runs through some spectacular gorges, with vultures and peregrine falcons flying overhead, and the rare European beaver living nearby. ▷

The Genetic Pollution of Native Species

In a half a century of disastrous neglect of our waterways, together with the evils of modern civilization (pollution, destruction of biotopes, dam building, etc.), we have destroyed a large part of the indigenous trout population, those termed as wild.

Over thousands of years, numerous native species had adapted almost perfectly to particular biotopes, but they have now all but disappeared. This is due more to the reckless introduction of young fish than the release of adults, although that too has had an effect. Millions of trout have been farmed or imported without the slightest thought for their origins. As a result, many young fish have come from the roe of Scandinavian fish or sires of unknown origins with several years of captivity behind them. These new species have competed too directly with our native wild trout in the rivers or they have interbred with them, producing an irreversible degeneration of the original species.

With hindsight, it would have been better for the genetic health of our trout to do what is now being done – albeit somewhat sporadically. Wild fish are electrically fished, their eggs and sperm removed, and their eggs artificially hatched. The success rate is nearly 95%. Rivers can be repopulated with trout which are genetically identical to native species. If only the money plowed into spawning trout of uncertain origin had been used in this way, trout fishing would not be in this state today.

companies who construct dams and run electricity generating stations, so as to ensure that reserved flow rates are respected. Similarly, agreements can be drawn up with local authorities to regulate water sports access to rivers and lakes. These activities should be banned from December through mid-April to prevent disturbance of spawning and to protect fish eggs and young. These sports could also begin two to three hours after sunrise and stop two hours before sundown, to give trout some peace at the beginning and end of the day, when they do most of their feeding.

• Prioritizing river maintenance

Banks should be cleared, but with care; not completely cleared of vegetation but by balancing the removal of undergrowth and allowing shade trees to grow, giving both shade and light. For water to flow correctly, waterways should be cleared of sunken tree trunks and the sort of debris which chokes them. By channeling large water veins toward areas originally used for trout spawning, with carefully placed rocks, silt will clear to reveal the gravel again and the beds will be freed of undesirable obstacles, creating perfect spawning areas. Slow-flowing and chalky rivers can be turned into ideal breeding grounds simply by breaking up accretions of rubble or pushing heaps of gravel which has accumulated on the banks back into the traditional spawning areas. Finally, in waterways where there is a lot of silting, only chalk treatment will mineralize the silt effectively enough to clear it and allow bottom-living life forms to return and trout to develop.

• Demolish Unused Dams

Wherever dams have fallen into disrepair and are no longer used, requests for their complete demolition should be made to the appropriate authorities. Free circulation of fish over large distances means that the breeding pairs can reach more favorable spawning areas situated upstream and more importantly increase the dynamics of the population, which is essential for a species' survival.

• Restocking

This is only a stopgap measure on rivers in which brown trout are in serious difficulties. However, it will only be truly successful if the river is properly improved and maintained. It has to be said that restocking with adult brown or rainbow trout is a heresy; such domesticated trout, whose genetic heritage is largely diminished, are nearly all captured in the first few days of fishing.

Even if they are not all caught that quickly, 80 percent of them will die in the rivers because they don't know how to fend for themselves in the outside world. Those that manage to survive are incapable of reproducing. The only advantage of these farmed trout is that they satisfy the heavy fishing demand at the beginning of the season, thus protecting to some extent our "real" brownies. Stocking with very young fish which still have a resorbed (approximately $^{3}/_{4}$ in (2 cm)) or resorbing ($1^{1}/_{4}$–$2^{1}/_{2}$ in (3–6 cm)) vesicle gives better results, as long as it is done in the right conditions. Nevertheless, even if the result is a fair proportion of good-sized fish two or three years later, it has been estimated that only 20–30 percent of them will be capable of reproduction. Each angling association should set up its own hatchery to produce young fish born exclusively from breeding pairs which have come from the relevant local basin. That is the only way in which a healthy brown trout population will ever manage to survive human and animal predation.

The fly fisherman has to have plenty of patience and know how to watch the water to understand the way insects act and their effect on fishes' behavior. ▷

NATURAL BAIT FISHING

This sort of fishing is ideal for trout, as it basically offers the fish a selection of bait identical or similar to its regular diet. At the start of the season, especially when the water is cloudy, the worm is the star bait for trout-fishing.

Mealworms, larvae, or grubs are just as tempting. In clearer and shallower water, especially where trout are regularly fished, the smaller the bait, the better your chances of getting a bite. Larvae of insects which generally live on river and stream beds give good results.

Natural bait fishing goes hand in hand with "reading" the river so you have a good feel for which spots may contain trout. The most likely places are close to banks, in deep hollows, downstream of rocks on the river bed, beneath branches and bushes overhanging the water, and around eddies created by waterfalls and whitewater. Basically, this means anywhere the trout may dwell for food or protection.

• Trotting

Trotting requires a simple rig and is a straightforward technique which is nevertheless highly successful and very subtle. Use it in streams, torrents, and rivers which are no wider than 33 feet (10 m). Make the most of clear banks by using a large rod (17–23 ft (5–7 m)) without a reel, simply tied with a 16/100 or 18/100 main line and a 10/100 to 14/100 hook length. On wooded banks, go for a shorter rod (12–13 ft (3.5–4 m)) with external or internal guide rings and a reel. This will let you control the line as required so you can navigate the vegetation.

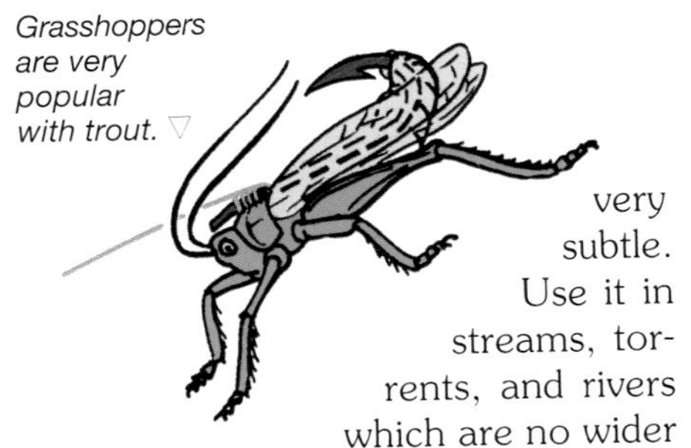

Grasshoppers are very popular with trout. ▽

Trotting involves presenting your bait exactly where the trout can be found; not an easy task, given the often complex flow of water. Your use of weights is the determining factor in this technique.

△ *Two houseflies on a no. 12 hook.*

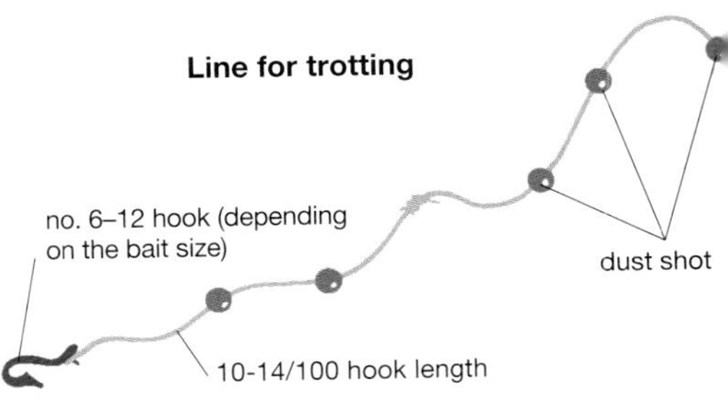

The size and spread of shot on your line will correctly present the bait and allow it to drift naturally. The slower the flow of water, the lighter the shot, and vice versa. Similarly, the more restricted the fishing space, the closer you should group your shot so the bait can be cast more precisely and drop more quickly. When fishing in more regular currents where trout habitats are less easily marked, spread shot out more so that the line can drift further. It's a matter of trial and error. Add a few shot, take a few away, and change their position as the river requires. No single rig can be used for every river and stream you fish.

Lobworm hooked on a no. 6-8. ▽

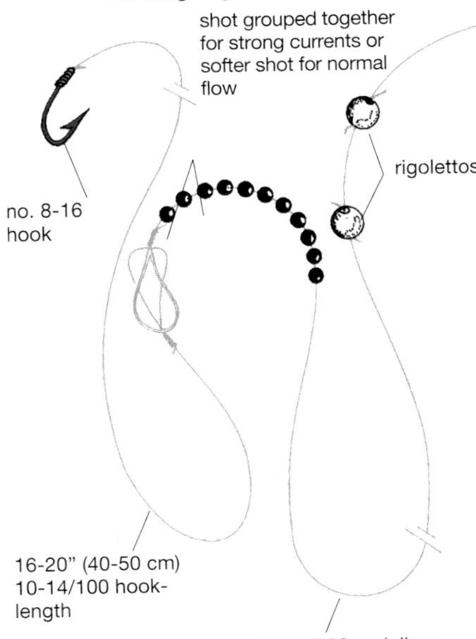

◁ *This fisherman has just captured a macrostigma trout with a tasty local bait – a bee larva!*

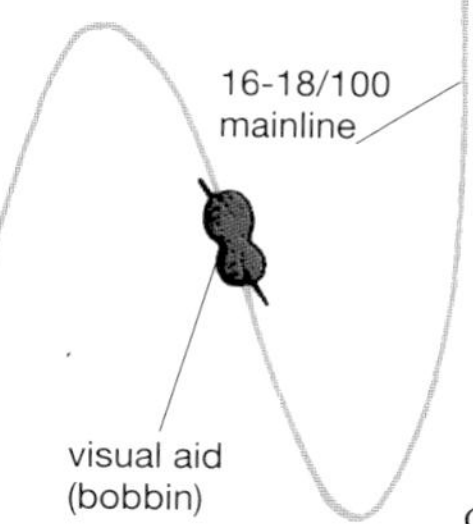

• Floating Line

Try float or long flow fishing where trotting is no longer effective, namely on rivers wider than 33–40 ft (10–12 m), with deeper pools which require a large amount of line, but also areas where very fussy trout can only be tempted by a floating line which drifts a long way downstream. An 11–15 ft (3.5–4.5 m) quivertip fixed reel rod and a reel filled with 14/100 to 16/100 line are perfect for this type of fishing. The float is all-important. It has to support the line and control its drift. Choose your float depending on the amount of shot needed and the strength of the current. Use a small float such as a Toulouse or Nicoise ball. This will provide minimum resistance to the fish when it bites. With float-fishing, all the shelves and areas closer to the opposite bank are within reach. As with trotting, weight your line with shot and spread the weights according to the type of river being fished so that the bait is presented as naturally as possible. For fishing in large deep pools, a sinking float sliding on a stop knot will allow you to cast, however deep or shallow the water. In shallow water during summertime, when trout are particularly fussy, use a float smaller than ½ in (10 mm) in diameter and a hook length without any shot, baited with a cricket or grasshopper. This is the only way of catching the wiliest trout on the river.

△ *When fishing on exposed banks, you may need to crouch down to avoid being seen by the fish.*

Genuine wild trout which have come from a stream into which no new young fish have been introduced. ▷

Fishing with minnow deadbait

Deadbait fishing with minnow or other small fish such as gudgeon is halfway between bait-fishing and rod-and-reel fishing and is becoming gradually more popular. The main idea of this technique is to present the small dead fish by dragging or maneuvering it so that it resembles a live fish that has been injured. Like most predators, the trout is a great opportunist and views a weakened specimen as ideal prey. The technique involves investigating all the possible trout haunts before lowering the bait into the water. Try hollow banks, uneven beds, and small waterfalls which are all ideal spots. Deadbait can be just as effective in rivers and streams of average depth where habitats may not be as obvious. For the best possible exploration, cast directly across or slightly upstream, giving the deadbait a good arc-shaped drift. Reel it in using jerky, irregular movements so the bait moves realistically near the bottom.

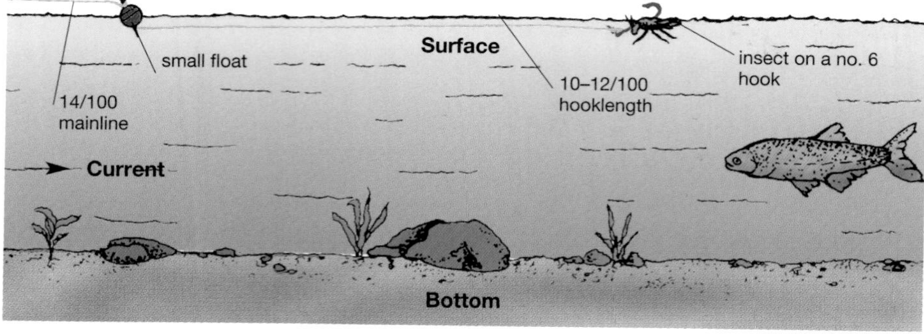

△ Angler pulling out a trout on the River Verdon in Provence, France, caught with a cleverly-maneuvered deadbait minnow.

Tackle is important here. Use a 8–10 foot (2.5–3 m) rod, depending on surrounding obstacles and the width of the river. It should be a light quivertip so you can quickly and easily transfer the type of movement you want to the bait. Make sure your reel is in perfect working order and that it balances the rod well. Load it with 20–24/100 nylon line. There are numerous rigs (shielded, Ariel, etc.) but the simplest is often the best. Just add a head sinker with a plastic disc then, using a baiting-needle, pass the line through the minnow's mouth and bring it out in the anal area. Then simply fix a fairly sturdy treble hook to the end of the line.
Unlike most rigs which use two trebles, this sort of rig is less likely to snag when reeled in. One fairly large treble is just as likely to catch trout as two smaller hooks, if not more so.
Finally, with this sort of rig, you will need to retie the hook knot every time the minnow is changed, which may seem like a waste of time but does avoid unnecessary breaks at the knot, which occur always at the worst possible moments!

• Catching and storing minnows

Before you can fish with deadbait minnow, you need to catch and store them. Some retailers sell minnows at a fairly low price – that's the lazy solution. Otherwise, spend a few hours stocking up on some livebait. Use a small floating line with a 8/100 hook length and a thin iron hook without a barb (so you don't harm the small fish). A maggot or segment of earthworm is ample bait for this sort of fishing. A minnow trap, carefully placed at the water's edge of a small river or brook where shoals of minnows swim is less sporting but can be just as effective. Do not use a trap with a capacity of more than 2 quarts (2 liters). Check with the local fishing association to see what the rules are for this sort of fishing. Minnows are generally fairly fragile and delicate, whichever way you catch them. Once caught, you then need to handle them carefully to make sure you keep them alive. A garden pond is of course the ideal place to keep them, as long as you make sure there is netting over it to protect it from herons. But not everyone has a house with a garden.

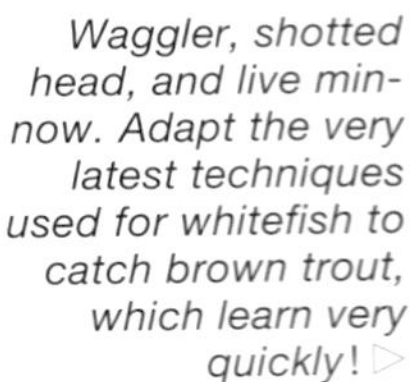

Other methods include:
– a freshwater aquarium with a good aerator;
– a simple 50-quart (50-liter) icebox or cooler, two-thirds filled with water and supplied with an aerator. The water should be changed every day and then you'll be able to keep around fifty minnows in it. Put a lid on the icebox to stop them jumping out, but don't seal it or they will suffocate.

Fishing with lures

Rod-and-reel lure fishing is a great technique for the tireless bankside angler, for whom fishing and sport are one and the same thing. Aside from being a way of burning off all that extra energy, rod-and-reel lure fishing is also a very efficient technique, as long as you observe a number of basic rules.
You quickly need to develop a hunter's eye for observing the terrain and a silent and discreet approach as you close in on the trout. As a predator among predators, the fisherman must disappear into the background, becoming one with the bankside vegetation and positioning himself in the ideal spot for each cast.
With the relevant tackle and many hours of practice, precise lure-casting will finally start to bring its rewards. Except in rare moments of excess when trout will attack anything and everything that moves in the water, they are not keen on mad chases.
The lure has to tempt the trout out of its personal hideaway. Often, 8 inches (20 cm) more or less when casting can make all the difference as

Waggler, shotted head, and live minnow. Adapt the very latest techniques used for whitefish to catch brown trout, which learn very quickly! ▷

LIVEBAIT TROUT FISHING

Livebait fishing is the poor relation for trout anglers while deadbait fishing has thousands of fans. Nevertheless, a nicely wriggling minnow, chub, or bleak will nearly always interest a trout. Often, livebait fishing can be the best way to catch large trout, which are much more likely to ignore small worms or lures! Both trotting and float-fishing are suitable with livebait, in exactly the same conditions: float fishing is especially useful for large rivers with deep areas or rocky crevices. Of course, if a river contains a large minnow population and it is easy to spot feeding trout, study the area, then place your livebait near to a bank. At the first attack, your bait will be the first to be taken, since it will be slower to escape, and with good reason! The trout's bite is usually very clear. Use a fairly thin no. 8 hook, impaled through the livebait's upper lip. On some days, however, trout will systematically kill livebait and spit them out immediately at such a speed that even the quickest hand cannot strike. Do they just want to eliminate any competition without actually feasting on them? In this case, two hooks can solve the problem. Having tied the first hook to the hook length, tie a second hook to the remaining end of the line, about 3/4 inch (2cm) lower. Hook the first through the mouth of the bait and the second though its back, just in front of the dorsal fin. Using this method, you'll often manage to hook a trout completely unawares.

◁ Livebait with two hooks.

to whether a trout decides to jump on your spoon or plug and give you a catch to be proud of.

• Light rod-and-reel fishing

Since rod-and-reel fishing can be used on all types of water, it needs to be practiced with tackle that suits the requirements of the current conditions. The rod is your main weapon and should be light and fairly flexible, with a semi-quivertip action. Carbon fiber or kevlar rods are perfect. They enable accurate casting and will be capable of holding the heaviest fish. Choose the length of your rod – between 6 and 8 feet (1.9 and 2.4 m) is a good length – depending on the surrounding bank conditions and average width of the river. Although they're more unusual, go for a larger rod 87–10 feet (2.5–2.8 m)) on wider rivers with a strong current. A large rod lets you control the lure better and, more importantly, manage all types of combat. This is an especially useful feature when the trout is aided by a strong current.

Your reel needs to be more than just reliable: no other fishing technique puts as much strain on this essential part of your tackle. Look for a reel that is sturdy, with immediate and careful bale-arm action and a progressive clutch. For most situations, use a 16–20/100 line and change it regularly so it retains all its good qualities.

Search the river by casting three-quarters or a quarter upstream, or even straight across to the other bank, and carefully comb each likely habitat. Fishing technique should be steady and rhythmic, with regular casting toward all likely spots. If the lure falls in the right place – near a rock, at the bottom of a crevice, between two counter-currents or right beneath or behind a waterfall, the trout will bite on the first or second cast. They will rarely do so after several casts.

A "bridge trout" – in this case, a typical stone bridge over a stream in the Millevaches plateau – is returned to the water. ▷

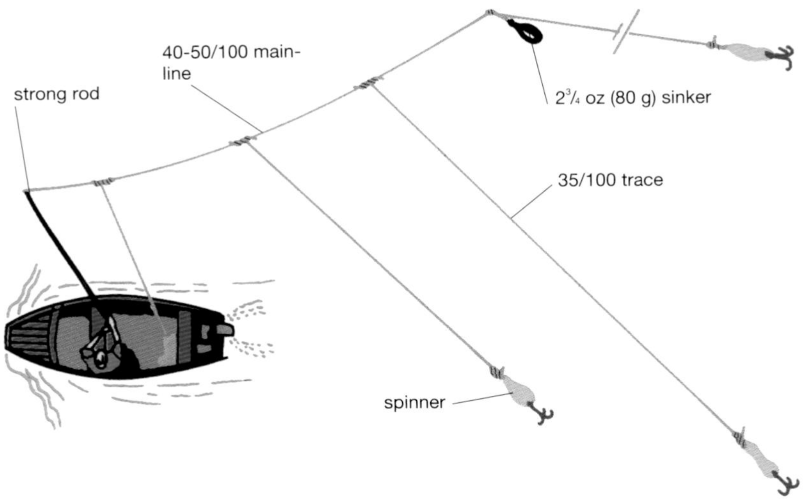

△ Salmo trutta lacustris *is a subspecies of brown trout which lives in various types of water. In large Alpine lakes in Austria and Switzerland, the largest specimens can be fished by trawling with special rigs, as shown above.*

In smoother, calmer waters, rod-and-reel fishing should be more concerned with the speed of reeling in (and therefore the depth at which the lure lies) and the angler should avoid using too monotonous an action for his spoon or plug. The lure should speed up, slow down to a near halt, and then shoot off again. This varied movement when reeling in often triggers the trout's aggression because, unlike previously mentioned circumstances, the element of surprise plays virtually no role in this specific context.

– Essential Lures
Nos. 1, 2, and 3 spinners (gold or silver, tinsel and other decorations optional) depending on the conditions and river width are the best to use for brown trout. Use only spinners whose blades begin turning as soon as they hit the water. Spoons which are 1½–2¾ in (3, 5 and 7 cm) long (silver in color, decorations optional) depending on water depth and current strength: these lures need maneuvering in a similar way to the dead minnow 1½–2¾ in (3.5 and 7 cm) plugs (silver, gold, realistic minnow or small trout colors) of a stocky (1¼ in (3 cm only)) or tapered shape. Floating and semi-sinking plugs are good for clear and fairly deep waters. Floating plugs are very useful for letting a line drift toward inaccessible habitats and when following the current. A plug is generally slower and less well adapted to small hits than the spinner.

• Ultra-Lightweight
This technique is intended for small rivers and streams where fishing space is very limited and the angler needs to be very unobtrusive and very accurate. This miniaturized light rod-and-reel fishing is however just as useful on larger rivers, in shallow water, and for tempting seasoned fish in "impossible" habitats. Fish when the trout are very active, especially from the end of April through June, and during the summer, preferably in the morning or evening. Ultra-light technique requires the use of small lures of negligible weight attached to very basic rigs. The ultra-light rod is extremely sensitive and rarely longer than 5 feet (1.5 m), making it perfect for fishing in very small areas. It shouldn't be too flexible however, otherwise battling a large trout becomes a very difficult task.
Given the restricted fishing space and the light rod, a small, light reel is essential. The mechanism needs to be even more trustworthy than for light rod-and-reel fishing, which is quite a tall order.

◁ *Trout are very sensitive to movement and waves, and so are often caught using a plug. The 1¼–6½ in (3–17 cm) sizes are the most popular.*

CHOOSING A LURE

Choosing a lure is not as thorny an issue as choosing a fly, but it still requires a lot of attention. Despite the ever more elaborate and attractive designs produced by manufacturers, you need to choose your lure by the type of signals it gives off underwater. Any object placed in the water is, of course, seen by the trout if it falls into its field of vision, but it is also detected by different sorts of waves. The lures which are of most interest are those which give off very clear vibrations and trigger the trout's aggressive instincts. The spinner's rotating blade, the wriggling plug or the waggling movement of the spoon are all designed for this purpose. Don't forget that lure manufacturers are more interested in catching anglers than in catching fish! That said, you need to be totally comfortable with what you put on the end of your line, so go for lures that look good to you. The other important factor is the size and weight of a lure, which obviously affect the way it moves through the water. For larger and faster water, you'll need a heavy lure to effectively fish at the bottom and one that is large enough for its signals to be seen from a distance by the fish. In very slow-moving water, the same lure would cause an enormous splash and disproportionate vibrations, frightening off your trout, so choose much more unobtrusive types.

△ The clear waters of the Jonte in the Cévennes are ideal for ultra-light fishing.

△ 1¼–2¾ in (3–7 cm) Rapala lures, floating or sinking, are trusty aids for trout fishing.

Finally, to complete the picture, use a 12–14/100 line. In streams or torrents, explore every possible habitat, along banks, behind every stone. under every shaded patch of water, in the smallest basins and at the bottom of the narrowest crevices. On larger swims, make the most of this technique's maneuverability in order to scan and sweep more unlikely spots where trout are almost never disturbed. An element of surprise is all-important!

– *Essential Lures*

No. 0 spinners (silver or golden), perhaps with a fly attached. Use 1¼ in (3 cm) plugs, which you should let drift with the current and against the banks and you can expect some amazing results. Feather or hair streamers which resemble a young fish, leaded with a little shot at the head. Plastic lures shaped like fish or flagella, 1¼–1½ in (3–4 cm) long, with a very small shot at the head of the hook are all excellent lures to use when you are hunting the brown trout.

FLY-FISHING

Fly-fishing is a subject about which countless books have been written. It is an essentially esthetic technique which is nonetheless supremely successful. Fly-fishing is based on two main principles – knowledge of the river and observation of the trout's feeding habits. The main reason for the development of fly-fishing was the importance of insects at all stages of development to the trout's diet. Sometimes as much as 80 percent of the trout's food intake consists of insects. The art of fly-fishing involves using the correct sort of fly at the right time of day and during the relevant season in order to imitate the trout's favorite dish. As most flies are extremely light, presenting them on the water requires very specific tackle.

• Dry-Fly-Fishing

Dry-fly-fishing involves presenting artificial flies which float on the water's surface. The flies consist of feathers, hair, and synthetic materials made up into realistic copies of the various sorts of insect which live on or by the water rather than beneath it.

Dry-fly-fishing is traditional and has been used for hundreds, even thousands of years (even the Romans used this technique). Nevertheless, it remains extremely popular – more popular than wet-fly or nymph fishing – because it is a very visual sort of angling. You can see the fly floating on the

decorated blade
"caterpillar" covering

◁ A Duborgel fly spinner.

water and witness the take in all its glory as the trout leaps from the water to catch the artificial lure. However, except during particularly frenzied surface feeding in the month of June, for every one trout that bites on the surface, there are another ten feeding below.

The price of the tackle required for fly-fishing used to make it a very exclusive pursuit, but this is no longer the case. The tip action or semi-parabolic rod is generally 8½ feet (2.8 m) long and made from carbon or kevlar. A 7-foot rod makes for easier casting, particularly on cluttered rivers. A 10-footer can be used on rivers and streams with exposed banks and fast-flowing water so you can control drift more easily and limit line drag.

The manual or semi-automatic reel should be made of a very light composite material which perfectly balances the rod. Automatic reels are often too heavy and not as predictable to work.

The synthetic silk used for the line is self-floating, and its size depends on rod action and the type of water being fished. The smaller the silk number, the lighter the line and the more delicate the presentation of the fly. The end part of the line or drop is very important and requires a lot of attention. Storebought lines, known as rat-tails, finish with a 10 or 12/100 line and are perfect for the job. You can obtain the same effect by attaching sections of 50/100, 35/100, 25/100, 18/100 and finally a 12 or 10/100 nylon.

A handsome brown trout caught with a small light fly. ▷

When the trout are being very fussy about their flies, they will often completely ignore a 12 or 10/100 line, in which case you need to resort to a 8/100. Some real experts go right down to a 6.5/100 but you would need a skilled hand to win any ensuing strike!

As for the type of flies to use, the greatest 19th-century naturalists spent years perfecting dry flies that came as close as possible to the real thing, sometimes even differentiating between male and female insects in their quest for realism.

Classic flies for trout include those which resemble the mayfly, black gnat, daddy longlegs, and flying ant. Dry flies are particularly successful in lake and reservoir fishing when used at times of year when real flies are hatching and hovering over the water's surface, making a tasty meal for a lively trout near the surface. That is why flies that resemble black gnats and mayflies are so successful.

It is important to remember that unless a dry fly is treated with a floatant, it will soon become waterlogged and need frequent changing. This is especially true of those made with woolly bodies to resemble caterpillars. A special substance called Permaflote is used to treat dry flies and keep them waterproof. Treat the flies and leave them to dry thoroughly if you want to get the best results.

New patterns of dry flies have recently been introduced, though some of them are merely variations on old themes. Some incorporate spinners, such as the USD polyspinner, others are designed to resemble different types of trout prey, such as shrimp or even minnow, but they remain "dry flies" nonetheless. The fly-fisherman is at liberty to buy those which are

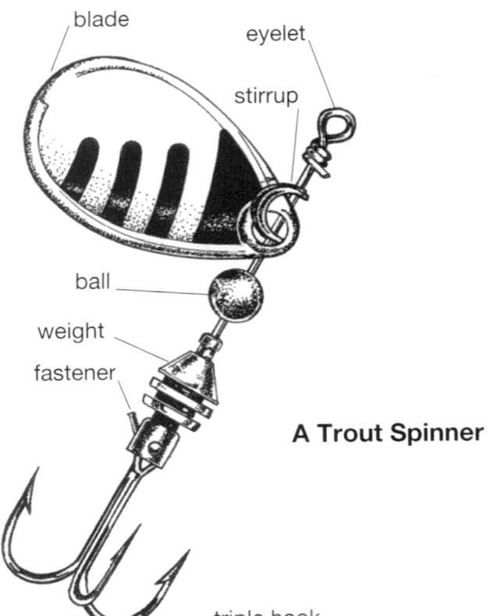

A Trout Spinner

Vertical Cast

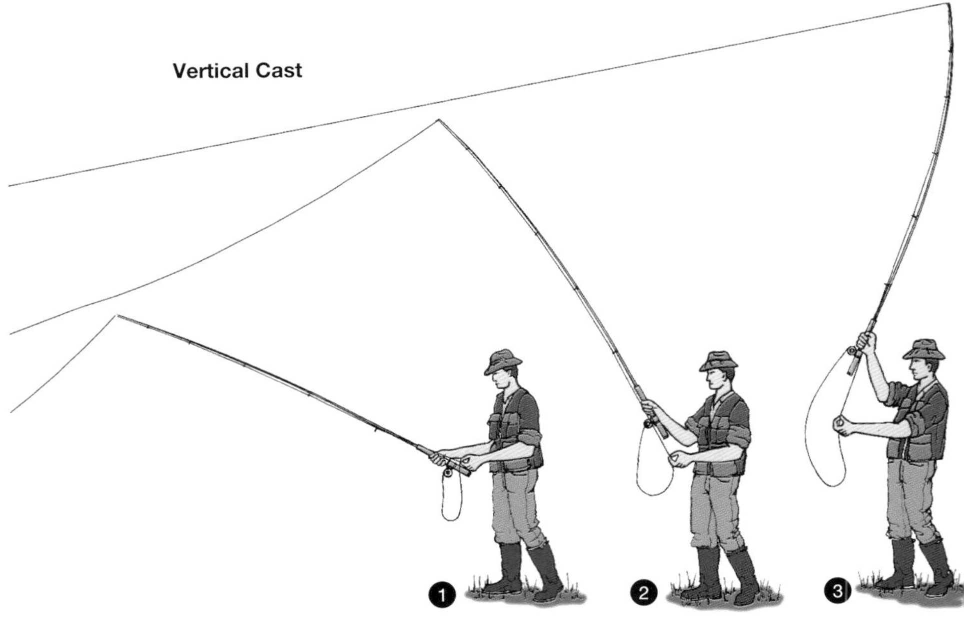

commercially available or try his luck at imitating nature, with help of silken and cotton thread and some feathers and wool. Of course, the result does not have to be lifelike because it is a trout which you are trying to impress, not a naturalist.

In dry-fly fishing, there are two main ways of presenting your fly: fishing for bites or fishing the swim.

– Fishing for Bites

This logical method of fishing centers around presenting an artificial fly to trout feeding on the real thing. The fly fisherman targets areas where the appearance of concentric circles on the surface betrays trout feeding areas. Obviously, you need to approach very discreetly, and you should position yourself on either side of the feeding fish and then cast diagonally upstream of that spot. After casting, the silk should be well away from the fish, so that the fly floats naturally toward it. The thickness of the drop plays an important part here: a 10/100 or even an 8/100 drop is often necessary so the artificial fly drifts along as naturally as possible. Particularly wary fish won't bite if there is the slightest hint of something amiss in the presentation of your fly, so fishing downstream has the advantage of presenting the fly to the trout without revealing the presence of the line. When fishing downstream, however, wait before striking because, as the fish is facing the angler, it is easy to simply snatch the fly from its mouth.

On the larger Irish lakes, fly fishing is often the best way of fooling a trout. ▷

– Fishing the Swim

Fishing the swim involves a completely different technique because takes come second. Instead, the rules of the game are to pass the fly over all possible trout habitats, particularly where a patch of still water ends, all small currents and near wooded or scrubby banks.

Very often, trout can be found fairly near the surface but they only rarely rise to feed, so you have to keep a constant watch for fish rising to the surface.

Once you have gotten a good feel for the swim and the trout's behavior in it, fish by methodically combing the water's surface, casting briefly and repeatedly.

In fast-running water, the type of fly used is less important than on slow-moving streams and rivers, because the trout has less time to study it and will often jump to the surface automatically. Don't be afraid to use a fairly bright dry fly which floats high

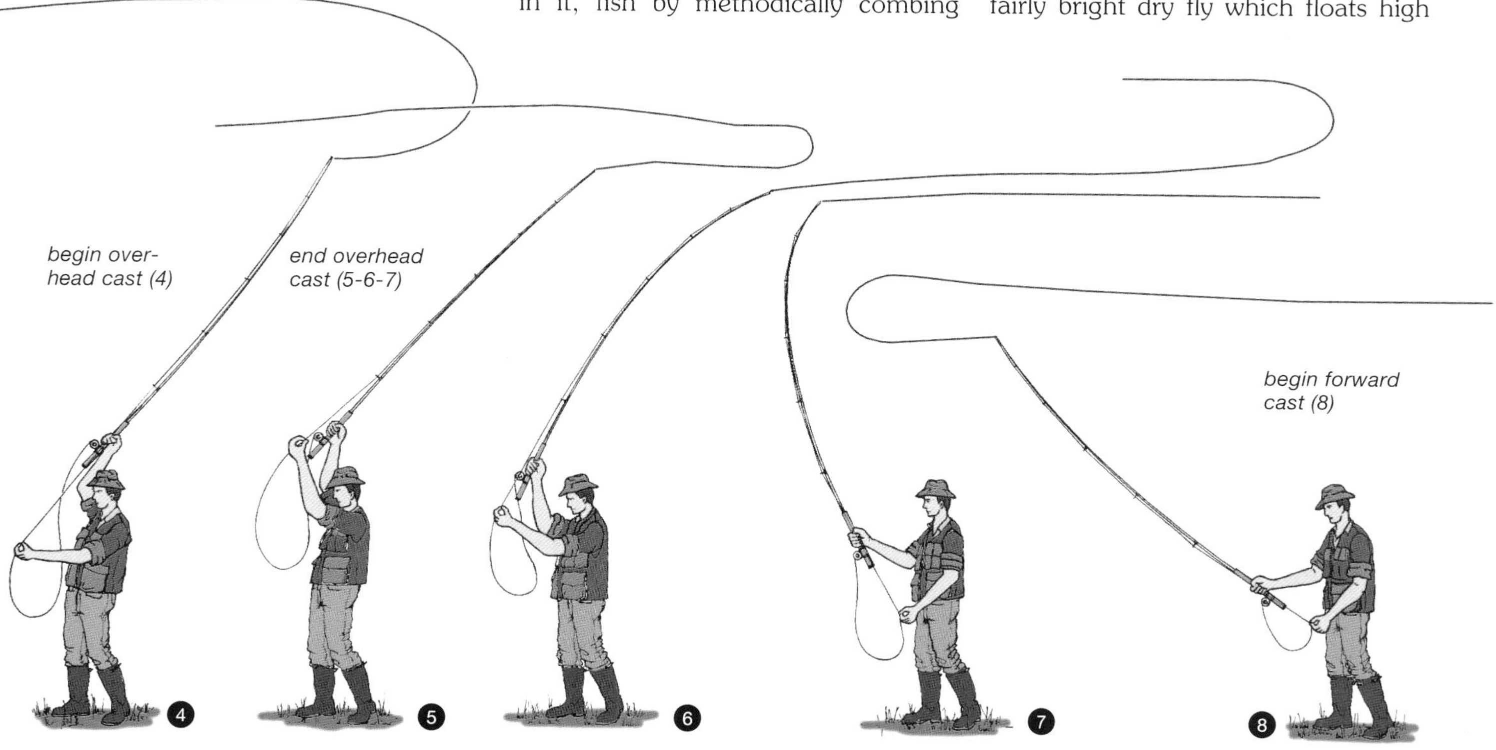

Choosing a Dry Fly

A fly fisherman's favorite subject of discussion is the type of fly to use. Followers of "accurate" fly fishing, which involves copying the insect that the trout love best in particular circumstances, mix angling and entomology. Others prefer fantasy flies, which bear no resemblance to anything living but can excite a fish's curiosity. Some anglers carry a hundred or so flies in their pockets, while others fish all season with less than ten different flies. You should go for general traits rather than specific details. Three main factors should influence your choice: size, shape, and overall coloring (rather than just "color" – a trout's perception of color is still a mystery).

in the water so you can easily pick it out in turbulence. During summer, dry-fly-fishing in small rivers and streams can often result in some spectacular catches.

• Wet-Fly-Fishing

As the name implies, wet-fly-fishing involves using a sinking fly at varying depths under the water. Insects nearly always die underwater and are rapidly submerged by the current, so trout will happily feed on them well below the surface as well as on top of it. That is why you should never presume that just because you can't see any activity on the surface, there are no feeding trout in the vicinity! Wet-fly-fishing is not as simple as some would have you believe. It is a technique which involves presenting one or more artificial flies underwater where trout feed more regularly. Wet-fly-fishing is far less visual and so requires a heightened sense of touch on the part of the fisherman.

Trout are very quick to detect a fly fisherman's ruse and can very quickly spit out an artificial fly, so you need to be able to detect a bite as soon as it happens. Fishing is done fully downstream or one-quarter downstream to get a larger and wider sweep with the fly. As the fly moves, the angler has to control the drift with a silk that is not too taut (to prevent dragging) and not too slack (so you can still detect the slightest pull or snag). No matter how slight, you should strike at the slightest take. A competent wet fly fisherman still only detects one out of every two actual bites. Despite everything, however, in most situations (cold water at the beginning of season, slightly muddy rivers, or fast-flowing streams), wet-fly-fishing is far more effective than dry-fly-fishing.

That's not to say that you shouldn't dry-fly fish when the conditions are right for it. For wet-fly-fishing on a river with a good current, you need tackle that is rather more robust than the tackle used for dry-fly-fishing.

When dry-fly-fishing, presentation and drift are the most important factors for success. ▽

You can use the same reel, but you will need a 9–10 feet rod which is rigid enough to give you effective strikes from a distance and easy reeling-in. Use a floating no. 4–6 silk if you are fishing in shallow water, because only the drop needs to go below the surface.

– *Types of wet fly*

Because they're intended to look like insects which have either "drowned" or are in the final stages of aquatic life, most artificial wet flies are fairly plain. Wings and legs are generally kept as simple as possible, made out of a few hackle fibers or flattened hairs (the so-called Spanish assembly), but the body is more elaborate. It is often bulbous or cylindrical, orange, yellow, red, or green, and circled with wire in a contrasting color. Gold and silver tinsel may also be added. Many wet flies do not resemble any known living thing. They are made of synthetic material and feathers in differing bright colors. However, this does not seem to deter the trout who often leap upon them anyway.

A few good examples of wet fly are Irish flies such as the Green Highlander, Claret Bumple, Bloody Butcher, Teal and Red, Duck Fly.

Wet flies tied with a full body hackle are known as "Palmer tied" after the original Red Palmer which is one of the classic British flies. Palmer flies include several winged flies with shoulder hackles, such as the Invicta and Wickham's Fancy. Some Palmer tied wet flies are designed to resemble spiders, in which case they have no wings and are referred to as spider-hackled flies.

The fundamental difference between wet and dry flies is the manner of tying and the softer more absorbent materials used for wet flies, which are designed to sink.

Which flies should be stocked in the Fly Box?

• High-floating artificial flies which resemble living insects floating on the water's surface or laying their eggs on it, especially spiders and Palmers in black, red, brown, and light gold. Flies such as the Panama, Indispensable, Mayflies, French Tricolor, or Double Collaret will get you a trout on virtually any water at virtually any time of the season. Sedges, which have long wings right along the body, are wonderful for tempting trout at dusk and just after dawn. It's a good idea to have different sizes of sedge on no. 10, 12, and 14 hooks. Once you get into summer, the trout become more difficult and the gnats take over (Blue Dun, Olive Quill, Wickam's Fancy, Red Quill, and so on). These much smaller flies are attached to no. 16, 18, and 20 hooks.

• Low floating artificial flies which look like dead insects floating on the surface are also known as spents. The previously mentioned flies are mounted with wings spread wide and flattened, depending on the size of the hook.

• Very low floating flies, resembling insects breaking through the water's surface during hatching, like the famous DAs. The overall coloring should be black, brown, yellow, and white, and they should be mounted on no. 14, 16, and 18 hooks.

These are just the basics, it is up to you to decide what works best for you. While these flies work best on still water, you may find that the new kinds resembling freshwater shrimp or larvae will be more effective in brooks and streams.

• Nymph Fishing

Nymphs are a form of wet fly, but the fishing technique involves angling at some depth beneath the surface of the water with more or less realistic imitations of insect larvae which usually live on or near to the bottom. Trout feed on more insects during their various stages of development than the definitive airborne adult. Most insects spend many months underwater, and only live for two or three days in the air, sometimes only a few hours, so there is much more chance of a trout getting a satisfactory meal from a larva or nymph.

Most artificial nymphs are the same shape, varying only in size and color. The "body" consists of silken thread, wound several times tightly round the hook to pad it out, and held in place with a shiny wire thread, leaving hackles, head, and "legs" to protrude front and back to disguise the point.

To make wingcases for nymphs, tie on turkey feathers with the pointed end of the feather facing the bend of the hook. Secure the feather

A racquet-type landing net, fixed or fold-away, is sometimes useful for wading or landing larger subjects. ▷

with a piece of wool of the same color as the feather which should be brown.

The great advantage of the nymph for the novice fisherman who wants to try his hand at making his own flies is that nymphs are much easier to make than wet or dry flies and are just as effective as wet flies.

They can be used in still water and flowing water alike, in all types of river and lake bottom and in all weather conditions, unlike dry flies which are best used at times of year when trout are snapping at the real thing. Nymphs were slow to gain acceptance but now even those who were most resistant to the idea admit that they work just as well as dry flies and fishing with nymphs can be just as rewarding and satisfying.

– Deepwater Nymphs

Like wet-fly-fishing, deepwater nymph fishing takes place much deeper, often close to the bottom. The tackle is the same as for wet-fly-fishing, except for the silk. As this technique requires a rapid descent and involves fishing so far below the surface, the silk should be sinking or semi-sinking (only the last few feet are leaded).

Deepwater nymph fishing is a very tactile technique and the line must be neither too taut nor too slack so the angler can feel the slightest touch or halt in the drift.

The nymphs can be leaded and their size should depend on the depth of water being fished. The best disguise in this case is a resemblance to water-fleas, trichoptera and other insect larvae which live on river beds. At the beginning of the season, when the waters are still cold and trout stay right at the bottom, deepwater nymph fishing may be the only way to get them to bite.

– Visual Nymph Fishing

This is a technique that has been fashionable for a number of years and has the visual aspect of dry-fly-fishing but it takes place underwater in clear swims. Although it can be extremely difficult to see a tiny nymph from several yards away, even in the clearest water and even with the best eyesight, this is a good way of spotting the fish. You can tell if the trout is following your nymph and spot it when it takes. The rules are the same as for any type of visual fishing, you need a careful and extremely discreet approach for this technique. You must not interrupt a trout at feeding time! You do need to get as close as possible to the fish however for the best results, so you can present the nymph precisely and judge the trout's reactions so you strike at the right moment.

The tackle used for dry-fly-fishing is perfect for this technique, including the floating silk. Because of the clearness of the water, the end of the drop should be 8–10/100. Use different nymph designs and sizes depending on the average depth at which the trout are swimming.

THE TEAM OF WET FLIES

With a team of two or three different types of wet fly, you can present each one at a different level in the water. The drop should be of decreasing diameter and the flies are tied to the last part of it. One, the leader, is fixed to the very end, obviously, with a second (or third) tied slightly higher, on a strand of line known as a trace. Given the sometimes violent strikes and fast-moving fishing technique, the tip of the team and the traces should never be less than 14/100, or 12/100 only if you are very careful when handling the line.

- The fly at the tip of the line is the one that sinks the deepest. It has a large and sometimes leaded body, with few hackles or hairs which are flattened to aid its descent.
- The middle fly is fixed to a trace about 20–24 inches (50–60 cm) from the tip for fishing closer to the surface. Its body is much thinner, and the hackles are drawn back very slightly to ensure it drops smoothly and not too fast through the water.
- The surface or leader fly is also fixed to a trace about 20–24 in (50–60 cm) above the middle fly and bobs about on the surface of the water. It has a spindly body with hackles sticking out, like a moderately mounted dry fly, to give it stability on the surface.

Of course, depending on the results obtained (most trout are caught on one or two flies, rarely on all three), you should change around your team of flies. You can remove the surface fly or the middle fly, or leave a larger gap between each fly, or even add more shot to the tip fly.

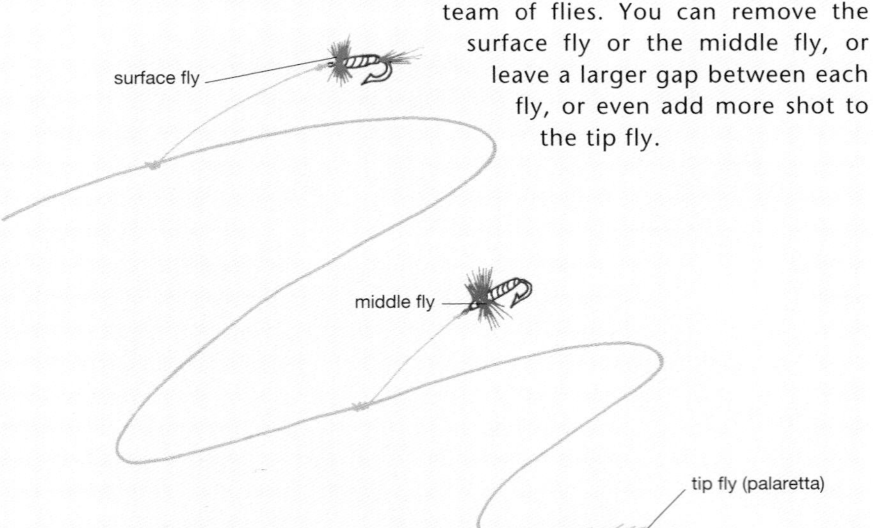

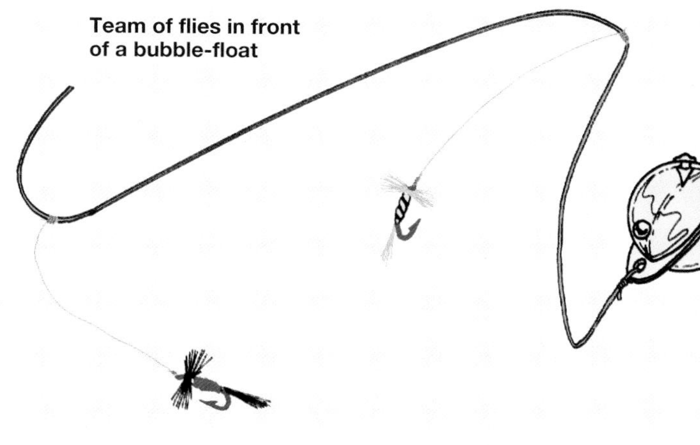

Team of flies in front of a bubble-float

Fishing in High Mountain Lakes

High mountains are the last bastion of almost unspoilt nature and a paradise for trout anglers who yearn for "the real thing" with a bit of adventure thrown in. In the Alps and the Pyrenees, some lakes are at altitudes of more than 6,600 feet (2,000 m) and you often have to walk for several hours up very steep mountainsides to get there. You will be richly repaid for your efforts with the extraordinary peace and quiet, beautiful flora and fauna, and, most of the time, trout which have hardly ever come into contact with civilization! Mountain lake fishing does not merely require a little physical exertion. You need to be very well organized, able to work with the bare essentials and have a healthy respect for nature. Walking for several hours, fishing, eating, living, and sleeping outdoors for two or three days requires careful preparation. You can't afford to forget your leakproof tent, warm sleeping-bag (even in July and August, the night temperature can drop below freezing), cooking stove, or high-energy foods – not forgetting your fishing tackle of course! A sturdy and reliable rucksack designed for hiking is essential for carrying all of your tackle. Your boots should be waterproof if possible, but more importantly, they should be comfortable. Lure and deadbait minnow fishing are always effective in high mountain lakes, but wet-fly-fishing with a bubble-float can be very handy during the middle of the day. Dry-fly-fishing, which requires a lot of re-casting, should be reserved for bank fishing in the mornings and evenings. Don't forget your camera! It is worth the extra weight on your back to capture the beautiful scenery and the spectacular catches!

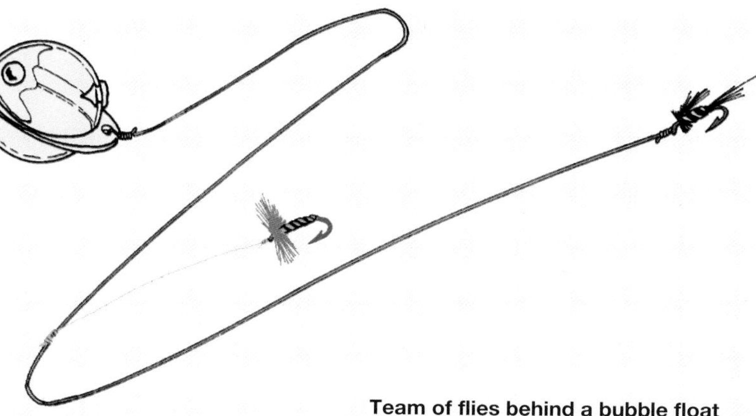

Team of flies behind a bubble float

On a mountain lake (Mercantour), summer storms can blow up quite suddenly. It's all part of the adventure. ▷

THE BEST TROUT STREAMS IN EUROPE

To list all the trout-fishing spots in Europe that are worth visiting would take a much heftier tome than this one! The following is a small selection of places where quality and size of trout are complemented by the beauty of the surroundings.

Game-fishing for trout and salmon is popular throughout the British Isles. Scotland is famous for its trout streams and salmon are to be had on the Tweed and the Tummel. In Ireland, the River Moy is famous for its salmon, where there are prize catches to be had. The lakes (loughs) of both Ireland and Northern Ireland are famous for their brown trout. Among the best-known are Emy Lough, White Lake and Milltown Lake, as well as Lough Nagarnaman in Castleblayney.

In England and Wales, trout rivers and streams abound, in all parts of the country. Perhaps the most picturesque are in the Chilterns and the River Wye on the Welsh borders.

In France, if you are after large brown trout, try the southeast, particularly the turquoise waters of the Verdon gorge in Provence. The coastal rivers of Brittany and Normandy are where sea-trout and salmon begin their journey.

Corsica is a little-known angling paradise where the native Macrostigma salmon *Salmo trutta macrostigma*, is to be found.

In Austria, the Teichel and Pielach are good trout rivers, as are the Soca and Sava in Slovenia. In Germany, the Wisent is famous for its brown trout.

△ *Fabulous mountain surroundings in Rizzanese, Corsica, where the sparkling mountain streams are home to a specific subspecies of trout, the* macrostigma.

Emerging nymphs or those mid-water which are aimed at trout feeding on the surface have fairly neutral coloring (beige, brown, red, etc.), large bodies, legs and wings (folded back or in an alar sac) made out of hair, feathers, or fibers. The gold-ribbed Hare's Ear and March Brown are excellent nymphs to use for visual nymph fishing. If you are making the nymphs yourself, whip them to the hook and finish them with a coat of odorless varnish such as metal varnish to give them a shine and ensure the trout will spot them.

Leaded nymphs in similar colors are sometimes more elaborate and obviously heavier, so they can drop to the bottom quite quickly. Water-flea and other imitations or a Pheasant Tail, which can look like anything from a damsel nymph to a large midge pupa, are very effective when fishing for trout at the bottom of a river. The same nymphs are also useful, of course, for deepwater nymph fishing when it is impossible to see the trout from the surface.

Finally, remember that when nymph fishing, you are pretending that your bait is an aquatic insect and fish accordingly.

The angler controls drift and manipulates the lure with tip movements. ▽

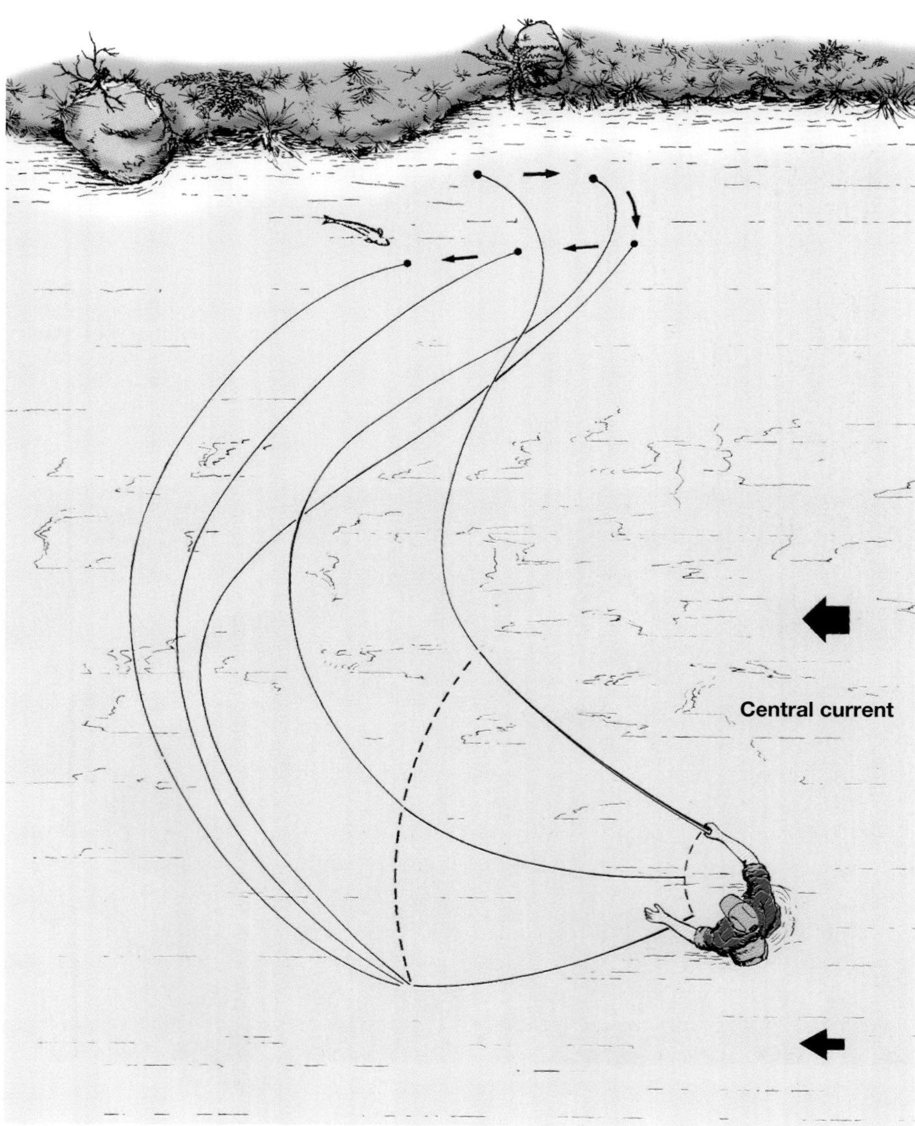

Rainbow Trout

*The rainbow trout (*Oncorhynchus mykiss*) is a real big-game fish, an unrivaled fighter that can make spectacular leaps out of the water. This American native is highly prized for the table, due to the flavor of its flesh, but it is also an extremely attractive fish due to the brilliance of its scales. The prospect of a wonderful "evening bite" involving a tussle on the lakeside also makes the rainbow trout a favorite game fish.*

A very distinctive fish, this rainbow trout was caught in a high-altitude lake, and has just been released back into its environment. Note that all its fins are intact, which means it is a truly wild rainbow. ▽

A Fighting Fish

The rainbow trout was introduced into Europe from its native habitat in the western coastal basins of the United States in the late 19th century and has had mixed fortunes ever since. Some countries which preferred quality to quantity took a lot of persuading before the rainbow trout was successfully introduced into their native waters. In most cases, this is a fish for farming, and rainbow trout are bred in great numbers for general consumption or to easily restock rivers or lakes. It has in fact become the favorite fish for the type of privately-owned waters on which angling has become more of a fair-ground attraction than a sport.

As a result, anglers are almost completely unaware of the rainbow trout's cautious nature, its beauty, and, above all, its magnificent fighting spirit.

Found Throughout Europe

The rainbow trout can now be found in the rivers and waterways of most European countries, from Italy to Austria to Scandinavia, from Spain to the British Isles. It has most recently been introduced into eastern Europe and Russia, where it is doing particularly well. A migrating rainbow trout known as the steelhead is found in Alaska, British Columbia and Argentina.

Aside from the artificially-bred products of fish farming, the rainbow trout, when introduced as fry, gives excellent results especially in mountain lakes and streams but also in well-oxygenated low-altitude rivers. The Sorgue in France has a healthy population.

Some French fishing associations, especially those in the Alps, have introduced rainbow trout fry into their local rivers and streams from the only natural breeding grounds in France, which occur in the Pyrenees. It remains to be seen how they will cope with the new environment.

A Well-Adapted Emigrant

Although the rainbow trout is in many ways similar to the brown trout, there are certain features that set the two species clearly apart. The rainbow trout has a longer body which is fairly high in proportion (equal to a quarter of its length) and its head is fairly small, with a wide mouth. Its silvery flanks have a middle band of pinkish-purple, and its back is generally a dark greenish-blue. The rainbow's body and dorsal and caudal fins are covered in small black spots, except on the underside, which is a pearly white. During reproduction or in fish over 4 years old, the operculum is a very luminous purple color, giving the rainbow trout an impression of being very powerful and lively.

• Power and Dynamism

Rainbow trout have similar behavioral patterns to brown trout, and are typically territorial. They can be found in mountain streams and lakes at high altitude as well as in low-lying rivers and ponds. Because they're more adaptable than other Salmonidae to fairly low levels of oxygen, rainbow trout can survive in water temperatures as high as 68°F (20°C).

Reservoirs

A reservoir can be either a natural or an artificial lake. It usually has very good quality water, in which Salmonidae can easily acclimatize.

Usually, fly-fishing is the only technique authorized on private reservoirs. Regulations often stipulate a very small number of daily catches and a minimum catch size, which usually means you have to immediately return any fish you catch to the water.

The rainbow trout, king of the reservoirs, adapts to these waters more easily than other trout or salmon. Its spectacular fighting spirit also makes it a favorite with game anglers.

Dry-fly-fishing is often overtaken by nymph or streamer fishing on reservoirs. The nymphs used are often copies of mayflies or caddis-flies, placed on no. 10-14 hooks. Streamers are much larger (mounted on long-shafted no. 1-5 hooks) with brightly-colored feather and hairs of synthetic material and should

be chosen for their mobility in the water. The best streamers are those which look like a small fish, but they often resemble no known living thing. Their purpose is to trigger the rainbow trout's aggressive instinct.

Experience shows that depth, reeling-in speed, and lure presentation are more important than the type of lure, as fish live at different levels depending upon the season or the time of day.

A change of family

The rainbow trout was previously classified in the Salmonidae family, like the brown trout and the Atlantic salmon and given the Latin name *Salmo gairdneri*. However, ichthyologists now place it in the *Oncorhynchus* genus, along with Pacific salmon. The shape, color, head, and jaw size resemble the Pacific salmon much more than the brown trout so it would make more sense to change its common name to "rainbow salmon". But by fishermen at least, it remains known as rainbow trout!

Nevertheless, this lively fish is at its best in Alpine lakes and hill or mountain streams (even above 7,300 ft (2,000 m)). The rainbow trout is less timid than the brown trout, and is constantly on the move, regularly changing habitats, even in a river. Thanks to the voracious appetite of the species, young rainbow trout grow very quickly.

In particularly rich waters, it is not unusual for rainbow trout fry 2½–2¾ in (6–7 cm) long to weigh more than 1kg after just three seasons. Several fish weighing more than 11 lb (5 kg) each are caught every year. A 22 lb (10 kg) monster was caught on the Roya, a river which runs from southern France into Italy. Our American friend will take insects, maggots, worms, small fish – anything within reason, as long as you fish on the surface or middle of the water. Unlike their brown cousins, rainbow trout rarely lurk in the depths.

• Spawning at 7,300 feet (2,000 m)

In North America, the rainbow trout reproduces from November through February, exactly like the brown trout, by burying its eggs (around 3,000 per kilogram (2¼ lb) of the female's bodyweight) in shallow gravel beds which are oxygenated by a fairly brisk current. Incubation is shorter than for the brown trout, about 310 degree-days (about two months in water of 41°F (5°C)). Sexual maturity is reached at the age of three in both sexes. In mainland Europe, rainbows only reproduce in mountain waters, often above 7,300 feet (2,000 m) altitude. Spawning generally takes place in June and July, especially in the mouths of rivers and streams or outlets on mountain lakes. That is what Pyrenees anglers witness every year and what can regularly be observed in the Alps, when having caught brightly colored males and females ready to release their eggs at the beginning of the summer near to tributaries on Mercantour lakes. However, it is difficult, if not impossible, to prove that this species is reproducing in the wild because of the continual restocking from fish-farms of young rainbow trout in European rivers and lakes.

• Incredible Acclimatization

The rainbow trout is faced with the same problems as the brown trout in most rivers and lakes (hydroelectric stations, silting-up of spawning grounds, limited migratory paths, pollution, etc.) but it is not aided by any wide-ranging acclimatization programs. In a few parts of France and the United Kingdom, attempts are being made to develop fish capable of reproducing, but in general, the rainbow trout in these countries remains a "starter" fish for the season, unloaded into the waters as an adult and easily caught in the days that follow.

However, acclimatization has succeeded in many other European countries including Austria, Slovenia, and Poland, and there's no reason why, with a little effort, the same shouldn't be achieved in western Europe too. By introducing young rainbow trout into mountain lakes fed by numerous rivers and streams as well as upper mountain rivers and streams, there's a good chance the rainbow trout will be able to reproduce in the wild in France, Spain, and the United Kingdom. By temporarily or permanently protecting these waters, the young trout or breeding pairs can then be electrically fished and used to extend the repopulation area of this species.

FISHING FOR RAINBOW TROUT

The rainbow trout's diet is as eclectic as the brown trout's, and so the fishing techniques are identical. Live bait, lures, deadbaits, and dry and wet flies are all perfectly suitable for hunting our American friend. However, rainbow trout in lakes at any altitude have adopted some strange habits and need to be studied carefully before using a particular fishing technique.

△ *Rainbow trout put up a fierce fight, which is all the more spectacular when they are caught by fly fishermen, as here on a reservoir.*

• Wet Fly Fishing in Lakes

During spring and summer, at the beginning and end of each day, but also in the middle of the day, mating intensifies and the rainbow trout spends most of its time feeding on the surface. While dry flies can often do the trick, with a wet fly, you're almost sure to get a take. If the banks give you enough room to move back, use a fairly sturdy 9–10 foot fly rod with a reel and a no. 6–7 silk attached to around 167 ft (50 m) of backing. If the banks are too steep or overgrown, use a bubble-float with a 10–12 foot (3–3.5 m) fixed-reel rod with a lure and a light casting rod with a 16 or 18/100 line. The bubble-float should be fixed to the end of the line and almost completely filled so it does not disturb the surface too much. The flies are then attached to very short traces (2¾–3¼ in (7–8 cm)) of very stiff nylon) so they stand well away from the main silk. The first fly should be attached about 40 inches (1 m) below the bubble float, and the second 2½ feet (0.8 m) below the first. With a whipped rod or bubble-float, reel in just below the surface, using irregular movements.

The slight choppiness created by the wind is a great aid to wet-fly-fishing on lakes. Artificial flies such as the palaretta, red-bodied blackfly, red-bodied redfly, flying ant, etc., can be very realistic but the rainbow trout is very quick to spot imitations, which are never perfect.

As a result, it is the more outlandish flies that generally prove their worth. Multicolored feathers and fabric, covered in silver or golden tinsel and

mounted on no. 8–10 hooks are used to create miniature salmon flies which are ideal for attracting the rainbow's curiosity and awakening its aggression. The lake-bound rainbow trout rarely stays in one place for very long, so it is essential to follow the trout as it swims so you can calculate your cast correctly.

Rainbow trout in any situation are much more prone to rise than brown trout and are far more active in their search for food, scavenging at all levels in their quest for flies, nymphs and even quite large fish.

A fish only 14 inches (35 cm) long can easily swallow a roach 3–4 inches (7.5–10 cm) long. Rainbow trout can become as predatory as pike, especially when they hunt in shoals and if their habitat is well-stocked with coarse fish. They have been seen to drive shoals of small fish, alevins or fry, into the shallows where they systematically devour their prey.

• Livebait Fishing

If you use a sliding float and shot on a trotting rig, you will soon witness first-hand the rainbow trout's incredible appetite for anything edible! The rainbow's other attraction is its tendency to feed near the surface. It is an opportunistic feeder and will happily swallow live and dead insects or feast on nymphs which are about to hatch, so nearly any kind of bait is suitable. The rainbow gives you the ideal opportunity to use both artificial flies and livebait, so forget those who swear the two should never be used together. You need a very simple rig consisting of a medium-sized bubble-float fixed to the end of a 16/100 line with a 2¾–3¼ in (7–8 cm) trace placed 40 inches (1 m) above it for the wet fly. Then use a 4-foot (1.2 m) strand of 14/100 line linked to a second bubble-float attachment, ending with a fairly thin no. 8–10 inverted hook. This long hook length, which does not use any shot, can hold a grasshopper, cricket, or horsefly on the surface.

The fishing technique involves casting along banksides, near shallows, and wherever activity can be discerned on the surface. As long as the insect floats on the surface, pull in the line with short jerks followed by long pauses, as rainbow trout move around very quickly and will soon snap up this appetizing morsel.

When the bait eventually sinks, reel in just as slowly but more irregularly. At this point, it is just as likely that your wet fly will attract the attention of the rainbow. Very often, the fly is rejected but a few seconds later, the bait is taken. Or it may occur the other way round.

If you are trotting along the straight-sided banks of deepwater rivers, the most attractive live bait may well be a grub or mealworm, which should also be used without shotting, and reeled in very slowly. Weather conditions are important when you are after rainbows. They seem to prefer overcast skies and will rise freely in high winds, even beneath the bows of a trolling angler's boat. Deadbait and live bait may well bring in a handsome rainbow trout. However, as with all game fishing, check first to ensure that bait fishing is allowed.

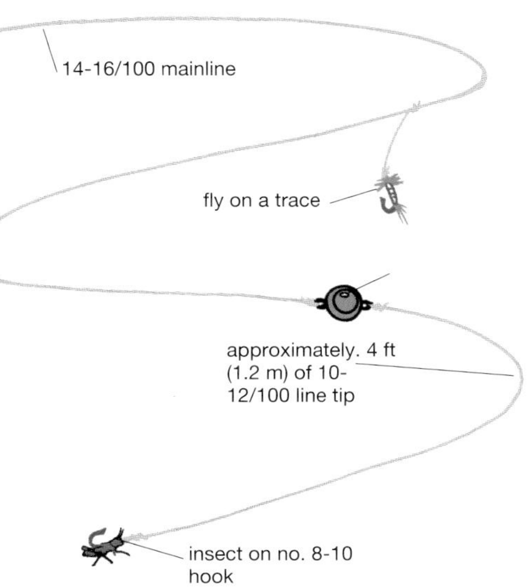

Mixed rig: wet fly and bait with bubble-float

The delicacy and sensitivity of fixed-reel angling have opened up a new world to natural bait anglers on lakes or shelved sections of large rivers.

Brook Char

This knight in shining armor of icy waters is the family glutton. Salvelinus fontinalis *seems to spend most of its time eating... and this is very often the cause of its downfall! It is not a very wary fish and is an easy prey for anglers. The brook char is also a major competitor of the trout, with which it shares the same diet and territorial behavior.*

A vermiculated blue-green back, pink and yellow spots on its flanks, white-fringed fins: the main identifying marks of a brook char. ▽

Stronger than the Rainbow Trout

This native North American char is often and wrongly called the brook salmon. Like the rainbow trout, it was imported into Europe at the end of the 19th century and it, too, has only occasionally adapted well to new environments. In France, with a few rare exceptions in Corsica, the Pyrenees and the Savoy, it remains a farmed fish which is introduced into the water as an adult and is intended to be fished immediately by novices and those anglers lacking in the patience which is the hallmark of the expert. However, given its incredible ability to survive in icy waters, at altitudes often unbearable for trout, over time this American char may well fill this vacant ecological niche.

A lover of cold waters

Apart from its native North America, the brook char is today present in the United Kingdom (almost exclusively in Scotland and Northern Ireland, where the water temperature conditions are right), Austria, Slovenia, Poland, and most other European countries. In France, it is mainly found in mountainous areas where, introduced at the young fish stage, it is generally very successful. In Corsica, for example, the brook char has flourished beyond all expectations and it has also successfully bred in the Alps and Pyrenees, to name but a few examples. It is an understatement, in fact, to say that the brook char develops particularly well in ice-cold waters. In the French Alps, young fish have been introduced into the upper reaches of mountain rivers, at altitudes of over 6,600 ft (2,000 m), where trout have difficulty surviving. Encouragingly, brook char remain in these high rivers, only rarely moving downstream, where they would almost certainly have to compete with brown trout. The brook char's natural reproduction cycle is even more sporadic than that of the rainbow

◁ *The brook char feeds on the bottom, in mid-water and also on the surface, depending on the amount of light, which controls its feeding habits.*

trout and up to now, only repeated introduction of young brook char has led to stable populations of the species.

THE TROUT'S VORACIOUS COUSIN

The brook char has a unique, though quite variable coloration, with its green or blue-green flanks splashed with yellow, pink, and white spots, and a darker and vermiculated back interlaced with clear wavy lines. It also has very characteristic orange fins fringed with white. The general body shape is much like that of the closely-related brown trout. The mouth is typical of a carnivore, in that it is very wide, with the corners well behind the eyes, which are large with a very narrow yellow iris.

• A Good Adaptor

The brook char is just as comfortable in rivers and streams as in lakes, and inhabits the same kinds of environment as the trout. It is a very active fish, and moves freely between the surface, mid-water, and the deep. While the brook char is very territorial in rivers, in lakes it is quite common to see small groups of brook char patroling the bankside or gathered below a small creek.

The brook char has an insatiable appetite for anything from nymphs at the bottom of a lake to minnows swimming in a river, or it will simply feed greedily at the surface on any sort of insect that happens to come its way. It has even been seen to swallow the entrails of a large trout that has only just been gutted – admittedly, with some difficulty and a great deal of effort!

• Extraordinary Development

On the rivers and streams of America and those European countries where it has flourished, the char spawns in the same way as trout, from October through February, and usually at night. The female reaches sexual maturity at 3 or 4 years (2–3 years for the male) and lays 1,500–2,000 eggs per kilogram (2 lb 4 oz) of bodyweight in shallow gravel beds which are well oxygenated. In these often icy waters, incubation can take up to 3 months. With its healthy appetite, the brook char develops very quickly in waters that contain plenty of food, and can reach weights of 2 lb 4 oz (1 kg) by its third year. The maximum size of brook char, in western Europe at least, doesn't appear to be very great, and specimens weighing 2 lb 4 oz (1 kg) are rare. Two brook char of more than 4 lb 8 oz (2 kg) were caught on Serre-Ponçon Lake in the High Alps, a wide mountain lake which is particularly rich in small fry. Recently, a 6 lb 8 oz (3.1 kg) brook char was caught using a deadbait minnow in Savoy, at an altitude of about 6,600 ft (2,000 m).

A fish that is easy to Catch

Like the rainbow trout, the introduction of too many adult brook char into foreign waters has lead to over-population which is not easy to manage. In mountainous regions, improved quality has been achieved by restocking with 2–3 inch (5–7 cm) alevins, although this has still not led to continued reproduction of the species in the wild.

The major problem for management of brook char is that they are so easy to catch. In most cases, regular re-introduction of young fish just about maintains useful population levels. By protecting small mountain lakes and the upper reaches of mountain rivers, which are usually ideal environments for the char, they could be left in peace to grow and reproduce, which would solve the problem. It would then be possible to remove some of these fish and use them to stock popular angling locations.

FISHING FOR BROOK CHAR

The brook char's voracious appetite makes it suitable for any technique used for catching Salmonidae. It will often come back to bite after one or two missed takes, making it an excellent customer, and one which almost impossible to scare away!

△ *During salmon spawning, brook char sometimes get together in great numbers on the spawning grounds to feast on the roe of the unfortunate migrating salmon.*

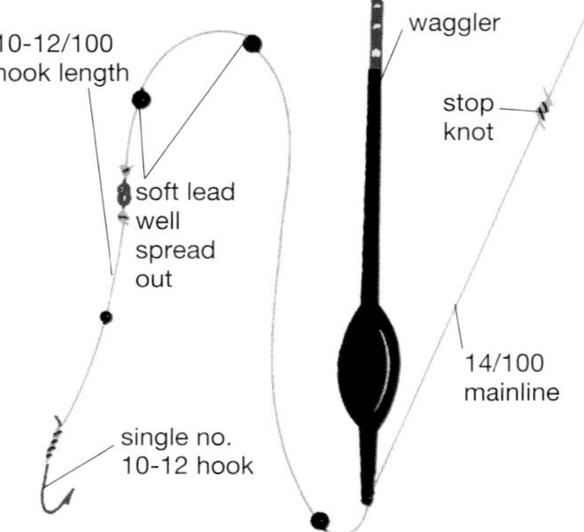

Trotting rig for floating line with live minnow

Brook char are strongly attracted to small fish. ▽

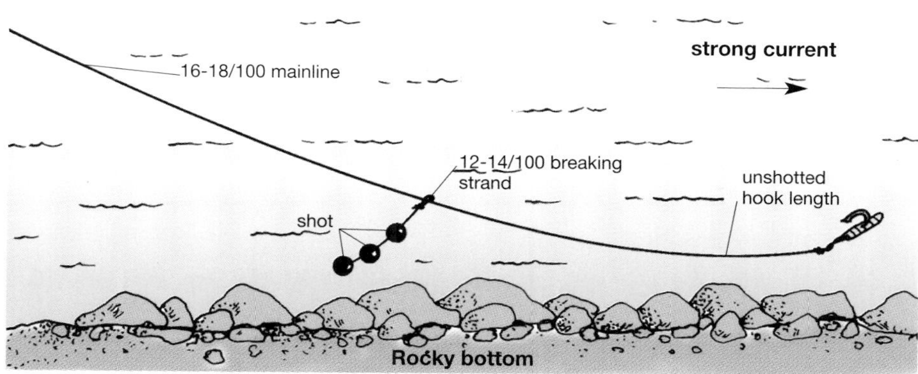

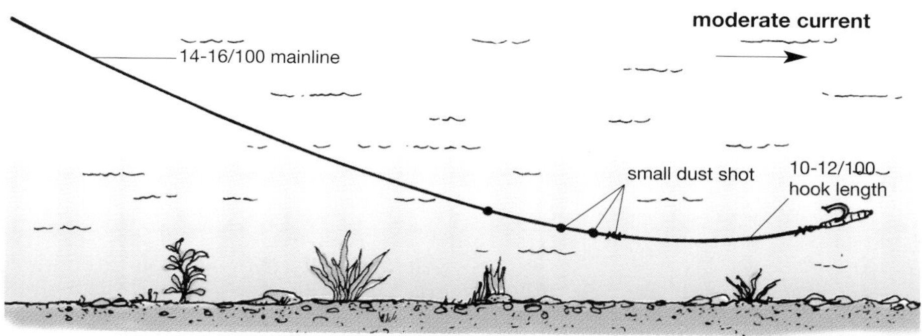

• Trotting on a River

The brook char is a particularly active fish, no matter whether it lives in still water or running water.

Unlike the brown trout, the brook char is not at all put off by water of only 34–35°F (5–6°C) which are to be found at the beginning of the season in lowland waterways, but which prevail year round at high altitudes.

In mountain rivers or streams with fairly exposed banks, go for a thin 13–16-foot (4–5 m) quivertip rod. Use a reel with a 16/100 line. For fast-flowing rivers, use a group of shot on a paternoster rig. Mount them on a breaking strand fixed above the hook length. If the shot gets snagged in stones on the river bed (a very common occurrence in mountain rivers with shingle beds), either the shot will fall off the strand, or the strand will break, without you having to reel your line back in. To save time, you should prepare five or six shotted strands beforehand and keep them in a satchel, so you can change them over if one does happen to break. This type of shotting, with a hook length that is not leaded, lets you present the hook naturally close to the bottom.

When the flow is slower, go back to a more spaced-out and lighter shotting of your line. This will give you a wider sweep, which suits the wandering char much better. Earthworms are the most suitable bait for fairly fast-flowing waters, and you can use them colored or fairly light. In clear and calmer water, a woodworm, grasshopper, or cricket will give excellent results.

Char are game fish, and so in many places fishing with live or dead bait is frowned upon and all that is permitted is dry-fly-, wet-fly-, or nymph fishing. Check out the rules before you start equipping yourself with the wrong tackle.

If you get a lot of bites which do not lead to catches, don't give up. Usually, all you need do is add a bit of weight to slow down the drift and persuade the char to bite more deeply.

Fish and... Release

If you are fishing on good char waters, play fair. Only keep a few fish per session and release the others, to give the char a chance to reproduce.

A catch of only one or two brook char is sufficient to take home. Let them grow up... and perhaps breed a few more healthy specimens! ▷

ARCTIC CHAR

*The Arctic char (*Salvelinus alpinus*), also known as the char or charr, is a relic from the last Ice Age and can be found in dark, deep lakes. It lives at depths of more than 130 ft (40 m) and very little is known about its habits. The Arctic char is also the only char which is native to France. Hiding from the light in caves and among roots, this voracious fish takes on a vibrant red livery when spawning. It can only be caught by using very specific fishing techniques.*

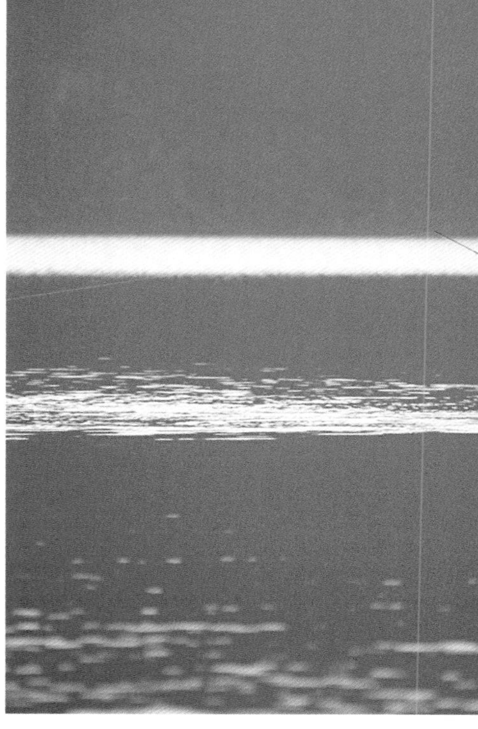

The Arctic char is often fished in all large lakes by dragnet. Here, a fisherman and friends trawl for char on Lake Pavin in Puy-de-Dôme in central France. ▷

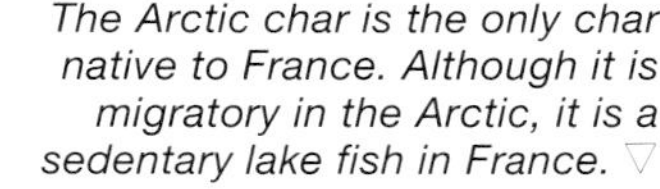

The Arctic char is the only char native to France. Although it is migratory in the Arctic, it is a sedentary lake fish in France. ▽

A VERY COLDWATER FISH

When the last glaciers of the Ice Age finally receded many thousands of years ago, some species of char – which must have been very numerous – became trapped in the Alpine lakes of Europe. These superb fish, which are considered a delicacy of the highest order in France and Switzerland, grew and flourished until the present day, where they are found only in particularly cold and well oxygenated waters, which offer conditions similar to those to which they have always been accustomed.

IN MOUNTAINOUS LAKES

Arctic char can be found in Russia, Siberia, Scandinavia, and Iceland. They also dwell in the arctic and subarctic waters of the United States, Canada and Northern Russia. In these waters, Arctic char are normally sea-dwelling, migrating up rivers in order to breed, like salmon. In the more southern parts of Europe however, they do not leave their freshwater habitat.

The Arctic char is also found in Ireland, Scotland, Switzerland, and Austria. The record catch in the United Kingdom is for a char caught in Loch Insh, Inverness-shire, Scotland in 1974 by a C. Imperiale which weighed 1 lb 12 oz (801 g), so despite their liveliness

and the fact that in France and Switzerland they are considered a great delicacy, the Arctic char does not grow to any great size.

In France, this coldwater fish is nearly always found in large mountain lakes, especially in the Alps. There are large populations in Lake Geneva, and Le Bourget, Aiguebelette and Serre-Ponçon lakes. French char are also found in Lake Pavin or the Tazenat gorge in the Massif Central. The introduction of alevins into high-altitude lakes such as Maurienne and Queyras has had disappointing results. The char is resistant and capable of reproducing but the introduced species appears to suffer from dwarfism and thus falls easy prey to other carnivorous fish.

△ *Returning a beautiful Arctic char to the Noatak River in Alaska. It has swum up from the Bering Sea.*

A Varied Species

The Arctic char, with its slim body, looks very similar to the brook char, a species introduced into Europe from North America, which is only native to the Northwestern United States but which looks very much like a trout, and is also a member of the Salmonidae family. However, given the number of subspecies (sometimes living in the same lake), only the commonest features of this fish are worth describing here. The flanks vary in color from one place to the next, but are generally blue-gray with small pale yellow spots. The back is green or dark olive, and the belly pinkish-white when not spawning. The pinkish fins are edged with white, like most char, and the caudal fin is darker and slightly jagged (the brook char's caudal fin is straight but the Arctic char's is very jagged). The head is usually small with a fairly wide mouth which is level with the eyes as in most predators.

During the spawning season the Arctic char comes into its own. Its flanks turn bright purple, and its belly and lower fins becoming orange or even red, highlighting the iridescent white border around them.

• Famous for its voracity

The lake-dwelling Arctic char found below the Arctic Circle in mountain lakes, nearly always dwells a depths of 73–133 feet (20–40 m), even deeper in cold and well oxygenated waters. Arctic char are fairly gregarious and dwell in large groups. Its diet consists mainly of larvae, shellfish, and mollusks living on the bottom. When it grows to a reasonable size, the Arctic char will happily turn cannibal, feeding on the younger and weaker members of its own group. This is another reason why restocking has so far proved to be unsuccessful.

• Mysterious reproduction habits

How the Arctic char reproduces in lakes remains a mystery. Only by catching brightly-colored breeders do we have any indication that spawning is taking place, or is about to commence. It appears that several colonies of Arctic char, inhabiting the same lake, will reproduce at different times of the year.

Spawning may take place in fall or in springtime. Hatcheries have been identified as generally being on beds of fairly large pebbles. The 3,000–4,000 eggs per kilogram (2¼ lb) of the female's body weight are laid among these uneven beds and immediately fertilized by the male. Incubation, which is often in waters of 34–36°F (4–5°C), takes 80–90 days.

The Arctic char's growth is directly linked to the amount of food in the environment, and thus varies greatly. Usually, it takes 6–8 years for an Arctic char to reach maturity, a size of 12–16 inches (40–50 cm). Similarly, the age at which it reaches sexual maturity varies depending on the environment, and can be anything between three and five years.

• Excellent adaptation to the environment

In the large lakes in which Arctic char dwell and flourish, fishing intensity does not seriously disturb this species, given the very spe-

North of the Arctic Circle, the char swims upriver in shoals to spawn. In this habitat, it will bite both flies and metal lures.

cialist techniques which the angler needs to use. Nearly every lake system seems to have one or more distinct subspecies of char which have developed to very precisely match their environment.
Reckless restocking with alevins is likely to be far less effective than farming local species which are genetically better adapted to survive in their environment. The same can be said with respect to introducing Arctic char into lakes which do not contain any at the moment. It seems that small lakes rarely make suitable homes for Arctic char. It is also important to ensure that the waters have high levels of plankton before they are stocked with these fish, otherwise they are likely to remain dwarfs. Arctic char from Lake Geneva seem the most popular choice for repopulating new lakes with alevins. For reproduction purposes, it seems that disused gravel pits offer the best conditions for the Arctic char. The pebbles on the beds of these artificial lakes are perfect hatching grounds for the char, and for once, gravel extraction actually does a species of fish some good! In fact, it may well be a good idea to add gravel to the beds of other lakes in an attempt to encourage the char to reproduce.

FISHING FOR ARCTIC CHAR

Except when the thermal layers are inverted and cold water rises to the surface while warmer water moves downward (a phenomenon which only occurs on a few days each year), the game fishing techniques employed for trout and salmon are unlikely to catch Arctic char.
Unless you are fishing on a bank with a very steep drop below, the only way to catch these deepwater fish is by trolling from a boat. However, trolling is not always permitted, so check the rules first.

• Spinning rigs for lake fishing

Although it is possible to fish for Arctic char from a boat using spinners or deadbait, you are better off opting for spinning with natural or live bait. This is a technique which, crucially, gives you total control over the depth of fishing. Whether fishing from a bank with an immediate drop (such as a cliff face, or scree on a steep slope) or from a boat, your first task is to determine the depth at which the fish are located.
Waggler floats with a single fixing point at the base of the shank are perfect for the job. In some cases, a sliding Chubber-type float with two fixing points will do just as well. Given that the fish are usually so far down, you will need to use floats that can support 4–5 g of lead, because a well shotted line will descend quickly to the required depth.
The fishing technique involves changing the stop-knot regulating the depth of fishing until you start getting bites. When the first bites come, you should note the exact spot at which you are fishing, as well as the season, time of day, and depth.
This information will be vital for future fishing sessions. For bait, try mealworms, larvae, water-fleas, and other small insects, not forgetting small fish, of course, because a live minnow will often attract a big char.

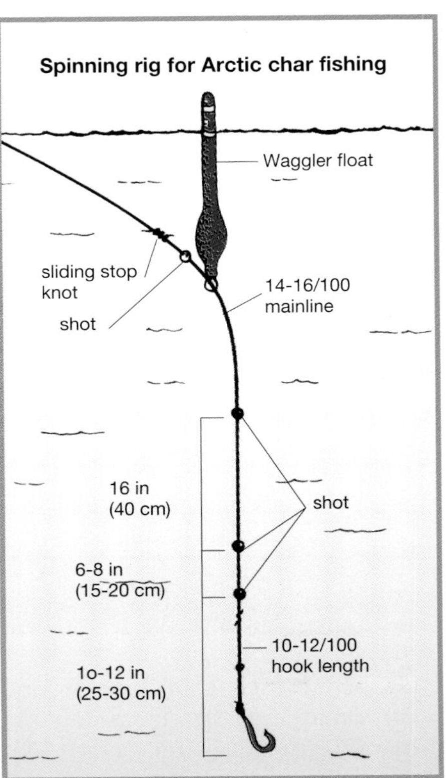

• Trolling on Large Lakes

On large Alpine lakes with heavy populations of char and trout, it is usual to fish for Arctic char using the dragnet method, the same technique as for lake-dwelling brown trout. Local fishing regulations generally permit this method.

Trolling is usually done from medium-sized boats, as storms are quite common on these miniature, inland seas. As the fish often live at depths of more than 100 ft (30 m), the technique involves using heavy sinkers which are dragged along fairly slowly. The sinkers, which are often homemade, weigh between 1 lb 12 oz and 3 lb 5 oz (0.8 and 1.5 kg) and are fixed to the bottom of a 70/100 or even 80/100 Dacron line. However, a wire braided line seems to be the most popular. Above the sinker, at intervals of 13–17 ft (4–5 m), the lures are attached to 30/100 nylon traces, each 10–13 feet (3–4 m) long.

Spinners and plugs are sometimes used, but spoons seem to be the most effective. These lures are carefully hand-crafted from thin sheets of alloy and decorated in gold and silver, pearlized, or painted a multitude of colors. Nowadays, faceted silver holographs are increasingly being used on spoons. The pirks and jigs introduced for sea-fishing are also becoming popular lures for game-fishing.

The major subject of discussion between anglers who practice spinning and trotting is how to make the spoon in exactly the right shape to enable it to swim through the water effectively and attract the fish lurking below. For example, many French anglers swear by spoons of their own making, while others travel as far as Switzerland to buy the famous Revelli lures. All would agree, however, that the key to success is finding the right depth at which to fish with your chosen lure. Indeed, the same goes for nearly every fishing technique!

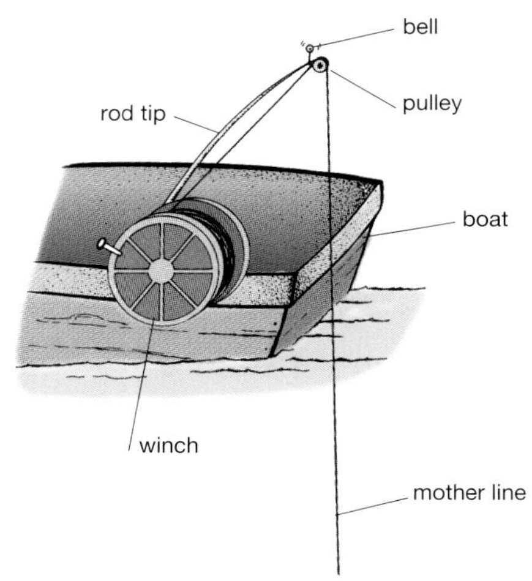

Winch for trolling

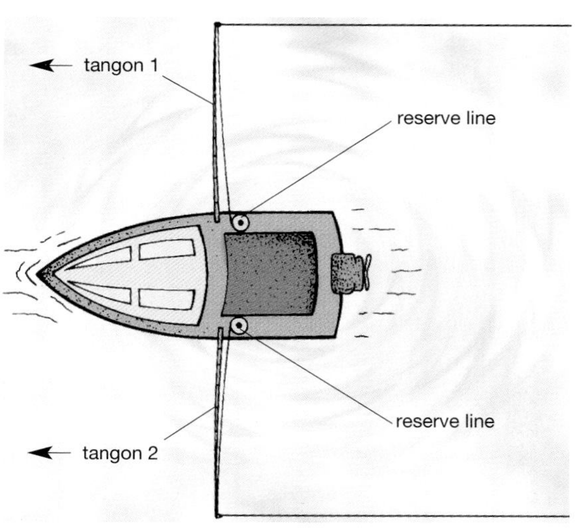

tangons for trolling (seen from above)

Boats setting off at dawn to go trolling on Serre-Ponçon Lake in the French Alps. ▷

GRAYLING

*There are those who claim that the Latin name for the grayling (*Thymallus thymallus*) refers to the smell of its flesh, which contains a subtle hint of thyme. The very special taste of a freshly fished grayling is due to one of its basic foods. It has a particular fondness for an insect which twirls around on the surface of the water and is known as a whirligig beetle. Whether from a culinary or angling point of view, the grayling is sure to get your juices flowing!*

A DIFFICULT FISH TO CLASSIFY

Biologists either class the grayling as a member of the salmonidae family or place it in a very different family, that of the thymallidae. Although the presence of an adipose fin could identify it as a salmonid, its sheath of large clearly visible scales and tiny mouth are more typical of a whitefish or char.

The grayling, especially the male, has a particularly large and prominent, flag-like dorsal fin, which has given the species the common name of "standard-bearer" in some languages.

The fin is used by the male to sweep its sperm over the eggs laid by the female. Spawning takes place in powerful currents, so the sperm needs to be waved into the right place and prevented from dispersing too rapidly into the fast-flowing waters.

MARKING A SPECIFIC AREA

The French ichthyologist Huet has identified four distinct areas of any type of water which are based on specific physical characteristics – type of substrate, current speed, oxygen levels, and so on, which can be classified as zones inhabited by particular species of game fish and coarse fish.

The zone furthest upstream is defined as a trout zone. The water is cold, fast-flowing, and rich in oxygen. The area furthest downstream is defined as a bream zone. It has slow-moving currents, deep pools, and watery hides which are rich in plantlife. This is a favorite habitat of whitefish and similar carnivores.

The grayling zone is in the intermediate section. It is characterized by a succession of currents, wide channels of smooth-running water, gravel pits, and pools where the bottom consists of stones, rocks, or gravel – essential for the bottom-loving grayling.

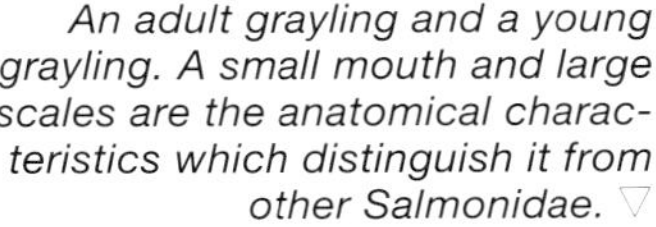

An adult grayling and a young grayling. A small mouth and large scales are the anatomical characteristics which distinguish it from other Salmonidae. ▽

How the grayling feeds

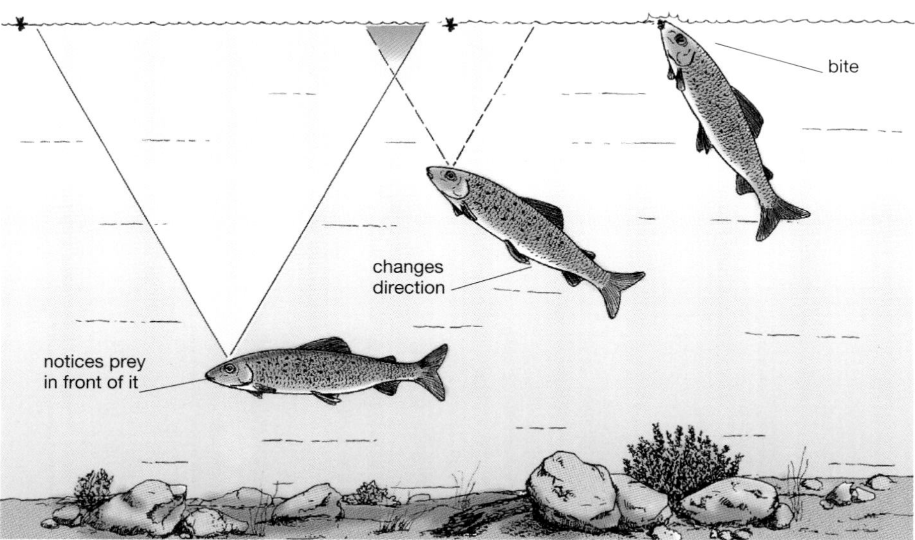

The grayling inhabits different zones depending on the season. In summer and midwinter, to escape the extremes of the weather or low oxygen levels, the grayling tends to favor the murky depths of hollows, gravel-pits, and deep pools. In spring and fall, it hunts in wide, clear waterways which are rich in plantlife and have cool, clear-running currents.

Above all, the grayling cannot withstand pollution and that is why this once-common freshwater fish has become something of a rarity.

An Opportunistic Predator

The grayling spends much of its time feeding near the bottom or in mid-water for small drifting invertebrates of all types. Its particularly narrow mouth and physical constitution are designed for this kind of diet.

In rivers where it is regularly fished (such as the Sorgues, in France or in the Tay and Tweed, in Scotland), it sticks obstinately to the bottom of pools, refusing to feed for insects at the surface throughout the fishing season. When spawning in fall or winter, and when the river banks are devoid of fishermen, it swims up to the surface to feed on insects as they drift downstream. As a result, this fish bites as late as December or January.

Spawning in Springtime

Unlike trout and salmon, which reproduce in late fall or during winter, grayling spawn in springtime, from March through May, depending on the water temperature. The grayling will only lay eggs in beds of pebbles and gravel. Each female lays 2,000–3,000 eggs per kilogram (2 lb 4 oz) of her bodyweight. The eggs are incubated for around three weeks in a temperature of 50°F (10°C).

The Arctic grayling (Thymallus arcticus)

The Arctic grayling is physically and behaviorally very similar to the grayling, and lives in great numbers in the waters of North America. The two types of fish are often mistaken for each other. The Arctic grayling found in Norway and Finland belong to our native species and not the American one.

The Arctic grayling distinguishes itself from its European cousin by its far more varied diet. Its small mouth does not prevent it from being an unrelenting predator of young trout, salmon, or whitefish. It rarely ingests insects and this is because, apart from mosquitoes, at this latitude insects are few and far between. The Arctic grayling is a fearsome hunter, but it is not particularly territorial, since it often swims in shoals of several dozen specimens. The male wears an impressive bronze armor of small scales, with bluish and blackish spots on its flanks.

During breeding, the dorsal fin is brightened with many golden patches. The Arctic grayling's opportunistic feeding patterns make it a good bet for anglers, who can fish for it with live bait as well as wet and dry flies, or even an ultra-light cast. It is a superb fighter, and its flesh has a delicious hint of thyme, like its cousin in the warmer waters. In the fishing camps of the Great North, on both sides of the Atlantic, broiled grayling is a favorite dish of the day at many waterside inns.

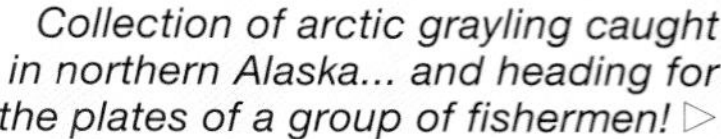
Collection of arctic grayling caught in northern Alaska... and heading for the plates of a group of fishermen! ▷

LIVEBAIT FISHING

In expert hands, livebait fishing for grayling can be just as effective as artificial fly-fishing, despite the claims of fly-fisherman that livebait is somehow beneath the grayling. The technique involves presenting examples of the grayling's usual diet, especially small insect larvae and caddis-flies, mayflies, freshwater shrimp, crawfish, and water-fleas.

This very delicate fishing technique will require an extremely sensitive touch and lightning reflexes, but it is the best way of catching grayling.

True specialists know to take only their fair share of these fish and not follow the example of the greedy fishermen who plunder our rivers.

Tackle depends not only on the conditions but also on personal preference. Although a trotting rod is fine, real experts opt for a 13 foot (3.9 m) fixed spool rod with a small reel that is used only as a line reserve. A Vivarelli-type reel will do just as well. The bobbin holds 167 feet (50 m) of 12/100, a thin line being necessary to fool what is a particularly fussy fish. You should go for fluorescent nylon so you can see the slightest take.

The rig includes a small barrel swivel followed by a 20 inch (50 cm) 10/100 line with a thin iron no. 12–16, long-shafted hook, depending on the type of bait used. The best bait are grubs, woodworms, water-fleas, and even a small earthworm for muddy water.

Another reason for using a thin line is that it is less likely to get carried away with the current, giving the bait a more natural drift.

The shotting should be light and very soft so that it does not stop the bait from drifting.

• Fishing Technique

You need lots of practice and eyes like a hawk! The idea is to control drift so the bait is always floating just above the bottom.

To do this, the rod gently brushes the current. You must get used to always having the nylon in a straight line from the tip of the rod. If your arm doesn't follow the drift of the line, the bait lifts from the bottom and becomes useless. It's very important to remember that you need to pay very close attention because you won't ever get a familiar bite. Instead, you'll see your line move slightly (which is why a fluorescent one is recommended) and you should respond with a supple strike.

FISHING WITH NYMPHS

Together with natural bait fishing, nymphs have become one of the most popular techniques for fishing for grayling. This type of fishing requires a great deal of concentration and can only really be practiced in crystal clear water, which is why it is generally only used in a few clear streams in the highlands of Scotland, or in the foothills of the Alps. Nymphs are

Such clear water is obviously ideal for nymph fishing. ▽

designed to resemble the larvae of aquatic insects on which the grayling generally feeds. They are often leaded and made in pale colors. The tackle includes a classic 5–9 foot fly rod with a no. 3–4 weight-forward silk, finished off with 17–23 foot (5–7 m) of 10/100. Other accessories, to cut down on reflection from the water's surface, include a large-peaked cap and polarized sunglasses. The technique involves casting far upstream of the fish you are after, so that by the time the nymph reaches the area of water occupied by the fish, it is at the correct level. As soon as the fish appears to be the fish, strike without delay!

DRY-FLY-FISHING

The grayling has become very fussy and wary of fishermen and it is more and more difficult to tempt it with dry flies, except during the fall or occasionally in the evening.

Basic tackle includes a 9 foot quivertip rod with a manual reel and a floating no. 3 or 4 double-taper or weight-forward silk. For a perfect drift, the line tip should be very long, at least 16 feet 6 in (5 m) and up to 23 feet 6 in (7 m) for very fussy fish.

Grayling flies are part classic dry-fly, part wet-fly. They are "emergents", with very little plumage. Most are on small (no. 16–20) hooks. One of the great classics is the Peute de Bresson, or all DA-type flies.

Fishing technique consists of casting upstream of observed feeding areas, and presenting the fly in a zig-zag motion across the current to limit drag. The drift should be impeccable. If the grayling has not noticed anything untoward, it will move up to the surface to seize your fly. Once the bait has been swallowed, you should strike immediately.

△ *This young angler should be very proud of his catch from a fly-fishing session.*

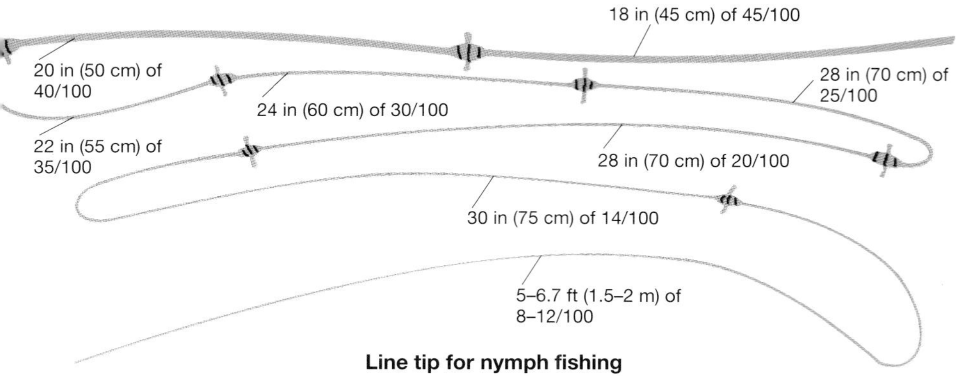

Line tip for nymph fishing

Whitefish

*Having retreated to cold water rich in oxygen and plankton during the last Ice Age, European whitefish can usually only be found in large deep lakes. The whitefish remains one of the least-known freshwater fish. In some Canadian and Alaskan rivers, there is a giant whitefish (*Stenodus leuchthys*) which is actually called "inconnu" (meaning "unknown") and which is said to reach sizes of 90 lb (40 kg) – a legendary fish which is revered by American fishermen and women.*

With its steely coloration and small scales, tiny mouth, and jagged tail, the whitefish is an usual species. ▽

The identity of the Mysterious Whitefish

The pollan (*Coregonus lavaretus*), and vendace (*Coregonus albula*) as well as the houting (*Coregonus oxyrinchus*) are all types of whitefish. This genus used to be classified in the salmonidae family because they have an adipose fin, but have now been brought into the Coregonidae family, the char family.

Species of whitefish are present in Russia, in the lakes of the upper Volga, in Norway and in several other European countries (Germany, Scotland, France, Ireland, Switzerland). There is even a migrating whitefish in some Alaskan rivers such as the Kobuk which can reach weights of more than 22 lb (10 kg) and are known as the "inconnu" (French for "unknown"). Lake whitefish are a great delicacy in the United States, as highly prized as the native sturgeon.

The common whitefish is well represented in Europe in the large Alpine lakes of Neuchâtel, Geneva, Aiguebelette, and Bourget and it is also found in Scandinavia and northern Russia.

Because of the large number of subspecies and frequent hybridization, it is very hard to distinguish between the various species of true whitefish. The family includes the Cisco, Peled, Houting, Arctic Whitefish, and Broad Whitefish.

A typical whitefish has a fairly long body completely covered in small shiny scales. The fairly small head is slightly rounded and downward pointed in the pollan, but pointed and prognathous in the vendace. The pale yellow eyes are very large, almost disproportionately so. The grayish fins are also quite large, especially the caudal fin, which is wide and very serrated.

Whitefish remain a mystery because they live in very deep water and only rarely come up to the surface. Whitefish are almost totally dependent on icy waters containing large reserves of plankton, seeming to prefer temperatures of 43–48°F (6–9°C), which is nearly always equivalent to a depth of 133–267 feet (40–80 m).

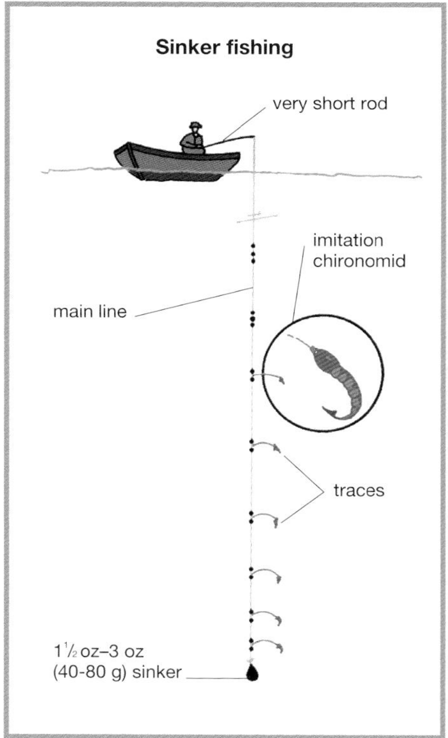

Although whitefish are caught commercially, whitefish angling requires techniques and tackle adapted specifically for the purpose. This denizen of the deep is rarely caught by accident.

SINKER FISHING

• A boat is essential for fishing the bottom

Sinker fishing cannot be done from the shore. The idea is to present artificial larvae like the ones whitefish feast on daily. A fairly heavy sinker is attached to the bottom of the line, while several nymphs are placed at stages along the line on separate traces. Indicators attached to the mainline allow the angler to see at exactly which depth he is fishing.

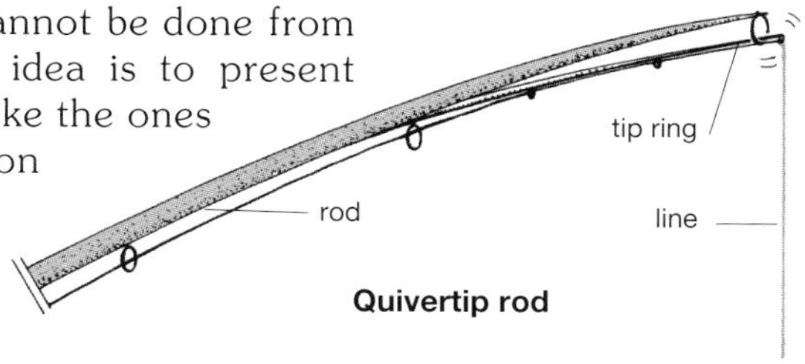

• Two Effective Techniques

There are two commonly-used methods for this type of fishing.

The first method involves holding the line in your hand then, once the line is steady and drops directly beneath the boat, constantly and slowly waggling the nymph up and down by up to 4 feet (2 m).

The second method involves using a fairly stiff rod, to which is attached a very sensitive rod-tip, one which responds to the slightest touch.

tip ring
rod
line
Quivertip rod

Whichever type of tackle you choose, you must strike at the slightest take because whitefish are quick to spit out an artificial lure. You need to be very persistent with this sort of angling, but sinker fishing is certainly the most reliable way of catching whitefish. When several anglers are fishing the water at the same time, as so often happens when fishing from a boat, it is a good idea for each angler to try different depths simultaneously using different baits.

Large, cold, deep lakes are the whitefish's favorite habitat. ▽

SALMON

THE TACKLE

△ This fly rod with a combat handle is ideal for fishing grylse.

According to Hugh Falkus, the famous British angling writer, salmon fishing was first mentioned in 1496, in the "Practical Treatise on Fishing", the first book ever printed in English. It says, "Salmon is the most important fish which man may catch in fresh water. You can catch it with an artificial fly when it leaps, in the same manner as one would capture a trout or grayling".

The red salmon has a reputation for not taking well, but it does go for flies if the drift is slow enough. ▽

BASIC TACKLE

Hugh Falkus, the notable British angler and author on angling, claims that the fishing rods of those days were very rudimentary. The base of the rod was made in two parts from hazel, willow or mountain-ash. It was as thick as a man's arm and up to 10 feet (3 m) long. The tip also consisted of two parts, the first of hazel wood, which was lashed to a 7 foot (2 m) length of blackthorn, crab-apple, or juniper. Once it was all fitted together, the rod might be as long as 18 feet (5.5 m). The line attached to the tip was made of horsehair. The first bamboo rods appeared in the early 19th century and reached their peak of popularity at the end of the Victorian era. Then there were the superb split cane rods, and finally the modern ultra-light fiberglass and carbon rods.

FLY- OR ROD-AND-REEL FISHING: SPECIALIST TACKLE

• Fly-fishing rods

You need to choose your rod not on the basis of the size of fish to be caught but based on the angling technique you are going to use, the type of lure and length of cast. Early in the year and during the intervening season, salmon will lurk near the bottom, whether they are Atlantic or Pacific varieties. As a result, you need to use wet flies, streamers, or tube-flies. To cast these fairly heavy lures, the ideal solution is a two-handed rod, as it gives you a longer cast, allows you to control drift more efficiently and handle the fish better when you've got a catch. Moreover, two-handed rods let you work the fly for hours without wearing out your arms and they help with spey-casting, which prevents mis-casts. The rods come in different sizes, in lengths of 12 through 15 feet, but they are the best multi-purpose rods available. Many American anglers, on the other hand, prefer short, one-handed rods. They may seem like a handicap when faced with a large fish, but the American minimalist fishing technique is probably due to the fact that their

△ Purple Shrimp (Ireland, Suir).

rivers are far more abundant in fish than their European counterparts. We would perhaps use a one-handed rod for catching small summer salmon or grilses, which happily snap at sedges bobbing along the surface. In that case, use a 9 ft 6 in to 10 ft 5 in rod with a no. 7 or 8 line.

△ *Monroe Killer (Spey River).*

• Spinning Rods

When going for larger fish, quality and strength are essential. In this case, go for a solid rod with a screw-on reel seat with a $\frac{3}{4}$–$1\frac{1}{2}$ oz or 1–$2\frac{1}{4}$ oz (20–40 or 30–60 g)

◁ *Cybele: the traditional spoon of the Allier.*

capacity. If you are fishing for summer salmon, which are rarely larger than 4 lb 8 oz (2 kg), you can go for a much lighter set-up, with a 1–3 g capacity, for example.

• Fly Reels

Reels were first mentioned in Thomas Barker's book, "*The Art of Angling,*" published in 1651. The unknown angler who first attached a reel to a rod with rings undoubtedly took the most momentous step in the history of angling.

From that time on, it was possible to catch larger fish much more safely, and salmon fishing took on another dimension, becoming a true sport. Manual reels are still the best, and you should only go for quality

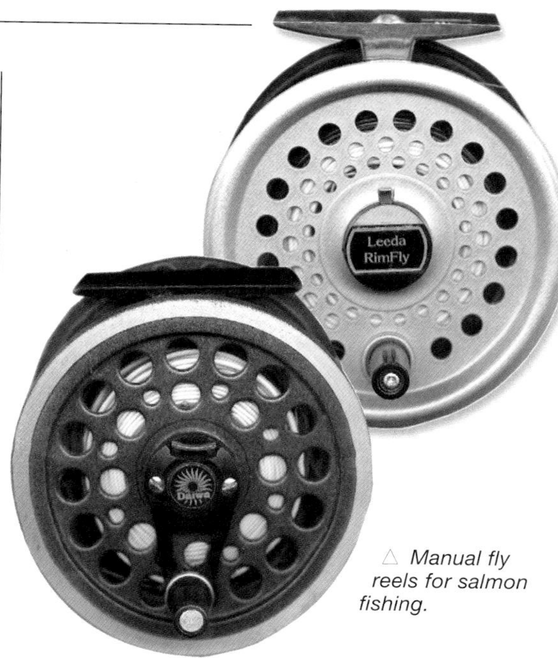

△ *Manual fly reels for salmon fishing.*

makes; the clutch, in particular, has to work faultlessly. In addition to the silk, the reel should hold 333 to 500 feet (100 to 150 m) of backing. The best reels are British makes such as Hardy, whose Hardy Marquis no. 2 (for two-handed rods) and Hardy Perfect Salmon (for single-handed rods) have a particularly high reputation.

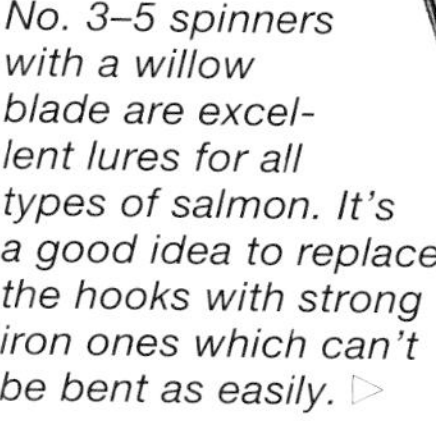

No. 3–5 spinners with a willow blade are excellent lures for all types of salmon. It's a good idea to replace the hooks with strong iron ones which can't be bent as easily. ▷

• Spinning Reels

There is a much greater range of spinning reels than of fly reels, and these are made in various countries. All are of good quality and reasonably priced. Yet again, it is resilience, clutch quality, and good reeling-in speed which count. Although most spinning reels used in Europe are fixed-spool, the Americans prefer spinning spools. In any case, the spool should hold 667 ft (200 m) of 50/100 line.

These silver salmon were caught with highly-colored flies. ▽

• Silks

Each type of rod requires a different type of silk, ranging from a no. 3 diameter (the thinnest type of line) to a no. 12 (heavy silks with the thickest diameter). In most cases, silks for salmon fishing are no. 7–8 (sometimes 9) for one-handed rods, 8 or 9 for 12-foot two-handed rods, and 10, 11, or 12 for 14-foot two-handed rods or longer. However, you sometimes have to "load" the silks. In the case of American rods (Orvis, Sage, etc.), you will get a better action by using a line with a

△ A spinning reel needs a clutch in perfect working order when salmon fishing.

diameter number higher than that given on the rod.

The use of the silk depends upon the type of fishing and the depth being fished. Seasoned salmon anglers usually have several reels or reels with interchangeable spools containing three types of silk:

– a floating line for dry-fly-fishing or fishing the shallows;
– a sinking-tip line for intermediate depths, the standard line used by most salmon anglers;
– a sinking line, used for deep water or slow-flowing pools at the beginning of the season.

For dry-fly-fishing, with a one-handed rod, it is better to use a double-taper line. Sinking tip lines on two-handed rods are generally "weight-forward" silks.

△ King salmon streamer.

• Backing

Backing consists of a Dacron line with 30 lb capacity tied after the silk. It is important when battling with a large fish which can easily swim off with all the silk in a fast current. Use 333–500 ft (100–150 m) of backing depending on the spool's capacity.

• Terminal Tackle

The line end should be short (5–7 ft (1.5–2 m)) for fishing close to the bottom. Making a rat's-tail line end is not necessary if you are using large tube-flies or streamers.

– Making up the line end

At the beginning of the season, if you're fishing near to the bottom or looking for king salmon, a very short line tip (7–8 ft (2–2.5 m)) on a single strand is all you need, as this will

The traditional Allier fly, which has been a hit on rivers across the world. ▷

allow you to present the fly at the desired depth. The tip diameter depends on the expected size of fish or the size of the fly. A large king salmon fly, for example, will only swim properly if fixed to a 45/100 or 50/100, while a smaller fly sitting under the surface on a greased line should be fixed to a 28–30/100 line end so it drifts unhindered. When fishing fast shallow waters with a floating line, many fly-fishing experts prefer a rat's-tail line end of decreasing diameter.

Fishing With a Well-Hooked Lobworm

The earthworm is a bait which is used by nearly all salmon anglers, except in the United States, where it is usually not permitted and France, where for reasons which are quite beyond us, anglers have never liked using it, even in mountain streams and on the Allier.

• The Gardener's Fly

This term is used for the lobworm or earthworm, which is prohibited on some waterways, simply because it is the most attractive bait for tempting a salmon when the river is in spate, at a time when all other lures or bait are useless. Lobworms are also useful in other circumstances, at the start of the season, for example, when the fish cannot yet be tempted to swim a few yards to grab a lure, or during the summer months, when salmon

A plus is an excellent salmon lure. ▷

DEVONS AND PLUGS

The traditional large brass winged devon, with its red- and black-striped sheath, has for a long time been the basic lure for anglers in opening waters, which are cold and at high altitudes, and large rivers like the Allier in France or the Tweed in Scotland, or even mountain streams.

It is certainly one of the few lures that can be used in fast-flowing water, as its weight (½-1½ oz (15–40 g)) and density mean that it does not need any shotting for it to reach the bottom. Nor does it need the angler to make any particular movement, apart from a few pulls and releases.

Pragmatic Irish anglers use devons made out of tractor tyre valves, ground down into a perfectly streamlined shape. These "leather eels" are 2–3¼ in (5–8 cm) long.

Devon fishing is similar to metal lure fishing, with even more emphasis on fishing downstream and leaving the lure to work away on its own without any reeling in.

In a sufficiently strong current, the devon will naturally move in an arc toward the bank on which the angler is standing. Once it reaches the bank, the lure should be reeled in slowly, keeping it close to the bottom, and varying the reeling-in speed. It is sometimes at this very moment that the salmon decides to bite!

△ *Brass devons, one with a traditional sheath.*

◁ *Salmon caught using a devon.*

reside at the bottom of deep underwater clefts. Worm fishing is unusual in that, even when fishing on American rivers, the bait will even manage to interest a fish which in theory never feeds in fresh water! This is yet another mysterious salmon behavioral trait which never fails to surprise!

Scottish anglers believe fishing with worms is a technique which doesn't traumatize the fish, or at least disturbs them less than using metal lures, such as the devon, in pools. Worm fishing in Scotland is permitted during periods of spate on some waterways which are otherwise exclusively reserved for fly-fishing.

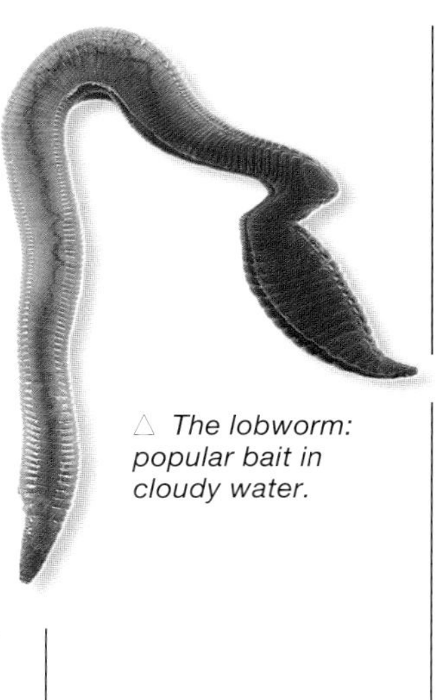

△ *The lobworm: popular bait in cloudy water.*

15-foot 2-handed rod: a rod for all seasons! ▽

• Rods

Some anglers rightly choose to use English-style carp rods. Their combat handles give precise drift control and are excellent for doing battle with a large, powerful fish. This big, 15 foot (4.5 m) rod is more classic but can sometimes seem a little heavy.

Fly-fishermen in Europe prefer to use 15–18 foot two-handed rods, which are perfectly balanced for the job.

• Reels

The fixed-spool reel (preferably a lightweight graphite type) should hold 670 feet (200 m) of nylon of a thickness depending on the size of the fish which are believed to populate the river. On rivers in Britanny, for example, a good 35/100 should do, but if you come across 33¾–45 lb (15–20 kg) salmon like those encountered on the Kola peninsula in Norway or in Iceland, you'd be better off with a 45-55/100 line.

△ A good control of drift, near the bottom, is essential for success.

• The Rig

Use a 5 foot (1.5 m) hook length attached to the mainline with a JB swivel of a good size. Only JB swivels are really reliable when dealing with very large specimens. If fishing deep water, you can add shot directly to the mainline. Use a small olivette on the swivel knot, protected by a silicon tube if necessary. When the riverbed is cluttered with tree stumps or contains a lot of large stones, you should use a paternoster rig with a bunch of shot pinched onto a breaking strand. Several types of hooks are suitable, including a solid little treble decorated with a cluster of worms wriggling like a little octopus, or a large single no. 1 or no. 2 hook. Some anglers prefer the Stewart rig, which includes two hooks, one no. 1 or no. 2 hook at the tip and another hook, such as a no. 4, for example, 2 inches (5 cm) above it. This rig gives better presentation and is more flexible. The bait is held more solidly and there are fewer missed takes. When rivers are in spate, the Irish and Norwegians use very heavy rigs for fishing a position. They fish in the deep hollows or clefts immediately downstream of waterfalls which salmon try to leap. This technique is used in summer especially, in small coastal rivers. Fish swimming in estuaries while they await a strong enough current try to rush upstream, and it is then that they will take a worm bait.

Lobworm cluster on a Stewart rig

The shot is placed on a breaking wire paternoster-style. ▽

A WELL-PRESENTED BOUQUET OF SHRIMP

Few other types of bait incite as much interest or aggression as the shrimp. That is why it is often banned in the United Kingdom, Ireland, and Alaska. Bait-fishing with crustaceans is forbidden on all waterways frequented by Pacific salmon. The fact that the shrimp always interests salmon is one thing, but whether it makes the salmon bite is quite another!

In a pool full of salmon, a shrimp often provokes unexpected reactions. The salmon begin by becoming excited by the sight of the shrimp and leap out of the water, only to completely empty the pool in a movement of complete panic!
That said, in midsummer, when water temperature climbs above 59°F (15°C), using shrimp as bait can be one of the best ways of catching a large salmon swimming in the semi-darkness in an area of deep water, or lurking in a cleft or crevice.

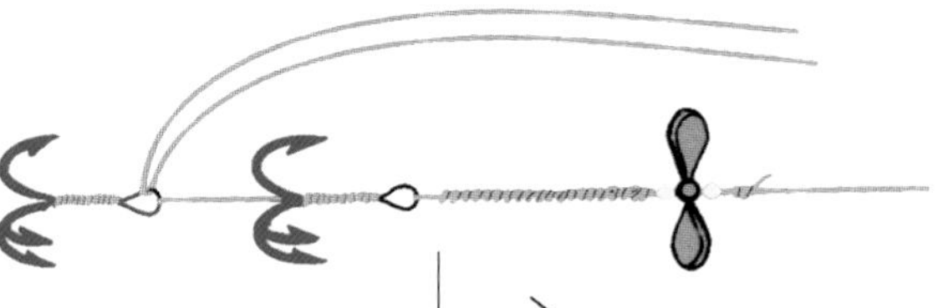

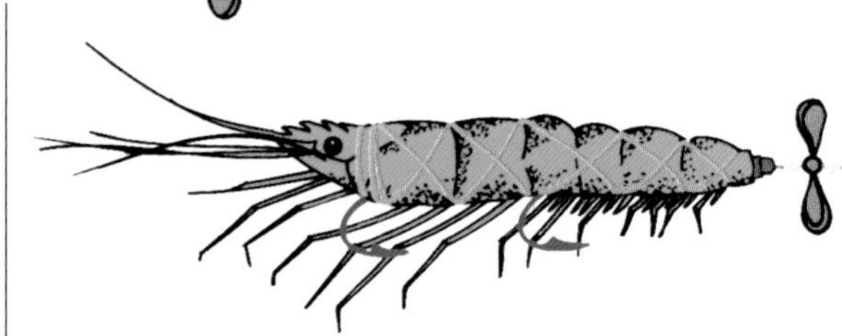

△ *The Big-Big, a small vibrating spinner can make the shrimp look even more attractive to a salmon.*

• Rod-and-Reel Fishing
A classic casting rod is fine, but it can be too stiff for casting and handling this fragile bait. Make the most of modern material and use a long English-style carp rod (13 ft (3.9 m)) with a fairly soft tip action, which will be perfect for fishing with prawn, or a rod intended for dead fish angling for pike. This obviously all depends on the size of fish you observe. The fixed-spool reel is loaded with 28–40/100 nylon, or even 45/100, again depending on the expected size of catch and surrounding obstacles.

• The Best Rigs
When fishing for salmon which have just swum back upstream, some British anglers use a floating line with large sliding wagglers. Others fish the swim with the shrimp immobilized on the bottom with an appropriate lead. The most traditional technique is the maneuvered deadbait technique. For this, the crustacean is fixed to an appropriate rig and then slowly worked, close to the bottom, in the same way as a dead minnow or other small fish.
Use several different species of shrimp, depending on the time of year, but remember that this technique is largely reserved for the summer season. From May through June, when water temperatures do not rise much higher than 54°F (12°C) and flow is normal, nothing is better than a large bouquet of cooked shrimp. Later on in the season, you're better off using small crustaceans like gray shrimp (bay shrimp) or a cluster of bay shrimp. When fly-fishing, use a "fly" that looks like these crustaceans.
Irish and Scots anglers color their shrimp to suit the atmospheric conditions, a precaution which is also taken by fly-fishermen, who abide by the same rule. They use dark colors such as purple and navy blue in overcast weather, pale colors such as pink and orange on sunny days. The color will also vary depending on the watery habitat – red in deep hollows, mauve or lilac in clear water.

Working a shrimp in a hollow

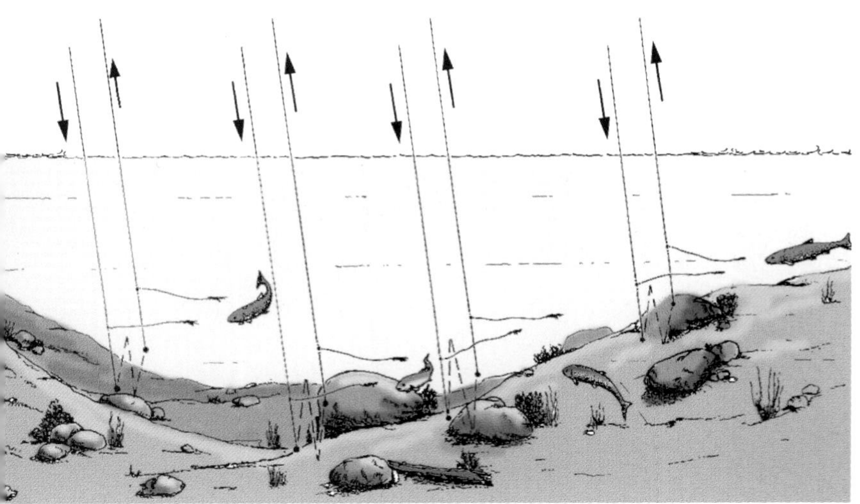

SUCCESSFUL FISHING TECHNIQUE

Salmon are often fished in hollows or pools, at the foot of waterfalls, where dark eddies lie alongside rocky falls, and near caves which are sometimes 33 ft (10 m) deep and regularly frequented by large salmon. Cast carefully so that the fragile bait is not damaged, and let it sink. As soon as it hits the bottom, move the bait around, up and down, like a tin fish. Strike as soon as you get a take, small or large.
In a typically wide, deep pool, cast straight across or slightly upstream, then reel in as slowly as possible, as for an impact-shielded deadbait minnow, with irregular quick jerks, which copy the unusual swimming motion of a shrimp.

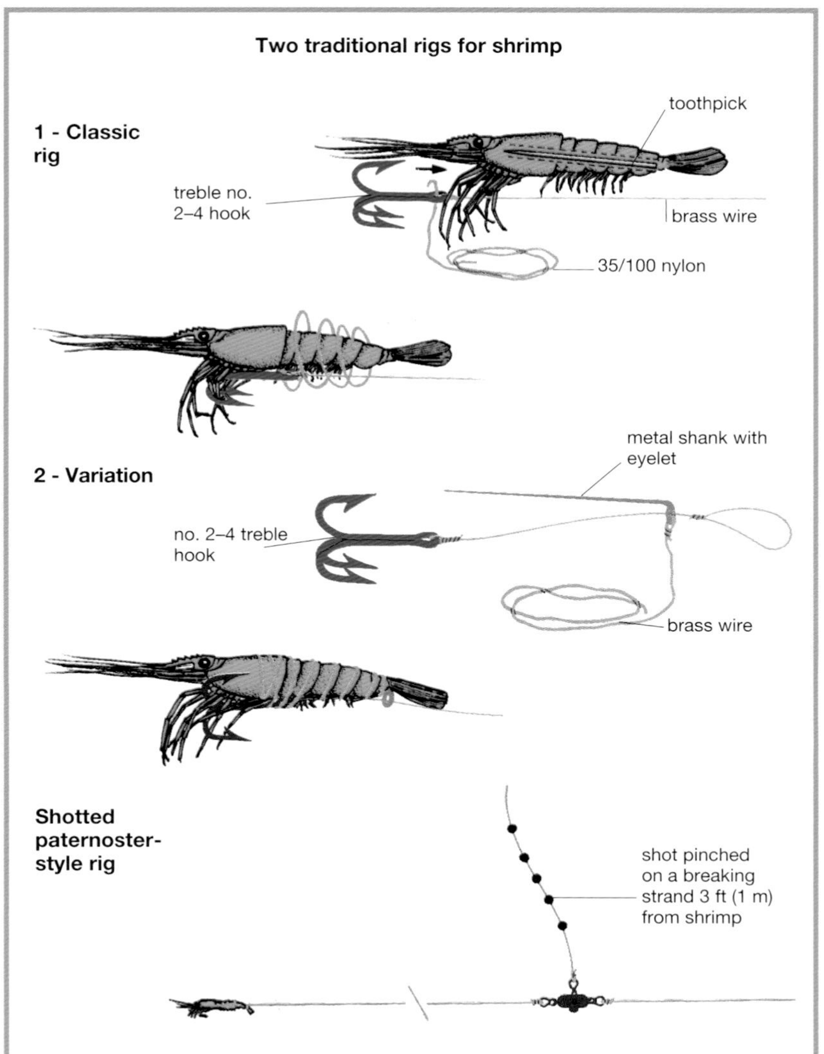

SALMON-FISHING ACCESSORIES

The typical salmon angler uses a wide variety of gadgets all of which will come in handy. The romantic will often cling to an old wooden fly-box which he wouldn't part with for all the fish in the world. Or perhaps he has a traditional old two-handed split cane rod fixed to the wall at home, and from time to time, for old times' sake, he will use it again to launch his silk across the water. Apart from the rod, a reel full of silk, and as large a range as possible of multicolored flies in our fly-box, there are a few other indispensable items of tackle, which no angler should be without.

Small Accessories

• Priest

This is used for putting the salmon out of their misery. A priest consists of a short length of weighted wood, metal or horn. Two or three firm blows should ensure that the fish has been "visited by the priest" to use an angling term. In North America, a solid block of wood cut down by a beaver making its lodge is commonly used. Due to its prolonged soaking, it is solid enough to do the job.

• Disgorger

This is another useful tool which prevents a lot of injuries (see the section on first aid). The hooks in spinners, lures, and wet or dry flies may become deeply embedded in the mouth or throat of the fish. The disgorger removes the hook very quickly from the fish's mouth, giving you more precious time if indeed you intend releasing your catch back into the water.

Beautiful clutch of silver caught with fly. ▷

• Swiss Army Knife
Choose one of the larger models, with all the interesting little extras, including scissors and a disgorger.

• Spring-loaded weigh scale
With a spring-loaded weigh scale, you can determine the exact weight of your catch without any arguments. This is particularly useful when you think you might have a record catch.

• Roll of Insulating (Duck) Tape
Use insulating tape, duck tape, or a strip of rubber from the inner tube of a bicycle to hold your reel tightly to the rod. Even the best screw-on or clip-on reel brackets will slip eventually – usually just at the wrong moment, i.e. right in the middle of a fight! There's nothing worse than losing your reel just as you get a massive salmon on the end of your line!

• Ball of strong twine
This will come in handy for carrying one big salmon, or a bunch of smaller ones, which can be strung together, back to your cabin or campsite.

• Sunglasses with polarized lenses
By cutting down on reflection from the water's surface, polarized sunglasses give you a better view of the fish. This is a useful advantage, particularly in summer when fishing on sight for salmon in clear, shallow water.

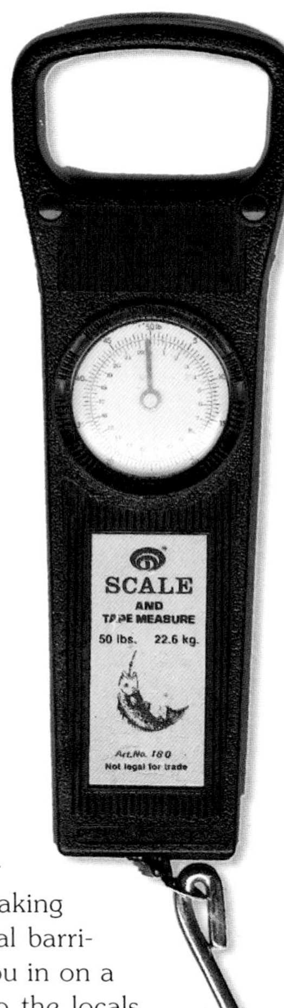

Weigh scale. ▷

• Wading Stick
This is essential for keeping your balance on slippery pebble beds in wide and powerful rivers. We know a few stretches of the Allier in Britanny, France which would be impossible to cross without this instrument!

• Hip-flask
When filled with the angler's favorite tipple, this item is very useful for engaging a local angler in conversation and "breaking down" language or cultural barriers, especially if he lets you in on a few secrets known only to the locals about where the find the best catches!

• Bag, satchel or wicker basket
For carrying home your catch and keeping it fresh on the way.

PRACTICAL FISHING GEAR

• Landing Net
Real salmon anglers prefer to land their fish by hand, for the beauty of it and out of a certain sportsmanship. However, a large salmon

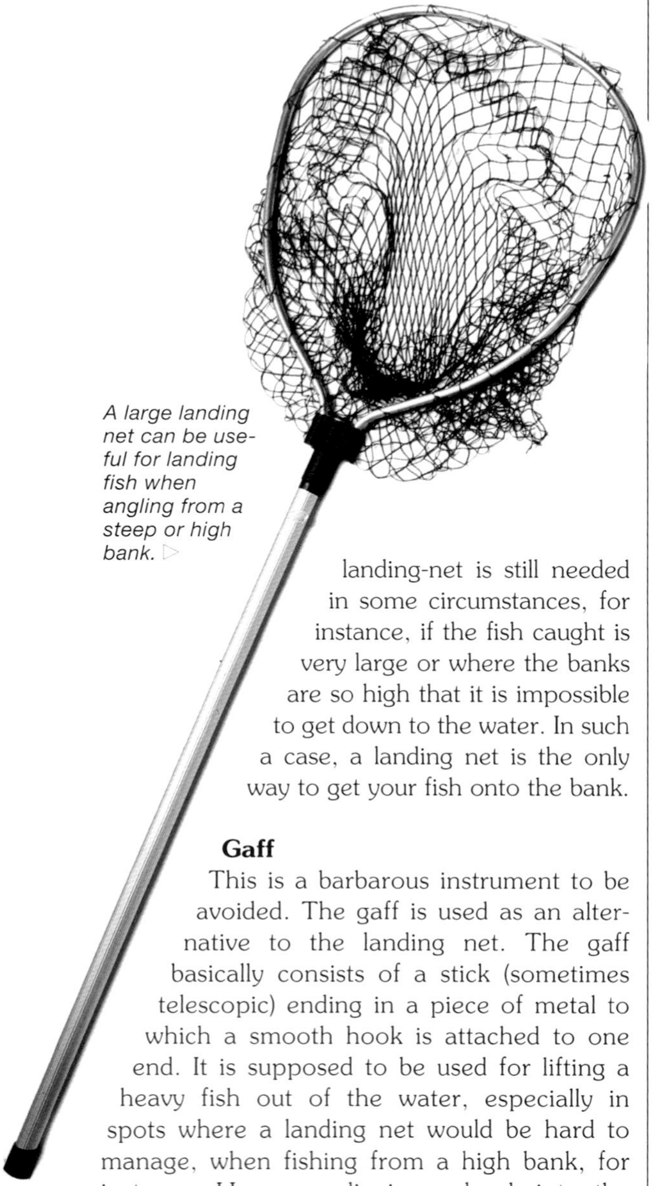

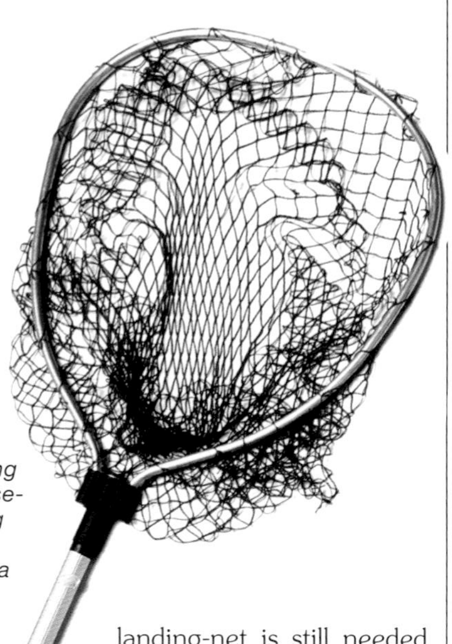

A large landing net can be useful for landing fish when angling from a steep or high bank. ▷

landing-net is still needed in some circumstances, for instance, if the fish caught is very large or where the banks are so high that it is impossible to get down to the water. In such a case, a landing net is the only way to get your fish onto the bank.

Gaff

This is a barbarous instrument to be avoided. The gaff is used as an alternative to the landing net. The gaff basically consists of a stick (sometimes telescopic) ending in a piece of metal to which a smooth hook is attached to one end. It is supposed to be used for lifting a heavy fish out of the water, especially in spots where a landing net would be hard to manage, when fishing from a high bank, for instance. However, digging a hook into the back of a live fish merely to remove it from the water damages the flesh irreparably, so the fish can never be returned to its element. Many fishermen consider the gaff an instrument of torture to be avoided at all costs.

Tailer

The tailer is a variation on the gaff, consisting of a thick handle with a loop attached to it. The fisherman is supposed to lasso the caught fish to lift it out of the water. The noose, once over the fish just in front of the caudal fin, should tighten, but not damage the fish, at least in theory. In practice, this is a difficult maneuver and the fish is bound to end up bruised and damaged, so, like the gaff, the tailer is best avoided.

Choosing lures. Everything depends on the circumstances – and on personal intuition! ▽

SPARES

There is nothing more infuriating than to spend days or even weeks on the water, miles from civilization – when your tackle suddenly breaks and you had not thought to bring along any replacements or spares! At the very least, you need a spare rod of each type (fly and lure), a spare reel, and, of course, plenty of line, lures, and flies.

• Sinkers and Shot
These are essential for weighting down a fly which is not trailing in the water at the correct depth.

• Lure- and Fly-boxes
All types of boxes are available, from simple plastic ones with compartments to splendidly crafted wooden or aluminum boxes such as the ones made by Richard Weathley. It all depends on your personal taste, and what you can afford. The main thing in the case of wet flies, dry flies, and nymphs is a box in which to carefully arrange the flies and protect them from the weather. Some boxes are magnetic, but this can crush dry flies if they are kept for long periods of time. Although foam deteriorates with use, it is simply and cheaply replaced and makes an excellent lining for a fly-box.
A box full of salmon flies is so beautiful, and colorful that the flies are best shown off to their advantage in a beautiful container, just as you would an expensive piece of jewelry!

◁ The fly-box, a rainbow of colors!

If you really want to travel light, especially if you are trotting, a zippered wallet especially designed for carrying flies will fit snugly in a deep pocket and is more easily and quickly opened with one hand.

CLOTHING

Because salmon fishing is a fairly static activity, clothing is particularly important, especially if you are going to spend many hours outside in the cold – or in the sweltering heat!

The classic fishing waistcoat, part of a salmon fisher's tackle. ▷

△ Leather-lined wellingtons will guard against wintry weather. Salmon anglers fishing at the beginning of the season, take note!

If you are fishing in the United Kingdom, for example, you should be well protected from the extremes of cold. Wear an oiled cotton jacket for humid but fairly mild oceanic climates, together with a hat of the same material, of course. Make sure you have plenty of layers underneath to keep out the penetrating cold, especially in Scotland and Ireland, but that you can peel them off if the sun becomes uncomfortably and unusually warm. In Alaska, however, where the weather is cold but drier, nothing does the job as well as a heavy sheepskin jacket.
You will need to wear waders for fishing salmon in any season. These days, plastic and rubber are slowly being replaced by neoprene but this material is very thick and becomes hot in the summer as to be unbearable. It is important to make sure that the stitching between the boot and trouser part is of good quality. Daiwa make a very tough wader with anti-slip felt soles, which are better than the old crampons or hobnails fixed to the bottom of the boots. The waders should have a stomach-pouch large and deep enough to hold a few accessories.
A fishing vest or jacket with pockets, is essential for carrying fly- or lure-boxes and a few handy tools. There's no point in a salmon angler having endless pockets; given the size of the boxes, you are better off going for a waistcoat with fewer but larger pockets.

With neoprene waders, you will be able to fish for hours in icy water. Felt soles will stop you slipping on pebbly riverbeds.

One extraordinary vest is the Shakespeare fishing vest, which combines the qualities of a fishing vest and a life-vest! It inflates either by blowing into it or by using a carbon gas cartridge set off by pulling a rip-cord, turning it into a life-vest.

At the beginning of the season, wearing gloves or fingerless gloves will prevent your fingers from going numb. Regardless of the weather, they are also useful for hanging on to the clutch of a fly-reel without burning your palm. In this case, the best kind are fingerless cyclist's gloves. To full appreciate how useful it is to fish when wearing gloves, you need to have experienced a bite and run in a strong current from a 45 lb (20 kg) king salmon!

FIRST AID KIT

Wherever the the salmon angler fishes, and whether he is after Atlantic or Pacific salmon, he often finds himself alone by a river, with no means of communicating with civilization. A first-aid kit containing the essential minimum of instruments, bandages, and medication is therefore essential. A microsurgery kit, in particular, can often be indispensable.

Angling is not the safe sport it might appear to be at first sight. For instance, an angler fishing for salmon in Alaska had a nasty accident. The fish he caught performed a violent leap, planting one of the treble hook's barbs firmly in the back of his hand. It then managed to struggle back into the water with a series of spectacular flips, the angler remaining firmly attached to the fish by another hook. You can imagine the incredible agony the angler was in, since he had been well and truly hooked. Luckily, a doctor who was a member of the fishing party removed the hook with a microsurgery operation, having injected the injured angler with a large dose of anesthetic which he had been prudent enough to bring on the trip.

Here is a suggested list of what a basic first aid kit should contain. Of course the kit should be as

light as possible, waterproof, air-tight, and well protected from extremes of heat and cold:

Essential Equipment

- scalpel
- scissors
- tweezers
- 5 ml syringes in sterile package with needles
- sutures
- range of antibiotics for all types of infection (dental, respiratory, etc.)
- anti-inflammatory medication
- creams (antibiotic, antiseptic, sunburn, insect repellent, anti-fungal against athlete's foot, etc.)
- arnica or aloe vera balm for bruising (sprains, strains, etc.)
- mild sedative
- anti-dehydration medication (salt tablets)
- anti-diarrhea tablets and laxatives
- vitamin-enriched aspirin
- cough and sore throat lozenges
- eye lotion
- rubber tourniquet
- crepe bandage
- roll of gauze and sterilized compresses
- safety pins
- thermometer
- box of Band-Aids
- absorbent cotton pads
- adhesive sterilized plasters (sutures for small wounds)
- sofra-tulle (for burns and deep cuts)
- total sunblock
- antivenom serum (depending on the country)
- 90° surgical spirit
- distilled water
- Mercryl
- surgical soap
- Mercurochrome

Finally, especially if you are going on a fishing trip abroad, don't forget to get vaccinated and inoculated against such nasty things as leptospirosis, hepatitis B, and tetanus.

◁ *An unloaded hydroplane prepares to take off, leaving this group "alone in the world" for several days. Under these conditions, a complete first aid kit is a must for inclusion in the anglers' tackle.*

A well-prepared expedition, a good day's fishing and, to top it all, hand-smoked salmon filets. ▽

THE CATCH

SALMON

Although so many rivers that once teemed with salmon are no longer full of these splendid fish, there has been an increase in awareness of the importance of this game fish, and the mid-nineties saw an increase in the population of wild salmon throughout Europe. Salmon fishing is no longer a sort of quest for the Holy Grail, with only shattered hopes and empty fish bags to look forward to. That is not to say that salmon-fishing doesn't require the utmost concentration, perseverance, and downright feistiness. You need to be active, have acute powers of observation, and an in-depth knowledge of the fish's habitats and habits.

Smolt ready to head downstream. The silvery coat now looks like that of an adult salmon's. ▽

A Myth

You never forget your first catch of a salmon (*Salmo salar*). Its defense is magnificent, and this fish is unrivaled in fresh water in terms of purity, beauty and hydrodynamics. Depending on the current, the season and especially the water temperature, salmon adopt radically different habits and live in various types of water. In any case, the results will not disappoint, even if you've been dreaming for many years of catching one of these beauties.

An Incredible Journey

The Atlantic salmon is an incredible traveler, and crosses the ocean in order to spawn in the same river in which it was born, sometimes swimming 3,000 miles (5,000 km) in the process.

• The juvenile stage in fresh water

On the spawning areas of a salmon river, at the end of winter, once the eggs have been through the equivalent of 420 degree-days (an incubation period of 105 days for a water temperature of 39°F (4°C)), young salmon finally see the light of day. The eggs are incubated in a gravel bed which is highly oxygenated and where the young fish remain for around six more weeks while their vitelline vesicle is reabsorbed.

At the end of their first summer, the salmon parr measure 4–4½ in (10–12 cm) on average. At this stage, they look very similar to trout, so be very careful not to confuse the two. Furthermore, they have identical feeding habits, with territorial hunting grounds. By the following spring, most of the parr are ready to begin their upstream migration and undergo various changes so they can adapt to marine life.

This phenomenon which involves a number of extraordinary physiological changes is called smoltification, which is why young salmon are also known as smolt. From a purely morphological point of view, the coloration of salmon changes dramatically. The fish loses its bright markings and develops a silvery coat. The scales contain a substance known as guanine. Smoltification is not induced by the length of time the fish spends in freshwater but by its size, and this depends on the quality of the environment in terms of food and the presence of minerals in the water. This is why in salmon streams and rivers, fish which develop more slowly (20–40% of all fish in any one year) stay for a further year (sometimes two) in the river before heading downstream. They move on to generally deeper water than in their first year of growth. Smoltification also occurs following certain hormonal changes involving endocrine secretions, especially from the thyroid, which are themselves dependent on external factors such as the amount of time the fish is exposed to light (known as the photoperiod) or the temperature of the water.

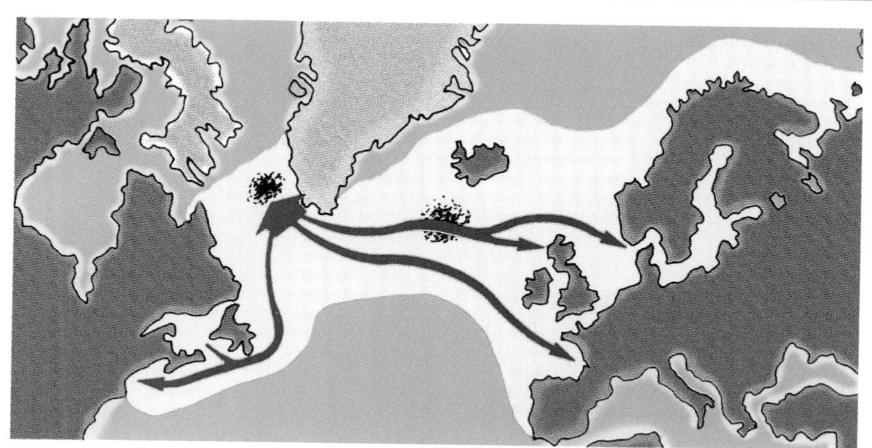

△ *Three main migratory paths for the Atlantic salmon, two of which are in Europe and one on the east coast of North America. Note the largest development areas: off the coast of Greenland and the Faroe Islands.*

• Downstream Swimming

Downstream migration of the Atlantic salmon begins in March on most European salmon rivers and can last until the beginning of the summer. There are also some fall migrations; Atlantic salmon caught in the fall and showing signs of pre-smoltification have been recorded. At night, the smolt generally form into shoals near the surface.

In France, experiments have been performed in marking salmon on the upper Allier and recapturing them on the Loire in the water supply of the Saint-Laurent-des-Eaux nuclear power station. This has shown that salmon swim downstream at a rate of 6 to 18 miles (10–30 km) a day. Increases in water temperature and spring floods appear to hasten their descent.

• The Journey to the Sea

For the salmon in many European streams, this stage remains a mystery. Observations on river systems in Scotland have shown that the fishes' transition into salt water can take place without any period of adaptation, although the smolt may still not be physiologically ready for it. Because they haven't adapted fully, there are large numbers of fatalities at this stage. The movement of the tides and the differences in temperature between fresh water and salt water are determining factors which affect the amount of time the smolts remain in an estuary.

• The Marine or Thalassic Stage

By marking young salmon on the Allier in Brittany, France, researchers have discovered that the fish generally develop around the Faroe Islands and off the west coast of Greenland. The young of other species may pass through the growing stage off the Lofoten Islands of Norway, and some even travel as far as the Baltic Sea. The little smolt's extraordinary journey of nearly 3,000 miles (5,000 km), from the gravel beds of streams of the upper Allier, remains a mystery and its migration paths are still largely unknown. Only one thing is sure and that is that these fish swim at speeds of around 30 miles (50 km) a day! Once it arrives at its growing ground, the young salmon feed on fish, such as sand-eel, pilchards, and herring as well as plankton, especially small crustaceans of the amphipod and euphausiaceae families. With such a rich diet, the salmon's growth rate is incredible, in the region of 4 lb 8 oz-10 lb (2–4 kg) a year!

The period of time during which the salmon lives in the sea is certainly dependent on genetic determinism and varies greatly from one breed to another. For reasons which are unclear, some fish – and this has been noticed in Scotland, Ireland, and Iceland as well as in salmon from the Allier – do not migrate to the traditional feeding areas and remain in coastal waters. These fish always ascend the river after only one year of living in the sea, at the grylse stage. Allier salmon remain for 1–3 years at sea (and very rarely 4 years), although the majority stay for 3. When they ascend the river, they weigh 10 lb –33 lb (5–15 kg) and are 30–46 inches (85–115 cm) long.

• Return to the Native River

Motivated by their reproductive instinct, which itself is dependent on particular hormonal secretions, the salmon decides to abandon its marine habitat.

This then gives rise to one of the most extraordinary phenomena of the animal kingdom. After several years of living at sea, thousands of miles from the river of its birth, the king of fish unfailingly finds its way back to the exact spot at which it was born. Extraordinary but also mysterious, because it is still not known exactly how the fish find their bearings. It appears that magnetic fields and the position of the stars guide the fish back home, as well as the chemical and physical composition of the sea, which changes far out from the mouth of an estuary.

◁ *Dams are major obstacles for migrating salmon.*

This all supposes, of course, that the fish have very finely-tuned senses. Researchers appear to have discovered how fish recognize the correct river by marking specimens at different stages of their development. The young salmon appear to recognize the right river by memorizing the smells of that river as they swim down toward the sea, a particularly clever way of adapting to this migratory way of life. Furthermore, these smolts mark their native rivers with particular secretions – pheromones – from their biliary salts.

The ability of salmon to systematic ally return to their native river, a phenomenon known as homing, has been questioned by some Scottish scientists. Their research has shown that in certain specific situations – severe drought, pollution, dams – which make it impossible for the fish to swim upstream, salmon were able to reproduce in waterways other than their native river.

Salmon from the river Allier arrive at the Loire estuary as early as fall in the case of the most adventurous specimens, and the arrivals keep coming until the beginning of the following summer. The fish begin their upriver journey at high tide, aided by a good sea breeze in overcast or rainy conditions, usually when it is dark. The tidal range seems to aid migratory movements. The Loire's flow levels which determine pollution levels linked to the presence of a silt bed are also important, as anadromous (sea to river) migration is aided by high water. Salmon never enter the estuary when water flow in the Loire is slower than 1,660 cu. ft per second (500 m^3 per second); and you will see peaks of upriver swimming at levels above 3 300 cu. feet per second (1,000 m^3 per second). The first fish, known as winter salmon, appear from October through January and are mainly females. These are the largest fish, but there are fewer of them, and they generally swim on their own upriver. On the Allier, they stay 13–15 months in fresh water and only reproduce the following year. Next come the spring salmon, which are greater in number but smaller in weight (10–18 lb (6–8 kg)) and they swim upriver in small shoals from March to May. Then the young salmon or grylse, weighing around 3 lb 5 oz (1.5 kg) each, migrate during the summer months. Some of these fish will not have completed their journey to the growing areas.

• Homing to the Spawning Areas: a Fighter's Journey!

Once it reaches fresh water, the salmon stops feeding. All its energy reserves are then used up to complete a journey of nearly 625 miles (1,000 km), to the upper Allier, and to wait until it has reached full sexual maturity. The fish undergo considerable physiological changes, with progressive atrophy of the digestive system, blockage of the kidneys, liver dysfunction, and thickening of the arteries. As a result, the fish loses 40 percent of its bodyweight by the time it reaches the spawning grounds. The rate at which the salmon swims upriver is largely determined by the temperature of the water, but also by water flow. So during the winter, when the temperature of the river is less than 40°F (3°C), virtually no fish swim upriver. Between 40–43°F (3–6°C) the fish manage to make small advances but they are easily stopped by small barriers for which extra effort is required if they are to be overcome. Above 41–43°F (5–6°C), they will make attempts to leap over such barriers. When the temperature rises above this level, migration gets into full swing, and fish have been seen homing on the Allier in very high temperatures. In August 1981, at the Vichy pass, three salmon were caught in river temperatures of 75°F (24°C)!

Reproduction: Spawning then Dying

Salmon spawn where the water quality is most suitable for their needs, i.e. an average of 100 miles (155 km) between the unbreachable Saint-

Etienne-du-Vigan dam upstream (which a "Return to Nature" project for the Loire plans to dismantle) and Issoire. Nevertheless, redds have been observed in some years at Clermont-Ferrand. Male and female fish assemble at the spawning grounds where they can get precisely what they need, namely plenty of oxygen-rich water and the right sort of gravel beds.

The males form a hierarchy whereby the largest specimens chase off the younger males. This is also seen between mating pairs, with the males being chased from the spawning beds by females. The females create a smooth circular area of 20–32 inches (50–80 cm) of gravel by lashing their fins, then they gouge out a groove, the redd, by making convulsive movements with their flanks and abdomen. They will even use the caudal peduncle to achieve this, and will repeat the operation at least once.

The female then deposits her eggs in three to five movements – a total of 2,000–3,000 eggs per kilogram (2 lb 4 oz) of bodyweight. These are then fertilized by the male. The eggs are immediately buried in gravel to conceal them from predators and protect them from sediment deposits which limit oxygenation and light. Egg-laying is usually done at night and the same female may start several redds at once some distance from each other, not always in the same current. The spawning season can last several days and the eggs of a single female are generally fertilized by several different males, thus giving a better genetic mix.

• Post-Spawning Migration

After reproduction, most salmon die of glandular deficiencies, covered with parasitic fungi, since their immune system breaks down. It seems that it is the males that pay the highest price for the physical changes required for reproduction. Thin and weak, with their lower jaw deformed into a beak-like shape (they're then known as kelt), they simply let themselves be carried away on the current, resting in the river's calmer parts, trying to reach the ocean to survive for another period of growth.

Only 1–2 percent of all fish which have reproduced once already manage to complete a second anadromous migration, and 5 percent of those fish survive to spawn again. This is a real miracle when one considers that most of their vital functions (urinary tract, digestive system, and so on) are completely atrophied during spawning, and yet become functional again immediately afterward. It gives them a sort of second lease of life, which even today biologists are still investigating, undoubtedly in the quest for the secrets of immortality.

FLY-FISHING

For the great American novelist Jim Harrison, "fly-fishing provides the ideal combination of exhaustion and esthetic joy. It is by far the most fascinating of outdoor sports". (*Just Before Dark*, 1991).

Fly-fishing is certainly the most noble way of catching the splendid salmon, and paying one's respects to this prestigious adversary.

In some ways, it is the best way of getting to grips with nature in a new way and getting to know the river and its complex structure. Fly-fishing today is incredibly popular in the United States and Scandinavia, with more and more younger anglers taking it up. For many salmon fishers, fly-fishing is much more than a fishing technique, it is a way of life. Entering the fly-fishing world is a bit like entering a new religion, with its own language and observance of secret rituals and strict moral codes.

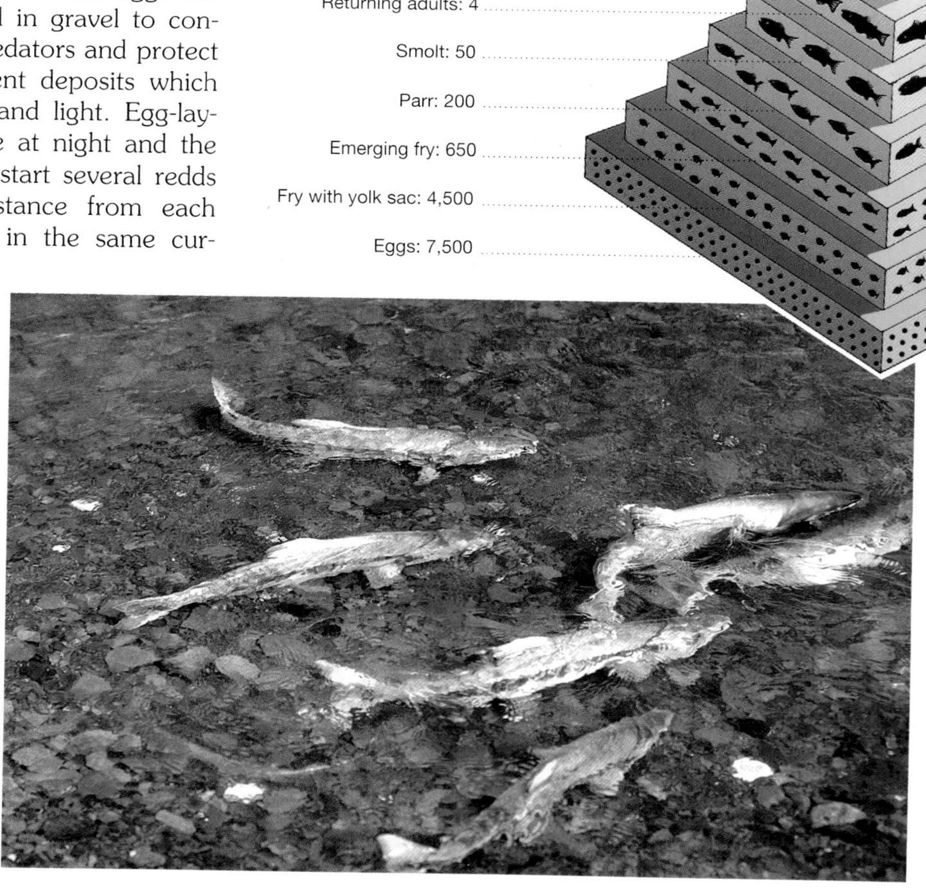

A salmon's destiny (after Gary J. Anberson and Ann E. Brimer)

◁ *Pacific salmon (chum pictured) gathering in great numbers on a spawning bed. A sight which has unfortunately disappeared from European waters.*

However, there is no reason to be hidebound by the unnecessarily strict rules of traditional fly-fishing, which was for many years the preserve of a few English aristocrats who would mumble their secrets in the smoky rooms of a few very private gentlemen's clubs.

In France, for example, fly-fishing for salmon is an old peasant tradition in Brittany. With the invention of the fixed-spool reel, all that changed. Still, the Brittany fly angler never worried about metaphysical considerations in catching their fish.

The clash of these two fly-fishing cultures is nowhere more clearly seen than in the type of artificial flies used. The Brittany fly is best represented by one created by the great salmon fisherman known as Father Clerc and is simplicity and efficiency itself. It may well look unexcitingly plain, coarse, and misshapen to the angler, but it is not the angler who will be biting the fly, and it certainly gets results!

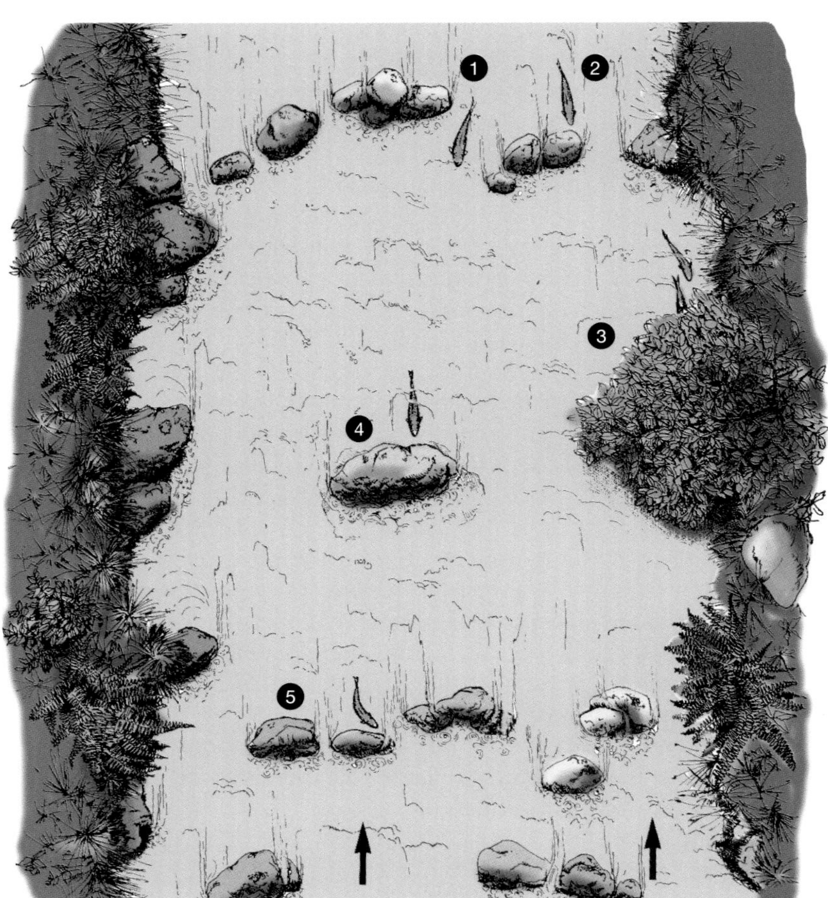

Salmon habitats

1–2 – Salmon arrive in the pool – often willing to bite.

3 – Salmon positioned along a bank: possible catch.

4 – Salmon positioned in the middle of a pool – unlikely to bite

5 – Salmon leaving pool – willing to bite.

English artificial flies, on the other hand, are miniature works of art, very beautifully made in bright colors. There are historical reasons for this difference.

British army officers who had been stationed in the colonies, mainly in the East, and who were fly-fishing adepts brought back the feathers of tropical birds they had caught (most famously, the jungle fowl), contributing to the creation of these multicolored creations which today are typical of the British fly.

American flies for catching king salmon are almost hallucinatory creations which look like small monsters from a science fiction novel, but they are also extremely effective.

Fly-fishing is a sporting challenge which combines the great pleasures of outdoor life with a good chance of catching something. The equipment and techniques you use will depend largely on the type and size of river, the current, and the expected size of the fish. (See pages 66–68 for information about equipment).

As for the rod, the Americans, in particular, swear by two-handed models which give a much wider cast, better drift control, and good presentation of heavily leaded lures. For large mountain rivers, a good 15 foot rod is ample, being an excellent compromise between a 12-footer (better for small Brittany or Irish rivers, women anglers or those of a smaller build) and the 18-footer, an enormous rod which only the body-builders among us could comfortably work with for a whole day. With a 15-foot rod, you should be able to catch any large fish, from giant salar on the Kola in Russia to king salmon on the Kenai in Alaska. Canadian and British fly-fishermen, however, prefer to use single-handed rods. These can be just as effective on smaller rivers in France but are not traditionally used unless you are dry-fly or greased line fishing. It has to be said that, despite the quality of the American one-handed rods, the length of cast is drastically reduced and struggling with a large fish can be distinctly dangerous.

Choose your line depending upon the area being fished and the prevailing water temperature.

For a two-handed 15-foot rod in medium to deep water, use a diving-point line. This is absolutely essential for catching large fish such as king salmon which only really ever bite at the bottom of a river. However, you should not use extra-fast sinking lines because they are difficult to snatch back out of the water

A handsome specimen caught by fly-fishing on the Kola peninsula in Russia, one of the few remaining havens for Atlantic salmon fishing. ▷

and are therefore only useful in particularly cold water of less than 50°F (10°C). In any case, use double-taper lines, a no. 9 for 12 foot rods, and no. 10–12 for 15-footers. When the water temperature rises above 59°F (15°C) (summer species) and you're using a greased line just under the surface, go for a floating line. The British and the Canadians fishing with one-handed rods generally use no. 7–8 silks.

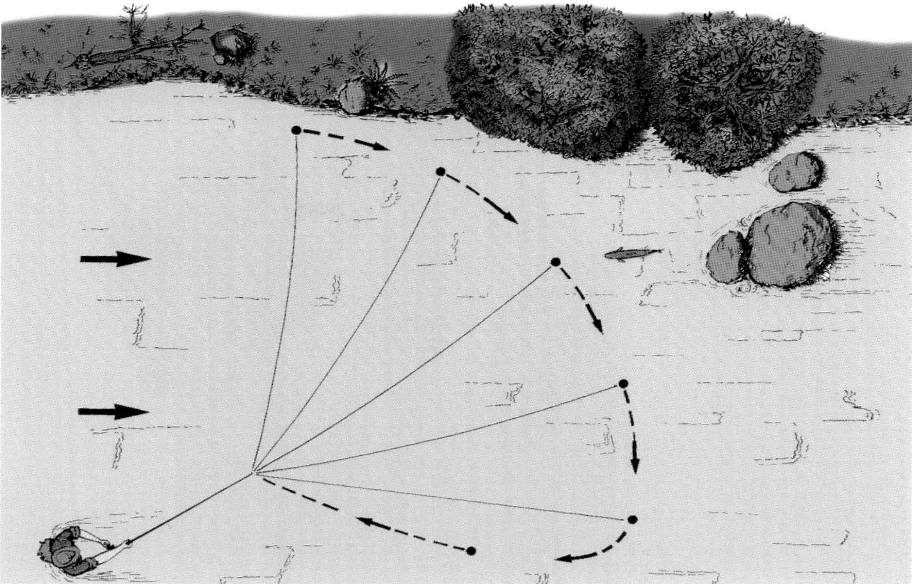

Fly-fishing with a downstream drift

• Technique

Fly-fishing is not as difficult as some purists would have us believe, and casting in particular is fairly easy to learn with either a two-handed or a one-handed rod. Cast 83–117 feet (25–35 m) in a straight line across or a quarter downstream, then let the fly drift with support. As the lure drops, you can waggle the tip of your rod to give it more movement and make it look as if it is alive. As the fly drifts, by moving it with your rod, you'll make it more attractive to any interested fish; slowly move the tip from side to side or up and down, pulling slightly on the line from time to time. Many experts argue endlessly over whether to strike as soon as you feel a bite. Without wanting to prolong the discussion, our experience has shown that you are better holding a loop of about 40 inches (1 m) of line in your left hand and letting it go as soon as the fish takes before it heads back down to the bottom. This delayed strike tends to produce more successful results than an immediate strike.

• Fighting and Landing Your Fish

Battling a large fish can be very dangerous on some rivers, especially when you are fishing in a pool which is cluttered with tree roots or between two powerful rapids. It is very difficult to control a large fish which has decided to shoot off with the current, taking all your line and backing with it. The only solution is to attempt to persuade the fish to return the other way by following rather than countering its movement with your rod.

Alternatively, follow its journey along the bank – not all that easy when the bank is so steep that you could easily find yourself taking an unexpected soak! And if the fish doesn't manage to escape in the first moments of a fight, nine times out of ten, it will manage to unhook itself as you bring it out of the water, either because the salmon reserves its energy to perform one last great leap or the hook has not embedded itself properly and falls out or opens up because it's made of poor quality metal. First of all, do not close the clutch as soon as the fish escapes because you want to prevent the line from breaking. As soon as the fish shows the first signs of exhaustion by rising to the surface, look around it for a calm patch away from the current and preferably near a gently sloping bank, so you can land your salmon more easily. In shallow water, try to push the salmon by its tail toward the bank, then lift it with a firm hold at the level of its caudal peduncle, on either side of which the salmon has cartilage which gives the angler a good grip.

Unhook the fish and, if you intend to return it to the water, let it oxygenate well before gently releasing it. You should never return a fish which is exhausted and gasping to the water, or you are as good as killing it. If you want to retain your prize, you have to club it to death with a sharp blow, using a priest.

Anglers wishing to smoke their salmon should then bleed it. We do not advocate landing salmon with the barbaric device known as a gaff. Salmon can also be landed with a tailer, which is a sort of lasso, or with a large landing net.

• Dry-Fly-Fishing

For many fishermen, salmon fishing with dry flies is impracticable. However, American and Canadian an-

A proud angler with his fly fishing catch – a handsome Irish salmon freshly arrived on the Moy River near Ballina, in County Mayo. ▷

glers manage to successfully fish this way, albeit in rivers which are well-populated with salmon. Jean-Loup Trautner, a man who moved to Ireland solely because of his love of salmon fishing, made some interesting comments.

Trautner claims to have caught many salmon with dry-fly imitations of caddis larvae. Most of his catch consisted of newly-arrived homing salmon who were feeding on surface insects. To prove his observations of the salmon's activities, he investigated the contents of their stomachs, and indeed found a high concentration of caddis larvae.

It is a mystery why some so-called experts proclaim so loudly that salmon never feed in fresh water after such a surprising discovery. True, all the fish caught in this way were grylse which had only spent a year at sea. Trautner thus concludes that the young salmon somehow "remember" their way of life in fresh water.

But it is not only grylse who feed in fresh water. Pierre Affre, another angling journalist, has caught salmon weighing nearly 33 lb (15 kg) by dry-fly-fishing in June on a recent fishing trip to Russia. Also in Alaska king salmon were caught by dry-fly-fishing. They were all caught in the same kind of waters, just at the head of a long and violent current preceding a large calm pool. We would sweep the surface, right across the flow, and just at the border between the "dead and live" area, with large floating Muddler Minnow or irresistible dry flies, whose bodies were made out of deer hair (the Americans use Virginia stag or mullet stag). It worked again and again, despite the unorthodox method.

Dry-fly-fishing by sight is very common on clear rivers like the Gaspésie or on Anticosti Island in Canada. The Canadians use a fairly light rig, a one-handed rod with a no. 7–8 line, using basic large sedge-fly imitations. The technique again involves sweeping the dry fly across the surface, near obvious salmon activity.

There is still a lot to learn about salmon fishing with dry flies in fresh water, and we will have to wait and see what anglers come up with over the next few years on the Kola peninsula when fishing very large specimens before we can learn more about this particular technique.

Rod-and-Reel Salmon Fishing

Metal lure fishing with rod and reel is certainly the most effective technique for catching salmon, no matter what the season. Nevertheless, it is still best practiced at the beginning of the season, when the water is too cold and too deep for fly-fishing. However, we should mention the very unpleasant practice of using very large leaded spoons during the summer, in low water, to "grab" salmon on sight, downstream of shelves where many of the fish are gathered. This is little better than poaching and unfortunately the practice is widespread. When people decide to behave in this way, it is better to ban lure fishing altogether, and only permit fly-fishing. In any case, fly-fishing results in far fewer accidental back hookings.

• Mastering a Light Rig

In rod-and-reel fishing, as in fly-fishing, equipment depends on expected fish size, river width, and current speed. During the summer months, for example, when fishing for 2 lb 4 oz–4 lb 8 oz (1–2 kg) grylse (often the case on Irish rivers in August), you can use a classic trout rig, with 18–20/100 nylon.

This light rod-and-reel fishing may well bring in a surprisingly good catch. When fishing for medium-sized salmon such as the silver, red, or pink salmon on small Irish, Brittany, or Normandy rivers, use classic pike fishing equipment. The rig is similar to that for spoon or deadbait angling: a ½–1 oz (15–25 g) capacity, an 8 foot (2.5 m) rod and a fixed or spinning reel with 667 feet (200 m) of 28-35/100 depending on clutter and whether there are any rapids. On large mountain rivers such as those found in Scotland, Norway, Russia or North America, where you are likely to have to deal with a salmon weighing up to 33 lb (15 kg) in rapid, deep, and rock-strewn water, choose a powerful set-up. Use a 11–12 foot (3.2–3.5 m) rod (more if you are using an English carp rod) which is perfect for this kind of fishing. It has a capacity of 1–2¼ oz (30–60 g), and should be used with a good quality fixed-spool, high-capacity reel with a reliable clutch. the reel should contain 667 ft (200 m) of 45–50/100.

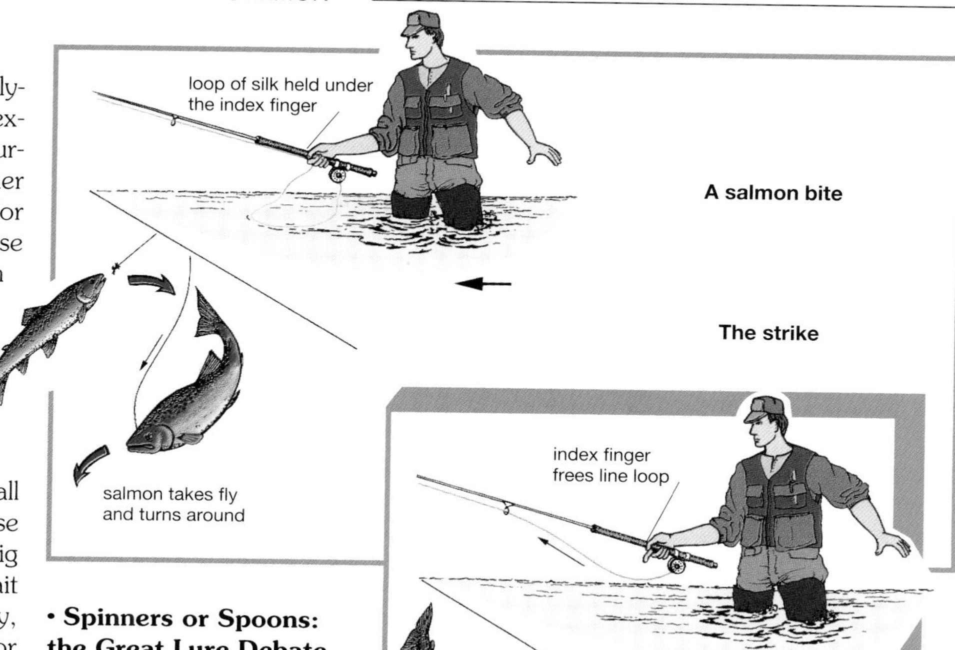

• Spinners or Spoons: the Great Lure Debate

Spoons and spinners are among the most popular lures in the world. Use spinners in mid-season and summer in deep water, calm pools, or slow-moving currents. In faster flowing water, where the current "pulls", spinners are not as useful because they tend to jump back up to the surface. Instead, use spoons (very popular in North America, Scandinavia, and the British Isles), which work better near the bottom. Everything depends on the circumstances, of course. Depending on the time of day and its ever-changing mood, salmon will often ignore a well-presented spinner but jump at a spoon straight afterward. The real art to this sort of fishing, especially when you are after Pacific salmon, comes in regularly changing the type and size of lure until you find one that works in those circumstances. Spinners we would recommend include Quimperloises, with their rubber skirts, golden, silver, or fluorescent-colored Mepps with a "nail" blade, or willow wood blade with a no. 3–5 hook for larger rivers and fish, no. 2–3 for grylse on small rivers and streams, and Blue Foxes (no. 4–6). A wide range of spoons is available. The classic Allier spoon is excellent, as is the Mepps Syclops, silver or copper Krokodil (½ oz (16 g)), a ⅛, ¼, ½, or ¾ oz (6, 10, 17 or 20 g) Loon, a ¼, ½, or ¾ oz (10, 12, or 18 g) Toby or an Orkla. If the current is strong or the river deep, extra shot can be added to the lures.

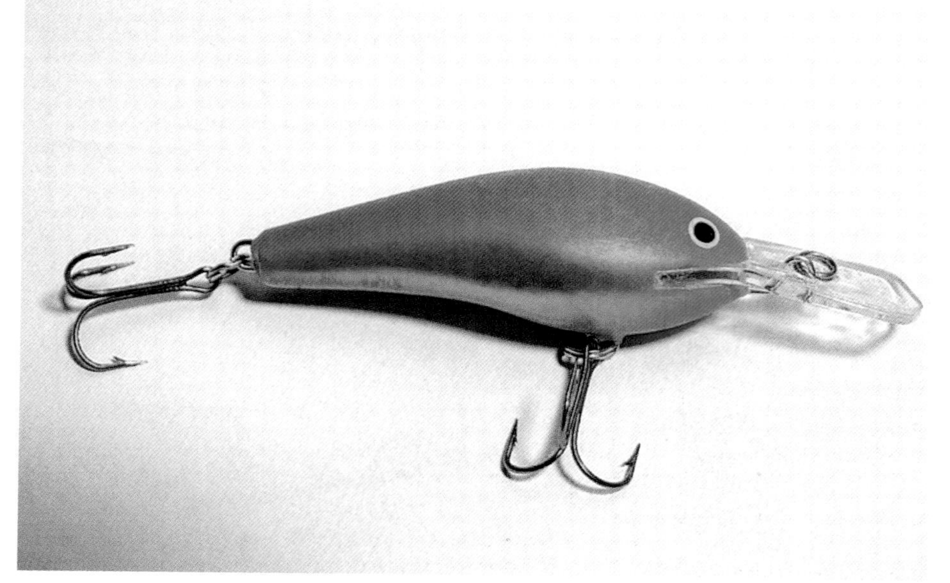

◁ *A well-presented Rapala can seduce the most wary salmon.*

• Fishing Technique

Although apparently simple, the fishing technique is particularly active requiring a good feeling for the water, the fishes' habitat depending on the season, and water temperature and rate of flow. You should generally start at the head of the pool and move down slowly, methodically sweeping each flow. Cast straight across or slightly downstream, and reel in as slowly as possible, just enough to make the spinner turn. Sometimes, you just need to hold the lure downstream without reeling in and the water flow will be enough to work the lure. The lure itself should literally brush the bottom, following its ups and downs. The earlier in the season it is, the slower you should work the lure as the fish will be still very apathetic. Success therefore depends on two things: slow-moving and the methodical investigation of the water (don't be in a hurry to move from one flow to another), and good knowledge of places in the river which could contain your fish. If necessary, animate the lure by reeling in and releasing irregularly, and moving the rod tip up and down or side to side to encourage even the most wary of fish to bite.

A bite can take on a number of forms: a sudden stop, extra weight on the rod, line moving upstream – sometimes at incredible speed – and more usually, a quick movement followed by small jumps. The most spectacular fights are usually with fish which are accidentally caught by the tail – they in particular will do everything to get free!

◁ The Quimperloise: a spinning blade and leaded body make this a formidable lure.

FISHING FOR PACIFIC SALMON

The western coast of North America – mainly the states of Alaska, Washington, Oregon, and Idaho are great places for the salmon angler to pit his wits against Pacific varieties. Pacific salmon can also be found on the other side of the Bering Straits, in Kamchatka, where rivers are only rarely fished (by rod and line at least – professional net fishing is another story!). Kamchatka was completely closed to foreigners under the Soviet regime and is only just opening up to visitors.

Five species of Pacific salmon inhabit coastal waters on the western shores of North America, notably the rivers of Alaska and British Columbia. In Alaska, nature has remained virtually untouched by man; it is a land of superlatives, with three million lakes, 3,000 rivers and streams, 3,300 miles (5,300 km) of coastline, mountains more than 2,000 feet (6,000 m) above sea level, and volcanoes by the dozen, all spread over a territory as big as the whole of Europe and inhabited by only half a million people. Every year in this angler's paradise, millions of salmon swim upriver to breed. It is interesting to study these species which regularly attract fishing fans from every continent of the world.

• King Salmon or Chinook Salmon *(Oncorhynchus)*

On the western coast of North America, from California to Alaska, the king salmon has always been treated with respect by all races of people who have fished it since time eternal throughout its anadromous migration. The Native American Indians called it *tyee*, which means "chief." Similarly, the Americans now call it "king" of all fish as a homage to its

△ American spoon specifically designed for the king salmon.

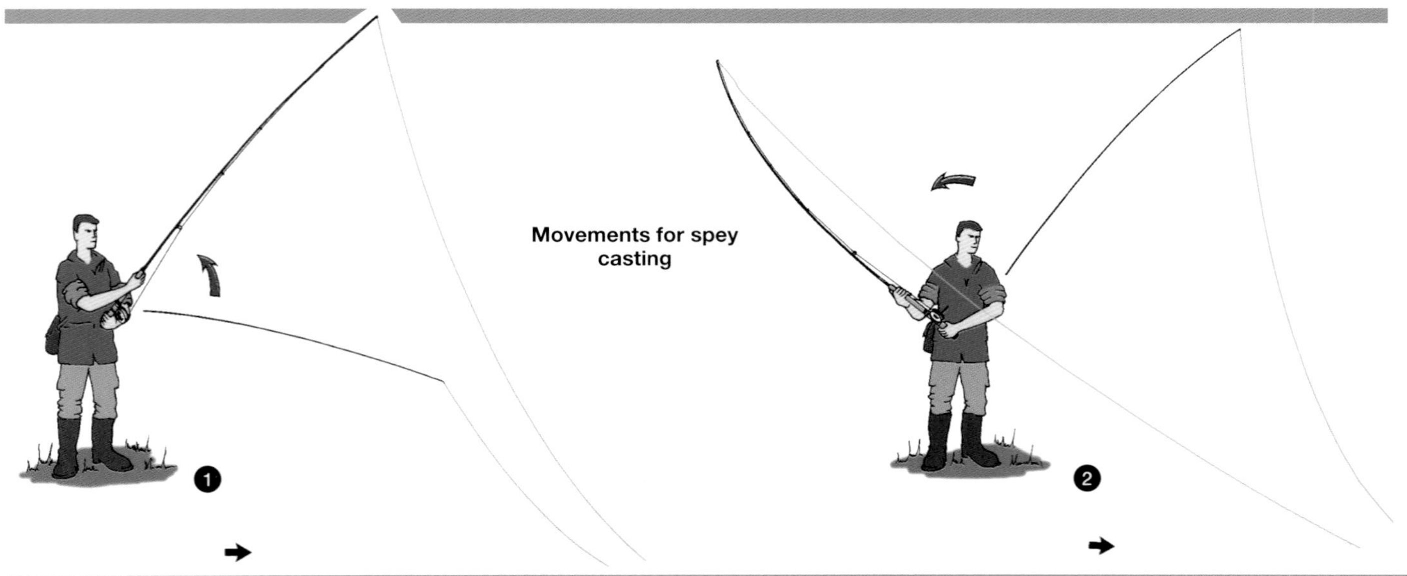

The Right Fly

There are countless types of artificial fly, all of which reflect local traditions or national traits. Some are dreamed up by creative fly-makers who have their own little preferences and secrets linked to particular fishing spots. The writer Pierra Affre claims that the first four artificial flies were described in 1496 by Juliance Berners in his *Traité pratique de la pêche* (Practical Treatise on Fishing) in the second edition of the *Livre de Saint Albans*. Since then, many books have been published on the subject of fly types, including one written by George Kelson in the late 19th century which mentions no fewer than 37 flies. Today, there are approximately 100 classic artificial flies which have been recorded and are used regularly across the world. Some of the first great classic flies were the multicolored English flies, one by-product of the British Empire. At the time, they were made out of the feathers of exotic birds such as the jungle fowl, toucan, macaw and Indian raven. Two good examples are the Jack Scott and the Durham Ranger, which are literally mini works of art. French artificial flies are much less flamboyant, made from the feathers of the familiar woodcock or pheasant, and hairs of the marten, squirrel, hare, or badger. Each type of fly has its supporters, but the important thing is to concentrate on fishing technique and respect a few elementary principles.

△ Sun Ray Shadow made by the Norwegian angler Brucks.

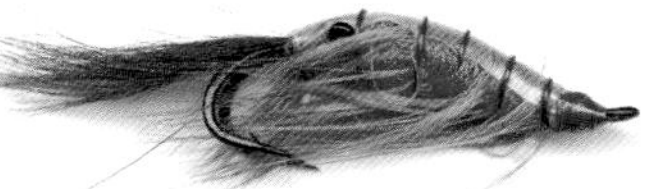

◁ Artificial shrimp.

Choose your fly depending on a number of physical conditions, including the flow, depth, and temperature of the water, air temperature, and light. As a general rule, use dark-colored, bushy flies, such as the Black Doctor, in poor light. Pale, thin flies, such as Lemon Gray, are best for good light, and medium-colored flies, such as Jock Scott, work best in overcast conditions. Similarly, less voluminous flies are good in clear, shallow water and the more bushy ones in cloudy, fast-flowing water. As a rule, the size of the fly should match the temperature of the water.

34–37.5°F (1–3°C): avoid fly fishing altogether, but for those new to fly-fishing, use a no. 2 tube fly.
37.5–43°F (3–6°C): 1 1/2 in tube-fly or fly on a no.1/0–2 hook.
43–46.5°F(6–8°C): fly on a no. 2–4 hook.
46.5–50°F (8–10°C): fly on a no. 4–6 hook.
50–54°F (10–12°C): fly on a no. 6-8 hook.
54–59°F (12–15°C): fly on a no. 8-10 hook and floating line. Then grease the line to fish just beneath the surface.

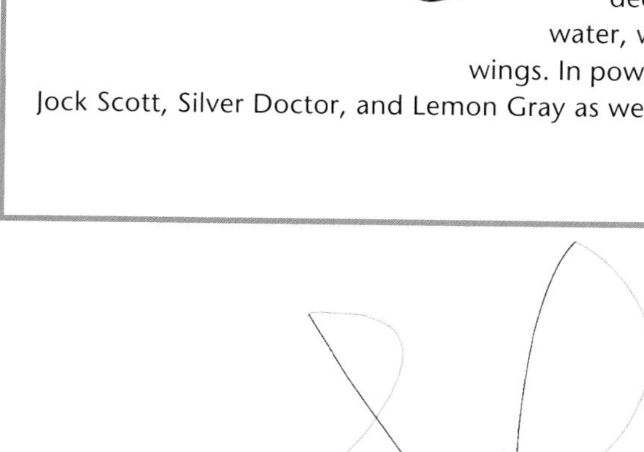

△ The Henri Clerc fly.

The Silver Doctor. ▷

Current strength is also important, as well as the topography of the river. In calm water, the best flies are obviously those which use everything to try and attract a fish. Because the rivers of Brittany are often deep and slow-moving chalk streams, Brittany flies are often perfect for calm water, with their boar's hair bodies, pheasant's feather livery, and peahen down wings. In powerful currents and fast flowing water, use the great English classics such as Jock Scott, Silver Doctor, and Lemon Gray as well as French flies made of fox, squirrel, or marten hair.

3

4

beauty and fighting strength. Biologists prefer to call it by its other name, the Chinook, out of respect for the Native American peoples of the region. A Chinook has an incredibly bright silvery coat which gradually reddens as spawning season approaches. It is impossible to confuse it with any other fish because of its sheer size. It is a truly enormous fish, one specimen having been caught on the Kenai River in Alaska which weighed nearly 112 lb (50 kg)! That is an exception of course, but still, most king salmon weigh in at 22 lb–33 lb (10–15 kg), depending on the river in which they are caught.

Fans of *Salmo salar*, the Atlantic salmon, look down somewhat on the Pacific salmon, which is to ignore this salmon's incomparable fighting spirit and supernatural strength. A large king salmon, when being landed, can snap the sturdiest rod in one movement, and with one flick of its caudal fin cut a strong 50/100 line or crush a hook between its powerful jaws. King salmon are fished with rod and reel and lures, flies or live bait.

A very strong salmon rod with a 1¼–2¼ oz (30–60 g) capacity is recommended, together with a very high-capacity reel holding 667–1000 ft (200–300 m) of 50/100 line. Again, the reel must be particularly high-quality with an excellent clutch which is well-adjusted – otherwise, something is definitely going to break! In the same vein, check your lure attachment knots regularly.

The use of spinners, spoons, or plugs depends on the circumstances of water depth and flow. When fishing on a dark night, for example, a no. 5 Mepps red or fluorescent orange spinner or a similarly-colored Mepps Syclops spoon will give excellent results. Similarly, Blue Fox no. 4, 5, or 6 spoons with small vibrating fluorescent bells are very effective, particularly on Kodiak Island on the Karluk River in Alaska, as well as red or golden Mepps willow blades.

One thing you must do is replace all treble hooks, which are often crushed by the king's powerful jaws, with strong single iron hooks. The swivel is another indispensable detail. Experience has shown that the most robust swivels long-term are the French JB clip-on swivels.

Let's talk about flies now. The Americans use lots of large fluorescent red and orange streamers. These are great when it is dark, especially on rivers which are not fished using salmon roe as a bait. A sprig of shiny tinsel can make the lure more attractive. Scottish flies are fine, as is the special Allier fly, which is yellow and black and made from jungle fowl feathers. Depending on your own preferences, your basic equipment should include a 15-foot two-handed rod with a manual reel and sinking point no. 10 line with 33 feet (10 m) of backing. Avoid extra-fast sinking lines – they sink well but are difficult to snatch out of the water – and lead with a strand of lead core or shot to give the depth required to the fly. You have to present your streamer very near the bottom, as you do with metal lures.

Some Americans prefer to fish with small, light one-handed rods, and they will often spend more than an hour battling to land a fish. Landing a king salmon under these conditions is far from a sure thing, especially if the riverbed is full of obstacles or if this fiendish fish suddenly decides to leave the pool and follow a fast current. A great king weighing more than 50 lb (22 kg) had the author running after it for a mile (3 km) down some rapids. After a battle lasting a whole hour and a half – it managed to unhook itself! American anglers also use live bait a

FISHING WITH WORMS

This fishing technique is similar to rolled worm fishing for trout. Investigate all the calm, deep flows in which salmon may be lurking, using a wide sweep while holding the line in your hand. Watch out for any unusual feeling – a small trembling in your hand, the drift stopping short, a series of almost imperceptible jerks – and let the salmon bite for a long time. The salmon often just snaps at the bait before deciding whether to swallow it. Only strike firmly when the line moves quickly upstream. The best spots to fish with worms during high water are deep pools, or channels immediately downstream of an obstacle, shelf, or waterfall. The fish remain in these areas for quite some time, especially if the upstream obstacle is difficult to overcome. This annoys them immensely and makes them much more likely to bite!

Superb king salmon weighing 30 lb, caught in the Karluk River, Alaska. Given the strict catch quotas on the river, this one will have to be returned to the water. ▷

lot, in this case a cluster of salmon roe attached to a bizarre lure called the clown. This is a sort of small, light, fluorescent red ball with two wings which turn in the current. The salmon roe attached to the lure are held in a little cheesecloth net. The rig floats downstream, near the bottom, or sits in calm, deep pools.
Despite the density of fish found in Alaska and British Columbia, fishing quotas are very strict and are rarely more than two fish per angler per river, with a total of five per season. Most fish must therefore be released carefully after they have been caught.

• The Red or Sockeye Salmon *(Oncorhynchus nerka)*
This small salmon has an average weight of 5 lb 8 oz–10 lb (2.5–5 kg), the heaviest recorded specimen weighing 18 lb (7.5 kg). Its beautiful silvery coat when it has just returned to the rivers gradually turns red as spawning approaches, hence the name. It returns in enormous shoals of several thousand salmon from June to the end of July.
It is one of the most popular fish caught for canning because of its economic importance.
It takes just as well with flies as with metal lures; however, it is only really aggressive when it is on the spawning grounds. The density of these fish can be so high that you can expect to catch several in one single run, near to the sea, when it still resembles an Atlantic salmon. It is a superb fighter which manages leap after leap and does not deserve its reputation as a lame sport fish. It attacks no. 3 or 4 spoons and brightly colored blue, red, or orange streamers. It is often accidentally caught with king salmon flies. If you are sure

The salmon angler's sportsmanship requires the salmon to be landed by its tail. ▷

An unexpected audience in Kodiak (Alaska), on the Karluk River. There is such pleasure in fishing in a nature reserve like no other, where thousands of salmon are a daily dish for the largest bears on the planet. ▽

you only want to catch reds, use a lighter rig than for the Chinook, similar to a spoon rig for pike, and don't use more than 30–35/100 nylon.

• The Silver or Coho Salmon (*Oncorhynchus kisutch*)
This fish owes its name to its extremely silvery coloring, with small black marks on the upper flank and tail. This is another "small" salmon – all the other salmon varieties are small, compared with the king, but it can still reach a respectable 5 lb 8 oz–11 lb (2.5–5 kg), with the record breaker found in Prince William Sound, Alaska, weighing 27 lb (11 kg). Together with the king salmon, the silver or coho salmon is certainly the most sought-after Pacific salmon, firstly because of its very energetic fighting spirit but also for its delicate flavor. Like the red salmon, it is unlikely to bite as it enters the river, but becomes more and more aggressive as it approaches the spawning grounds. It is rarely found in large groups, and often mixes with other varieties of salmon. The silver salmon swims rivers on the western coast of North America and Kamchatka, from the beginning of August through mid-September, with a peak during the last half of August. It takes at the same lures as the red salmon but, as spawning approaches, it seems to respond to dry flies. A very enjoyable salmon to fish!

• The Chum or Dog Salmon (*Oncorhynchus keta*)
This is another much-maligned salmon. Although during spawning it does not have the spectacular fighting nature of its close relation, the king salmon, the chum is a formidable opponent, despite its relatively small size. It has an average weight of 11–27 lb (5–12.5 kg), and the record is a formidable 34 lb (16.5 kg) chum caught in Alaska. The reason why the chum is also known as the dog salmon is because during the breeding season, it develops an extraordinary extended lower jaw which reveals its impressive array of teeth. It is undoubtedly a strange fish but it cannot be said to be ugly, with its striped flanks and large, sad eyes. Like all Pacific salmon, it is a superb, sleek, silvery fish before it begins its post-spawning endocrine transformation. The chum or dog salmon is very willing to bite with fly- or rod-and-reel-fishing and its defenses are as formidable as those of any king or coho salmon. The chum is the only salmon found in Alaska's Arctic regions, where it is a very important commodity for the local Inuit people, who use dried salmon filets to feed their huskies.

△ *Large "feather duster" for fishing king salmon.*

There is a story about chum salmon on the Noatak River in Alaska, where these fish were formerly the cornerstone of the region's economy. The Inuit believed that salmon were a race of special men, immortals, who lived in underwater homes during winter. At the end of spring, they would turn into scaly beings, when they would swim upriver in tight shoals to offer themselves as food to the "people of salmon and caribou". This sacrifice did not destroy the man-salmon. All the fisherman had to do was remove its skin and throw the bones back into the river, and they would swim back to the ocean where they would give new life to the men who would again inhabit their underwater homes – so that the cycle could begin again in just the same way as the life cycle of the chum, red, pink, king, and Atlantic salmon.

• The Pink Salmon (*Oncorhynchus gorbuscha*)
Also known as the pinky or humpback salmon, this

◁ Red salmon caught with a fly on the Kenai River in Alaska. A large streamer managed to whet the appetite of a fish which is usually reluctant to bite.

small fish weighs between 3 lb 5 oz–6 lb 8 oz (1.5–3 kg). Many anglers look down on this salmon – or at least those who catch it near its spawning grounds when, after mysterious physical changes, it acquires a rather unattractive shape. The lower jaw curls up into a kind of beak, and an enormous hump appears on its back extending right up to the back of its head. This appearance hides the fact that the pink salmon is an interesting fighter, especially when fished at sea and when it is still silver in color with the same sleek shape of all the other salmonidae. Most of the canned Pacific salmon is pink salmon, which just goes to show its economic importance. The pink salmon is worth fishing, as are all Pacific salmon. For the angler who is new to the west coast of North America, this is a species which is present in great numbers during August and offers as much sport to the salmon fisher as the king, red, or silver varieties.

Magnificent male silver salmon caught with a fly on Clear Creek, Alaska. As spawning approaches, the fish loses its beautiful silver coat. ▽

FISHING DESTINATIONS FOR THE ATLANTIC SALMON

There are plenty of hospitable European destinations, such as Ireland, Scotland, or Norway, while others are much more remote and exotic, such as the Kola peninsula in Russia, which has been opened to anglers from the West for some years.

• Ireland

Ireland is one of the least expensive angling destinations in Europe, much loved by the French. The best times to visit are April to June for spring salmon, which weigh between 10 lb–18 lb (4 and 7.5 kg), and mid-June to September for small grylse. Ireland is a very pleasant country, and angling tourists are particularly welcome. The only problem is the often treacherous weather conditions, with rain and wind being the norm even in high summer. But this is soon forgotten when you discover this country of a thousand lakes and rivers. Ireland has some beautifully set rivers such as the Moy, with its famous Rich Pool in Ballina, which is open to all but has to be reserved years in advance. The Moy, the Black Water, and the Suir are among the most beautiful rivers in Europe.

• Scotland

In this picture-book country of lochs and castles, where the landscape is wild and magnificent, you can find very large salmon to battle against from the first day of the fishing season on famous rivers like the Spey, Tay, and Dee. It can sometimes be an expensive destination, but it's worth every penny. Again, the weather is a force to be reckoned with, even in high summer. May you hook a salmon like the one caught on the Tay in 1922 by a Miss Balantine, aged 18, which weighed 67 lb (29 kg)!

• Norway

Many Norwegian rivers are open to fishermen, with relatively low daily fees, and they contain some lovely fish, both sea-trout and salmon. The most accessible rivers are around Stavanger, the best being the Orkla, Gola, Aidal, Aerdal, Vorma, and Sand. The upper reaches of the Tana, contains some real prize catches, and it has been fished by the most famous people in the angling world, including Hemingway, who in 1928 landed a record catch of 90 lb (39.5 kg)!

• Iceland

Iceland is expensive but excellent! It offers incredibly clear rivers in whose waters you can detect the unmistakable outlines of a thousand great salmon, who swim among the

◁ *Chum salmon are not popular with American anglers. The chum, however, is a magnificent fighter which, contrary to popular belief, bites very well with fly fishing!*

geysers and boiling lava pools, at the bottom of inaccessible canyons. Iceland is a real Eldorado, but it is for anglers who already have their pot of gold!

• Kola Peninsula, Russia

The rivers of the Kola peninsula, on Russia's border with Finland, have only recently been opened to anglers from the West. Because they haven't been fished intensely for decades, the Kola is an unexplored fisherman's heaven. You should however, avoid visiting in August, when low water levels can prove disastrous. The rivers of the Kola peninsula can be divided into two categories. Those which run from south to north, into the Barents Sea, include (from west to east) the Rynda, Khanluka, Litza, Sodoruka, Varzina, and Jokanga. Then there are the rivers which run from north to south, into the White Sea. From west to east again, rivers include the Umba, Vareuga (and its tributary, the Pona), and the Strelma. Finally, there is the Ponoy, which bisects the peninsula. The rivers on the north coast are very similar to those in Iceland, cutting through canyons and rocky gorges. Those on the south coast run through a landscape of steppes and scraggy pine forests. The largest fish (the average weight is 33 lb (15 kg)) swim through the rivers of the north coast from mid-May to June. Having spent up to four years at sea, some weigh as much as 45 lb–67 lb (20–30 kg).

IS THE SALMON AN ENDANGERED SPECIES?

We have decided to devote a large part of this chapter to salmon conservation, but also to the tortuous and sometimes contradictory regulations concerning spawning. The salmon continues to be a victim of absurd regulations which permit new dams to be built in places where they are totally unnecessary; and of pollution and barrier nets in estuaries. To say nothing of the fact that the salmon is the victim of widespread poaching. It is a miracle that a few of the salmon of Brittany still manage to find their way back to the rivers in which they were born. Despite all the steps taken to try and protect it, this particular European salmon is in danger of extinction. With the extinction of the wild Atlantic salmon of Brittany, French angling would lose its soul.

• Hope in Brittany

For many years now, Brittany fishermen have made a number of improvements to their rivers. They have fought pollution, restored and cleaned rivers, and cleared migratory paths, and finally, they have got a result. In the mid 1990s, salmon in spectacular numbers were seen homing in several rivers in the Armorican peninsula and Lower

△ *The pink salmon is a superb, sleek and silver fish during its thalassic journey, but acquires a prominent hump as it approaches its spawning grounds.*

Normandy basins, as well as in rivers such as the Blavet, Ellé, Scorf, and Aulne.

• Nets remain a menace in the Garonne-Dordogne basin

Twenty years ago, operations began to bring wild salmon back to the Dordogne salmon, and in 1994, a significant number of breeding pairs returned to the Argentat spawning grounds for the first time. The fish ladder in the Tuillères dam, the last obstacle before the large dams of upper Dordogne, was jumped by 331 fish, enabling them to reach the unblocked part of the river. Forty-three mating salmon were caught in the trap on the Bergerac ladder for egg-laying at the Vitrac fish-farm.

On the Garonne, 134 salmon were noted in the Golfech ladder near Agen, and, for the first time, 55 fish traveled upstream from the Bazacle dam in Toulouse. Today, breeding salmon swim home up the Garonne, Aveze, Aveyron, Tarn, and the Lot.

It may well be asked why there has been a sudden resurgence of the wild salmon population, giving hope to the continuation of the Atlantic salmon species. It is due to the exceptional climatic conditions which favor the migrating fish, namely the very high levels of cloudy water all year round which has meant that a lot of them managed to avoid the nets still being laid for them in the Gironde estuary. The practice of netting wild salmon, whether legal or illegal, have so far ruined the efforts of anglers to repopulate and revive the traditional French salmon rivers.

• Nets still in the Adour Basin

For the past 10 years, anglers on several rivers around the Adour Basin have worked hard to encourage migrating fish to return and breed. Forty-three dams have been equipped with fish-gates which have allowed the salmon to swim up mountain rivers such as Ossau, Pau, Mauléon, and Aspe. Unfortunately, yet again, poaching continues to be rife, with nets being laid in the Adour estuary, which is supposed to be a marine protection zone for about 12 miles (20 km) of its length.

▽ *This beautiful Scottish salmon has made its last journey up the Spey.*

• Salmon returning to the Rhine

In the 19th century, the salmon population of the Rhine was measured at being more than 200,000 breeding fish. Then, like most rivers that acquired hydroelectric dams with no migratory fish-gates or fish-ladders and due to growing industrial pollution, this large silvery fish completely disappeared in the 1950s.

Then there was the spectacular pollution of the Rhine caused by the Sandoz plant, though this had at least one positive consequence. It was suddenly realised by the countries through which the river runs – Switzerland, Germany, France, Luxembourg and Holland – that the Rhine might remain sterile forever. They consequently decided to take steps to improve its water quality. In the early 1980s, the scientific authorities which formed the International Commission for Protecting the Rhine Against Pollution recorded the first arrivals of sea-trout. They then devised a regional plan intended to see the return of migrating fish – especially salmon – to the river by the year 2000.

• Catastrophe on the salmon rivers of France!

In 1985, 573 redds were counted on the Loire-Alier basin, the site of the best salmon fishing in France. By 1994, the number had fallen to 26. Given that each female breeding salmon makes at least two redds, that's a very small number of breeding pairs – so small that specialists already see the species on this basin as extinct.

The reduction in the number of salmon is due to an accumulation of reasons. For this reason, the only effective measures which can save the Atlantic salmon in western Europe must be comprehensive and multi-national. Although the 18 physical obstructions on the Loire-Allier waterway are the major obstacle to homing fish, and the Loire's silt-laden estuary can sometimes constitute an unbreachable barrier for the fish, there are other more bizarre obstacles to anadromous migration. Because the estuary has become choked with silt, the fish arrive in the river late in the season and have to pause for long periods in the intermediate sections. By that time, it is summer and the water is warm and low in oxygen. The fish therefore cannot reach their spawning grounds in time and will die en route unless they reach the mouth of the Allier at the beginning of the summer.

Fly-fishing on a river on the Kola peninsula in Russia, which runs through a magnificent gorge.

• The guilty parties: Hydroelectric dams

In less than a century, hydroelectric dams have reduced breeding grounds by more then 90 percent. Saint-Etienne-du-Vigan was the first hydroelectric dam built on the Allier in 1898, blocking off 30 percent of the best spawning grounds on the river. It is due to be dismantled as part of the Loire "Return to Nature" project. The dam would never have been given planning permission today, because it is on a river classified as one inhabited by migrating fish and does not have any fish ladders.

Poutes-Monistrol, built in 1941, was the final great blow dealt to salmon on the river, which had already been excluded from three-quarters of the Allier's best spawning grounds. The dam holds 6.6 million cu. ft (2 million m^3) of water and diverts nearly the whole river through $4^1/_2$ miles (10 km) of magnificent gorges by means of an artificial conduit to the Monistrol hydroelectric plant. Although it has a perfectly good fish-elevator, which was built in 1986, salmon rarely take the "old Allier" up to the dam since its waters are now so shallow, and are forced to spawn beneath the power station, where the water is much too powerful. It is a particularly unsuitable spawning ground, since sluicing can wash the spawn away. The positive action group SOS Loire Vivante managed to increase the reserved flow rate from a paltry 125 gallons (500 liters) per second to 11 cu. ft (3.3 m^3) per second, which was reduced to 8.3 cu. ft (2.5 m^3) from 1st June 1993, after they had occupied the dam in 1991. Let us hope that this will encourage a few more salmon to take the elevator and reproduce in the strong currents situated above Pont d'Alleyras. Since then, yet another power station, Naussac I, has been built, fed by the diversion of the Chapeau-

roux (formerly a wonderful salmon river) and Naussac II is now planned to replace Naussac I, as the Chapeauroux did not provide enough water to fill the reservoir. This dam will be built on the Allier's riverbed near Langogne. Naussac I and II will provide enough water flow in the Allier during the summer to irrigate the Limage plains and provide water for the nuclear power plants. Other dams like the one at Grangent on the Loire prevent migrating fish from ever reaching the upper reaches of the river.

• The Deadly Silt Dam

Although silt build-up due to the arrival of fine sediments is a natural phenomenon in most estuaries, it is reaching worrying levels in the Loire estuary, which is on the receiving end of all the industrial, agricultural, and domestic pollution from the whole basin. Although the silt covered only 32 miles (20 km) in 1960, it now reaches as far upstream as Nantes.

Between Nantes and Saint-Nazaire, 500,000 tonnes of toxic mud with a high concentration of heavy metals, such as lead and mercury, can be seen when the tide is low. In low water and very hot weather, the centre of the silt dam is completely devoid of oxygen, forming an impossible barrier for salmon, and of course for all the other freshwater fish, such as mullet, of which thousands die every year in the estuary, where they come to spawn. American-style dredging, which involves scraping the mud from the bottom and dispersing it in the water, means there is a constant suspension of the sediment, which only contributes to this silt barrier. Today, it would need a flood with a minimum flow rate of 6,600 cu. feet per second (2,000 m^3 per second) to push this muddy barrier out into the sea once and for all. Furthermore, the destruction of rocky outcrops to aid navigation on the Loire has allowed the estuary's putrid water to reach much higher upriver, aided by high tides. There are other obstacles in this catalogue of horrors: nuclear power stations and their water supplies (acting as real traps for descending salmon, who get stuck in the turbines), gravel extraction which decimates the spawning grounds, and poorly designed structures such as the Vichy bridge dam. Two fish-ladders, one on each bank, will soon be constructed with the help of a local government grant. As if all this were not enough, overfishing, by legal and illegal fishermen alike, is reducing the salmon population even further. It is a wonder that any salmon manage to reproduce in the upper Allier at all!

FRIENDS OF THE SALMON

The British Waterways Authority was recently brought to task by anglers who claimed that the rivers were being made too clean! Since so many fish shelter beneath and behind obstructions, fishermen felt they were being endangered. However, clean English and Welsh rivers are good news for salmon fishermen. Bad news, however, comes from Scottish salmon farms, which have been hit by a new virus. If the virus is allowed to escape and attack wild salmon, the consequences will be dire indeed. It is not known if infected fry have managed to get into the rivers and streams.

• Ed Chaney

Ed Chaney is Mr American Salmon. His campaigning and research have led to the spectacular return of migrating fish, particularly on the Columbia River, between Oregon and Washington states. Today, only 350,000 salmon of the various Pacific varieties swim home to breed on rivers that 50 years ago contained 16 million salmon! According to Chaney, 80 percent of the blame can be attributed to hydroelectric dams, and in the United States, 10 percent is due to agriculture and deforestation, the rest being caused by pollution, watersports and fishing.

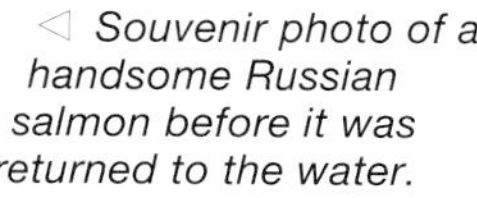

◁ Souvenir photo of a handsome Russian salmon before it was returned to the water.

SEA-TROUT

THE TACKLE

The tackle you choose depends largely on the average size of the fish in the river, the type of obstacles cluttering its bed and, of course, the current and flow. The larger the river, the stronger the currents, and you will have to equip yourself with sturdier tackle.

When rod-and-reel fishing, reliable tackle, especially clutch quality, is essential. ▽

A one-handed rod is perfect for smaller rivers. For fishing in wide and deep water, choose a 12-foot two-handed rod which will give you better control of drift. ▽

In this chapter, we will be discussing the delightful little coastal rivers of Ireland, an angling paradise where the sea-trout have a fairly small average size of 16 in (40 cm) and weigh 14 oz–1lb 2 oz (0.4–0.5 kg). When fishing for these trout, which are nonetheless good fighters, ultra-light or fly-fishing with a classic trout rig will give you the best results. And a pound of sea-trout squirming at the end of a 12 or 14/100 line is a sporting as fishing can get!

ROD-AND-REEL FISHING

We recommend ultra-light fishing for great sport since it gives a good feel for the trout's fighting spirit. To do that, you need to choose your rod and reel very carefully.

RELIABLE TACKLE

You will need a rod of a reasonable size (at least 7 feet (2 m), with a maximum length of 8 feet (2.4 m)) so you can control any sudden leaps and rapid departures the trout may decide to perform. Most ultra-light rods are, unfortunately, far too short but some manufacturers do have some excellent models. Hardy, for example, has a 8 foot (2.4 m) "insect fishing special" rod which is unparalleled for dealing with larger fish. Then there is the Vega 0.5–3 g by Sert, made by Taboury and Boileau.

The reel is the centerpiece of tackle for fishing large sea-trout on an ultra-light rig. The spool should hold 500 feet (150 m) of 14/100, and the clutch should be more than just OK. It's worth noting that most reels have back clutches which can sometimes catch.

A clutch placed on the spool, on the other hand, will work perfectly but unfortunately there are few reels these days which are equipped to take this mechanism. The Mitchell 308 and Penn ultra-light special are cream of the crop and virtually indestructible. Shimano, Dam, and Daiwa reels are also excellent choices.

• Classic Casting Rods

To control large fish and fish on large rivers, you have to go for strength and reliability in your rod: an 11 lb (5 kg) sea-trout can run off with 333 ft (100 m) of 35/100 nylon in one movement. All 8–10 foot (2.5–3 m) light or semi-light rods are good. Makes available include Garbolino, Mitchell, Sert, Dam, Shimano, and Daiwa, to name but a few. Some of the coastal rivers in which sea-trout

△ *Fly fishing is a sure thing for night fishing.*

are fished have very high banks, and to give you control of your fish during a fight, you will need a rod that is long enough to cope. Bubble-float rods for bass are very useful in this case, or even Mitchell's Super bubble-float, which is 14 feet (4.2 m) long ($1\frac{3}{4}$–4 oz (50–120 g) capacity).

• Light to Semi-light Reels
These should contain 500 feet (150 m) of 28, 35, or even 40/100 nylon, depending on debris and obstacles. They should have the same properties as those listed for ultra-light reels.

SEA-TROUT LURES

• Spinners
If you are using an ultra-light rig, small no. 0–1 spinners will be fine. Use silvery blades for slightly cloudy water, and golden blades for clear water. It gets more complicated when fishing for larger trout, in which case you should use larger no. 2 or even no. 3 spinners.
Normandy fishermen prefer the white no. 3 Mepps with black dots, replacing the treble with a stronger single iron or steel hook.
White spotted spinners are also very popular and great for fast flowing or slightly cloudy water. Some swear by tandem spinners, with a smaller blade at the top, near the eyelet.

• Spoons
Because they fish more deeply than spinners in whitewater conditions, spoons are indispensable for fishing in the strong currents of large rivers. A silvery spoon with a thin, streamlined blade looks like a sand-eel to the trout, and since sand-eels constitute a large part of the sea-trout's daily diet when it is at sea, the spoon is an effective lure. Heavier blades are useful for fishing the deeper waters in which trout hide during the day. The Orkla, for example, is very popular with Scandinavian anglers. As a general rule, light spoons should be leaded by placing a sinker on the mainline, around 3 feet (1 m) from the lure.

• Devons
Devons are not much used in game fishing because they can cause twisted lines, especially with thin nylon, but they are an essential item in the Irish or Scottish angler's tackle box and are used at the beginning of the season and in fast flowing water. The devon is very effective in rapids because its shape and weight mean that it sinks quickly to the required depth, swims very attractively in the water, and gives precise casts. Some devons are made out of brass or bronze, but Scottish ones are made of wood.

• Plugs
Some sport anglers use plugs and nothing else. The favorite is a small $\frac{1}{16}$–$\frac{1}{8}$ oz (3–5 g) hand-painted Rapala, resembling a young trout.

△ *A handy box for organizing your lures.*

FLY-FISHING

As soon as night falls, sea-trout go hunting in the current, and this is when they are most likely to snap at an artificial wet or dry fly.

STURDY AND RELIABLE TACKLE

• Fly Reels
Although fine for trout or grayling, automatic reels are strictly not advisable for sea-trout fishing.
An automatic reel only has enough capacity for the silk, not for the backing, and backing is indispensable when fishing for large sea-trout. Go instead for a manual reel which is well adjusted and has sufficient capacity for 167–500 feet (50–150 m) of backing, depending on the average size of the catch.
English reels, particular those made by Hardy, are generally the best, but unfortunately they are also among the most expensive!
Special mention should be made of the Daiwa Osprey, made in the United Kingdom, which offers almost unbeatable value for money.

△ *It is important to fish near the banks, where sea-trout often gather.*

• Fly Rods

Going back to our small coastal river in Ireland with its stock of medium-sized trout, a classic trout rig is perfect. Everywhere else, you will need to rig for strength and robustness.

The 9-foot rod is a good all-rounder and perfect for small rivers that do not necessitate long casts.

Choose rods for no. 7–8 silks such as the Sage GFL 796, the Sourdot Voyager by Astucit (very practical lightweight option), or 9-foot Daiwa Super Samurai. Still on the subject of one-handed rods, if you are fishing from a high bank, an 11-foot rod is useful but difficult to handle for long periods of time.

For large fish, and high banks – when fishing in a large river, where you have to cast very far out – the best option is a 12–15-foot two-handed rod with a no. 9–11 line.

For those on a budget, Silstar rods are an excellent low-cost choice. Anyone who can afford top-of-the-range tackle should consider a Hardy Favourite Salmon (no. 9 silk) or Shimano Twin Power Salmon (no. 9–11 silk).

△▽ *Hugh Falkus flies for sea-trout.*

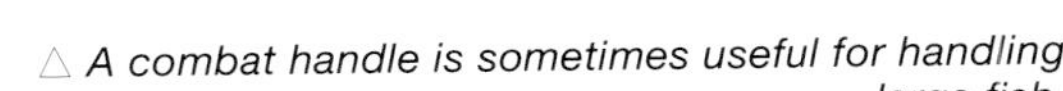

△ *A combat handle is sometimes useful for handling large fish.*

TYPES OF FLY

The superb collection of trout flies includes more than a hundred different types, all of which are a beautiful sight. However, with ten basic flies, you can fish in nearly all types of river, as long as you have a good range of sizes to match the type of water being fished, with hooks ranging from no. 4 through no. 10.

• British Flies

Here is a basic list of flies suitable for all occasions: Lemon Grey, Zulu, Peter Ross, Silver Blue, Black Pennel, Blue Doctor, Blue and Claret, Jock Scott Special, Connemara Black, and Hairy Mary, all of which are British flies.

• French Flies

Of the major French flies – or rather, Brittany or Normandy flies – the Perruche and Touques are

JB SWIVELS:

Whether fishing for sea-trout, salmon, or any other game fish, takes are often lost due to unreliable tackle. One accessory to which too little attention is paid but which is extremely important is the swivel. The swivel has to be in perfect working order and is an essential part of the rig. Anglers fishing for prize catches in the United States will all tell you the same story. Most cases of breakage, especially when fishing with rod is due to the swivel either breaking or bending on the line. Today, there are a large number of swivels made in the Far East which are relatively inexpensive but not up to scratch when it comes to holding a large fish which has decided to make a break for it and swim away rapidly. One exception to the rule is the JB swivel, which is made in a little village called, Jaligny-sur-

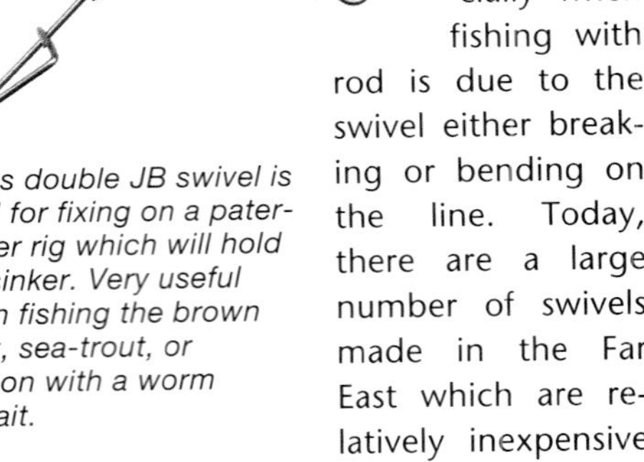

△*This double JB swivel is used for fixing on a paternoster rig which will hold the sinker. Very useful when fishing the brown trout, sea-trout, or salmon with a worm as bait.*

light versions, with the darker Prenante, Seulles and Divine flies.

• Other dry and wet flies
It is worth remembering that artificial shrimp make an excellent bait in May (on the rivers of Donegal for instance). Hugh Falkus lures, with several hooks, such as the Silver Corte, All Black or Dressed Quill, all in their blue versions are also effective.
For wet flies, Hugh Falkus adds the Medicine, again in its blue version. The Medicine is tied on a low-water salmon hook and lightly dressed. After some time, the Medicine is replaced with a lure on a sinking line. Hugh Falkus's own fishing ground is in Cumbria, on the borders of Scotland, but his methods work in almost any sea-trout environment from west Wales to Ireland, and even in the United States where they have been used with great success to catch migratory rainbow trout.

A Strategy for Quality

Besbre, in Britanny which happens to be on the Allier, one of France's most famous trout rivers. It is the only truly reliable swivel we have ever found. The triangular head distinguishes it from the flimsy Far Eastern imitations, as does its polished finish. However, where it really scores is in the exceptional resistance of the components, especially the stainless steel fastening.
Proof of its quality was provided recently in Finland, where the JB won a prize for best swivel.
Jean and Alain Masseret, the two co-directors of JB, are only interested in providing the best possible quality. JB swivels are handmade individually on a series of small specially designed machine tools which are themselves marvels of ingenuity.
The production cost of an Asian-made swivel is around 30¢, as against $1.60 for a JB. But on the water, what angler would regret paying a few pennies more when trying to land a large catch!

△ Small double swivel, for trout fishing with worms.

△ Sea-trout become active at nightfall.

Worms, flies and maggots
The worm is one of the hardest ways to fish for sea-trout. When freelining with a single lobworm, it has to be cast way out in midstream, almost to the opposite bank. A premature strike may result in a mangled worm and a lost catch, so cast, retrieve slowly and do not let the bale arm close. The fish needs to be able to maneuver, letting it assume for a short time that it has a genuine catch.
When fishing with maggots, load a single maggot onto a forward single hook, then add a treble, to which a cluster of wriggling maggots it attached. A sea-trout may nibble half-heartedly on the single maggot, but this will arouse its appetite and it will enthusiastically grab the cluster attached to the treble.

Irish flies for sea-trout. ▽

THE CATCH

In many European rivers, the sea-trout bears a strange resemblance to the salmon, especially as it can reach similar sizes, often more than 11 lb (5 kg). It is also true that its silver coloring can add to the confusion if you do not notice the few anatomical differences – which aren't that easy to identify – separating the two species.

Irish sea-trout are generally quite small on the rivers of Donegal, but very pleasant to fish! ▽

The rapid departure of a sea-trout as soon as it bites – makes it look as though we're in for a fight! ▽

A CLOSE RESEMBLANCE TO THE SALMON

A newly arrived sea-trout can measure from 14 inches (35 cm) (finnock) to 36 inches (90 cm) or even up to 40 inches (1 m) for the largest specimens. These fish can weigh more than 22 lb (10 kg). Adult trout have a rounded, stocky body, with a thin lengthwise stripe and are covered in several cross-shaped marks especially above the stripe. The sea-trout is silver in color at the beginning of the season, turning orange as the breeding season approaches, especially the male.

The sea-trout also has a thick caudal peduncle, a straight or convex outside edge to the caudal fin and 13 through 16 scales (often 14) between the thin stripe and the adipose fin. The sea-trout is actually a member of the same species as the brown trout (*Salmo truita*), but it is a migratory fish and this fact explains the reason for the distinctive coloring.

AN ANADROMOUS MIGRATING TROUT

The sea-trout also bears remarkable similarities to the salmon in its life cycle. Both fish are born in fresh water but develop out at sea, returning to reproduce in their native river, which is why they are known as anadromous migrators. The only way in which they differ from salmon is the fact that the trout spends very little time in the sea, and even then it stays close to the coastline. The fish live mainly close to estuaries or in the breakers of sandy and rocky beaches.

Some large trout which breed in the rivers of Normandy in northern France, such as the Orne and Bresle, move erratically around the sea, sometimes as far north as the coast of Denmark. The trout, then, are born in rivers, where they live for up to three years.

During this time, they look exactly like brown trout, adopting the same solitary and territorial behavior. They feed on various invertebrates or young fish in the water, eating at the surface as well as beneath it.

Differences Between the Sea Trout and the Salmon

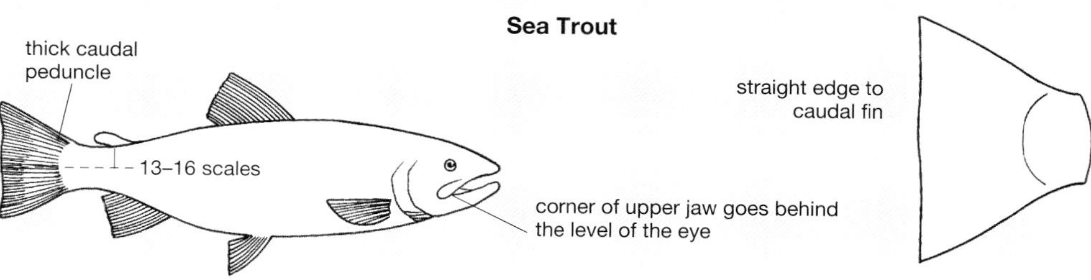

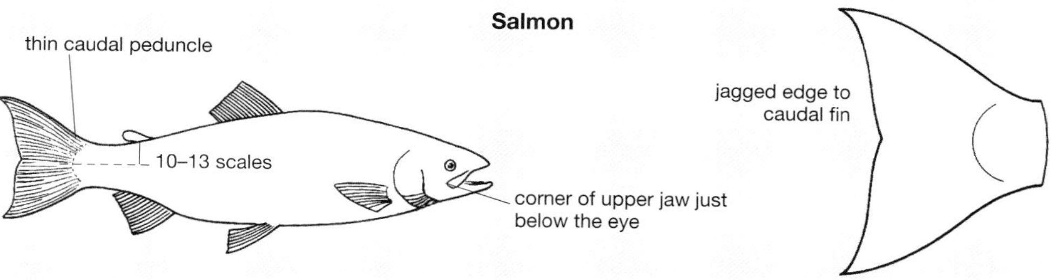

	Sea Trout	Salmon
Caudal fin	*The edge of the caudal fin is straight or slightly convex and thick. The absence of cartilage means that it is difficult to land; hold the fish by the tail.*	*The outside edge of the caudal fin is jagged, thin, and ends in two bony knobs giving a good grip when landing.*
Head	*Very large, with well developed jaws.*	*The snout is thin and long.*
Jaws	*Corner of the mouth goes well behind the eye.*	*The corner of the mouth reaches just below the eye.*
Scales along the lateral line	*14 on average (between 13 and 16).*	*11 on average (between 10 and 13).*
Coloring	*The sea trout is generally more brightly colored. The largest spots can be found below the stripe on its flank.*	*Except during spawning, when it is brightly colored, the salmon has very silvery flanks, covered with small black spots.*

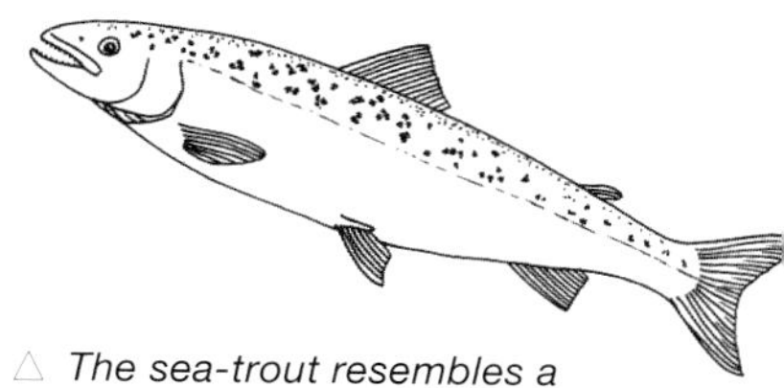
△ *The sea-trout resembles a miniature Atlantic salmon and is almost as delicious.*

Once they reach a size of 5–11 inches (13–28 cm), the sea-trout undergoes smoltification. It has a richly colored silver coat, and there is a gradual loss of pigmentation on the flanks, leaving a few red spots. All its fins lose their color, with only the adipose fin retaining an orange-red border. In many rivers, this phenomenon, which precedes the sea-trout's journey to the sea, takes place in the spring following birth. Then, from January through April, the fish swim in small shoals towards the tidewater (estuary). According to Hugh Falkus, the British angling authority, several things may then happen:

– migration to the sea followed by a return to the river the next summer and then a return to the ocean whether or not the trout have spawned;

– migration to the sea and return to the native river the same summer, followed by winter in freshwater and a return to the ocean in the first few months of the following year, whether or not the trout have spawned;

– migration to the sea and return to the river the same year in winter, then return to the ocean during the same winter or during the following early spring, whether or not the trout have spawned;

– return to the river after a stay of 1–4 years at sea.

The fish which return to fresh water the summer following smoltification and descent to the sea are known as finnocks or herlings. They have an overall silver livery, with black marks which are sometimes cross-shaped. Their average size varies from 10 through 16 inches (25 through 40 cm), and their weight rarely exceeds 1 lb 12 oz (0.8 kg). The fins are often colorless and only a light orange-red border remains on the adipose fin as a reminder of the trout's former river life. These fish migrate, often in great numbers, from July 15 through August 15, having stayed at sea for only three months. The shoals of fish contain individuals of an average size of 2 lb 4 oz–4 lb 8 oz (1–2 kg) in weight, accompanied by a few larger fish. The latter return in October through November, just at spawning time, and can weigh up to 22 lb (10 kg), depending on the breed and type of river. They will have spent 1–4 years at sea. All these figures are given as a guide only, as the periods mentioned can change depending on the state of the water, currents, tidal range, and atmospheric conditions.

THE MOST LIGHT-SHY OF THE SALMONIDS

The sea-trout's habits are similar to those of the large brown trout which only hunts for food at night. The sea-trout is mainly active during dusk. As the sun sets over the ocean, this predator leaves its gloomy refuge to pursue young fish, worms, and various insect larvae, rising to the surface to find whatever insects may be floating past. The sea-trout feeds from sundown to around midnight, with a further burst of activity at daybreak. This is not always the case, however, as the sea-trout will happily feed during the day too, as long as light levels are not too high. The best fishing times are on rainy days or when the sky is totally cloudy.

On the other hand, on hot and very sunny days, the fish remains in hollows and deep pools or sits still in the darkness of shelving banks and crevices; it may be completely apathetic and will refuse to take any lure or bait, no matter how well presented.

A SEA PREDATOR

At the fry stage, the sea-trout has the same diet as its close relative, the brown trout, consisting of large numbers of invertebrates which vary in type depending on the season and area. During the summer, the sea-trout hunts in the currents and still water, happily swallowing any insects which come its way, of which there are many at this time of year. While at sea, the sea-trout eats almost non-stop and grows spectacularly in size, putting on several ounces in less than three months. For the sea-trout – an unforgiving predator which happily ventures into the breakers to satisfy its hunger – anything is a next meal: sprats, sand-eels, sardines, shrimp, and other food picked from the bottom. While diving in an Irish creek at the break of day, we have observed several large trout gathered in groups, chasing sand-eels to the bottom of a hideaway where the small fish, backed into a corner, were the victims of a real massacre. The only escapees managed to get away by leaping desperately out of the water, some even jumping onto dry land in order to escape the jaws of these seafaring predators!

△ *Two peak times – June and October – for trout homing give the angler a chance of a good catch.*

REPRODUCTION: THE RETURN TO THE NATIVE RIVER

Anadromous migration takes sea-trout gradually toward their spawning grounds, situated on the upper parts of rivers where the fish live.

In some Irish or Scottish rivers, the breeding pairs take to small tributaries, spawning in a few inches of water, but in places where the physical and chemical quality of the water and the type of substratum are perfect.

While hunting for snipe on a bog in Donegal, Ireland, along the Crow river, we noticed a strange stirring in a tiny stream leading from a river several yards away. The surface of the water seemed to be boiling on and off, occasionally revealing large fins, which turned out to belong to sea-trout busily preparing their redds.

Reproduction takes place during the winter months, usually November through December, although it can start as early as October. The fish gather in small groups, in areas rich in oxygen and with very clean small pebbles on the bed. Although they can be very aggressive toward other fish in the river, they ignore each other, or at least avoid contact with one another.

The female chooses where the redd should be and she creates it by making a small 8–10 inch (20–25 cm) depression which is more or less round and with a diameter of no more than 40 inches (1 m).

The eggs number 2,000 per kilogram (2 lb 4 oz) of bodyweight and are fertilized by the male as soon as they are laid, then covered in very clean gravel. To do this, the female makes powerful movements with her caudal fin and by flipping her body.

Spawning beds can be easily identified in clear water, because they form a light and clearly visible mark on what is usually a darkened river bed. The incubation period for the roe varies from 90 through 120 days, depending on the temperature of the water (70–80 days for water of 50°F (10°C)), during which time the eggs are as vulnerable as that of the brown trout and attractive to the same predators.

SUCCESSFUL FISHING FOR SEA-TROUT

It seems that every region and every country has its own techniques for sea-trout fishing. More than for any other fish, the sea-trout requires specific techniques which truly reflect a sort of cultural heritage, and sometimes ancient traditions, as in Scotland, for example.

• The Best Times

Success or failure is dictated by a number of factors, some of which are completely independent of each other. One thing remains constant: the sea-trout does not like the light and only bites at night or at dusk. Hugh Falkus gives the percentages of takes during night hours in his admirable book, *The Sea-trout Angler's Bible*:

– 60 percent of takes happen from dusk through to midnight, just below the surface, using a floating silk;
– 10 percent from midnight through 1:00 a.m.,
– from 1:00 a.m. through daybreak, 30 percent of takes occur in much deeper water. The angler needs to use a fast sinking line and reel in slowly as close as possible to the bottom.
Falkus is one of the greatest angling authorities in the world and his figures are beyond reproach, since they have been compiled from many years of practice – and many nights spent by the water!
Of course, you can try fishing for sea-trout during the day, as long as the circumstances are right. First of all, it seems that the best weather conditions are an overcast sky, warm but humid weather with even a little light drizzle. Water depth is also important and cold, muddy (chocolate-colored) water is of no use.
The ideal situation is a very slight lowering of the water level, which begins when the levels drop and the river clears following a moderate rise – after a storm, for example – itself preceded by a period of drought, though the dry weather should not last more than a week. This magical moment, together with a certain clearing of the water, can, if it coincides with a high tide in a coastal river, produce some great results.

△ *A trout fishing specialist shows his fly-fishing catch on a Scottish river.*

Floating line rig with livebait for tidewater (estuary) fishing

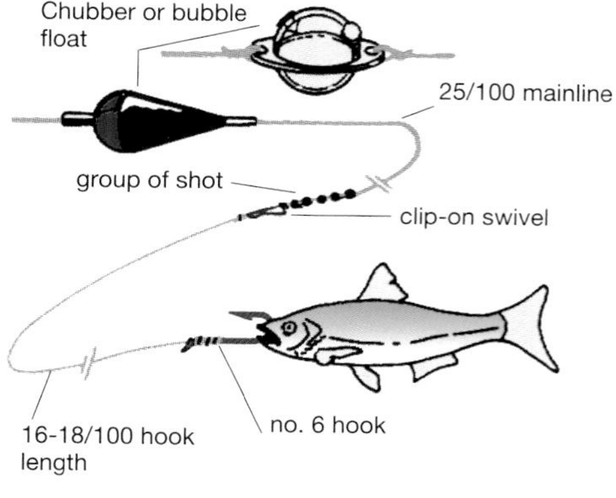

• Good Fishing Spots
Sea-trout follow water flow from tidewater (estuary) to river, and the fish are more likely to bite if they have just made the journey up from the sea. Some of the larger sea-trout simply wait in pools for the end of the season before swimming upriver, when they continue their migration. Some decide to stay where they are and spawn in a small stream near their chosen spot. Those sea-trout which stay in the same place for several months are diabolically fussy!
Several local authority regulations allow anglers to fish for sea-trout with a good chance of success. Permits allow anglers to fish for at least two hours after sundown (which can be midnight in June) and two hours before sunrise. In Normandy, for example, you can fish in October, giving you the chance to pit your skills against the largest fish of all, which swim upriver at this time of year.
Although sea-trout fishing can be disappointing for the novice, your first catch will put up a great fight – ample reward for the effort required for capturing the fish.

DEADBAIT MINNOW FISHING

This technique is practiced in very different ways in different countries where sea-trout swim up the rivers. Although Scottish anglers prefer rod-and-reel fishing with spoons, Normandy fishermen swear by deadbait fishing with minnow at any time of year, as long as the water is clear enough.

• Tackle Adapted for Efficient Rigs
Your rig will depend upon the expected size of fish, and less importantly, the river's strength, water flow, and any apparent obstructions. On some small Irish rivers where finnock weighing no more than 1 lb 12 oz (0.8 kg) swim, the most enjoyable way to fish is

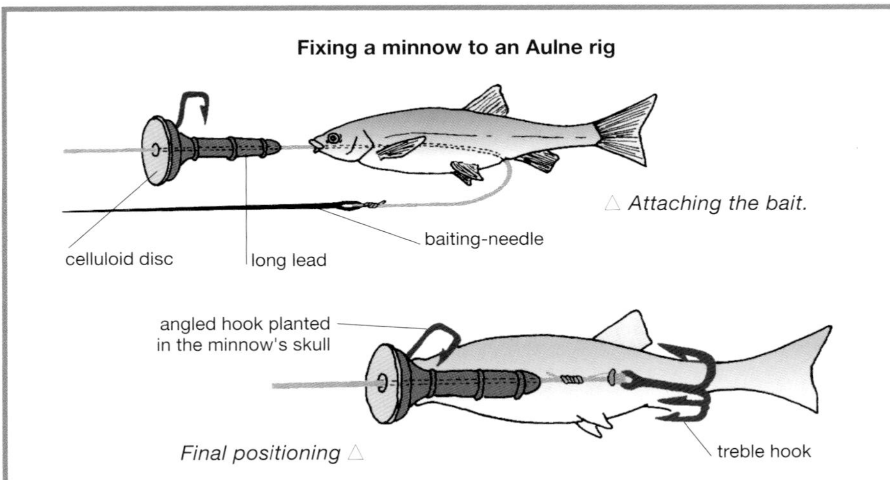

Fixing a minnow to an Aulne rig

△ *Attaching the bait.*

Final positioning △

with an ultra-light rig. On the Touques or Orne in France, where fish measuring up to 32 inches (80 cm) and weighing several pounds swim, you're more likely to need "special salmon" fishing tackle. But for finnocks, or when fishing on rivers in which the average fish weight is around 2 lb 4 oz (1 kg), use a light or ultra-light casting rod with a 1.5–4 g capacity and an excellent fixed-spool reel with a reeling-in capacity of 28 inches (70 cm) per turn and holding a solid 16/100 line. Choose your tackle carefully. With such tackle, you could use a small Aulne rig with a vibrating disc. Another rig we have tried out on lake trout is also very effective. It consists of a small Ariel with three small treble no. 16 hooks, leaded at the head with some shot. This rig keeps the minnow well stretched and it swims gently from side to side, which makes it very attractive to the trout. Very few anglers, with the exception of some experts on the Pavin in Auvergne, fish this way – it is another sea-trout fisherman's secret!
With a large trout, you have to be able to strike with force. A "special minnow" rod such as the Sert Phoxi by Olivier Plassereaud is both strong ($^1/_4$–$^3/_4$ oz (12–20 g)) and lightweight. With this excellent rod, you should be able to cast the minnow on an Aulne rig with precision and control its drift with ease.

Fixing the treble hook on the line loop

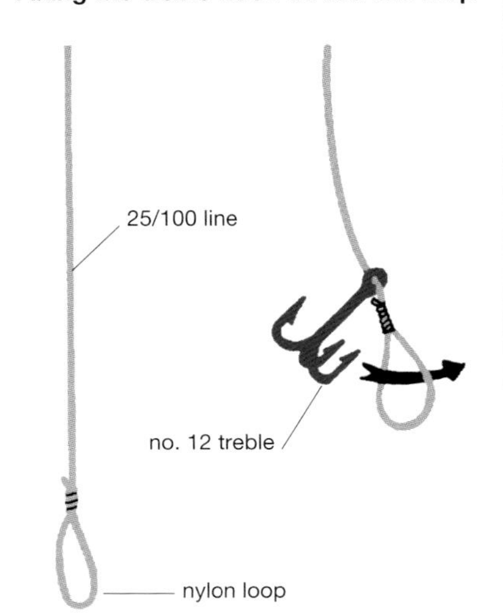

When fishing from high banks for sea-trout weighing up to 22 lb (10kg), you need a stiff 11–12 foot (3.4–3.6 m) rod with a $^3/_4$–$1^1/_2$ oz (20–40 g) capacity. This will help control the sudden departure of a big catch and fishing in deep pools and hollows, beneath the rod tip, using an impact-shielded minnow. Line diameter should also be adapted to the conditions, with a 30–35/100 line being the minimum for retaining hold of the largest catches.

• Rigs and Technique

The Aulne rig, a French rig, consists of a small celluloid disc which causes the minnow to move irregularly as soon as it hits the current. It has a treble no. 8–10 hook, or a single no. 1–2 (see diagram above).
Fishing technique involves casting at right angles to the opposite bank or one-quarter upstream, then maneuvering the minnow into the current, so it drifts in an arc. With a few pulls and releases, you can make the bait more attractive to any waiting trout. This technique and the rig itself are good for fishing current, pools and in still water when the trout are active.
In the middle of the day or during high water, the fish are often to be found at the bottom of deep pools or hidden under concave banks, in the calmer parts of a river. An impact-shielded minnow waggled under the rod is a recipe for success at these times.
Deadbait minnow fishing is a peculiarly French technique for fishing for sea-trout. Most angling authorities in other countries prefer worms or maggots, as well as the traditional dry and wet flies.

FISHING WITH WORMS

During day or night, this technique, which can be practiced from the beginning of the season, is considered by British anglers to be one of the most effective for catching sea-trout.
Elsewhere in Europe, it is reserved for cold and cloudy water, sometimes unnecessarily. Although a large lobworm is certainly the only bait which can tempt a sea-trout when a river is in spate and is thick with chocolate brown mud, it can also be very useful in clear, shallow water. Fishing with worms can be quite difficult during the night, however, as the worms are almost systematically devoured by eels before the sea-trout gets near them.

• Anglers' Worms

There are many types and species of worm, all of which are of a specific use to the angler:
– the lobworm (*Lumbricus terrestris*) is ideal for very high and cloudy floodwater;
– the large blackheaded worm (*Allolobophora langa*), which is good for medium-to-strong currents;

– the small blackheaded worm (*Allolophota caliginosa*), for normal water depths and flow levels;
– the redworm (*Eisina foetida*) and the brandling (*Lumbricus rubellus*), as well as the earthworm, are recommended for shallow and clear water.

• How to Prepare for Worm Fishing

The Irish fish during high water, placing their bait, leaded with an olive sinker, in the water downstream of a waterfall or similar obstruction which is difficult to jump. The fish, using the fast flowing water to start their ascent, swim in the hollow for a long time before trying to jump the waterfall – where they will eventually take a bunch of lobworm presented for their attention.

On many Scottish rivers, where only artificial fly fishing is allowed, a dispensation concerning the use of worms is occasionally given when the river is in spate.

Anglers then use a fly-fishing rod – usually 10 ft 6 in through 11 foot long – which gives excellent drift control and a good handle on the largest fish. Two-handed rods are also very useful.

In France, the most commonly used rod is a telescopic version with guide rings, 15–20 feet (4.5–6 m) in length, robust, and with a quivertip. If the fish are not too big, a fixed-spool rod, such as those used for fishing lake-bound trout in the high mountains, is an excellent compromise and makes the most of very refined methods needed to catch this tricky fish. The fixed-spool reel contains 500 feet (150 m) of 24–35/100 line.

Lobworm. ▷

• Rigs

The best rig, given the number of casts and sinks required, have two no. 1/0 and 2/0 hooks with barbed shanks, and is known as a Stewart rig. This holds the bait well, even when it is buffeted by the most violent currents.

The hook length, with a diameter 2/100 less than the mainline, should be 24–32 inches (60–80 cm) long and attached with a JB swivel. The lead can be a little olive sitting on the swivel's eyelet, or a better option for cluttered riverbeds is a group of shot pinched onto a paternoster rig.

Use soft shot which can easily be removed and added to so you can adapt the weight to the depth required.

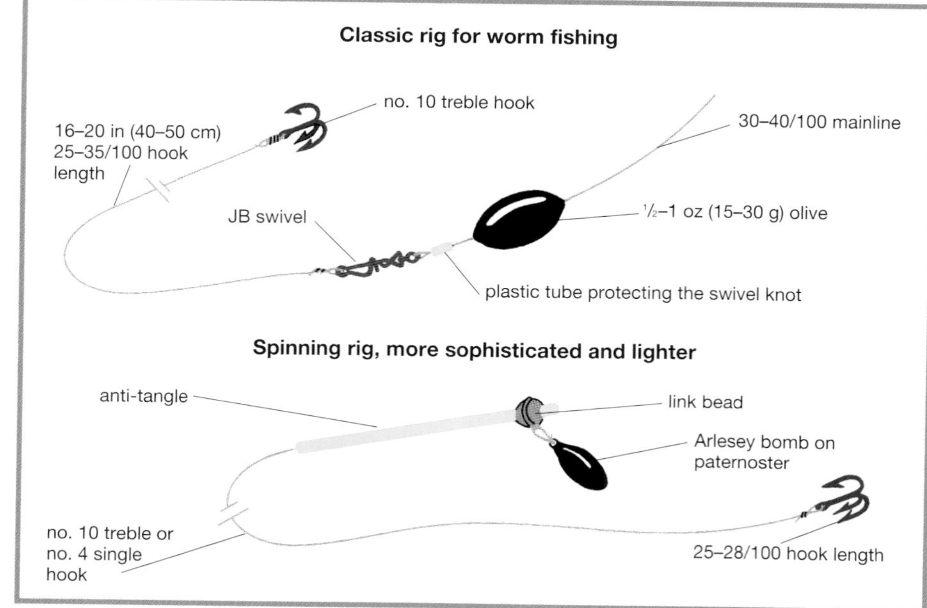

• Fishing Technique

This will vary depending on the water type. In shallow, clear water, during the day, fish at the beginning of the day downstream of rocky beds and other obstructions, proceeding upstream, exactly as if you were trotting for brown trout. The worm needs to roll slowly across the bottom, in the right current. When the water is fast-flowing, it is better to use slower, smaller drifts, in an arc, casting at right angles to the opposite bank. All areas of the river should be swept using this method, passing just above the gravel bottom. Watch out for any unusual snagging or a sudden stop as the bait drifts. Once you get a bite, let the line go for a few moments before striking energetically.

ROD-AND-REEL LURE FISHING

Lures have their own particular followers, especially for fishing on the coastal rivers of Normandy or Brittany. It is true that in any season, as long as the water is not too high and especially not too cloudy, this technique is very effective during the day. Experience has proved, however, that at night and at dusk, fly-fishing still reigns supreme.

Those keen on new tackle should go for a rod with a more flexible tip and a softer action which gives more precise casting, the key to success when fishing for the very fussy sea-trout.

• Spoon and Spinner Fishing

Spoons and spinners are, without a doubt, the most popular lures for sea-trout. Depending on the conditions, you should use:

– *Undulating spoons*

These have their own advocates and are unequaled in deep, slightly cloudy, cold water. The ⅛ oz (6 g) Toby is excellent, as are all spoons with a long blade. Use heavy

OTHER LIVEBAIT

Another very effective livebait is the shrimp. Two small, live shrimp are hooked through the last few tail segments – and for this, you need to use a floating line – or are fixed to an identical rig, smaller than one used for salmon. In a tidewater (estuary), a live sand-eel can also be a very effective bait.

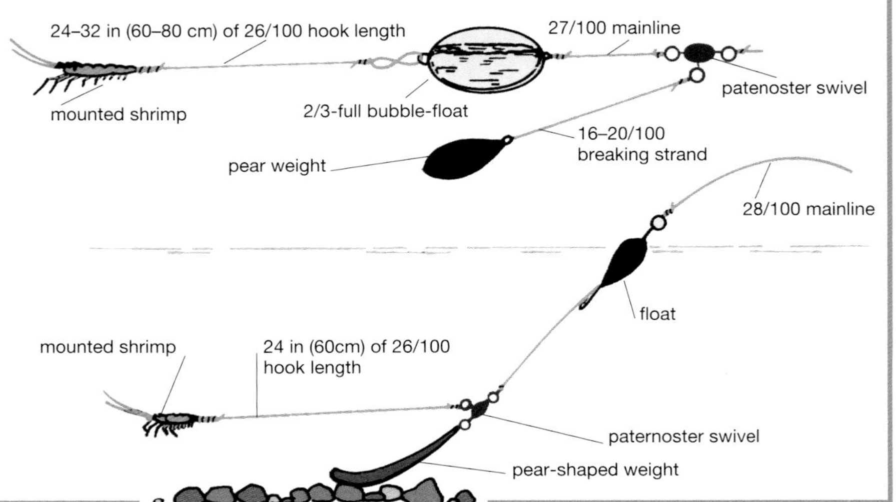

Two rigs for fishing with shrimp in deep hollows

spoons for deep water, light ones for fast-flowing currents.

– *Spinners*

Once the weather improves, when the water temperature rises and clears, the spinner comes into its own for the sea-trout angler. Spinners can be used at any hour of the day, but the best results appear to have been achieved at dusk and dawn. Traditionally, anglers in Normandy and Brittany use no. 2 or 3 spinning "nail" blades with black marks. The small no. 2 Quimperloise is excellent for fishing in slow-moving, deep pools and hollows; its rubber-covered lead makes the lure sink quickly for working on the bottom of the river. When fishing for finnocks or smaller fish weighing no more than 3 lb 5 oz (1.5 kg), an ultra-light rod is really effective, especially with a small no. 1 Mepps with a golden "nail" blade.

• Jigs

The jig is another kind of lure. It is used extensively in the United States, mainly for catching coarse fish, but it is just as effective on sea-trout, especially in trying to lure them out of a hollow or crevice in the bank.

• Fishing Technique

When the fish are active, proceed in the same way as for brown trout, in other words fish upstream. The sea-trout is a very fussy fish, so take care in your approach and the way you cast, and keep a good distance from the spots you want to fish.

However, as a general rule, cast straight across, one quarter through three quarters upstream. Reel in slowly, making the lure run along the riverbed. Move the lure at each habitat with sideways tip movements, accelerating and releasing the lure as you go.

DEVONS

Devons are traditionally used in France, but are also very popular with British anglers.

This type of lure appeared in Scotland at the end of the 19th century. The 1½–2 inch (4–5 cm) devons for sea-trout fishing, which have defied time and fashion, are still incredibly popular because they fish at great depths in fast currents and are indispensable at the beginning of the season wherever the current drags strongly.

Small devons for trout can be used in shallow, clear water, but it seems to be a better idea to use the real Scottish devons, often made out of wood. They are very light, and rotate even at a very slow reeling-in speed. Hugh Falkus recommends bluish-gold or golden-brown colored devons for sea-trout fishing.

FLY-FISHING

This is one of the most successful methods for fishing at night or during dusk or dawn. Only streamers, wet flies, or tube-flies should be used: a dry fly is only rarely taken by a sea-trout, and why it does so at all remains a complete mystery to us.

For your choice of rod, see page 100 and take care to choose your rod on the basis of the width of the river and the expected size of the fish.

Some one-handed rods with detachable combat handles, such as the Globe-trotter by Marc Sourdot can be used as two-handed rods.

Use a curved cast and avoid miscasting, which can be catastrophic when fishing for sea-trout. An unfurling silk above the water can make this wary fish even more suspicious. Use a manual reel with enough capacity for the line and 50 yards (45 m) of backing line.

• The Right Silk

The type of silk used for the line depends on fishing conditions. For example, the lower the temperature of the water, the deeper the fly needs to sink. At the beginning of the season, therefore, when the water is deep and very cold, use a completely sinking line. In shallow, warm water, on the other hand, you need a floating line so that your fly can be presented near the surface. In any case, the best

◁ *An Irish grand slam! Brown trout, sea-trout and castillon make up a memorable evening's catch.*

all-rounder is a floating line with a sinking tip.

Finally, a heavy, quick-sinking line is extremely useful for fishing in weeds in shallow water. The line falls among the vegetation, while the lure sits above the bottom.

With a wet fly, you don't need a very sophisticated line end: a simple 8 foot (2.5 m) trace in a small river and 10 feet (3 m) in a wider river is quite sufficient.

Purists can make up a rat's tail line end, using a series of nylon strands in the following order: 50/100, 40/100, 35/100, 30/100, and a 24–26/100 tip.

Light fly for clear weather. △

• Choosing your Flies

(See also p.101)

The merits and demerits of the various flies are discussed in the chapter on salmon fishing. As a general rule:

– the warmer the water, the smaller your fly should be – use a no. 4–6 at the beginning of the season, and a no. 8–10 during the summer;

– in overcast weather, strong currents, and cloudy water, use bushy, dark-colored flies;

- in clear weather and shallow, clear water, use small pale-colored flies.

• Fishing Technique

Depending on the condition of the water, slow-moving, deep pools offer the best prospects early in the season, and smaller currents and eddies when the weather becomes warmer. Casting should be three-quarters downstream and one quarter upstream. Slow reeling in should make it possible to sweep the bait in a circle, right up to the bank on which the angler is standing. The fly will then be brought in slowly, parallel to the bank, right up to the angler's waders, because a fish may well be following the lure throughout the reeling in process before deciding to bite at the very last moment.

Surface swims can be fished as well as any sighting of a fish leaping out of the water. Watch out for the attack, which may come as soon as the lure touches the water!

Falkus recommends fishing systematically in this way, using a floating line tipped with a teal blue and silver sea-trout fly. This type of fly is known as the 'medicine'. It is attached to a low-water salmon hook and is lightly dressed. A small double hook is fished slowly through the pool, and may attract the attention of a sea-trout who will tweak the fly, if only through irritation!

Dark fly for darker weather. ▷

Plugs

Floating plugs are used at night or during dusk or dawn, when sea-trout hunt in the currents, stillwater or on the riverbed. Small $1^1/_2$–2 in (4–5 cm) plugs are very effective for this sort of fishing.

For deep areas in a river, use a "big sinker".

FISHING WITH MAGGOTS

Maggots can be used on their own but the traditional sea-trout bait consists of a fly-and-maggot combination. Again to quote Falkus, the traditional fly-maggot combination, where two maggots are attached to a lure, often fails to bring results and above all, a fish may peck at the maggots and eat them without swallowing the hook. Falkus uses something that he calls his "secret weapon" for picky fish who take tiny bites. A cluster of maggots is loaded on a forward single and the sea-trout which makes a grab at them is inevitably impaled on the tail-end treble.

Shrimp. △

A DIFFICULT FISH

Fishing for sea-trout is never easy and it is certainly unpredictable. It is one of the easiest fish to lose off the hook, because it is not really hungry at the very time when it is most accessible to the angler.

However, if you find the right combination of rod, reel, bait, and rig, you can be incredibly lucky and that is sure to turn you into a sea-trout addict!

PREDATORS

THE TACKLE

With simple techniques and equipment, livebait and deadbait fishing are the most successful types for these fish. French anglers have discovered over the years that a maneuvered dead fish which has been correctly leaded, hooked, and played can be an unbeatable fishing method.
These techniques also leave most of the imagination and talent to the angler himself. Lure fishing with a rod and reel is just as efficient, and will get you some good catches, as long as you cast accurately and move the lure correctly.
Finally, fly-fishing has a charm all of its own – providing you use reliable equipment which is well adapted to the various angling conditions in which you will find yourself.

△ Use a strong rod for livebait, especially when fishing from a boat.

Livebait fishing is classic and traditional. It is also constantly progressing, both in terms of equipment and rigs. ▽

LIVEBAIT FISHING

Effective livebait fishing relies on one core requirement. As carnivores feed on small coarse fish, all you need to do is present them with their favorite dish. By attaching a live fish to a hook and making it drag the lead, line, and float, you will make it slower, less mobile, and therefore less active than its fellow fish who are not impaled on your hook. All this makes it the ideal prey! But before you get to this stage, you have to mount your bait correctly and unobtrusively enough for it to fool a wary predatory fish. It is a matter of presenting your bait in the right place at the right time.

TACKLE

A vast amount of tackle is available for fishing the larger predators among the coarse fish. Anglers have come a long way from white horsehair lines attached to hazel poles!

• Rods

Use a 10–13 foot (3–4 m) rod with guide rings. A telescopic rod is easiest to pack and carry. Tip action is the best for casting the livebait and handling larger fish. Your rod cannot be too powerful, you can always cast a light bait with a rod that's too heavy, but the opposite is impossible, and is likely to cause your expensive rod to snap. A DAM Telepike rod is the best there is for classic livebait fishing. If you are fishing exclusively for pike or catfish, your carp rods will be just as effective.
Always clean and store your rods carefully. When carrying the rods, even over a short distance, keep the heaviest parts at the bottom of the bag. You will damage the rods if the weight is put on the tip.

To slow down a carnivore after a strike, your reel should have a reliable clutch. ▷

• Reels

Use a classic fixed reel with a good smooth-action clutch, and fill it with 22/100 nylon (for difficult zander in clear water) to a 30 or 35/100 line for pike in tricky water.

• Floats, Weights, and Swivels

Basic floats for fishing for carnivores are fixed for fishing in shallow water, or sliding for reaching depths greater than the rod length. Sliding floats, stopped by a small knot or plastic or rubber line stop, are more practical for casting long distances. Generally go for tapered floats (such as DAM, Cureau, or Water Queen) which are more sensitive and easier to balance correctly. The most popular leads for balancing floats or sinker fishing are olives, which are long and round and slip directly onto the line, sitting on the knot attaching the line to the swivel (the knot should be protected with a small silicon sleeve). Catherine interchangeable olives are even better, because they let you vary the weight of your tackle as required. Flat leads, sometimes with small bumps on them, are more for sinker fishing. Finally, shot, which are fat leads with a split, are handy for balancing a line. Simple barrel or pin swivels link the mainline with the hook length and prevent kinks in the line when the bait spins during reeling-in or casting. Clip-on swivels link hook length with a loop, which is essential when baiting with eels. Finally, paternoster swivels have three branches for mounting a bait on a paternoster rig – i.e. a separate trace off the mainline. Some have a fastener on the lateral branch, or a long metal arm which terminates in a fastener.

Livebait Fishing with a Sinker

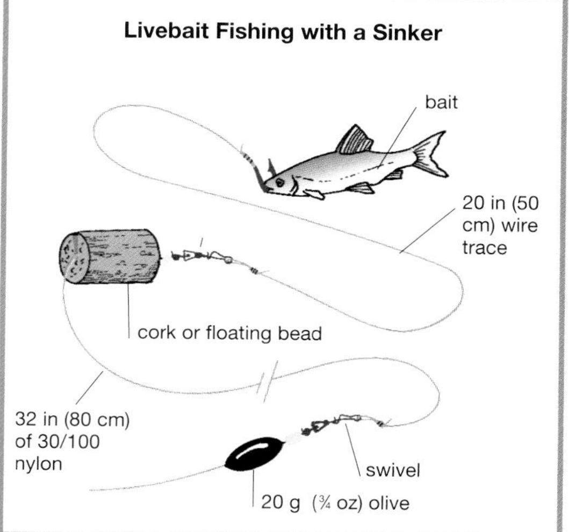

△ "Predator special" lines are often produced in fluorescent colors so you can easily spot very slight takes. Some are also "non-memory" lines, which means they do not stretch at all easily, which is very important for landing a fish from a distance.

△ A hair rig is becoming popular with zander anglers.

• Special Line Ends

Wire lines and traces, which are sold in reels or cut into sections, sometimes with a hook, are the only types which guarantee good resistance to the sharp teeth of a voracious pike. They are sometimes braided with nylon or with kevlar, for even greater flexibility. Two good makes are Tortue and Ragot. These lines can also be made up of hundreds of microfiber lines which give incredible flexibility and can be knotted directly. Kevlar, which is a very soft material, is perfect for zander but not advisable for pike. Braid, which is also very flexible, is excellent for zander – especially on cluttered riverbeds, where it resists abrasion. However, it is totally unsuitable for pike.

• Hooks

Single hooks, with just one tip, are unobtrusive and preserve the small deadbait fish better. Use hooks with an eyelet, which are easier to rig, and reversed hooks, which penetrate better when striking. The Ryder double hook has two branches of different lengths: a small one for placing through the livebait's nostrils, and a longer one for hooking the carnivore. The most commonly used double hooks are of the parrot's beak type, which have not only a barb but a small kink in the metal which holds the hooked fish better. Treble hooks allow you to bait in many different ways, particularly when using sand-eels. Pin hooks give a very solid grip on your bait. Open the pin, slip the hook under the skin of the fish, and close the pin again.

Positioning a livebait in mid-water

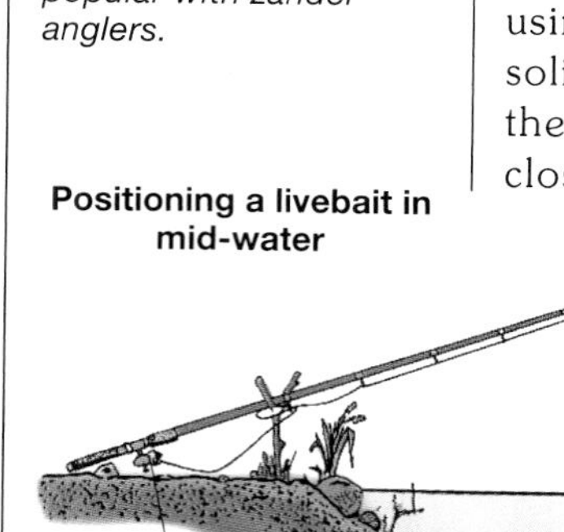

DRIFTING DEADBAIT FISHING

Unlike maneuvered deadbait fishing, drifting deadbait fishing is a very static kind of angling. It is best reserved for large zander, eels, and even large pike, which can be so lazy as to make do with dead prey. Tackle and rigs are the same as for livebait fishing. The bait has to rest on the bottom and often very near to habitats containing lots of obstructions where the big fish hang around, and so you need to lead your line well and use a sturdy rig which can withstand the powerful and sudden departure of a big fish that you absolutely have to prevent from reaching a hideaway. Wire lines are not essential for zander. Use Kevlar or nylon instead. But for pike, you need wire or a steel-Kevlar braid.

MANEUVERED DEADBAIT ANGLING

This really started in France with the arrival of the zander and the creativity of several renowned anglers such as Albert Drachkovitch, who built what is now an indispensable rig. The zander soon became used to this technique, however, and it was then that anglers began using it on pike, thus discovering the virtues of a technique which was very popular with our forefathers when they tried to track this large and fearsome coarse fish.

The principle is very simple: giving life to a dead fish by moving it so it looks like a live fish in pain, and therefore a potentially easy prey for any predator. To do this, the most important parts of the equipment are the rod, which transmits the angler's movements, and the rig, which has to present the fish freely in the water.

Deadbait is also used for pike rigs. It can be paternostered or trolled on the end of a line weighted with a barrel weight, swanshot and a swivel above the bottom line. Deadbait is also used in sunken float ledgering, where it is attached to a bed and pilot float. The danger posed by rough ground is alleviated by attaching the bottom line to a swivel.

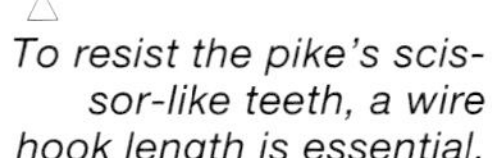

△ *To resist the pike's scissor-like teeth, a wire hook length is essential.*

TACKLE

• Rods

As an extension of the angler's arm, the rod should transmit all movements as faithfully as possible, even in a current or under more than 50 feet (15 m) of water. The rod should also be strong enough to strike effectively and hold up to the thrashing head of a large zander or the sudden departure of a big fish more than 40 inches (1 m) long. For these reasons, tip action and good rod capacity ($^1/_2$–1 oz (15–30 g at least)) are indispensable. The length depends on the area being fished: 9–11 feet (2.8–3.3 m) for fishing from a bank, with enough leverage to keep control of the line in a strong current and remain in contact with the rig; or a shorter 8–9 foot (2.5–2.8 m) rod for fishing from a boat, which will let you fish closer to the area inhabited by the fish without having to cast too far. Most specialist rods for deadbait angling are fine. We recommend the following: Daiwa Shogun, Jacques Chavanne, Garbolino Garbostick, Sert Sanderman, and Astucit Drachko Pro.

MOVEMENTS FOR PIKE FISHING

Deadbait fishing for pike requires a particular technique. First there is the rig, which has one lead at the head of the deadbait and the other inside the fish's body. Fuse wire is wrapped around the carcass so the bait drops less directly. For movement, fish a bit higher up in the water and more slowly, letting the deadbait glide back down through the water, which obviously requires a little less leading. Finally, remember to fish at different levels in the water. The pike's physical shape means that it is particularly aware of what is happening above its head.

Movement diagram for pike fishing

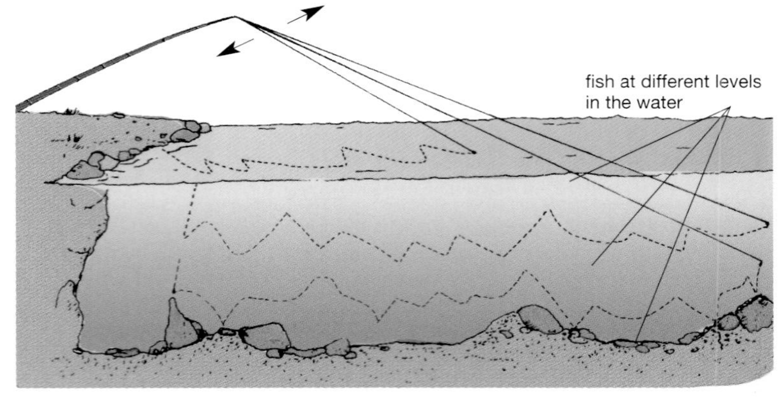

△ *The zander is a canny fish and requires a light rig. Use nylon or even braided line or kevlar.*

• Reels
Use a sturdy reel with a wide, long-cast spool and a progressive clutch. An additional Full Control clutch by Mitchell gives more comfort, although it is not essential.

• Line
For deadbait fishing, you always need to know what's going on! The ideal solution is a fluorescent line which will remain visible whatever the light conditions. With a fluorescent line, you can follow the line during casting, control the depth of the fish and then see the slightest movements or releases in tension of the line, which are usually signs of a bite. Good diameters go from 22/100 in clear riverbeds when angling for smaller fish, to 28 or 30/100 in difficult conditions when fishing for powerful fish which you need to reel in straight away so they don't manage to hide among obstacles.

• Rigs
The Albert Drachkovitch rig is the undisputed king of rigs for deadbait fishing of carnivores. The rig is marketed by the Astucit company and consists of a piano wire line forming a sort of fastener which is slid through the dead fish's body. The dead fish is then armed with one or two trebles, hooked through the flank. This arrangement is then held together with a copper or brass wire trace which is fed through the small fish behind the opercula. The original lead is at the head of the fish, on a joint, which gives the fish a good amount of flexibility. This joint is what makes all the difference when fishing with a Drachkovitch rig.

Control the line as you cast

BASIC TECHNIQUES

• First of all – a good cast ...
Maneuvering deadbait begins with the cast. Just before it hits the surface, slow down the line feeding from the reel with your finger so the fish drops as discreetly as possible. As it sinks, do not close the bale-arm; instead, leave it open and, again with your finger, control the line with each turn of the spool. This gives the fish a vertical descent, and stops it drifting from the spot at which you want to fish, as well as keeping the right amount of tension on the line. This is also necessary so you can notice a bite as the bait is sinking. Indications are a premature stop, sideways movement of the line, etc.

• ... then good movement
Once the rig touches the bottom – the line will suddenly release, showing that the fish has touched the riverbed – close the bale-arm or basket handle, tighten the line with a few turns of the reel, and begin to move the fish, with the rod held high, by tapping the tip section in the air. The fish should literally take off and land again. Still with the rod held high, accompany the fish as it descends. Just before it hits the bottom, start over again with a new series of taps, and then let the fish sink again, always with the line held fairly taut so you can see or feel a bite. Once the fish hits the bottom again, open the bale-arm and let the line give a bit. These basic movements

Movement for zander deadbait fishing

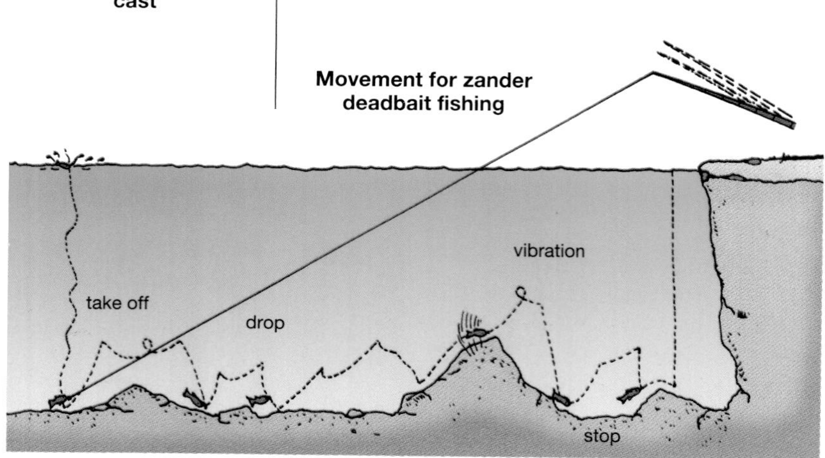

△ *Easy to set up and without too much preparation, lure fishing is one of the most popular forms of angling. It is ideal for trying out a new river!*

can be combined with sideways rod movements. You can also vibrate the rod as you hold it tightly, which will make the fish look more like it is in spasm.
Reel in slowly with the rod held low so the fish slides across the bottom, kicking up small clouds of mud. As you can see, maneuvered deadbait angling involves using a considerable amount of imagination!

ROD-AND-REEL FISHING WITH LURES

The main objectives of lure fishing for carnivores are to copy the signals given out by an ill or injured small fish and to stimulate the predator's aggression. Spoons and spinners, plugs and plastic lures are all combined with rod and reel, adapted to the size of catch expected. Although lures can, in most cases, work on their own, their success still depends largely on the amount of "life" you give them in the water.
Spoons, spinners, and plugs are aimed mainly at pike and perch. The zander, which lives in deeper water, is sensitive to plugs worked slowly close to the bottom, or spoons when they are moved around on the riverbed.
In all cases, a precise cast, which is certainly less essential than for trout fishing, is still very important. The lure needs to fall just below the bank, behind a falling branch, or in the center of a small passage between water lily pads. You also need to be able to see or feel the speed at which it is moving, whether it is going too fast or too slow, and whether it has snagged on an obstacle or become lost in weeds. All this depends on the quality of the tackle used.

Horizontal cast

TACKLE

• Rods

Whether fishing from the bank or a boat, use a rod measuring at least 7 feet (2 m), with a maximum of 9 feet (2.7 m) for most baits, a bit more for plastic lures, which can

also be used with tackle for deadbait fishing. The rod should be strong enough to cast tackle of 1/4–1 oz (10–30 g). Tip action is preferable for a good cast and proper lure positioning.
If you like, you can use rods which are not so stiff and will work over greater distances: these quiver-tips are very interesting for deadbait fishing in that they give more a distilled touch. There is unfortunately a very small range of good casting rods for carnivores. Garbolino Feeling and Sert Jet Spin are our favorites.

• Reels
Reels need to be sturdy, with a wide long-cast spool, a spinning roller, accurate and progressive clutch, and good reeling-in speed of at least 28 inches (70 cm) per turn of the handle. For perch-fishing, make sure the reel is not too heavy.

△ *The classic fixed-spool reel, which French anglers prefer to the spinning reel so loved by US anglers.*

• Line
Even though it is important to be able to see what is happening at the end of your line, a fluorescent nylon line isn't essential, unless you are fishing with plastic lures, which is similar to maneuvered deadbait fishing. Avoid line that stretches too much and go for 20/100 line for clear riverbeds and smaller fish, and 28–30/100 for cluttered beds and large pike.
Braid is very effective, being both strong and very flexible: you can go down as far as a 14 or even 10/100 diameter with no worries!

LURES

French anglers prefer to use spinners when lure-fishing, but these are not the only types of lure to interest carnivores. Spoons are great for large pike, plugs offer endless possibilities and plastic lures are quite simply brilliant, so pack a few of each in your box, along with some jigs and pirks which are becoming all the rage for coarse fishing.

• Spinners
These consist of a blade spinning on a metal axis, usually on a vane. Spinners are real precision mechanics, and their brightness

Light or ultra-light rod-and-reel fishing with metallic lures is perfect for perch. ▽

Spinners

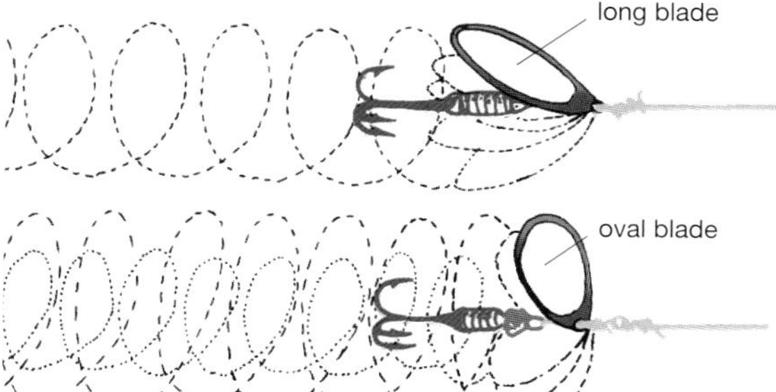

and vibrations attract carnivores and encourage them to bite. The blades can be separated into two distinct families:
– *Long-bladed*
These turn rapidly close to the axis, and move irregularly in the water. They are particularly effective in rivers because they offer little resistance to the current. They are also very useful for working very slowly close to the bottom. In this category, you will also find soft-bladed spinners from Ragot, which are generally more elongated and turn closer to the axis in a fast current or when reeled in quickly;
– *Round or oval blades*
These revolve much more regularly, further away from the axis, which makes them turn faster and produce larger vibrations underwater. They are easy to "feel" in the rod because of the vibrations they make and are the most popular type at the time of writing.
There is a vast range of colors and decorations. For trout fishing, dark spinners are better for clear weather and water, and brighter lures are good for dark conditions and cloudy water; the same applies to coarse fishing. Do not choose your lures through any preconceived notions. Trust your imagination and your individual preferences. Fishing with complete conviction is still the surest way of catching a fish!
Another important point to note is the location of the shot on the spinner. Placed under the blade, on the axis, it gives a more regular movement, in a straight line. When fixed to the head of the spinner, it produces a more unpredictable movement, which is an important advantage for pike fishing in particular, because it also makes the blade spin at the slightest release and while it sinks.
Although a spinner can, by definition, work alone, it is a good idea to help it along. As soon as you've cast, control its drop, like deadbait fishing, by placing a

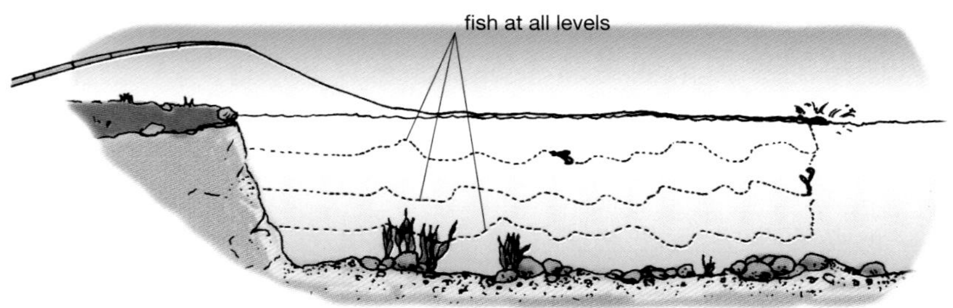

Fishing with a spoon

finger on the spool to keep the line taut. If you use a spinner with the lead at the head, it should turn as it sinks, so be ready to react to the slightest take (shown by a sudden stop in its descent, sideways movement of the line, etc.). Once the lure hits the bottom, begin to reel in, varying the speed and pausing from time to time to allow the lure to sink again. Add a few changes of direction by moving the rod left or right.

For zander, keep close to the bottom. For pike or perch, explore all the different levels, one after the other.

• Spoons

The principle is simple: a blade held on each side by a split ring, attached to a treble hook on one end and a small swivel or the line on the other. Depending on the curve and shape of the blade, the spoon moves by waggling in quick movements.

– Classic blades

The classic blade looks a bit like a soup spoon, and has a hesitating and fairly slow movement in the water. They are best reeled-in slowly, with little rests to stop it snagging on objects and let it drop towards the bottom like a dead leaf, which will often provoke a take. It is useful in deep water.

Spoons

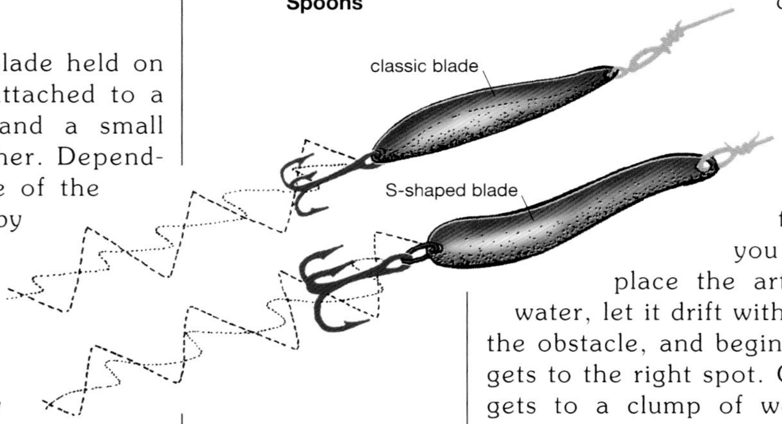

classic blade

S-shaped blade

– S-shaped blades

These blades are very curved and move much more quickly through the water. They are good for producing a much more dynamic movement, and should be accelerated and decelerated sharply, without bringing the lure to a halt. If heavy enough, these spoons are good for fishing at depth or for almost vertical movement, a bit like dapping.

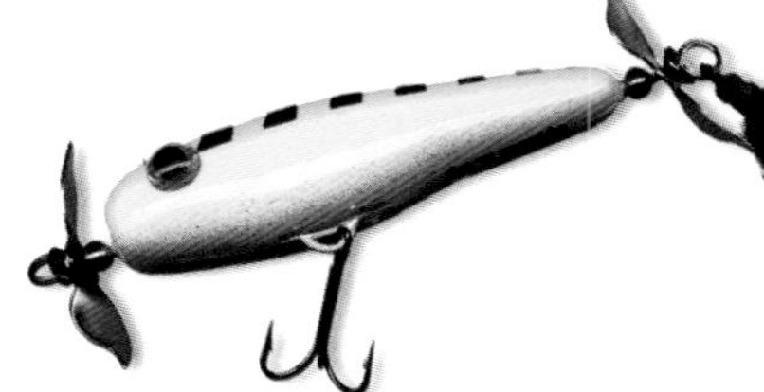

The Big-Big, created for bass works very well with pike too. ▷

• Plugs

These are supposed to imitate fish and can be found in an astounding range of shapes and colors. In France, Rapala are the most famous lures of this sort and by far the most popular. Two factors need to be taken into consideration when choosing your plug:

– Density

In other words, whether it floats or sinks. Floating plugs are useful in cluttered rivers, where you simply need to place the artificial fish in the water, let it drift with the current under the obstacle, and begin to reel in when it gets to the right spot. Otherwise, when it gets to a clump of weeds or above an obstacle, stop reeling in so the plug floats to the surface, thus missing the danger zone. Sinking plugs are of interest in deep water, where they will drop as soon as they are released. Because they all sink at more or less the same rate, with a bit of

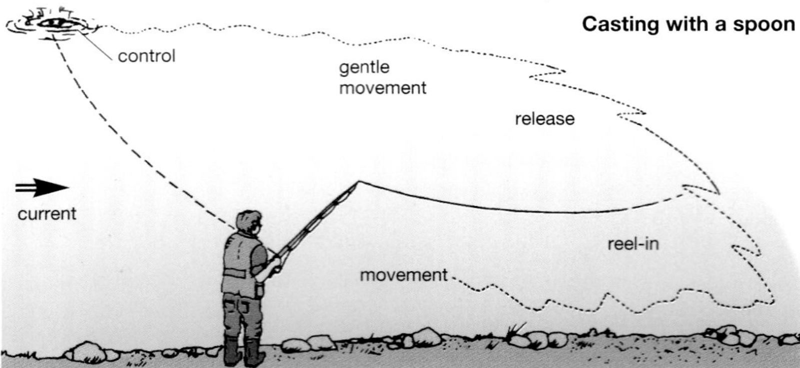

Casting with a spoon

Plug

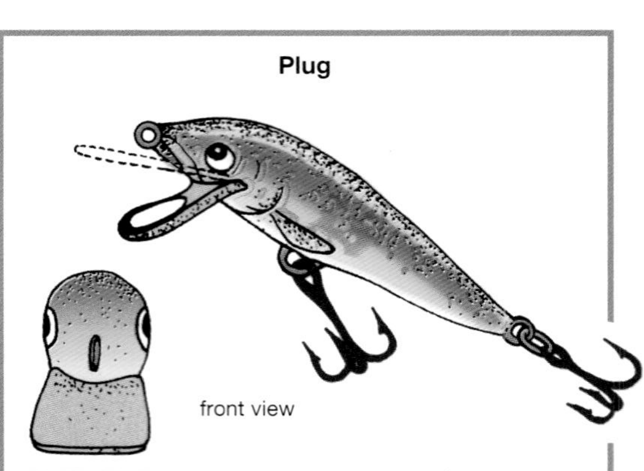

TROLLING

Trolling is very popular with American, British, and most other European fishermen, who use it on large artificial or natural lakes. Trolling involves fishing from a boat with the engine idling, so you can fish over very large areas of water, "dragging" your line behind you. Use larger sizes of lure, generally spoons or plugs. The movement of the boat often works as a stimulus, if it attracts the attention of nearby predators. Bites always occur in the boat's wake, and are often quite brutal, so stay awake!

△ On all large lakes, trolling is very effective in capturing large fish. However, check that this type of fishing is allowed by contacting the local fishing authorities.

practice, you can even get an idea of the depth of the water simply by counting how long they take to drop. This is why certain Rapala plugs are called Countdowns.

– Shape and direction of the tab
These determine the speed at which the plug drops and, to a lesser extent, the size of waves produced by the lure when it is moving. Near-horizontal tabs make the lure sink more quickly, almost straight down. Near-vertical tabs practically prevent the lure from dropping through the water. Flat tabs give off virtually no vibrations, while round ones cause large waves. Use jerky movements as you reel in, accelerating as if the artificial fish is fleeing danger, and then pausing, allowing the lure to sink – or rise.

△ Floating or sinking, Rapala plugs are among the best lures for predators.

Casting a plug

Moving a floating plug

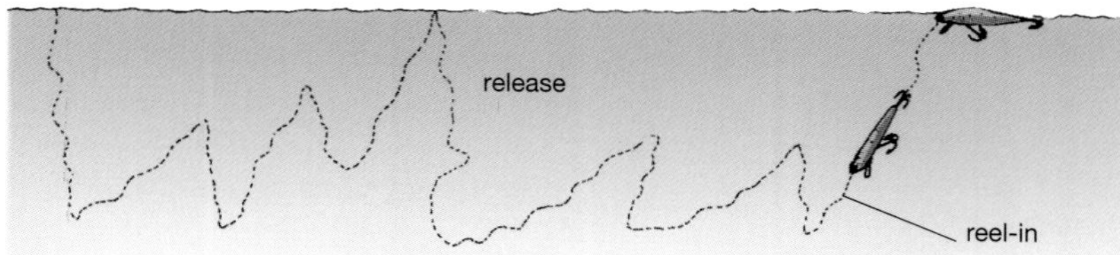

Moving a sinking plug

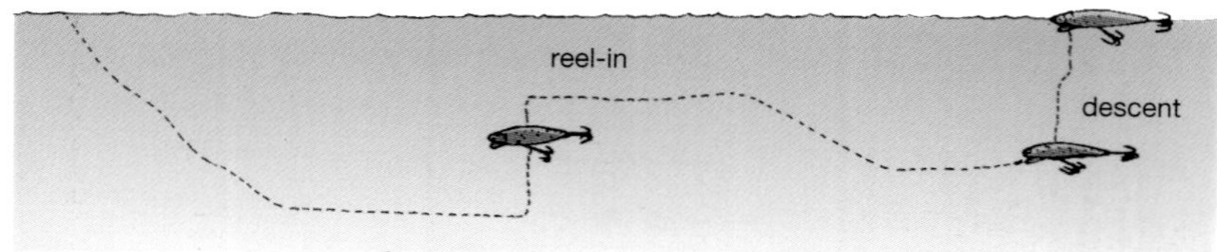

• Plastic Lures
These lures have only been around since the 1980s but are constantly acquiring new enthusiasts. They are inexpensive, easy to use, effective, and offer all sorts of possibilities. New shapes and colors come out almost every year, and all are efficient, as long as they're properly presented in the right place and at the right time!
Another advantage of plastic lures is their adaptability. They can be used on a leaded head (a large hook with the shaft covered by a lead of varying weights) and on a more elaborate rig, directly inspired by deadbait rigs (again, the most famous rig being the Astucit Drachko LS). They come in the following shapes:

– Commas
These are great for larger perch and pike. They are used on a leaded head or mounting.

– Fish-shaped lures
Their movement is largely dictated by a little flat appendage at the end of the tail. They can be directly swapped for deadbait on a rig, but are also very good with a leaded head.

– Worms
These lures are designed to mimic a lobworm or bloodworm, and are the best for

◁ Comma.

trotting; they are attached to a large hook or are impaled on a leaded head, completed with a small length of nylon and a treble hook, placed through the last third of the worm.

– More fanciful shapes

Frogs, crayfish or salamanders are all excellent for both pike and zander, as

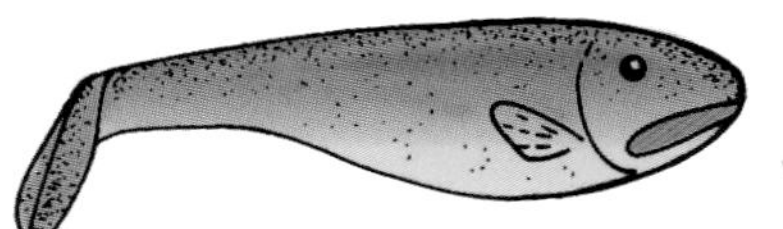

Fish. ▷

long as the real thing is present in the same stretch of water. They are used with a leaded or floating head but, for crawfish, they can also be mounted.

Plastic lures should be manipulated in the same way as deadbait. Acceleration should be slightly weaker and releases more restrained, so the lure performs a series of small jumps on the bottom, interspersed with frequent changes in direction and fast vertical climbs.

It is important to remember that trolling is only allowed on a few large lakes in Europe, although it is a popular fishing method in Ireland, for example. It is essential to consult the local fishing authorities for details. In parts of Europe, it is strictly forbidden on all rivers, streams, and small lakes.

◁ Crawfish.

FLY-FISHING

Although they're not habitual surface feeders, carnivores can fall for the charms of an artificial fly! The best flies are in fact streamers, which resemble small fish and provoke the predators' aggression. An amusing and exciting technique.

A Wels, caught with a soft lure, is a large adversary. ▷

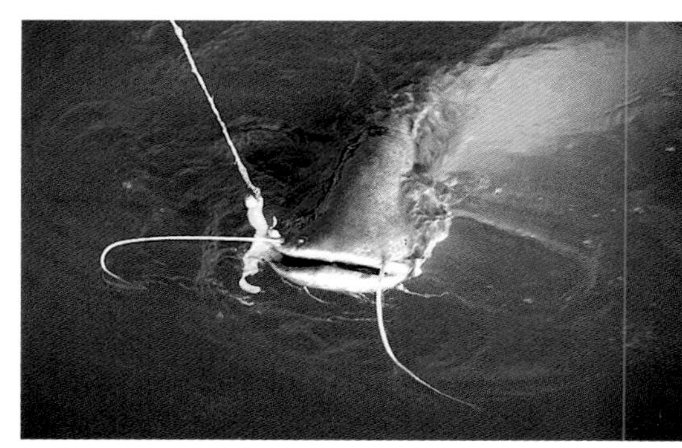

A tackle box is very practical for holding lures. ▽

△ Plastic lures like the frog or crayfish have an anti-weed system which allows you to fish in weedy areas for zander, pike or black bass.

AN ORIGINAL TECHNIQUE

As with many new techniques, this one has come from abroad, perhaps from the United States, where all fish (black-bass above all) are systematically fished using flies. It is more likely this came from Britain and the Netherlands, where pike and even zander hunting with a fly rod and a handful of artificial flies is becoming increasingly popular. In France, this sort of fly-fishing is still rare – largely out of trout fly-fishermen's reluctance to use the technique for the pike. There is certainly

PERCH AND TROUT SIMILARITIES

Because it is so much smaller, the perch is a very different kind of predator, at least in terms of fishing technique. To fish it with rod and reel, you can simply use equipment normally reserved for trout. A 6–7 ft (1.8–2.2 m) rod with a 1/8–1/2 oz (4–12 g) capacity with tip action or quivertip, as you prefer, and 16–20/100 line.

The best lures to use are spinners and plastic lures. Use no. 0,1 or 2 spinners (as you would for trout), preferably colored or golden and with or without decoration. Use small plastic lures too, but in whatever shape and color you like. The curious and aggressive perch will probably give a warm welcome to your imagination!

no shortage of equipment, technical bases or fishing opportunities. However, fly-fishing for predators with lures made of feather and hair is in for a bright future.

TACKLE

• Rods

Use "predator" rods or reservoir rods, which are normally reserved for game fish, of 9–10 foot for casting no. 7,8 or 9 silks. Tip action is essential, given the capacity required to cast large silks – and catch large fish!

The new carp rods known as float rods can also be used, especially as general purpose float rods, such as the Graphlex made by Don's of Edmonton are becoming popular.

• Reels

Reels have to be manual, and they should have several spools which are compatible with the large silks used and which can hold several dozen feet of backing.

• Line

Use a range of silks of different densities, both floating (F on the packaging) and fast sinking (noted S or FS), which are useful in deep water. Wherever possible, use shooting heads, which are very short, around 30 feet (9 m) long, and give weight to the rod so you can cast a long way out.

Terylene and dacron are not strong enough, especially not for trolling.

• Hook length

Whether fly-fishing, live bait, deadbait or lure fishing, if you're looking for pike, you need some protection! Use 12–20 inches (30–50 cm) of wire microcable or kevlar and steel braid.

MOVEMENT

Once the fly has reached the required depth, move it by making a number of short and sharp jumps of around 8–12 inches (20–30 cm). Between each jump or series of jumps, nothing is stopping you from pausing; this is actually necessary when fishing deep so the fly can sink and find the right depth. You must pull with the hand holding the line, not the reel, and the speed of these tugs is up to you. Slow fishing is better in winter, but fast fishing gives a succession of quick jumps. Either is fine. At the beginning of a fishing session, vary the speed, add a few changes of direction, waggle the fly and move to a different depth. As with all lures, originality constitutes the essential element of surprise.

◁ Trout, perch, and black bass.

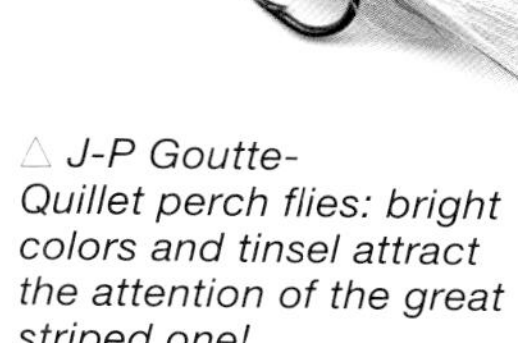

△ J-P Goutte-Quillet perch flies: bright colors and tinsel attract the attention of the great striped one!

Alevin (Alewife). △

FLIES

To attract a predator, flies have to be brightly colored (red and blue seem to be the most successful), voluminous and with a fairly shiny body, covered in tinsel. To increase their efficiency, add some hair, which will give the fly more volume and movement in the water. By inserting a few strands of tinsel, your fly will shine more brightly. For black bass, American fishermen have for many years used poppers, which are halfway between a plug and a streamer. Most French importers offer a good selection of streamers and poppers suitable for catching predators. But with a little imagination, you can make your own.

△ Two pike flies. The one on the right has an anti-weed system. ▷

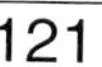

THE CATCH

PIKE

*The pike (*Esox lucius*) is the traditional predatory fish. Together with the perch, it has always been responsible for maintaining the ecological balance of European fresh waters, as it mainly preys on fish which are weak, ill, injured, or poorly adapted (victims of genetic defects, for example). However, for several years now, the pike has had to share this role with some new arrivals like the zander, wels, and black bass. However, there seems to be plenty of prey to go round, and the pike does not seem to be suffering any real competition from the newcomers. The only problem facing the pike is man's reshaping of its waterways and banks, thus slowly depriving it of its natural spawning grounds.*

With its unusual coat, the pike can hide in weed on the bottom. It can stay still for hours before deciding to leap upon its prey. ▽

A FRESHWATER MONSTER?

Pike are to be found in all the slow-moving rivers and large lakes of Europe, as well as in Asia and North America. In fact, pike have one of the largest ranges of any freshwater fish. The fish has an enormous mouth and teeth, and camouflage markings of green and yellow which help it to hide among aquatic vegetation while it awaits a prey to swim by.

Pike are generally despised as food for the table in countries such as the United States and the United Kingdom, in which sea fish have traditionally been readily available. They are something of a delicacy in central Europe in countries far from the sea, such as the Czech Republic, Slovakia, and Poland. Even in Eastern France, with its Polish influence (Lorraine) and its distance from the sea in olden times, pike is considered a delicacy, especially in winter.

Pike have been wrongly suspected of eating their own bodyweight in fish every day. The pike is actually a very economical fish which eats quite frugally. In summer, when it is most active, it is rare for it to eat more than two or three small fish a day.

In the winter, when it is numbed by the cold, it lives at a slower pace to reduce its need for food, like most freshwater fish. It only eats once every two or three days.

Pike may come to feed in considerable numbers at roughly the same time each day, but they will only feed for a short time.

This economical feeding habit does not stop the pike from reaching an impressive weight, up to 45 lb (20 kg), and occasionally more, as proved by the French magazine *La Pêche et les Poissons*, which witnessed a 56 lb (24 kg) pike catch! However, sometimes a young pike in the pink of condition can put up a tougher fight than a weary old warrior which has spent many years in the pond or stream.

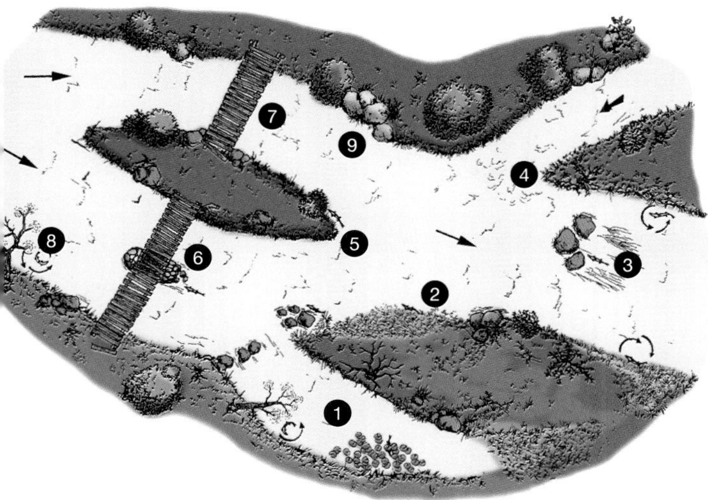

Some typical pike habitats in a river

1 – Inlet or sidestream: excellent all year long, but especially in winter, sheltered from the main current.

2 – 8 – 9 – Wooded banks and overhanging branches: big pike can be hiding in the shade of foliage and among submerged roots.

3 – 5 – Downstream of obstacles barring the current: excellent in summer.

4 – Tributary mouth: very good during the summer, as pike come here to hunt fry which gather in great number.

6 – 7 – Pike can also hide in the shade of a small bridge.

A VERY PECULIAR HUNTING METHOD

The pike is different from all other predators in its hunting methods. It rarely chases after prey or launches savage attacks after a carefully orchestrated group effort, like sea-trout for instance. Instead, our old friend is a master of the art of ambush.

When it is hungry, the pike moves close to the small fish it prefers and then displays its talent for lying still for many hours at a time. When the prey has forgotten about it and is no longer wary and moves within hunting distance (rarely more than 7 or 10 feet (2 or 3 m)), the pike launches a blistering attack on the group.

The small fish instinctively scatter in all directions, confusing the pike which can no longer get a fix on its target. That is why the pike actually misses far more prey than is often realized. If it manages to catch a fish at all, it will certainly be the weakest of the group, the one that could not swim away as fast as the others and ended up stranded on the battlefield. Luckily for the pike, nature has given it a camouflage coloring which merges into the background when hiding among submerged branches or among aquatic vegetation or water-weeds on the bottom.

According to scientists, the pike's position in the water provides a lot of useful information about its level of activity. That is if you can see the pike, which is not always the case. Research performed in an aquarium has shown that an inactive pike holds its head toward the bottom. A hungry pike which is looking for food and ready to attack points its head toward the surface so it can see everything that is going on around it. The eyes of the pike are situated above its head and give it a very wide field of vision especially in the upward direction, which is why it is so difficult to catch as it can see exactly what is happening on the surface, except for the blind field directly behind it.

PIKE HABITATS

To be certain of finding pike, all you need is to locate one thing – the tiny coarse fish on which it

Shallow water at the edge of ponds or lakes where lots of vegetation grows is an excellent spot for pike fishing, but do it from a boat! ▽

loves to feed! Whatever the pike's habits, it has to follow these fish to be in with a chance of getting a decent meal.
Once you have located the small fry, begin to look around them for areas where a hungry pike could be lurking. Logic should guide you: the pike will look for a place where it can hide while protecting itself from those who constitute its own predators (anglers, of course, as well as fish-eating birds) and wait without expending too much effort. There are several typical spots where pike love to lurk and which should help you fish with a good chance of success, even if you are fishing in unfamiliar waters.

• Good Places to Hide

In flowing water, the pike's first concern is to find shelter from the current. This is why it can nearly always be found in eddies near to banks (even when they are only a few square inches), on the inside of a bend, or behind large submerged obstacles such as rocks, blocks of stone, branches, or tree roots. When fishing for pike with maneuvered deadbait, it is not unusual to catch handsome pike right out in midstream, because they have been lurking behind a rock where, one would have thought that only trout would have considered hiding. These pike have undoubtedly sought out this spot in order to keep temporary close observation on a shoal of minnows! Another possibility is that this is a specimen which moves from one habitat to another, stopping at the first comfortable spot it finds in order to catch its breath.
In midsummer, when the water is calmer, pike fishing becomes more difficult because the fish tend to stick to areas of very deep water, particularly water lily pads, reed beds, or thick clumps of waterweed which give them the shelter they seek.
Only by searching systematically for the pike, and exploiting their natural aggression during the summer months, will you manage to come up trumps. Under these conditions, active fishing techniques such as lure or deadbait fishing using a rod and reel are obviously going to be the most successful.

• Good Fishing Spots on Lakes

In a pond or lake, a pike's behavior is more straightforward. In winter and when the water is cold, it tends to hide in the darkest and calmest areas, which are often even better if they are near steep banks covered in roots, branches, and submerged trees to hide amongst. In summer, you will find pike lurking in reed-beds and among clumps of weeds, although the largest specimens are to be found out in the open water, where they feel calm and safe. Do not fish too close to banks or in shallow water, or you could end up damaging a lot of small fish, no matter how careful you are when unhooking them. Again, you will improve your chances by fishing a large number of possible habitats.
Pike will react quickly if they are in the mood for biting. After ten minutes of casting in different directions and at different depths, if nothing has happened, it is time to change your fishing position.
On a natural lake, pike generally remain at the outer limit of the bank shelf at the edge of the deep. There, on very steep slopes which are often very uneven, the pike play "elevators", descending to depths of 27–33 feet (8–10 m) in winter and rising to less than 7 feet (2 m) of water in summer. On certain lakes, you will also find shallow water at the tip of a lake (near to the main tributary) or near beaches where the slope is very gradual. These are generally very good places to fish in summer or at the beginning of fall, but only if they are at least 5 feet (1.5 m) deep. Otherwise, as in ponds, you will probably only catch small fish. However, remember that catches of these little fish are the key to the success of future fishing trips. Furthermore, the small fish can be deep-frozen and used as deadbait for catching pike on a future occasion. As already mentioned, pike are quite happy with deadbait, as long as it is manipulated realistically.

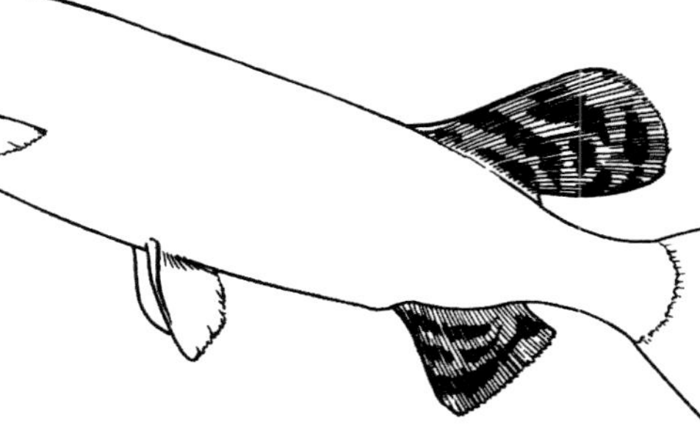

△ The pike remains a superb adversary in terms of muscle and nerve, and will shoot off as soon as it is hooked.

• The Particular Case of Dam Lakes

On dam lakes, which are extremely complicated environments, finding pike is even more tricky. These artificial lakes are a mixture of different watery "worlds". These include a river upstream of the lake and, near the mouths of all its major tributaries, a pond in its calm bankside areas and a lake everywhere else, except that the bank shelves are more clearly defined. To begin with, find submerged obstacles under a few feet of water which are likely to act as shelter for the pike throughout the year. This

GRAVEL PITS:

These artificial lakes are wonderful, created by repeated gravel extraction which lowers the level of the soil below the ground water level, as long as they are linked with the neighboring river. They are also quite disconcerting. The relatively poor quality of the bed (basically just gravel) makes it difficult for weeds to grow, and it is weeds which attract small fry and therefore predators. But the holes made by the quarrying machinery and the roots and other plant remains often abandoned in the water

Fall and winter and traditionally the best times for pike-fishing. But spring and summer, which is suitable for the most active techniques are also excellent, and can bring in some handsome specimens.

is where you are most likely to find at least a few fish. If the water level in the dam lake drops, take the opportunity to make a map of the obstructions and debris on the lake bed. It will come in handy later, when the water rises again, for finding the sort of places in which pike tend to lurk.

In summer, concentrate on areas containing lots of weeds and banks which are well covered with vegetation, and which are not too deep. In the fall, go for eddies which form upstream of the lake or near the mouths of tributaries, in the middle of bankside plateaux, just where the slope sharpens, or near wooded sloping banks. In winter, pike-fishing becomes much more complicated. The best specimens sometimes live up to 33 feet (10 m) below the surface, near obstructions which are completely invisible from the surface, and which you could only know well after several years' experience on the lake. To avoid wasting too much time, concentrate your efforts upstream of the lake, in the calmer areas of water. This is often where small coarse fish gather to feed on the debris brought downstream from the river. Other interesting areas in which pike may be lurking are scree, the foot of cliffs near very deep water, or near submerged trees or logs.

It is all important with pike to work out where they are hiding and when they are feeding. Once you have studied your quarry carefully, it is just a matter of time before it will be hooked. But it means a lot of careful preparation, and timing is everything.

THE RIGHT TIME OF DAY

Pike does not seem to have a particular preference for a particular time of day when it is most likely to hunt. Everything depends on its appetite and the availability of the prey. However, as for many species, the most interesting times of day are dawn, midday, and dusk.

Anglers have identified particular times of year which are good for pike-fishing. In January, when fishing is still permitted in some European waters, it is never very good. The pike are relatively inactive because of the cold, which slows down their metabolism, and also because they are only a few weeks away from spawning at this time of year. The pike has the same egg-laying capacity as members of the salmonidae family, in that the female is able to lay 2,000–3,000 eggs per kilogram (2 lb 4 oz) of her bodyweight. The fish has difficulty finding suitable courting grounds (mostly submerged land vegetation), and is best left alone from February through May when it spawns.

• Spring and Summer

The season begins once spawning is finished, which is April in southern Europe, May in the north. This is a time of year which is generally quite good for fishing. Pike change habitat to spawn and are sometimes moved from regular spots by spring floods, and they often find themselves temporarily in unusual places, which makes them much more vulnerable than usual. If you cast your lure or deadbait over areas which could shelter a pike, you may stand a good chance of catching some beauties. In summer, from June through mid-September, things get a bit more uncertain, because the pike have all the food they need easily available to them. But by methodically fishing with livebait, lures, or deadbait near weeds or along banks, you can still catch some pretty good specimens.

• Fall and Winter

The period from the end of summer through mid-November is the best time of year for pike-fishing. With the cold weather and high water, coarse fish gather near banks and in

A LITTLE OF EVERYTHING !

create a number of possible habitats for the pike and other carnivorous fish, which can then be found all over the lake.

In such cases, unless you have specific information from local anglers or have managed to spot pike hunting-grounds, systematically explore the lake, concentrating on areas around obstructions and major changes in depth. Also try to have enough tackle with you to cover every eventuality: pike, perch, and zander can all easily inhabit the same territory.

warmer waters, while reducing their activity. The pike will follow but, yet again, find itself on unfamiliar territory where it does not have the time to investigate good hiding places, thus making itself vulnerable. Food has now become scarcer, so the pike is forced to remain active for longer during the daytime in order to hunt. Be persistent and fish in different areas if you are interested in quantity, or work the same area if you want to catch yourself a big fish. Finally, winter is still a fairly good time for the pike angler, especially at the beginning of a big freeze. In these conditions, the coarse fish

△ The largest pike are often caught during the first frost.

retire to calm areas of a river and will even temporarily dig into the mud, resurfacing if the temperature or the water level rises. The pike, however, has not got the same freedom of movement. Since it does not hibernate, in order to survive, it has to continue to eat, one way or another, however sparsely and slowly.
By fishing from the same spot and persisting in the most likely areas, you will stand a good chance of catching the pike. If you know that a particular place is frequented by a large specimen, it is a case of now or never for tempting it to bite. Cast in all the places it loves to haunt. With a little perseverance (you may need to come back to the same spot for several days in a row), it would be very surprising if you didn't end up hooking your catch. Then you can serve pike on Christmas Day, as they do in Eastern Europe, where pike is the traditional Christmas fare.

LIVEBAIT FISHING

The arrival of the zander changed European coarse fishing habits completely. The mood-swings of this fish, its fantastic adaptability, and its extreme wariness when faced with our most elaborate traps have led to a sharp increase in elaborate fishing techniques. The second the float starts to sink, after a series of leaps and movements, you will begin to wonder how big the fish on the other end of the line could be. It's all part of the wonder of angling.
Livebait fishing is also a technique which happens to suit the pike's hunting habits very well. When the pike snatches at a group of small fish, it will only manage to catch the weakest, which cannot swim as fast as the other fry. Weakened by the hook, handicapped by the taut line, the heavy weight and resistance of the float, your little livebait is more than likely to be one of the last fish hanging around and therefore an ideal victim for the pike!
Pike are not always hunting, as was explained at the beginning of the chapter, their dietary needs are quite modest. Consequently, there are many periods when they are sleepy or at least very hesitant. Again, this is another advantage of live bait. Even when presented to a sleeping pike, a fry wriggling on the end of a carefully concealed hook will provoke some sort of reaction, whether it is out of annoyance or hunger. This same reaction may not be as forthcoming when the pike is faced with a lure or deadbait, as they will not necessarily be presented at a time when the pike is available – or they will not stay long enough in the right place. All the more reason to take your livebait

onto the river or lake and place it carefully no more than 7 or 10 feet (2 or 3 m) from where you believe the pike to be lurking. Move the bait around from time to time, even if only slightly. This will set the bait squirming again, and could be just enough extra movement to arouse the pike's interest.

• Types of bait

Except in very rare cases, feel free to use large livebait measuring 6–8 inches (15–20 cm) for catching pike. Large bait is the best way of attracting large pike! You will also distinguish yourself from other anglers, as most only use 2½–4 inch (6–10 cm) fry for livebait. Here are a few species of fish which are bound to be of interest to the pike.

– *Bream*

These fish can be found in great numbers in medium-sized rivers and lakes and are very active livebait. Bream are excellent for livebait fishing on a floating line, but difficult to use as maneuvered deadbait, because their oval shape makes them difficult to rotate or manipulate underwater.

– *Young carp*

Carp is a real fighter which can swim about for more than an hour on the end of a line and cover several square feet without giving any hint of tiredness. Just try stopping a carp, even a young one, from swimming to the bottom! However, the fairly dark, dull coat of a carp seems to make it relatively unattractive to the pike. Despite this, a young carp is an all-round bait, though it is only to be used with a floating line.

– *Chub*

The chub isn't satisfied until it has patrolled the whole area – a real hard worker! With its very shiny coat, good resistance, and the fact that it is easy to use (unhooking happens rarely),

◁ ▽ *Baiting methods for an immediate strike.*

the chub is a favorite with many livebait fishing experts. Chub makes an excellent pike bait, especially for larger specimens, and it is particularly well adapted to paternoster and similar rigs.

– *Roach and rudd*

They are the favorite bait of tackle sellers. With a good shine on its coat, above-average resistance, easy to use when hooked, the chub appears to have several advantages. They are excellent all-rounders which could find their way onto any pike rig.

– *Gudgeon*

Despite its fairly dull coat, the gudgeon has always been a favorite with pike-anglers who like its persistent nature. The gudgeon is always trying to reach the bottom, no matter what the circumstances. It will hide in the weeds if you let it. Gudgeon is a very good livebait, but should always be used with a float.

– *Perch*

With its competitive nature, the perch has a gift for inciting aggression in any predators it encounters. At the end of your line, this beautiful striped fish is very active – but tires very quickly. Even without an attack, you will have to change the bait every 20-30 minutes. Nevertheless, perch remains an excellent pike bait. The variety known as sun-perch is a restricted fish in several parts of Europe and cannot be used as bait in free waters. The same rules apply in other countries, check with the local angling authority.

– *Tench*

The tench has more than average resistance when on the hook, but it does have a habit of heading to the bottom and hiding under weeds. If it is no longer visible to a pike, whose range of vision is mainly above its head, the tench becomes completely useless as a live bait. Thus, as a bait, tench is only of average quality, but it can provide a useful service when other food is scarce.

– *Minnow*

Minnow is a great trout bait which can also attract pike, especially if it is used with a handful of other minnows at the beginning of the fall, when young fish gather in enormous shoals.

• Baiting Techniques

– *Baiting for an immediate strike*

Although it may seem barbaric to use fish fry as live bait, live bait fishing is just as barbarous when practiced by the carnivores, such as pike, who swallow the bait whole only to find a large hook embedded deep in their throats! To avoid this happening and to catch more fish, there is only one solution, namely, baiting for an immediate strike, which lets you hook the predator in the mouth and not at the back of the throat. Consequently, you can safely return the fish to the water and generally provide much more sporting combat. This method of baiting is also useful from a technical point of view. When chasing difficult fish, you can react earlier, before your trap is exposed to any other potential catch.

◁ *Double hook on the back.*

– *Double baiting on the back*

This excellent baiting technique leaves the fish free to swim. The first of two trebles is hooked by just one branch in front of the dorsal fin, on the fish's back or slightly to one side. The second hook, which should slide on the line, is fixed at the correct place with a length of silicone sheathing which also slides on the line. Just force it onto the treble hook's eyelet and shaft to hold everything securely in place. One single point of the treble should be firmly embedded in the bait, as this is the hook which "carries" the bait on casting and when reeling-in.

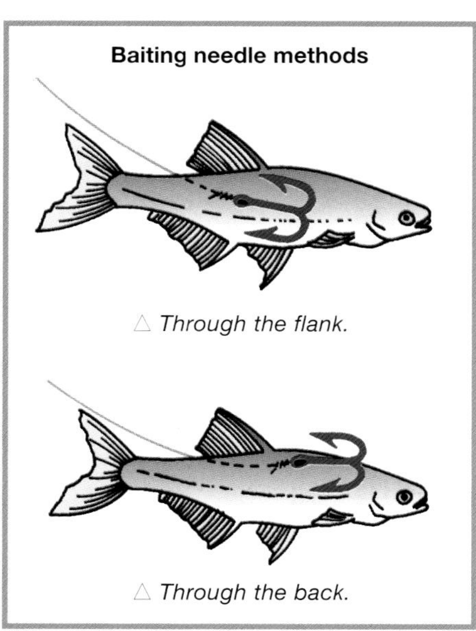

Baiting needle methods

△ *Through the flank.*

△ *Through the back.*

– *Adjustable two-hook rig*

This lengthwise-adjustable mounting (due to the silicone sheath) can be a large single-headed hook (no. 2–4) or smaller treble hook (no. 10–12). It is ideal for a current or for fishing from the bank of a lake and each time the fish is placed in a real current or one caused by reeling in. By keeping the fish's mouth shut, it will live longer and be more active as you work the line.

– *Baiting for a delayed strike*

With this sort of baiting, you must not react as soon as you get a take. You need to be patient. Wait for the pike to turn its prey over in the right direction and swallow it headfirst. Then when you do strike, the carnivore will be well and truly hooked and very unlikely to escape.

– *Baiting a fish through the nose*

Hooking livebait through the nostrils gives the advantage of being unobtrusive and you can save the little fish for when you really need it. Use a large single hook, a double Ryder, or a small treble. Do not forget to also hook the bait's lips, or you will stop it from breathing normally.

– Baiting with a baiting-needle

Although this is the most barbarous way of baiting a fish, it is also the most reliable and efficient in preserving a hooked fish. Whether you are using a single or a treble hook, you also need a hook length, finishing in a loop which is then linked to a fastener. Baiting is performed by passing the baiting-needle through the livebait's flesh to thread it through the hook length and sink the hook's shaft. Whatever the type of baiting you use, do not forget to position your hook with the point directed toward the live bait's tail. When eating its prey head-first, the pike will not catch the hook in its throat and if it decides to spit the livebait out, the hook will catch almost automatically.

Classic floating line rig

Sliding float line

• Rigs

– Floating line

In the floating line rig, the float is fixed directly to the mainline, with the sinker sitting on the swivel attachment, protected by a piece of plastic tubing. For the hook length, use 20 inch (50 cm) of steel wire.

– Sliding float line

For depths of 10–13 feet (3–4 m), use a sliding float, stopped with a small knot or a stop-float placed on the line. During casting, the float sits on the lead, which allows you to pay the line out without any problems. Once the tackle is in the water, the line sinks freely through the float until the stop. The float will then right itself, keeping the live bait at the height you want.

– Bubble-float rig

Although it is not very popular with coarse fishermen, except those who fish for black bass, the bubble-float is nevertheless very useful for dealing with pike. Its main advantage is that it gives you enough weight to cast as far as you want, without dragging the line and bait right to the bottom. You can therefore fish in weed beds and the edge of reeds where pike often lies in wait near the bottom, looking up toward the surface. It should be half-filled to keep it from drifting in a high wind and be used with a gudgeon, minnow, or similar live bait.

– Shotted line

Slip a sinker or a piece of plastic anti-tangle (as used by carp anglers) with a lead attached to a clip-on swivel. Add a very flexible wire hook length. The anti-tangle lets you cast very far out without worrying about line tangle. At a take, the line will slip easily through the tube, and the pike can bite down on the bait without feeling the slightest resistance.

Bubble float rig

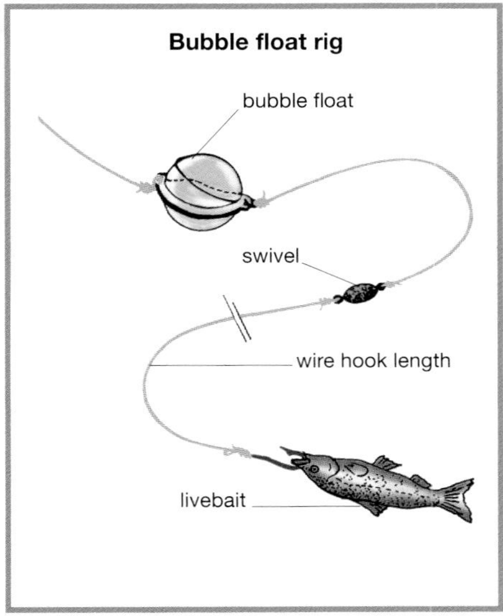

Leaded line

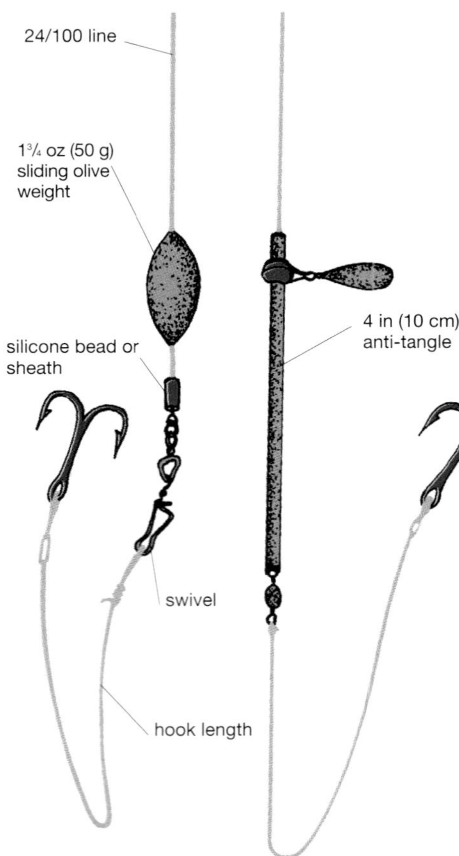

– Paternoster rigs
Place a sinker on the end of the line which is heavy enough to stay where you cast it, no matter what happens (livebait movements, current, wind, etc.). At the level at which you want the livebait to move, add a three-way paternoster swivel. The bottom part should go to the sinker, the upper part to the mainline and the side-piece to the hook length. To avoid any nasty surprises, such as the bait hiding itself in weeds, or snagging your tackle, the line between the swivel and sinker should be longer than the hook length.
– Breaking strand paternoster
The line carrying the sinker should be at least 4–6/100 thinner than the mainline. In stead of lead shot, use metal nuts, small pieces of scrap metal, or similar weights – anything you will not mind losing on the bottom of the river if the line breaks.
– Sliding paternoster
This rig is useful in depths of more then 5 feet (1.5 m). It uses a simple or clip-on swivel slipped onto the mainline, where it can slide freely between two stops. The lower stop has to leave more line than the hook length you are using.

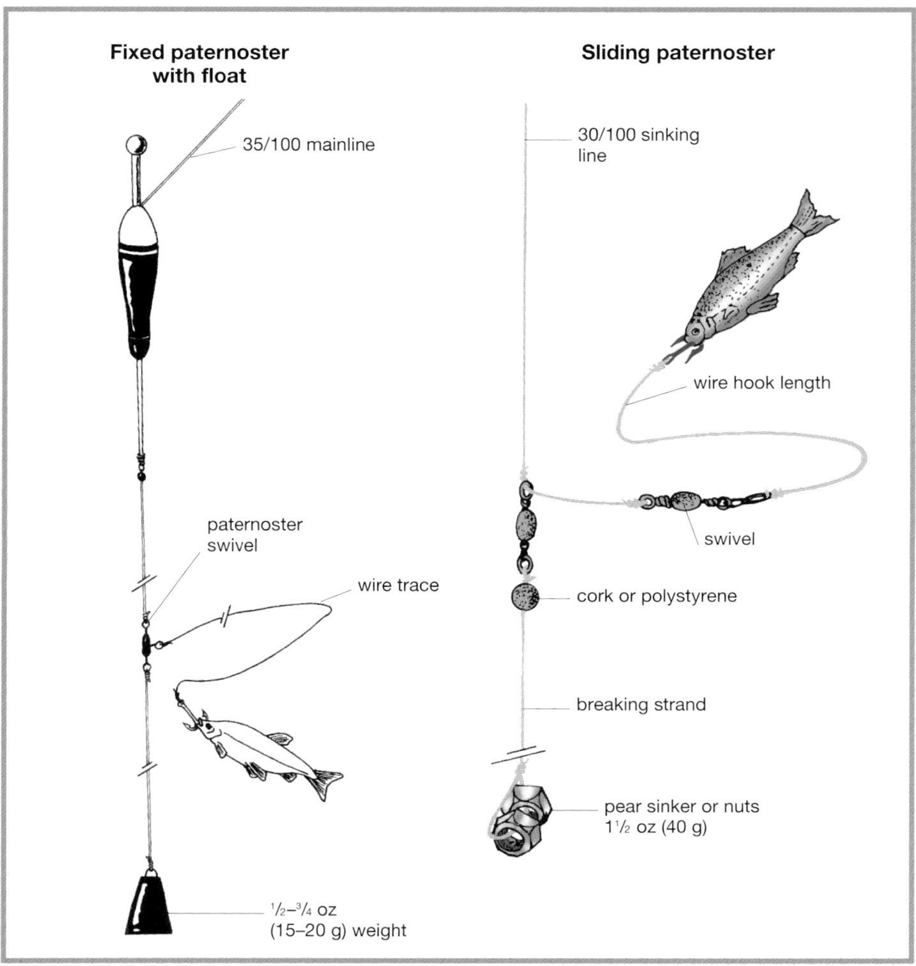

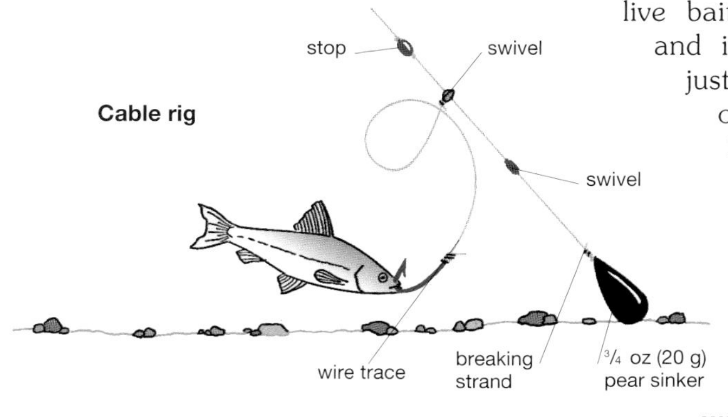

The stop-float needs to be played around with in order to determine where the live bait will be shown off to its best advantage, thanks to the sliding sinker on the bottom line.

– Cable mounting
This is a simple adaptation of the sliding paternoster. It is a leaded line with the weight at the end of the line and the hook length on a trace coming off a swivel which can slide freely along the line between two stops. This sort of rig allows the live bait to move around and is ideal for fishing just outside a reed bed or clump of weeds in the open water. The results are even better if the lead is a long way from the rod and the tip section is placed just by the surface of the water, so the line forms a very obtuse angle, allowing the livebait a very wide area in which to move.

• Choosing your rig and fishing technique
– On a large fishing position
Go for a floating line in a large clearing among some weeds, beside a reed bed, beside a wooded bank, or in an area of scree, for example, or on a plateau or a shallow which seems to be "inhabited". By allowing the live bait to swim around, perhaps drifting in the current or wind (a sailing float is very useful here), you can sweep a very wide area. Try to keep the float well balanced. It should sink slightly as the livebait moves around. To keep the bait active, you should hook it very delicately, either through the nose with a single hook or a small treble (when you can give the pike the time to swallow) or with two hooks (one single through the nostrils and a treble through the back). The latter is useful for striking on the take if you can catch small fish, or more simply if you intend to return all or part of your catch to the water. Beside a reed bed or a large clump of weed, a bubble-float rig can be extremely successful. It will give you casts of the length you want, and you will be able to fish near the surface

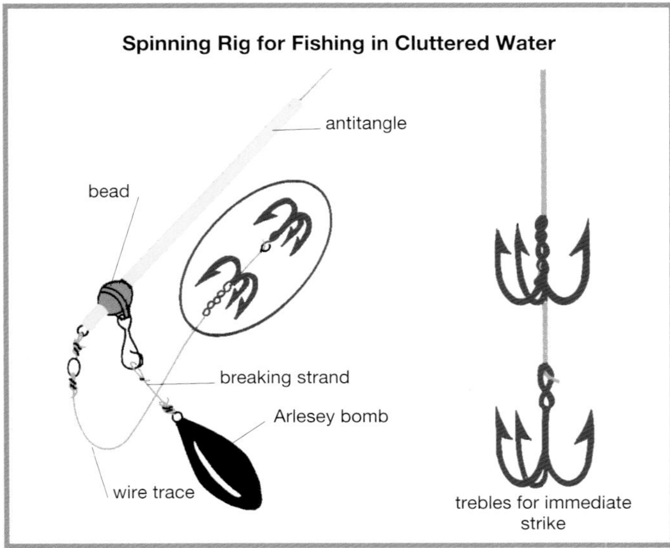

△ Very flexible, perfectly resistant to a pike's teeth, a line end in Kevlar braided wire is indispensable, including for rod-and-reel fishing.

△ To get a pike to bite, don't ever worry about using too large a bait !

KEVLAR BRAIDED WIRE: A MUST-HAVE

To guard against the pike's scissor-like teeth, all anglers know they need a special wire line-end. But since the days of our grandfathers' wire traces, angling equipment manufacturers have made enormous progress, ending up with a near-perfect product – kevlar braided wire. It is so flexible, it is almost as easy to use as nylon yet very resistant to a big pike's teeth. It is a must for any pike rig.

without any danger of snagging. You then need to "work" the line by slowly reeling in over 3.5 to 7 feet (1 to 2 m) with pauses in between. The bubble float's wake will attract the pike, which will often snap at the live bait dangling below it. In any case, do not be afraid to place your livebait "a little too high", and certainly never less than 20 inches (50 cm) from the bottom. You should never forget that the pike has its eyes on the top of its head and is more sensitive to prey swimming in the upper water levels.

– On a smaller spot

Near a submerged or semi-submerged tree, a clearing among weeds, or a small eddy, use the paternoster in all its forms (cable, reversed, etc.). It has the great advantage of holding the livebait "on a leash" over an area of your own choosing and you can define the depth at which it swims by making the necessary adjustments and using the right hook length. When fishing near an obstruction (which is where paternoster rigs are most useful), your baiting method must give as immediate a strike as possible.

Should You Fish Subtly?

"Subtle" can be quite surprising in a pike angler's terms. However, most anglers will remember numerous occasions when the fact that the rig was not particularly sophisticated was enough to deter an active pike. To prevent that happening, here are a few tips. Make use of a 25/100 line (for clear spots and "normal" pike) or a 35/100 maximum (for very cluttered water). For the hook length, flexibility is the deciding factor, and wire traces should be avoided in favor of microcables or kevlar braided wire. The float and sinker, which need to complement each other, should be light. Use a thin float with careful balance, so the bait pulls it under from time to time. In difficult situations, where finesse and a light rig is impossible to achieve, bait so you can strike as soon as you get a bite. You can react immediately and hook your fish before it has time to drop the bait.

Another solution for fishing near a shallow which is a long way from the bank is the classic leaded line which allows you to cast very far and with the maximum amount of discretion. If the bale-arm is open and the line held under an elastic band or small pebble so it can be released on a take, even the most wary pike will have a problem in seeing through your trick.

In any case, you should intelligently fish each area. If nothing bites in 30–45 minutes, and if the live bait is not giving any particular signs of distress, change your position. You are probably fishing a position that is completely devoid or pike, or any pike that are there are completely apathetic, in which case, there is not much point in going on and you should try your luck elsewhere.

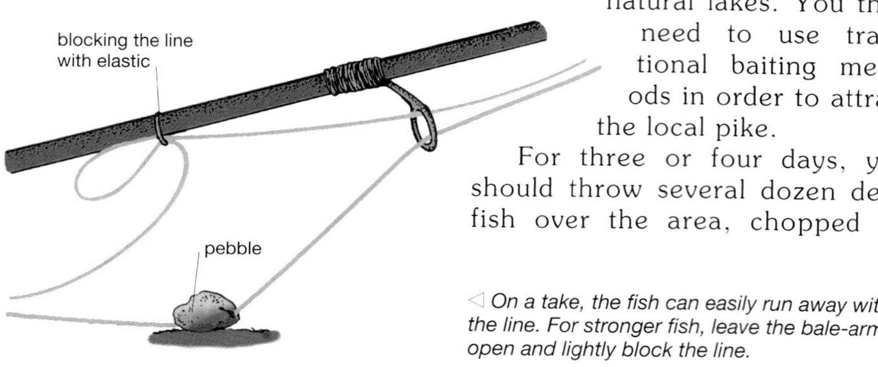

◁ *On a take, the fish can easily run away with the line. For stronger fish, leave the bale-arm open and lightly block the line.*

POSED DEADBAIT FISHING

For a long time, anglers believed that pike were only interested in live prey.

But then the ever-inventive British had the idea of fishing with very carefully baited parts of dead fish – sea fish, in fact, which have a far stronger odor than traditional freshwater fish.

Although this type of posed deadbait angling is not very frequently practiced outside the British Isles, it remains one of the most promising methods for fishing the larger pike. With age, these venerable fish become lazier and lazier, making do with carrion, a dead fish or part of a fish, as long as it is fresh enough for their liking.

• Bait carefully

For this sort of fishing, you should limit yourself to dam lakes or natural lakes. You then need to use traditional baiting methods in order to attract the local pike.

For three or four days, you should throw several dozen dead fish over the area, chopped up into slices. Baiting will be even better if you use sardine or mackerel, which emit a very strong and long-lasting odor in the water – although they are quite expensive!

Alternatively, grind up a few of these fish, mix them with some molehill earth, and fling it all into the water together with some fish parts. This will spread the smell and attract the carnivores more quickly and reliably. Fishing technique requires a classic shotted line. Since you do not have the problem of keeping the bait alive, you should hook deeply. Use a piece of fish slipped onto a big no. 2 or no. 0 single hook or baited with a baiting-needle on a good-sized, strong iron treble (no. 2 or no. 4) that you can hide inside the fish.

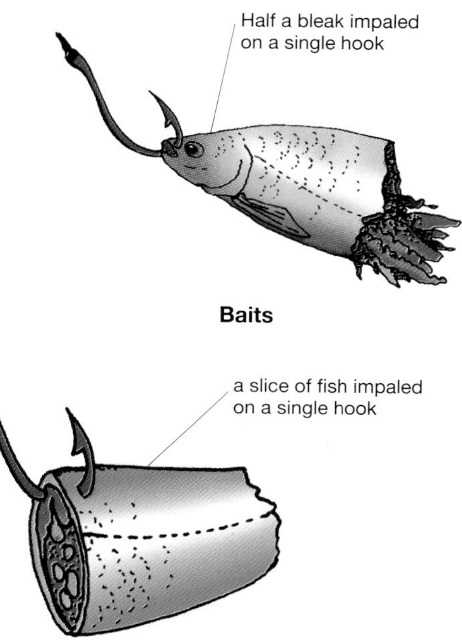

Baits

Maneuvered Deadbait Fishing

Although this method is traditionally reserved for zander fishing in France, maneuvered deadbait is also a classic pike angling technique.

It uses two types of rig, both of which should be preceded with 20 inches (50 cm) of wire line (microcable or kevlar) to prevent line cutting.

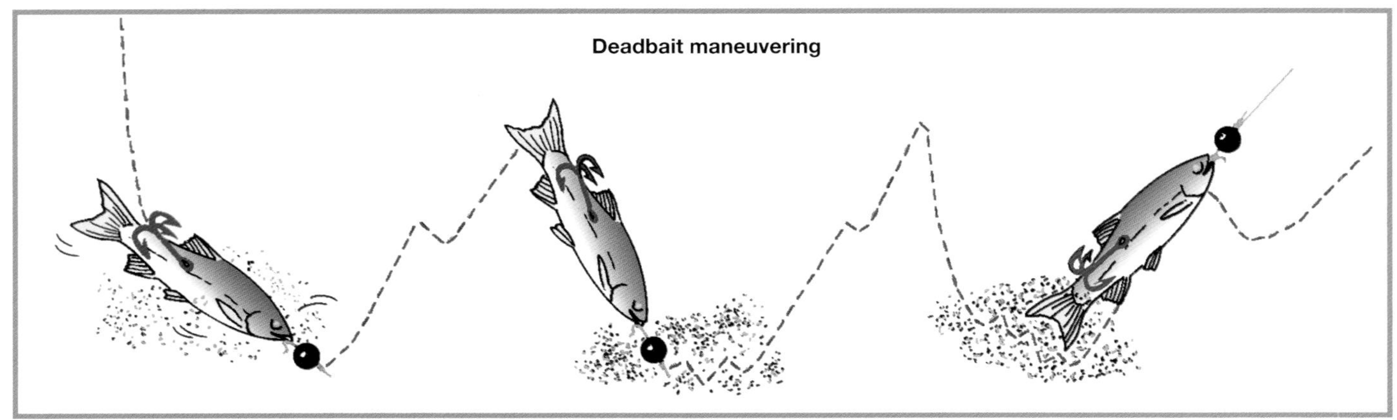

△ *This animation of a maneuvered deadbait, with alternated tugs and releases, should imitate the hesitant swimming movements of a young fish in pain moving with small leaps on the bottom.*

Fixing a deadbait to a Drachkovitch rig

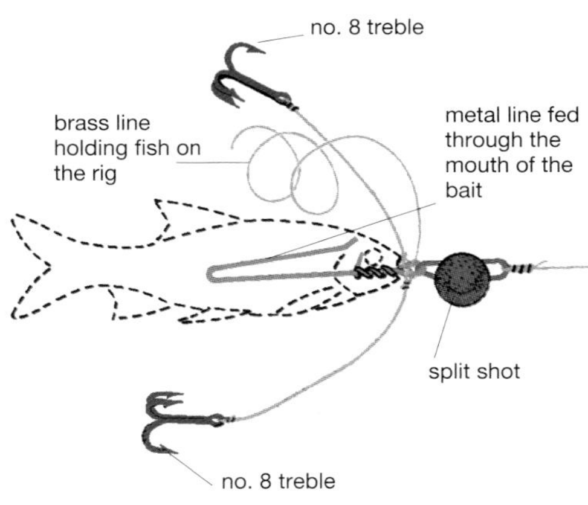

Probing

Probing is a fishing method which is halfway between live-bait and maneuvered deadbait fishing. It is used by many zander anglers these days.

Using a classic sinker rig (preferably with an antitangle tube) set up for an instant strike, you need to move a live bait around near to all main pike areas. The trick is to move the live bait around quickly at different levels.

By holding the line with your free hand, monitor the livebait's movements (if it moves hurriedly, a pike will not be far away!) and when you get a bite, release the line by opening the bale arm, then strike a few seconds later.

• Swimming Rigs

These use a plastic deflector (usually a disc or flap) and give the fish very realistic swimming motion. As soon as you accelerate, it looks as if the fish is flapping its tail more quickly, exactly as it would do if it was trying to make a quick getaway from an approaching predator. The deadbait should thus be moved in a series of fast and slow movements so that it rises and falls in the water.

Swimming rigs are basically maneuvered in exactly the same way as spoons and that is exactly what makes them attractive to a number of anglers.

• Articulated Sinker Rigs

These are more or less inspired by the famous Drachkovitch rig, and remain the most widely used. They provide more varied animation, with sharp drops and changes of direction. These rigs are also more demanding for the angler, who has to constantly think about the movements made by the deadbait. As the articulated sinker rig is not usually designed for catching pike, you will have to modify the leading on this sort of rig.

Reduce the head lead by changing shot and use a complementary lead on the hook (and therefore inside the fish), by adding a few turns of fuse wire. This way, you will get a steeper movement from the fish, which will drop more quickly and glide more easily, a maneuver which the pike finds particularly attractive!

• On the River

You can easily troll for pike from a boat. Cast near the fish and monitor the deadbait's drop once it hits the water. Nothing is stopping you from closing the bale arm and starting to move the bait straight away, a decision essentially dictated by the type of rig used. Pass the

For good rod-and-reel fishing, use a long and sensitive rod which can easily transmit the movements of the lure used. ▽

bait near to the surface, then further down, and then 12–16 inches (30–40 cm) from the bottom.

• On a Lake

You are much better off fishing from a boat for this. That way, you can access all the habitats and avoid a number of snags while fishing in the best possible conditions. Cast as close to the expected habitat as possible and monitor the bait as soon as it is in the water. Keep an eye on the line: if it moves even slightly or if the bait's drop is stopped prematurely, strike immediately. For habitats offering shelter to the fish, such as dead trees or underwater branches, some pike anglers recommend dapping the dead fish on the water's surface, making it "water-ski" just before it reaches the required spot. This is, apparently, a great trick for waking up sleepy pike and exciting those which are on the hunt. Try it and see. Pass the deadbait through the water at least three times at different depths and, if the areas are not very large, cast a few times in various directions, which will give you a larger field to work with. If this does not get any reaction, then either there are no pike in the vicinity, or they have just had a good meal!

ROD-AND-REEL FISHING WITH A LURE

Spinners or spoons, plugs and plastic lures – all of which are easily found in all angling suppliers, and are particularly pleasant and easy to use – are still remarkably effective with pike. Obviously, they are not all as good as each other, but they do allow fishing throughout the year (subject to regulations, of course) and with very great chances of success.

△ *Pike lure with two treble hooks.*

• Spinners

The most common are also the easiest to use. Rounded blades give a relatively fast swim which is useful for shallow and calm water. Conversely, longer and thicker blades give a heavier and more hesitant motion underwater which is excellent in deep and fast-flowing water. As regards blade colors, numerous theories abound. It seems, however, that silver is the best for dark weather and cloudy water, while copper is good for all situations.

Gold is good for sunny days and clear water. Decoration is another matter and is an added extra, entirely at the angler's discretion, with skirts, pom-poms (a "blood" signal which fixes the attack at the level of the hook) and other "eye" signals which are supposed to make a difference. It all depends on your taste, and the results you get with your chosen lure.

The technique involves casting across the spot fished, waiting for contact with the bottom, and slowly reeling in, moving the rod about to vary the lure's direction.

Insert a few irregular pauses so the lure can drop a bit. Avoid monotonous, regular reeling in, which is not really compatible with "real" lure fishing. To ensure you are using good lure action, you should be able to feel the lure working in the hand holding the rod. Reeling-in speed should decrease to the point where the lure stops turning and increase to produce large vibrations in the rod, but never over a very long distance. The pike is fast but neither courageous nor sporting and it will never swim very far to catch your lure; it should pass within its reach and seem provocative but not too far away. As with deadbait fishing, make several passes at different depths, carefully sweeping each area.

• Spoons

Still little-used in France, spoons are however favored by many European anglers when fishing for large pike. They are often used for trolling from a boat, which is not as common in France, since it is generally prohibited except on a few lakes on which it is permitted due to special regulations.

Non-leaded pike spinner. This can work near the surface or on the bottom if used with a lead weight. ▷

Blade colors and decorations follow the same rules as spinners. The shape, however, has a specific role. Rounded spoons give a very slow and hesitant movement underwater. S-shaped spoons move more quickly underwater and are famously less predictable. Fishing technique is very similar to that for maneuvering deadbait, i.e. a series of small rod movements and quick, jerking stops which successively set off the spoon or make it drop while waggling or gliding.

◁ *Large plugs, up to 7 inches (18 cm) long, are great pike traps.*

On a river, overhanging branches are excellent spots. Fish these areas from the bank, from a boat, or by wading. ▽

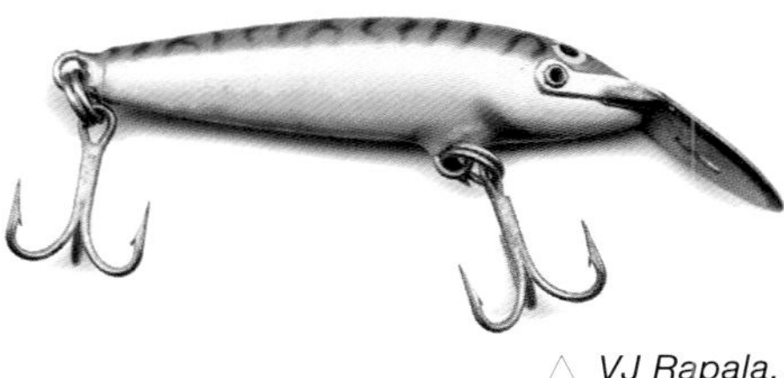

△ *VJ Rapala.*

• Plugs

Plugs are made out of balsa wood or plastic and are always little marvels of ingenuity. It is a shame that they are usually so expensive (often costing more than $15.00 each!) because they prevent you taking as many risks of losing them, which you may have to do if you "fish well".

Floating plugs are perfect for fishing in shallow water or weeds, while sinking plugs are great for deep water or light currents. For shape and color, do not shy away from a bit of originality, because it is often true that you need to surprise a pike to attract it!

The fishing technique involves passing the lure near all known or expected habitats, moving the rod around and constantly changing the speed of reeling in while making it jerk rapidly (the lure works from side to side, rising and dropping) and pausing occasionally (the lure will drop if it is a sinker and float if it is a floater).

• Plastic Lures

While popular for zander and perch fishing, plastic lures are still not widely used for pike. However these fish-shaped lures are excellent on deadbait rigs and

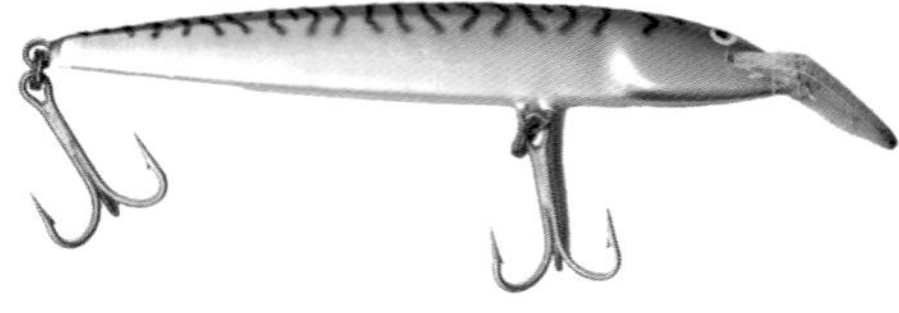

△ *Pike Rapalat.*

the larger "Comma" types with several tails are excellent on a shotted head, when used together with a treble on a small steel pin or a deadbait rig. They need to be moved carefully, basically dropped with the rod held high. Use dapping movements near obstacles and zigzagging movements at different depths near the best pike habitats.

△ Pike take very well to flies when they are hidden among weeds.

FLY-FISHING

Often posted near the surface, aggressive if awake, and a bit of a fighter, the pike is an ideal prey for the fly-fisherman in summer. In winter and colder periods, pike live deeper, but luckily they tend to stay near the banks in rivers, which makes fly-fishing easier at these times of year too.

• When the pike is near the surface
Use a classic floating silk and a short line tip: 20 inches (50 cm) of 45/100, 20 inches (50 cm) of 40/100, 20 inches (50 cm) of 35/100, 40 in (100 cm) of 30/100, with 16–20 in (40–50 cm) of wire to prevent the line being bitten. If you have the good fortune to notice a hunt or recognize a large pike, cast nearby and move the fly without allowing it to sink.

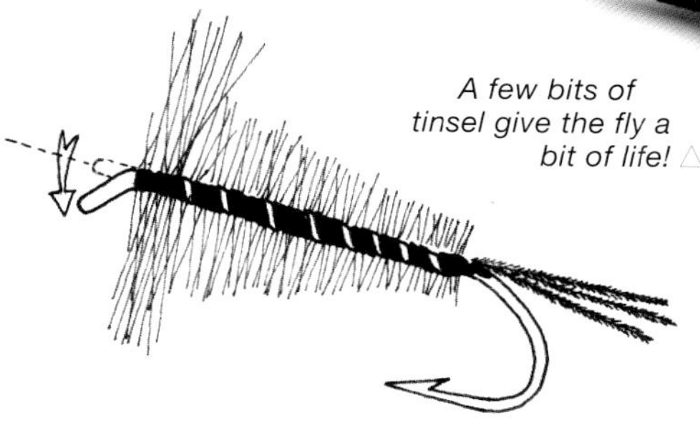

△ A pike tube-fly, skinny but efficient.

A few bits of tinsel give the fly a bit of life! △

Fish systematically and sweep the area, casting once every 3 feet (1 m) or so. Fish near the surface, using the fly's weight to allow the line to sink during pauses.

• When the pike is deeper down
You cannot avoid using sinking lines for rational fishing. With the different densities of silk, some of which sink very rapidly, you will not have any problem adapting to all habitats. If you are worried that your streamer will not sink enough, use a small floating olive on the line-end. Move the fly with longish jerks, alternated with pauses of varying lengths. Change direction often and, if possible, fish at different depths without forgetting that the pike is always more sensitive to what is going on above it.

The decisions of what to put on the end of your line, which kind of rig to use, the type of lure, and all the other decisions to be taken in coarse fishing, are of no importance when compared to the wiliness of the pike, and the extreme importance of remaining hidden from the gaze of this fish which is constantly combing the surface of the water and its upper levels for potential prey. That is why it is essential to cast wide, and to ensure that you are outside its line of vision.

The bite
This is always an emotional moment. It is indicated at least by a sharp stop, perfectly well detected by the hand holding the silk. But the attack is often brutal! If you are fishing in shallow water, you may also have the rare pleasure of seeing the swell produced by the pike as it launches its attack. The following seconds, just before the full attack and the bite which leads to your longed-for strike, are the longest you will ever experience. The hardest thing of all is to have the necessary patience. The only solution is to control all your reflexes and wait until you feel the fish in the hand holding the silk, without ever trusting what your eyes see. Copy the pike, and lie in wait!

Pike flies are often very sparkly, and look a little like fish fry. ▷

PIKE FLIES

Artificial flies for pike fishing have to be brightly colored (reds and blues are the most attractive), thick, and with a sparkling, tinsel-covered body. To increase their efficiency, use longer hair, giving the fly more volume and movement in the water. By adding a few bits of tinsel among the hair, you will make the fly shine more brightly.

ZANDER

Zander (Stizostedion lucioperca), *also known as pikeperch or pike-perch, is a popular catch which is now to be found throughout mainland Europe and in eastern England. Once found exclusively in Eastern Europe, the fish extended its natural habitat as the Danube was linked to the Rhine and the Rhone via canals. It was introduced to East Anglia, mainly into reservoirs, and there has also been extensive restocking in France, Germany, and the Netherlands. Zander is still confined to eastern France, however, and has not yet moved into the Iberian peninsula. Wherever it is found, it is a highly popular coarse fish.*

△ *The zander, a subtle, cunning, and disconcerting fish.*

The zander learned at a staggering speed how to adapt itself to all the traps that anglers set for it! ▽

A SHREWD, GREGARIOUS HUNTER

The zander is a close relative of the perch, as its other name implies, and has similar habits. It is a gregarious hunter, living and feeding in groups which diminish appreciably in number as the fish put on weight. The feeding tactic of the two species is similar in a number of ways. Both zander and perch like to locate and then encircle schools of coarse fish, and at a certain moment, all of them start the chase at the same time, whether or not they can actually see their prey. All this suggests that biochemical communication, a phenomenon common to many fish, is particularly well-developed in the zander. Once the attack has been launched, the zander will remain active for several minutes, chasing and killing with a bite any prey within reach. Zander do not necessarily consume their prey straight away. Studies of the fish have shown that, in fact, they return later at their leisure to consume the dead or dying fish lying on the river bed. However, it took anglers some time to understand this behavior, which explains the persistent reputation of this magnificent and exciting fish as a bloody murderer that "kills for pleasure". Research shows that only young zander continue to feed in groups. The older (and thus larger) specimens would much rather live a more stay-at-home existence, which means that they hide in sheltered places which they hardly ever leave except to get close to the feeding zones of their fellows, in the secret hope of profiting from their work by devouring corpses and even pieces of fish which may fall to the river bed or drift away on the current.

However, it is not only scientists who have studied zander and their habits. Anglers, too, have watched them closely, making observations which tend to prove that this member of the Percidae family has shown an astonishing ability to adapt to changing circumstances. In rivers which have been intensively fished for many years, it seems that the zander has been able to modify its behavior, to the extent that it will no longer visit the more dangerous places (in other words, those which are fished most regularly.) Some experts in the use of moving dead bait even claim that the most cunning zander choose to live only in very small groups so that they can communicate rapidly amongst themselves. This allows them to escape at the slightest warning, or to keep watch if one of them happens to be caught or momentarily hooked. At all events, you will be lucky to have more than two or three zander in the keepnet by the end of the day, unlike the huge catches of ten fish or more which were common in the late 1970s and early 1980s. Yet records of catches kept by professional anglers, or for stocktaking purposes, tend to prove that there are still as many zander around as ever there were. The inevitable conclusion is that they have become more difficult to catch or that they no longer frequent the same haunts.

△ *Zander flies are best used close to the bottom, made to move in small, hesitant jumps, and they are a good way of provoking the curiosity and aggression of the fish. This is an excellent way to trap difficult and over-fished zander.*

Favorite haunts of the zander

Just like any self-respecting member of the perch family, the zander loves to hide in the depths, on riverbeds where there are a lot of rocks or dead wood. This phenomenon is further enhanced by the physical characteristics of the fish. Its eyes, in particular, are well adapted to conditions of very poor light and can barely endure strong illumination. This explains why, on sunny days, zander often stay several feet below the surface of the water or in shady spots, in order to protect themselves as far as possible from the rays of the sun. Unlike other carnivores, the zander does not dislike the current, in fact it enjoys "playing" in the fast-moving waters as soon as the milder weather arrives.

The zander is easily recognizable by the shape of the head and two dorsal fins, the first of which has easily visible rows of spines. △

• The best spots in the river

In rivers and canals, the best positions for fishing for zander are always downstream of weirs and locks. This applies particularly to summer and for most of the fall, or until floods and frosts come and drive the zander toward safer and quieter places of refuge. For the rest of the year, you will find them in the eddies which form close to banks where the water level is high, near rocks, downstream of bridge pilings, alongside calm, deep, wooded banks, and more generally lurking in any deep, wide trench where a lot of submerged objects provide good cover and a safe refuge from the force of the current. The wide eddies that form downstream of bridge pilings are particularly popular winter haunts. Entrances to moorings and gravel pits, downstream of overflows and locks are also excellent.

Apart from these known and generally very popular haunts, there are others, some barely noticeable, which may equally provide some pleasant surprises for the alert angler. You may be fortunate enough to make your best catch from a small eddy close in to the bank. That may be because nobody ever thought of fishing from that particular spot, even though it happens to be a favorite haunt of the wily zander.

• The best spots on a lake

– In ponds and gravel pits

Zanders always inhabit the deepest trenches of lakes, ponds, and gravel pits. However, when they are on the hunt for prey they may stray far from these shelters, though, like carp, they will take quite specific routes. You may encounter them at sunrise or at dusk during the summer, opposite clumps of aquatic plants, close to wooded banks, near dykes, or even on small beaches, especially in places used for swimming. The particles stirred up by swimmers attract other coarse fish, so it is logical that zander searching for food are never far behind.

– In reservoirs and dammed lakes
Here the hunt for popular zander haunts often becomes a real brain-teaser! It must be said that among the scree, the submerged remains of bushes and forests, former pathways and the walls which run alongside them, windmills, houses or whole villages engulfed under several feet or many fathoms of water, there are particularly large numbers of possible hiding places for a fish whose movements are so unpredictable. Fortunately, when feeding, zander tend to move toward floating reed beds, lurking on the steep shelf which separates the underwater plateaux from the deepest trenches, the foot of bluffs, or from scree at the lake's edge, unless they swim alongside steep wooded banks with overhanging vegetation. If following these basic precepts proves unproductive, all you can do is to patiently and meticulously inspect all the places that seem likely to offer one of these accidents of underwater topography, from small pools to hump-backed mounds, which zander seem to like so much.

△ *Fall and winter often provide regular catches of some handome specimens of zander.*

THE BEST TIMES OF DAY

Because of their sight problems, zander are especially keen on the times of day just before dawn or dusk, at least during the six hottest months of the year. Days when the weather is overcast or rainy are equally good, due to the weak daylight. January is never a good month in still waters, even though a few individual anglers who are particularly well acquainted with the fish's behavior will manage a few catches anyway (even of big fish) by using moving dead bait, and more rarely with live bait, or grounded dead bait. On the river, floods cause the zander to congregate near the banks. This is often an excellent time for fishing, except when it coincides with some frosty weather, which is as fatal to the activity of fish as it is to that of anglers! The months of February and March, with the arrival of the first mild days of the year, the presence of fry which demand a lot of energy (and thus feeding) and the spring floods which often provide lots of food, are generally quite productive times of year.
But taking into account the end of the pike season and the whole series of bans which then come into force (on use of live bait, dead fish, lures, etc.) you may not have much choice on the technical front. The only way left to sweep the bottom of the riverbed is to fish with worms.

• Spring and summer
Leave zander alone in April and May, as this is the breeding season and they will emerge from it hungrier and more active than ever in June, which, along with the first two weeks of July, is definitely the best time of the year for catching zander. Fishing with live bait using a floating line, or with grounded dead bait, as well as with moving dead bait or flexible lures, are the most effective ways of ensuring a catch. In spring and summer, you will certainly catch a lot of fish, but rarely any large specimens. Don't expect too much in August, apart from a few catches in the early morning and evening, unless you are lucky enough to be around during a storm – storms turn zander totally crazy – of which you should take advantage, preferably using moving dead bait, or flexible lures.

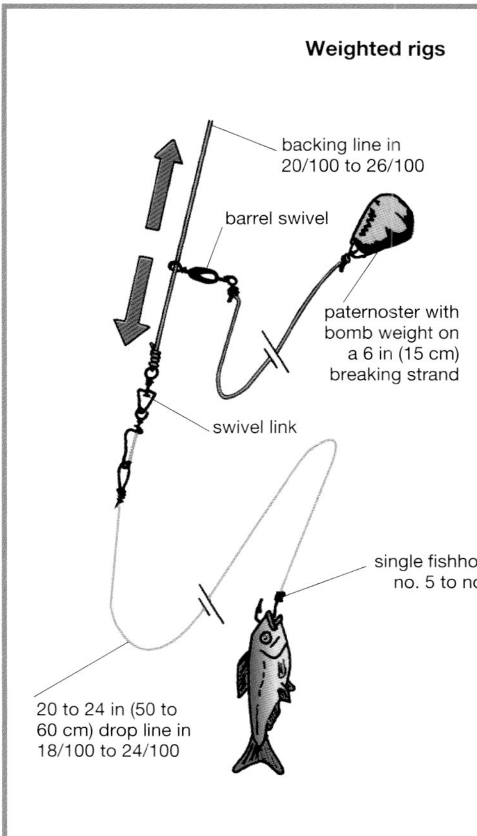

• Fall and winter
With the return of cooler weather and sometimes the arrival of the first floods, September and October are generally excellent for all the techniques. If you are patient enough to place dead fish or pieces of fish in deep spots that are full of obstacles, you might be lucky enough to get a bite from a monster weighing 18 lb–22 lb (8–10 kg). If the weather is relatively mild in November and December, you may also be lucky, but only if you search for zander quite deep down in lakes, using moving dead bait or flexible lures, or try the eddies which form in rivers when the water level is high, using live bait or flexible lures. When the weather is cold or the water is very

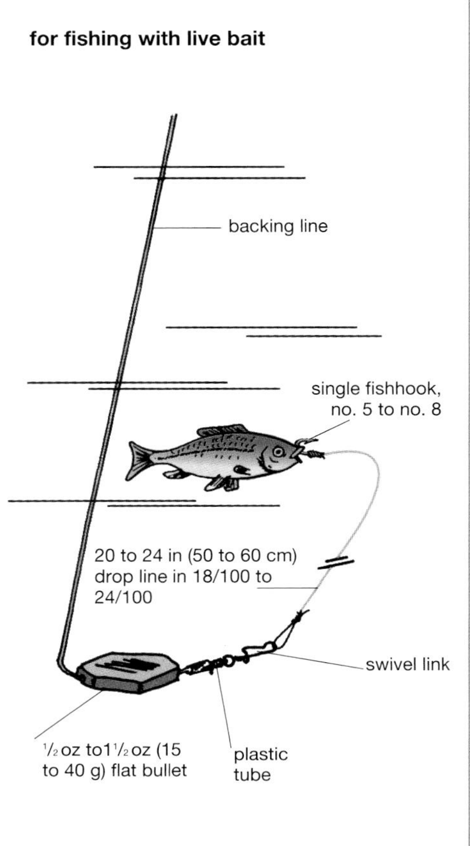

still, you could still persuade a few decent zander to bite by perch-fishing with a tin fish.

Fishing with live bait

Even when it is sulking, apparently deserting its favorite haunts and obstinately refusing anything that is offered to it, the zander must still continue to feed. By presenting it with little fish, which make up the basis of its diet, you will have a good chance of enticing it anyway, as long as you put the live bait in the right place and do so discreetly enough to ensure the trap is not discovered.

• River fishing

In running water, if you are able to position yourself upstream of the place at which you want to fish, do not hesitate to do so. For example, position your rowboat at the edge of a large area of calm water or downstream of a bridge piling (be very careful here when sinking the weights) or use long rods in order to reach the best flows. The aim of the maneuver is to take advantage of the current in order to fish with a floating line. By adjusting the depth so that the live bait wriggles when only inches from the bottom, you will be ideally positioned for a bite. Incidentally, you will be quite free to explore the area if you let the line move with the eddies. If you are not able to use the current to its best advantage, you can still use leads. Classic rigs are all very well, but when fishing for zander in eddies, nothing compares to the breaking strand mount. Not only does it limit the damage if it gets caught on an obstruction, it also guarantees a much better positioning of the live bait, which remains more easily visible.

• Lake fishing

– In large lakes

Live bait fishing can be quite tricky whether you are doing so on a reservoir lake, a natural lake, a pond, or a gravel pit. The spots may be innumerable, as on a reservoir lake, or it may be impossible to find somewhere suitable, a problem that often occurs on a natural lake. Faced with such a problem, users of moving dead bait and lures have a slight advantage, because their active technique of moving from place to place allows them to increase the number of places in which they can search. The live bait fisherman needs to try and achieve the same ubiquitousness, for which purpose a rowboat is indispensable. On windy days you can just let yourself be carried along by the breeze, dropping the weights from time to time to explore the position. Your lines must be stretched out behind on both sides of the boat, and must be able to reach different levels of the lake, but always close to the bed (you will need to check the depths regularly). Levels to explore include wooded banks, the foot of the slope and the center of the lake, as well as source river

◁ *A rowboat is indispensable for reaching the best spots, which are often deep, cluttered, and far from the banks. It is far more comfortable and above all allows you to fish more effectively.*

△ These very mobile, colorful lures, capable of withstanding many different movements, are definitely the best zander lures currently on the market.

channels of dammed lakes. In winter, and especially during cold spells, you should still favor the deep-water areas where zander seem to prefer to lurk at between 30 and 90 feet (10–30 m) below the surface.

Certainly the most difficult part of this operation is preventing the lines from getting caught up and especially from breaking. Although there is no miracle solution, you can limit the damage here, too, by using the breaking strand method.

All you need do is fix the weighted rig to end of the floating line. However, if you do so, the paternoster weighted with the lead (which is always thinner) should, in this case, be longer than the drop. If everything goes well, you will be able to fish by skimming the bottom of the lake without doing much damage to your tackle. As soon as you get a bite, thoroughly search the level in which you found the fish. It is unlikely that this nibbler was lurking there all by himself.

– On small stretches of water

Fishing from a rowboat looses some of its attraction on smaller stretches of water, and, in any case, it may not even be allowed. However, as the suitable spots are even less easy to distinguish than they are in large expanses of water (they may be little more than a hollow or a submerged branch on a bare bed), finding them can become a real headache. The solution here, too, is to use the floating line, which is more mobile. Cast the lines in a fan-shape configuration over the spot and reel back three to six feet (1 or 2 m) of them regularly, so as to comb the area thoroughly. If the fish appear to be wary – a common situation in gravel pits – the best idea is to resort to thinner lines, keeping them as light as possible. The whole trick is to make the trap practically

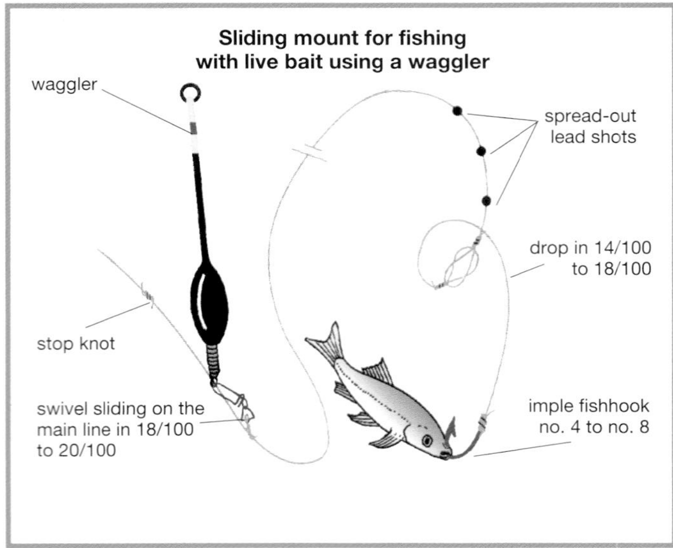

impossible to detect, first by using 18/100 or 20/100 for the main line, secondly by making the bottom line as flexible as possible (16/100 or 18/100 nylon, braided or kevlar) and above all by ensuring as far as possible that the weight does not cause the bait to lie inert. You may well be surprised at the results. It might be a good idea to copy these principles in all the spots where there is enough clear water to allow you to reel out some more line to a struggling fish.

• Live bait
Not all live bait has the same characteristics. Some types are irresistibly attracted to the vegetation and other obstacles that cover the bed; others, in contrast, see the only means of escape as flight toward the surface. These are all possibilities that a skillful angler must take into account and use to his advantage, depending on which rig he is using. Small fish have a tendency to nose-dive, so use a floating line set up in such a way that the live bait can never reach the bottom, and use a weighted line placed on the bottom for any types of bait which, in contrast, are strongly inclined to aim upward toward the surface. The type of fish you are angling for and the nature of the area you are surveying must equally be taken into account.

– Bleak
This is by far the shiniest of all small freshwater fish and is recommended for fishing at great depths. When attached to the end of a line, the bleak has a natural tendency to swim toward the surface. This determination, combined with its extreme fragility, means that it is very soon overcome by exhaustion. The other major problem is keeping it alive, which becomes problematic as soon as the air temperature exceeds 59°F (15°C). Despite of these problems, bleak is still a first class live bait for zander on account of it shininess, which makes it very easy to see, even in the feeble light of the murky depths of a pond or lake.

– Bream
These fish may be found in profusion in most waters, but have never been popular among coarse fishermen. This is a mistake, because small bream or "skimmers" swimming in shoals are very easily caught and when hooked they remain extremely active. On the other hand, they tend to pull toward the bottom, where they take advantage of the slightest obstacle to attempt to free themselves from the hook. Nevertheless, they make useful live bait for catching zander.

– Chub
The chub is a tireless worker and very hardy. It has a smooth and shiny skin and is useful for survey fishing with a floating line.

– Roach
Shiny and hardy, it is also capable of working for hours when hooked, and as it is so common, all sizes are available, normally in tackle stores and at fish farms, which makes the angler's task easier. The roach is the supreme all-rounder.

– Gudgeon
This prey lives near the bottom and is ideal for zander. It compensates for its dull skin by its stubborn and constant desire to return to the bed. It is live bait that should be reserved for fishing with a float.

– Minnow
Small but strong, the minnow has been used to lure thousands of zander. Although it will not survive every ordeal, it is able to cover a large area from the end of the line, especially when combined with a small weight and a float.

• Hooking the bait for striking at the first sign of a bite
If your live bait are regularly attacked and then released before they are fully taken, the answer is to strike at the first sign of a bite. In practice, all you need to do is to attach your live bait using two fishhooks. Set up in this way, you will be able to react to a nibble immediately, and give yourself a much better chance of hooking a difficult fish.

– Double-hooking the back of the bait
The first of the two trebles must have one hook piercing in front of the dorsal fin. The second should be fixed in the correct place by a silicone tube strand to enable it to slide along the bottom line, which should be made of nylon, or better still, of kevlar or braid. In order to fix it firmly in place, you will need to force it onto the ring and shank of the treble.
The technique of always hooking at the same point is much more secure, and this is important as it actually holds the live bait in place while the line is being cast and when it is being reeled back in. This method is suitable for using a floating line of any type.

Floating line for wary, picky zander

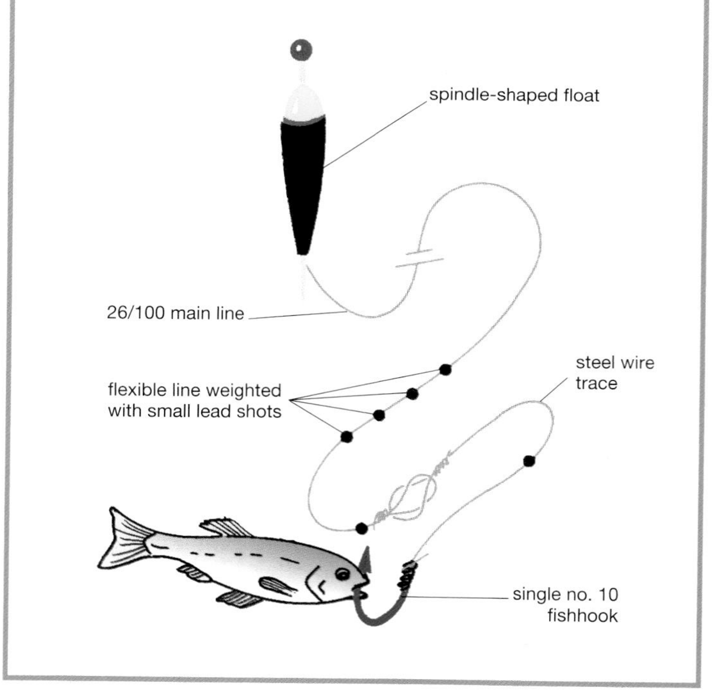

– The Stewart hooking method
Here the mobile fishhook is a single hook with an eyelet ranging in size from nos. 2 through 6, which will slide along the bottom line. Once it has pierced the mouth of the live bait, fix it with the help of a piece of silicone tubing, and thread it onto the line. The second fishhook should be a treble. Attach it to the end of the line and allow it to pierce the back of the small fish. This is the only really worthwhile hooking method when using a weighted line, and also works well when using a floating line.

• Hooking the bait for varied strikes

– Hooking through the nose
Hooking the bait onto a large fishhook is more subtle than the hooking methods suitable for striking a nibble, and is also the method that best shows off live bait to its best advantage, by allowing it to remain more active. It is excellent when using a bleak or a minnow, for example, and also for trotting or for using a leaded line over a very great distance.

– Hooking the bait using a baiting-needle
Originally designed for pike, the baiting-needle can equally well be used for zander, particularly when using large live bait, as in deep-water fishing. It is just as effective when used with grounded dead bait, such as a whole fish or one cut into pieces. You can insert a treble on to the back of the live bait in front of the dorsal fin, or a double (parrot-beak) in one of its sides.

• The rigs

– The floating line
To fish at any depth, attach a sliding float blocked by a stop knot or a ledger stop. Use a long bullet weight, together with a few pieces of split shot which are easy to detach and allow you to adjust the weight. The ideal float is one that is barely submerged by the movements of the live bait. For the drop, choose between nylon, braid, or kevlar, the latter two being more flexible but also more expensive. The fishhook should be a treble or single, depending on which hooking method is being used.

– Floating line with sliding float
The sliding float is ideal for fishing a bed that is covered in roots or dead wood, if you are using a weighted line and angling from a bank at the foot of a scree slope or in a clearing, or even when fishing from a rowboat over a cluttered bed, perhaps close to submerged trees. All you need to do is to fix the stop of the sliding float at least three feet (1 m) above the actual depth. Once in position, the float will stay flat while the lead weight and the mount, lying on the bed, prevent the

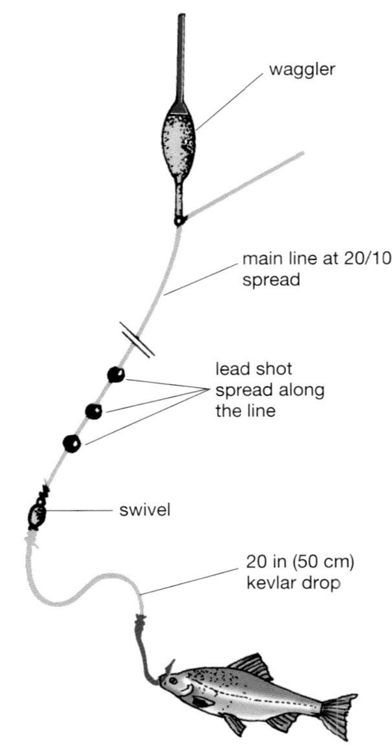

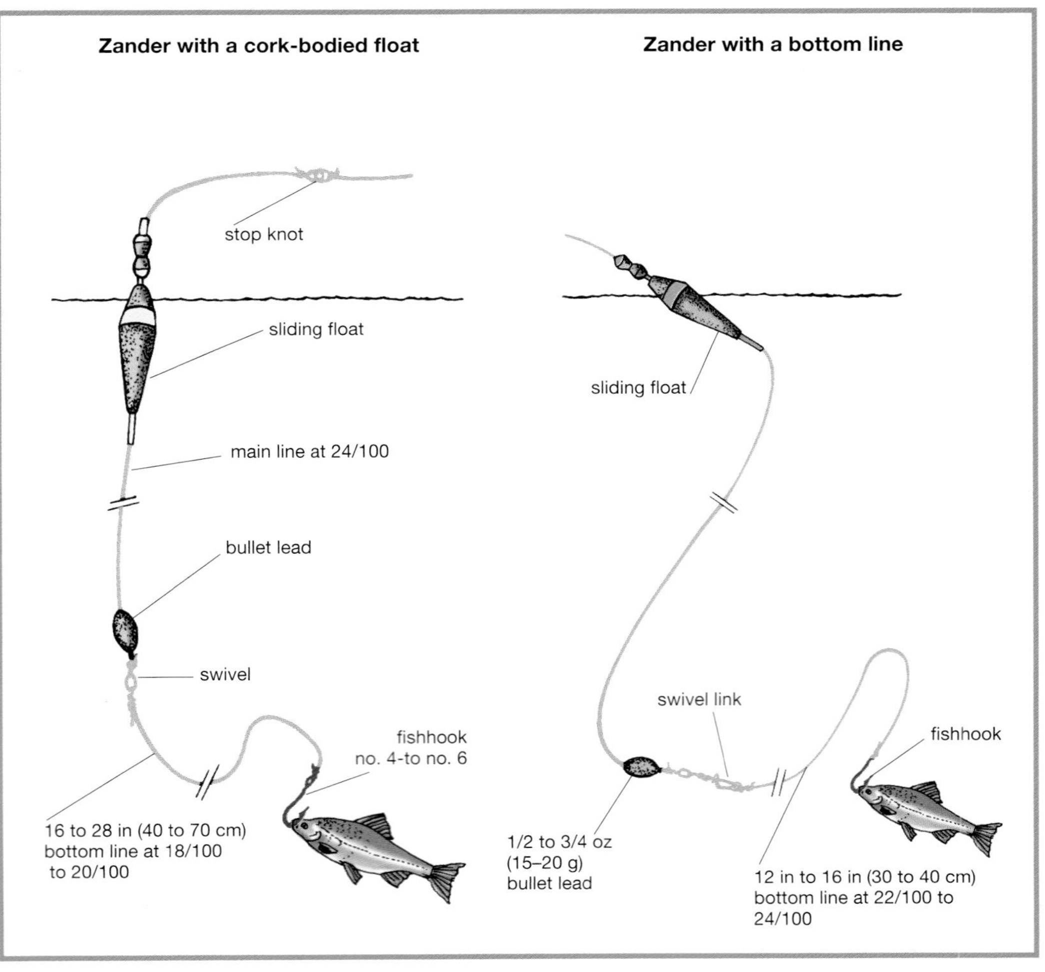

livebait from straying and getting lost among the debris. When you retrieve, the float will work as a relay on the surface and, if you reel in quickly, it will enable you to lift the live bait and mount sufficiently high off the bottom to prevent them from getting snagged.

– Floating line

Here the main innovation is in the float, which is far more sensitive than a float for fishing with live bait. Wagglers, which may be changed in an instant thanks to their special attachments, are excellent. Their sliding action means that you can sink the backing line without difficulty in order to avoid the effect of the wind. But large "wind-beater" fishing floats, which are just as sensitive and sometimes easier to see, are also very effective. For the weight, use round leads which grip the line, as these are even more flexible – and therefore less easy to detect – than a solid weight.

– The classic weighted line

Slide a 1/4 oz to1 1/4 oz (10 to 40 g) bullet onto the 18/100 (for clear beds) up to 24/100 (for cluttered beds or very large fish), backing line with a piece of plastic tubing to protect the knot of the swivel. For the bottom line, choose kevlar or a piece of braided line, which are distinctly more flexible than nylon. A single fishhook is preferable for live-bait, while a treble using a baiting needle is best for grounded dead bait. When fishing over a long distance, add 8–12 inches (20 to 30 cm) of anti-tangle tubing above the swivel.

– Sinker with breaking strand

Attach the weight to a paternoster line that is thinner than the bottom line. If it gets snagged, which happens to weights nine times out of ten, the breaking of the strand will prevent you from having to reel the whole line back in. The principle is the same as the fuse wire for electricity. To reduce the cost, recycle useless old bits of scrap iron. The short length of anti-tangle tubing will allow you to cast the line without having to worry too much about it getting snared, which is practically inevitable at distances greater than 50 feet (15 m) without this device (which was invented by English carp anglers). To make it even more efficient, slide a floating bead two-thirds of the way up from the swivel on the bottom line. This will stop the live bait from reaching the bed and force it to make desperate attempts at escape, which is more effective.

△ *Their increasing rarity should encourage anglers to limit their fishing of carnivores.*

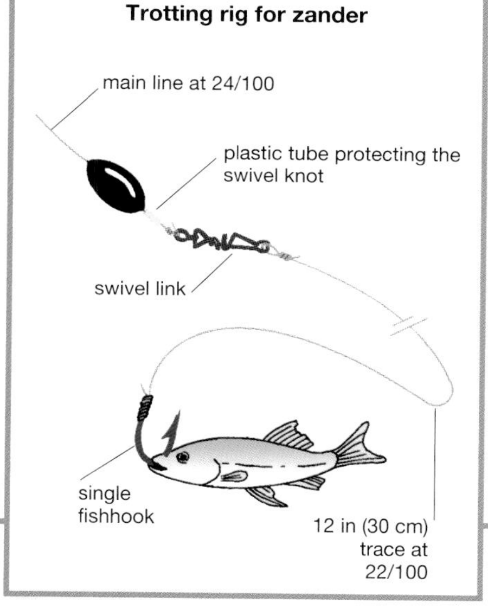

Trotting

Trotting is a method of float-fishing whereby the tackle is allowed to travel along with the current in a controlled manner. This fishing method has been practiced for a very long time and is highly effective for zander.

Since you will be using a small fish (preferably live) as bait, carnivores will definitely be attracted. On the other

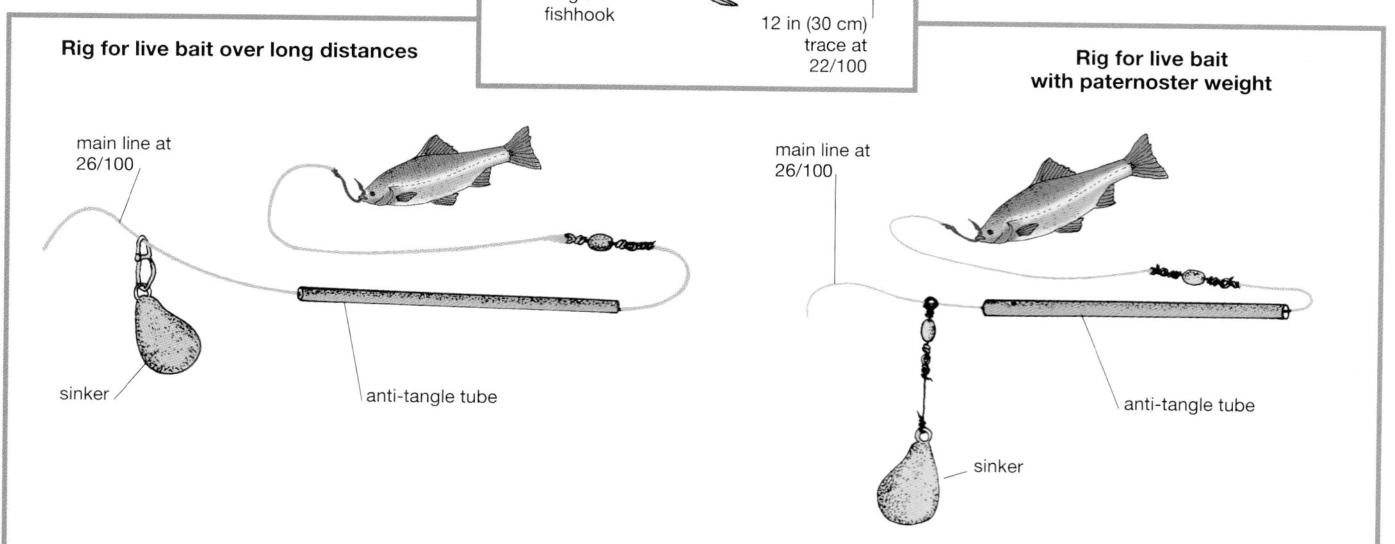

hand, the rig must be discreetly sited enough so as not to arouse their suspicions. Avoid lines that are too thick and limit the weight to what is strictly necessary.
On the practical front, the main difference between trotting and ordinary fishing with live bait lies in the movement. It is important to move the live bait around the bed, using little jerks interspersed with pauses of various lengths (you are the best judge of these). There is no point in resorting to trickery. Quick movements of the tip of the rod and shaking are useless in this case, as it is the live bait which does the work, but by moving it, you increase its chances of being attacked.

• The rig
Trotting is well suited to the weighted rig. To improve upon it for beds covered in debris, attach the weight to a paternoster, to form a loop inside the ring at the top of the swivel, and clip

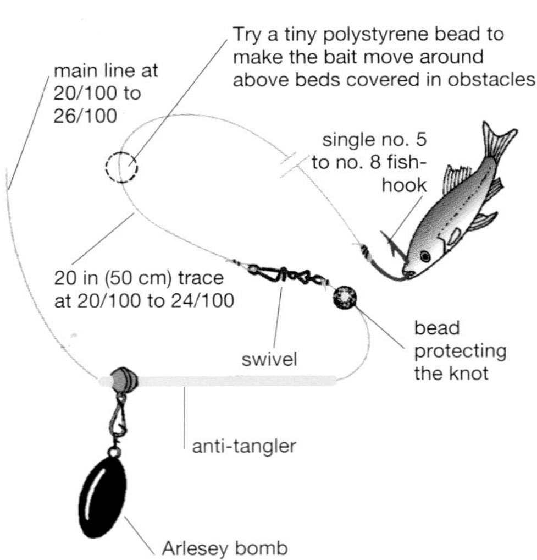

Rig for zander using grounded dead bait

on as many lead shots as are necessary to drag the mount down to the bed. Add or remove the shot, using a knife-blade and pliers, in order to adapt to the different places in which you fish.

FISHING USING GROUNDED DEAD FISH

Bleak and small roach are the shiniest and most frequently used, either whole or in pieces. The line, generally a

Trotting rig with dragging lead

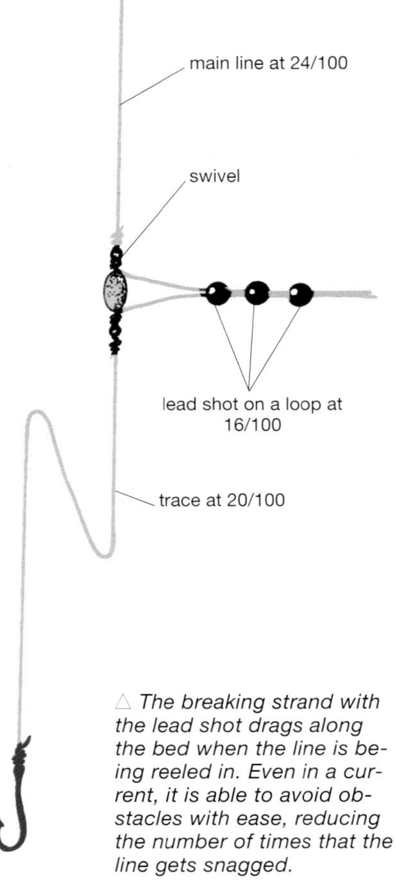

△ *The breaking strand with the lead shot drags along the bed when the line is being reeled in. Even in a current, it is able to avoid obstacles with ease, reducing the number of times that the line gets snagged.*

classic sinker, should be cast immediately next to a popular spot for zander, one with plenty of submerged wood, eddies, etc. Since you no longer have to worry about the movements of live bait, you can take advantage of every nook and cranny in an obstacle. But be ready for a struggle, even if your nylon line is very strong!
If you are fishing for zander on a reservoir lake, you may also use a mount with relay float. When the bait, lead, and bottom line are resting on the bed, the float will lie on the surface, but when there is a bite it will start jumping around, before bobbing under. For fishing over beds with a lot of obstacles or weeds, the British have perfected some small balsa rods that they stick right into the dead fish, which raises them slightly above the bed and obviously makes them easier to see. Another British trick (see page 131) is to use sea fish because of the stronger odor. When they are mashed up and mixed with dirt as a binding agent, these fish also make good surface bait for carnivores. There is no reason why you should not adopt the same technique using freshwater fish, simply by throwing small pieces of fish onto the bed (even when fishing with bleak or roach), just as you would with seeds when coarse-fishing.

FISHING USING MOVING DEAD FISH

Thanks to such experts as Albert Drachkovitch and Henri Limouzin, fishing for carnivores using moving dead bait has progressed extensively over the past twenty years. So much so that in certain lakes, as more and more people are adopting this technique, zander are beginning to turn their noses up at moving dead fish. But fishing with moving dead bait remains overall one of the most reliable and rewarding ways of fishing for zander or pike.

Moving a dead fish

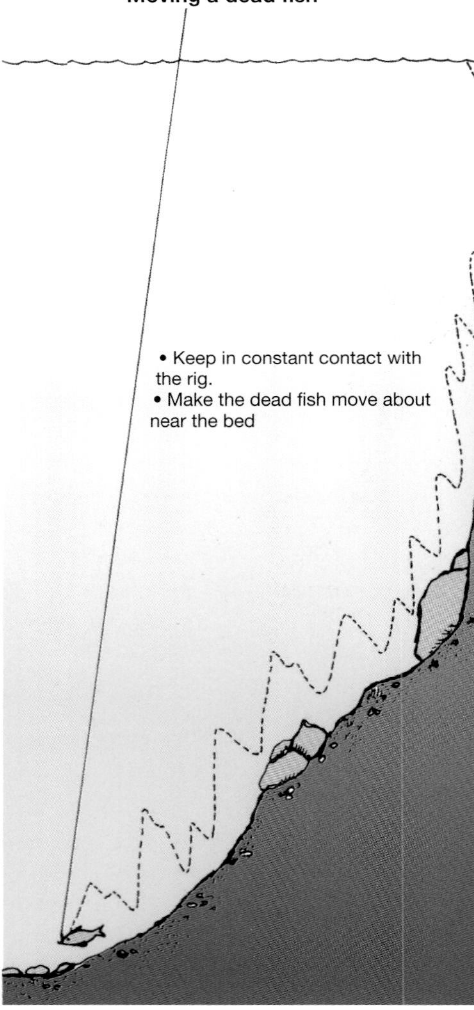

△ Zander may grow to and exceed 22lb (10 kg). Small fish at below the legal limit of 16 in (40 cm) must be returned to the water, while taking great care to keep them alive.

• Fishing action

As soon as the dead fish is in the water, place your index finger on the spool of the reel and keep the line slightly taut while you are letting it out, releasing the line with single turns. If the line momentarily stops sinking, or if there is the smallest jerk or sideways movement, this could signify a bite and you must strike immediately. When the fish has reached the bottom you can start to reel in, holding the rod high, accelerating in quick bursts with short pauses in between. You should use the pauses to retrieve the surplus slack line. At the same time, make sure to move the rod from side to side so that the small fish can tempt prey over a wider area. When there is a bite, the line will generally stop sharply or move sideways, but the hand holding the rod will not necessarily be able to feel this (which is why a fluorescent float is so useful). Bring your hand back before striking firmly, and reel in quickly so as to compensate for the sluggishness and elasticity of the line.

• Fishing in deep water

Things get more complicated when you need to fish deep down or, worse still, at the base of a steep slope. In the latter case, you must fish from a boat and position yourself opposite the bank from which you intend to fish, otherwise it is almost inevitable that the line will become entangled and something will break every time you cast. It is a good idea to jerk the tip of the rod a few times. Be ready to reel out the line, or even open the bale arm, using your finger to stop the line from running out too quickly, so that the bait can sink right down to the bottom. This is because it is important, if not essential, that your small fish visits all of the obstacles. Remember, too, to reel in slowly, and from time to time, to make some controlled jerking movements by shaking the rod tip violently whilst keeping the line quite taut. On certain days, this strange behavior will be enough to persuade the more persistent fish... Here, too, you must keep a close watch on the line so that you can detect a bite that is too imperceptible to feel through the wrist. If it happens, you must strike immediately and very forcefully, even if you are not sure what you have seen. It is actually better to strike out at nothing a few times than to miss the smallest fish.

In rivers, the hunt for zander using moving dead bait is similar to the technique used for trout-fishing using a dead minnow. Exploit the current, which will carry your bait and make it roll along the bottom, so you have nothing to do but to liven the bait up with a few jerks of the rod tip of varying degrees of sharpness to make it look like a dying, very tempting fish. Do not hesitate to sweep the same place time after time, for an hour or so, because zander often begin to feel restless after a while. Or it may be that the sight of your small fish going by again and again gives them the illusion that there is a sudden abundance of food of which they had been unaware hitherto.

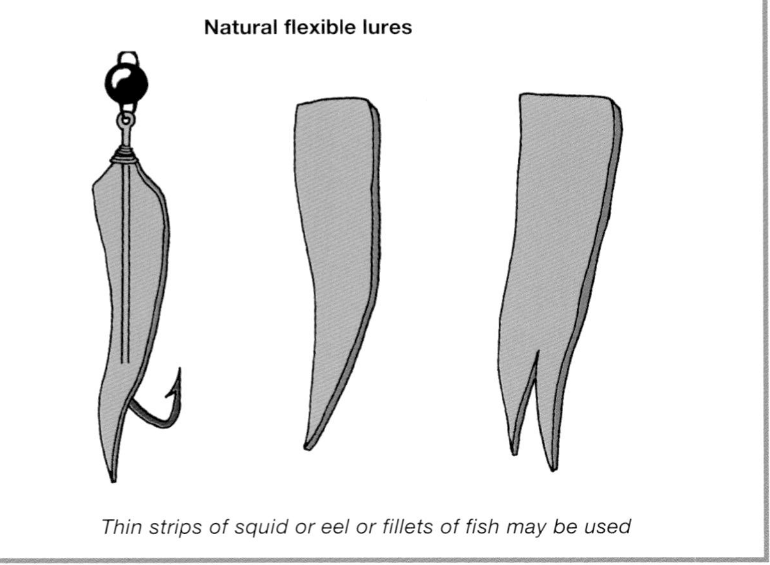

Thin strips of squid or eel or fillets of fish may be used

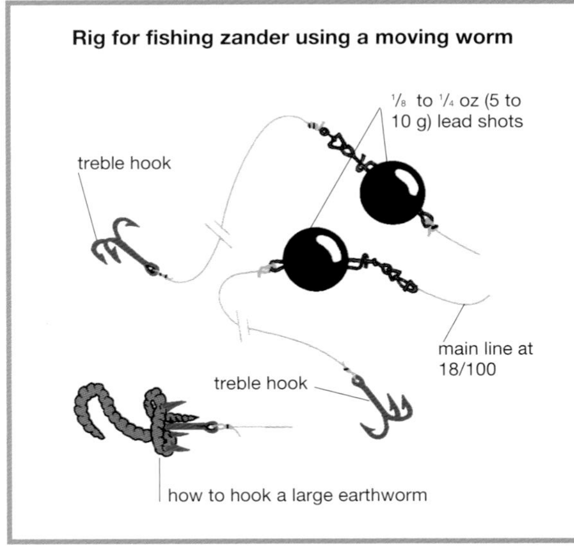

WORM FISHING

When the pike season is closed, many forms of angling such as casting, fishing with moving dead bait, and with live bait, are forbidden. So to fish for zander the only method left is to use a large earthworm as bait. The moving worm technique has been providing great catches for a long time, but over the last few years tougher regulations have virtually outlawed movement of the worm. So now you just have to make do and just count on the intrinsic qualities of the bait.

Slide a long olive (or a few large lead shots) on to the backing line, restricted by a small swivel that will hold 16–20 inches (40–50 cm) of bottom line. If using one large single hook (no. 2 through a reversed no. 6), tie a small hook (no. 14 for example) to the line $^3/_4$ to $1^1/_4$ inches (2 or 3 cm) above the big hook. (You can also use a hook with an eyelet, through which you should thread the line twice, so that it is still possible to slide it up and down.) The smaller hook will hold one end of the worm, while the rest of it will have already been carefully threaded on to the first hook and on to the line, in the same way as when fishing for trout with wet flies.

The fishing action is similar to that of free lining. Cast in a fan-shaped pattern over the spot, wait for contact with the bed, and move the line regularly as you would when fishing for roach with a floating line. When there is a bite (which could be from one of the more unusual carnivores such as the chub, or from a fish of the carp family, such as carp, bream, tench, or roach), pay out for about a minute before striking.

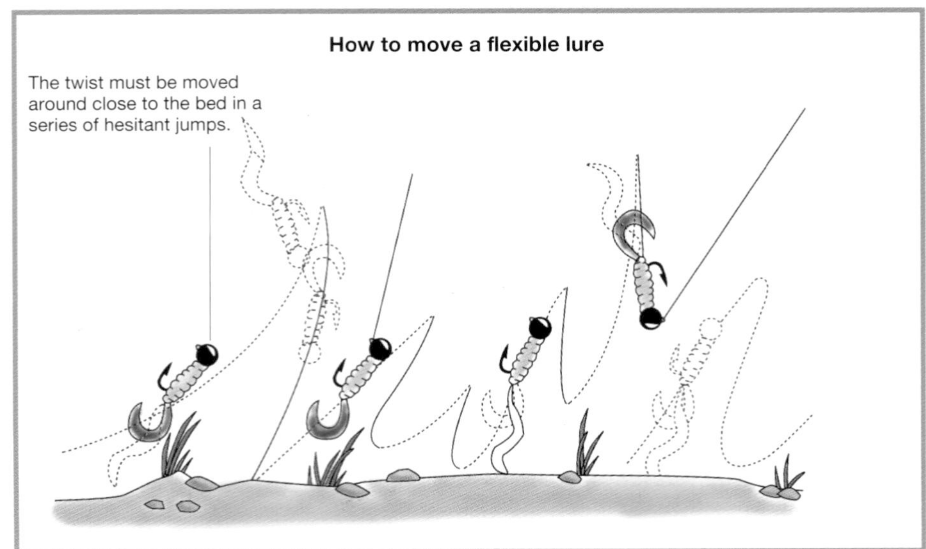

IMPROVE YOUR SINKING PLUGS

Store-bought plugs are the plainest mounts imaginable. From the strict point of view of effectiveness, however, they suffer from a slight lack of hooking power. The solution to the problem is to improve them by adding a small trace attached to a no. 12 to no. 10 treble hook (the size should increase with that of the lure). Use some steel cover with kevlar and you will be untroubled in the event of an attack by a pike.

Fishing with flexible Plugs

Supple lures cost pennies, their effectiveness has never been faulted and they are perfect for finding zander. This surely explains why there has been such a craze for them over the last few years. You must have noticed the mountain of flexible plugs that we have to choose from in the stores nowadays. There are weirdly shaped ones whose main aim is to surprise, and those which are quite faithful copies of nature – the choice is enormous. So, until you are able to make an informed choice on the basis of personal experience, rely on some infallible criteria, such as fish-shaped plugs, commas, twists (these are the most common shapes and on average the most effective), plus a few freshwater crawfish, worms, and lures with multiple tails (two or four). An all-purpose selection will enable you to fish for zander with a good chance of success. As for color, white and yellow seem to be the best, but shiny ones are highly prized as well (dark colors for worms, almost translucent for crawfish).

– The rig

Store-bought sinking plugs are inexpensive, and are ideal if you use them right (see box on the preceding page). With the fish shapes and the largest lures, rigs such as the Drachko LS, which offer the same characteristics as a dead bait rigs, are very effective too.

– The movement

Tugs, changes of direction, and pauses, which will make the lure work while giving it the appearance of struggling prey, are very well suited to weighted heads. Vertical movements (jigging), may irritate the fish and thus cause it to bite. Using a Drachko LS, the movement becomes much closer to that for moving a dead fish. Always use the fan-shaped cast and explore every possible hiding-place carefully.

Spinners and spoons: not the easiest method

Even though it is possible to hook a handsome zander with a spinner, plug, or spoon, it must be recognized that these are not always the most effective lures. Try and use an undulating plug or spoon. You will need to crisscross the lake or river bed thoroughly, and it may sometimes be worthwhile to persist for a long time. Proceed in the same way with the spinner, always using types with long blades, such as fly spoons and bar spoons, preferably rotating blades, that float along slowly and heavily. The best plugs are those with flowing shapes that swim horizontally or dive slightly, but again it is important to fish very close to the bottom, and to do so slowly, in such a way that the head of the plug scrapes along the sand or gravel.

When fishing in large lakes, flexible plugs allow you to explore the bed rapidly, and thus find biting fish more quickly. It is then up to you whether to continue with the flexible plug or to opt for another method. ▽

PERCH

*Unpleasant, aggressive, and sometimes very cruel, the perch (*Perca fluviatilis*) also has an insatiable appetite, which leads it to investigate any prey that comes within its reach. It is therefore active all year round. It will eat anything – fish fry and aquatic larvae, as well as earthworms and insects. It is the ideal companion for a very enjoyable fishing trip!*

When they are feeding, perch are particularly adept at swimming around unnoticed, which is how they are able to position themselves a few feet away from their desired prey. ▽

A VORACIOUS, AGGRESSIVE FISH

Of all the freshwater carnivores, the common perch is certainly the fish with the most varied diet. Although small fish (mainly fish fry born that year) are its main article of diet, it is also ready to gobble up any aquatic larvae that pass within its reach, and sometimes it even eats insects.

Another characteristic of the perch is its patent aggressiveness when feeding, a time when it becomes exceptionally violent.

It always attacks in groups of varying sizes, depending on the size of the individual fish (like pike-perch, the largest perch tend to live alone) and on how much food the lake or river contains.

As soon as the perch find a shoal of young fish, generally close to banks or to a large clump of aquatic plants, they form a perfect circle.

They move slowly at first, their striped sides helping their concealment. Then, as soon as they have cordoned off all possible escape routes for the school of young fish, they launch the attack. The onslaught is brutal and unpredictable, involving all the perch from a group, even if some of them are several yards away, which suggests the existence of a sophisticated means of communication. All the evidence suggests that, as with the pike-perch, it is a question of a biochemical exchange; the fish that makes the decision to attack releases a substance which its fellows are able to detect and interpret in record time.

During the chase, the perch surge forward onto the shoal of young fish, encircling them from every direction so that they have nowhere left to flee.

The only fish that remain calm and composed are the perch themselves; they are capable of singling out a victim which they will then chase with exceptional relentlessness and ferocity. For proof of this, you need do no more than watch one of the giant chases that make lakes and ponds seethe and boil every year between late August and early October. There is noisy clashing of teeth, splashing, and persistent chases some of which end up tight against the bank. Perch really is a very nasty character indeed!

FAVORITE HAUNTS OF PERCH

Like all members of the Percidae family, perch love places where there is a lot of underwater debris, among which they can hide more easily. A few of their most typical haunts, where they spend the better part of their time, are around stone quoins and floating or anchored wood. This includes tree roots, branches, or dead trees, pilings and the remains of landing stages, or even rotting rowboats that have been more or less abandoned. They may also lurk in thick underwater vegetation. When they are at their most active (especially the smaller specimens weighing 7–10 oz (200–300 g)), they may abandon these shelters for the purpose of mounting attacks on beaches and in the shallows, which are the preferred habitat of the fish fry and larvae of which they are so fond.

Perch are fond of natural or man-made shelters in which they can hide or keep watch. Footbridges, landing stages, and jetties make very desirable hideouts. ▷

Fishing in winter is often very successful, this is a time when large perch can be caught. So don't hesitate to cover a lot of ground and try persistently in the best places. ▽

• The best areas

On the river, look first in the deepest, calmest patches of water (perch are not very keen on current), close to steep banks, especially if the banks are thickly wooded and have overhanging branches.

In ponds, look near the sides of the pond and by any outlets, especially close to pieces of submerged wood (such as old roots or dead trees in former gravel pits, for example).

Natural or artificial lakes (reservoir lakes), contain even more suitable places, but these may be much more difficult to find. At ordinary times of the year, perch may be found well away from the bank, several feet below the surface of the water, lurking near clumps of aquatic plants. They can also be in clefts in the bank, or where rocks or large lumps of stone or concrete litter the lake bed, as well as among dead wood or roots, where the bottom slopes steeply, near large logs, or even at the foot of a bluff which provides shade by the bank. Try and think like the perch, where would it position itself in order to grab an innocent passer-by?

◁ *The handsome perch is very fond of the deep water of large reservoir lakes. It may be found at the foot of scree or lurking within dense clumps of vegetation.*

• How to find a shoal

The only way to locate perch when they are not having one of their famous big chases – at which time you can spot them from yards away – is to patiently angle in every possible spot until you record the first bite.

Perch live in shoals, so once located, you can be sure of having found a spot where they congregate. But be careful, if you miss just one of them, or worse still, if a fish succeeds in unhooking itself from your line, this may cause the whole shoal to flee in a mad rush!

If you are lucky, the perch will only move a short distance away and it will not be too hard for you to locate them again. But they may swim off, or hide right in the deepest water, lurking there without making a move, remaining stock still for an hour at a time.

Perch seem to prefer to gather at natural underwater features, such as the point where a tributary joins the river, sharp changes in the slope of the bank in gravel pits, among sunken logs, and generally around other natural obstacles – anywhere, in fact, except in long straight stretches of clear water. No doubt this is because they can more easily hide from their prey, ready to leap out from the shadows as it passes by.

WINTER FISHING

Of all the carnivores, perch are definitely the most active during the winter months. Since perch has not been given any particular form of legal protection, the fishing season is open all year round. When the pike season is closed (and occasionally when pike-perch also cannot be fished) there is a simultaneous ban on live bait and lures, but you can fish without a problem, if you use worms and real larvae.

Of all the possible fishing methods for perch in winter, fishing a position with a floating line is by far the simplest and most effective. Always cast the line slightly to one side of the most sensitive point, making sure that the bait moves around in the top third of the water. As soon as the float is in position, reel in about 3 ft (1 m) of it and start over, guiding the line well so that it passes as close as possible to where you suppose the perch to be. Repeat the maneuver to sweep the whole area if it is large enough, moving progressively nearer to the bed. First do so halfway down, then two-thirds of the way down, and finally on a level with the bed.

A typical fishing method for winter is jigging which, when practiced with a special type of line, allows you to use the latter to thoroughly explore all the spots along the edge or bank. It is not a particularly quick method, and may be seriously boring when the bites are slow in coming, but it still remains the most effective technique. A spot that has given you nothing when you have jigged it may be considered empty or devoid of interest for that day!

In practice, all you need do is sink the line right to the bottom and then bring it back up again slowly and jerkily (with short pauses all the while it is being raised) until it reaches the surface, before sinking it again. If there is a bite, the line is stopped more or less abruptly and should be paid out before striking.

The last option is the trotting method, using brightly shining little fish. This rig will catch you some beautiful fish if you reel it in slowly in deep pools, in eddies near the bank, or right beside submerged debris. If the bites

VERY LARGE PERCH

The oldest perch, which can weigh as much as 4½ lb (2 kg), live in very deep water and are solitary, or gather in groups of two or three which stay well apart from each other. With age, they seem to have an increasing need to feel safe, and their taste for small fry increases... as does their fondness for dead wood and old stones! In reservoir lakes, for example, the best spots are regularly to be found at the foot of screes or among submerged trees and bushes that were not cut down before being covered with water. To fish for them you will thus have to rely on live bait, or on moving or jigging dead bait, rather than using natural bait. You must also be ready to take risks since you might be caught at an inopportune moment!

are slow in coming, scrape the lead weight so that it shines or use an added attraction, for example the bowl of a spoon, which may succeed in arousing the interest of the perch and make them react.

SUMMER FISHING

In summer, you must rely more than ever on roving, always remaining alert to the slightest sign of activity. Small frightened-looking fish, young fish leaping out of the water, a violent eddy close to the surface or next to the bank – all these are signs that should prompt you to start angling there and then.
Even though jigging may provide you with a few fish in narrow places or at the banks, the floating line and trotting are greatly preferable. Do not hesitate to rely on live bait, which will allow you to select the most beautiful fish. By fishing around obstacles, large cluttered beds, and dense clumps of aquatic vegetation, and even inlets and outlets, at dawn and dusk, you will certainly manage to achieve some great catches. When perch are in their feeding frenzy in early fall, you can take advantage of the situation, using the same techniques, by fishing at hardly more than three feet (1 m) below the surface with the first line, having the others positioned slightly to one side but always in a much deeper place. This ploy should tempt any perch that are still inactive, or the largest ones that often stay in the background.

THE BEST TIMES

January and February are generally very good for perch fishing, and more particularly during very cold spells, which drive the small fry into hiding in the warm sludge of large holes. Like all carnivores, perch are ravenous at this time of year and are ready to jump out at any lures or bait that come within their reach in the deep hideyholes, in which they take up residence. It is the ideal time for jigging fishing, using red threadworms, young fish, or pupae (if you can manage to keep them alive in the cold!), and above all for fishing patiently and persistently using tin fish.

• Spring and summer

March and April, which are more or less the spawning season, are not good months. In any case, the perch are quite inedible at this time, so it is preferable to leave them in peace while they spawn.
The summer, from June through the end of August, is a poor time for river fishing, but it is quite good for lake fishing. The difference is actually due to the behavior of the fish, which spread themselves out in rivers but are more gregarious in lakes, making them easier to find.
You will usually catch perch by fishing various positions in rivers, near steep, wooded banks, for example, and cast fishing or using miniature live bait in lakes. Stick to clefts in the bank or to the outside edge of dense patches of water foliage.

• Fall and winter

September and October, early fall, is by far the best time for perch-fishing. In large lakes, conditions can become favorable from mid-August, especially if a few storms bring some cooler air, causing the young fry born that year to gather near the banks or in dense clumps of aquatic plants. Whatever technique you are using, whether you are fishing with miniature livebait, casting with very shiny little lures, or ledger fishing with small multi-colored rubber teats or flexible lures, you are likely to be lucky. As long as you manage to locate the perch (by spotting them feeding) and can follow them as they move from place to place, you have every chance of filling your basket to the brim!
November and December are still good months, and especially so for the largest specimens of perch, which ought to be pursued with live bait and jigging with natural bait (page 152). As soon as the first spell of cold weather hits, start using a flexible or jigging lure.

In summer, fishing right along the banks, under floating branches, or even at the foot of overflows, produces excellent results. ▷

THE GREAT CHASE

The dawning day gradually reveals the beautiful foliage of the aquatic plants which grow out about a dozen yards from the bank. The boat advances slowly and silently, cleaving the mist that enshrouds the surface of the reservoir. The sky is perfectly clear, the weather is still mild, as it is early September, there is not a breath of wind. Everything seems to have come together to make it a great day for fishing.
Suddenly a terrible commotion from under the water shatters the tranquility of the surroundings. The water foliage, which had been so still just a second ago, is now surrounded by seething water. Overcome by frenzy, young fish fly in every direction, visibly panic-stricken. Here and there, a ferocious feeding frenzy finally reveals the cause of the whole uproar. Perch, in their dozens, even in their hundreds, have combined to launch a ferocious attack on a group of small fish. It is spectacular sight and one which causes great excitement to anglers like us, because we can count it as a huge bonus! Since the perch are are in a highly excited state, they will strike at anything that moves, so we obviously have every chance of getting lucky.

FISHING WITH NATURAL BAIT

Small fish are one of the favorite foods of perch, but worms, aquatic larvae or even, on occasion, insects figure in their diet too, and may consequently make excellent bait.

• Types of bait

Perch are inquisitive and aggressive and may be interested in any edible prey, or even just in those that dare to enter its living space! But to fish sensibly and effectively, there are certain definite principles that must be observed.

– Pupae

The larvae of the great mayfly are well known for being real "perch magnets". It is true that the beautiful striped perch is excessively fond of them, whatever the time of year. The hardest task is to find the larvae, for example on silt and gravel beds, near the banks or close to watering places, in rivers where currents and calmer sections alternate. Note too that they are particularly difficult to find in winter... and frankly unpleasant to collect! To hook them, use fine, iron hooks (no. 14 to no. 16), delicately thread through the last segments of the creature's body, near its tail. You can use them jigging, but the standard technique is with a floating line. If there aren't any mayfly larvae, you may also use other aquatic larvae that give good results, yet not as good.

△ *Damselfly pupae.*

– Earthworms

As perch have a small mouth, bright red, wriggly compost worms are distinctly preferable to large lobworms. They are easy to find, especially at angling supply stores, and should be hooked on to a no. 12 to no.14 fishhook, if possible one with a fine gauge and a long shank. You may opt for the trout fishing way of hooking bait, with two thirds of a worm threaded on the fishhook, or perhaps better, the classic pole fishing hooking method, with one worm pierced twice near the center. Worms are excellent for jigging and are also very useful when hooked on a floating line.

△ *Compost worm.*

– Live bait

Here too, taking into account the mouth and size of perch, only the smallest live bait are useful. Minnow, which are easy to catch and to take care of, obviously make ideal bait. But young coarse fish are occasionally better, in particular at the end of summer or the beginning of fall, when they are the targets of those famous perch poles. The most difficult part is catching the bait. You could always use a light, ultra-fine pole fishing line and miniature no. 24 or no. 26 fishhooks, but the ideal way is to just to net them, using a large, fine-meshed landing net, or a square dipping net, in a privately-owned pond. Do not forget that netting in public lakes and rivers is still considered to be poaching. Live bait may be used with a wobbler, but is especially useful with a floating line

EVERYBODY WANTS SOME!

Young fish may congregate in shoals so dense that they form an almost opaque cloud on the surface of the water. Perch of all sizes hunt almost tirelessly among these shoals – nothing else is needed to attract the attention of other carnivores, whether they be pike or perch-pike! It is not known whether they are attracted by the fish fry or by the perch, the important thing is that they are there and more accessible than ever!

When perch fishing, do not forget therefore to cast a few times (with dead bait or a large flexible lure) just off where they are feeding, or deeper down if you are fishing in a lake. All you need is a second, more powerful rod at your disposal in a corner of the boat, or in your hand if you are fishing from the bank. Another solution is to fish with live bait a little way beyond the point where the feeding is taking place. The best live bait? Another perch, of course.

▽ *Current British fishing techniques allow very skillful perch fishing using live bait.*

or when trotting, and dead bait may be used, though this is most effective only with the largest specimens.

• Rigs

– Jigging

The lead weight, preferably a bullet or torpedo which is nickel-plated so that it shines more brightly in the water, is attached to the end of the line. Two very short paternoster links are attached above the lead weight. The first may be actually fastened to the lead, in order to benefit directly from the fish's fascination with it.

However, care is needed. This rig may cause you a few problems when it is the closed season for pike. It is

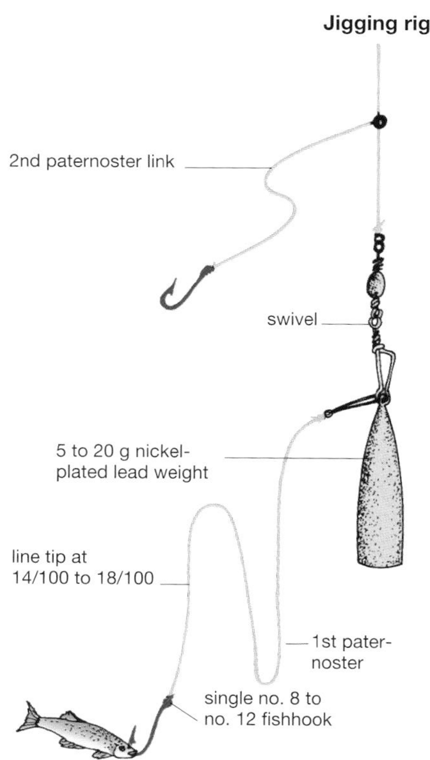

therefore better to avoid bright lead weights and not to move the rod around too quickly, as this could be interpreted as a method likely to transform the mount and bait into a lure, as it is now defined in law.

– Floating line

Connect a tapered float to the 14/100 or 16/100 reel line, sliding if necessary (look at shapes for the English method, which are more sensitive than the standard designs for carnivores), if you are to fish in more than 6 or 7 feet of water. The sinker may be divided up (using small lead shots) or solid (using a long olive, which could be scratched with a knife to make it more alluring). The trace should be nylon,

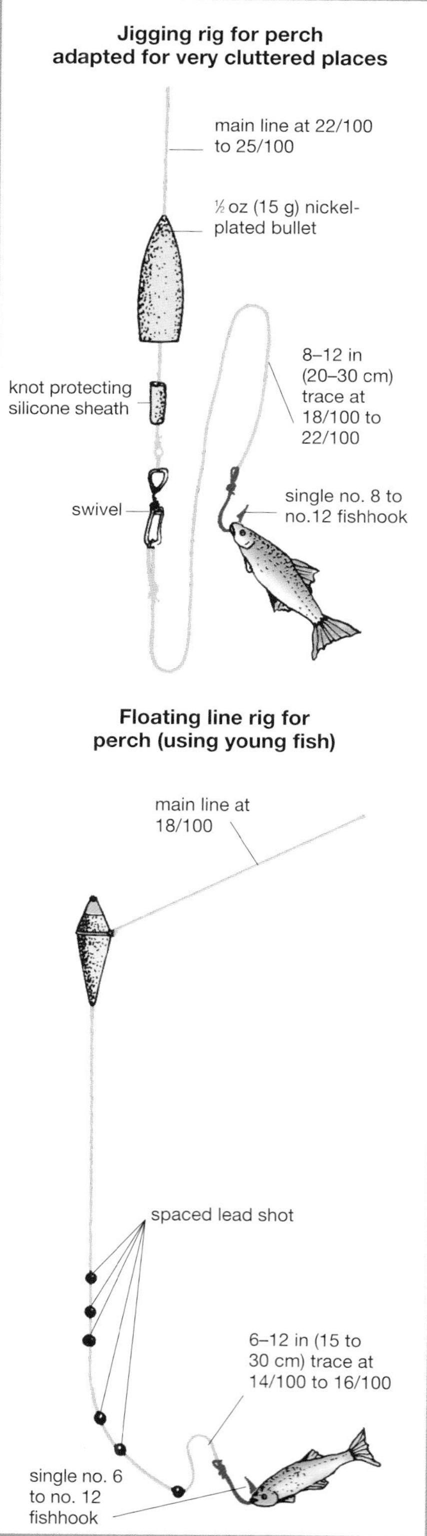

No. 1 and no. 2 turning spinners are still formidable traps for perch. In summer, try angling around clumps of aquatic vegetation. In winter, stick close to the banks.

braid, or kevlar, finer (or not as stiff, in the case of kevlar or braid) than the main line. The size of the fishhook, which should be no. 6 (live bait) through no. 12 (nymph), should be suited to the bait which is being used.

– Trotting

Connect a long olive, scratched with the blade of a knife, directly over the 16/100 or 18/100 reel line, restricted by a swivel whose knot is protected by a piece of silicone tubing. The trace, which must be finer than 2/100, should carry a reversed no. 6 through no. 8 fishhook. The young fish is usually hooked by the nose, though certain experts recommend killing it and passing the hook through the eyes. When you use dead instead of live bait, you must move the mount around more actively and hardly pause for a second.

CASTING

Perch are common, inquisitive, aggressive, and never too wary, so they are ideal fish for casting. The prime season is summer, when striped perch are at their fittest, spending their time on the prowl or feeding. But lures can result in catches of large fish in winter too, if you patiently angle close to the banks and at the best spots.

• Trolling

There is always one exception, and when it comes to carnivores, the smallest lures are the best. For spinners, choose a no. 0 and a no. 1; for spoons you need tiny blades, which are not necessarily easy to find but exist all the same, for example in the ranges made by Mepps. Trolling spoons with flexible blades deserve special mention. When reeling in slowly, the blade spins hesitantly, but as soon as there is acceleration, the blade tends to lengthen, thereby spinning faster and more regularly. They are in fact genuine moving trolling spoons that remain just as active when the line is relaxed (due to the lead weight at the tip), which are marvellous for perch.

– In Summer

You must move around a lot in order to hunt down perch in all the places where they could be (of which there are many!). Always begin with a few castings in a fan-shape, reeling in close to the surface. If nothing happens, repeat the fans halfway between the surface and the bed. If there is no reaction, nor bite, nor fish following the trolling spoon, change places. As a general rule, rely on lures with quite a fast, fluttering spin.

△ *Comma or sickle flexible lures, when simply connected to a sinking plug, work just as well when casting as when jigging.*

– In Winter

The choice of lure is only of secondary importance, as what counts above everything else is the fishing method. You must cast precisely so that the lure falls exactly a few inches away from the bank or an obstacle. Go over the same spot a few times but at different levels and reel in slowly but continually changing the speed, with many pauses and changes of direction. Do not hesitate either from persisting at each spot for a long time, as in winter, even ravenous perch are occasionally slow to react.

• Fishing with flexible lures

Activated by the slightest movement and perfectly adapted to variations in speed and direction, flexible lures are really marvellous for perch anglers. For the mount, use a small comma, a Kat, a Vitala, or a Shad with a weighted head, or even a Pisciflex, and you are all set.

– In Summer

Fish all the likely spots, and even in open water, moving the lure around at the halfway depth. Get the lure moving with a series of strokes of the rod tip combined with changes of direction, and intersperse with pauses with the rod held high, so as to slow the lure down.

△ *A very effective flexible lure: the Kat.*

– In Winter

Fish close to the bed using the same action, but moving much more slowly and sometimes staying still without reeling in. Often merely by relying on the perch's aggressive nature, an angler can lure a fish to bite.

• Fishing with a plug

The only plugs that are really useful for catching perch are 1¼ in (3 cm) and unfortunately, these are quite rare. Floating designs are useful in the summer, while in winter sinking ones are better, since you will then need to be fishing close to the bed.

How to take advantage of the big chases

When you have located a chase, position yourself at a suitable casting distance – about 50 yards (15 m) away. If there is no movement, sweep the area using the fan method. If the chase continues, help yourself from the mass of fish! Although striped perch are single-minded, there are always a few that have no identified prey, or are tempted by your tiny trolling spoon, flexible lure, or streamer. Even though comma-type flexible lures and Agila no. 1 spinners are by far the best choice, any lure will produce a result during a chase. If lures do not work, try fishing a run with a very simple line. For bait, the first choice is thread or compost worm, followed by live minnow and aquatic larvae (though these are rather fragile.) Explore around the spot and do not hesitate to drop to a depth of 7 feet (2 m) from the bed, or even further if bites are slow in coming. Even when casting, it is always prudent to leave one or two lines with live bait trailing behind the boat, so you can fish at the sides and deeper down. The first line should be made of kevlar or nylon, and should trail with a minnow halfway between the surface and the bed, to tempt any large perch that may be passing. The second, baited with perch on steel, should trail deeper down, aiming for the larger specimens that are hoping to get some easy catches from the chase!

As regards the movement, you should alternate reeling in rather quickly with pauses, while constantly jerking the rod tip and changing direction. The tactic is the same as for trolling, so the method is the same.

FLY-FISHING

Because perch are smaller in size, classic trout fly-fishing equipment can be used. You will need to connect a paternoster link to the trace (as you would for wet fly-fishing), to which you fix a second lure. Here you have the choice between simple little pupae that are brightly colored and shiny (wrap a few bits of tinsel around them, or varnish them well), small, more evocative streamers, colored plastic teats (used for leger rigs in lakes), tiny flexible lures (commas connected to a link fishhook) or simply a fly hook with a strip of household aluminum foil round it. The essential thing is in the fishing action, which is only really effective if you guide your flies close by a school of perch or, even better, into the middle of one of the chases that stir up the surface in early fall. Be sure to make the flies move jerkily, accelerating abruptly and stopping very quickly, like frightened young fish. Bites are usually sudden, almost always sparing you the need to strike, yet there is nothing stopping you from adding a solid jerk of the wrist to be sure of your catch.

Perch flies made by J.-P. Goutte-Quillet.

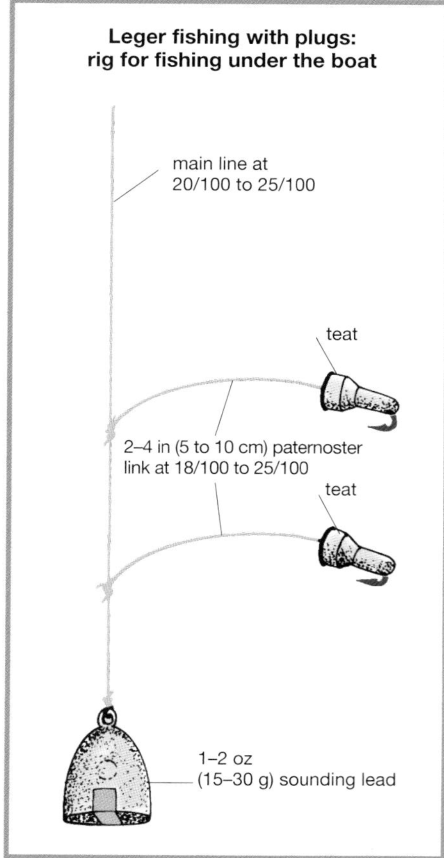

SPECIAL TECHNIQUES USED FOR PERCH

• Leger rig

Place a bullet or torpedo nickel-plated lead weight at the end of the 20/100 to 25/100 reeling line. Attach the fishhooks above it on a paternoster, either carrying a small rubber teat (plugs clear to Swiss or Savoyard anglers), or tiny comma flexible lures. The movement is similar to trotting and basically consists of repeatedly pulling the rod right back with pauses in between to gather in the excess line. You must cover the whole area of the water, right over the chase. The law only allows the use of two fishhooks, but some large lakes are subject to bye-laws covering large inland lakes which may permit a greater number of fishhooks, and therefore more paternoster links for your legers. Find out the angling rules from the local angling federation, especially if it is abroad.

• Fishing with a tin fish

The tin fish method may also be used with more modern jigging lures, or even flexible lures attached to a weighted head. It relies more heavily on the aggressiveness of perch, and has more dynamic movement. Open the reel and allow the lure to float away. Contact with the bed is indicated by a slackening of the backing line. Now reel in the excess line until the rod tip is around 12–16 in (30–40 cm) from the surface; then bring the rod up again by at least three feet (1 m) and finish with a firm strike; repeat immediately by taking the lure down, which will glide to the bottom. To do it well, you must begin the next, identical movement just before the tin fish touches the bed. This method is most effective in winter, producing the best results during prolonged periods of frost, which reduce the water level, sometimes making the water clearer than in mid-winter. The only drawback is that perch often get hooked by the head or body, not through the mouth, since tin fish behave unpredicably. Comply with the law, which requires the release of catches that are not hooked through the mouth.

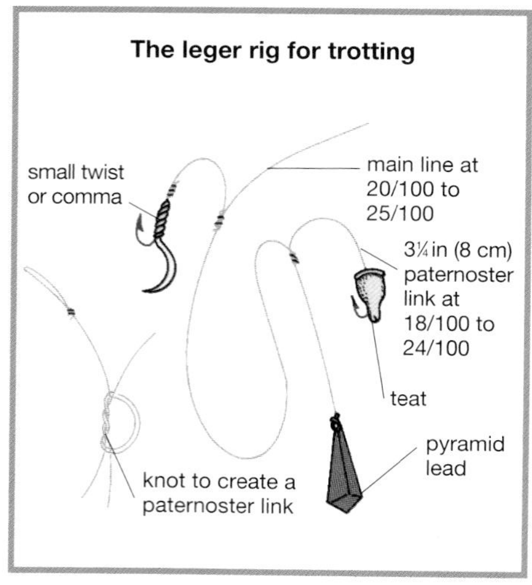

WELS

This snakelike, whiskered monster that inspires fear in some and admiration for its gallant fighting spirit in others, leaves no one indifferent. The Wels is a large, likeable catfish which is found mainly in southern Europe. There are extraordinary stories about this giant fish, claims having been made that it has swallowed poodles and even children! The "freshwater ogre" has featured more seriously (and far more interestingly) in the angling press, with claims of catches of wels weighing well over 50 lb (23 kg)!

A very peculiar face...Four short barbels beneath the lower jaw and two very long ones just above the upper jaw. ▽

A MONSTER FROM THE EAST

Wels appear to have originated from the Volga Basin in Russia, but they have now spread throughout central and southern Europe and have been introduced into some parts of western Europe, such as France and England, in recent years. They were introduced into France in the late 19th century, when a few fish farmers on the upper Rhine, near the German border, indeed attempted to breed them in ponds. In the 1950s, a few individuals introduced some into privately-owned ornamental lakes. In heavy rains, a few wels swam down to the Rhine, the Doubs, the Saone and, inevitably, the Rhône and into the downstream course of most of their tributaries.

Today, the giant catfish is found in many French lakes that are not linked to any of the rivers in which it lives, such as Lake St. Cassien in the département of Var, where a specimen 7 ft 9 in (2.4 m) long and weighing 220 lb (100 kg) was caught in 1985. This tends to prove that the illegal introduction of these fish is more widespread than is generally admitted.

WHERE DOES IT HIDE?

Endemic in most of the tributaries of the Black Sea and the Caspian Sea (the Danube, the Volga), the Wels (*Silurus glanis*) is plentiful in most eastern European countries (Russia, Poland, Bulgaria, Romania, Slovakia, and the Czech Republic, and in former Yugoslavia). It is also found in Turkey, Scandinavian countries, England and Spain (where its recent introduction by German fishermen has given rise to some spectacular catches on the Ebro, Segre and Cinca). Most large rivers in France conceal sizeable established populations, since fish weighing between $6^1/_2$ lb (3 kg) and more than 28 lb (60 kg) have been caught in the Saône, Seille, Rhône, Doubs, Loire, and Seine. It will not be long before the downstream course of most of the tributaries of these rivers (page 157), even those that are only 50 feet (15 m) wide, as well as the lakes linked to these streams, will soon have a wels population of their own.

△ *A 5½ foot (1.65 m) wels weighing 16 lb (35 kg) caught with a spoon in Mequinenza, Spain.*

Surprisingly, only 20 years ago the thousands of anglers of carnivores in France, using live bait or lures, hardly ever caught any wels, while nowadays a catch weighing 45–65 lb (20–30 kg) is almost commonplace. Anglers who specialize in this fish are unanimous in their opinion that a catch of around 100 wels a year, even on a broad stretch of a large river, requires the wels population to be very dense. Yet more proof that the Saône, Seille, Rhône and recently the Loire are abundantly populated with these whiskery fish.

Some scientists claim that there has been a change in the external structure of the roe, which over time could have slightly increased the reproductive potential of the wels. The difficulties that most carnivorous fish face, when confronted with the destruction of many of their habitats (and the resulting reduction in the coarse fish population), may well benefit the wels, since it is a scavenger and will feed on dead and even rotting fish. It is the perfect example of an ecological vacancy being filled.

ONE OF THE LARGEST FRESHWATER FISH

The wels bears a slight resemblance to the Brown Bullhead, a catfish found abundantly in France but which is of little interest to anglers. It also resembles the Horned Pout, an American catfish which has not been introduced into European waters.

The body is very long and the skin is covered in mucus like an eel. The sides are mottled with brown and greenish patches, contrasting with the almost white belly.

The wels is a good swimmer and has highly developed fins, especially the caudal and the anal fin, the latter running along almost half the length of its body. This enables the Wels to accelerate extraordinarily quickly.

Even if you only see it once in your life, you will never forget the face of a wels. It is flat in the front, split in two by a huge mouth, with two tiny eyes on either side of the head, and it is adorned with six barbels. The four shorter ones are positioned under the lower jaw; the other two, very long ones, sprout from above the upper mandible, just behind the corner of the lips. These two longer barbels are incredibly sensitive feelers, enabling the wels to hunt in the depths of night and in very turbid water. The wels' lower jaw is very strong with a grip so firm that it leaves prey with little chance of escaping from that fearsome mouth.

• A shade-loving fish

This big cat is not particularly fussy about where it lives. Large lakes and wide rivers, whose waters are well shaded, offering a combination of quite deep patches and reaches dotted with dead trees, islets, or various manmade objects, with an abundant population of coarse fish, suit it perfectly. The wels dislikes bright light and spends a large part of the day settled at the bottom of a pool, concealed in a jumble of submerged wood or under floating roots. It leaves its lair under cover of darkness, at the end of the day or when the weather is particularly dark and the sky is overcast, and makes for sheltered, often quite shallow, places in order to hunt. However, the wels is an extremely unpredictable fish and may be found at any time of day, though always in warm weather. That is why the fish has been successfully introduced into northern Europe now that summers are becoming hotter.

• A varied diet

The wels has eclectic tastes, feeding on roach, bream, tench, crayfish, and frogs; occasionally a small aquatic mammal or a moorhen will do. Wels are especially active from April through October, slowing down marginally at the hottest time of the year, but in northern climates they are rarely caught in waters colder than 65°F (18°C). In winter they become sluggish and often congregate in sizeable groups in pools 40 feet (10 m) or more deep.

Many anglers and the authorities responsible for administering the lakes and waterways of Europe are displeased with the way the wels has been introduced to waters outside its native habitat. They claim that its gigantic appetite could damage the coarse fish populations, especially those of the carp family. We beg to differ. If the wels is colonizing French and Spanish lakes and rivers and the reservoirs of southern England to this extent, it is because they contain everything it needs for food. There is no example in nature of a predatory species proliferating without adequate prey being available to feed it.

In most European lakes and rivers, zander (pike-perch), perch, and pike flourish without diminishing the population of other coarse fish. Furthermore, two eastern European researchers, Varsarmelyi and Popova, who based their investigations on a study of the stomach contents of more than 100 fish, showed that the wels only consumes about 4½ lb (2 kg) of fish per 2.2 lb (1 kg) of its own body weight, about the same as the zander!

So when all is said and done, the wels is without doubt a blessing for recreational fishermen.

• Late reproduction

The wels becomes sexually mature at 4–5 years for the female and 3–4 years for the male, breeding between May and July, providing the water temperature has reached 73°F–77°F (23°C–25°C) and does not drop below 65°F (18°C) at night. Mating takes place beneath wooded banks, among roots and aquatic vegetation. The male builds a crude nest by making large sweeps of its tail. The roe (about 30,000 per 2.2 lb (1 kg) body weight of the female) are expelled over this nest and immediately fertilized by the male. They attach themselves to vegetation or wood thanks to their sticky coating. Hatching requires about 140 degree-days, that is to say 7 days in water with an average temperature of 68°F (20°C).

After one year the young wels are around 8 inches (20 cm) long. Depending on how well-stocked the habitat is with food, they will grow to 40 inches (1 m) in 6 to 8 years when they will weigh 16–22 lb (7–10 kg). In most places, the wels frequently reaches an optimum length of 6 ft 8 in–7 ft 10 in (2–2.3 m) and weighs 110–150 lb (50–70 kg). Individual specimens have been caught in Russia and eastern Europe which were 10–13 feet (3–4 m) long and weighed 330–440 lb (150–200 kg)! The record, a fish weighing more than 660 lb (300 kg), was set on the river Dnieper in Russia.

Before long, wels weighing around 220 lb (100 kg) will be caught in waters into which they have been introduced, especially in the lower reaches of major European rivers like the Loire or the Rhône, where large quantities of grey mullet swim upstream, providing easy prey as they swim into its huge, ugly maw. In northern Europe, a favorite prey is the freshwater mussel.

This is quite a small specimen of wels. Some grow as big as 13 feet (4 m)! ▷

• The future of the wels

The wels has already taken up residence in the majority of large western European rivers, especially in France and Spain, and the lower reaches of a great number of their tributaries. In the United Kingdom, the fish do not seem to grow as large but they are flourishing as waterways become cleaner. Furthermore, the range of sizes caught strongly indicates that *Silurus glanis* populations are well balanced and that natural reproduction will be enough to ensure the species continues to thrive. This may not be true of lakes and reservoirs where the wels has never lived before. The first concern of anyone managing angling sites with a view to increasing the wels population would be to make certain of an abundance of coarse fish, which alone are able to contribute to the steady growth of wels without it having to compete too fiercely for food with other carnivores. After all, the wels is a slow-moving and lazy fish compared to these competitors. It is thus a good idea to introduce wels into ponds well-stocked with bream and smaller catfish. If the pond has a clear bottom and banks denuded of vegetation, it is important to add dead logs, create some overhanging plants, and to introduce aquatic plants and other types of shelter where the wels can lurk and hopefully reproduce. As in so many cases, the introduction of large individuals is definitely not recommended. The odds are that more mature wels have already become accustomed to a certain habitat and will not be happy in a new environment. On the other hand, a shoal of fry consisting of specimens around 8 in (20 cm) long will be able to adapt to a change in their habitat and do well under slightly different conditions to those into which they were born. By stocking water with specimens so young that they are only a few inches long you expose them to predators, of course. However, this method has proved to be extremely successful with the (illicit) introduction of wels using alevin 1³/₄–3¹/₄ in (4–8 cm) long transported in insulated cool boxes.

Fishing with fish bait

When dealing with a carnivorous catch, fishing with fish bait is almost always the answer. Offering the wels the kind of food it eats normally has its advantages. Contrary to popular belief, using fish bait weighing as much as 2¹/₄ lb (1 kg) does not automatically guarantee catching a correspondingly large wels. It has been proven scientifically, as well as empirically by anglers, that wels of all sizes most often attack fish that are only about 6 in (15 cm) long. Roach, chub, tench, and gudgeon, as well as freshwater (swan) mussels, are therefore best suited for persuading them to bite.

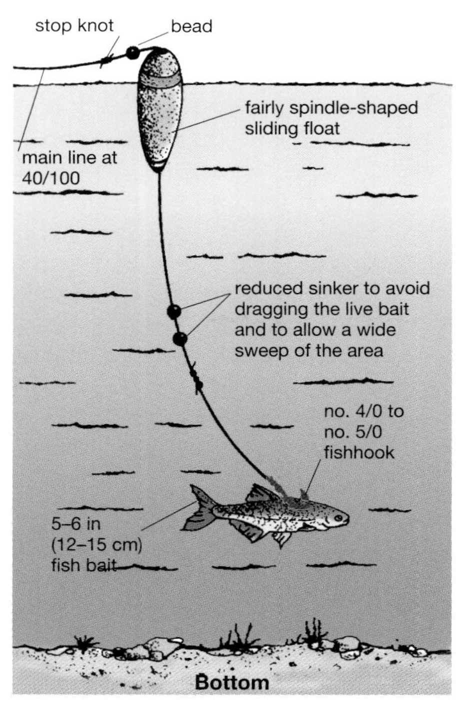

• Robust tackle

You must not skimp over the sturdiness of your tackle. Tackle devised especially for catching this fish, or very powerful carp rods are ideal for fishing with natural bait. A 12 ft (3.3 –3.6 m) rod with a test curve of 3 to 4 lb will help you land this formidable adversary. Ensure that the fixed-spool reel can hold around (200 m) 225 yards of 40/100 line and that its running order and clutch system are foolproof. Reels equipped with a robust clutch, or a releasing mechanism enabling you to release the clutch in a split second, are very useful because the initial rush of a wels can be quite spectacular!

• The rig

A classic floating line of the kind used for pike (but without the steel trace), with a fairly ripe-smelling bait attached to it is ideal. However, this method should be reserved for shallow areas at times when wels are very active, especially in early summer. The use of a fairly spindle-shaped, controller-type float is less resistant to the dive when there is a bite. A reduced sinker is very useful, however, so that you do not restrain the live bait too much, and will also permit you a wide sweep of the banks and shallows, which increases your chances of finding something. Moreover, this tactic is the obvious one to adopt when chasing wels which are close to the surface.

In deep gullies, or in pools of around 40 feet (12 m) deep, it would be tedious, even impossible to make fish bait move around where you want it to using a floating line, the drift of which is very difficult to control.

• Setting up the rig

If you have the use of a boat, rather than casting from the bank, it is preferable to set up the rig in the exact spot at which you intend to fish. Not only do you increase your accuracy, but if the bait is live, it will retain all its original liveliness. In this instance, rather than using a lead weight connected to a breaking strand, complete the line with a solid metal link to which you attach two rubber bands. When you lay the rig, wrap the bands around a stone about the size of your fist and let it drop to the bottom.

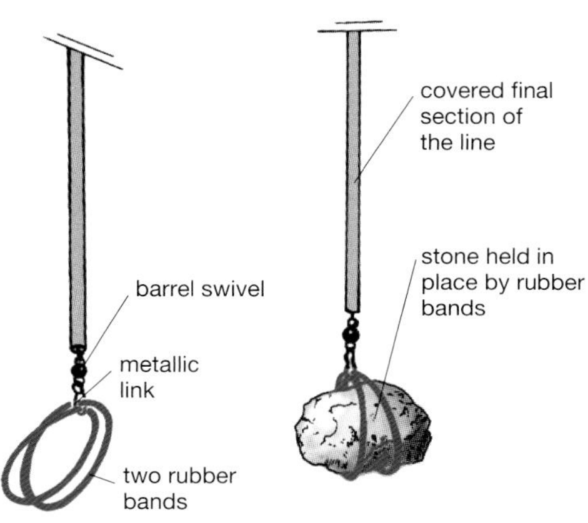

FLOAT PATERNOSTERING

Float paternostering is well adapted to the behaviour of the wels and has the unrivalled advantage of being able to make the live bait move around at a precise distance above the bed and exactly where you want it.

These mounts are very simple to assemble, present live bait well, and seldom become tangled. You will need a silicone sheath about 1 mm in diameter in order to make the end of the main line rigid at the point where the rig is attached to it, thereby preventing the live bait from becoming tangled in the line. Of course, a fairly short hook length (about 12 in (30 cm)) will greatly reduce the risk of tangling.

The ideal is to sheathe the last three feet of the line, with the hook length inserted 2–2ft 8 in (60–80 cm) above the bottom. The lead weight that completes the mount works better when connected to a breaking strand (25/100 nylon) so that the line can be released quickly if it gets caught.

The paternoster mount can be used without any other accessories when fishing straight above your target, from a boat or by a deep pool or gully.

Holding the rod high helps to create an angle as close as possible to a right angle and ensures that the live bait moves around well above the bottom.

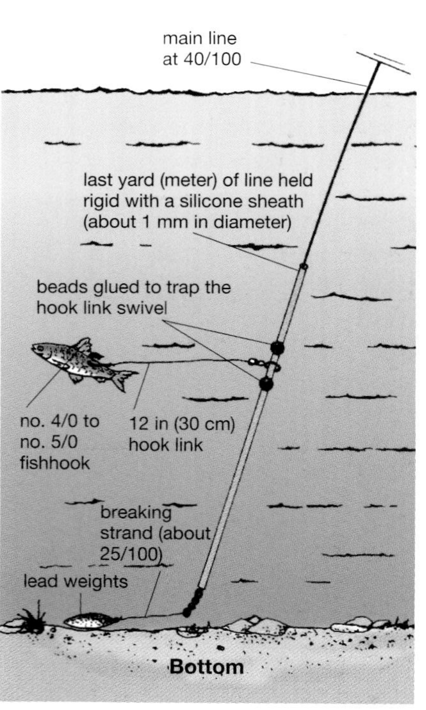

Paternoster with float

If a wels bites or when the battle begins, the stone will normally be ejected and the line will become totally free throughout the whole struggle, which is distinctly more pleasant, and thus reduce the risk of breakage. Best of all, stones cost absolutely nothing! On the other hand, over shallow spots, when the line may come into contact with reed beds or other impediments, and generally when you are angling from the bank, it is better to rely on a float.

If the float is actually used to indicate a bite, you must perform a meticulous sounding in order to position the stop knot correctly for positioning the float as dictated by the depth at the spot.

If you are fishing with the pick-up open (with deferred striking), the float is only used to guide the line to a point immediately above the rig.

• Choosing the right fishhook

The wels has an extremely hard mouth, so it is imperative to make the right choice of fishhook. The treble hook, where the three hooks are designed to enable better penetration, should be avoided because in most of these hooks the tips are not sharp enough. Furthermore, if two hooks of the treble accidentally get stuck in both jaws, you will find it very difficult to seize your fish by the mouth!

A single no. 4/0 to no. 5/0 fishhook, with maximum strength and hooking power, is much more suitable. The hook can grasp the live bait directly in the mouth, back, or near the tail. This type of strong, iron fishhook often perceptibly causes fish bait to become less lively, which may make it less attractive. Hooking the bait by a hair, popular with carp fishermen, provides an inspired solution in many respects. Attach a hair through the eye of a no. 4/0 or no. 5/0 fishhook and knot a no. 6 to no. 8 fishhook to the end of the hair. The fairly fine iron hook enables you to hook the live bait without damaging it and to keep it "fishing" for longer. Your main hook is thereby freed from any restriction and thus has the highest potential effectiveness. This method of hooking the bait is good at withstanding a strike at a bite, preventing the wels from taking the whole bait right down, while nine times out of ten it still becomes properly hooked.

Traditional hooking of fish bait

no. 4/0 to no. 5/0 fishhook

Hooking through the mouth. △

Hooking through the back. △

▽ *Hooking near the tail.*

• Haunts of the wels, for fish bait

The wels often occupies radically different types of habitat, depending on the time of day and, especially, the season.

In the middle of the day, and generally from October through March, it tends to favor deep pools or holes, or very cluttered areas even if they are as shallow as 10–25 ft (3–4 m). A careful sweep, using a lead weight cast with a rod, will allow you to determine the nature of the bed – clear, covered in plants, littered with plant debris – as well as the deepest spots. Otherwise, as long as you are not actually fishing (as this is forbidden by law), an echo-sounder will give you a very precise indication of the contours of the bed. In other areas, such as close to man-made objects or directly below deeply shelving banks covered in overhanging trees (providing plenty of shade, and generally not visited much), it is worth casting a line at the deepest point. For all these conditions, paternostering is the most suitable method for fishing with fish bait. If you fish using three rods, you will multiply your chances if you work at three specific types of haunt. For example, the first mount could be positioned over a deep gully or hole, the second near the largest

Hooking the live bait to a hair

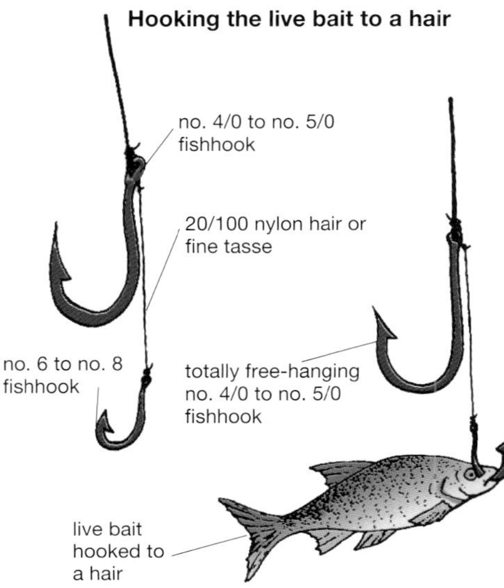

WORMS AND LEECHES ON THE MENU

The wels does not have refined tastes, and its diet is so varied that any living and moving creature that attracts its attention will end up in those formidable jaws. Worms and leeches are no exception to the rule, far from it. But the major drawback to these bait, when fishing on or just above the bottom, is their lack of drawing power, quite apart from the fact that thick aquatic vegetation debris will partially or totally hide them from view. Again taking our inspiration from carp fishermen, the problem may be resolved by positioning the bait at a distance from the bottom so that it moves around in open water. The trick is to knot a hair to the curve of a no. 4/0 or no. 5/0 header fishhook, threading a ⅛ in (12–15 mm) polystyrene bead onto the hair, with a no. 2 to no. 4 fishhook attached just behind it. Worms or leeches hooked on to the fishhook are thus held well above the bottom thanks to the float consisting of the polystyrene bead. Since the header is linked to a sliding sinker, it is essential to place a stop on the line in order to adjust the height at which the bait moves around, which should generally be 20–32 in (50–80 cm) above the bottom.

◁ *The wels can be tempted with the help of almost any type of living bait.*

obstacles, and the third halfway between them on the side of the gentlest slope leading down to the pool. In the coldest spells of winter wels often gather in quite large shoals, so it is a good idea to bring all the mounts close to where you get your first bite.

At dawn and dusk – fishing for wels at night is forbidden in some countries so check local regulations – in times of flood, from April through June, and to a lesser extent from July through September, the wels becomes a much more active feeder and it changes its haunts entirely. You will frequently find it under a reed raft near the banks, always close to obstacles and aquatic vegetation. Studying the outline of the banks plays a very important part in locating wels. Coves, places where the level of the bank changes sharply, immediately downstream of sills, in cross-currents, and channels – in short, anywhere that attracts most coarse fish often causes the big cat to lie in wait for them. In general, dawn offers some chance of success, but our whiskered friend soon (often less than an hour after sunrise) settles on the bottom to digest its food and doze for a few hours. It becomes active again from the middle of the afternoon, and it is during the two hours before nightfall that the best opportunity of finding it hunting will arise. One of the most productive tactics involves spreading out

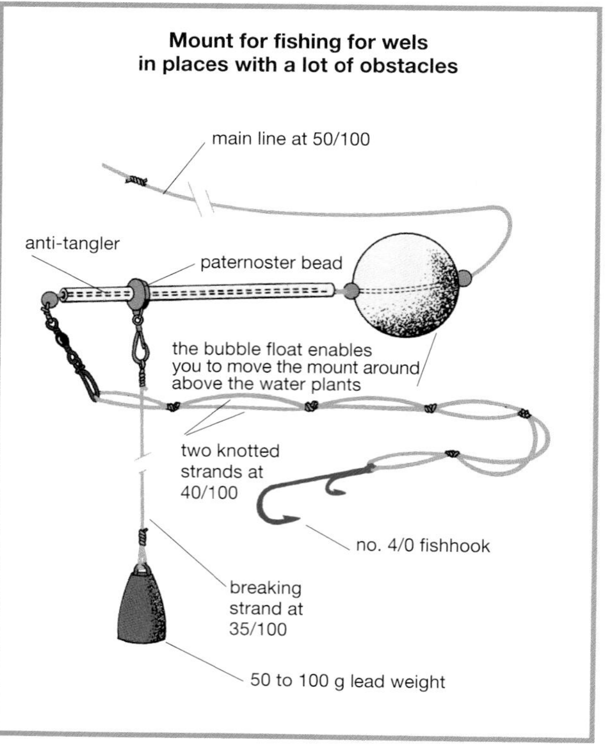

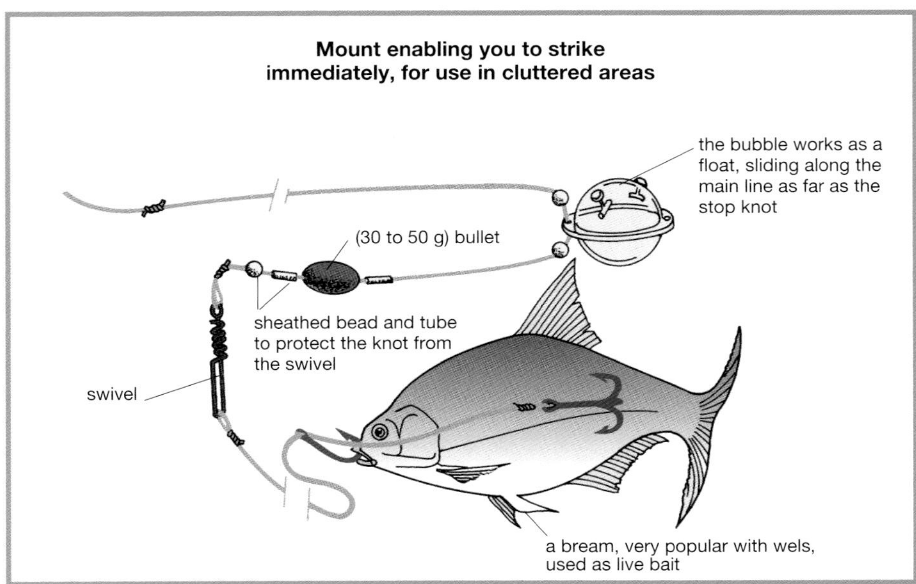

the rigs close to where a lot of fish of the carp family are gathering, choosing shallower areas as evening approaches. Similarly, blocking off a bay that is popular with coarse fish almost always pays off.

FISHING WITH LURES

Although a fishing-pole with live bait can lend itself very well to the lure technique, the pole ought generally to be much shorter. A 10-foot (3 m) rod with a 3 to 3.5 lb action for fishing from the bank, or 9 ft 4 in (2.8 m) long rod for fishing from a boat, if possible with a semi-parabolic action, will enable you to cast $^{1}/_{2}$ oz (15 g) without a problem and to set yourself large targets.

• Rippling trolling spoons and supple lures

Any kind of lure can be used for fishing for catfish, but in this large family, plugs and spinners are not the most wildly attractive bait. On the other hand, gently moving trolling spoons and flexible lures are worthy of attention because they move in the same way as the wels' favorite prey.

As in the case of live fish bait, avoid large items. Trolling spoons of around 3–4 in (8–10 cm), weighing around $^{1}/_{2}$ oz (12–18 g), are lethal, especially if they are predominantly silver in color, perhaps enhanced with a red pattern. These are actually lures made to attract pike, but wels as big as 7 ft (2 m) long regularly attack this type of trolling spoon, even on very dark nights, so sophisticated are their processes of detection!

Thomas Flaüger, a specialist in this technique, actually believes that the older wels get, the more skilled they become at noticing minute wave movements in the water. Experience tends to prove this theory, as small lures often attract the best wels! Flexible lures, which are suited to being reeled in more slowly, or even left in one place when used from a boat, should be kept for the deepest spots that need to be swept methodically.

△ Flexible lure and rippling trolling spoon: two excellent lures for wels. Make sure that the fishhooks are strong and sharp!

A rippling trolling spoon valued highly by anglers of wels. The best size often seems to be 3–4 in (8–10 cm). ▽

• Fishing action using lures

Fishing with lures, which goes on in roughly the same places as fishing with live bait, should be reserved for times when the wels is constantly active, generally from April through September. Aim mainly for spots that are fairly shallow.

Cast fishing is characterized by its sweeping method, enabling you to cover a vast surface area and move the lure around to test different depths. The reeling in and movement are quite complex. It is best to adopt a slightly jerky style, interrupted by gliding descents of the rippling spoon and wobbling of the flexible lure.

At nightfall, and especially if you find a wels on the prowl, keep beside large reed-beds, next to partially submerged trees, and around small islands, even if the water is only a few feet deep. It is often in these places that, with a huge swirl of the water and a violent bite, Mr Wels comes along to swallow the lure.

• Plundering in the dark

Wels are confirmed nocturnal creatures. Although they are quite active in the daytime, especially at dusk, they prefer to grab their prey in the dark. The hunting technique does not rely much on sight. In

A flexible lure produces excellent results. ▽

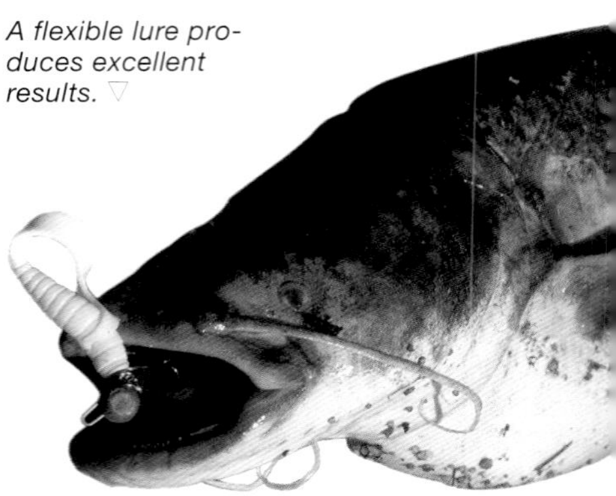

those countries in which night fishing is permitted, it is glaringly obvious that bites are far more frequent than during the day. This is the case in Spain, where it is occasionally possible to hear a hundred or so hunts in one night, the vast, almost disturbance turbulence of the water being sure to produce some worthwhile catches for the waiting angler!

The vibrations produced by a lure or live bait are quite strong enough to be just as effective at night as they are in daytime. So those only allowed to fish for wels during the day must be content with the fishermen's stories of the spectacular hunts. Even in countries where night fishing for wels is not permitted, there are privately owned lakes in which nocturnal fishing is permitted.

FISHING WITH DEAD FISH BAIT

The technique of using dead moving fish bait is midway between that of fishing with live bait and using a lure. The use of moving dead bait is totally feasible, and the tackle is the same as that required for fishing with lures. This method is ideal for exploring large pools, especially during the colder months, and works better when performed from

LANDING THE WELS

There is no landing net big enough for the often huge size of the wels. The biggest landing-net, designed for carp, will only hold a fish which is 4½ ft (1.2–1.3 m) at most. As for the gaff, this an out-of-date piece of tackle that is better not to use. A wels should be gripped by hand, though a few precautions need to be observed. First of all, if at all possible, do not fish alone, especially if you are in a boat. Grasping your first wels in your hand when all alone in a boat is no small feat. Try to have a friend with you, especially if he or she already has some experience of wels fishing. Always bring along a pair of gloves and a few pieces of rope about 10–15 ft (3–4 m) long and about ⅛ in (10 to 15 mm) thick. When the struggle is over, as the exhausted wels is gaping on the surface of the water, locate the exact part of the mouth that has been pierced by the hook (especially if it is a treble!) Seize the lower jaw firmly with your (preferably gloved) hand, endeavoring to raise the head about 8 inches (20 cm), which is usually enough to immobilize it totally. Next slide the rope just behind the gills, knotting it to prevent the loop from tightening. Never use a slip-knot as this will damage the fish.

▽ *Grip the wels by its lower jaw.*

The often phenomenal size of the wels (These two fish are 5 ft 6 in and 6 ft 4 in (1.65 and 1.9 m) long) is attracting more and more anglers in search of a thrill. ▷

△ *To keep a wels alive, for example while you are waiting for the opportunity to photograph it, the best method is to rope it up.*

a boat, as this makes it possible to move the dead fish around slowly over a limited surface area for a long period of time. When shoals of wels are very localized (as is often the case between November and March), using moving dead bait with heavy mounts is definitely the recommended tactic. The impressive statistics recorded every winter on the rivers of France and Spain are eloquent testimony.

For the rest of the year, it pays to investigate the shallower spots, a tactic that works well if you reel in regularly. Rigs that are very lightly weighted, used as you would a rippling spoon, work wonders at nightfall in all spots along the bank where the water is shallow and where the catfish has plenty of cover under which to hide and leap out at passing prey, its favorite hunting method.

• What size fish?

An eternal topic of concern to anglers is the size of the fish to attach to the rig. Dead fish bait should be approximately the same as live fish bait, say 5–6 in (12–15 cm). Having caught a wels more than 5 ft (1.5 m) long in shallow water just a few yards from my boat, using a dead roach 3–4 in (7–8 cm) in size (unfortunately, with my small pike-perch rod and 22/100 line, I couldn't hold it for long!), I can vouch for the fact that wels do not turn their noses up at small prey. It is probably the very occasional waterfowl that they swallow from time to time that make anglers think that they are fond of large bait.

• The rigs

These are inspired by the set-ups used for angling other carnivorous fish. Rigs for wels must not only be adapted to the size of live bait you are using (that is to say, the equivalent of a large pike rig) but above all, made of very sturdy tackle and accessories.

The piano wire should be of good quality, and the fishhooks must not bend or distort and should be able to pierce the fish almost perfectly. Do not forget that the wels' mouth is extremely tough.

Some wels hunters, inspired by mounts usually only used in the sea, hook their dead fish on to a very large single hook (no. 6/0 to no. 7/0) which they bind to the dead fish.

Although this method enables you to use fishhooks on any occasion, you must take great care when striking. You must defer the strike, which means paying out at the slightest bite so that the whole bait is taken properly, and strike very forcefully to ensure that the hook pierces thoroughly.

It is possible for the hook to get flattened against the dead fish when you cast the line, which is why many catches are missed if you strike as soon as there is a bite.

For a similar reason, you should cast smoothly so as not to disturb the position of the hook too much.

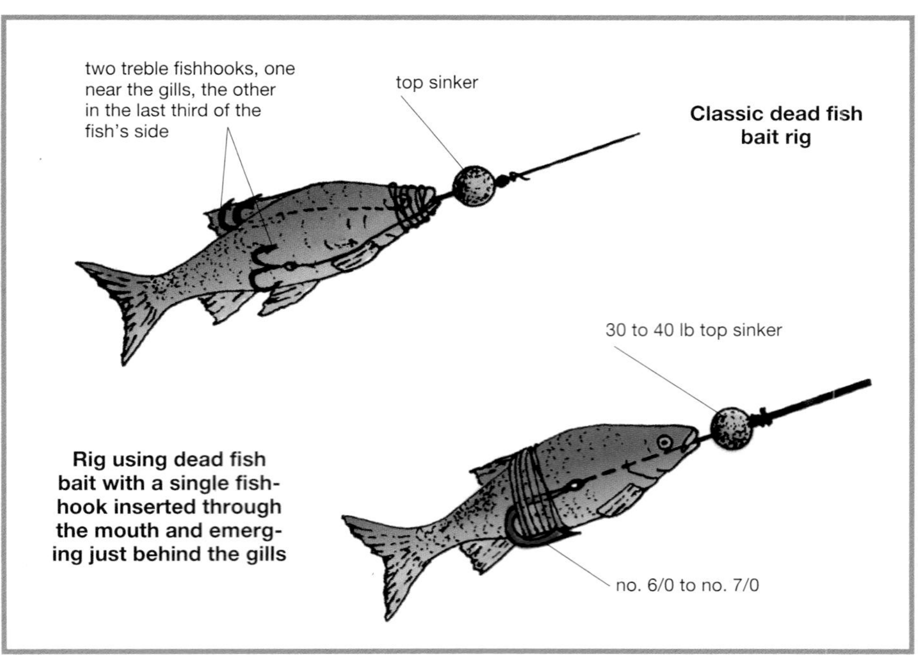

Where to find wels

In France

• *The Saône.* From immediately downstream of Chalon-sur-Saône where it meets the Seille until the point where it joins the Rhône in Lyon, this river has high potential. The use of a motor-boat is recommended in order to investigate a number of areas quickly.

• *Le Rhône.* From Lyon to Valence, and especially downstream of Avignon from where it meets the Gardon down to the delta in the Camargue, the Rhône (as well as the little Rhône) contains without doubt the biggest wels in France. The difficulty of access to its banks means that fishing on this river is still private, but professional anglers regularly net wels weighing more than 110 lb (50 kg), of which a few weigh nearly 198 lb (90 kg)!

• *The Loire.* More and more wels are being caught in this river, in the Loiret and in the vicinity of Gien, as well as in some of the sandy pools in the district. Further downstream, especially in Nièvre, the big cat seems to be colonizing the waters of the Loire at an alarming pace.

• *Lake Saint-Cassien.* This lake in Var, famous for its enormous carp and for the largest wels ever caught in France, could quickly become a favorable stretch of water for wels. That is mainly because a thousand fry around 8 in (20 cm) long were introduced into it in late 1992. These specimens now weigh between 6½–8 ½ lb (3–4 kg.) It is only to be hoped that coarse fishermen give them a chance to grow even bigger!

In Spain

In the Ebro and where the Segre meets the Cinca, about 20 miles (30 km) from Lerida, wels are abundant even though they were only recently introduced there. The section between Mequinenza and La Granja accommodates an amazing density of specimens 5–6½ ft (1.5–2 m) in length, frequently reaching a weight of 88–110 lb (40–50 kg). Spanish law requires one fishing permit for fishing from the bank, and an additional permit for using boats. Fishing is generally tolerated until midnight.

In Germany

The largest wels populations, of which some individuals may reach 220 lb (100 kg), live in Bavaria, in the rivers Regen (near the point where it flows into the Danube) and Naab, and generally in the many lakes in the region of Regensburg.

In Romania

The Danube Delta is one of the best places in the world for fishing for wels, as are most lakes and rivers of this country. Freshwater fish are a popular dish in Romania and there are many professional fishermen.

In the former USSR

The Volga and Dnieper basin, birthplace of the wels, offer fabulous opportunities for fishing for wels and the opportunity for catching some very large fish. These regions are opening up more and more to tourism, but you need to have good connections in the area, or arrange your trip through a travel agency that specialises in angling vacations.

In Turkey

The reservoirs built along the Euphrates hold wels weighing over 220 lb (100 kg), and some are said to weigh up to 330 lb (150 kg). No specialist travel agency as yet organizes angling trips to this country, and the political instability of the region, especially in eastern Turkey, requires the traveler to be very cautious, especially the traveler from the West. It may well be wise to wait a while, until the catfish of eastern Turkey grow even bigger!

◁ *A great rarity! An entirely yellow wels, totally devoid of dark pigmentation (Spain, the Ebro).*

Black bass

*The black or largemouth bass (*Micropterus salmoides*) is another import from North America, being introduced to European rivers a few decades ago. The black bass is the favorite sport fish of American anglers. It has not yet become as popular in Europe, due to the fact that black bass are still few in numbers there. However, recent restocking initiatives have given it a new lease of life, much to the delight of coarse fishermen.*

The family of Centrarchidae, to which the black bass belongs, is distinguished from that of the Percidae by the presence of two separate dorsal fins, the first of which is supported on an array of spines. ▽

An American who finds it hard to acclimatize

At first glance, the black bass with its gaping mouth bears a superficial resemblance to the common perch, notably the body shape and stripes on the sides.

However, a closer look will dispel any doubts. The black bass is longer than the striped perch and has no red fins, while its spiny dorsal fin is distinctly smaller. Furthermore, it has a neat black band which runs almost all the way along the flank.

Black bass was introduced into Europe from the United States in the mid-twentieth century, mainly into the lakes and rivers of France and Spain, with small pockets in southern England and northern Germany. However, only in the south of France are there spots where black bass proliferate, as the water there is warmer than in the rest of its European habitat. In fact, in order for the fry to survive, black bass must find water at a temperature of between 64°F and 68°F (18 and 20°C) in June or possibly early July. This difficulty in breeding is the real problem in populating lakes and rivers with this excellent coarse fish. European waters are unable to consistently reach the right temperatures and combination of conditions on an annual basis. As a result, although quite common in the 1970s, black bass have tended to disappear from European waters since then. Fortunately, the popularity of the fish among the angling enthusiasts in the

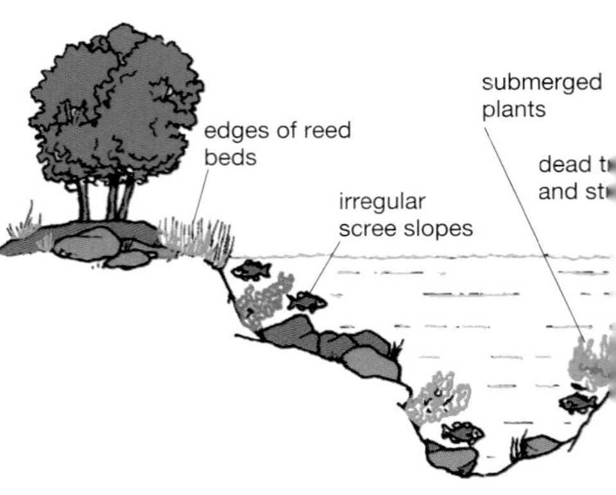

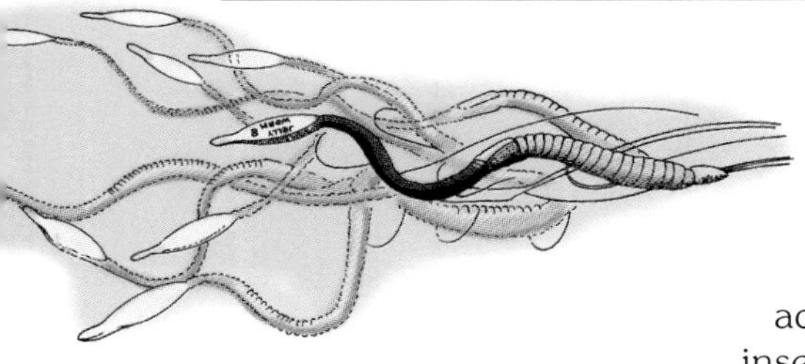

△ *The 'Slimy Slug' has a rippling swimming action. Its lead-weighted head enables it to penetrate the thickest colonies of aquatic plants.*

United States, and in those parts of Europe and North Africa where it has become popular have ensured that it will continue to be fished even where it is currently scarce. Anyone who gets the chance to fish for black bass on vacation will want to continue doing so at home. So the fish ought to continue to be found in northern Europe, even if it entails maintaining the populations artificially by regularly restocking with young fish. Many private pond owners have already managed to provide their angling clients with lakes that are well stocked with black bass. Anglers have been willing to pay quite highly for the benefit from good-quality fishing conditions. Angling associations and federations have also taken a shine to the black bass, with more and more of them restocking with black bass alevin or even breeding fry in their fish farms. There is every indication that black bass will become an important sport fish in Europe by the year 2000 and beyond.

Typical black bass haunts in a reservoir lake

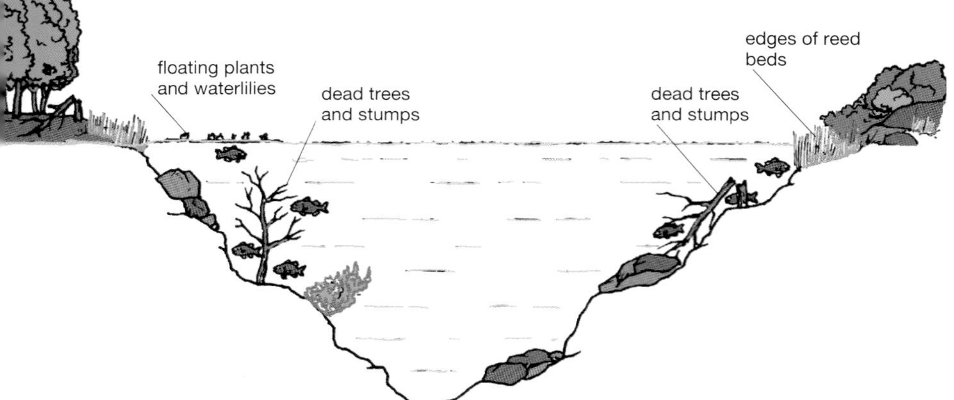

A VERY VARIED DIET

Rather like perch, black bass eat a very wide range of foods, from small fish to frogs, including crayfish, aquatic larvae, and even large land insects that fall into the water. Anything serves to feed their voracious appetite. Even small waterfowl may occasionally be gulped down in a huge swirl of water! While on the subject, it should be said that specimens as greedy as this are still rarely found in Europe, but videos shot in the United States bear witness to these kinds of frenzied attacks on small vertebrates by large black bass.

◁ *A surprising lure: a mouse.*

BLACK BASS HAUNTS

Black bass are quite good at throwing anglers off the scent, and are just as likely to hide in a clump of aquatic plants or somewhere where there is a lot of submerged wood, as to move off in a group to attack a school of small fish. As a general rule, the best spots by far are calm waters that are not too deep and where there is a lot of cover in the form of aquatic plants or dead wood. For instance, it is quite common to catch sight of a huge black bass remaining quite motionless under a waterlily pad.

In the river, look for them in backwaters, upstream of mill-ponds, and in the quietest parts, where aquatic plants and submerged obstacles proliferate.

On lakes, look near the banks and shallows or close to where the current peters out in ponds or lakes, even if there is not a lot of vegetation cover. When locating your prey, never forget to use your polarized glasses to help you see beneath the water.

△ *The black bass bites very well on surface lures as soon as the weather turns nice.*

THE BEST TIMES

Black bass are particularly unpredictable. They are capable of being totally listless for hours on end, and then almost feverishly active in the next few minutes. A change in the weather, a cloud that hides the sun, a break in the clouds, or a gust of wind, may be just some of the reasons for their sudden bursts of activity but these are quite difficult to predict. However, as with most carnivores, dawn, midday and evening are still quite good times to fish. Winter is never the right season. Since the native waters of black bass are warm or at least temperate, they react quite badly to the cold. They slip away to find shelter in the deepest pools and hardly ever emerge. So can they be made to bite in cold weather? The experts used to say that it was impossible, but over the last few years some anglers have apparently been able to persuade some quite large fish to venture out. The techniques used are fairly similar to those which work with perch, including casting with natural bait, spinning with a perch spoon, and fishing with live bait, using a sliding float. All the same, don't expect miracles ...

Frogs and crayfish – great delicacies

When fishing for black bass, it is most effective to use two flexible lures to imitate frogs and crayfish. The former work on the surface as they have a floating head. When you reel in, the frog slips underwater, bobbing back to the surface immediately if you pause even slightly. Crayfish work better when they are descending. They must give the impression of returning to the bottom (don't forget to ensure they are always moving backward!), and doing so in several stages. When the crayfish has reached the bottom, move it around over 40 or 80 in (1 or 2 m) of the bed, then bring it up sharply, then repeat the downward movement.

• The best season

The high season begins in mid-April, perhaps a little earlier in the southern parts of Europe and the U.S., where it is always sunnier. Like all carnivores, black bass feed a great deal at this time, no doubt to restore their reserves of energy. Later on, in June through July, the mating season begins, so the male prepares a nest in which the female lays her eggs. The male stands guard during the whole incubation period and until the young fish are able to manage on their own. It chases away intruders, oxygenates the eggs with its fins and gives the young their first lessons in the hard rules of life in fresh water. The male is extremely aggressive during this period but sport fishermen must make an effort to leave the black bass alone, as curtailing their reproduction would ensure that future fishing trips for black bass are doomed to failure!

Genuine fighting fishing

If black bass are becoming so popular in Europe, it is because of the extraordinary fight they put up as soon as they are hooked.

Ploys used to escape the hook include fleeing desperately, changing direction, nose-diving, dramatically shooting upward, jumping and twisting in every direction, taking the line around plants, or around the first obstacle

Shady spot favorable for fishing for black bass

they encounter. Black bass are cunning fish and will not admit defeat until they have tried everything and have no strength left. However, there is no shortage of ways in which to lure this wonderful fish.

If you are using natural bait, try a maggot or other small live bait, fishing very close to the surface (preferably with a bubble float, so that you can manage to cast a long way without the hookbait being dragged deep underwater), and if possible right in the middle of the cluttered spots which black bass favor. Reel in over a short distance from time to time, in order to create a small swell on the surface with your bubble float. This movement will be enough to attract the attention of any fish in the area, and it will dash

A real frog may be replaced by a realistic-looking plastic lure ▽

Pond fishing for black bass using a frog

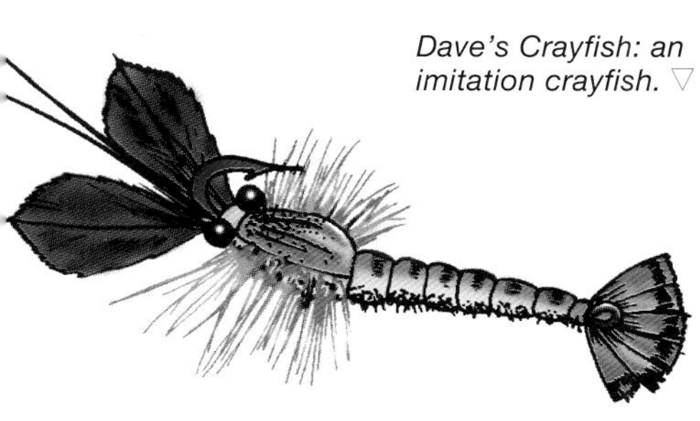

Dave's Crayfish: an imitation crayfish. ▽

over to your bait and throw itself onto it like mad. It is up to you to control your reflexes, so as to be certain the fish has taken the bait before you strike.

• Casting

Casting is another possibility, and perhaps a more interesting one in view of the struggles involved. You can use ordinary spoons, plugs, flexible lures, or those very distinctive American lures known as poppers because of the pop-

△ Featherwings.

ping noise which they make when there is the slightest pull on the line. What all these lures have in common is their lightness, or more precisely, their ability to work very close to the surface, as well as having something truly weird about them, whether it is their color, their action in the water, or their size. Never be afraid of surprising a black bass! As for the fishing action, it all takes place near the surface and, as far as possible, close to plants or obstacles. This is why poppers and floating plugs are so useful, as they too enable you to create the slight swell on the surface that is the best way to arouse the interest of a black bass.

◁ Gold popper.

△ The popper: a classic lure for black bass.

• Fly-fishing

Fly-fishing is the last possibility and obviously the most spectacular and sought-after method. There should be no need to remind you that the rods must be of a very particular design and markedly more powerful than trout rods, firstly to deal with the strength of the fish, but equally because you will have to cast and manipulate poppers, and some of these are quite heavy. Poppers require you to cast more slowly and in a wider arc than when using classic artificial flies.

This battery-powered frog starts croaking as soon as it hits the water. ▷

If you do not have poppers, choose the most colorful, bulkiest, and craziest streamer designs from the range used for pike, and these will be perfectly adequate. Using a floating silk line and a short hook length, place the popper or streamer right in the middle of plants and water lilies, then reel it in in an irregular fashion, so as to create a series of noises and movements on the surface of the water that will attract the attention of the carnivore and provoke it to attack. Whether the bite is revealed by a fierce, noisy chase or by a sudden obstruction when reeling in, there is no room for the slightest uncertainty. In certain specific cases, such as hooking a fish that you have managed to locate, a more subtle angling technique is also possible. Using a large dry fly, or even a large, shiny, brightly-colored nymph, you may have the pleasure of seeing your black bass getting caught. It may swim slowly up toward your fly and take it almost casually as would a chub, or on the other hand, it could take off like a jet plane, gulping the dry fly or nymph in one movement like a flash of lightening. You may often feel like you are in the midst of a battle, so good is the black bass, a tireless fighter, at taking off in an instant.

When there is a tug on the line, it sinks in a cloud of bubbles. ▽

CARP

THE TACKLE

Carp (Cyprinus carpio) has been fished for centuries, proving its popularity and instinct for survival. The fish populates every type of pond, lake, and slow-moving river. In recent times, interest in carp has declined sharply, and has tended to be fished only by specialists. However, the fish has made a recent comeback, thanks to the introduction of new types of tackle, mainly from England. Carp fishing has also become very popular in Canada and the United States, where the fish have been introduced and restocked on a regular basis. The coarse fisherman would do well to remember that carp-fishing is the only way, practically every time, for the angler to pit his strength against a wily, lively fish that weighs more than 22 lb (10 kg). No wonder carp has made such a spectacular comeback!

Having rigged his set of rods and baited the tackle, this carp fisherman is now preparing to cast. ▽

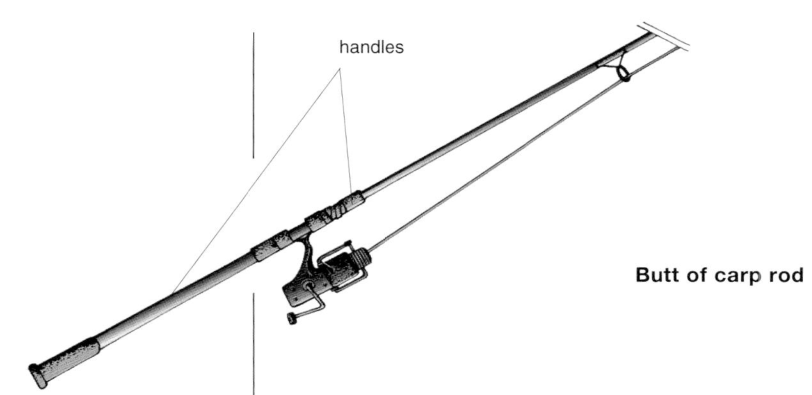

Butt of carp rod

CARP FISHING ENGLISH-STYLE

This new technique, which originated in England, uses extremely sophisticated equipment and synthetic bait. It is now being adopted throughout the angling world.

PRECISION EQUIPMENT

• The rods

These are usually used as a set of three, even four in regions where local regulations so permit. Modern rods have nothing in common with the old-fashioned cane rod. Light and fast-acting, their construction is based on carbon fiber often in combination with kevlar. They enable the angler to cast a 3-ounce (80 g) lead weight 400 feet (100 m) and tackle any size carp without spoiling the pleasure of the fight.

Rod length is expressed in feet and varies between 12 ft (3.60 m) and 13 ft (3.90 m). Models 11 ft or 14 ft (3.35 or 4.30 m) in length are only used occasionally. The butt of the rod usually comprises two cork or foam handles, one at the very end and the other about 16 in (40 cm) higher, giving a good grip for bringing the fish in. Between the two handles there is a screw-winch reel-seat, which will hold the reel securely in any situation.

Rods are tending to have fewer and fewer rings (6 to 7) though their diameter is increasing, in order to reduce friction on the line and maximize the length of the cast. The power of the rod depends upon the requirements of the fishing method used and is expressed in pounds.

For short – to medium distance fishing, (less than 20–23 ft (60–70 m)), in open waters stocked with medium-sized fish, a rod weighing $1^3/_4$ to $2^1/_4$ lb is quite adequate. When casting further than 230 ft (70 m) or in rivers, especially near obstructions which require you to exert full control over the fish, a $2^1/_2$ to 3 lb rod is fine. Very powerful $3^1/_2$ to 4 lb rods are used only in special conditions, such as long-distance casting to 400 ft (100 m) and more, in rivers where the current is very strong, or in lakes renowned for their very large fish.

• The lines
A 30/100 diameter monofilament line is generally accepted to be the best solution for carp fishing. Of course, this is very dependent upon fishing conditions. The thickness of the line can be reduced to 26/100 if the waters are unobstructed and the fish of average size. On the other hand, it is vital to move up to a 35/100 when the waters are cluttered with debris and the current is strong, especially if the carp are of a respectable size.
Multi-strand, anti-abrasion, braided lines are used increasingly and make it possible to fish in obstructed waters, near river-mussel beds or in rocky areas. However, it must be remembered that braided lines use ordinary rings, so they can only be attached to a rod equipped with "sic" (carbon silicate) rings, which are virtually indestructible.

◁ *To fight carp effectively, the diameter of the line must be between 28 and 35/100. Buying in bulk (about 1000 m) is economical and allows you to fill the spool accurately without wastage.*

• The reels
Medium-weight, modern, fixed-spool reels work wonders, as long as you opt for a foolproof, very robust model, able to hold 240 yards (200 m) of 30/100 line. A second spool is useful to allow you to change the diameter of the line rapidly as you change position. Double oscillation reels allow for a perfect reeling in of the line and thus keep it in good shape for longer. The smooth, controllable unreeling of the line also makes it possible to cast further. Models with a slipping clutch are the most practical since they allow you to put the line in stand-by mode (with shut bale arm) while waiting for a bite and then brake gently while you bring in a fish.

The rod pod (or portable support)

This accessory consists of a set of rests and supports linked by a central bar. The rod-pod, which does not need staking into the ground, holds the rods efficiently on any type of bank, be it rocky or concreted, and even on wooden decking. It is easy to carry when changing position, However, care must be taken to anchor it firmly in place on windy days.

• Rod rests
To avoid leaving the rods lying on the bank and prevent snagging when the fish takes the bait – which it may do violently – it is best to rest them on tackle specifically developed for the job. These rests are made of metal, alloy or stainless steel, attached to stakes planted in the bank. The height is adjustable, and each rest supports a single rod. The forward rod is equipped with the bite indicators; the plastic or metal forks holding the butt of the rods are fixed on the rod which is furthest back. Not only do these rod-pods undeniably tidy the set of rods, but they also help to prolong the life of the tackle and keep it safe when the fish bites.

• Bite indicators
The bite indicator, which is not the same as the buzzer, is a visual indicator which reacts to the slightest bite. The indicator is referred to as a bobbin and consists of a small plastic or Teflon (rarely metal) cylinder which slides up and down a metal pole about 20 in (50 cm) long. The guide at the top holds the line against the metal pole, which is stuck in

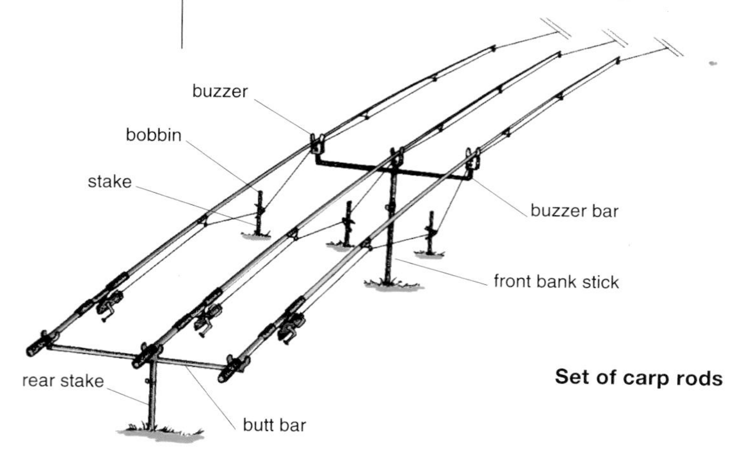

Set of carp rods

◁ *Bobbins are visual bite indicators which keep the line tense as it passes through the guide, and move up or down the stake to indicate the direction of the fish when a carp bites.*

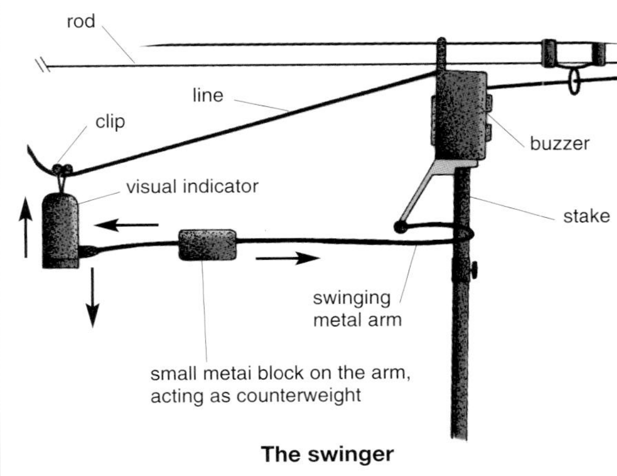

The swinger

the ground right under the rod. When the stake is placed between the reel and the first ring or between the first and second ring, the bobbin makes a vee-shape on the line. If a carp bites and then swims away from the bank, the bobbin will climb up the stake; if, on the other hand, the fish swims toward the bank, the bobbin drops down. Furthermore, by acting as a counterweight, the bobbin guarantees perfect tension every time on the line and this enables the buzzer to work, even if the line is slackened. The bobbin may not be of much use when the carp leaps powerfully when biting, but it is an extremely useful tool in detecting half-hearted or gentle bites, which occur most frequently in waters where carp are fished regularly.

role of the Monkey climber

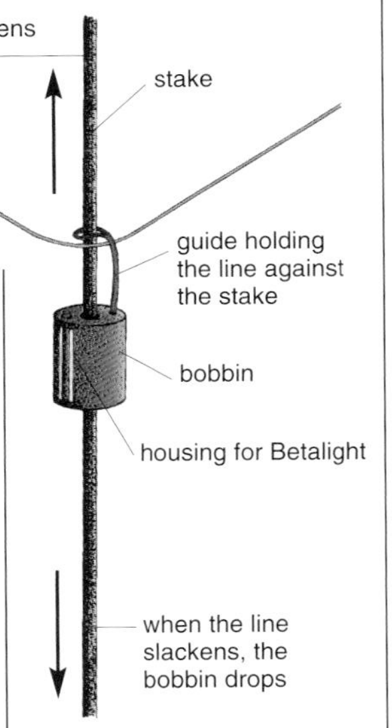

• Various types of visual bite indicator

Bobbins are found in various colors and weights. They enable you to adjust the tension on the line to the weather conditions, the current, and the fishing distance. On some models, you can add dust shot or additional weights, in order to regulate the total weight of the bobbin. Most of the visual indicators also have housing for a Betalight (luminous apparatus), which is very much appreciated when fishing at night. Recently, another type of indicator has become fashionable. This is a type of visual indicator consisting of a rod clipped to the line with a metal arm at right-angles to it, articulated under the buzzer. The light is at the tip of the arm. A small lump of metal slides along the arm, enabling you to adjust the counterweight to its ideal position.

• The buzzer

This is a metal or plastic housing on which the rod rests. It produces an audible signal every time the line moves. There are various systems of detection (photoelectric cell, electromagnet, pendulum, etc.) all using a 6-volt or 9-volt battery and an amplifier. Most buzzers are fitted with volume and tone controls as well as a memory lighting system for the key which is lit for up to 15 seconds. A reliable waterproof buzzer guarantees that you will be made aware of the slightest bite, without having to sit watching the line for hours on end in a constant state of alert. However, it really comes into its own in those places where night fishing is allowed.

GROUNDBAITS AND MOUNTS

• Paste balls

Apart from vegetable and animal bait, which will be discussed in detail later on in this section, the paste ball technique is another idea for carp-fishing which originated in England. Paste balls are small multicolored spheres which are around all the tackle shops now, and if you have not spotted them there, then you will surely have noticed carp fishermen

The swinger is a visual indicator attached to the tip of a horizontal rod clipped to the line. A weight slides along the arm to give the line the correct tension. ▷

using them. They are very easy to find ready-for-use, even if good quality products are rather expensive. The much more popular, and cheaper, alternative is to make your own paste balls.

– Making paste balls

The first option is to use a ready mix combination of ingredients which you buy from a tackle store. You can also acquire the various ingredients and make your own dry mix, following specific recipes. Whichever method you choose, beat eggs in a bowl, add a flavoring (complying scrupulously with the manufacturer's instructions), then stir the ingredients until the paste is smooth and does not stick to your fingers. Roll the paste into balls the size of mandarin oranges and use them to fill the magazine of the paste-gun. This gun resembles the type used for extrusion molding. Press the trigger until the paste comes out as a long roll. Cut the roll in lengths suitable for the rolling-table. Put the rolls on the bottom part of the table, press with the top part and move it forward and backward. This will do the trick!

When all the paste balls are rolled, put them in boiling water (cooking time depends on the diameter of the paste balls). As a guideline, paste balls with a diameter of $^5/_8$–$^6/_8$ in

△ A buzzer sounds each time there is a pull on the line. Choose a type that is reliable, waterproof and robust, rather than one that just looks good or has lots of additional features.

INGREDIENTS FOR PASTE

Some anglers prefer homemade paste to commercial mixes. Here is a selection of the various products used in the preparation of paste.

- Protein-rich ingredients (85 to 90%) such as casein, calcium caseinate, or lacto-albumin, all of them milk derivatives. These are energy rich (and quite expensive), but they should not constitute more than 30% of the mixture.
- Ingredients with an average protein content of 40–50%, such as soya flour, ground birdseed, bone meal, or fish meal. These can account for 40% of the mix.
- Ingredients low in protein (10–15%) such as cornstarch or wheat flour (both of them very inexpensive) can make up 50% of the mix.

Wheat gluten or egg albumin are excellent binders for ingredients with a coarse texture, such as ground birdseed or granulated fish food for farmed trout. They should not account for more than 5%, or the paste will be too rubbery and difficult to roll. Sugar is used essentially for binding and sweetening and can make up to 10% of the mix.

△ A shelf full of flavors! There are hundreds of flavors on the market to tempt a handsome carp, but rather than try and find the miracle flavor, be sure the product is of high quality.

CHOOSING A FLAVOR

Amongst hundreds of flavors available on the market, the angler has yet to be found who can prove the superiority of strawberry flavor over chocolate or that honey works better than any synthetic flavoring (or vice-versa!). There is nothing romantic about the factual explanation, it is the molecular combination of flavors which acts on the carp's sense of taste.

So the quality of the product is more important the specific flavor.

Having said that, here is a list of the flavorings that appear to systematically trigger a positive feeding response: tutti frutti, strawberry, honey, maple syrup, chocolate, spices, garlic, banana, caramel, and condensed milk.

Bon appetit !

△ *A different shape of lead weight is best suited for each type of bed or bottom, depth, and the rig used.*

(14–18 mm) require $1\frac{1}{2}$ to 2 minutes cooking time. Be careful to choose a gun with a nozzle of the right size for the rolling table (8, 10, 12, and up to 24 mm).

• Rigs and drops

Rigs for carp fishing use sliding weights on the main line. The sliding mechanism is a pierced bead through which the line passes. A lead weight is attached to the bead with a metal link. Beyond a fishing distance of 164–197 ft (50–60 m), it is advisable to use an anti-kink device instead of a bead. This consists of a piece of flexible tubing 16 inches (40 cm) long, through which the line passes. The tube has a bead attached to it which has a device for holding the lead weight on it. It is possible to stop the weight from sliding by fixing a stop on the line just above the bead or the anti-kink tubing.
The basic principle of this rig, in which the mass of the sinker acts as a counterweight to the movement of the carp as soon as it is hooked, is that as the fish swims away, it increases the depth of penetration of the hook, in a sort of self-striking action. The drop is made of braided 15–20 lb line, which is flexible and very resistant. A barrel swivel is attached to one end of the drop to link it to the main line. At the other end, a very strong and extremely sharp hook is attached by a knot next to the eye. The size of the hook may vary between a no. 2 through a no. 6, depending on the size of the bait and of the potential catch. The drop should be short – about 10 in (25 cm) – to reduce the risk of kinks.

Tackle for carp fishing

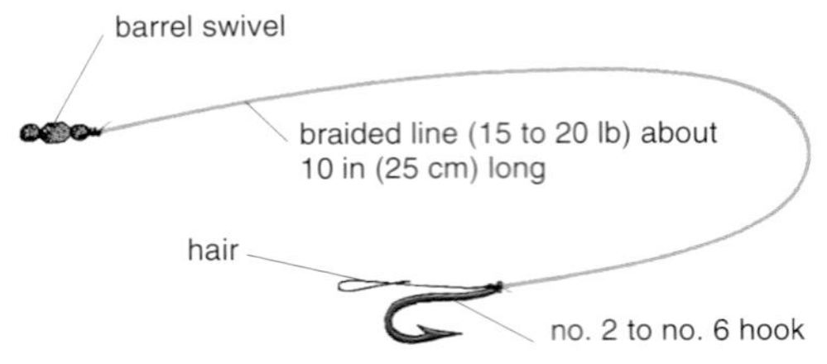

Main types of lead weights for carp fishing

Bullets and bombs are aerodynamic lead weights which are suitable in all situations.

Sphere: compact shape with a lot of inertia, suitable when the fish swims away.

Stealth: streamlined shape, ideal for casting on windy days.

Flat-bottomed: as it planes through the water, it is particularly useful when you need to place the bait delicately on the mud.

12/100 to 14/100 nylon strand attached to the eye of the hook

terminal loop

Hair mount

• The hair mount

The hair mount was the most important English innovation in carp-fishing and was the cause of the revival of interest in carp-fishing in the mid-1980s. English angler, Lennie Middleton, was tired of having to deal with a very wily bunch of carp, which had been caught and released so many times that they disdained any bait which they suspected might be fixed to a hook. One day, he had the bright idea (though Kevin Maddocks has also laid claim to the same thought) of separating the hook from the bait. He attached one of his own hairs to the bend in the hook (hence the name of the device), and threaded the bait onto

A FEW RECIPES

It is vital to take fishing conditions into account when opting for a particular recipe. Fish have different protein requirements, depending on the season. In general, from mid-spring through mid-fall, carp feed intensively, especially after spawning. For the rest of the year, and particularly during the coldest part of winter, the carp's metabolism slows down and the feeding activity is limited.

All-purpose recipe (47.5% protein)
To make 2 lb 4 oz (1 kg) mix:
$10\frac{1}{2}$ oz (300 g) of casein + 14 oz (400 g) of soya flour + $10\frac{1}{2}$ oz (300 g) of wheat flour + 2–3 eggs + flavoring + coloring (optional)

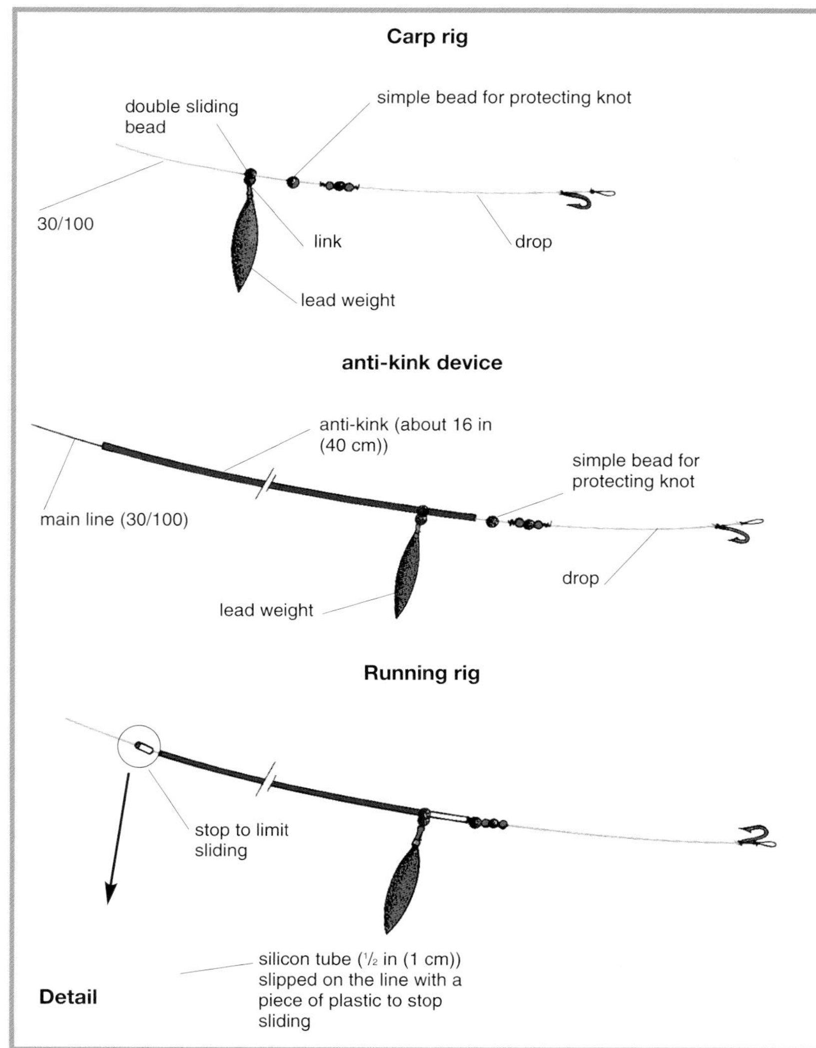

this makeshift extension. The idea, simple but brilliant, was that as the carp sucked in the bait with its powerful mouth, it would have to suck in the hook as well. If the carp blew on the bait, as carp are in the habit of doing as a precautionary measure to check their food before eating it, the hook, being completely free, had a good chance of pricking the lip of the carp. Today, the hair mount, in its various forms, is a practically indispensable item of carp-fishing tackle.

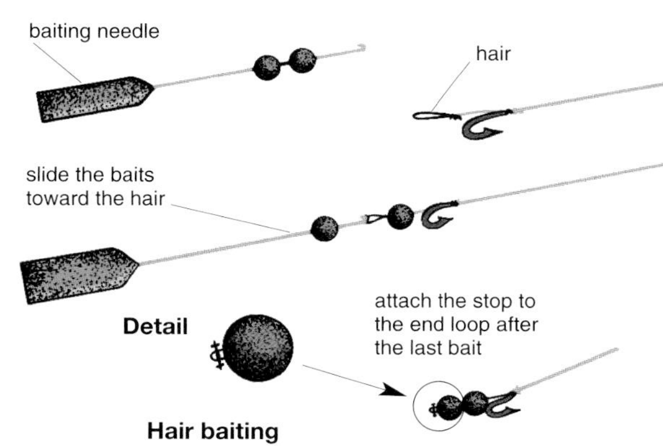

• Constructing a hair mount

To make a hair mount, simply tie a few inches of 12/100–14/100 nylon thread to the eye of the hook, making a loop at the other end. After tying on the hook, you may have too long a drop line to be able to attach the hair directly to the hook. The length of the hair depends on the number and size of the baits required. To load the hair, use a special baiting-needle to thread the baits (seeds, grains or paste balls), then pass the bent end of the needle through the loop at the end of the hair and slide the bait onto the hair itself. Once you have done this, all that there is left to do is to place

FOR PASTE BALLS

Hungry Fish Recipe (82% protein)
To make 2 lb 4 oz (1kg) mix:
14 oz (400 g) casein + 7 oz (200 g) lacto-albumin + 7 oz (200 g) calcium caseinate + 7 oz (200 g) soya flour + 2–3 eggs + flavoring + coloring (optional).

Winter recipe
(37% protein)
To make 2 lb 4 oz 1kg of mix:
14 oz (400 g) ground birdseed + 14 oz (400 g) of wheat flour + 5½ oz (150 g) casein + 1¾ oz (50 g) egg albumin + 2–3 eggs + flavor + coloring (optional).

The soluble thread allows you to place a few seeds or paste balls near the bait. It dissolves completely after one minute in the water. It would be difficult to improve on this arrangement for ground baiting. ▷

a small plastic stop in the loop of the hair to prevent the baits from flying off the hair as you are casting.

• Groundbaiting

Carp spend a lot of their time digging in the muddy bottom and among aquatic vegetation in order to find worms, water snails, shoots, and all the other foods of which it is fond. The main concern of the angler will therefore be to tempt the carp with the baits he has prepared for them. Whether they are seeds, grains, or paste balls, the offerings must be deposited accurately and spread evenly over the whole fishing area to induce the carp into making a methodical inspection of the fishing zone and eventually come into contact with the hooked baits.

• Groundbaiting accessories

The ideal solution is to have a boat of some kind, even a simple raft, which allows you to get into midstream and drop the groundbait opposite the fishing position. Groundbait needs to be spread thinly in order to cover the bottom evenly. Don't just dump it in the water in fistfuls. A boat may not be available, however, and some waterways do not even allow fishermen to use any kind of boat, so the alternative is to spread groundbait from the bank.

◁ *Groundbaiting with a catapult is ideal for middle and short distance (up to 82–98 ft (25–30 m) for seeds, 230 ft (70 m) for paste balls).*

SOLUBLE THREAD

As the name indicates, this consists of a tie that dissolves in a few seconds (one minute maximum) in very cold water. It is useful in that it allows you to increase the attractiveness of the bait by groundbaiting in a very specific location. You just cut about 6 in (15 cm) of soluble tie, then you thread bait onto it using a baiting-needle, in the same way as for hair baiting, then to tie the lot onto the hook. A few seconds after casting, the tie will dissolve, leaving only the bait near the hook.

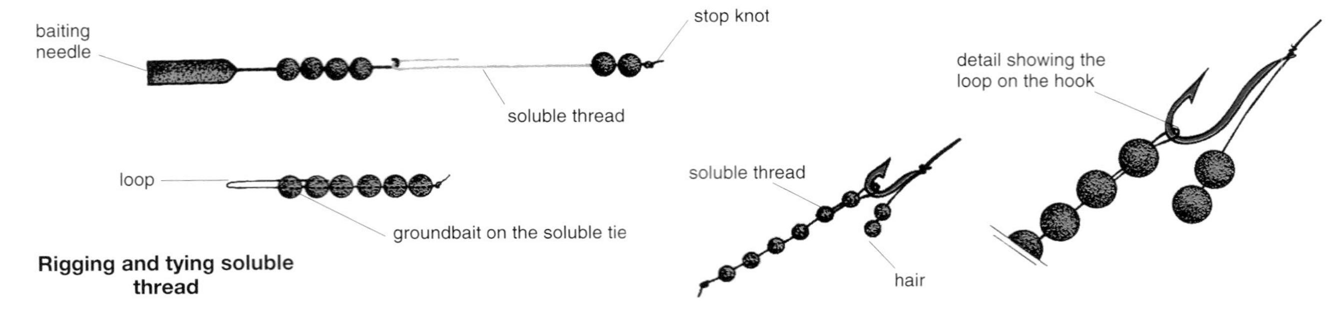

Rigging and tying soluble thread

◁ The most economical and one of the best seeds for carp fishing is plain corn.

– The catapult

The old-fashioned catapult, equipped with powerful elastic bands and a good size cup, serves well for groundbaiting. However, it cannot be used for ejecting seed further than 100 ft (30 m) or paste balls more than 230 ft (70 m). Some powerful models with a large rigid cup allow you to throw bait balls containing seeds or grain to a distance of about 197 ft (60 m).

This common carp was fished in the River Rhône in France and finally gave in...The landing net must be large to avoid the need to aim during the final phase. ▽

Carp landing nets

The carp is an impressively large fish. Moreover, it never gives up totally and keeps enough energy in reserve for a last attempt to escape. So the landing net had better be large and deep. The side arms should be at least 40 in (1 m) long. Make sure the netting is strong and robust. Choose a model with very small mesh, as this avoids snagging the rig and will not catch the spiky dorsal fin of the carp inside it.

– The tube

With a bit of practice, the groundbaiting tube called the Cobra enables you to throw the paste balls up to 328 feet (100 m) from the bank. Unfortunately, it is not designed for seeds or grain. Groundbaiting tubes are available in different sizes and diameters, which are suited to the various sizes of paste ball.

MARKING OUT THE FISHING LOCATION

polystyrene block 4 x 6 in (10 x 15 cm)
surface
rubber band to hold excess thread
thread thinner than the fishing line
marling in place
$5^1/_2$ oz (150 g) weight
bottom

Making a marker buoy

In order to maintain accuracy during an angling session (which may last several days) when groundbaiting or casting, it is prudent to mark the fishing area with a buoy.
Wind 49 ft (15 m) of thread around a block of polystyrene measuring about 4 x 6 in (10 x 15 cm). Attach a lead weight weighing $5^1/_2$ oz (150 g) to the end of the thread. Take a rowboat to the fishing area and unwind the thread until the lead rests on the bottom. Stop the thread running out by securing the remainder with rubber bands. Make sure that the thread of the marker is thinner than that of your fishing line, so that if it snags during a fight with a carp, the marker buoy thread will break, rather than the carp line!
Besides, as soon as the marker buoy is in place and you are back on shore, it is a good idea to check the position in line with a marker of your choice on the opposite bank (a house, tree, rock, etc.), when standing just behind your rods. This will enable you to position the marker buoy in exactly the same place next time.

– The ground catapult
Some anglers will stop at nothing in their determination to catch carp and will go to any lengths. These fishermen may well delight in using a gigantic catapult firmly anchored in the ground and equipped with huge, tough elastic bands. The ground catapult makes it possible to throw a paste ball to distances of up to 328 ft (100 m).

THE TECHNIQUES

• Casting and waiting for strikes
Looking for the right position, marking out, and groundbaiting the fishing area, are all hard work. It is therefore essential to cast with care, in order to be sure that the rig ends up in the ideal position. Overhead casting is easy to learn and allows for a great precision after only a few practice runs. To cast overhead, stand behind the rod rests, facing the groundbait marking. Hold the rod with one hand on the rear handle and one on the front handle, lifting the line away from the reel with your forefinger. Lift the rod up until it is exactly over your head, letting the rig hang down about 8 in (20 cm) from the ground, and cast with a whipping movement. Analyze the impact of the lead weight on the water and allow for any corrections that are required – a longer or shorter cast, one that is more to the left, and so on. Repeat until you are satisfied with the result. As soon as the lead touches the ground, shut the bale arm, and tighten the line just enough to prevent the backing line from arcing on the surface but not so much as to move the rig along the bottom. Place the rod on its rest, not forgetting to set the clutch, and do not set it too loose or the hook will not penetrate the lip of the fish when it pulls. On the other hand, if it is set too tight, your rod will fly away with the carp! Thread the line through the guide on the bobbin, making sure that the bobbin itself is two-thirds of the way up the stake. This precaution is to give the bobbin far enough drop if a carp swims inshore. Finally do not forget to check that the buzzer is switched on and working properly.

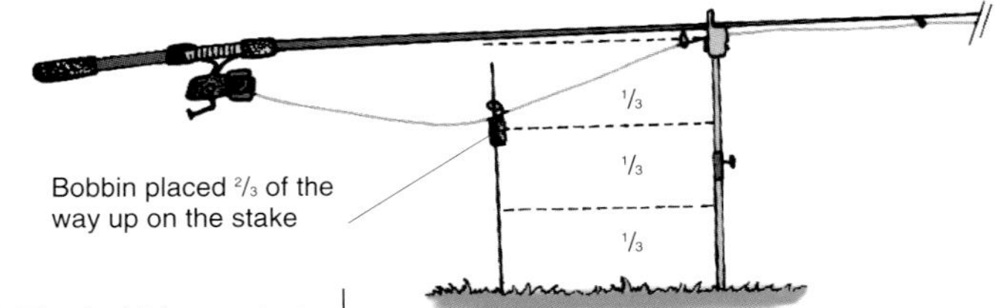

Rigging the bobbin

△ *The bobbin needs to be able to move two-thirds of the way down the stake to indicate a bite, even a casual one.*

• The fight
When the carp bites violently, and follows this up by thrashing around wildly, the bobbin will rise rapidly and free the line, the clutch will scream on the reel while the buzzer will be buzzing away for all it is worth. All this cacophony and motion is part of the explanation of why carp-fishing can be so exciting.

The bobbin may sometimes move up and down jerkily, to the accompaniment of a few bursts from the buzzer. Whichever way a bite registers, the strike must not be delayed if the hook is to catch the mouth of the fish. Remember that the hair rig leaves the hook totally clear of the bait and that hooking the carp is a separate event which only occurs subsequently. It is therefore important not to strike wildly and shakily, but to pull firmly on the line using a wide movement. Quickly raise the rod straight over your head to create the most favorable angle. Then, using the palm of the left hand (if the rod is held in the right hand) keep a constant pressure on the reel to counteract the first jolts from the carp, which are always violent. As soon as it turns and quietens down slightly, start pumping, ready to free the clutch instantly, in case the fish reacts suddenly. When you see the first signs of a ripple near the bank, you know that the end of the fight is near. Crouch down to avoid frightening the carp and bring it toward the landing-net which should be submerged in the deepest part of the water and wide open, ready to take the fish. When the fish is in the correct position, lift the net firmly and bring the catch in toward you. Never try to chase a carp with the net, the angler never wins that particular battle!

• The correct handling of carp

Inasmuch as the carp is fished much more for sport than for the table – even in those countries in which it is prized as a delicacy – it is imperative to give it its freedom in such a way that it has every chance of surviving and fighting another day. That is why the fish must be placed on a wet mat, so as not to damage the layer of mucus with which its body is covered. Remove the hook quickly, with a disgorger if necessary. To weigh the catch, put it in a wetted weighing bag, which fastens with a drawstring, and attach the bag to the hook of the weighscale. You can take photographs of your catches, but always remember to keep the body nice and wet, especially when the weather is hot and windy.

◁ This carp fell for the grains of corn on a hair rig. Note the position of the hook, always caught in the lip, which makes it easy to remove and leaves the fish in excellent condition for being released.

RELEASING THE FISH BACK INTO THE WATER

After weighing the fish and taking photographs, wrap it up in the wet mat, and lower it carefully in the water. Support it in the swimming position until it moves away. If necessary, help it with forward and backward movements to facilitate the re-oxygenation. The more relentless it was during its fight, the more this has weakened it, and the more stressed it will have become. Take this into account when releasing the fish. It may take several minutes before the fish recovers entirely. Jack London put it this way: "The pleasure of killing is great, but the pleasure of letting live is greater." Releasing a fish back into the water is a great joy, knowing how to restrain our predatory instincts in order to spare the life of a living creature. This must come from deep inside, not to satisfy some sort of fad or snobbery. However, there should be no criticism of the angler who, from time to time and by tradition, will take out a small carp for the table. It is only if this is done to excess that it is reprehensible. If too many carp are taken at once, just for the glory of it, most of them will end up in the garbage. What a waste!

△ This 40 lb ½ oz (18 kg) mirror carp is being released back into its element. That way it will give pleasure to another angler on another day, when it will be even bigger!

THE CATCH

It would be hard to ignore the carp, since it is found in so many watery habitats, from the most inconspicuous pond to the largest man-made lake. The literature about the fish has often been wrong, characterizing it as being dumb, ancient, cautious, melancholy, and mysterious... It is also said to hibernate in the mud. If some of these attributes are accurate, it is a pity that the relentless fighting qualities of the carp and its consequent fascination for anglers have usually been omitted! The record catch in England was of a carp weighing 44 lb (20 kg). This 1952 record, by David Walker fishing in Redmire Pool, still stands, although Walker was using tackle which would be considered totally inadequate by today's standards.

A BEAUTIFUL ORIENTAL

It is generally accepted that the carp originated in Asia and was introduced into Europe in Roman times, about two thousand years ago. Carp were brought in from Asia by ship and were destined to be farmed, but some of the fish were accidentally released into the river Rhône, in France. In the lower third of its course, the carp population closely resembles the wild carp found in China.

Some ancient Chinese engravings representing carp are reminiscent of the common carp. They show a very long fish with a massive head and large fins, a type which is still often caught in the Rhône and in some small coastal French rivers. There are many references to the import of carp in medieval manuscripts. The fish were generally brought in from eastern Europe. Medieval fish farms were usually tended by monks and the sale of fish was a rich source of revenue in the days when it was the law that no meat could be eaten on Wednesdays and Fridays.

Carp has spread throughout Europe, but as a delicacy for the table, most of the dishes originate from Poland, Russia, Hungary, and Romania.

Despite all that has been said above, the theories of the origin of carp were completely turned on their head when in late 1991, while digging in the former bed of the River Seine east of Paris, archeologists unearthed not only rowboats and flint tools, but also fossilized carp, all dating from around 6000 BC. The only possible conclusion is that even western Europe had a carp population more than 8,000 years ago. Did carp die out completely in France, only to be reintroduced during the Roman conquest 6,000 years later?

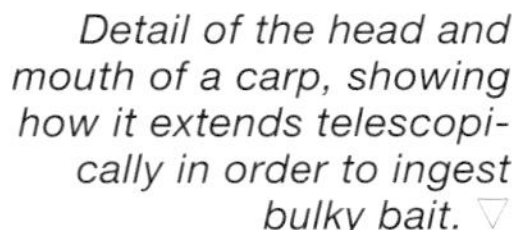

Detail of the head and mouth of a carp, showing how it extends telescopically in order to ingest bulky bait. ▽

AN OMNIVOROUS OPPORTUNIST

Carp is endemic to Central Asia and Asia Minor, and can be found in all the Black Sea tributaries. It is found in almost every waterway, in China and Japan of course, but even in the United States, Canada, Australia, and South Africa, throughout southern Europe and in Scandinavia. It is also found in England, Wales, and Ireland, though not in Scotland. It has been introduced into Israel solely as a farmed fish, where it is considered a delicacy, thanks to the large population of East European origin. Although not generally found at altitude, the fish has been found in lakes 4,000 feet (1,000 m) above sea level.

• A massive fish

The body of the carp is massive and supports powerful fins, in particular the pectoral fins and the tail, often bright yellow to orange. The dorsal fin is long, concave, coarsely serrated, and very sharp. Although carp are normally slow-moving and even sluggish, thanks to its powerful build, it is capable of huge bursts of speed and has a great stamina. That is why it is such a formidable adversary. The head of the carp is massive and its slightly prominent eyes are golden yellow. The upper lip is adorned with four barbels, two short upward-pointing ones and two longer, thicker ones at the corners of the mouth. The true sensory organ of the carp is its mouth which is telescopic, the lips stretching and retracting as it searches the bottom and palpates the aquatic vegetation, to find its preferred food. The carp has pharyngeal teeth that can crush the toughest prey (crayfish, freshwater mussels, etc.). These are indispensable because its digestive system is rudimentary.

DIFFERENT VARIETIES OF CARP

– *The common carp* is characterized by a body that is entirely covered with scales. It is a hybrid resulting from extensive crossbreeding and it may be long and slender or thick and sturdy, with a variety of intermediate body shapes.

– *The mirror carp* is normally rounded in shape, almost bulbous. The flanks are smooth as leather and are adorned with a few very bright scales.

– *The leather carp* differs from the mirror carp only because it completely lacks scales. Some writers on angling use the term "leather carp" for all mirror carp with only a very few scales.

Carp belong to the goldfish family, as can be seen by the brilliance of the scales and general body shape.

△ *Synthetic paste balls, colorless and odorless, are very practical as a base on which to stick corn or seeds (in this case, hemp seed), enabling the angler to offer carp a generous mouthful.*

• Habitats closely linked to the distribution of food

Although most waterways of interest to anglers are stocked with carp, the fish develops best in the most temperate waters, that is at low altitude (less than 1,500 feet (400 or 500 m)). Ponds, natural lakes, gravel pits, and artificial lakes, wherever they are located, will all harbor some carp. When it comes to waterways, whether they are rivers hundreds of feet wide or narrow lowland creeks, all are suitable for the dynamic carp. The carp is omniverous and is happy to eat lugworms, watersnails, freshwater mussels, crayfish, young shoots of aquatic plants, and occasionally, even fish spawn

◁ *Catching a handsome specimen (this one weighs 41lb 1/4 oz (18.5 kg). It is a mirror carp, caught in the Durance near Avignon. For some anglers, the quest for such a catch can become an obsession!*

or fry. The carp is thus often to be found close to rich supplies of food, amongst the vegetation, near submerged trees, beside reed beds, and under overhanging branches. It also favors muddy trenches near the piers of a bridge, inside locks, even near shoals or weirs. The diet of carp varies enormously from one season to the next, because its digestive cycle is closely linked to the water temperature. It is estimated that, in waters in which the temperature is around 68°F (20°C), it takes between three and four hours for the carp to digest its food, which means it has to spend most of its time eating. On the other hand, in waters whose temperature is around 48°F (8°C), digestion is much slower, and 24 to 30 hours may elapse between feeding periods. However, it has been shown that even in waters whose temperature is as low as 36°F (2°C) carp continue to feed, though sparingly, thus putting paid once and for all to the legend of carp hibernation.

• A seething mass of fertility

In early May, as soon as the water temperature reaches 64 to 68°F (18 to 20°C), carp congregate, often in massive groups due to the approach of the spawning season. They then make their way toward shallow spots, such as water-meadows, near thickly-wooded banks, or shallows rich in aquatic vegetation. Several hundred individuals may be seen crowded together, throwing caution to the wind, in an area no bigger than a couple of acres. The females patrol the waters in all directions for several days, relentlessly pursued by the males. Large eddies, broken

SPECIFIC

Here are a few of the names given to the various sub-species of the common carp. The same English names are used throughout Europe, since it was the English who proved themselves the past-masters at this type of coarse fishing:

– *Scaled* is the term used to describe a mirror carp where large scales are scattered sparsely over the body.

– *Linear* describes a mirror carp whose scales are aligned in a strip along the top of the body just below the dorsal fin. Sometimes there is a

Common carp from the Rhône, weighing 29 lb (13 kg), a wild variety of the fish. Notice the length and the size of its fins. Dynamite on the end of a line! ▽

TERMINOLOGY

corresponding strip on the lower part of the body.

– *Fully scaled* is used for a mirror carp whose body is almost entirely covered in scales, but their arrangement is still unmistakeable and cannot be confused with that of the common carp.

– *Wildie* is used for a common carp, generally a river-dweller, which is similar to the original wild stock. The body is very slender, with a massive head and almost abnormally enlarged fins, a body-shape adapted for life in strong current.

with washes and churned-up waters, transform the whole spawning area into a large aquatic turmoil. The splashing from this mass of fertility, at its height, can be heard from quite a distance! Very often the female, exhausted by the long chase and the act of spawning, remains motionless on her side in only a few inches of muddy water. The spawn (about 70,000 eggs per pound or 150,000 per kg) soon adhere to the aquatic vegetation or to roots in the water and hatch after about 212 degree-days (100°C) (i.e. five days in 68°F (20°C) water). The alevin feeds essentially on animal and vegetable plankton and soon turns into a young carp. Under normal conditions, the young carp will grow to a size of 2 lb 4 oz (1 kg) in 2 to 3 years. It reaches sexual maturity in 3 to 4 years for the female and 2 to 3 years for the male. Even though the hundred-year-old carp only exists in the collective imagination of anglers yearning for a legend, this fish can nevertheless live to the respectable age of 25 to 30 years, and even exceptionally 40, and frequently weighs up to 45 lb (20 kg). Several specimens weighing over 67 lb 1/2 oz (30 kg) have been caught with a rod and line. The French record is held by a Mr. Rouvière who caught an 83 lb (37 kg) mirror carp at the confluence of the rivers Yonne and Seine. Perhaps the next western European record will be for a 90 lb (40 kg) specimen. Carp of this weight have reportedly been netted in Serbia & Montenegro and Hungary, and two more were harpooned in South Africa.

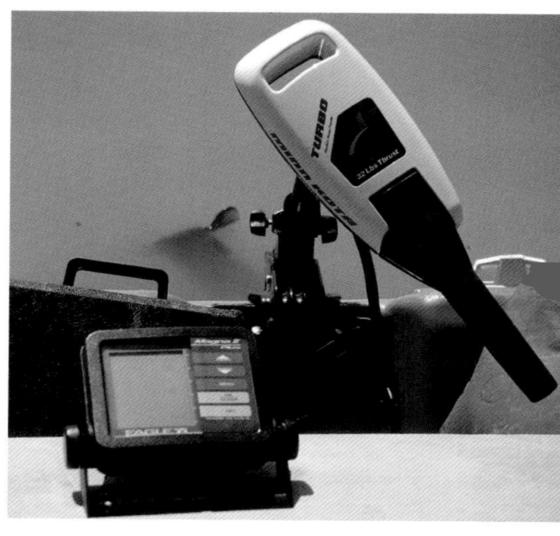

Boat, electric motor and echo-sounder... The winning trio for finding the optimum fishing position.

STOCKING AND BREEDING

Most of the smaller waterways of temperate mainland Europe and North America are sufficiently well-stocked with carp to allow restocking to be left to nature. Man's involvement is thus limited to restocking waters where there are few fish and improving the spawning conditions.

• Stocking

Experience has shown many times that the best results are obtained when the fish used are young. The metabolism of young carp (weighing between 10 1/2 oz and 2 lb 4 oz (0.3 to 1 kg) actually adapts more easily to the physical and chemical characteristics of the water (range of temperatures, current, exposure, pH, etc.). Furthermore, when introduced as alevins into a stretch of water, carp are more likely to breed and replenish the waters by their own efforts.

• Improving spawning conditions

In stretches of water in which there are significant variations in water level, particularly in artificial and reservoir or dammed lakes and millponds, the spawning areas are sometimes inaccessible or even worse, the water level drops just after the fish has spawned, thus wiping out the entire spawn. The remedy is to install floating spawning areas. These consist of a raft made of empty plastic drums, covered

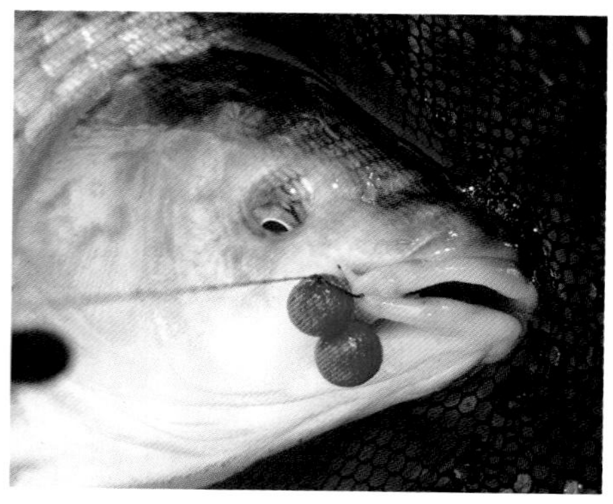

This carp has fallen victim to a hair rig baited with paste balls. Being hooked in the lip, it is possible to remove the hook and free the fish leaving it in excellent condition.

ACCLIMATIZATION OF LARGE CARP

To increase the value of private stretches of water, many authorities stock with fully-grown carp (weighing from 33 3/4 to more than 56 lb (15 to 25 kg)) in order to attract "trophy" fishermen. Nine times out of ten, this short-sighted policy results in failure. Either the fish are caught soon after they were introduced, or these carp, which are mature and have a metabolism which has grown dependent on a habitat elsewhere (natural food, exposure, the specific physical and chemical composition of the water), will rapidly go into decline, loose weight, and even die.

Such large specimens are netted and then sold on live by professional fishermen (often completely legally), but also by anglers who know the price that some owners of angling waters are ready to pay for a 45lb (20 kg) specimen. This is an environmentally unsound practice, and the elementary ethics of the sport require fish not to be moved out of their native habitat.

A FEW GROUNDBAITING STRATEGIES

When the carp are in a feeding frenzy, from April through October, groundbaiting consists in distributing seeds and/or paste balls on the position that you have chosen. The spread of the bait, covering an oval area of 50 to 70 sq. ft. (15 to 20 m²), must be quite homogenous so that when searching determinedly for food, the carp is guided toward your rigs. When the carp are following various specific routes, T-shaped or X-shaped groundbaiting paths are more selective but they require more precision when throwing the bait. Where the fishing is intense, the carp are not slow to associate the plentiful distribution of food with a latent danger... In such a case, it is better to considerably limit the amount of groundbait and to spread the rigs out, each having no more than twenty baits attached to them.

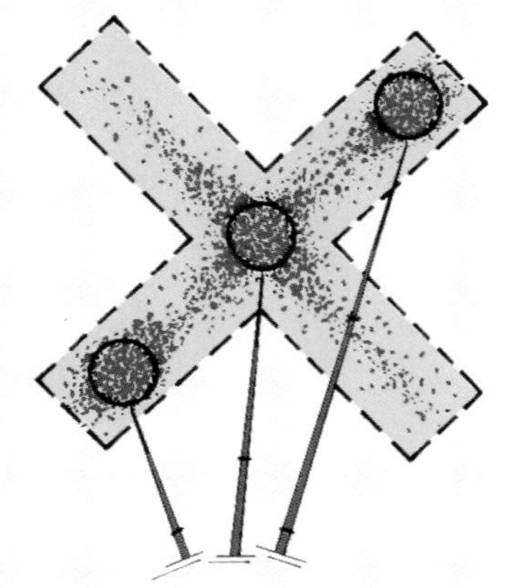

△ *X-shaped path.*

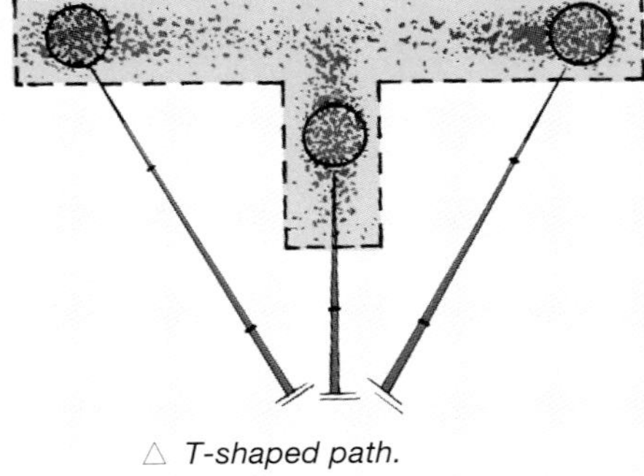

△ *T-shaped path.*

Paths for groundbaiting

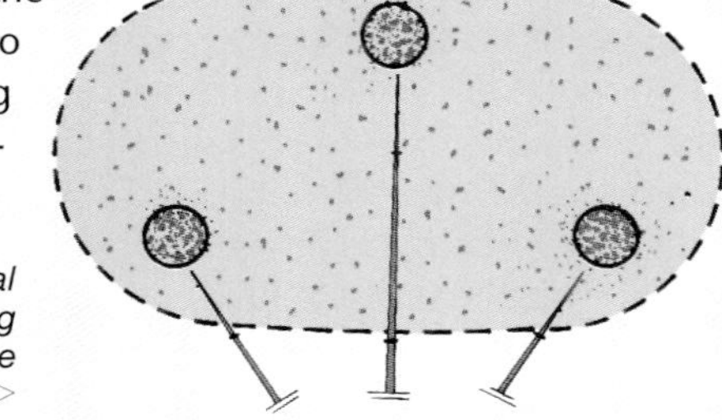

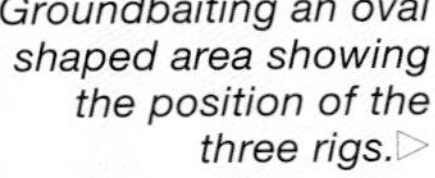

Groundbaiting an oval shaped area showing the position of the three rigs. ▷

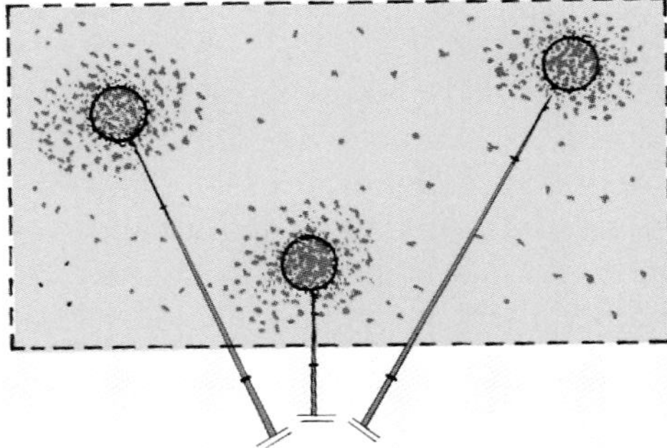

△ *Very light groundbaiting with three concentrated points (one for each rig).*

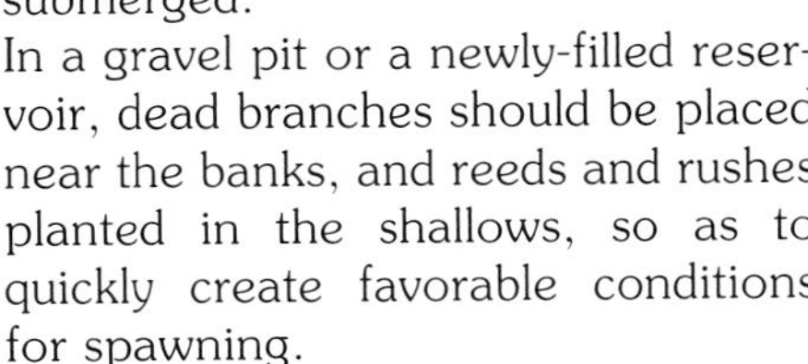

with branches. By mooring this raft in mid-stream, the rig will move up and down with the water level and the spawn will always remain submerged.
In a gravel pit or a newly-filled reservoir, dead branches should be placed near the banks, and reeds and rushes planted in the shallows, so as to quickly create favorable conditions for spawning.

FISHING IN LAKES AND RESERVOIRS

Whatever the area covered by the water, whether it be tiny pond, large gravel pit, or gigantic artificial lake, your first concern is always the same, namely, to find a good position. To achieve this, it is essential to meticulously observe everything around you, so that you clearly

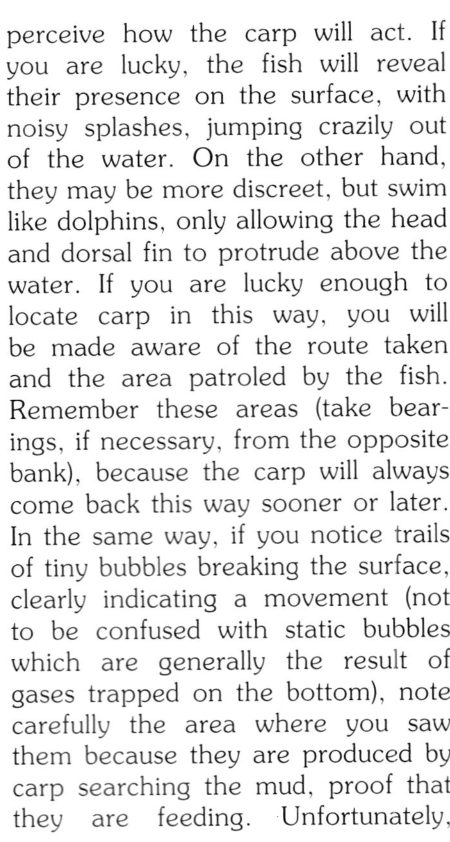

perceive how the carp will act. If you are lucky, the fish will reveal their presence on the surface, with noisy splashes, jumping crazily out of the water. On the other hand, they may be more discreet, but swim like dolphins, only allowing the head and dorsal fin to protrude above the water. If you are lucky enough to locate carp in this way, you will be made aware of the route taken and the area patroled by the fish. Remember these areas (take bearings, if necessary, from the opposite bank), because the carp will always come back this way sooner or later. In the same way, if you notice trails of tiny bubbles breaking the surface, clearly indicating a movement (not to be confused with static bubbles which are generally the result of gases trapped on the bottom), note carefully the area where you saw them because they are produced by carp searching the mud, proof that they are feeding. Unfortunately,

◁ *The carp is an outstanding fighter. It is only with adequate equipment and a good retrieving technique that it will reach the landing net.*

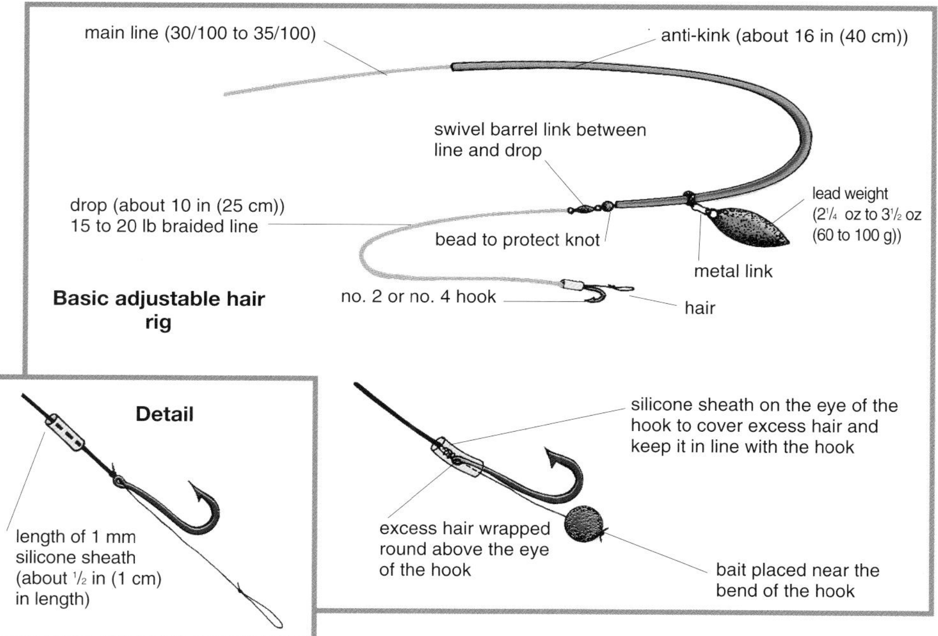

carp can sometimes be very discreet. If this is the case, you must then rely on other methods in order to determine the positions favored by carp, which are likely to be places in which natural foods abound. Banks that are rich in aquatic vegetation, even better when wooded, the areas around islands, submerged, decomposing wood, and reed beds constitute a first-class food source in which the carp can find water snails, larvae, spawn, and young shoots in large quantities. Promontories and meadows that slope gently down to the water are almost always indicative of an underwater shelf and a gentle incline, favored by crawfish, freshwater mussels, and other freshwater shellfish. Deeper trenches allow for the mud to accumulate and are inevitably bristling with worms. Shallows benefit from photosynthesis and it is common to see small grassy areas with an abundance of benthic fauna developing, even away from the banks. But, while the water's edge and anything protruding above the surface are easily identifiable, the layout of the bottom always remains a mystery. That is why it is essential to take methodical soundings to get a precise idea of the topography. Cast a lead-weighted line in various directions and at different distances. Close the bale-arm as soon as the lead touches the water and count the seconds it takes for the lead to get to the bottom, which will give you an indication of the various depths. Remember to drag the lead weight slowly along the bottom. If it moves smoothly and easily, the bottom is hard, if it trails heavily, the bottom is muddy.

• The rigs

– The basic adjustable hair rig

This rig, which uses a sliding group of lead shot on a length of anti-kink tubing, includes a short drop-line of about 10 in (25 cm) made of very flexible 15 to 20 lb braided line. A barrel swivel is used to join the drop to the main line. The size of the hook, which should have a large eye and be very sharp, should be between a no. 2 and a no. 4, depending on the size of the bait used. The hair, attached using the braid left over from the knot or a short length of 14/100 nylon, is an extension of the hook, ending in a loop through which the bent end of the baiting-needle is passed. The size and the number of baits may vary, so the length of the hair must be adjustable.

– The run rig

The design here is the same as in the basic rig but differs in that the bunch weight is stopped from sliding. This enables the inertia of the lead weight to counteract the pull of the carp and act as an instant self-striking mechanism with deeper penetration of the hook into the lip of the fish. Several methods are used to hold the weight in place, the most common of which is to place a stop above the weight or the anti-kink tubing. This rig is suitable for ninety percent of the fishing conditions you are likely to encounter.

• The bait

The most productive rigs owe their efficiency to the hair mount.

The hair is usually an extension of the hook, because it presents the baits beneath the bend (see p. 177).

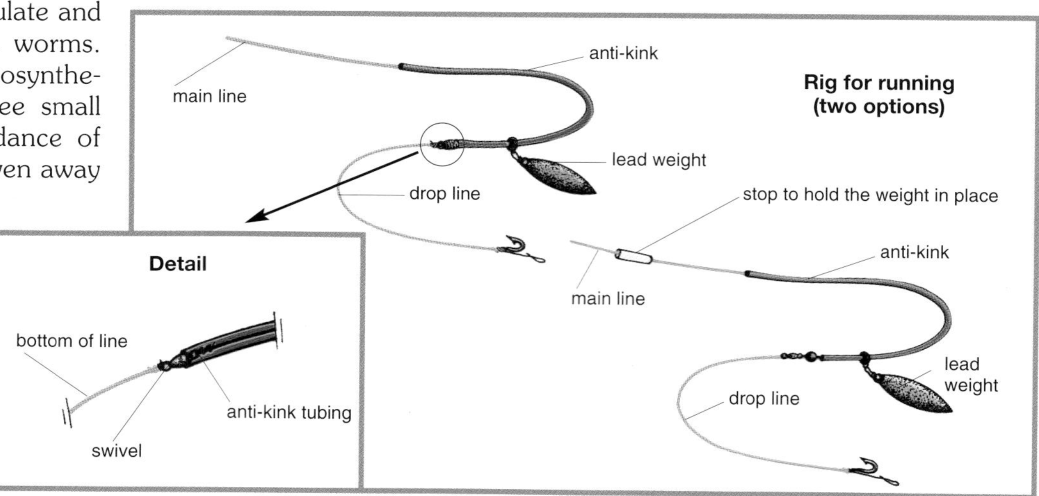

However, under certain conditions the bait must be adapted. For a better presentation of a floating bait, the hair may be lateral, in other words, fixed to the middle of the shank of the hook so that the paste ball is tight against it. The use of a powerful elastic band allows for the perfect lateral presentation of the hair. However, in situations in which the carp are highly experienced at escaping the angler and thus very wary, they may tug lightly on the bait and give up at the slightest resistance. The trick then consists in threading the bait onto the hair and then tying the end of the latter just before the bend in the hook; this forces the carp to grab the hook whether it wants to or not.

△ *To lay the groundbait near the area marked by the buoy (polystyrene block), this angler uses a boat to drop the seeds and paste balls with precision.*

– Free presentation

On muddy bottoms or where the vegetation or the litter is dense and there is plenty of clutter, classic baits are often hard for the fish to see and thus do not attract carp. In these circumstances, the solution is to use floating bait that moves around above the bottom, but well below the surface.

There is a special type of mixture called a floating mix which can be used to make floating paste balls. You can also bake your usual paste balls for 3 minutes in the oven; this will also have the effect of enabling them to float. Do not forget to put a string of shot on the drop line, to act as a counterweight, so that the bait moves at a specific distance from the bottom, normally about 2½ to 4 in (6 to 10 cm) above it. To make corn or seeds float, just tie a small cube of foam to the hair to lift it up from the bottom. Whatever the type of bottom you are fishing in, it is often a good idea to rig at least one of the 3 hooks with floating bait, because occasionally, for no apparent reason, carp seem to prefer to have their food presented in this way.

River fishing

In rivers between 40 and 400 feet (10 m to 100 m) wide, the behavior of carp is dependent upon the current. Where it is slow, or even non-existent, it allows for the growth of natural foods and the fish can move effortlessly. That is why in rivers where the current is stronger or quite fast, carp prefer to swim along close to the banks.

Consequently, anything that contributes to breaking up the flow and creating an area of calm waters is a possible carp haunt and should be noted precisely at once. Sharp bends, downstream from islets, near submerged trees, spots below manmade dams, bridges, shelves, etc. are first-class positions. This is where you must set up your rigs, often very close to the bank, but you must be extremely discreet in doing so.

In winter, carp seem to remain more active in rivers and streams than they are in lakes and ponds, probably

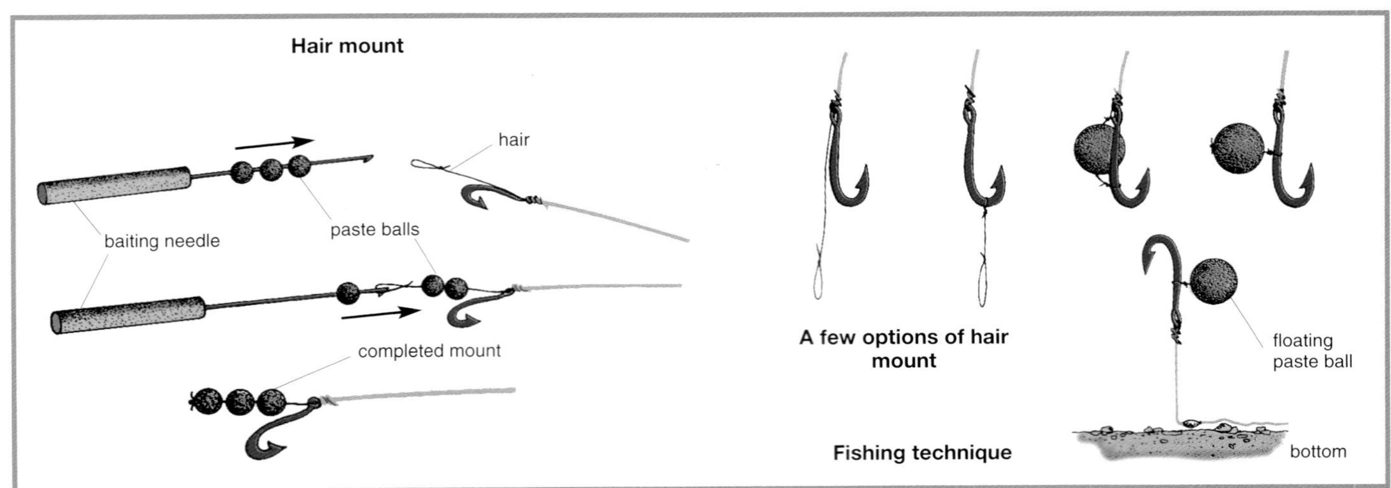

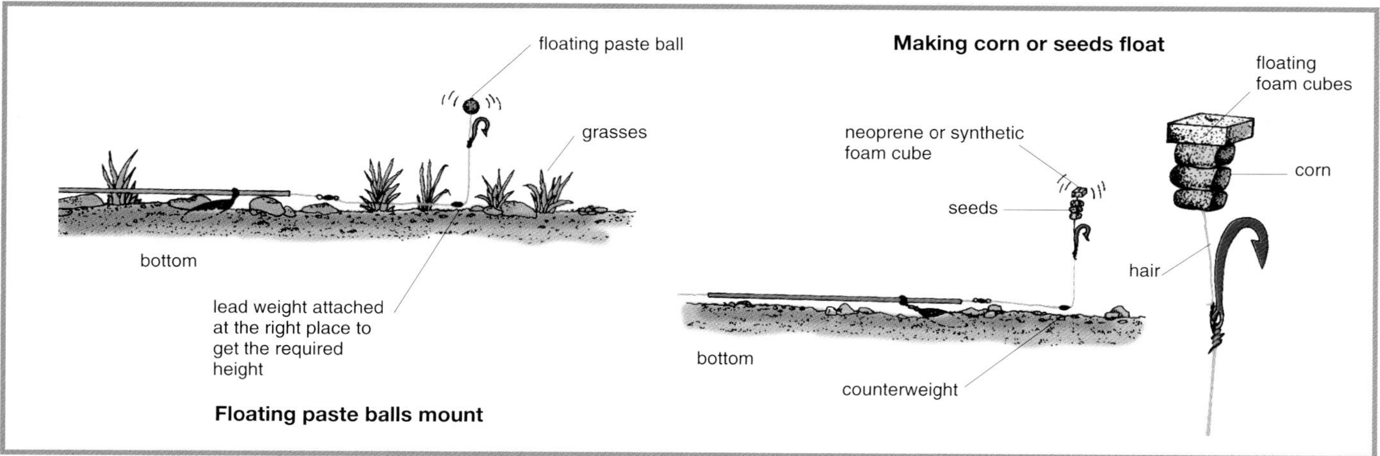

Floating paste balls mount

Making corn or seeds float

because they need energy in order to fight the current of even a slow river when it is in full spate.

In summer, in rivers in which the current slows down considerably, shelves are the favored haunts because the water is more heavily oxygenated just below the surface. Failing this, the deepest waters, where it is cooler, will harbor more active specimens, even in hot weather. Due to the fact that eighty-five percent of rivers have a reasonably strong current, and because most of the time you will have to fish near obstructions, you will need to use 35/100 line. This way the largest fish can be brought swiftly under control.

As far as the rigs are concerned, they can be any of the various types we have described, all of which are perfectly adapted to river fishing. There is still plenty of room for the up-and-coming carp angler along the river banks. Although intensive groundbaiting is becoming less recommended in reservoirs because of the pressure of fishing, it still has a future in running water, especially in fast-flowing, fairly straight rivers such as realigned sectors), in which carp patrol the shore, never staying still for an instant; a generous spread of groundbait will keep their interest for longer in one place. The formula, consisting of 10½ to 18 lb (5 to 8 kg) of seeds or grain, added to 200 or 300 paste balls gives excellent results.

Bait your rigs with these paste balls and the carp will often make them their first choice.

• The floating line

In sluggish rivers and in ponds or gravel pits, the floating line technique, which is hardly ever used for carp – fishing, may nevertheless be very effective if soundings have been carefully taken as to the topography of the bottom. The first option, suitable for when the bottom is quite clean, consists in lengthening the drop until the leaning position of the float indicates that the line is partly resting on the bottom, in other words, among the groundbait. When the fishing

Rigs for "fiendishly clever" carp

In areas which are overfished, carp which have been returned to the water many times become very sly and makes lots of careful tests on the bait they are offered. If there is the slightest resistance when they pull on the bait, they make a rapid escape... Anglers in England having been faced with this situation for a long time have created very crafty rigs to deal with this problem. Where the carp are more accessible, these mounts are too finicky to be suitable, unless the waters are heavily fished.

Discreet rig

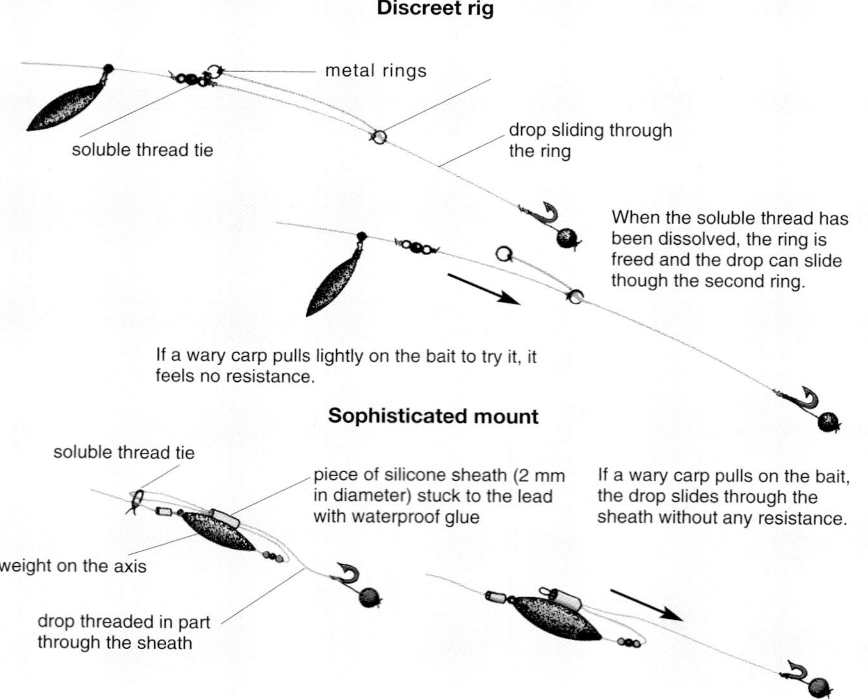

Sophisticated mount

position is littered with grass and detritus (this often being an excellent spot!) but where there is considerable risk of snagging, the operation is more delicate as you have to use the same technique before reeling in enough line for the bait to float above the obstructions. Redworm, clusters of maggots, as well as bread or grains of corn are the best baits for fishing, slightly above the bottom.

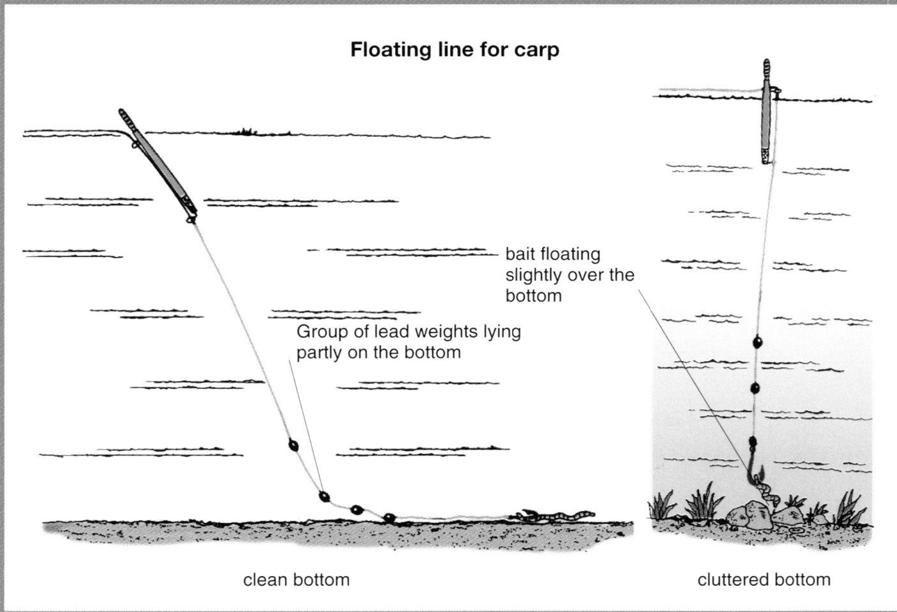

• The sliding sinker

When an angler is after roach, bream, or tench he frequently spots a shoal of carp, which attract his attention when they come leaping to the surface or when they leave a trail of bubbles on the surface while searching the muddy bottom, or simply because a massive specimen has hurled its body at the line, breaking it effortlessly! The way to get around this consists in using extra lines. After groundbaiting with potato, corn, and pieces of worm, cast one or two 30/100 lines rigged with a sliding weight and a 28/100 drop with a bait of the same type as the groundbait. The clutch must be correctly set or you must fish with the bale-arm open. This type of complementary technique allows you to carry on fishing for roach or other coarse fish while keeping an eye on the carp rods, which must be kept by you at all times, so that you can react as quickly as possible...

FISHING IN CANALS

Many canals in mainland Europe are well-stocked with carp, yet surprisingly they are hardly fished at all. The current is generally slow, enabling the fish to explore the whole length of these waterways, but the banks, locks, and rare obstructions are the refuges of choice for carp. Unfortunately, they are difficult to locate because of the uniformity of the canalside landscape. However, in these localities, since carp are not familiar with the wiles of

Fishing for carp in winter is becoming more popular, but groundbaiting must be restricted because the fish are feeding less than at other times of the year. The proof is this 20 lb 1/4 oz (9 kg) common carp caught in the river Rhône, near Vaucluse, in France in February, in a water temperature of 45°F (7°C). ▽

LEAPING CARP?

It is worth asking why carp leap about with such gusto on the surface of the water and stop doing so just as suddenly. One of the theories has long been that this maneuver was an attempt by the fish to rid itself of parasites. However, this is unlikely, because some larvae attach themselves to a point near the mouth or at the base of the fins where they are extremely difficult to shake off. Another theory is that by falling back heavily on the surface of the water, the fish manage to expel internal gases caused by the fermenting of certain foods in their stomach. This theory is also not very credible, because carp often perform their acrobatics at feeding time. Perhaps the leaps are a means of communication among the shoal, because the shock waves created by this activity can be sensed at a great distance by other carp. Or could the carp simply be playing and enjoying themselves?

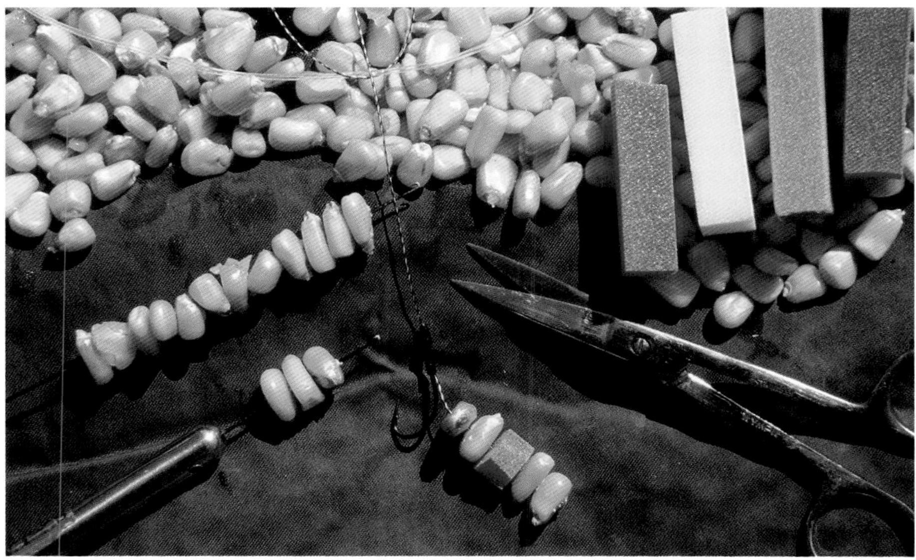

◁ *Grains of corn, buoyant pieces of foam, and scissors...That is all you need in order to make your corn or seeds float.*

anglers, they are not so frightened of groundbait, all the more so because they have little natural food at their disposal. In shallow waters, intense groundbaiting in a triangular pattern will enable you to intercept carp with a degree of certainty, whether they come from up or downstream. Where the carp are more wary, it is more rewarding to fish near the banks, in particular where bushes and trees overhang the water.

NIGHT FISHING

In many countries, night-fishing for carp is not allowed. In France, for example, night fishing was not allowed but due to a fierce campaign led by angling clubs and the carp section of the French Angling Federation, the law was amended in 1994. Carp fishing is now permitted in France at any time, day or night, as it is in England, and to a lesser extent in Belgium, Holland, and Germany.

△ *Two grains of corn.*

Night-fishing for carp opens up new horizons. This technique allows the angler to maintain a position 24 hours a day, without being forced to leave at nightfall.

Earthworm. △

This is a considerable advantage if one considers the amount of equipment involved in carp fishing. But above all, night fishing offers the chance to catch carp that have adopted a night feeding cycle, which is often the case.

△ *Cluster of maggots.*

Night fishing cannot be improvised: everything that is taken for granted and considered as routine during the day soon becomes an exciting adventure as soon as you operate at night. You will soon notice that, under the cover of darkness, the carp tend to feed near the banks, assuming they will be able to do so undisturbed. Choose the closest position possible in order to be as accurate as you can be in casting, because sooner or later you will have to cast again, as soon as it becomes pitch-dark. Do not forget either that you will need to use the same precision when boosting the groundbait.

△ *Potato cube.*

Most of the time, non-stop fishing involves two different positions, one for the day, generally out in midstream, and one nearer the bank at night. Note carefully the direction of

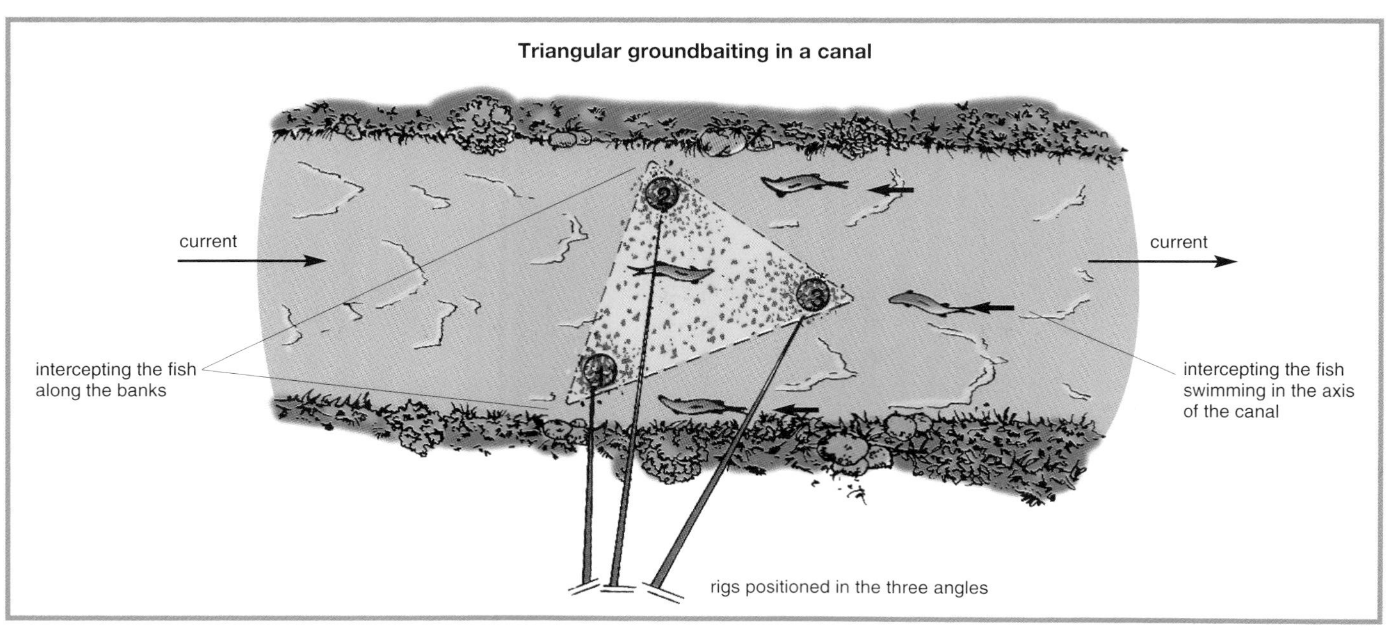

NIGHT-FISHING IN FRANCE?

Although the ban on night-fishing for coarse fish in France has now been lifted, it would be an impossible situation if thousands of carp anglers suddenly took up a spot wherever they felt like angling throughout the French network of waterways (secondary rivers, streams, canals).
Permission is therefore given, on a gradual basis, for a section of waterway in each Département (administrative region). After all, French waters are extremely popular with visiting anglers from abroad, several thousand of whom arrive in France every year. In practice, what this means is that soon two or three stretches of water in each of the carp-fishing locations will be open to night-fishing.
The best way to prepare for a night-fishing trip in France is to contact the local Fédération de Pêche, the angling federation, by telephone, in writing, or by email, in order to obtain accurate information.
Although there is no specific regulation in this respect, you are strongly recommended to release the fish back into the water if they are caught at night, so that the fish stocks are not depleted by this extra pressure.

△ Carp anglers are rarely alone and like operating in harmony, only to try out various fishing methods (baits, depth, fishing distance...).

the splashing, indicating that the carp are jumping. As soon as you hear them during the first night, spread the groundbait over an area which you will be able to cover after dark.
If you do not observe – or rather hear – any surface activity, then choose spots which are close to aquatic vegetation, promontories, headlands, and deep bays. It would be most unusual for a carp not to swim into these sheltered spots at some time during the night in search of food. Be methodical. Always pack your tackle away carefully in the same place, and always set your landing net down in the same spot. Keep a wetpack for holding everything you need for building a new rig at night. It should contain all the small items of equipment, such as a flashlight, baiting-needle, ready-made drop line, lead weights, soluble thread, and so on. Nor should you neglect your own comfort. Make sure you have a warm sleeping bag, a spacious waterproof tent, and cooking equipment to make a hot meal at the waterside.
Although there is so much new tackle around, this does not mean that tried and tested tackle should be abandoned. The traditional techniques are still proving successful in hooking carp. More important than expensive and sophisticated rods, lines, hooks, and rigs is a keen eye and ear, as well as a thorough knowledge of the area in which you are fishing, so that you can locate the fish and make just the right choice of angling position.

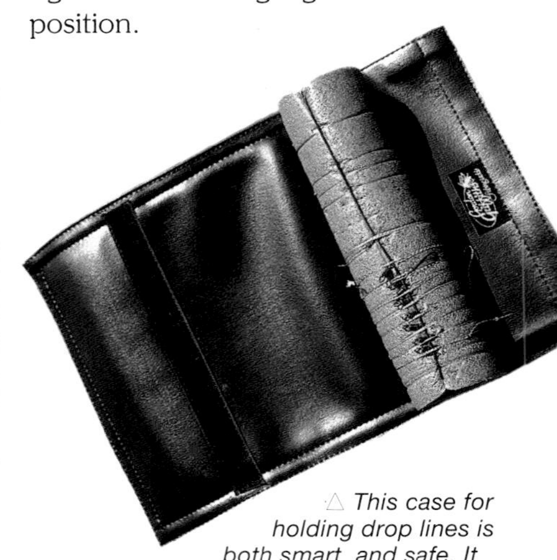

△ This case for holding drop lines is both smart and safe. It enables the angler to wind the lines around a foam cylinder and these are then held in place by a protective cover.

Where to fish for carp in France

It would be easy, and partly true, to say that carp are found throughout France. However, a few places of interest are worth a special detour, either because the carp are particularly numerous in that location or because they reach such impressive proportions.

Reservoirs and lakes

* Saint-Cassien Lake. This is the pick of the bunch. This stretch of water in the Var covers an area of 1375 acres (550 ha). It has very rugged banks and varied depths, and harbors an average quantity of carp but those that are there reach such a huge size that it has gained the reputation of being one of the best carp-fishing lakes in Europe. Dozens of fish weighing more than 45 lb (20 kg) are caught every year. To date, the record stands at 78 lb (35.5 kg).

* Der-Chantecoq Lake. This lake is used to control the flow of the River Seine. It is a shallow reservoir covering 1200 acres (4800 ha) in the départements of Marne and Haute-Marne. The stock of carp averages 30–32 lb (13–14 kg) in weight, though there are plenty of specimens that weigh 45 lb (20 kg) and more.

* St-Geniez-d'Olt Lake. This dam on the river Lot covers 545 acres (218 ha) and stretches along a deep winding valley in the département of Aveyron. It harbors what may be one of the densest populations of carp in the whole country, perhaps in Europe. The average weight is about 22 lb (10 kg) but some 45 lb (20 kg) specimens have been caught there.

* The Lake of the Forêt d'Orient. This is a new mecca for carp anglers, consisting of a gigantic stretch of water covering 10,000 acres (4,000 ha). It owes its success to the size of its carp. Mirror carp weighing more than 67 lb (30 kg) have been caught there, as well as a 72 lb (31.8 kg) common carp which was landed in 1993!

* Salagou Lake. This reservoir in the département of Hérault, covers 2,000 acres (nearly 800 ha). The shining, blue waters against a backdrop of red hills is reminiscent of a Moroccan landscape. There is not only a huge carp population, 30lb to 33 lb (13 to 15 kg) specimens are numerous, and those weighing more than 45 lb (20 kg) are by no means rare.

* Sainte-Croix Lake straddles the départements of Alpes-de-Haute-Provence and Var. This reservoir lake on the river Verdon extends its turquoise waters over 5500 acres (2200 ha) amid a mountainous landscape. The carp density is only average and they are not easy to catch but large specimens are numerous.

* The Lake of Villeneuve-de-la-Raho. This 500-acre (200 ha) lake in the Pyrénées-Orientales, only a few miles from the

Spanish border, is worth a visit. Even if the carp rarely exceed 20–22 lb (9–10 kg), it is often possible to catch 20 a day.

The best carp rivers

* The River Seine south of Paris is best for carp, mainly near the cluttered banks. There have been some formidable catches of fish weighing 33 lb–45 lb (15–20 kg), including a common carp weighing 65 lb (28.5 kg) and an 83 lb (37 kg) mirror carp, a French record, caught at the confluence of the rivers Yonne and Seine.

* The Saône. Between Dijon and Lyon through Chalon-sur-Saône, this wide river offers enormous potential for carp anglers, with a preponderance of common carp. There are plenty of 13 lb to 22 lb (6 to 10 kg) specimens.

* The Loire is very rich in carp all along its course, especially from Nevers to Tours through Gien and Orléans. They are not particularly big, but they are very numerous and possess a remarkable fighting spirit.

* The mighty Rhône between Lyons and Port-Saint-Louis-du-Rhône, via Montélimar, Valence, and Avignon, is one of the richest carp waters in France, especially where it meets the rivers Ardèche, Durance, and Gardon. Common carp (often from wild stock) predominate but there are also some large mirror carp.

* The river Gardon. This tributary of the Rhône is worth prospecting in its lower reaches below Rémoulins. It has many common carp of average size alongside some hefty 45 lb (20 kg) mirror carp.

* The river Dordogne. The course of this beautiful river, which is interrupted by many weirs and dams, offers great possibilities between Bergerac and St-Jean de-Blaignac. It has common and mirror carp of average size, as well as a few large specimens.

COARSE FISH

THE TACKLE

Pole fishing is still the favorite fishing technique for European anglers, with nearly 60% of them practicing the sport. It is rich in possibilities and offers a challenging learning curve. You start with fry and small fish and end up entering competitions and using state-of-the-art equipment! Casting with a reel is most suitable for those trying to catch larger fish in the deepest waters, furthest from the bank. Such fish seek a quiet spot away from the shores where they can lurk undisturbed. Innovations in tackle, baits, and techniques are being imported all the time from countries like England and Italy, and they are truly taking carp angling to new heights.

Pole fishing for small fish is easy and a favored means of introducing youngsters to the sport. ▽

POLE FISHING

Classic pole fishing takes place from a fixed position, on a stretch of water normally chosen for its average depth, its tranquility, the evenness of the bottom, and the density of the fish available. Once settled comfortably, the angler should spread the groundbait, by throwing paste balls made of a mixture that is bound to attract fish, which may have to come from far away, and keep them interested in the fishing area while tempting them to feed. The quality of the tackle, the pole, the lines, the groundbait, and the bait, must all be of the best if you want to make the best of the situation and enjoy it.

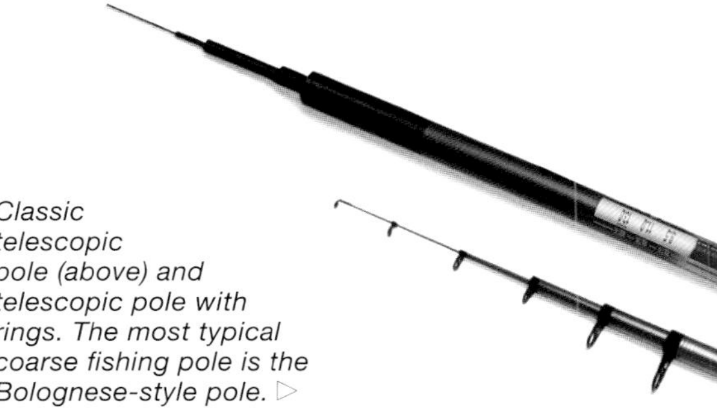

Classic telescopic pole (above) and telescopic pole with rings. The most typical coarse fishing pole is the Bolognese-style pole. ▷

QUALITY EQUIPMENT AND FAULTLESS GROUNDBAITING

• The poles

Whether telescopic or in sections, poles have made technological leaps forward these last few years. Since the arrival of carbon fiber and kevlar, they are a lot lighter and more rigid, enabling their length to increase without gaining weight or having to be thickened at the butt end. They can be as long as 60 feet (18 m) but regulations to restrict the length to 43 ft 6 inches (14.5 m) in competitions should put an end to this race for length which the manufacturers have been conducting over the last few years.

– Poles in sections

These are the pride of French and Belgian anglers and, still favored by competitors in fishing contests, are even becoming popular in England. They allow you to fish at a distance using a short backing line, just beneath the pole. However, when you have to retrieve the line to change the bait, or just to unhook a fish, you have to disconnect the section (see box on opposite page). This means removing the sections one by one, starting with the butt end, and assembling them to cast the line again. There are special rests on the market now which you

△ *This angler is using different types of rod and pole in order to fish with a floating line and a weighted line.*

can use to roll or slide the whole pole backward so you can get right to the section you need to disconnect to get to the best part of the drop. To avoid oversized butt-ends on sectioned poles, which make for awkward handling, the manufacturers have devised a system called reversed fitting, in which each part (starting from the butt) fits into the section above. The tip and the last few sections are telescopic. For storage and transportation, the sections of pole can be pushed inside each other through the base. This saves a lot of space but it is rather a finicky job to pack up the pole.

– *Telescopic poles*

These poles, whose sections slide into each other are indisputably the most practical. They have the added advantage of taking up less room and of being easy to set up as the sections just need pulling out one by one and the pole is ready for fishing. It used to be said that telescopic poles lacked smoothness of action, but nowadays this disadvantage has disappeared, thanks to the new materials used and much more sophisticated manufacturing techniques. In modern, so-called flexible tip fishing, in which the whipping action of the pole propels the line forward, telescopic poles are absolutely perfect! Fast rods, known as whips, are always telescopic and very short. They have a cork handle for a better grip and a very fast action designed for the particular requirements of those angling for small fish.

FISHING WITH KIT

As soon as you use sectioned poles 30 ft (9 m) long and more (sometimes up to 60 ft (18 m) in length), the sections have to be disconnected. To make fishing easier and to remain effective, the backing line must stay relatively short between the tip and the float. Therefore, the length of the line cannot be allowed to exceed 10 to 14 ft (3 to 4 m). In other words, it should be as long as the last few sections of the pole (which is called the kit in competition fishing). To hook the bait or to bring the fish back to land or to the landing net, the last few sections must be removed; meanwhile, the rest of the pole may be laid on the ground behind you, or better still, it should be laid on one or several rests especially rigged for this purpose. To carry on fishing, fit the rest of the pole back onto the kit and scatter the groundbait as you would normally do. When you strike at a bite, bring the fish toward you by rolling the pole behind you until you can reach the first section of the kit and retrieve the line and catch, and replace the bait as usual.

• The thread and the line

The nylon line used for pole fishing must be adapted to the specific requirements of the pole, as regards the regularity and consistency of the thickness, as well as the resistance (and especially resistance to kinking and crushing). Elasticity is also an important point, there must be as little "give" as possible in the line. Every movement of the angler must be sent down the line perfectly and instantaneously to ensure a clean strike. Most manufacturers now offer brands of "competition" line which are generally recognizable by their diameters. A pole angler should not use a line thinner than 8/100, unless it happens to be his favorite thickness.

To make a good line, it is important to adhere strictly to basic principles. Lines made of one piece of nylon, from tip to the hook are rare and are reserved for fishing for bleak or for stalking chub. Otherwise, it is better to opt for a line and a drop, the diameter of which must be smaller than that of the main line. Plan for a 2/100 difference as a general rule, except in the case of diameters of less than 10/100, when the difference can be 1/100. To attach the line to the tip, the simplest way is to make a loop which is tied into a special tip-end, called Ivo, made by the Italian firm of Stonfo.

By sliding back the collar, you can attach or change a line in a fraction of a second and best of all this does not damage the nylon in the slightest! To tie the line and the drop together, the simplest way is to add another loop to the line and drop line. You can then pass the drop line loop through the line loop. The knot is easy to undo, for instance, if you want to change the drop line. The best anglers trust this system which enables them to prepare the line and the drop line separately. The lines are stored wound around plastic spools (make sure the spool is large enough to hold the length of line and protect the float). Drop lines are stored on cards or in special boxes.

How to attach the line

sliding ring

△ *Stonfo's Ivo system.*

△ ▷ *The 18/100 is only suitable for the largest coarse fish.*

• The floats

A float for pole-fishing usually consists of three components: the antenna which varies in length,

ELASTICATED TIPS

Elasticated tips are commonly used in areas where pole-fishing is popular. The elastic used to be attached to a hook-shaped tip end, but nowadays it has become an integral part of the tip, on which it plays the role of shock-absorber.

Without doing anything to change the composition of the line, it reduces risk when hooking a large fish – or limits the adverse effect of an excessively powerful strike! It is indispensable when using a sectioned pole, especially if the fish is relatively powerful. The elastic may be replaced with a flexible tip for small fish or when using a telescopic pole, which is more flexible than a classic sectioned pole.

Tackle stores and mail order sources sell tips of various strengths, as well as special tip ends, which are fixed inside the tip and guarantee to hold the elastic securely.

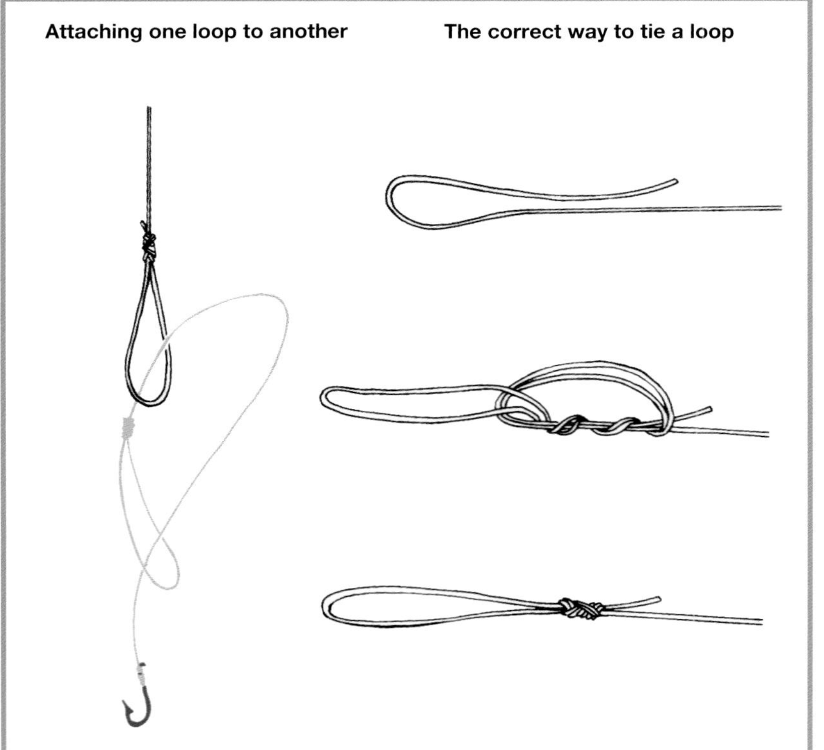

the top end, which is frequently colored, and is the only part sticking out of the water during angling, and the body. The body of the float can be of various shapes and the keel may vary in length, the antenna extending downward to give it more stability.

The float is attached to the line by small eyelets through which the line slides freely. They are generally located on the body of the float or below the keel). Small plastic rings are slipped over the line which, once in place, stop the float from sliding up or down on the line, and enabling you to position the float precisely.

The choice of the right float for pole-fishing is made essentially on the basis of prevailing fishing conditions. First there is the water to consider, where the strength of the current and the depth are major considerations, but weather conditions, the amount of wind for instance, are also factors that must be taken into account.

– The carrot float

The carrot float is by far the most common and most popular float. It is cylindrical, tapering toward the bottom like a carrot. The carrot float is also the most versatile since it makes it possible to deal with just about any situation. Since carrot floats are generally small, they are excellent for fishing for small fry on the surface.

– The stick float

The longer and larger carrot floats are called stick floats. They are best suited to deeper fishing positions for bigger fish. Although stick floats are very useful in the calm waters of ponds and canals, and on windless days in more open water, but their disadvantages are soon revealed when the wind gets up. As soon as it starts to blow hard, a carrot float will keel over or sink in the current, making it extremely difficult to detect a bite, and thus negating the whole point of using a float in the first place.

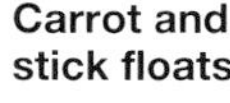

Carrot and stick floats

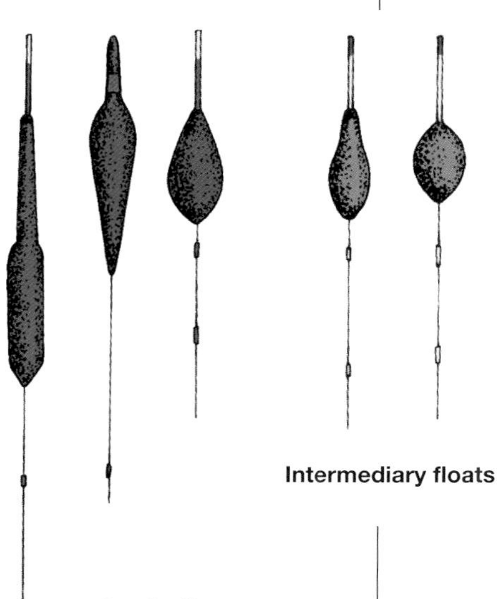

Stocky floats

Intermediary floats

△ *For coarse-fishing in its widest sense and for catching small fish, telescopic poles are the perfect solution.*

– Thicker floats and wagglers

Thicker-bodied floats, such as the Avon, are known for their stability and their capacity to hold a large amount of lead shotting. They generally have a long antenna and keel, and exhibit exceptional sensitivity without being overly influenced by the outside environment. They are marvellous for fishing in rivers on windy days. Those with the longest antennae are often known as wagglers from the way in which they bob about on the surface of the water.

– Intermediary shapes

Between carrot and stick and the waggler-type floats there are quite a few intermediary shapes of float. These are normally teardrop- or pear-shaped and may look topsy-turvy (in other words, the fat end is at the top). These floats generally offer a good compromise between stability and sensitivity. If they have a long keel, they hold up well in the wind, current, and waves (on navigable waterways and canals for example). They are useful for catching particularly tricky customers or large fish that lurk near the bottom.

The shape, size, and brand of float determine its buoyancy, that is to say, the weight it can

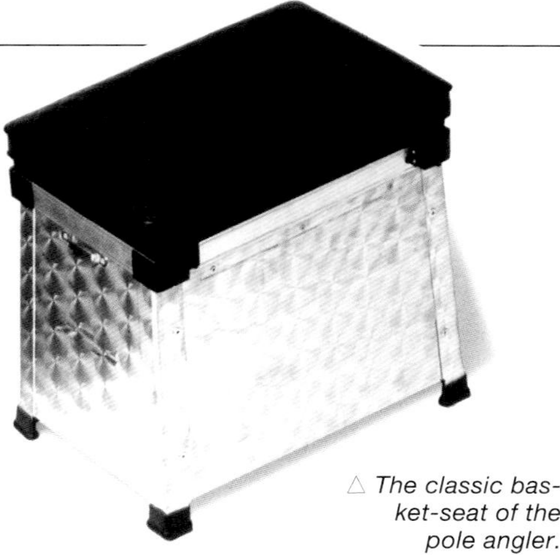

△ *The classic basket-seat of the pole angler.*

support before sinking. These features are generally marked on the body of good-quality floats, and may be given in grams or a reference number may be used for the weight (which is generally shaped like an Arlesley bomb or an olivette).

• Shots and shotting

– *Spherical lead shot*

The most common weights are lead shot which are split to facilitate their fixing on the line. The smallest shot is known as dust shot. All shot must be carefully split so that it is perfectly centered on the line. Use a pair of pliers to squeeze the lead around the line, ensuring the line passes exactly through the middle of the shot to retain the balance of the line. Lead shot is numbered from 13

◁ *Unhooking a beautiful tench caught on a floating line.*

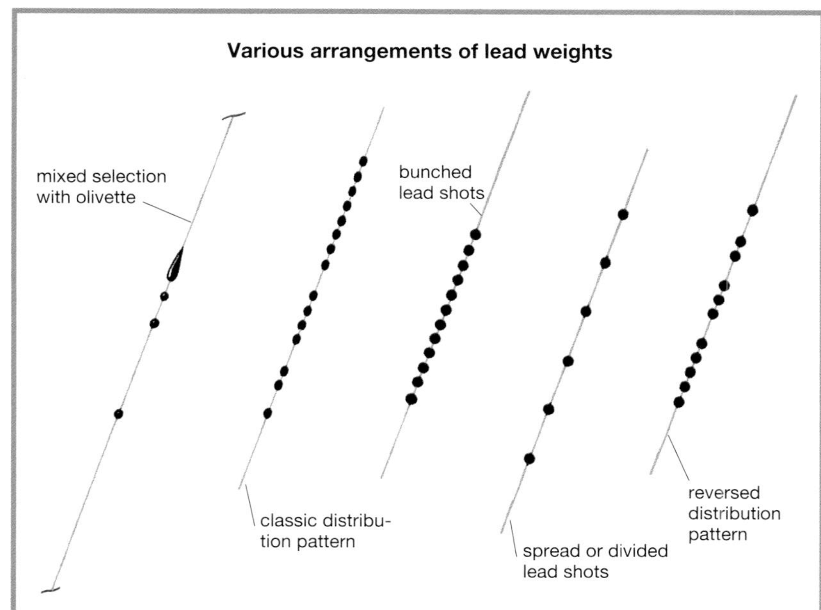

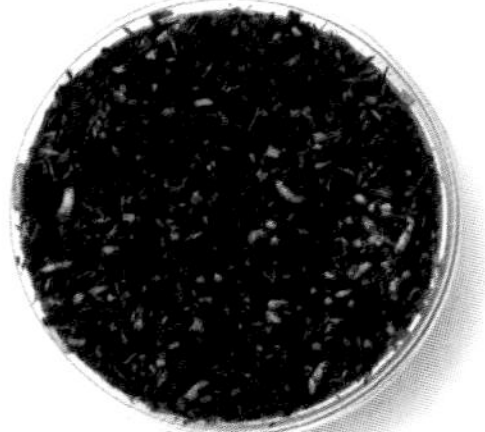

△ *Colored maggots. The bream, in particular is very sensitive to the attraction of a variety of colors.*

(0.009 g) to 5/0 (1.08 g) and is sold in assorted weights and sizes in boxes, or in small tubes containing a single weight of shot. There are a large number of types and shapes of shot which reflect their size and appearance, from dust shot through mouse-droppings (!), to...

– *Cylindrical leads*

Another type of sinker favored by anglers when pole-fishing, are the cylindrical lead weights, the best known of which are made by Styl. These are also split and must be squeezed carefully around the line, using a special pair of flat-tipped pliers. The shape is more streamlined than that of the spherical leads, and they have a following of ardent enthusiasts. They are sold in boxes.

– *Olivettes*

The olivette is a larger lead weight with a central channel to enable it to slide up and down on the line. It is stopped with a split shot, a knot, or a piece of silicone tubing. It is the prime example of a heavy sinker. It is important to get the weights arranged in an even pattern on the line. Bunched split shots will make the line sink rapidly, especially if they are near the drop and hook, but they are useful in fast-flowing waters where the bait must drop quickly to the right depth and also when dealing with very active fish or when fishing in deep waters.

The more spread out the shot pattern, the slower the descent. This is perfect in calm waters and if the fish are finicky. There are anglers who prefer to use a reverse pattern, in other words, they arrange the shot in decreasing size up the line, in order to get a really slow descent. This makes it possible to explore the water at various depths.

Due to the danger of lead poisoning, shot made from lead substitute is now available. In the United Kingdom, the Control Pollution (Anglers' Lead Weights) Regulations 1986 has made it illegal to import or sell any lead weights weighing less than 0.06 g and more than 28.35 g. Lead may still be used for the core of the line, for swimfeeders, self-cocking floats and flies.

• The hooks

Hooks for pole-fishing are almost always single hooks. They consist of a shank with a spade end at the top (less often with a notch or an eye) which is used to hold the whipping on the shank so as to attach it to the bottom line; the bend is dependent upon the width of the throat and therefore the size of the hook (the larger the hook, the lower the number, although the manufacturers cannot agree on a single coding system). The point may be barbed with a tiny backward-facing point that penetrates the flesh of the fish on striking and prevents the hook from falling out. The gauge of the metal forming the hook also varies. Fine gauge hooks are small and light, suitable for holding fragile bait and for difficult techniques. Medium- and heavy-gauge hooks weigh more but have the advantage of being more robust. Even the color of the hook is important because it enables you to match the hook to the color of the bait being used. You have a choice between copper, gold, silver (nickel), red, blue, and black.

Barbed hook. ▷

Barbless hook. ▷

GROUNDBAIT

Manufacturers sell thousands of tons of ready-to-use groundbait every year. However, judging by the reaction of the majority of anglers, the subject of groundbait remains shrouded in mystery! Good anglers, especially champions, are suspected of having recipes which they jealously guard as a deadly secret. Furthermore, they are believed to know the secret of adding miraculous powders which are solely responsible for attracting the fish.

• Ready-to-use groundbait

Champion pole anglers, scientists, and manufacturers of bait have long been working together, putting all their ingenuity and creativity into devising the best groundbait formulas for anglers. Manufacturers now take great care in choosing and measuring the ingredients and are making use of the latest scientific discoveries as regards the diet of coarse fish, in order to improve the quality of their products and make their mixes even more attractive to the fish. Ready-to-use groundbait usually consists of a mixture of ingredients, chosen for their effectiveness, but they are not necessarily easy to get hold of and they are often difficult to store in optimum conditions and to keep fresh. An angler resorting to these ready-made mixtures will find he is required to use a different product for almost every type of coarse fish tackled! Despite the expense, how can one resist the time-saving aspect of using a ready-made product? Instead of spending hours slaving away to get the mixture just right, all you have to do is open the bag and prepare the wet mix by following the manufacturer's instructions.

Several of the knots used to attach the hook to the bottom line

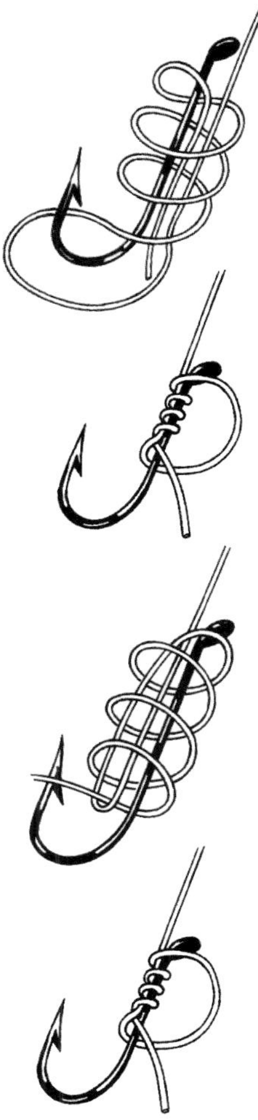

△ *A special 'coarse fish' groundbait.*

ROAMING

Coarse pole-fishing does not mean sitting stock still for hours on end. By roaming, you can also go out to find the fish while discovering many varied positions. The catches are most likely to be chub, rudd, and dace, as well as tench, small carp, bleak, and roach. The best equipment for the purpose is a 13 to 16 ft (4 to 5 m) ringed pole. The line should be the standard 16/100 nylon line with a buoyant, stick-type float. Consider spreading the weight pattern of shot along the line, as this will help make the descent gradual and will allow the bait to move more easily along the bottom if necessary.

Wear a shoulder-bag of the type shown opposite for small items of tackle, extra line, and cans of bait, and so on.

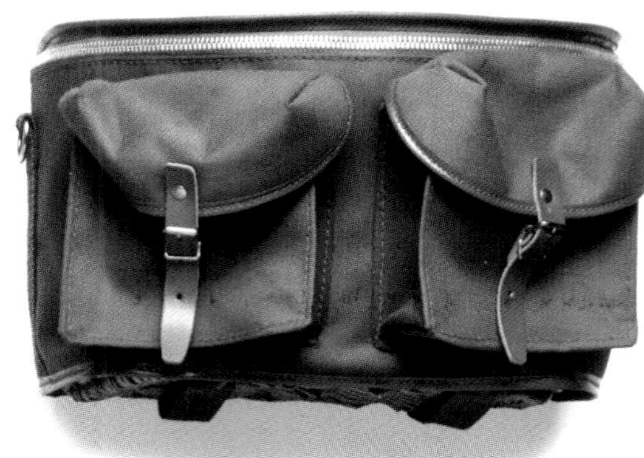

△ *Bag suitable for the roaming angler.*

With a few exceptions, such as inexpensive groundbait aimed at coarse fish in general, without any particular fish being specified, most of the store-bought and mail order baits are strictly targeted and accompanied with clear instructions and advice. This enables the angler, even the beginner, to sort it out quickly and to use his bait to the best possible advantage.

– *Light, surface baits*

These are designed for fishing for bleak and small fish near the surface of rivers or in lakes.

△ Groundbait plays a vital role in pole-fishing. The aim is to attract fish to the spot at which the angler wants to practice his skills!

A package of groundbait created especially for bream. ▷

– *Bait for small fry*

They are versatile mixtures aimed at the sort of fish which end up most frequently in keep-nets (roach, bream, rudd, etc.). They are suitable for rivers as well as lakes at whatever depth you choose. It all depends on the wetness of the mix (if it is very wet it will stay near the surface) and the firmness of the balls (the firmer they are, the more likely they are to sink to the bottom).

– *Groundbait for large fish*

These differ in their size and the choice of ingredients, which are primarily destined for bottom-fishing, where the largest fish normally lurk. It is important to make an informed choice of groundbait by first carefully reading the manufacturer's recommendations. Some groundbaits are indeed specifically made for river, pond, canal or long distance fishing, amongst others.

Spreading groundbait

• Home-made groundbait

If you prefer making your own mixtures, if only for the pleasure of it, some precautions are necessary. The quality of a groundbait clearly depends on its ingredients and the proportion in which they are used, but there is more to it than that. The quality of the ingredients themselves, especially the freshness, is also extremely important. Try and get in fresh ingredients on a regular basis, rather than making a large batch and storing it for a long time, with the exception of seeds and grain which can be ground up as required.

To spread the groundbait correctly

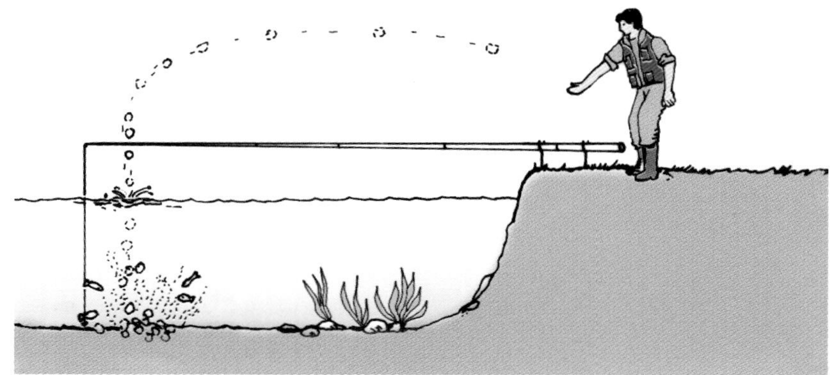

• Method

– Wetting

Wetting is an important stage in home-made groundbaits. It must be done gradually, through continuous and prolonged mixing in a large bowl. Do not forget that many ingredients, especially bread crumbs, take a certain amount of time to absorb water and swell up.

– Sifting

The final operation prior to groundbaiting is to sift the mixture, in order to eliminate any impurities as well as break up the lumps. The gauge of the mesh in the sieve must be appropriate for the fish targeted – large mesh for big fish so that the groundbait consists of large granules, fine mesh for small fry, producing fine groundbait.

– To spread the groundbait correctly

The next problem is how best to spread the groundbait. For surface fishing, there are two options. You can either wet the groundbait excessively to produce a sort of soup that will hang around like a cloud, or make it drier than you would normally so that it is well aerated and breaks up as it hits the surface. For classic coarse fishing, where the groundbait is needed half-way down or near the bottom, the paste balls should not be too tightly compacted. For fishing in deep waters to catch large fish, prepare large balls, that are very compact so that they descend quickly to the right level and take time to break up.

Finally, the timing for groundbaiting is all-important. For small fish, you must throw the groundbait in small quantities but do so frequently if you want to keep the fish hanging around your fishing position.

For large fish, on the other hand, it is best to strew the groundbait generously and in large quantities right from the start, followed up with well-spaced, regular, and discreet top ups, composed mainly of pure bait.

△ *Groundbait for bleak.*

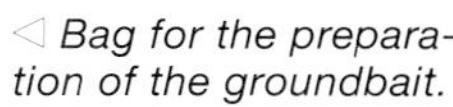

◁ *Bag for the preparation of the groundbait.*

A groundbait bucket is very useful for making your own groundbait mixtures. ▷

◁ Apron for fishing a position.

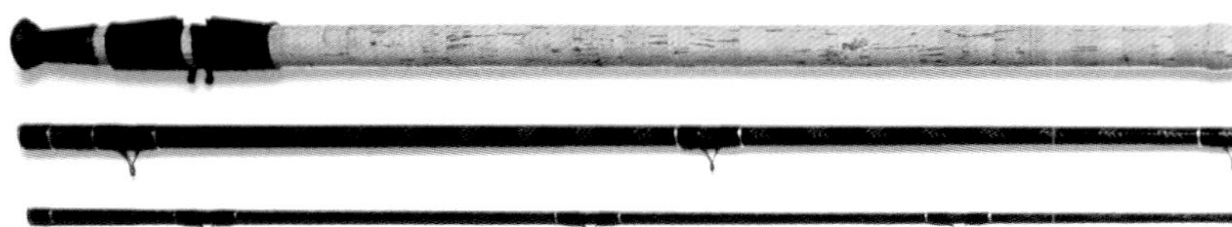

△ Classic British rod with flexible tip.

REEL-FISHING

British anglers in the 1970s inspired European fishermen to use a reel and line, and this technique has been adopted extremely quickly over the last ten years.
At first, the British technique, which used a float, was preferred throughout Europe, but gradually more sophisticated techniques for drop-fishing emerged.
At the same time, the Italians set a trend in fishing a position with a reel, using the "Bolognese" technique which was much closer to the traditional technique using a long run, which is still used by anglers fishing for trout and all those who are keen on white waters and roaming.

Drifting groundbait

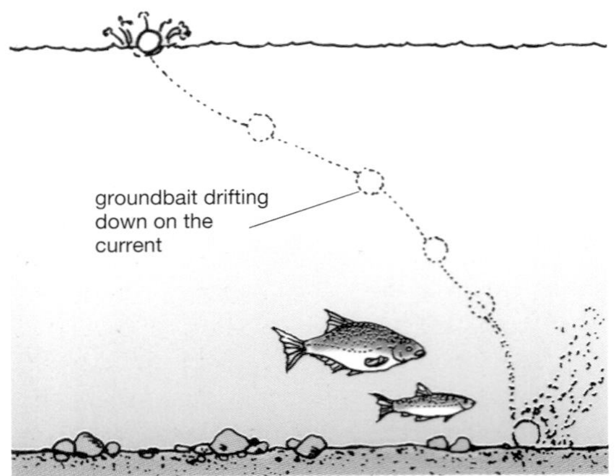

FIXED-SPOOL REEL FISHING

The fixed-spool reel is an English invention, first patented by Alfred Illingworth in 1905. Nowadays, the British make excellent fixed-spool reels with the popular slipping clutch, but equally good models are manufactured in Sweden and France.
Spinning rods with fixed-spool reels are known as English rods on the Continent. They are around 13 ft (4 m) in length, and are now available in different styles adapted to the various types of fishing techniques. They all share careful construction and manufacture and are generally made of carbon fiber in most cases, a lightweight material (because they have to be handled for hours on end) and the rod has numerous rings, well offset so that the line does not stick to the rod.
Rods used for fishing on the drop also have a device for attaching a special tip. This tip may be a swing-tip (articulated) or the quiver-tip (a small, very sensitive tip), which is attached either to the top ring with a thread, or directly to the top section of the rod (for the quiver tip).
Rods for fishing with a feeder are equipped with a more powerful tip, which is especially designed for casting and retrieving a feeder filled with groundbait and bait.

BOLOGNESE FISHING

Rods for the Bolognese technique are also made of carbon fiber and are telescopic to facilitate storage and transport. The length of the most popular of these rods varies

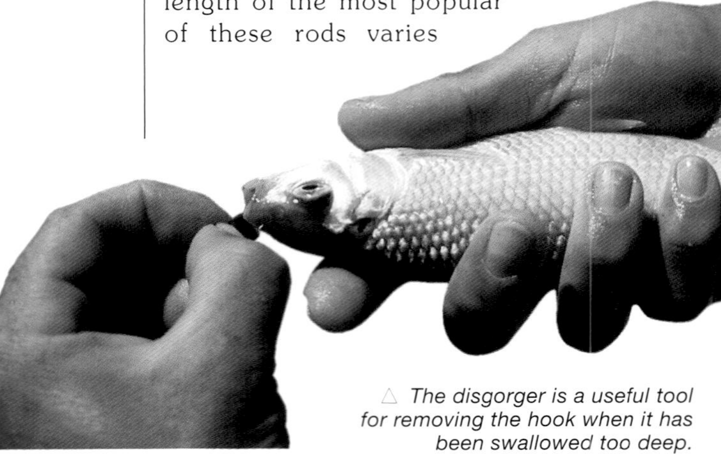

△ The disgorger is a useful tool for removing the hook when it has been swallowed too deep.

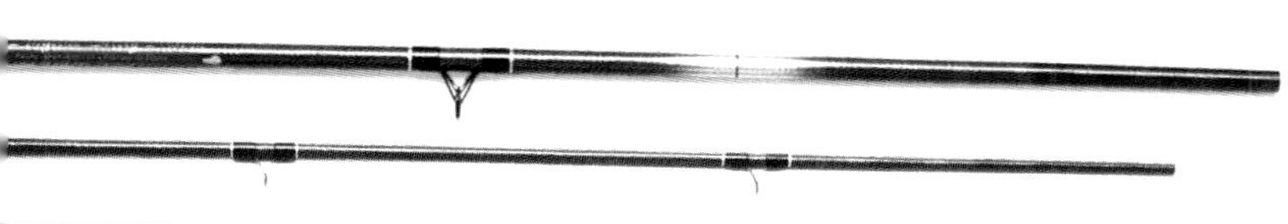

between 20 through 26 feet (6 through 8 m). The rod is suitable for all fishing conditions. The Bolognese rods do not generally have a separate handle, but the butt-end of the rod is sometimes reinforced where the hands grip it. The reel is firmly attached to the rod, generally at a distance from the butt-end about equal to the length of the forearm. The rings are light and raised, and whipped at the end of each section. There are more rings toward the tip and these are adjustable so as to achieve the best distance for holding the line tight. Arcing actions suit fishing for small fry, whereas a straight pull is required when river-fishing for big fish.

Beautiful rudd caught using the spinning rod technique. ▷

A well-made fixed-spool reel, such as this one, is suitable for spinning rod and Bolognese techniques, since it is light enough to balance the rod properly. ▽

Tackle is sometimes very specific to the type of fish

• The lines

The lines suited to the so-called Bolognese technique are the same as those used for fishing a position. When fishing in good conditions, you should make sure that the line floats well (even to the point of greasing it), in order to keep it under control without experiencing any difficulties when striking.

On the other hand, when using a spinning rod with a fixed-spool reel, the line needs to have been specially treated for sinking rapidly. The specific products offered by most of the main brands purposely provide reduced elasticity, to get a faster response and above all to have better control when striking from a distance. The low friction which this surface treatment produces makes it possible to cast further for the same amount of effort.

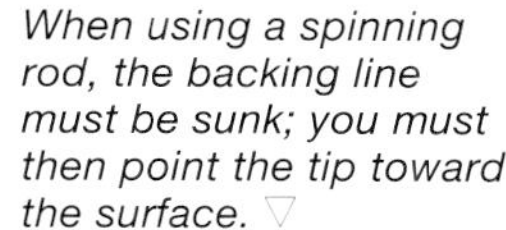

When using a spinning rod, the backing line must be sunk; you must then point the tip toward the surface. ▽

• The reels

Regardless of the technique used, the reels for fishing a position must have been designed, above all, for using with fine lines suitable for coarse fishing. The quality of the clutch is absolutely vital. It must be sufficiently sensitive and gradual to allow for precision adjustment. This precaution is basic when you consider the thinness of the lines.

Another interesting feature of the Bolognese method is the way that it enables you to change the spool rapidly, so that you can handle any situations that arise while fishing.

When it comes to reels used with spinning rods in the British fashion, the experts are of two minds as to which type of reel is best. On the one hand, the closed-faced reel, in which the spool and the line are protected from the wind by the casing considerably reduce the chances of snagging or kinking when using thin lines. On the other hand, the traditional fixed-spool reel, with its reduced friction, allows you to cast further without having to use excessive force on the rod. Thanks to the quality of modern reels and lines, the risks of snagging and kinking are greatly re-

CASTING CORRECTLY

Bring the rod to the vertical position above the head or shoulder, and whip toward the fishing area using a generous gesture. To relocate the area in which you spread the groundbait more than 50 ft (15 m) away, aim toward a fixed spot (such as a house or tree) on the opposite bank. Don't worry about overshooting the area. That way, you won't frighten the fish and it is easy to come back to the right distance by using a small trick. When you first throw the groundbait, mark the line with a felt-tip marker pen or white correcting fluid. Then after each cast, all you have to do is retrieve the line until the mark reaches the ring or the section you used to check the length. When using the "Bolognese" technique, the casting movement is the same, but because of the length and the relative fragility of the rod, you need to use less power when whipping.

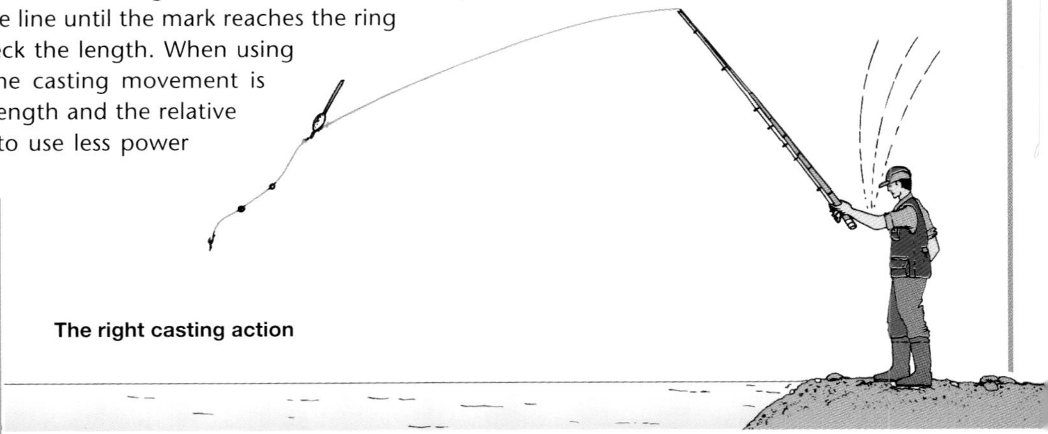

The right casting action

Controlling the line with your finger as you pay it out enables you to be as accurate as possible. ▽

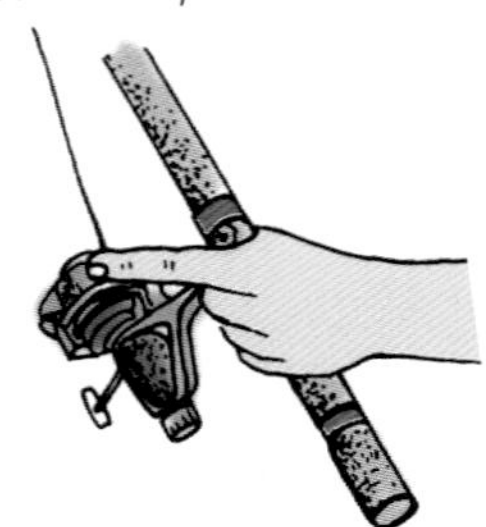

duced, so it has to be admitted that those who favor the traditional fixed-spool reel are becoming more and more numerous.

• **Floats**

The same types of float that are used for pole-fishing are also suitable for the Bolognese technique. As for the fixed-spool reel and spinning rod technique, the so-called British technique, specific shapes and types of float can be bought in the stores or by mail order.

– *The "straight antenna" types*

Shapes similar to the spinning-top and the carrot, which are used by pole-anglers, are recommended for good weather and stretches of water on which there is no surface drift. Their use is nevertheless limited to fishing small fish at short distances.

– *Wagglers*

These can support a fair weight and allow for powerful casting while remaining very sensitive; on the other hand, they are more difficult to use in windy conditions and in the current. The bulbous ones, which are round at the base, are more stable and are suitable for fishing in a strong current or on windy days.

– *Stick floats*

These are very hydrodynamic and buoyant, and are at their best in rivers, when fishing close to long runs, at short or medium distance.

– *The Avon float*

The stocky body of this float makes it extremely flexible for river-fishing, where it works wonders in eddies and rough spots. As the name implies, it is of British manufacture.

Floats for the "Bolognese" technique

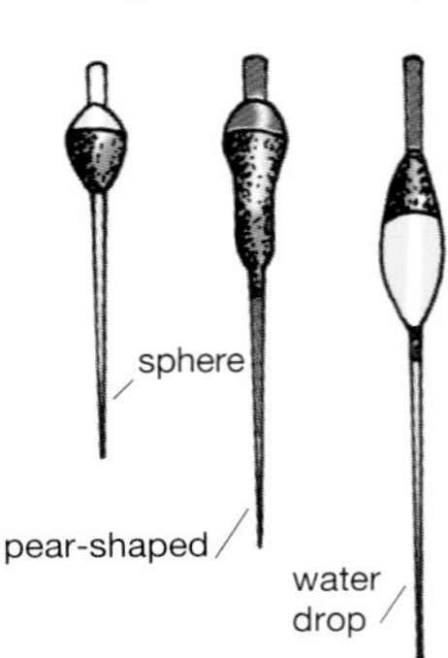

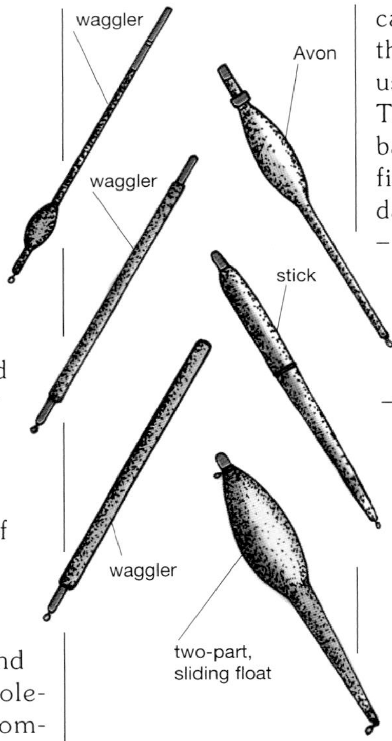

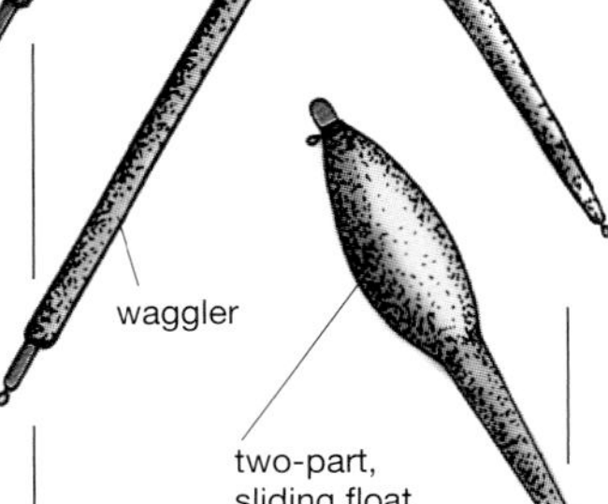

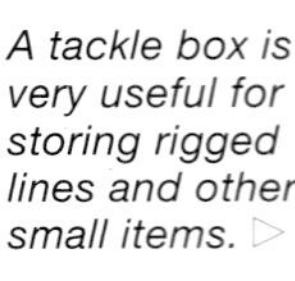

Floats for the British technique

A tackle box is very useful for storing rigged lines and other small items. ▷

• Lead weights

Like the lead shot used for pole-fishing, the weights used with spinning rods are spherical and made of a material soft enough to be tightened easily and removed or loosened without damaging the line. They are only available in a few sizes. They may be sold in boxes all of the same size or, as happens more and more often, in boxes of assorted sizes.

• Feeders

Most feeders are cylindrical and made of plastic. They are about 2–2¾ in (5 to 7 cm) long for a diameter of 1⅛ in to 1¼ in (25 to 45 mm). They are used more and more frequently for fish on the drop, such as small carp, bream, or barbel, particularly in wide rivers or on very large lakes. The feeders are closed at both ends, but have lots of small holes punched in them so that the fish can get at the bait. They are usually designed to be filled with a small quantity of groundbait (preferably a very coarse mixture) or with bait (maggots, seeds, or grain for example). They are attached to a link at about 4 in (10 cm) from the hook, and serve the purpose of semi-automatic groundbaiting that will attract the fish, even if you are fishing in the current or changing position regularly, as in roaming or trolling.

swivel
anti-kink
14/100 to 16/100 main line
sliding bead
feeder
12/100 to 14/100 bottom line 20–28 in (50 to 80 cm)
no. 14 to 16 hook
breaking strand 2 in (5 cm) long

Rig for fishing on the drop using a feeder

◁ Frenchman Philippe Jean, world pole-fishing champion, Finland, 1995.

THE QUIVER-TIP

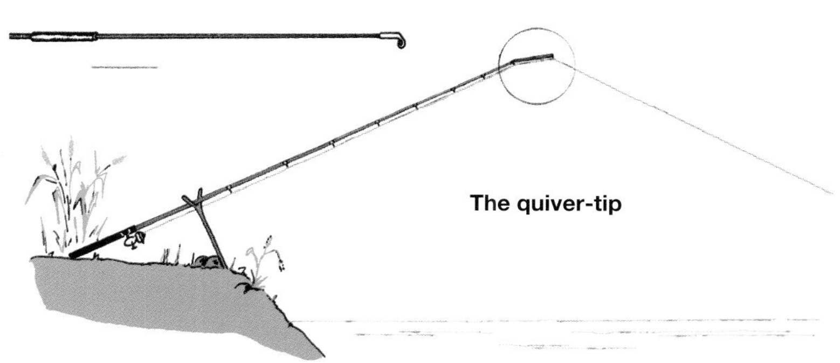

The quiver-tip

Pole-fishing on the drop relies essentially on the efficiency of the bite-indicators, such as the quiver-tip and swing-tip.

• The quiver-tip is the most popular nowadays. When the fish bites, it reacts with vibrations that can be more or less amplified. To help with the observation, there are now some pale-colored graduated cards which are positioned behind the quiver-tip. The rod is then placed parallel to the river, the tip pointing to the surface when the water is calm or slightly upward in fast-flowing current.

• The swing-tip looks like an articulated arm. It must be rigged so that it hangs about halfway up its range. When the fish bites, it will rise to the horizontal or drop to the vertical. The swing-tip is more sensitive than the quiver-tip but it is strictly for use in calm water and on windless days. If you have to deal with current and wind, you should opt for the quiver-tip.

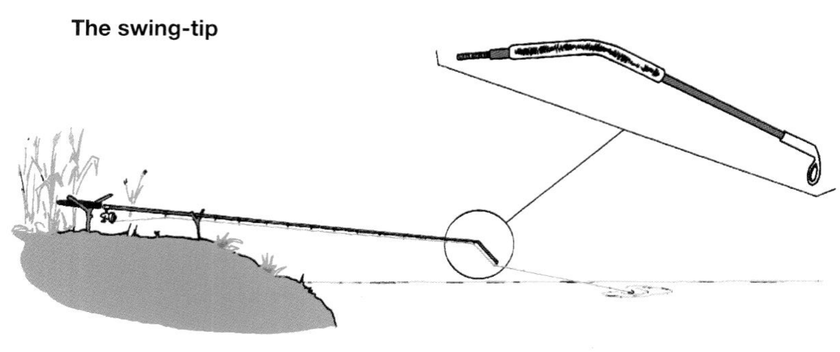

The swing-tip

THE CATCH

ROACH

*Roach (*Rutilus rutilus*) are something of a cult with anglers, despite the fact that it is one of the commonest European freshwater fish. Roach are attracted by most animal or vegetable bait and are quite easy to catch. They are thus a particularly good target for novice anglers. Whatever your favorite technique, try it out on this popular catch.*

Roach can be differentiated from the closely related rudd by different clues. One is the position of their dorsal fin, which is exactly in line with their pelvic fins. ▽

THE POPULAR FISH

Roach are fully fledged members of the Cyprinidae family, and one of Europe's most typical coarse fish. The body, covered in shiny scales, is easily recognizable. The fins are brownish, sometimes with a tinge of red on the pelvic and caudal fins. The rather tapered body is quite variable in shape, due to frequent and repeated cross-breeding with rudd or bream. Originally, the "true" roach may have been rather longer, unlike rudd and the cross-breeds that can be distinguished by a more rounded back.

The roach's back is quite dark in color, shading from a very deep brown to a pale greenish-blue. The lower part of the body and the belly are lighter, almost white in color.

In the spawning season (May through July), the male displays white nuptial tubercles that cover the head and part of the body.

The female lays as many as 100,000 eggs. She spawns among waterweed in very shallow waters. Weedy margins and thickly vegetated waters are the favorite breeding grounds in rivers. The bottom of ponds, bankside shelves, reed beds, and shoals in pools are also popular.

Once the eggs have been fertilized, incubation lasts from 10 through 20 days, before the fry hatch. Growth is relatively slow. A young roach will only be 4 inches (10 cm) long by the time it is two years old. However, the fish does not stop growing in adulthood. Record fish even exceed 16 inches (40 cm) and weigh in at 4 lb 8 oz (2 kg).

THE BEST BAIT

When it comes to food, roach have catholic tastes. They are completely omnivorous, and are happy to munch on the young shoots of aquatic plants, seeds, grain, insect larvae, and worms of every kind, and even insects, whether they are water-dwellers or whether they have fallen from waterside vegetation.

The following is a non-comprehensive list of the most effective baits for roach. Many of these can be used for most coarse fish.

THE BEST TIMES OF YEAR FOR FISHING FOR ROACH

- Roach are sluggish in the winter. At times of flooding, fish a river, because chances are limited in pools and ponds.
- Spring is excellent, because roach have to get their strength back after winter and build up reserves for the spawning season. Fishing prospects are better in small pools and canals, which warm up quicker after the winter frosts.
- Summer is also a very good time. This is the most intense period of activity for roach. Fishing prospects still seem best in rivers, canals (except during heat-waves) and deep pools. Ponds are frequently choked with weeds which causes them to overheat in summer, and this makes them less promising.
- Fall is more of a gamble, due to unpredictable weather conditions. Fishing prospects are still good in canals and rivers, however, where the best roach are often caught.

• Grains of wheat

Because wheat has a rather neutral flavor and scent, it readily tolerates the addition of flavoring, either directly added to the cooking water, or before soaking. For hook-baiting, use no. 12 to no. 16 hooks, golden, crystal, or round, with a medium or long shank. To do the job properly, choose a brand new swim, and ground-bait one or two days beforehand as a preliminary. Then make provision for loosefeeding every ten minutes or so. The best time for using wheat is from early June through late September.

△ Grain of wheat.

• Corn

Canned corn kernels, baby corn-on-the cob are undoubtedly the most popular of all the vegetable baits. They're easy to store (baby corn will keep for 10 days in the refrigerator) and are ready for use. Corn makes excellent bait for large coarse fish, and is increasingly popular, particularly when using a reel. As with all cereals, corn is best during warm weather, but if you're willing to feed at regular intervals, you can use it throughout the year.

• Bread

The best bread for fishing is undoubtedly whole-wheat bread. It is unquestionably firmer and thus stays on the hook better. Angling stores also stock special bread for fishing, which retains its shape and texture for a very long time.
Small lumps of bread, crusts removed, are one of the most versatile baits. Bread is an excellent lure for all members of the Cyprinidae family throughout the year, with a preference for the summer months.

△ Bread cube.

△ Bread lump.

• Pasta

With fishing in mind, angling stores sell specially shaped noodles that won't fall off the hook (two sizes are available, sizes 1 and 2). A small hole is pierced through the center enabling it to be fixed to the hook more easily. There are also pasta types called "heavy pasta", which are round and have no hole. They should only be cooked until they are "al dente", which is relatively firm.
To stop them sticking together, add a drop of hemp-seed oil to flavor them, or some cornmeal. The tiny particles of cornmeal bond around the pasta, and then spread the loosefeed all around when they break up on contact with the water.

• Maggots

Maggots are now sold at fishing tackle stores, and increasingly in refrigerated vending machines. They are actually bluebottle larvae, bred on dead meat. For some time, maggot breeders have concentrated on breeding different varieties of maggots, suited to the varying needs of anglers.

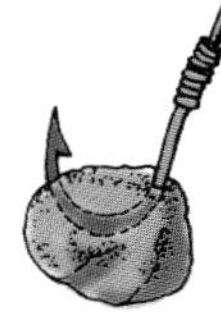
△ Bread crumbs.

– Jokers

As might be expected, these are the smallest: they have a slim, hard, ringed body not unlike that of a bloodworm, mainly because of the red coloring they are given.

– Pinkies

They look like small maggots in shape, but with a slightly darker shade of pink. Pinkies are particularly active, and the ideal bait for small fry. They are gradually replacing jokers in popularity. Most importantly, they are an ideal solution for ground-baiting. All you have to do is add a few handfuls to the mixture you are using, and any fish go wild for the maggots!
Again for ground-baiting, it is also possible to use broods of maggots, that are known as spats. These consist of thousands of tiny maggots, harvested very early in their development.

△ Maggot.

△ A cluster of maggots.

– Traditional maggots

Nor should the most popular bait of all be forgotten. Both pole-anglers and those who like spinning rods have created a great demand for the standard maggot which is a truly general purpose bait, since all fish are attracted to it. Maggots are used for catching the finest specimens.

– Gozzers

These are very large maggots, which are heavier and plumper than the standard maggot. They are the favorite bait for reel-fishing, because they will truly attract the finest fish. Gozzers lend themselves readily to baiting by catapult, because they are more compact than ordinary maggots. However, they are difficult to store. They can only be refrigerated for a few days at the most and there must be no movement as this might stir them up and hasten their transformation into flies.

– *Jokers*

Jokers are the young of flies in the bluebottle family which lay their eggs in the dark. They are even larger than gozzers. They are hard to obtain, and very tricky to handle.

– *Casters*

Casters are particularly popular with reel-fishermen. Casters are actually maggots in the pupal stage of development. They are very effective on large fish, although not all are good for fishing. Some sink, others don't. To be absolutely sure they will sink, place them in a bowl and discard all those that stay on the surface. Angling stores and mail-order companies deliver them in a water-filled container.

• Bloodworms

When they say bloodworm, anglers actually mean the larvae of various winged insects. Bloodworms are members of the Chironomus and Glypotendipes families. They have a more or less translucent body, which is often colored with a ruddy pigment, making them an attractive ruby red. They are harvested with a fine mesh sieve from mud in quiet reaches of rivers or in pools. They are most likely to be found downstream of minor sources of organic pollution, such as villages, sewerage outlets, and so forth. Smaller bloodworm are used for ground-baiting, while the larger ones are reserved for hook-bait.

Angler with traditional tackle. ▷

◁ *Two hook-baits for bloodworm on a no. 18 to no. 24 very fine gauge hook.*

From the point of view of roach or most coarse fish, this is undoubtedly one of the most appetizing baits around.

POLE-FISHING WITH A FLOAT LINE

The most typical fishing for roach is in a swim, in a fixed position. Ideally, you need to locate a swim where the bottom is smooth bedded or one that is slightly bowl-shaped. It must be clean, with a sand or gravel bed, rather than mud. If possible, the swim should not be too far from feeding grounds, with water-plants growing near the bank or near shoals.

• Still water fishing

Ponds are excellent after the first signs of spring, and are still worthwhile when summer is on the doorstep, only weeks after the roach have bred. From then on, the build-up of water-plants and the increase in temperature make fishing more of a hit-and-miss business. The best thing then is to move on to larger and deeper lakes

▽ *Teeming maggots, the universal bait!*

Still water fishing

8/100 or 10/100 main line

olivette

locking shot

swan shot

6 in to 12 in (15 to 30 cm) 6.5/100 to 8/100 drop line

such as reservoirs or large natural lakes.

In ponds, start off around banks sheltered from north winds, fishing along the front line of water-plants or close to shoals situated further out in midstream. Then, look out for deeper hiding-places, such as places where aquatic vegetation is growing in 7 to 9 feet (2 to 3 m) of water.

In reservoir lakes, there are two promising types of hide for coarse fish. The first are the outside edges of shallow shelves three to six feet deep (1 to 2 m) where water-plants grow close to inlets. They are excellent in summer because the water is cooler, and in winter because the water is warmer. Always study the topography of river beds carefully. It is often very uneven, especially the slope from the bank, and this could spoil your ground-baiting.

In natural lakes, marginal shelves are good for small roach (1.1 yd (1 m) deep) or medium-sized fish (1.1 to 2.2 yd (1 to 2 m) deep). The finest specimens often keep further out, on the slope leading down to the depths of the lake or on any level sections there may be, often under 4.4 to 5.5 yd (4 to 5 m) of water, or even a little deeper.

• Canal Fishing

Canals are excellent in mid-season and still very good in winter, but are more difficult to deal with in summer. Nuisances such as warm water, an endless stream of boat traffic, and the activity of catfish, sunfish, and stickleback, make coarse fishing just that much less attractive.

Canal beds being by definition very regular, the best hides are often near locks (where the water is churned about), near water-side landing-stages and jetties and, more generally, at any place where there is a break in the regular course of the waterway.

• River Fishing

In running water, roach can be fished throughout the year. The only thing that changes are the hides where they're found. In winter, deep slacks are excellent, near the bank or behind obstructions, and ports, basins and other dead channels, or close to water inlets.

In spring, early water plants and still waters offer the best prospects.

In summer, gravelly bottoms close to currents and waterfalls are perfect, and so are deep pools when there's a heatwave. In Autumn, it's best to fish in deep venues, slacks and quiet reaches when levels are high or the current is strong.

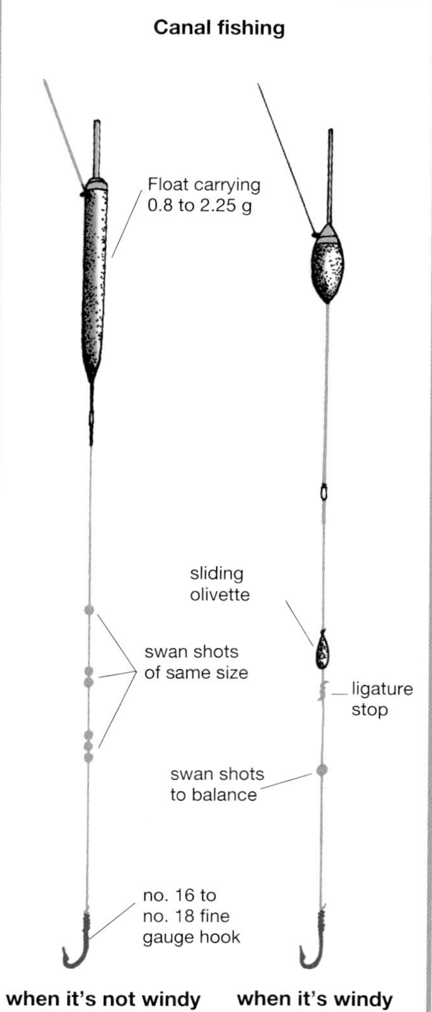

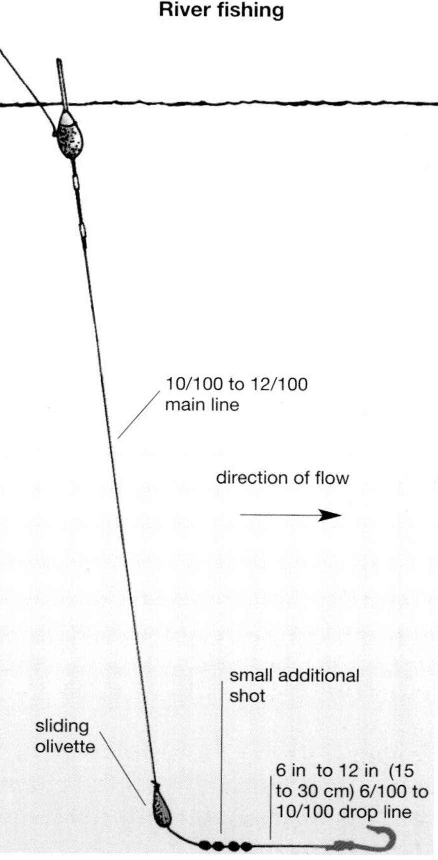

• Finding the depth

The first job you have to do on reaching your hide is to find out the exact depth. You need to attach a very heavy plummet to the end of a line so that you can make two different measurements. First, identify the shape of the river bed and any obstructions that may be present. Second, calculate the exact depth, so that you can adjust your float. Your bait should be positioned between 2 and 4 inches (5 to 10 cm) above the bottom.

• Ground-baiting

After plumbing, begin ground-baiting. If you use a mixture of meal or commercial bait, don't forget to add some of the hook-bait you are using.

Start by initial ground-baiting quite generously (several large balls or handfuls of hook-bait if you use seeds or maggots), at the same spot where you're going to fish. To aim straight, the best idea is to place your rod on its rest and to cast the bait balls slightly to the near side of

STORE-BOUGHT MIXES

Sensas 3000 Big Roach, Van den Eynde Nature, Rameau Plus Roach, Sensas 3000 Bottom, Rameau Plus Bottom, Flash X21 Bottom, Tesse Rameau Ground-bait, Van den Eynde Secret

Sensas 3000 coarse fish ground-bait. △

the tip of the end section. Then when you fish this side of the rod, you will have the benefit of your ground-bait. For running water, increase the binding agent, such as soil, clay, or fullers' earth. Make it up into large balls that are heavy and compact. This way, they'll sink more quickly to the bottom, stay in place, and take time before they break up.

In canals and more generally on silty deposits, you can also use the "carpet of earth" technique perfected by canal anglers in France's Northern regions. Just throw in balls of pure earth before the fishing starts. These form a layer at the bottom of the water, on which your bait will be able to land and do its job, with no risk of it disappearing into the mud, which can be very soft.

After the initial ground-baiting, top up regularly. Use small balls of bait with meal, or a pinch of hook-bait if you are fishing with grains, seeds, or maggots. You could start with initial ground-baiting using a mixture of meal, and then top up exclusively with hook-bait.

• Choice of bait

Generally speaking, meat-based baits such as blood or giblets and creatures such as larvae and worms of every kind are preferable in cold weather and out of season. In contrast, plant-based baits (seeds and grains) are especially effective during the summer months, sometimes prolonged into fall. But maggots, brandling, and bloodworms are so effective that you'll be using them throughout the year.

TWO GROUND-BAITS FOR ROACH

• Recipe for still water fishing:
2 parts dark (rye or whole wheat) bread crumbs, 1 part white bread crumbs, 2 parts rich cookie, 2 parts sticky PV1, 1 part natural copra.

• Recipe for river fishing
3 parts dark (rye or whole-wheat) bread crumbs, 1½ parts sticky PV1, 1½ parts rich cookie, 1 part yellow coloring, 1 part corn cake soaked in warm water, 1 part cooked ground hemp seed, 1 part scalded pigeon droppings, added last.

• Tantalizing movements

While you are fishing, you can increase the number of bites by waving your hook-bait tantalizingly around, to make it more tempting. Fish are attracted by anything that moves in an unusual way. In rivers, the current does the trick, if you hold the line in check slightly for a few seconds. With the force of the current, the hook bait will then lift off the bottom, and then slowly fall back down when it is released. It's often at that point that a bite occurs. For still water fishing, these movements are a little more com-

◁ *Roach abound in European waters, and are the ideal quarry for younger anglers.*

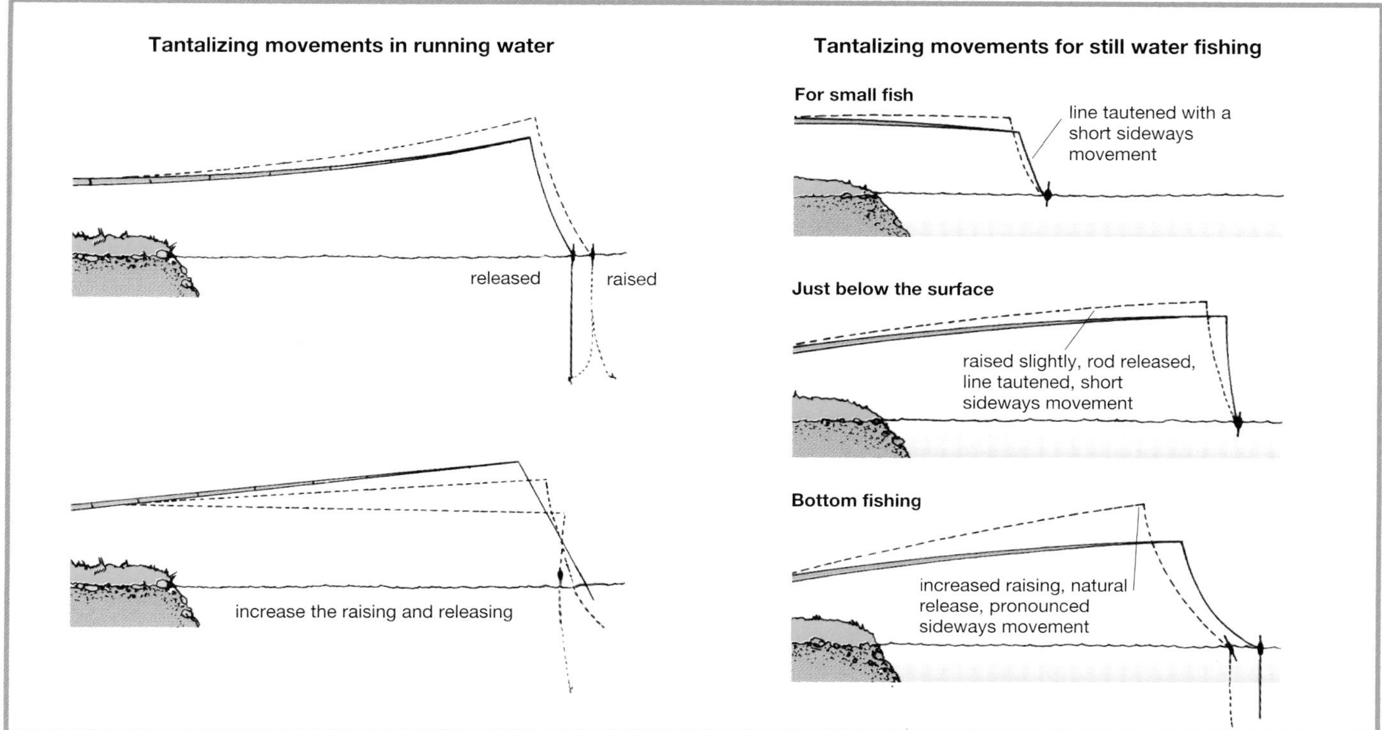

plex, because of the absence of current. You therefore have to combine lateral movements of the float, that are going to increase the field of exploration of your line, with a more vertical movement, that will also lift the hook-bait off the bottom slightly.

HEMPSEED FISHING

"Seed fishing", as it is known to its fans, is often regarded as the best of all fishing methods in a swim for roach and coarse fish in general. You will soon have to admit that hempseed makes for very special fishing. It demands highly specialized techniques, but can produce amazing results throughout the period from early July through the end of September or even later if you are able regularly to ground-bait a swim.

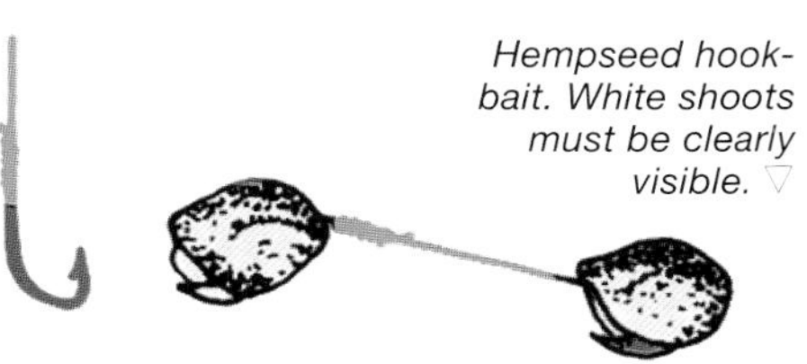

Hempseed hook-bait. White shoots must be clearly visible. ▽

• A highly specialized technique

Whether your rod is telescopic or sectional, it should have a length of between 13 and 24 feet (4 and 7 m), with a flexible tip that will help you to strike.

The line should be 8/100 or 10/100, with a long, tapering, carrot-shaped float for still-water fishing, and a bodied and well-keeled float for choppier waters, a float that will remain upright and buoyant in strong current or waves. The weights must be partially or fully spread out for still-water fishing, but low down on the line and bulky (olivette plus additional swan shot) in fast-flowing waters. The drop line must be short (8–10 inches (20–25 cm)) and thinner by 2/100 than the main line. The hook itself must be a no. 16 or no. 18, round, black, fine gauge, and long-shanked, to make hook-baiting easier, since this is always rather tricky. You need to guide the point inside the husk and bring it out again at the bottom of the seed. This gives you a better chance when you get a strike. Make sure that you ground-bait regularly, throwing in a small pinch each time you cast the line. Don't forget that frequency is always more important than quantity.

Adjust the float so the seed drifts a few inches above the bottom, and be sure to move the bait backward and forward at regular intervals.

HEMPSEED COOKING TECHNIQUES

Hempseed comes from a textile fiber plant used in the manufacture of rope and other strong fabrics. It is sold at any fishing tackle store. Choose the larger and shinier seeds for fishing, and keep the others for ground-baiting. Place about 6 cups (1.5 liters) of seed in 8 cups (2 liters) of water and bring it to the boil. As soon as the seeds start to split and white shoots appear, after 40-50 minutes, stop the cooking by rinsing the seeds under cold running water. This will stop germination and help the germ to be clearly visible.

◁ *Hempseed can be stored in a vacuum pack. This does not adversely affect their ability to germinate.*

◁ *Disgorgers are used to remove a deeply embedded hook.*

Preparing hempseeds

Allow the seeds to swell until they are soft enough to go on the hook and release the unique flavors that will attract fish from quite a distance away. To achieve this, you can choose either to soak them or to cook them.

– *Soaking*

This is the equivalent to what happens in nature when seeds fall into the water by accident. However, soaking is a long and tedious process, and you'll have to be patient for a few days! Soaking may not even be adequate to soften all types of seed, including hemp. The ideal solution is a combination of pre-soaking and cooking. If you soak seeds in water for a day or two first this considerably reduces cooking time.

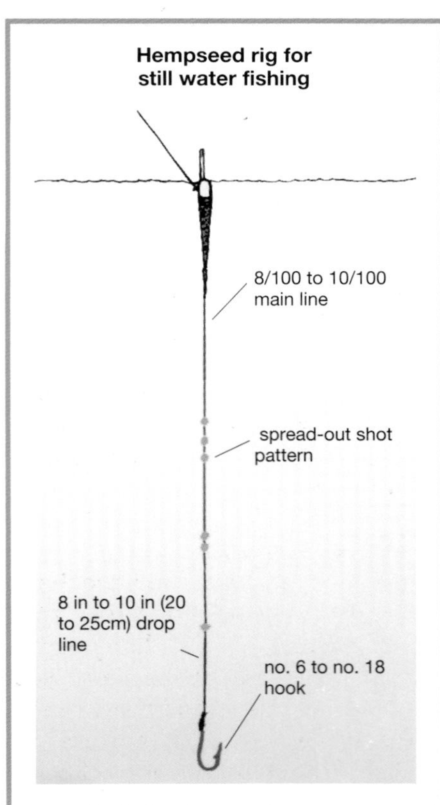

– *Cooking technique*

Don't use metal or aluminum pans. They give the seeds a taste which may be undetectable to humans but which fish find unpleasant and frightens them off. Use glass, heatproof ceramic, non-stick, or enamel cookware and stir with a wooden spoon or spatula. As soon as the water starts to boil, reduce the heat. Keep your eye on the seeds so they only swell and soften. Do not let them actually burst. If you are using seeds other than hemp, stop cooking as soon as the first seeds begin to split. For hemp seeds, rinse them under cold running water as soon as the first shoots appear. Reserve the rinsing water and use it as a broth in which to cook your ground-bait. If you are adding flavoring or fragrance to your seeds, do so a few minutes after cooking stops, while the water is still warm but not too hot, or much of the flavor or fragrance will evaporate.

– *Storage*

Once cooked, seeds do not keep very well, so let them cool until they are perfectly cold. Then refrigerate them and use them within 24 hours. When you are at the water's edge, avoid casting too many seeds at one time. The worst possible thing is to empty any leftover seeds directly into your swim. That is because if there are not enough fish to eat all the seeds within a few hours, the seeds will putrify and pollute the water, so instead of ground-baiting the fish you'll end up poisoning them!

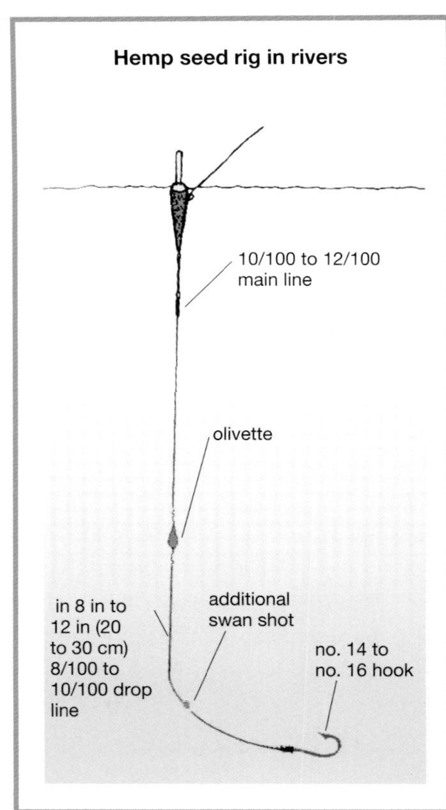

– *Cheese*

A popular bait among British anglers is cheese. It has a strong odor and is easily molded to the hook. Furthermore, it is an inexpensive bait, useful for beginners, as any old piece of "mousetrap" will do, as long as it has not become moldy. All non-predatory fish are attracted to cheese, including roach.

△ *Seed-caught roach ready for the skillet.*

Bream

*Bream (*Abramis brama*), both the large common bream and the smaller white bream (*Blicca bjoerkna*), are one of the most universal fresh water fish in Europe, particularly in large rivers and streams, where they now constitute the predominant species. This poses ecological problems, since larger bream readily devour fish roe, especially in the spawning grounds of other carnivore species. Bream can be found from the British Isles (except Scotland) and Scandinavia to as far south as the Black Sea.*

This is the common bream, which is smaller than the white bream, and found in the same waters. ▽

"Slabs" or "garbage can lids"

The common bream has a very flat body, barely an inch thick. The mouth is very fleshy and telescopic, so that it can stretch out its lips and forage along the bottom in search of the larvae and rotting vegetation that constitute its daily diet.

The dorsal fin is quite small, and is situated to the rear of the protuberance formed by its back. In contrast, the pelvic fin, anal fin, and tail fin are very well developed. The body is covered in tiny scales, themselves protected by a very thick, sticky slime. This slimy coating is often found on the drop line, and at hides frequented by large schools of bream.

The coloring ranges from dark brown on the back to white on the undersides. The flanks have coppery tints on their flanks, that become pronounced as the fish age. They can exceed 6 lb 8 oz (3 kg), with the average fish varying from 14 oz through 3 lb 5 oz (0.4–1.5 kg).

White bream (Blicca bjoerkna) is not very easy to distinguish from the common bream but for the angler the most significant difference is the size, since it very rarely weighs more than 3½ oz–7 oz (0.1–0.2 kg) and is only 8–12 inches (20–30 cm) as against 12–20 inches (30–50 cm) for the common bream.

Bream can easily cross-breed with other Cyprinidae, such as roach. This sometimes makes identification even more difficult.

Fishing a swim

If you fish a swim near the bank, you are likely to find only small white bream. The techniques and ground-baits described for such small fish as bleak and roach, especially the former, are therefore particularly effective (see pp. 208 and 220).

△ *You can fish bream either using a spinner and reel style or in a swim with floating line.*

If you want to find common bream in large numbers, you will need to do so in midstream, at least 50 to 65 feet (15 or 20 m) from the bank. It is as though the fish have learned to distrust banks, since it is where anglers are likely to be sitting in wait for them.

That is why the rod used for catching bream is at least 30 feet (10 m) in length, with removable sections and using a line that is noticeably shorter than the rod.

TWO GROUND-BAITS SUITABLE FOR BREAM

• Recipe for stillwater fishing
3 parts whole-wheat bread crumbs, 2 parts white bread crumbs, 1 part coarse cornmeal, 1 part fine cornmeal, 2 parts cornbread, 1 part peanut flour.

• Recipe for river fishing
4 parts white bread crumbs, 1 part sticky PVI, 2 parts rich cookie, 1 part cornbread, 1 part farina (cream of wheat), 1 part bentonite, 1 package of the additive Brasem.

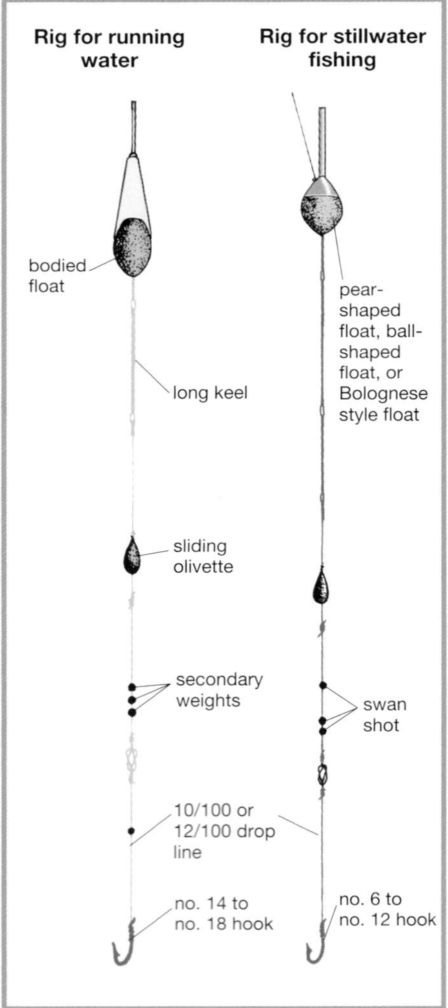

Maggots, single or in a cluster, are unquestionably the favorite bait of common bream anglers. But brandlings are just as good, especially when dealing with tricky fish.

In summer, wheat grains, and corn kernels are very effective. In the fall and spring, the fish still find them attractive, but only if there has been some pre-baiting. In pools, you should have some luck among waterplants along the margin, where there is a cleft in the bank, in a hollow, and almost always at depths greater than 5 feet (1.5 m). In canals, the hides are even more difficult to find, due to the evenness of the bottom. Look in canal-side locations, wide bends, or close to locks. The safest thing is still to ground-bait regularly and repeatedly. In rivers, try and find the deepest swims, especially in the central channel in channeled rivers. That's where you are most likely to find the largest number of common bream.

• The need for ground-baiting

Generous initial ground-baiting will always necessarily be followed by more subtle loosefeed, until the first bites occur. Straggly streams of bubbles rising from the bottom often betray the presence of a large or small school of bream – as with tench – and you can then increase the frequency and the amount of loosefeed. Bream are particularly gluttonous and don't take long to clear a swim that is being fed with generous amounts of ground-bait. As soon as they realize that the food has gone, they will desert it very swiftly. Should you find that bites are going quiet, try being more generous with feeding.

• Pre-feeding

Another possible tactic, especially in reservoirs, lakes, or large rivers, is to groundbait a swim the night before you go fishing. The best place to choose is a shelf or a large clearing surrounded by water-plants.

Any bream that are around – along with large roach, tench, and young carp – will thus have the chance of finding your groundbait during their nocturnal sorties, and will invariably be induced to move nearer to the banks, among the water plants which supply them with food. The following morning at dawn, they will still be foraging among the ground-bait if you supplied enough of it the night before. When you get to the water, avoid plumbing the depth. Find the depth the day before or proceed by trial and error. Now throw a few pellets of ground-bait or handfuls of hook-baits into the swim. Then, all you need to do is to fish using the still line technique described for tench, scraping the bottom. The bream bite is very characteristic; the fish raises itself up to swallow your hook-bait. This move takes the weight of some of the shot, causing the float to lift up and even lie horizontal, before it moves along the surface and slowly sinks.

FLOAT FISHING WITH A REEL

Using a reel with a float line, the distance fished and the depth no longer pose a problem. Your first job is to chose the right spot. In rivers, this means a swim with a rather slow and very regular current. In pools, you will want a peaceful area not too far from water plants, and not with a bed that is fairly even. As always, the ideal is a small hollow. Groundbait your swim using very compact balls. They get to the bottom quickly and stay there longer. Don't try to economize on quantity. Be generous with the loosefeed, and top up with a regular supply of hook-bait as soon as you get your first bites. In most cases, you will need a catapult. Look for one with pre-adjustable elastic. They are much easier to use, and deliver balls of bait or hook-bait to the distance you want. In rivers of any depth, make allowances for drift. Drift can carry your ground-bait quite a distance downstream. As with traditional angling in a swim, only ground-bait with the line in position. This gives you better aim. Always ensure you are about 20 inches (10 cm) or so away from the float. If bites are slow, try casting a bit further out or spreading out your casts, to see whether the fish has moved because of some problem with the ground-bait. The hook-bait

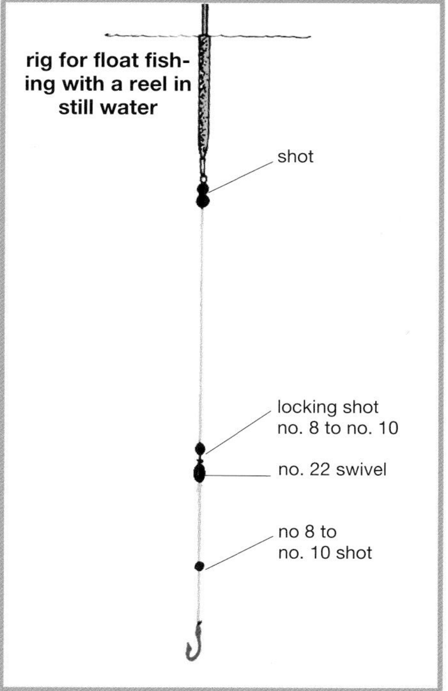

Thanks to increased imports from Europe, new ground-baits are becoming available.

STOREBOUGHT MIX

3000 Sensas Bream, Van den Eynde Record Silver, Drachko Fine Rameau, 3000 Sensas Reel, 3000 Sensas English, Clip-fish Rameau.

When fishing for roach with a floating line, you can sometimes catch a common bream.

must practically roll along the bottom, which means the float needs to be adjusted until some of the hook length trails along the bottom. Cast a few feet upstream of the feed area and, if possible, slightly further out. This will counteract drift from the current or any pull-back when the line sinks. For this purpose, one little trick is to find a landmark on the far bank, and mark the line at the proper distance. This will always enable you to cast into the same spot and to fish at more-or-less the same distance from the bank, within the feed area.

Then let the line go with the current, tightening up regularly to make the bait rise up, then slackening off again. For fishing in ponds and lakes, give one or two turns of the handle from time to time, with the rod-tip and shock leader always submerged, modifying the direction in which the rod is pointing so as to troll the surface of the swim more efficiently. If you are fishing in deep waters, such as an impounding reservoir or natural lake, add a sliding float with one or two fixing points, blocked by a slip knot on the line.

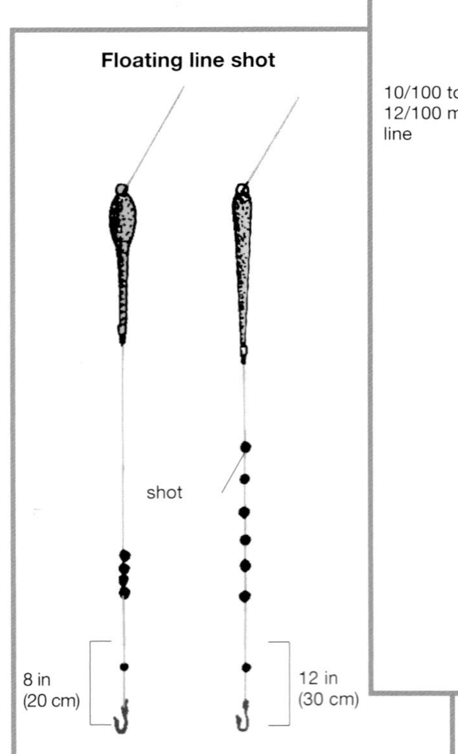

Bolognese-style
for still water fishing

bodied float
10/100 to
12/100 main
line
shots
no. 22 swivel
no. 10 to
no. 18 hook

Long line fishing

To fish at long-range, way out in midstream using a rod of reasonable length and price, try long line fishing. This actually involves using a typical pole, combined with long float-line.

The rod has to be telescopic to retain a certain springiness in the top sections. It must allow you to cast with a whipping action, and this cannot be done with sectional classical poles. The standard length of long line poles is around 33 ft (10 m) and they have to be made of carbon if they are to be light enough to handle.

The line itself is almost as long as the rod, so that you can grab the hook in your hands, as they rest on the grip. The float is either a straight waggler when the water is calm and there is no wind, or on slow-moving rivers, or a more bulbous one, such as an Avon on windy days and/or strong current in rivers.

The Bolognese-style float is deliberately oversized, as are the floats used for reel fishing. The very big float serves two purposes. It supports heavy weights for casting over distances greater than 50 feet (15 m); and it provides greater stability and better line visibility. Long line fishing is attractive in slow-moving rivers, but is equally useful in pools, where it enables bream to be fished at greater depths, and is comparable to fishing a swim. Let the hook-bait move along the bottom, regularly moving it backward and forward by tightening the line and slackening it again at intervals.

△ *Float line fishing with a reel for bream.*

Bolognese-style fishing

In a strong current with lots of eddies and swirling water, you may also prefer Bolognese-style rods to spinning rods with reels as these become practically unusable in such conditions. Furthermore, a long rod can be quite difficult to handle. Bolognese rods have a lever-arm of 20 to 23 feet 6 to 7 m). This helps you to get the barking out of the flow, and maintains the right drift on the line and bait without sacrificing the comfort of your fishing. If you are fishing a pool, you will also manage to get to greater depths than with sliding floats, which are never very easy to use.

The only drawback with Bolognese-style fishing is that it is practically an impossibility on windy days. That is because the line offers considerable wind-resistance when the rod is raised. In rivers, always cast to the front and fish downstream. Control the drift constantly, tightening up and slackening off from time to time. This keeps the hook from snagging, because it normally drags along the bottom.

Whatever the distance fished, the technique and the backward and forward movements are the same for pools as for fishing in a typical swim.

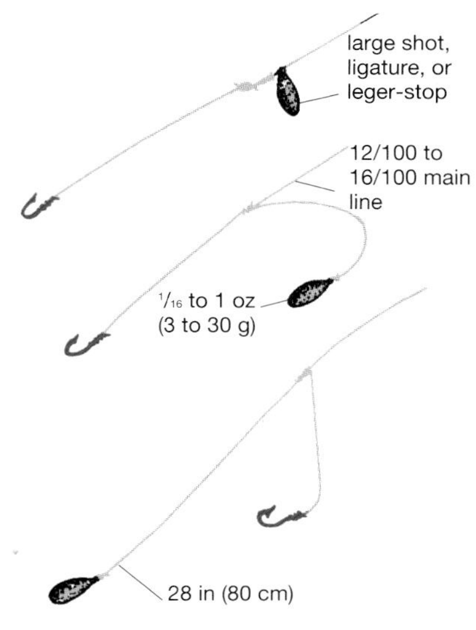

Rig for legering

Rig for Bolognese-style in running water

LEGERING ENGLISH-STYLE

When bream are present in a swim, whether in rivers or in pools, it sometimes happens that they stuff themselves so full with the ground-bait and loosefeed you have generously provided, that they are no longer tempted by the bait on your hook. Experiment by changing loosefeed frequency, making tantalizing movements, fishing on or slightly above the bottom. Sometimes, despite all your efforts, nothing seems to work. And yet the garbage can lids are down there all right; they give themselves away with the streams of tiny bubbles rising from just about everywhere in the swim, as well as those beads of white slime that you are constantly bringing up on your drop line.

This state of affairs is more common than might be imaged. You can start by giving brandling a try. That often does the job. Otherwise, go for a leger as well as brandling. We prefer the English method, which is more subtle, more unobtrusive, and more effective.

Swing-tip fishing (see p. 225) is particularly sensitive. It can give good results in still waters on windless days. However, bream are practically always fished in large rivers or reservoirs where it is almost always windy. Quiver-tips are therefore preferable.

QUIVER-TIP FISHING

Without changing your ground-baiting strategy at all, cast your leger well beyond the fishing zone, to avoid frightening the fish with the noise of the impact, and bring the line in as far as the swim itself. Ideally, you should try and find some landmark facing you and mark the line accordingly.

When the rig is in position, place your rod on its rests, parallel to the river pointing downstream, or at the lake (with the wind behind you). Keep your rod-tip toward the surface in pools or slightly raised in rivers (except where there's wind of course). Tauten the line with a few turns of the handle, to bend the quiver-tip slightly. If the wind picks up or the current becomes stronger, change your rod-tip (rods are always supplied with several quivers of assorted sizes and strengths) until you find the one that suits the prevailing conditions. Bites are signaled by vibrations, though these are never very strong with bream. After three or four minutes, if you have not had a bite, give the handle one or two turns to reposition the hook-bait. This trick will stir up a small cloud on the bottom and often does the trick.

FEEDER FISHING

In this technique, the weight is replaced by a feeder, also known as a swimfeeder (preferably attached to one of the rigs shown opposite). There are several types of feeder, but all should be attached in such a way as to prevent them tangling the rig. The feeder is filled with ground-bait laced with hook-bait. Small holes in the feeder enable maggots to wriggle out a few at a time.

Without altering the fishing technique – only the quiver-tip needs to be modified because of the extra weight added by the feeder – you can thus deliver loosefeed almost automatically to the exact spot at which you are fishing. This is very useful for fishing at long-range or in difficult conditions that make ground-baiting impossible or too inaccurate to be effective. Try not to make too much noise with the feeder when you land it in the water. Cast it as far as possible beyond the position being fished.

Rig for feeder fishing

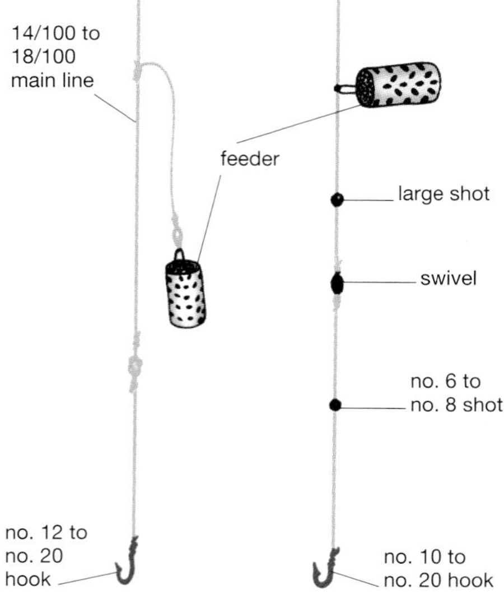

BLEAK

*Brilliant, in every sense of the term, extraordinarily volatile and endowed with an astonishing appetite for such a small fish, bleak (*Alburnus alburnus*) is a favorite species for competition angling. Bleak live in very dense shoals that respond particularly well to groundbaiting. They move in thick clouds of fish that offer truly impressive catches.*

THE SILVERY FISH

Although bleak are able to cross-breed with other Cyprinids, they are quite easy to identify due to their tapering body that is slightly compressed laterally, but especially thanks to the bright, shiny scales that are its most outstanding feature. The color of the back may vary from brown to green. The flanks are silvery and very shiny, with gray fins and a white belly.

Bleak is found in smaller rivers and canals and in stillwater (ponds and lakes, whether natural or artificial) throughout central and southern Europe, and in Sweden and Denmark. It is also found in southern England. It is a gregarious fish. In winter and in times of flood, shoals of bleak shelter in slacks and the quieter parts of rivers. They seek out such places as tributary outlets, canals, or landing-stages, basins, and gravelly bottoms, where they often gather in massive numbers. In summer, shoals of bleak are more scattered, continually crisscrossing the surface in quiet reaches and river backwaters or close to turbulent areas. Breeding takes place in spring, on sandy or gravelly bottoms.

A variety of the bleak known as the Schneider (*Alburnoides bipunctatus*) lives in whitewater, exclusively in central and southern Europe. It has a more rounded belly but an even more distinctive feature is the flanks which are underscored with two rows of small black spots. It lives alongside minnows, stroemling, and dace, at the mouth of streams or in slacks.

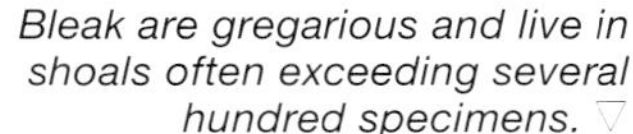

Bleak are gregarious and live in shoals often exceeding several hundred specimens. ▽

FISHING A SWIM

Winter is the best season for fishing a swim for bleak. Hungry with cold, bleak form immense schools, congregating away from the flow, often close to small roach and rudd which tend to live at deeper levels than bleak. The places to find them are in small creeks, along steep earth or stonework embankments, or even in the shelter of islands. They also like to hide near banks that are well

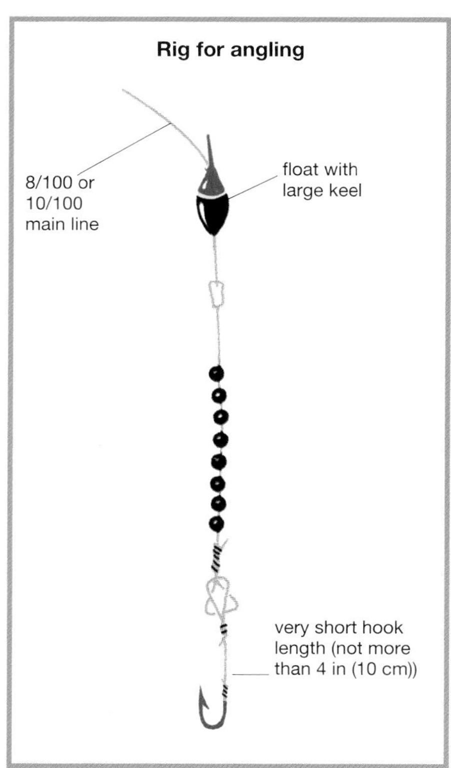

△ *In lakes or in wide rivers, you sometimes need to use a long rod.*

protected from the current. When the river is in flood, concentrate on deep slacks or the places where tributaries flow into the larger river. These waters will be more temperate and more nutritious than those of the main river and will exercise an irresistible attraction for small fish. Prospects are good in the deepest pools and hollows, or near banks that are more exposed to the rays of the sun. Generally speaking, you'll catch larger bleak (so long as you ground-bait generously) than in rivers, but there will definitely be fewer of them. In summer, go downstream of weirs instead. Look out for disturbances in the water, and spot any counter currents that form along the banks. In quieter spots, choose a bottom that is clear of sand and gravel. In pools, springs and little streams provide very good hides where they join the main body of water.

Failing that, you can round up small bleak quite quickly near the bank, even in relatively shallow water. Larger bleak will generally keep further out toward midstream and it will be difficult to attract them to the ground-bait for any length of time.

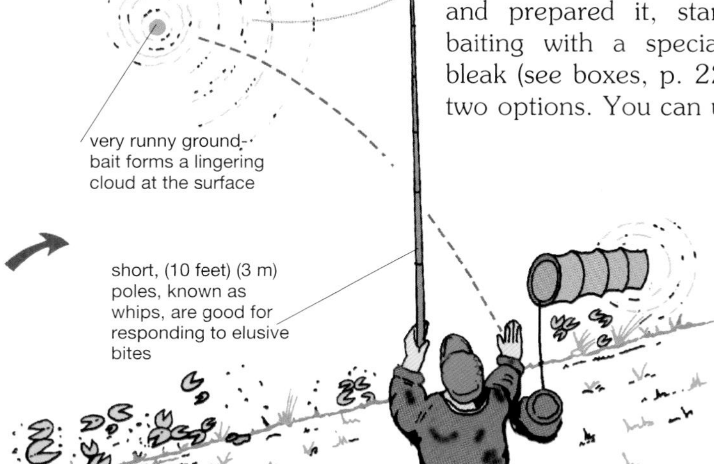

Angling for bleak

• Ground-baiting

Once you have selected your pitch and prepared it, start by ground-baiting with a special mixture for bleak (see boxes, p. 222). There are two options. You can use a fairly dry ground-bait that is rather grainy so that it disintegrates on contact with the water. Or you can choose a very runny ground-bait with a soupy consistency which will expand rapidly on the surface, creating a thick and lingering cloud. Be sure to add color to the mixture first so that you can easily spot it. If you use the colored cloud, get yourself a ladle or a really long serving-spoon to ensure better delivery of your ground-bait.

The main feed should be delivered before you start fishing, as this will attract the fish to the swim. Then deliver an ounce or so of ground-bait at regular intervals and with each cast. This loosefeed tops up the cloud that forms near the surface and keeps the fish interested. All you need to do then is to cast the line into the cloud with the certainty that the fish that are ready to bite.

As for hook-baits, you are spoiled for choice. There are bloodworm, jokers, clotted blood, diced bacon, bread crusts, maggots, chopped brandling, caddis fly larvae – the list of hook-baits to attract bleak is endless.

Bloodworm is definitely the most successful bait, but if you want an easy life, get yourself some pinkies or maggots, and you may well catch several fish at a time without having to change your hook-bait.

TWO GOOD GROUND-BAITS

• Bottom ground-bait: ground rusk, light cream, copra, cornmeal, and roasted ground peanuts in equal quantities.
• Surface ground-bait: 4 parts of copra, 2½ parts graham flour, 1½ parts roasted flours,½ part concentrated binding agent.
• Other substances that attract bleak include powdered milk, rice flour, Alba 2000 (a very strong white coloring), and Ablettix (a particularly effective and stimulating flavoring).

STORE-BOUGHT MIXTURES

3000 Surface Sensas, Surface Plus Rameau, Van den Eynde Special Match, 3000 Bleak Sensas, Plumm X21, Record 515 Red and Yellow Sensas, Rameau Gazza, Corsaire X21.

• The basic line
10/100 main line, spherical float with a long keel and a small antenna, balanced by an olivette and additional swan shot where necessary. Very short 8/100 hook length, no. 18 through no. 22 fine steel hook.

– Line for tricky fish
8/100 main line, float identical to that of the previous rig, balanced by round shot. Very short 6.5/100 hook length always, with a no. 18 through no. 22 fine gauge hook.

– Twin hook line
This is an effective rig for winter fishing at a particularly well-stocked hide, where the bleak are really biting. The line is 10/100. Use a spherical float with a long keel and a small antenna, bulk shot (a few large round shots) placed right at the end of the line. The no. 18 through no. 22 fine gauge hooks are placed on a trace above the shots, on drop lines no longer than 2 inches (5 cm).

• Frozen bleak
The best live bait for zander is bleak but they are such a headache to keep alive, being so delicate and sensitive to handling. Make the most of any leftover small fish and freeze them at home to use later for deadbait fishing, either moving or still. As soon as you get home, place your bleak flat on a sheet of plastic film (freezer-safe type), making sure they are not touching each other. When your bleak have turned into zander ice cream, carefully store them in a container or a bag, being careful not to break their fins. When you go on your next fishing trip, all you have to do is to take along as many fish as you need.

SPEED FISHING

Patrick Burckenstock, a French champion angler, is the holder of an amazing world record. In one hour, he managed to catch 590 fish! Speed fishing the way he does it leaves nothing to chance. The rod, the lines, ground-bait, hookbait, even the un-hooking movement, are all calculated to be done in the most speedy and time-saving manner.

All speed specialists are unanimous in their opinion that the best time of the year is in late winter, in February and March. They fish near outlets of tributaries, at the entrance to landing-stages, canals, or ballast works. Once the right location has been identified, the next stage is ground-baiting.

Because the fish are generally present in the swim, they don't have to be lured in from a distance. On the other hand, they have to be corraled into the exact spot at which you're going to be casting your line. You need to keep them almost continually interested so that they will throw themselves onto the bait from the moment they spot it.

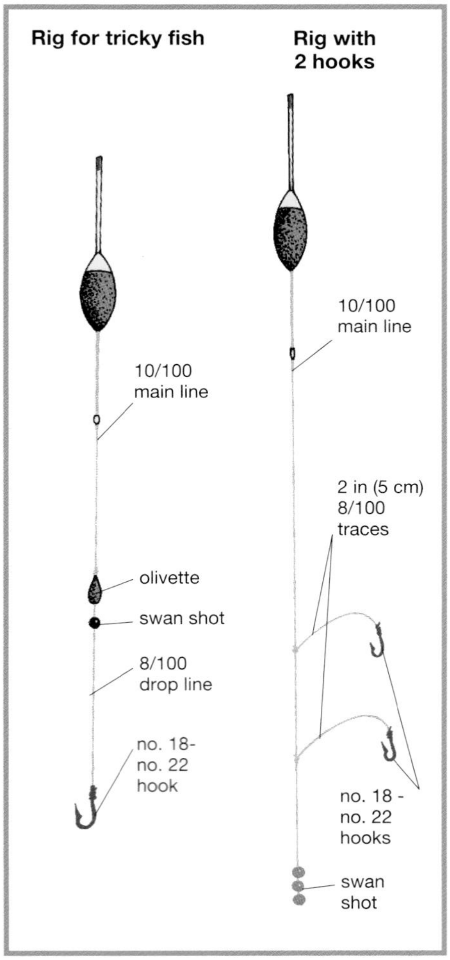

• Some tricks for an impeccable technique
To save time, competition anglers use very short rods, known as whips. They are light and rigid, with a length of 5 through 6½ feet (1.50 to 2 m). They have a small cork grip like a casting rod, which is very useful for landing a catch. The shorter and more responsive telescopic rods (7 to 13 feet (2 to 4 m)) are also very good and are often a lot less expensive!

The line, one single length, is generally 8/100, possibly 10/100 if you're after large bleak or some nice roach, or if you want to be on the safe side. The float is preferably pear-shaped or teardrop-shaped. It must be balanced as accurately as possible with bulk shot (either large cylindrical shot, round shot added side by side, or an olivette) placed very near the hook (no. 20 or no. 22). This will very soon move the line into its proper position, about 8 to 20 inches (20 to 50 cm) below the surface of the water.

◁ *Bleak will give children the opportunity to sharpen their reflexes for strikes.*

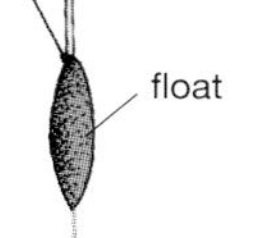

Rig for speed fishing

Nothing compares with bloodworm as a hook-bait, but it is expensive and difficult to hook. Small maggots (pinkies), jokers, or a small quantity of Mystic Red seem preferable to start off with. In certain cases, champions also use a small red bead that they thread onto the hook. When the bleak are really excited, they just see red and fight over the bait, saving you the trouble of having to change hook bait between catches!

The rest of the fishing is just a question of rhythm, and for that you have to be perfectly set up at the water's edge. Your bucket or keep-net must be within reach, your ground-bait box close at hand, hook-baits ready in a container, or on a board that is within easy reach.

As soon as the line is in the water, a pellet of ground-bait must land on the float. The bite can sometimes be just a quiver on the line or a small movement to one side of it. You have to strike and pull the fish out decisively. Unhook quickly, re-bait, and the line should already be on its way into the water, followed by a new pellet of ground-bait.

SURFACE FISHING

As soon as the faintest sign of the sun appears, bleak and schneider spend the best part of their time prowling a few inches beneath the surface and gulping down anything that remotely resembles something to eat.

Their behavior is governed by curiosity. Nothing escapes their attention, including insects, small leaves, or plant debris: everything is meticulously examined.

No properly presented artificial fly or insect will have any difficulty in achieving success for its owner.

• Fly fishing

You evidently need to keep to the smaller sizes of artificial flies (midges, ants, and small palmers, their bodies enhanced by a few wisps of silver tinsel); do not use a hook bigger than a no. 18 hook. The tip should be fine with an average drop of 11½ through 13½ feet (3.50 to 4 m), 8/100 or 10/100.

The technical side of things does not present any major problems either. Bleak rarely prove difficult to catch. In moving water, just position yourself upstream from where you have seen them rising and leave them to it as always! In still water, on the other hand, you will have to increase the number of casts and follow the fish rising. Bleak often live in small schools that are almost constantly on the move in odd patterns. You have to work out where they are going to be so that your fly cuts across their path and holds their attention.

Fishing for bleak, you will soon notice there is no shortage of bites. In fact, there's even a risk of it becoming boring! If the catch is small, this can lead to disappointment. It all depends on the speed of your strike. Bleak may well display an unbelievable curiosity, but they are capable of lightning speed when it comes to spitting out something they don't want to eat. So sharpen your reflexes.

At this game, you can count on three or four catches for every ten fish you see rising. By the fifth near miss, you will be just about ready to go back to trout and salmon just to prove to yourself how infinitely easier they are to take!

• Insect fishing

In practically identical conditions, you can fish bleak with a bubble-float and artificial flies, although the strike is always a problem. You can also use real insects, such as houseflies. The best are red ants or winged ants.

There is another way to fish with insects, namely using a float line and the special float described in the section on chub. If you do not add any shot to the line, you will be able to cast far out and to fish the surface unobtrusively.

The final possibility discussed here is freelining (see the section on rudd), using an unweighted maggot, a grasshopper, a small cricket, or the head of a large grasshopper.

Tench

*If there's such a thing as a modest and retiring fish, it has to be the tench (*Tinca tinca*), This handsome copper-flanked fish is timid and suspicious, spending most of its time among the deepest clumps of water-weed, where it finds its food (plants and insect larvae) and above all the peace and tranquility that it craves. However, once you have a tench at the end of a line, you will realize that once hooked, it instantly turns into a raging fury. This fierce fighter can weigh more than 6 lb 8 oz (3 kg) and will defend itself with ferocious energy!*

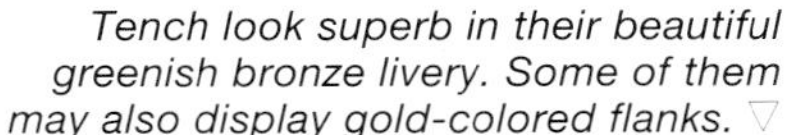

Tench look superb in their beautiful greenish bronze livery. Some of them may also display gold-colored flanks. ▽

A peace-loving fish with a copper-colored body

Tench can be recognized by their greenish bronze color, which is shot with yellow, particularly on the underside. The back itself is darker, almost gray. The body is bulky, solid, and thickset, covered in very small scales and a thick protective slime that makes it extremely slippery to handle. The fins are very well developed, with the exception of the caudal fin which is short but extremely thick and powerful. There are two small barb on either side of the thick, fleshy lips.

Tench are found in most waters, and even in some quiet, deep sections of trout and grayling rivers. They are especially active in the summer months, with two major peaks, before and after the breeding season, between late June and late July. They hide among water plants and are sometimes to be found very near the bank.

In winter, toward mid-November, tench cease all activity and go into a sort of hibernation, hiding in the mud. Heavy floods in rivers can force them out. They then feed for a few days, especially if the weather is mild.

Ponds and small canals full of duckweed and vegetation are their favorite habitat. If you intend to fish for tench in canals, have a look at slacks or canal-side landing-stages and moorings, where barges and boats provide shade. Rivers are excellent spots near reeds, such as in big muddy slacks or mill-ponds and small dams.

Fishing a swim with ground-bait

You will need three rods. Spread them out in a fan, securely anchored on their rests, but closely watched at all times.

The main line should be 14/100. The float should be tapered but quite buoyant, so you need to use enough weights to immobilize the line. It is best to use round shot rather than olivettes. Ensure that they are carefully distributed, just above the knot joining it to the 12/100 drop line. The hook (no. 10 through no. 14) must be strong enough to become attached to the fish with no danger of unhooking.

When fishing, the drop line and some of the weights should rest on the bottom. This results in the float resting in a slightly inclined position. This gives you an ideal presentation of the hook-bait, which the tench will locate while grubbing around on the bottom. Supply a generous initial amount of ground-bait, containing a considerable amount of hook-bait. The bite of a tench is characteristic. The float will quiver slightly at first, and then submerge slowly but deeply. The strike should not be rushed. Tench takes a long time to take the bait properly.

Rig for big fish in still waters

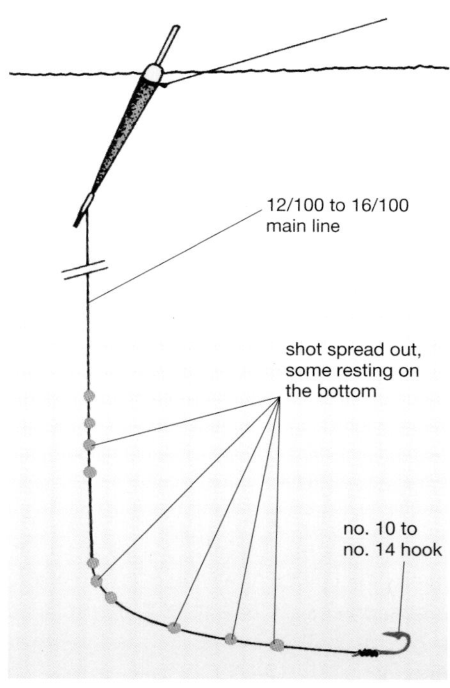

Bubble fishing

At nightfall and at daybreak, tench often emerge from their dens among the vegetation. They venture out further along the bed of the river or lake, on the lookout for any prey they may find on the muddy bottom.

So you need to look out for small streams of bubbles. The bubbles will be close together and don't make a lot of noise. Tench expel these bubbles when they stir up the mud, sometimes only a few inches from the weeds or the bank. If the bubbles are moving around, they clearly point to the presence of one or several tench who are lurking in the vicinity.

Using a line similar to the previous rig, adjust the float well beyond what is needed for the hide in question, so as to be certain that the hook-bait and some of the weights rest on the bottom. Don't worry if the float lies horizontally. Hook up some small brandling, a cluster of maggots, termites, wheat berries, corn, or stale gingerbread or ginger cookies. Submerge them slowly. After a few minutes, reel in slightly in the direction of the stream of bubbles and sit tight. As with a still line, a bite is confirmed by the float slowly moving away from you, after a series of quivering movements.

Store-bought mixtures

Sensas 3000 Tench, Sensas 3000 Big Fish and Carp, Rameau Big Fish, Van den Eynde Carpano, Sensas 3000 "Bottom", Rameau Plus "Bottom".

Legering with a swing-tip

Swing-tips are hinged, ultrasensitive rod-tips. If you use this technique, you can easily spot a bite, even if you are fishing at a distance of about 66 ft (20 m) or more from the bank such as near an island, next to some shoals, or on the opposite bank if it is inaccessible, as well as on the bottom. Put some 15/100 on the reel, place a 1/8 to 1/2 oz (5 to 15 g) Arlesey bomb-type weight on a paternoster above a small barrel swivel. The 12/100 drop line should measure 12 to 16 inches (30 to 40 cm). The no. 10 through no. 14 hook should also be strong and very sharp.

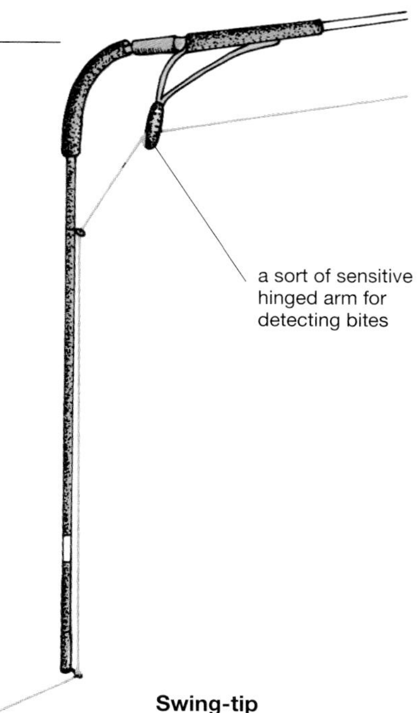

Swing-tip

Start by ground-baiting generously (using a catapult, to throw it a good way away), possibly topping up while you are fishing with a loosefeed of hook-bait on its own. Always cast the line well beyond the fishing area and then bring the rig back to the position itself (make a mark with a felt-tip pen on the line to act as a guide). Place your rod on its rests, facing the position fished, rod-tip pointing toward the surface. Turn the handle a few times to tauten the line, place the swing-tip in the half-way position (at an angle of 45° to the vertical) and keep your eyes open. A bite may be indicated by a straightening of the jointed rod-tip if the line tightens. On the other hand, the tip could point downward as the tension slackens. Take the rod, wait a second or two, give the reel a few turns to tauten the backing and strike, not too sharply. If you have to wait some time for a bite, take the rig in 3 feet or so, wait 5 to 10 minutes and repeat the operation.

Gingerbread mad!

Gingerbread drives tench wild! Whether crumbled or soaked then crushed, gingerbread and ginger cookies deserve a place among all your ground-bait. For the hook-bait, a no. 10 through a no. 12 steel, bronze, or golden, a no. 14 through no. 18 hook straight or treble, is the most suited. Dice it into cubes 1/4 to 3/8 in (6 to 8 mm) in size. Attach them to a single hook, or use small pellets molded onto a treble hook.

CHUB

*Chub (*Leuciscus cephalus*) are found throughout Europe in all types of waterway, from brooks to major rivers. The chub is a wary, suspicious fish with a savage nature and an insatiable appetite. However, it can be capricious and unpredictable. Sometimes it refuses hook-bait or lures which it will suddenly seize avidly a few minutes later.*

Some anglers dislike chub. They do not like its omnivorous diet, the ravages it causes to the roe and alevin of trout, and the flesh which is rather flavorless and full of bones. Other anglers love to fish for them. These anglers like the fact that chub are so widespread and easy to find and their violent response to a strike, which means that bringing them in is quite a skill. No angler is indifferent to the subject of chub.

The chub has been called "poor man's trout" in Europe. It is a remarkable coarse fish, found in most waters. ▽

AN ATTRACTIVE ADVERSARY

Chub can easily be identified by the massive head with a wide flat forehead, large mouth, and the streamlined body which is covered in large, shiny scales. The pelvic and anal fins are russet-colored. The back is generally very dark and the underside is quite pale. The flanks are shiny, and in older specimens they are sometimes tinted bronze.

The largest specimens of chub can exceed 2 feet (60 cm) in length and weigh 6 lb 8 oz (3 kg) and sometimes more. Chub live in shoals which are often composed of fish of different sizes. Larger specimens, however, have a tendency to isolate themselves from the pack.

Breeding takes place in spring, from April through June. The roe consists of 100,000 and 200,000 eggs, that become very sticky once they have been fertilized, and are laid in relatively calm areas, such as gravelly or pebbly bottoms, or possibly on a bed of weeds.

Certain varieties of chub are found in very specific European locations, such as the Black Sea and the Caucasus. Another close relative is the blageon (*Leuciscus souffia*) which is found in the River Rhône, in France. Like most members of the Cyprinidae family, chub can cross-breed with other species, especially dace, and this can cause an identification problem.

CHUB HIDES

Chub are particularly adaptable and live in many watery environments, from still, deep waters to trout rivers involving a switchback of currents and less turbulent sections. In winter, however, they tend to take refuge in the quieter parts of rivers. They prefer deep hollows and the inside of sharp bends, mill-ponds or dammed lakes, where they live as close as possible to the bottom. During summer months, they do the opposite, moving into fast currents and shallower areas. Some chub, often the larger specimens, may also remain in quiet, deep areas, where they will take up their position near the surface. They prefer the proximity of banks and land-based vegetation, because they are on the lookout for insects and other land-based prey. At midday, in the warm weather, it is not unusual to see dozens of chub absolutely motionless at the surface, right in the middle of a deep hollow or of a mill-pond. In reservoirs and lakes, chub are more infrequent. Though some impounding reservoirs or natural lakes stock up with chub or have a good supply from rivers flowing into the expanse of water. In summer, chub live near banks and at the surface, but then in winter they go deeper or stay close to streams flowing into the lakes which will supply them with a good source of food. Chub are even found in brackish water, such as the very slightly salty waters of the Baltic sea.

In summer, midday fishing for chub can mean full nets. ▷

The best hook-baits

Michel Duborgel, one of France's greatest writers about the sport of angling, rightly describes chub as the cafeteria rats of the fish world. Anything that is edible will at some time or another be on the chub's menu. Chub have huge appetites and an extreme curiosity. This means that any of the standard hook-baits can be used. Depending on the type of angling you are practicing, you can also rely on a number of goodies that are guaranteed to drive them wild.

• Fruits

– Cherries

The small wild cherries which grow beside river banks and fruit in July attract fish the most, because they are naturally there. But, like ourselves, chub prefer the larger hybrid cherries because they are sweeter. So cherries make an excellent hook-bait for the summer season. Their effectiveness will be distinctly increased by sparing loosefeeding. The other trick is to work the same section day after day, so that the fish get used to the taste of fruits. Depending on the size of the bait, choose no. 2 – no. 6 hooks, or no. 8 – no. 12 trebles.

– Blackcurrants, redcurrants, and gooseberries

This small berry of the Ribes family is smooth and shiny, black, white, or red. Blackcurrants, redcurrants, whitecurrants, and even gooseberries are excellent for chub and relatively easy to use, because of their thick skin. In July and August, use them with no. 6 through no. 12 hooks. Bronze or steel hooks are fine either bronzed, or steel. Use simple hooks for redcurrants and whitecurrants, or a no. 14 treble for gooseberries.

– Blackberries

The fruits of the bramble bush are common from late summer through early fall in northern Europe and the northern United States. Blackberries found growing wild in scrub and on heaths are by far the best. To make them easier to hook, choose firm fruits, leaving the soft, ripe, fragrant ones for ground-baiting. Use either steel or bronze no. 4 through no. 8 hooks. No. 8 through no. 10 trebles are the best for a good hook-bait. If you feed your ground-bait properly and choose a section with plenty of overhanging bushes, blackberries make a hook-bait that will enable you to have some superb late-summer fishing. This is a chub bait with a long-standing reputation.

– Grapes

Grapes grow throughout southern Europe and certain parts of the United States from mid-August through late October. Grapes are a fantastic hook-bait for chub, even out of season. The fresh fruit is used as it comes, cut in half to help to spread the aroma. Raisins can also be used, straight from the package or after soaking it in sweetened water for half a day. The ideal hook is a single no. 6 through no. 10, of steel or bronze. Use a no. 10 through no. 12 treble hook for grapes and a no. 4 through no. 10 reversed steel or bronze hook for raisins.

• Insects

*– Red ants (*Formica rufa*, a member of the Formicidae family)*

These are among the largest ants around. They live in anthills which they build into huge mounds using twigs. You find them in forests, especially in coniferous woodland. In the summer months, you'll also find winged ants that are bigger than the workers. Red ants, winged or not, keep very well in small containers with air holes. They like to have some twigs from the anthill. To bait them, hook them gently through the abdomen (the bulkiest and softest part). Red ants make an extremely productive bait throughout late spring, summer, and fall, and more particularly in August and September. You can also use ants for fishing on the move. Use a line fitted with a bubble float or a small float, that does not have to be weighted.

△ *Dead cricket bait.*

– Crickets

The commonest crickets are $\frac{5}{8}$-$\frac{3}{4}$ in (16–20 mm) long. Those that are most useful for fishing are quite dark, almost brownish-black in color. Generally speaking, crickets live in fields of

Live cricket bait. ▷

grain and grasslands but you can also find them under stones in the hot dry hills of southern Europe and the United States. If you want to use crickets live, you have to hook them gently between two rings, to the back of the head. For fishing on the drop, you can also kill them and insert the hook into the head, so that it protrudes under the body. Use a no. 8 through no. 12 hook. If presented at the right spot, under branches or beside a deep bank, crickets will rarely leave an alert chub indifferent. You can also use them with a float line or legering for fishing along the bottom, in potholes and deep slacks. They may even attract other large-sized Cyprinidae. They are good throughout the summer period right up until late September.

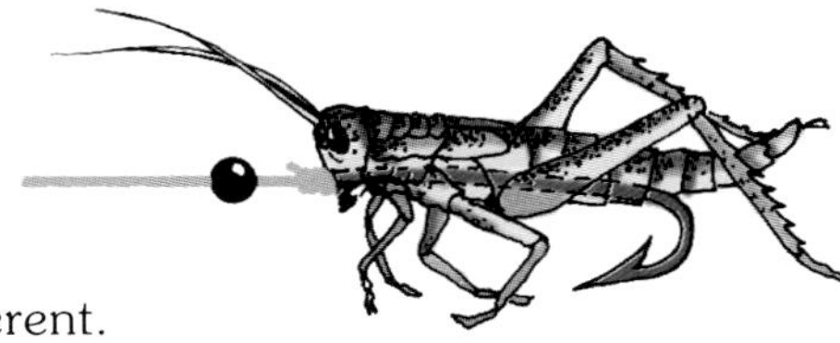

◁ *Dead grasshopper as bait.*

– *Grasshoppers*

The best grasshoppers for fishing are green grasshoppers that live in pasture and grassland, probably because they would be more likely to end up on the surface of the water under natural conditions. Depending upon the required effect, there are two main types of possible hook-baits. To keep grasshoppers alive and make use of their movements at the surface, slip the hook into the rear of the head, just under one of the harder rings that cover the body. Alternatively, for a more robust hook-bait and for drop-fishing or fishing at depth, introduce the hook into the middle of the head and allow it to exit below the body of the insect.

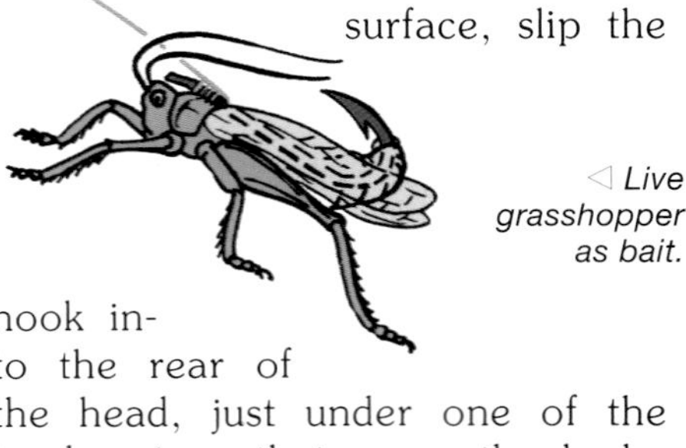

◁ *Live grasshopper as bait.*

Fishing on the move is a simple technique, ideal for streams and creeks. ▷

FISHING ON THE MOVE

Fishing on the move is simple and quick by definition. You need an 20 through 23 foot (6 to 7 m) telescopic pole, or a telescopic rod with rings, adjustable as required, from 13 through 16 feet (4 to 5 m), with a small reel (fixed or revolving spool) fitted with a 12/100 to 16/100 line. Then all you need are your bait boxes, spools of line, shots, floats, and replacement hooks, a few indispensable accessories such as a plummet or a disgorger – and you're ready. Bring a pair of waders, that will enable you to walk into the water, or even to take a few steps a few feet down the river. For storing your fish, keepnets designed for carrying around the waist are very useful, but only if you are certain of regular strikes while you are in the water. Otherwise, keep your catch in a creel. Models fitted with pockets on the sides are perfect, because they also enable you to carry spare tackle. Obviously, you will not need this if you are sporting enough to give the

fish back their freedom on the spot!
In spring and fall, the most interesting rivers for fishing on the move are of a modest size, not more than 200 to 250 feet (10 to 12 m) across. The features of such rivers should be varied, with small areas of fast-flowing water giving way to quieter and shallower areas, broken up by a few deep hollows. If the section is heavily wooded and there are backwaters and millponds, so much the better.

• The rig
Fit a 14/100 backing and a pear-type float, balanced by an olivette and a few additional swan shots on the 12/100 drop line. For hook-baits, brandlings and maggots are a real asset, but aquatic larvae (caddis and nymph essentially) are even more attractive.
In fast-flowing and slightly muddy waters, head down the river as you fish. However, in shallower and clear waters, fishing upstream is almost a necessity. Fish along the bottom in the quieter areas and just below the surface close to moving water, especially downstream of weirs.
In summer, shallow, warm, very clear waters are undoubtedly best for fishing on the move. Whatever the type of river you deal with, you really will be able to find a way to catch fish, sometimes even plenty of them!
In large rivers, fish downstream of weirs and moving water and place yourself at the head of deeper areas where you will be able to let out your line and practice casting at range. Adjust the float so that the hook-bait moves along the bottom, and check it while keeping your rod high so that it is always presented first. If you use a cluster of maggots, a brandling, aquatic larvae, a grasshopper, or a cricket, you will catch good chub and lots of other fish.
In rivers of more modest size, use the cunning float described in the box, mounted on a 12/100 with a 10/100 drop-line that will enable you to fish unobtrusively very near the surface. Houseflies, small grasshoppers, and ants are the best hook-baits, along with maggots and aquatic larvae. You can also get rid of the float and go for freelining.

A CUNNING FLOAT

To make a float that will go unnoticed among the spume and twigs floating downriver with the current, take an ink cartridge, cut off the two ends (retain just 2 in (5 cm) of tube) and rinse thoroughly. Cut two small pieces of cork to block the two ends. To slide your float onto the line, just remove the plugs and pass the line through the cartridge. If you want more weight to make it easier to cast, fill the cartridge completely with cork. To remove it, just push it out with a stick.

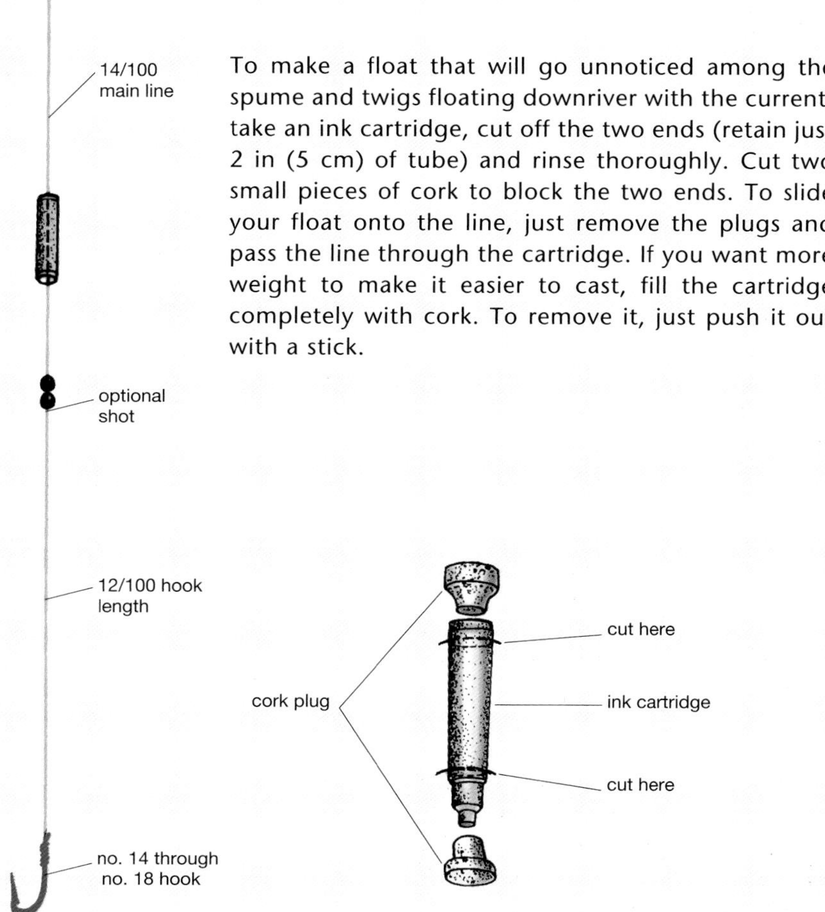

FREELINING

For freelining, the hook must be directly attached to the end of a 16/100 or of a 18/100, connected to the tip of a rod without rings. Make sure this line is distinctly shorter than the rod itself, and use this rig to present a grasshopper, a cricket, or a large fly, alongside bushes with submerged branches, under overhanging trees, or even right in the middle of deep holes. The best times are midday or mid-afternoon, when big chub rise to the surface to sunbathe.

FISHING WITH FRUITS

At the end of the summer, the most attractive hook-baits are undoubtedly different fruits. Do some groundbaiting and you will get very big catches. You may land chub as big as 4 lb 8 oz (2 kg) and more, that will provide you with wonderful memories. One day they may find a place in your personal record book.
The most attractive rivers alternate between deep holes and shallower areas, possibly stirred by a gentle current. Wide rivers may be equally suitable, but where there are lots of hides suitable for chub, you will have more trouble in luring them out.
Position yourself upstream of the section that you have chosen and set up at the first suitable hide. Depth is important, and the presence of a deep bank washed by the

Rig for fishing with fruit in still waters

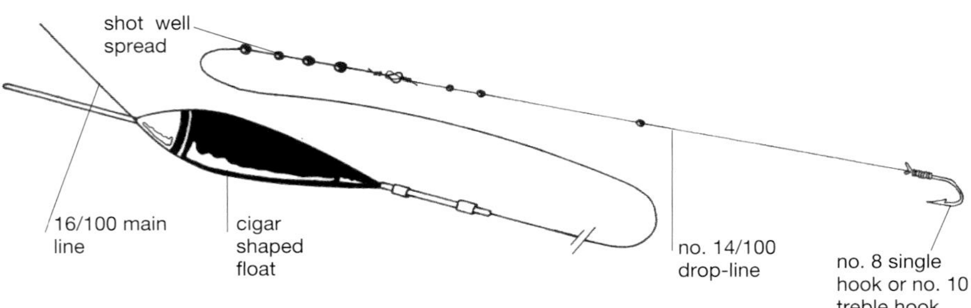

current, with submerged branches or blocks of stone, is a really good sign of a swim with big chub.
In quieter rivers, fish downstream of bridges, alongside embankments, riverbeds strewn with large blocks of stone, and heavily wooded banks overlooking deep water (at least 5 feet (2 m) deep).
A rod with rings measuring 13 through 16 feet (4 to 5 m), a reel of 16/100 line, a tapered – but well buoyant – float, a few well-spaced shot and a 16/100 drop line, that's all the tackle you need. Since you will not need to make powerful casts, use single hooks, as they will make hook-baiting easier.
Plumb the position for depth as usual (your hook-bait should be deployed 4 inches (10 cm) from the bottom), and feed your ground-bait. On average, two handfuls of fruit should be thrown before each cast. When ten minutes have passed, make an empty strike at the end of a cast to free the hook-bait and loosefeed automatically, throwing a handful every 7 or 8 minutes.
When there is a bite, strike quickly and immediately throw out some more fruit, then cast again. After a few catches, you may notice that the bites drop off a little. That's normal. Instead of persisting with fish who are now wise to your game, move downstream and set up at another position. If the current has managed to wash down some of your ground-bait, your chances will be that much better.

LEGERING WITH SLUGS

Whether it's because their color is particularly easy to detect on the bottom or because their softness makes them easy to play them, big chub go wild for slugs. The best times of year to use slug-bait are from the first floods of April through late October, with a peak in June and September, so long as the weather isn't too hot. An excellent way to rid the garden of a pest!
The best time for fishing is easy to identify. When it's dark and overcast, catches come in quick succession all day long. When the barometer is set to fair, however, you will have better luck in the early morning and at nightfall. At sunrise, chub are far too busy at the surface to be attracted by hook-baits presented on the bottom. Water levels are also very important. Prospects are excellent when water levels are rising or after a flood. Stable or normal levels are attractive, no more than that, while variations in level are very negative.
The depth of the swim should be no more than 5 to 6 ft 6 ins (1.50 to 2 m), and the best bed is a clean, sandy or gravel bottom.

• Classic legering

Slip a 1/8 – 3/4 oz (6–20 g) olive onto a 14/100 to 20/100 line long enough to fill the reel, and let it run freely. Simply fit a length of silicone tubing about 12 inches (30 cm) long over the connecting knot to protect it, at the eye of the swivel link on the drop-line (12/100 to 18/100). The hook is a no. 2 to no. 4 reversed.

• Rig-fishing with a quiver-tip

If you are after more intense sensations during the fight, kit yourself out with one or more quiver-top rods. For these, the rig is as follows: the main line (reel line) should be 16/100 or 18/100, while the weight – a 3/20 - 1/2 oz (3.5–14 g) Arlesey bomb – should be on a paternoster. The barrel swivel anti-kink of the weight is passed through the link of a rigid 1 1/2-inch (4 cm) anti-tangle tube that should slide freely along the main line. A barrel swivel link then serves as a stop for the anti-tangle tube and receives the loop of the drop line (14/100 to 16/100) 16 to 20 inches (15 1/2 to 20 in (40 to 50 cm)) to which a reversed no. 2 to no. 4 hook is attached.

Two rigs for legering, with slugs

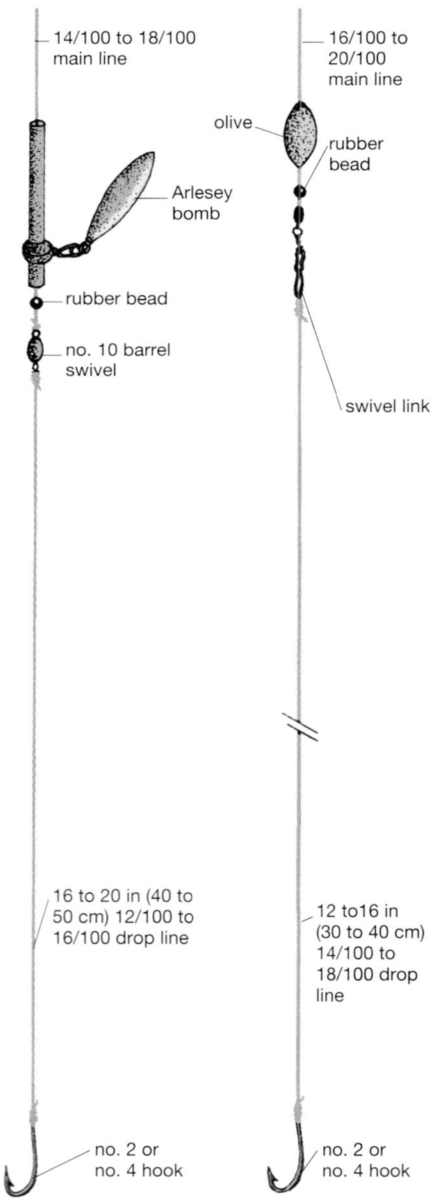

• The fishing action
Whatever the chosen technique, it is important to cast accurately. Place the slug preferably along banks edged by overhanging bushes. You need a slow current, downstream of some eddy, where there are vertical banks, or scattered rocks, or choose a spot downstream of weirs and turbulence, where fishing is allowed.
Next, place your rod on its rests, rod-tip pointing upward if you are fishing in classic leger style, rod parallel to the river and rod-tip pointing toward the surface for quiver-tip rods. To increase your chances, always place two or three legers within a narrow area. You could also cast a few slugs there and then, right at the beginning of the session, to sharpen the appetite of any chub in the vicinity.
If you get a bite, you will feel a powerful jolt on the line. You must strike immediately, sufficiently but not too sharply. Keep a gentle control over the clutch, in readiness for the struggle which is sure to be violent when you are dealing with chub.

THE BEST SLUGS FOR CHUB

Always use the biggest slugs. The bigger the meal at the end of the hook, the larger the fish you will catch. The best color for slugs is brick-red. The slug should be hooked through the back, from the rear to the front, in the part that's smooth and bulging, and harder than the rest of the body, where the shell would be if it were a snail.
To remove the slime that these horrible pests will inevitably leave on your fingers, rub your hands with wet grass. Don't forget to include a nail-brush in your fishing box or basket-cum-seat, to remove the last traces of slime.

FISHING WITH BLOOD

Maggots, earthworms, bloodworms, pasta, or bread can all be classified as classic baits for chub. They make top quality hook-bait, summer and winter. During the cold season, however, the ideal bait is still blood and variety meats, including liver, milt, and tripe or chitterlings. Their appeal for chub is unequaled.
Ox-blood is not always very easy to find, nor is poultry blood. If your butcher visits the abattoir regularly, from time to time he should be able to bring you a bucketful.
Otherwise, find out where there is an abattoir near you, and go along. If you explain what you want and if you know how to respond to someone doing you a favor, your supplies shouldn't be that difficult to obtain.
Blood deteriorates quickly, always keep it refrigerated and always use or discard it after two or three days. When you are ready to prepare your hook-baits, set aside one or several good clots of blood of a uniform color. Place them between two pads of absorbent cotton (cotton wool) pressed between two boards and weighted down with a large stone or a bucket of water.
Prepare a container for collecting any serum that might be released by the clot of blood. Overnight, you will obtain a sheet of blood hard enough for you to cut out cubes of any size you wish. A few experiments will enable you to decide the size you need to fill your hook properly.

• The rig
With customers like chub, you have to use a relatively strong line. With a classical or reel rod, the main line should be between 14/100 and 18/100. The drop-line needs to be 12/100 to 16/100, so that you always leave yourself some margin. The float needs to be of a type that can bear the weight of the shot, which are often numerous, to bring the line down to its right depth. One thing that has to be stressed if you are fishing with blood is that you must distribute your shot very evenly. This will make the descent as gentle as possible, and protect your hook-bait which is very fragile. The hook needs to be a single no. 10 or a treble no. 12.

• The fishing action
In rivers (prospects are practically nil in pools), areas that are relatively calm and deep offer the best opportunities. The same goes for slacks that form at the edge of the main stream or downstream of obstacles. To fish for chub as effectively as possible, use tackle light enough to enable you to fish on the move: use a rod with rings, a haversack containing line-repair equipment and your hook- baits, a landing net, maybe a small keep net, and a ground-bait bucket. Whatever hook-bait you use, the blood-based formula shown opposite is a force to be reckoned with. Find a hide that you feel is suitable, check the depth as usual, and ground-bait generously (use four or five ladlefuls). Then loosefeed every two or three casts with just half a ladleful. When the bites are felt, increase the frequency, especially after a noisy catch. With blood bait, you will need to strike without delay. Otherwise, the fish may well just slip off the hook. Be prepared also to change your bait at each cast, or just about. Liver, milt, and especially chicken guts, are excellent hook-baits for large chub. You can allow them to play a little for a little longer. In any case, if there has been no bite after fifteen minutes, change position, but always go downstream. This will allow you to derive the greatest benefit from your ground-bait. The smell of your ground-bait carried on the current will have already

Rig for fishing with blood

awakened the interest of any fish that may be lurking downstream of you.

• Special hook-baits

Using similar, blood-based groundbait, you may also fish using liver, milt, guts, and any types of inexpensive variety meats. If your supermarket or butcher does not stock them, look for this type of meat in street-markets and farmers' markets. Raw meat is very attractive for chub. If you are using blood, cut a cube from a very hard clot of blood. Insert it gently onto a single hook. If using a treble, attach the hook-bait with a needle. This is very tricky. For liver and milt, cut the meat into dice the size you want and prick them onto the hook. Leave the point protruding slightly.

If you are using tripe, chitterlings or chicken guts, cut small pieces from the intestines. You then have to prick and twist the piece of gut around the points of the treble hook, so as to hide it and offer an appetizing mouthful. When you have removed the clots of blood to be used as hook-bait, mix the congealed blood and the serum. Add well-aerated, crumbly, dry earth to it, such as molehill earth or fuller's earth. This will give the mixture a bit of weight and will help it to sink swiftly. If you add bran, it will tend to rise towards the surface, bringing particles of blood with it. These will then more easily spread out in the water and churn up the loosefeed for the fish you are after. Deliver this mixture with an old ladle or a large spoon. For quantities, use two parts of the blood-and-serum mixture to one part earth, and one part bran.

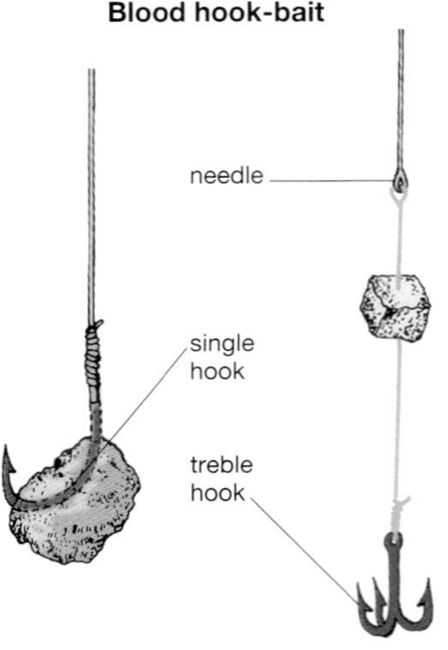

FLY-FISHING

When you get the chance, all surface-dwelling coarse fish prove to be particularly attractive adversaries for any fly fisherman. They are suspicious, timid, moody, capricious and particularly perceptive. You are liable to experience some very hard times. But as an adversary for the fly fisherman the best of all, the most attractive, adversary is definitely the chub. Chub are also the biggest and the toughest fighters. The best prospects are offered in the summer months, preferably in shallow waters. At that time of year, chub haunt every part of the river or pool.

The best positions are located in slacks that are not very far from an inlet or an oxygen-rich current.

From the technical point of view, you will soon see that the main difficulty is when there is no current, because this makes the presentation of the fly infinitely more complex. If you want to avoid problems, you don't have much choice. Watch your approach, always face into the sun, being careful not to make any wavelet or to crunch the gravel if you are forced to enter the water.

During heatwaves, in big deep hollows, you will often find dozens of chub, remaining completely motionless, a few inches below the surface. You will observe that they gather in small packs of four or five individuals on average. Your tackle needs to be have an ultrafine tip with a very long drop line that ends with a maximum of 10/100. The size of the artificial bait must obviously be perfectly matched to the delicacy of the line. The hooks should be no. 18, or no. 16 at the very most. They may well seem rather disproportionate in comparison with the wide mouth of the beast you are after.

• Be unobtrusive – chub are suspicious

As unobtrusively as you can, cast your fly into one of these small shoals, and if possible slightly to one side of it. This will give you another chance for a repeat if you get a catch. If you can aim with sufficient precision, you may even land near the biggest fish, but only if you aim for the middle of the shoal. Since chub have some competitive instinct, you should very soon provoke a reaction. Keep your wits about you and don't miss that strike!

Other interesting places include deep, shady banks under branches. You can't resort to trickery here. You may reduce the drop-line to the same size as if you were trout-fishing. A good average is between 10 and 13 feet (3 and 4 m) long, with a 12/100 tip.

When fly-fishing, the same general rules apply as for fishing with live bait, in that the rig must be carefully planned and set up. Do not use a hook larger than no. 14. A bi- or tricolor palmer will do the job perfectly. If you spot a fish, or the sign of a fish rising, cast out, aiming slightly upstream, or just to the rear of the fish if the water isn't moving. Otherwise, simply trust your instinct and cast the fly just about anywhere against the bank, behind a submerged branch, where shade meets sun.

△ *When chub are lying at the end of a slack, at the head of the next stream, fly fishing becomes a delight.*

• Dry fly

Because coarse fish are distinctly less demanding about the accuracy of the imitation, you can quite comfortably rely on any type of fly as bait. And because chub are also attracted to land insects, palmers logically top the list. Black, red, and gray are the three favorite palmer colors. It is a good idea to add a few wisps of tinsel to the body. The silver flashes are bound to awaken the curiosity of chub.

Midges and ants continue to be effective after mid-August, and represent other interesting alternatives. On very sunny days, you'll sometimes find that bait is repeatedly refused. There are two ways to counteract this, either by reducing the size of the fly, possibly choosing a lighter color, or alternatively by submerging the artificial fly and adding a little spit to it. The cul-de-canard prove by far the best for this trick.

In overcast weather, on the other hand, choose thicker, fatter flies that float well on the surface.

• Nymphs

When we talk about coarse fish, we rarely think of fishing well below the surface. This is the wrong attitude. The best way to fish at depth is to use the nymph stage of an insect. If you use the simplest type such as Pheasant Tail, you will find it very easy to attract fish that are apparently indifferent to every prompt. The sole requirement is not to set up too near the fish you're after, and to be careful about the sound of the fly entering the water. It is pointless to overweight the nymph.

If nothing comes your way, don't despair. Wait a few seconds before raising the nymph again, using a few slight flicks of the rod-tip. This ought to provoke a lightning attack.

SPINNING FOR FISH

Chub are willing carnivores when the occasion arises, taking alevin and minnow, for example. They may also be easily fished with a spinner, and more rarely using moving deadbait and livebait. These last two techniques are used to attract the very largest specimens of chub that from time to time take bait meant for the larger carnivorous fish.

For spinning, use spinner no. 0 and no. 1, with silver or gold colors and a treble hook, which can be adorned if necessary with a teaser or a fly, and some wagglers, such as comma, worm- and fish-shaped lures.

In summer, wind in slowly at the mouth of streams, preferably early in the morning and late in the afternoon, or even on narrow beaches along the edges of these streams. At midday, it is preferable to explore deep holes and quieter positions, where strikes can sometimes be fierce. In mid-season, look for deep, obstructed sections on the outer curve of a bend, where the banks are wooded and the bed is littered with blocks of stone. Don't forget bridges and dams where fishing is allowed, they are truly excellent spots. In winter, prospects for spinners are distinctly reduced, but all the same you can catch a few fish, often very big fish, in deep holes and hollows. Fish slowly along the bottom, preferably using a flexible lure. However, under these circumstances it is best to see what you can catch in the way of any coarse fish, rather than aiming for chub in particular.

△ *Black palmer with a red hackle for chub.*

Chub are surface fish and take a fly very well. ▽

BARBEL

*Barbel (*Barbus barbus*) feel equally at home if they hit a strong current, where they make the most of the smallest stone behind which to hide, or in a deep hole amid a turmoil of eddies. They are generally so inconspicuous that they manage to go practically unnoticed by the majority of anglers! So much so that there are now plenty of rivers in which barbel have been present for a long time, but where they have long been forgotten, although they have been there among the currents and in deep trenches. If you love intense excitement and fishing that is both traditional and high-tech at the same time, it's high time to rescue the barbel from oblivion.*

Barbel are famous for their mustaches, which consist of four prominent barbels located at the corners of their mouths. ▽

A SPORTSMAN'S FISH

The common barbel is a member of the Cyprinidae family. They are to be found in most waters, mainly in the middle reaches of rivers which are sometimes classified ecologically as the Barbel Zone. The common barbel is found across Europe from eastern England to the Black Sea. It colonizes the deep pools that open up at the mouths of streams, slacks, and even more turbulent areas. Their massive heads taper down to a slim body, enabling them to shelter from the current almost as well as a common grayling or a trout. They make use of the tiniest pebble lying on the bottom as a hide. Their large fleshy mouths are strongly downturned and there are two pairs of barbels, one at each corner of the upper and lower lip. Their bodies are covered in scales that vary in color from greenish-brown on the back to yellowish white on the underside. They have large, powerful yellow-orange fins. Average fish measure between 12 through 20 inches (30 through 50 cm), and weigh between 1 lb 2 oz and 3 lb 5 oz (0.5 and 1.5 kg). Pools in deep rivers shelter even heavier specimens, sometimes exceeding 11 lb (5 kg).
The barbel is a fish that has numerous close relations, many of them highly specific to a particular area. The most widespread is the Mediterranean barbel (*Barbus meridionalis*), sometimes referred to as the southern barbel or trout barbel because of the small spots along its flanks. This barbel is much smaller than normal barbels. Other varieties of barbel are found exclusively in Spain, Portugal, Greece, Albania, and in the rivers which run into the Aral Sea.

BARBEL HIDES

Find barbels by searching first at the mouths of wide streams, especially if they finish in a bed strewn with large pebbles. In such spots, barbel can be found in a hide from early May. They start off sheltering behind lumps of rock on the river bed, as long as the water remains cold and choppy. They may, however, venture right out into the current during long hot spells. You will then find them on the bottom,

△ *Iberian barbel caught in a lake of the River Ebro at Caspe.*

busy searching for the larvae of which they are so fond.

Other attractive positions include deep pools that form downstream of weirs or bridges. The crucial point is that the flow of the water must not be uniform. The best option is a fairly narrow channel with eddies forming on the banks. Very deep holes in general, on a bend for example, are equally attractive.

THE BEST HOOK-BAITS

Barbel are archetypal bottom-feeders. They love to stir up the gravel or flip stones over in the search for larvae, crawfish, alevin, and fish roe lurking underneath, that constitute their daily fare. But, when the opportunity arises, they may also be tempted by more classical hook-baits, whether animal or plant.

Maggots, aquatic larvae (nymphs and termites in particular), and cheese are the best. But brandling, for example, or even crickets and soft fruits at the height of summer deserve equal mention. You can attach them to a strong wire, single-eyed hook or needle-mount them (especially in the case of fruits and cheese) on a smaller sized treble hook with points only just larger than the size of the hook-bait. In view of the barbel habitat, ground-baiting is never very easy. If you are fishing in a relatively quiet hole, meal and cake or pastry with a very coarse crumb, weighted with earth or sand, may be of some help. Ideally, however, you should use hook-bait on its own, regularly distributed at the head of the hide. This will attract any barbel in the sector and really sharpen their appetite. In moving water, the only alternative is to cast the hook-bait quite a ways upstream, in the hope that this will be enough to attract the fish to you.

FISHING FOR BARBEL

There are three techniques for fishing barbel: the long run using a floating line; legering, that offers different variations, and fishing with a feeder, made of soil or a tube. All these techniques require a rod with rings of 13 through 16 feet (4 to 5 m), maybe a little less for legering, and a reel filled with 16/100 line for shallow fishing or 20/100 line for fishing where there are obstacles on the bottom or where the current is particularly strong.

• The long run

The line used for the long run differs only in the diameter of the nylon used (never use less than 12/100) and the shotting pattern. Shots must be mounted in parallel, on a small breaking strand that you can secure, for example, where the line meets the drop-line. If the shots are crimped onto a wire trace noticeably finer than that of the drop-line, they can easily be trawled along the bottom. The length of your hook – on which you will place one or two swan shots as required – and your hook-bait will be more unrestricted in their movements and should be able to sway and spin round in the current. An additional advantage is that if your line gets tangled – a problem that happens nine times out of ten – at least it's the string of shot that will be involved. Your very fine line may well break but you won't have to replace the whole line.

• Legering

For legering, the classic rig continues to be perfectly valid. On the reel line, thread a $\frac{1}{4}$ to $1\frac{1}{2}$ oz (10 to 40 g) olive (depending on the strength

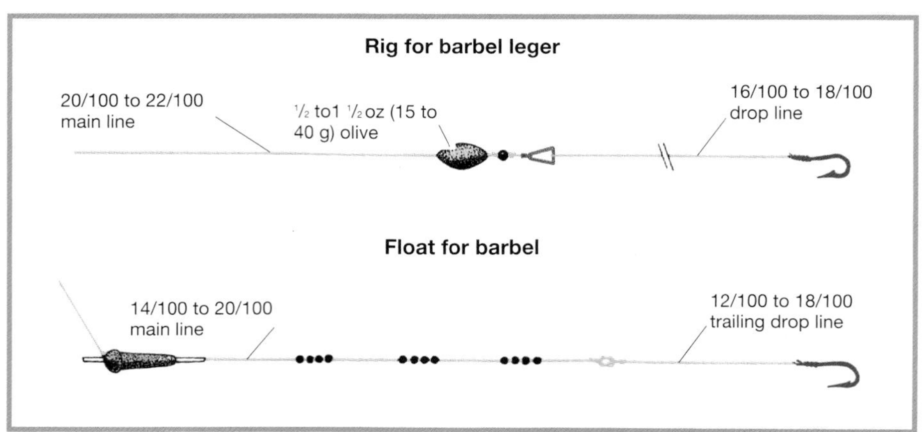

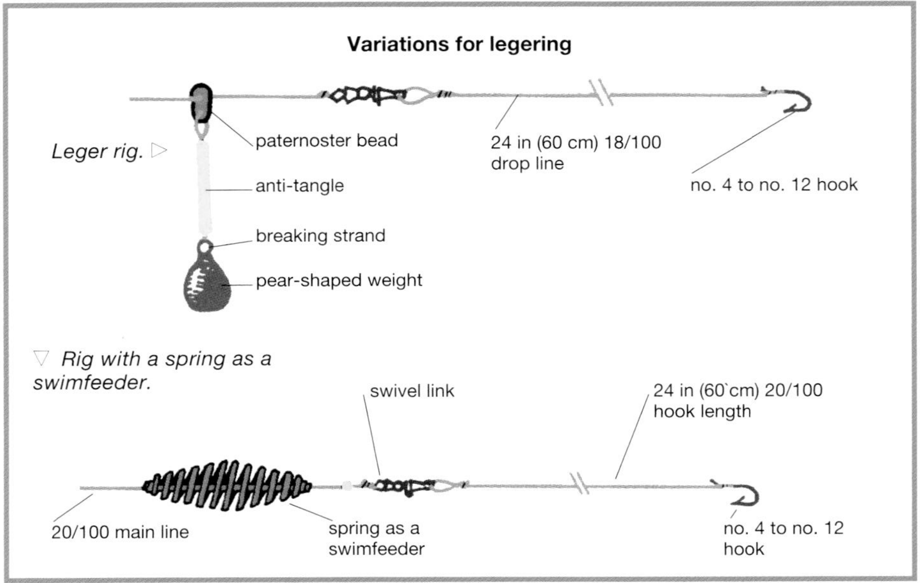

of the current) that will connect to a small swivel protected by a length of silicone tubing. Attach this to a hook length, a good 12 inches (30 cm) long and with a diameter that is always at least 2/100 less than that of the main line (in this case, the reel line). In addition to this basic rig, there are evidently many variations. To begin with, one variation consists in mounting the weight on a paternoster on a breaking strand (a line finer than the drop-line). On bottoms covered with obstructions, you will thus avoid losing the line every time it gets tangled, and you can also save money by replacing the shot with an old metal nut.
Finally, there is also a type of rig where the weight is at the end of the line, while the two hooks are mounted on a trace, leaving a space of 12–16 inches (30–40 cm) in between.

Cross-section of a baitball

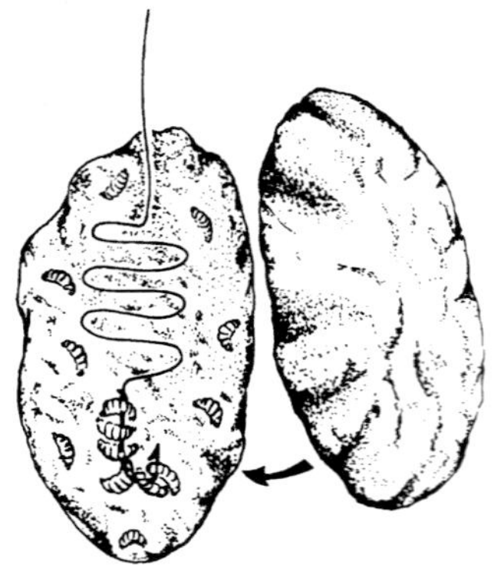

• Baitballs

Baitballs are used with the traditional weight described above. But just before casting, the weight, drop-line, and hook-bait (a cluster of maggots in most cases) are squeezed inside a ball of clay or mud that you have stuffed with maggots. To make a good job of it, try to position the cluster of maggots filling your hook so that they touch the baitball. As it slowly disintegrates on the bottom, the earth will progressively release a cloud of particles, along with one or two maggots, which will infallibly attract any marauding barbel.
One important point is that the feeders available today in tackle stores and by mail order can be used instead of baitballs. Choose weighted models and top them up with maggots.

• The fishing action

If you are fishing in moving water, the long run is going to give you the most satisfaction. Always position yourself at the head of the run that you wish to fish, adjust the float so that the drop-line and shot trawl easily along the bottom, and cast slightly upstream. The drift should then be just around the edge of the most powerful stream of water.
Keep your rod high. Control the drift, so that the hook-bait is presented before the shot and the line itself. If you feel a bite, lower your rod and wait a few seconds before striking.

In deep runs, downstream of weirs or the piers of a bridge, the long run and legering come to more-or-less the same thing. If you are certain that the position is well stocked, go ahead and ground-bait it. Loosefeed handfuls of hook-bait quite far upstream, leaving it to ride on the current. For the long run, place yourself as high as possible at the head of the hide and do as described above.
For legering, position yourself somewhere toward the middle of the hide and distribute your lines to take in the whole position. If the bottom is clean (sand or gravel, without too many obstructions), you can also decrease the weight and leave your legered lines to trundle slowly along the bottom when possible. This “roll-along fishing” is undoubtedly the most productive. When you get a bite, always release the line for a few seconds before striking.
In deep holes, legering, whether stationary or “roll-along,” baitball and feeder fishing are the best. But in positions notorious for the size and the number of fish they contain, it is best to use baitballs and feeders, since these will enable you to attract any fish in the sector more swiftly.

Heavy barbel rig for deep and powerful rivers

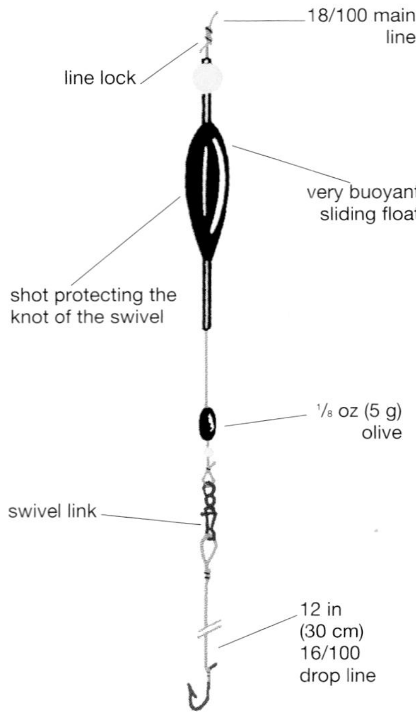

Nase

For a very long time nase were on the official list of fish pests kept in France. This has not been true since 1984. It was long believed that they lived off the eggs of trout and grayling. The confusion arose presumably because nase are bottom-feeders. Several scientific investigations have proved that nase are, in fact, one of the few fish that have a very restricted diet. They scrape the bottom and live mostly off diatoms, the microscopic algae that cover the bottom and stones, in rivers where there is the least pollution, but in which the water content is high in organic matter and mineral salts. It can therefore be said with certainty that nase keep the rivers and lakes clean for the Salmonidae species.

Nase are bottom scrapers, equipped with a prominent snout that enables them to scrape-off pebbles. ▽

A river's own cleaner

Nase (*Chondrostoma nasus*) are recognizable because of their snout-like noses. The mouth is small and strongly downturned, with very rubbery, almost cartilaginous lips. The body is strongly tapered and covered in tiny scales, reminiscent of the common grayling. The back is quite dark, but the flanks are lighter in color with grayish tints, while the underside is paler, almost white. The fins are slightly orange-colored and well-developed. The common Nase and its relatives are found exclusively in central and eastern Europe. Unfortunately, these natural cleaners are very sensitive to pollution, and in many rivers, their numbers are declining or even disappearing. All the more reason, therefore, to carefully release each catch. The flesh of the nase is so flavorless and riddled with bones, that it is of no commercial value.

Stalking your fish

The most classic style of fishing for nase is by trolling. This is performed with tackle and rigs that are identical to those recommended for chub (see pp. 228–229). Adjust the float so the drop line and even some of the shot are free to trawl along the bottom, and concentrate on deep pools and counter-currents. For hook-bait, use maggots (where permitted). Termites and brandlings are also excellent. But green algae (*Cladophora*) found at the edge of the main stream, covering stones or on the bottom, are even better. You just need to place a few strands on the hook and trawl along the bottom until you get a bite.

Fishing a swim

Nase can be fished in small rivers and certain reservoir lakes. They are also to be found in the quieter and deeper zones frequented by grayling and barbel. Ground-bait quite generously. Add some maggots or chopped brandling to the ground-bait but do not expect any bites for the first hour or even two hours. For your line, the rigs described for bream or tench, using still line, are perfectly adequate.

GUDGEON

Gudgeon (Gobio gobio) *are regular visitors to silty and sandy bottoms. They are now coming back in force in most lowland and medium altitude rivers, due to increased protection and the efforts of numerous fishing associations. But they still have a long way to go. Indeed, in the 1970s and 1980s, local gudgeon populations experienced very serious problems. Targeted protection became necessary in certain districts during the breeding season. Very fortunately, the situation has very noticeably improved and to catch one now, you only have to put your feet in the water! Gudgeon are tiny fish which many anglers catch merely to use as bait for more interesting coarse fish, but they are great practice for beginners and young anglers.*

Gudgeon, fish that resemble a miniature barbel, are now tending to recolonize Europe's rivers. ▽

A DENIZEN OF SMALL RIVERS

A quick description of a gudgeon is that it looks like a miniature barbel. The main difference is that the gudgeon only has two barbels to the barbel's four, and a tapering head and body. The body is covered with dark scales on the back, bluish-silver on the flanks, with prominent black markings in a line along flanks, and white on the underside. The underside of the head and downturned mouth is often slightly pink.

The common gudgeon is found throughout Europe and Ireland, with the exception of northern Scandinavia, Scotland, and the Iberian Peninsula. Related species are found in central and eastern Europe.

The best gudgeon positions are located on bottoms covered in fine gravel and occasionally in bottoms of coarse sand, but without too much mud or silt. The ideal situation for this type of hide is at the mouth of a small stream that you can then use to attract and contain the fish you are after. Positions that are generally successful include downstream of weirs, the inside of a bend, and tributary inlets, whatever the type of water course. In the few ponds or impounding reservoirs that contain populations of gudgeon, stick to the narrow beaches of gravel or sand. Proximity to water inlets also often provides first-rate positions.

HOOK-BAITS

Aquatic larvae are best, because the fish find them naturally in the groundbait that you're going to put together. Termites and crawfish also give good results but you need to find large quantities, and be aware that they do not hold the hook particularly well. All things considered, maggots are by far the best baits, preferably red ones, pinkies, or jokers. They all belong to the same family and can easily be found in fishing tackle stores.

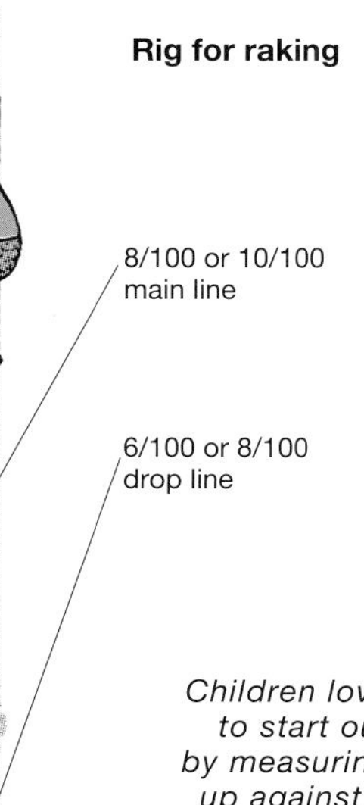

Children love to start out by measuring up against a gudgeon, on the banks of a shallow river. ▷

Raking a swim

For this simple and inexpensive method of fishing, you need a small 4-foot (3 m) rod and a keep-net, a creel or bucket, hooked to a belt at your waist while you fish, standing in the water. If the weather is cold or if you don't like the wet, add a pair of waders to your kit. Wellies will also do the job, just to stop you hurting your feet on the gravel of the bottom.

• The rig

The line is not at all complicated. Use a 8/100 or 10/100 line slightly shorter than the rod, a 2/100 drop-line, a small spherical or inverted pear-shaped float, and few small round shot, spread out along the hook (one shot in the middle) and on the main line below the float. The hook must be fine gauge and barbless if you want to keep your gudgeon to use as a great live-bait for zander or pike. Hook size may vary from no. 18 through no. 22, depending on the size of the bait used.

• The fishing action

Even if gudgeon appears responsive to most store-bought feed, with a preference for the feed designed for ground-bait or small fish, the trick simply involves using the most natural feed you can find. Use grit, particles of plants, and larvae found in the sand and gravel of the bottom. There are two ways of obtaining this kind of bait. The first can be used anywhere. You will need a garden rake or a long pole for stirring up the bottom. The second is for when the water is shallow enough to enter, and is the most acceptable in summer: Indeed, what you do is to stand with your back to the current and slowly shift your feet and drag them along the bottom, thus bringing up an endless cloud of particles. Get to know the bottom, either by plumbing it or quite simply by feeling your way, so you can adjust the float so that the hook-bait, drop-line, and some of the shot can drag directly on the bottom. Place the line upstream of the feed area and let it go with the current, so long as it is strong enough. Whatever you do, regularly liven things up by slackening off a bit, which will also disentangle the hook-bait a few inches above the bottom. The impression of flight that this gives, followed by a very slow descent to the bottom are often enough to arouse the appetite of any gudgeon that happens to be in the neighborhood.

In rivers whose waters are very clear, it is sometimes possible to see the gudgeon on the bottom, when they are busy stirring up the gravel or sampling any particles that float by. If you wear polarized sunglasses, to eliminate reflection, you will have the fish in your sights. Use the same rig, and just do away with the float. Group the shot together, so as to make the line easier to handle.

Although gudgeon are small; they are not only acceptable as bait but are good for making up the catch in coarse-fishing competitions, so even champion anglers do not turn up their noses at gudgeon!

ARE YOU BREAKING THE LAW?

Fishing regulations in some parts of Europe have banned stirring up the bottom to attract fish in game-fishing rivers. This technique may only be used in rivers, lakes, and reservoirs which are not considered prime for trout-fishing.

Gudgeon hides in a small river

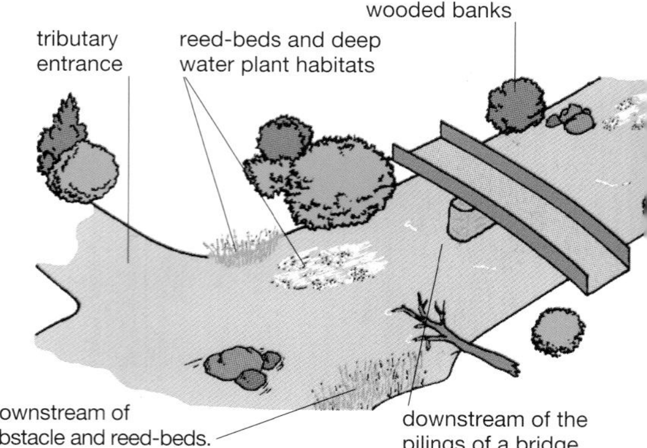

Minnow

*The Minnow (*Phoxinus phoxinus*) is the favorite fish of youngsters and of all beginners. Minnows are actively sought after by trout, who consume vast quantities of them, so they are equally popular among trout anglers to use as bait. This shared passion for minnow consumption has led to the little fish becoming an endangered species in some regions. Minnow populations are also decimated by drought and by pollution – to which they are particularly sensitive.*

Minnows may be small fish but they are still ferocious predators! ▽

A whitewater fish

Minnows have an almost cylindrical, tapering body. The back varies from black to dark green, and the flanks are smooth and heavily mottled with black. The background color of the back varies considerably from yellow to silver. The belly is paler, almost white. In the spawning season, the males change color until they are almost scarlet and yellow, and nuptial tubercules appear on their heads. Their size varies on average between 2–4 inches (5–10 cm).

Breeding takes place between early April and late May and causes the fish to congregate in large shoals on fine gravel bottoms that are well aerated, near the current. At this time of year, minnows form a seething mass which appears to be fighting a constant battle against the current.

Each female lays around 1,000 eggs which adhere to stones or gravel. However, the spawning season is a boon for trout, often lurking a few feet away, which wreak havoc among the minnow population and their roe, of which trout are particularly fond.

Minnows are found all over Europe; there are some varieties which live just below the Arctic ocean.

Line fishing

At the start of the season, minnows lurk in hollows and in the quieter reaches. However, as soon as the weather begins to warm up, they launch their attack on the streams that they will colonize until the first frosts of the fall.

The best tackle for minnows is a plain 4 to 6 foot (3 to 4 m) pole, a bait-box, and a small bucket or a miniature keep-net, if you want to keep your catch alive.

For hook-bait, you have a choice between small maggots, jokers, pinkies, or chopped brandling, a drop of Mystic, or a bread crumb pellet. Use any of these and you can't go wrong!

The line should be an 8/100 or 10/100 main line, with a small, very visible and very buoyant inverted pear-shaped or ball-shaped float counterbalanced by a few round shot that are quite spread out. The shot should sink gradually because min-

Making a minnow jar

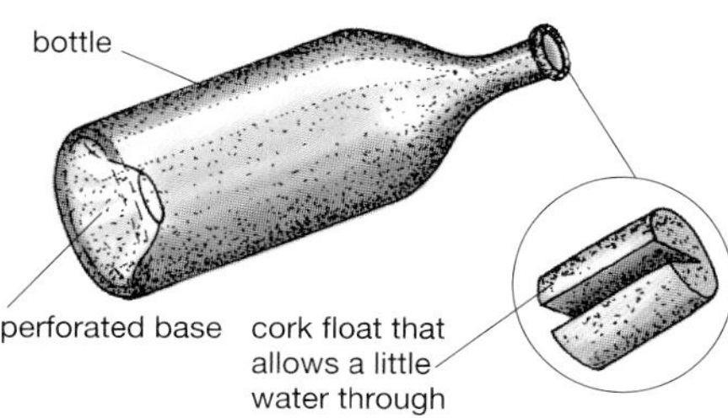

nows may be stationed at various levels. The drop line should be 6/100 or of 8/100, with a fine gauge no. 20 through no. 22 hook.

FISHING WITH A MINNOW JAR

A good way to catch minnows is with a jar, but this method is forbidden in some places, so check first with your local angling association. The minnow jar principle is simple. A gentle current is allowed through the container (a plastic cylinder or a large glass bottle) to attract the fish. They enter through the narrow opening in the perforated base. Once inside, very few find their way out. To increase the effectiveness of your minnow jar, place some bread crumbs, egg shells, or wheat bran inside. They will give it a shine that is attractive for the fish.

△ *Minnow fishing with a floating line.*

GREAT LIVEBAIT

If you are fishing minnows as bait for trout or carnivores, a certain number of precautions are necessary. If you use a line, always choose barbless hooks. That way you will prevent your protegés being seriously wounded. Whatever the technique you use, place your catch in a livebait bucket, from which you can easily remove the basket and place it directly in the river. During the trip home, a small ventilator, operated by battery or the car cigarette lighter will be welcome.

At home, keep the minnows in a large tank or aquarium with a mains-operated ventilation system. Don't forget to change the water from time to time, especially on days following the arrival of new inmates. Minnows do well in aquariums and are often kept as pet fish or for research purposes.

△ *Minnows are highly valued by large trout, as deadbait or livebait.*

Rudd

Rudd (*Scardinjus erythrophtalmus*) are a close relative of the roach. From an angler's point of view, the important difference lies in their behavior. From spring onward, they position themselves near the surface, where they unremittingly prey on any creatures that might come within reach. This also betrays their one major defect, their curiosity.

Rudd have more compressed and distinctly more rounded bodies than those of the roach. The mouth is distinctly upturned and their fins are reddish in color. Roach fishing techniques work just as well for rudd. Furthermore, the two species very often live together, and a whole keepnet can frequently be filled with a mixture of roach, cross-breeds, and rudd. Since rudd show the greater interest in insects and surface prey, they are worth a more targeted hunt, since they provide particularly enjoyable coarse fishing.

Freelining

• Wooded banks and water lilies

In ponds and quiet rivers, the best positions for rudd fishing are normally located right in the center of water lily pads. Half-hidden by the large leaves, the rudd are able to lurk

Dace

Dace (*Leuciscus leuciscus)* are built for whitewater and fast-flowing streams. They are fairly similar to chub, with which they quite regularly cross-breed, though endowed with a more streamlined body. The head is smaller and narrower. The mouth is smaller and more noticeably downturned, and the scales are thinner and shinier. The back is quite dark, almost black in some cases. The flanks are lighter, often with a touch of green, while the bellies are paler. Dace weigh a lot less than chub, usually 7 through 10 ½ oz (0.2 or 0.3 kg), and very occasionally up to 1 lb 2 oz (0.5 kg), or more. Dace live in clean, clear water. Sometimes they can be found at the lower limit of and watch their surroundings while being completely invisible to the angler and most passing fish. Another of their favorite positions is heavily wooded banks, where overhanging branches sometimes reach right down into the water. Under cover of the leaves, you will often observe shoals of fish, and here again, rudd are to be found consorting with dace or chub.

The best rudd positions are definitely located near heavily wooded and inaccessible banks fringed by thick clumps of water lilies. To make the best use of the fishing position, you need a flexible-tipped reservoir rod, 12 to 15-foot (3.50 to 4.50 m) long at the most. The springiness of the rod-tip and rod-tip holder is vital. This is what makes it possible to deliver your hook-bait all that distance, without any weight.

The line itself is very simple. Use a 6 to 8-foot (2 to 2.5 m) flexible-tipped rod with 14/100 to 16/100 nylon line (you need sufficient strength to test the response of the rod) all in one piece, and directly connected to a no. 12 through no. 16 hook, depending upon the size of the hook-baits.

Reservoir fishing for rudd

You would be better off using hardier hook- baits. With one or two maggots, a small brandling, or a termite securely attached to your hook, you are likely to get just as many bites.

• The best hook-baits

Given the rudd's curiosity and eclecticism, the choice of bait is huge. Land-based creatures appear to be of enormous interest, including houseflies, horseflies, cockroaches, Mayflies, June bugs, small grasshoppers, and ants. On the other hand such baits are very fragile, and therefore not well-suited to freelining.

• The fishing action

The fishing action for rudd is very simple. Try your luck just about anywhere in the river or pond. Deliver your hook-bait very accurately, so that it just makes a small "plop" when it hits the surface: watch out for those lightning attacks! Your strike should be just as quick! You can also position your bait on a water-lily pad and let it slide gently into the water.

Traditional paternostering and link-leger float fishing are also used for rudd. Rudd may even rise to a well-cast fly, wet or dry. Some anglers attach a maggot or a piece of white leather to the end of the fly.

the trout zone, the grayling zone, and the barbel zone, and more infrequently in the choppier waters frequented by bream. You will find them at the mouths of streams or downstream of weirs. They live in groups and feed off insect larvae taken at the surface, though occasionally they will eat plant debris.

FISHING ON THE MOVE

Trotting is a popular way of fishing for dace as it is for chub, and the tackle and rigs are similar, although there are some slight variations. To tackle a shoal of dace, place yourself at the water's edge and try your luck at the mouth of every stream. Pay out your line, with your float adjusted so that your bait is deployed halfway down it. Use aquatic larvae, maggots, brandlings, and insects that are not too bulky.

FLY-FISHING

Dace are active fish and ready eaters, which makes them a favorite quarry for fly fishermen. And because they live in reaches where the current is not strong, in depths rarely exceeding 3 to 7 feet (1 to 2 m), this makes them easier to fish and more accessible than chub. It's more like fishing for trout or grayling. If you come across a shoal of dace, you can get some very good fishing out of it. Even when some have already been caught, they are still active and don't seem at all bothered by your presence, no matter how conspicuous. But don't let that fool you! They will still do whatever they can to escape your clutches. Avoid following them, and either wait for them to move closer or change position completely, even if it means having to come back later to the more attractive swims. If you coax them too hard, you'll soon be forced to fish too far away and miss some good catches. This could cause the whole shoal to move away. Always use small flies that are not too thick, such as culs-de-canard, small spiders, midges, ants, and palmers. This will save you lots of wasted time.

GRASS CARP

Grass carp (*Ctenopharyngodon idella*) originate from the Manchurian-Russian border, specifically from the River Amur. This Chinese carp species was introduced into Europe because of its extraordinary appetite for plants. A grass carp is like an underwater lawn-mower, which is pretty useful where stretches of water are choked with weeds. You can recognize grass carp by its cigar-shaped body covered in shiny, very conspicuous scales, that are also very fragile. Other even more reliable identifying marks are the very small mouth and eyes that are located almost level with the corners of the lips. The fins are well developed and grayish in color. Only the particularly jagged caudal fin has a hint of brown.

Another variety of carp which has been introduced into Europe and is of Asian origin is the large-headed grass carp or silver carp (*Hypophtalmichthys militrix*) which lives almost exclusively off plankton. It has no commercial value and presents practically no interest for anglers.

SUNFISH

The Pumpkinseed, calico bass, pond-perch, or sunfish all refer to the same iridescently colored fish. Many anglers dream of taking one home to keep in an aquarium. Others, sadly, have nothing but contempt for them. They are related to black bass, and can upset the ecology of a pond or a river.

The sunfish (*Lepomis gibbosus*) is undoubtedly the prettiest denizen of the pond. It is native to North America and has only recently been introduced into mainland Europe and some fishing lakes in southern England.

The body is flat and almost disk-shaped. The two dorsal fins are connected, the first being spiny. The coloring is bright, the back varying from brown through bluish-green. The flanks are speckled with yellow, orange, and blue, and the belly has a distinctly golden yellow tinge.

Sunfish reproduce in May through June and the eggs and fry are guarded

Grass carp live as a group and feed almost exclusively on water-weeds. In China they are farmed for the table

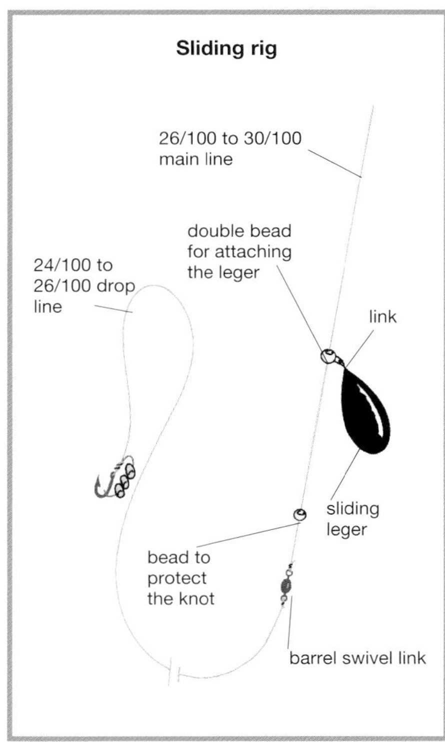

and they usually weigh around 45 lb (20 kg). Record weights for catches in Europe are around 112 lb (50 kg).
Grass carp have been imported into many European countries but they are still unwelcome in open waters where their introduction is banned for ecological reasons, in case they become a pest.
So in additional to fish-farms, you will find them in reservoirs and lakes where they help in the reintroduction of fishing by eliminating many of the weeds in the summer months. Their average weight of between 33 lb and 45 lb (15 and 20 kg), makes them a fierce adversary for the reservoir angler.
When fishing for grass carp use the same techniques that are specific to all varieties of carp. Grass carp happen to be fond of seeds and boilies. Track them down close to large clumps of weeds, the obvious place, since this is their feeding-ground. For competition angling, use ground-bait containing corn kernels, peanuts, or hearts-of-palm.

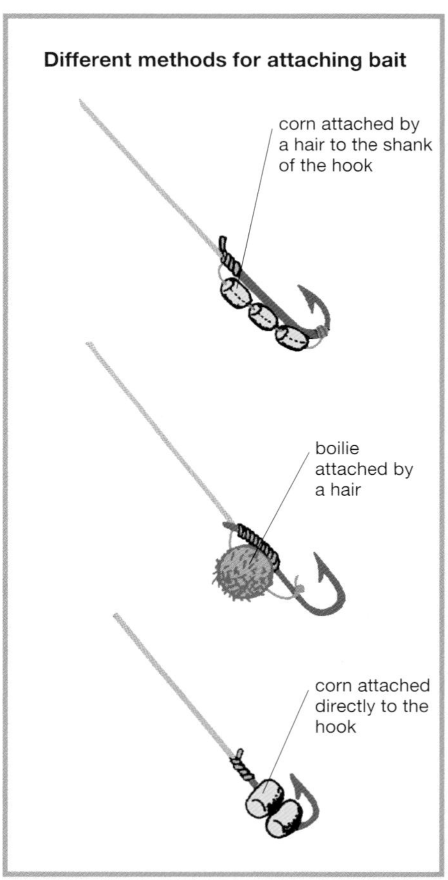

by the male. There are several related varieties of sunfish, including the redbreast sunfish and the green sunfish, all of which are native to North America, but only the sunfish has been introduced to Europe.
To find sunfish, keep to banks with a gentle slope, and to shoals and shallows with an abundance of weeds.
The angling technique is the standard one for fishing in a swim with a floating line. Bear in mind that the sunfish is a territorial fish, so you cannot rely too much on the effects of ground-baiting. Where catches are large, it is more a matter of luck, or a consequence of the prevailing density of the fish.

VISUAL FISHING

For a more targeted hunt, get yourself some polarized sunglasses. These will help you to spot sunfish. With a 13 to 16-foot (4 to 5 m) pole and a 12/100 or 14/100 one-piece line ending in a no. 14 hook, preceded by a small weight, position yourself facing the sun and go after all the fish you have spotted.
You will only need to position your bait (maggot, chopped brandling, colored bead, fly-fishing nymph) close to any sunfish and leave it to run. If nothing comes along, bring the line in slightly and waggle it. It would be astonishing if such a nasty piece of work as the sunfish resisted this ploy for any length of time. When removing the hook, bend back the spiny dorsal fin as it can cause very painful injuries.

◁ Sunfish are insatiable windfall eaters, and respond well to a floating line with natural bait.

Catfish

The Ictaluridae, the catfish family, contains five members, all of which are exclusively native to North America. Two species have been introduced into central and southern Europe, probably in the last century, of which the favorite for anglers is the common catfish, also known as the black bullhead (*Ictalurus melas*). These fish have proved to be a pest, devastating the spawning grounds of other fish while evading carefully laid traps, and often too small to be worth keeping in a keep-net. Some catfish are so voracious that they will swallow the bait along with the bottom line! So catfish are not popular with European fishermen. Nevertheless, they deserve credit for having certain qualities, in that they have bred well and are very easy to catch, as well as being considered a delicacy, particularly in the Deep South of the United States.

An undesirable guest

Catfish have a very characteristic shape. The head is large, broad, and slightly flattened. The mouth is a wide slit with no fewer than eight highly developed barbels, reminiscent of cat's whiskers, hence the name. The pectoral fins and the first dorsal fin are equipped with poisonous quills. The skin is absolutely smooth, and almost black on the back and more greenish on the sides, with coppery and golden highlights on the belly.

Catfish breed in early summer. The female lays her eggs in a sort of nest hollowed out of the river bed or lake bottom. The parents then take it in

Sturgeon

All the varieties of sturgeon are hunted for their caviar, though the eggs of the Beluga sturgeon (*Huso huso*) and other sturgeon varieties that live around the Black Sea are the most widely consumed nowadays. The common sturgeon (*Acipenser sturio*) is native to the coastal river areas of western and central Europe, from Spain to the Black Sea. However, the sturgeon has been so heavily fished for its roe that it is now a rarity turns to guard the clutch, a factor which explains how this species has spread so fast in alien waters. Once hatched, the young catfish remain in shoals, forming moving black clumps which can be seen near banks, in all the catfish haunts.

A good means of controlling the population consists in eliminating these tight shoals of fry, using a fine-meshed landing-net.

The catfish is a fish of warm, still waters, which is why it remains inactive, snuggled up in the mud, during the winter months. Only temperate floods can attract them out of their hibernation and tempt them to the eddies close to the banks, where they then feed actively. From the middle of spring you will find them in holes, oxbow lakes and the calmer locations in rivers, and more or less everywhere in lakes and canals. Smaller catfish venture closer to the banks, while the large ones remain in the deep zones.

Pain-free unhooking

In order to avoid painful stings which take a long time to heal, inflicted by the pectoral fins and first dorsal fin, use a thick rag when grasping a catfish catch. Make sure to take them with the thumb and index finger placed just behind the pectorals, and slowly pull down the dorsal fin using the inside of your hand. You can then unhook the fish without a risk of stinging yourself.

△ *Sinker fishing is perfect for catfish. If you use pieces of dead fish as bait, you can even go after the bigger specimens.*

Float fishing

Once you have chosen your fishing position, try dragging the bottom, using the same rig as you would when legering for tench, to see if catfish are lurking in the depths. If they are, a few baitballs will suffice to draw in a few more specimens and make them active. If you can't find anything, don't do anything until you have done some serious ground-baiting. Any store-bought mixes will attract catfish. You may need to mix the bait with some fuller's earth or clay in order to make it heavy enough to sink to the bottom. Distribute it all in one go. You can also use the mixtures sold for bait specifically for catfish. These contain dried blood, bone meal, and fish meal (the odor is pretty strong!).

Another type of bait which catfish seem to like is cattle feed or chicken feed, probably because these also contain a high proportion of bone meal and fish meal. Catfish also like the granules developed for farmed trout, but these need to be heavy enough and compact enough to float down to the bottom and stay there.

Many catfish anglers swear by the traditional earthworms, clusters of maggots, and crawfish tails.

Sinker fishing

Another solution, which is often more effective for large catfish, involves using a sinker line with a very simple assembly (see p. 235). You can then fish slightly further from the shore and above all deeper.

When the line is in position, place the rod on its rests, keeping the line moderately tense. As bait, use an earthworm pierced several times, to make it into a fat ball, which may deter the smaller fry from taking the bite. You can also try a piece of dead fish held firmly on a large single no. 2 hook, or threaded onto a treble hook, using a baiting-needle. The bite will take the form of a series of jerks. Be patient, until these occur continuously, just sit it out or you will lose the catch.

---

in France and Spain, where a few pairs spawn in deep rivers.

A huge rescue operation has been mounted in France by angling associations to encourage sturgeon-farming and replenish the vastly depleted stocks which are only a fraction of what they were a hundred years ago. It will take time, however, before the first tangible results can be recorded, since this fish take more than ten years to become fully grown and reach sexual maturity. Consequently, sturgeon fishing has been outlawed in western Europe, and there is every reason to suppose that this will be the case for many years.

If you happen to catch a sturgeon on your line, you will recognize it instantly by its body, which is devoid of scales but which has several rows of bony, shield-shaped plates. It has an almost pointed snout with four barbels in front of the mouth, level with the eye. The body shape is almost tubular. The tail, which is also quite distinctive, has a substantially developed upper lobe.

Another variety of sturgeon (*Acipenser baeri*) is also starting to appear in lakes, having been bred in fish-farms. Sturgeon feed mainly on grubs and worms on the bottom. For this reason, they may bite on a line, on a sinker in most cases, or even on a floated line.

The most effective baits are earthworms, maggots and aquatic grubs.

SEA-FISH

THE COASTAL MARINE ENVIRONMENT

Freshwater fishermen who decide to try sea-fishing for the first time, will be disconcerted by the absence of landmarks and the great volume of water, both of which will tend to encourage them to drop their lines all over the place. In addition, the currents change direction every day and the water level changes hourly! So there is no truth in the rumor that sea fish are abundant and easy to catch. What all this means is that an angler moving from a pond to an ocean needs good advice more than he needs a bundle of rods.

Rocky points and other outcrops, which mark a creek sheltered from prevailing winds, provide excellent opportunities for all types of fishing. ▽

THE VARIOUS COASTAL FEATURES

The geology of the location, the topography, and other coastal features, lend themselves to different types of coastal fishing technique.

• Chalky cliffs

The famous White Cliffs of Dover and their opposite numbers across the English Channel are, in fact, difficult to fish from because they are so steep and sheer. To reach the coast, you need to seek out the erosion cones which cut gashes in the cliffs. These are called "chines" in England and "valleuses" in France. They are the best way to get access to the pebble beaches which are uncovered at low tide. The wave-lashed rocks just offshore are rich in microscopic food and thus frequented by many fish.

All the traditional coastal fishing techniques – surf-casting, rod-and-reel, support fishing – can be used in this kind of environment.

• Granite cliffs

Granite cliffs are typical of the coasts of Brittany and southern Cornwall, which become broken down into coves and small bays through erosion. Fishermen can best exploit the rocky outcrops in the sea, which are washed with strong tidal currents.

Many game fish, such as bass or pollack, frequent waters where there is a permanent swell. These should be fished with rod-and-reel, using support fishing or a floater line in the deepest waters, especially in creeks that are sheltered from the full force of the waves.

• Low rocky coasts

These are all the more full of fish if the rocky outcrops are located near an estuary. Provided escarpments alternate with sandy beaches, a great variety of fish will be found here, such as bass, turbot, conger, sea-bream, and wrasse.

Surf-casting on the beaches, rod-and-reel fishing with lures from the outcrops, or float fishing at the feet of large on-shore rocks are all techniques that will work here.

• Flat sandy beaches

Wide, flat beaches washed by huge breakers, such as the coasts of Landes, northern Cornwall, and the Pacific coast of the United States, are ideal for surf-casting. Even Mediterranean beaches which are relatively deserted and flat, especially those which have been created by coral reefs, are suitable for this type of fishing.

HOW TO READ A BEACH

The illustration above shows the best fishing positions, collected onto one hypothetical

A sandy and rocky beach

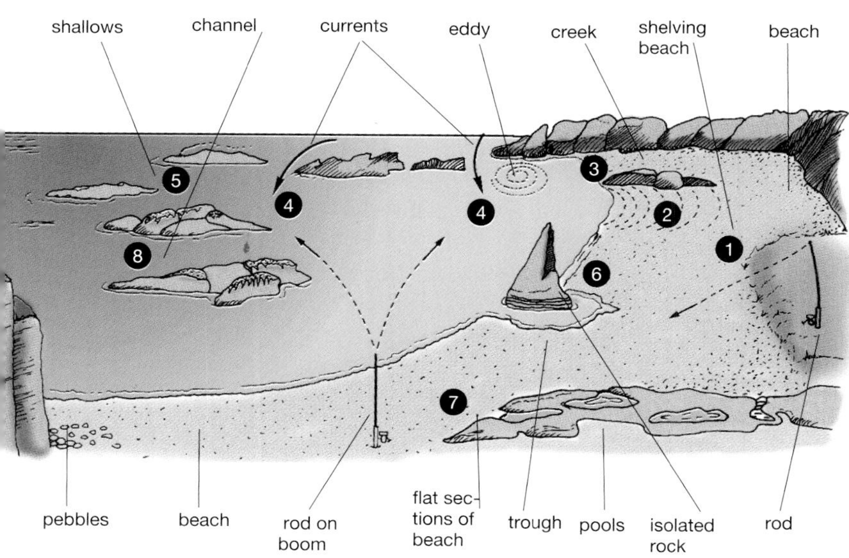

beach. It is most unlikely to find them all in one location, but several of these features can be found along most coasts.

1- A shelving beach covered by the waves at high tide. The swell rakes this slope, disturbing sand-eels, lugworms, and the other invertebrates that fish love.

2- Ripple marks, the favorite haunt of sand-eels; these should be fished at ebb tide.

3- Rocks offshore from an outcrop; the fast current that forms a channel between two such obstacles is a favorite swim for mullet, which should be fished with a float rig.

4- The tidal current that surges around half-submerged rocks, marking a deep fissure.

5- Shallows are highly sought-after by bass fishermen, who fish here using a rod and reel with lures (big-big or plug), over carpets of razor-shells.

6- An isolated rock beside a beach. The leeward side of such an obstacle will have a pool or trough crammed with worms, shrimp, or crabs, and this will attract predatory fish.

7- Flat sections of beaches that are covered in seaweed, especially bladderwrack. This is the best place to find soft-shell crabs in summer which can be unearthed at low tide.

8- A channel between two rocky escarpments, will have a large population of predatory fish.

Tides and their effect on fishing

Tides, whether they are neap tides or flood tides, and whether they are ebbing or flowing, have a considerable influence on the behavior of fish which means that each type of tide requires a different fishing technique.

• Tidal factors

These are percentages of between 20 and 120 which are used to measure the daily tides.

In addition to tidal factors, the depth of the water at low and high tide. The difference between them, the so-called tidal range, is highest with fast-moving tides. Conversely, they are lowest in the case of still water tides.

Sea anglers need to be aware of what these factors mean for them.

– *Factors between 20 and 50*

A weak tide will mean that fishermen will be unable to reach the far end of the beach.

The weak current will be less favorable for lures, but better for baits.

Conversely, fishermen will be able to remain for longer on positions like flat beaches to fish the channels, or in the center of the beach for surf-casting.

Generally speaking, fishermen consider that predatory fish "work" less hard when the tides are flat and the sea is calm. However, flatfish and congers are more inclined, with this type of tide, to emerge from the sand or the caves in which they hide.

– *Factors of between 50 and 75*

Average tides are suitable for all sorts of fishing. Gray sea-bream are particularly fond of them.

– *Factors over 75*

This is the time of the month of fast-moving waters corresponding to new or full moons. These high tides make it possible to fish at positions far from the shore at depths which are normally inaccessible from land. The canny fisherman

A typical sandy beach beaten by breakers, the ideal location for surf-casting fishing. ▽

knows that he will not be able to stay in such positions for too long, since the tide changes very quickly when there are high factors, and the incoming tide will quickly force an angler to move back. He should have just enough time to snatch a few bass, however. Along with the tide factor, the current will also be fast-moving, an advantage, as has been shown, for rod-and-reel fishing using lures. Similarly, in the case of intermediate positions such as flat sections of beach, anglers are in danger of quickly being swept away by the tide. The best beaches with strong tides are the rockiest, since they will contain more strategic outcrops from which you can cast, provided you change position frequently. Overall, strong tides are a good time to fish, especially in the case of the most predatory fish.
The currents promote greater activity in the fish. Unusual, little-fished positions can be prospected and the mass of water causes a pressure on the bottom and disturbs normally cautious prey. Everything tends to encourage angling on the move, to the detriment of static fishing (surf-casting, especially at night, or fishing from jetties, piers, or harbor entrances).

• Outgoing tide

In this introduction to tides, incoming tides have been discussed at length, but the outgoing or ebb tide has not been mentioned, although it is nonetheless of interest.
As the water recedes, it is accompanied by a suction which vacuums up small prey and debris originally swept in by the incoming tide and pushed right up the beach. These include sand-fleas, sea-ice, lugworms, razor-shells, clams, cockles, not to mention the many blow-fly maggots which have emerged from eggs laid in the belts of seaweed stranded on the beaches by the sea at ebb tide. After fermenting in the sun, this seaweed contains sea maggots, which fish love. Even bass feed on them.

The tides directory

Fishermen in straw hats and fishermen in waders will all have consulted the tides directory before setting off with their rods across their shoulders. This sea fishermen's bible indicates the day factor, times of the low and high tides, and the corresponding sea heights. It is absolutely impossible to do without this little marine calendar.

To fish successfully during an ebb tide, try and find a sloping beach with clear relief, and do not be afraid to explore the sands where the tide has gouged out channels with lures or baits, and the deeper rock-pools.
This is particularly true for bass, which are not at all afraid to return to the sea through shallow waterways.
It is worth noting that another delicious fish, the turbot, is better fished on the outgoing tide. Ebb tides are also particularly suitable for night-fishing.
Whenever you are fishing from a fixed position or trolling from the shore, ensure you wear thick boots which will grip the foothold firmly, as slippery seaweed can cause accidents.

Weather

Atmospheric conditions play an important role in fishing. Wind is usually a friend of the fisherman, in the sense that it is the

◁ *Waves and breakers are two different things. Waves affect the mass of water deep down and consequently sweep the bottom powerfully, where prey often seek refuge. Breakers are the result of a distant disturbance and are characterized by large, smooth swells, the troughs of which commonly reach 7 to 15 feet (2 to 4 m) in depth. When breakers come inshore, the bottom part of the water decelerates, and turns into a wave. On some beaches where the swell of a breaker is broken on submerged sand bars parallel to the beaches, a large, perpetual wave is created. This wave formation has a strong undertow which is particularly dangerous for swimmers, but very favorable for surf-casting.*

THE RULE OF TWELFTHS

In addition to the spring tides which force fishermen back to shore, especially on flat beaches, there is also the rule of twelfths. Under this rule, the tide does not rise uniformly but in unequal stages. The incoming tide rises by 1/12 of its total height during the first hour, 2/12 during the second hour, and 3/12 in the fourth hour, when it moves fastest. The tide then slows down and only rises 2/12 in the fifth hour and 1/12 in the sixth hour, until the high water slack, which does not last long in a strong tide.

underlying factor behind wave formation. A light wind registering no more than 2 or 3 on the Beaufort scale (approximately (6 to 9 m.p.h (10 to 15 km/h)) will form wavelets which will act as distorting mirrors and hide the presence of the fisherman from the fish.
A wind which rising to 4 or 5 on the Beaufort scale will create a choppy sea, but the waves will not yet be high enough to prevent bait or heavier lures being cast. Bubble-float fishing is still practical, as is fishing with sinkers, and also fishing with rubber eels.
The most important thing is simply to avoid fishing in a cross-wind, and to take up a position in which you are facing into the wind, even if this means that the casts will be shorter, a not insignificant problem.
When the wind speed is 5 to 6 and over (very rough sea), fishing becomes difficult.
However, there are cliffs which will "break" such a wind, as well as sheltered bays and inlets. Otherwise, when surf-casting, use 5 1/2 oz to 7 oz (150 to 200 g) sinkers, and cast heavy spoons of 3 1/4 oz to 3 1/2 oz (90 to 100 g), which are still light enough to fly up into the air.
As for wind direction, this is very much dependent on local factors. The fishing method depends on the outline of the coast and the technique used. Although European bait fishermen do not like north and east winds very much, European bubble-float fishermen love them, because they cause the little bubble-floats to travel far out to sea, thus giving them plenty of opportunity for deep-water fishing.
In the Mediterranean, opinions are divided as to the efficacy of the seasonal Mistral wind. In the Atlantic, southerly or westerly winds tend to be favored by anglers. For flatfish, sandy beaches, sheltered from the wind, and quiet, sandy coves and inlets are good for angling flatfish.

THE TACKLE

Sea spray, surf, the sea pounding on the rocks, and the powerful fish which are the angler's quarry all require the tackle to be capable of withstanding difficult, or even extreme, conditions. So sea-tackle needs to be utterly reliable and extremely robust. No detail should be overlooked. The nylon line must be just as sturdy as the rod or reel and all metal parts must be treated against corrosion. The fishing technique used will require a different type of tackle for specific conditions. A long rod of 15–16 ft 6 in (4.5 m–5 m), is needed for surf-casting, and a 10-foot (3 m) casting rod is required for bass or pollack. In this chapter, all the various types of sea tackle which are on the market will be reviewed.

Rocky coasts pounded by surf provide ideal positions for bass fishing. ▽

△ *Surf-casting rod.*

SURF-CASTING

Surf-casting literally involves casting into the waves. This definition is succinct but not very helpful. In practice, surf-casting involves a technique consisting of casting a weighted line, while offering natural bait for the fish on the sea-bed. The bait is thus all-important as everything depends on its attractiveness, and the way it tastes and smells to the fish. The odor is borne by the water over surprisingly long distances, and can be smelled by the fish, so well-developed is their sense of smell. However, this does not mean that the fisherman should choose anything other than the best possible fishing position, quite the contrary.

EQUIPMENT

• Rods

Surf rods used to be made of bamboo, a material which has many good points, especially flexibility. They were subsequently made out of solid glassfiber, then hollow fiberglass for lightness, and now they tend to be carbon. It is still possible to surf-cast fish with glassfiber rods, which are substantially less expensive than currently available carbon fiber or composite (a mixture of fiberglass and carbon) rods. The most desirable type of rod is made of carbon fiber mixed with kevlar. These rods combine lightness, resistance, temperament, power, and action. Surf-casting rods are over 13 ft 6 in (4 m) in length and may well be 14–15 ft (4.50 m), so that a cast will go far offshore and extend well beyond the ship's bow waves when fishing from a boat. Another indispensable piece of gear is the rod-rest, and a very robust model should be chosen. The rod-rest for sea-angling consists of a simple post or stick supporting a pot in which the butt of the rod rests, which should itself rest on a two-legged stand. The rod should have a power of 3 1/2 oz–7 oz (100–200 g). Apart from a few luxury models, most rods start to suffer when weighted with over 6oz (175 g) of sinkers, plus the weight of the bait. The diameter of the rod-tip, close to the head ring, should be around 1/8 inch (3 mm). If it is less than this 1/16 inch (2 mm)), the rod may break. As for the thickness of the fiber where it emerges from the reel-holder, this may be anything between 7/8 to 1 inch (23 to 26 mm), which is only just capable of handling the violent struggles of a large fish.

– *Reel-holders*

Another point which is often overlooked when purchasing a surf-casting or beach-casting rod is the position of the reel-holder in relation to the knob, which should ideally be made of foam. Manufacturers arbitrarily set this distance at around 36 inches (90 cm). Since everyone is made differently, this distance does not always suit the arm length of the fisherman. It is an important point, since the cast depends very much on the grip, and particularly on the distance between the right hand, placed near the reel, and the left hand, which holds the knob. For this reason it is sometimes preferable to have a reel-holder with a mounting-ring, rather than a screw-type reel-holder which cannot be adjusted.

– Rings

The main purpose of the rings is to guide the line without slowing it down excessively (if the rings are too small), or allowing it to drift along the rod (if the rings are too large). In modern rods, the first ring is quite far from the reel, with a diameter slightly less than that of the coil, and often folding (practical for transport, but more fragile). The other rings, of which there are four or five, are usually made of aluminum. The head ring must be of high quality, and made from silicon carbide. The intermediate rings should, if possible, be made from the same material, especially if the new braided lines, which are very abrasive, are being used. Three-stand rings may be recommended (two rear-mounting stands and one front stand), which have less effect on the bend of a rod under flexion than the traditional four-stand rings. As for spreading them uniformly along the rod, this can be judged by wedging the butt in the corner of a wall; supporting the rod with the left hand, press hard on the ring in the head of the rod-tip, using the right hand. Well-positioned rings will perfectly follow the curve of the rod.

△ The ray is a favorite catch of the surf-casting angler.

– Rod weight

The final area of importance is the weight of the rod. Weights range from 1¾ oz to 2 lb (50 to 900 g), depending on the material used. However, for surf-casting rods, the weight is of only relative importance since casts are not made very frequently, and the rod is not held in the hand during the fishing action. The lighter the rod the easier it will be to make clean, classic casts.

• Two casting techniques

In a nutshell, these are two techniques which will improve performance without too much effort.

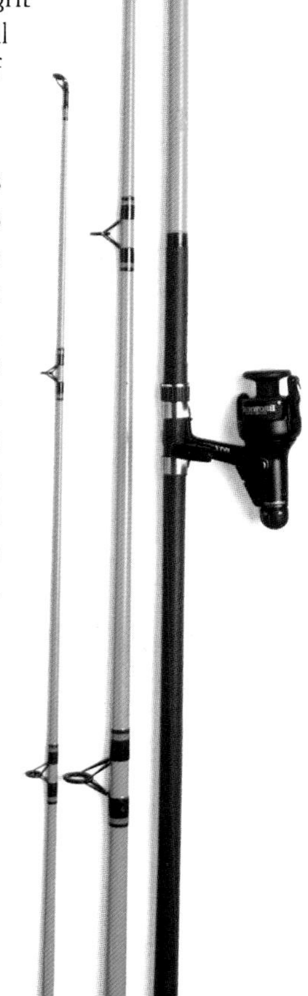

A traditional surf-casting rod fitted with a fixed drum-type reel. ▷

VARIOUS ROD ACTIONS

Here, summarized in the diagram, are the four dominant rod actions, although the action of a given rod may fall somewhere between two of these.

• In A, the bend of a fast action, or so-called "point", rod. The bend on casting, or on striking, only affects approximately one third of the length of the fiber.

• In B, a faster, semi-parabolic action: the rod bends more, almost to halfway.

• In C, the bend can be felt along two thirds of the length of the rod, with a parabolic action.

• In D, the entire rod is bent: a slow parabolic action.

For surf-casting fishing, use a B-type rod as long as it is no longer than 13 ft 6 in (4 m), and also the parabolic C-type rod, which is the one most used for casting baits, which should be kept on the hook in a good condition until cast into the sea. Some fishermen prefer a D-type rod, which may perhaps be less effective, but the extreme sensitivity of whose rod-tip is an excellent bite indicator. Bites would go unnoticed with a stiffer rod.

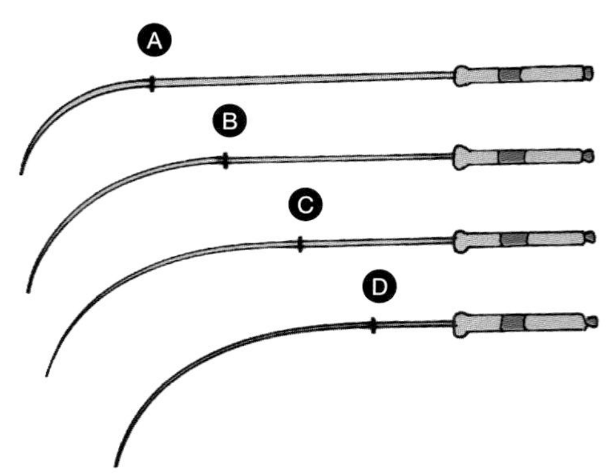

– Still sinker or "South African" casting
This is very effective and easy to learn. The sinker is placed on the ground behind the caster, with the rod parallel to the shore, and with a backing of approximately 4 feet (3 m) (A). The fisherman walks toward the sea. When the line is tense enough, the rod butt is brought back to the left hip (B). Simultaneously, the right hand projects the rod forward very hard whilst pushing with the arm (C). The sinker passes over the fisherman's head in the direction of the target, with the rod maintained at a 45° angle when the line is released (D). This cast, which is powerful and precise, requires an even sandy beach.

– Swing-casting
This is derived from grounded sinker casting where the ground is congested, for example on a rocky beach. The start (A) of the grounded sinker cast is eliminated, and replaced by swinging the sinker under the rod held at 45° (with a shorter bottom line). The rest of the movement is identical, with first the left arm and then the right arm pulling. Swing casting, which is less effective, has the merit of doing as little damage as possible to fragile bait. It may be improved by twisting the body as the sinker is thrown back (A), and by bringing it back while facing the sea, using a sustained action which puts it through a three-quarter circular movement in a rising trajectory (B).

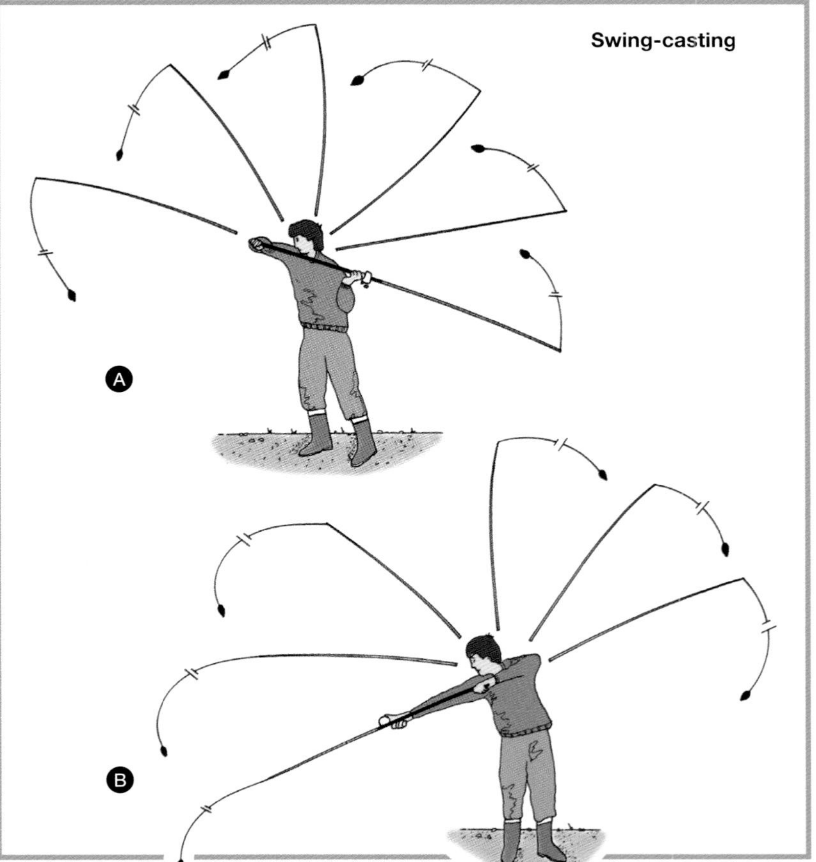

Swing-casting

• Reels
A good surf-casting reel should be a heavy model, which does not mean that it weighs 2 lb (900 g) when the rod only weighs 1 lb 5 oz (600 g). Although this is not too important, since surf-casting does not involve frequent casting, a modern reel, with a lighter graphite frame, is more comfortable for the fisherman.

– Capacity
The reel should be able to hold around 1000 feet (300 m) of 50/100 nylon line to be able to cope with lunges by big fish. The greater the capacity, the larger the size of the reel, which means fewer turns for unwinding line on casting, and thus a better range in terms of distance. To gain a few more feet, the coils often have conical, oscillating hubs to cross the line on recovery to ensure that the turns do not overlap one another. A bronze-coated enveloping coil is ideal.

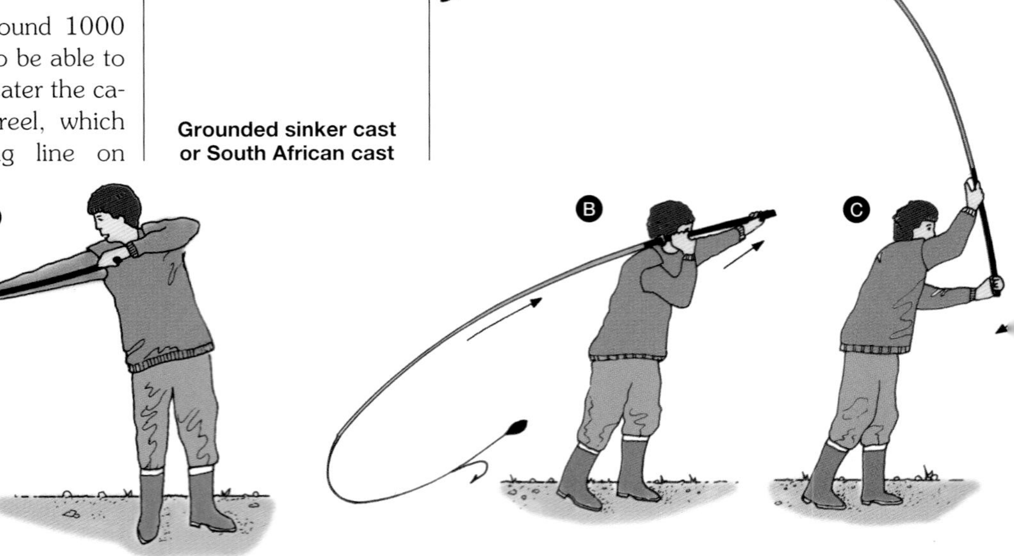

Grounded sinker cast or South African cast

– The clutch

This consists of springs and a series of washers. A good clutch pays out line under lower traction (sensitivity) and responds gradually to heavy adjustments, when the control button is pressed.

– The pick-up

Two systems are used for winding the line onto the reel. These are the automatic pick-up with basket handle and the manual pick-up using the finger. Generally speaking, with surf-casting, for the sake of simplicity, and thus reliability, finger pick-up is preferred. The important thing is that the pick-up should be fitted with a very durable roller, which can rotate for a long time without effort. A roller mounted on a sealed self-lubricating bearing will deal with the hazards of sea angling (salt sprays, sand-laden wind, rod dropped into the water). It acts as a pulley, sparing the nylon from wear and tear, and preventing overheating, which would soon sever the line.

– Good recovery speed

When there is no fish to reel in, but a heavily weighted bottom line must be recovered, you have to work quickly if you want the sinker to rise before it drags for too long on a fairly bumpy sea bottom. You should be able to reel in 3 to 4 feet (0.95 to 1 m) of line with each crank of the handle. This depends on the ratio, often around 4, which means that for a complete turn, the pick-up will need to revolve four times around the coil. Clearly, 4 feet (1 m) of line for each crank turn will seriously stress the mechanism, which should be large and as simple as possible. The gears must be adjusted (up to 1/100 on good reels). The mechanism is mounted on stainless steel ball bearings; the fact that there is a large number of them is not necessarily a proof of their robustness. A Mitchell 498, for example, which is virtually indestructible, has only two bearings, one ball bearing on the plate axis, and a needle bearing in the crank axis. Quality is the most important consideration.

Finger pick-up reel

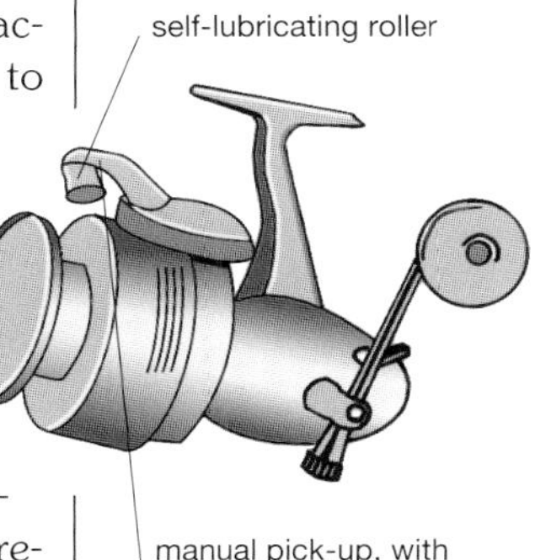

Basket handle automatic pick-up reel

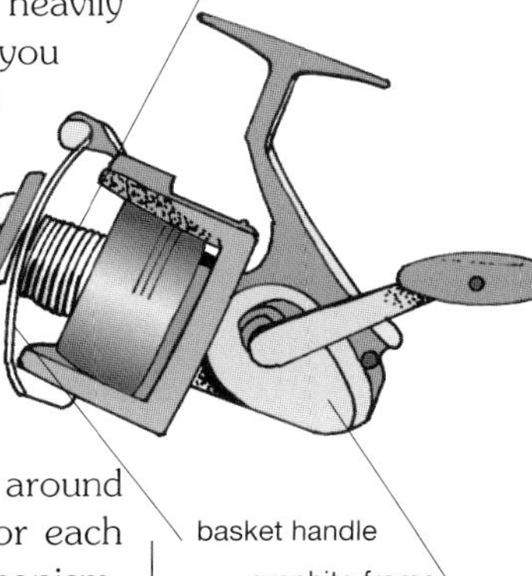

• Lines

The quality of the reel holding the line is crucial. It must be resistant, flexible, "invisible", incapable of distortion, anti-abrasive, and able to hold knots. It should not buckle when twisted, nor be damaged by the ultraviolet rays of the sun.

The surf angler needs a highly resistant line. Releasing a traditional, clawed sinker from the sand or tearing it out of a clump of seaweed requires a lot of strength. When a line needs to be broken after hooking, ordinary stretched nylon loses its initial resistance. We believe the right resistance is 40/100 (about 30 lb (13 kg) resistance) in a calm sea, and 45/100 or 50/100 in a rough sea. You can go as low as 30/100, provided you use a snatcher, 36 feet (10 m) in 50/100, to prevent the nylon from

Support or surf-casting fishing on large sandy beaches lets you catch many flatfish, such as this plaice. ▷

splitting when cast. It might be an idea to use monofilament lines which are not too elastic, given the great length of the line used, which requires good striking. Similarly, too fine or too flexible a bottom line will always tend to wrap itself around the backing line. A new and tempting solution is to use multi-filament line. These lines consist of a multitude of braided filaments, making them extraordinarily resistant. For example, an 18/100 line has a resistance of 24 lb (11 kg), or the equivalent of a high quality 35/100 nylon line. For surf-casting, a 20/100 (30 lb (13 kg)) multi-filament line would be particularly suitable. There are many other advantages, such as greater distance, less pressure on the line, a lighter sinker, and sensitivity to the bite. To this should be added great flexibility, and perfect sliding along the rings. Nevertheless, although the complete absence of elasticity is an advantage for instantaneous striking at a great distance, it is less so for the tip of a parabolic rod, which must absorb part of the impact if the clutch is not perfectly adjusted. In addition, multi-filament lines require complicated knots, doubled with many turns and, ideally, glued using cyano-acrylic or hydro-glue. Finally, these lines are still expensive.

If many traditional knots are used, there is a loss of a third or half the initial resistance. One of the safest knots which is also relatively easy to make is the Palomar knot (see illustration). Multi-filament lines have other faults, including a propensity to saw through ordinary rings, especially the head ring, as well as the pick-up rollers. There is also a tendency to become tangled at the head of the rod-tip and to become tangled up in the spirals of surface lures. In addition, you are forced to use a crossed turns line rolling reel, otherwise they will become tangled up in the coil. If a blockage occurs at the start of the cast this can be very painful; hence the need to protect one's index finger with a finger-guard, which is an absolute must for small diameter reels.

In conclusion, there are pros and cons to using multi-filament lines. Although they are now very much the fashion, only time will tell whether they will replace monofilaments, and for which types of angling they are most appropriate.

Palomar knot for multi-filament line

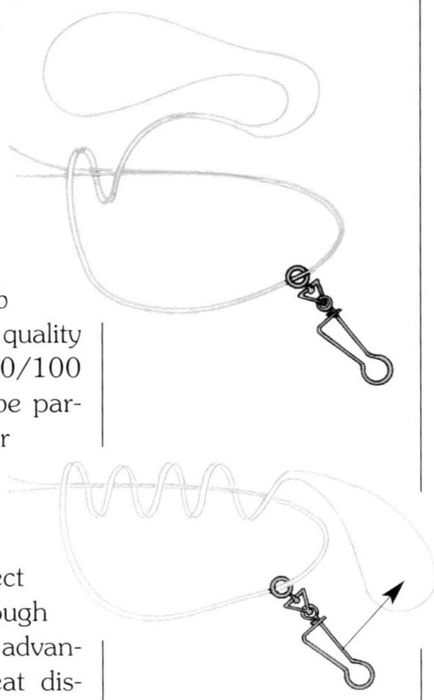

Watch sinker. △

• Sinkers

Sinkers are having ever greater demands made on them. They must have good air penetration on casting and water penetration on immersion; sufficient holding on the bottom to keep the line taut, but not too much so, so that bringing them back up is easy.

Clawed brass sinkers are still used – no doubt due to their low price – but, increasingly, sinkers with

Star sinker. ▷

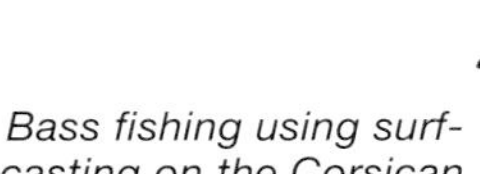

Bass fishing using surf-casting on the Corsican coast. ▽

unlocking claws, which turn over when pulled, are appearing on the market. Sinkers with small wings, which maintain a good trajectory in the air despite wind, come up easily due to their streamlined shape. A long rod prevents the sinker turning back on the line during casting. These are very good sinkers.

△ Anti-tangle, four-bladed sinker (Lemer).

If the condition of the sea permits, sinkers without claws can be used. They can move lightly, either with the current, or under the fisherman's guidance. These drifts attract fish, due to the sliding movement and the small, accompanying cloud of sand. The best are watch sinkers, which slide very easily, star sinkers or chestnuts, both of which stay better on the bottom. There are also anti-tangle sinkers with three or four blades (four-blades), through which the line is threaded. They do not roll around on the bottom, are easy to cast, and come up without sticking.

Anti-tangle sinkers are suitable for beaches with rocks and sand, and for wary fish, since the bottom line slides.

• Bottom lines

Traditionally, bottom lines for surf-casting are of two types, paternoster rigs for rough seas, and drag rigs for calm or slightly choppy seas.

– The paternoster rig consists of approximately 4 feet (3 m) of 45/100 bottom line, and has two or three short (8–20 inch (20–50 cm)) snoods mounted on a paternoster loop.

– A drag rig, also called a straggler, consists of a three-loop swivel called a "paternoster" 10 to 12 inches (25 to 30 cm) above the sinker, to which a snood approximately 8 feet (2 m) in length is fixed. The drag rig is more sensitive than the paternoster rig, and gives better presentation of the bait on the bottom. These typical rigs may be improved in ways which will make them considerably more effective.

– There is a variant of the paternoster rig which is intended for rough seas with breakers or strong currents. For this, the snoods are shortened to 8 inches (20 cm) and reduced to

80 in (2 m)

12 in (30 cm)

Traditional drag rig

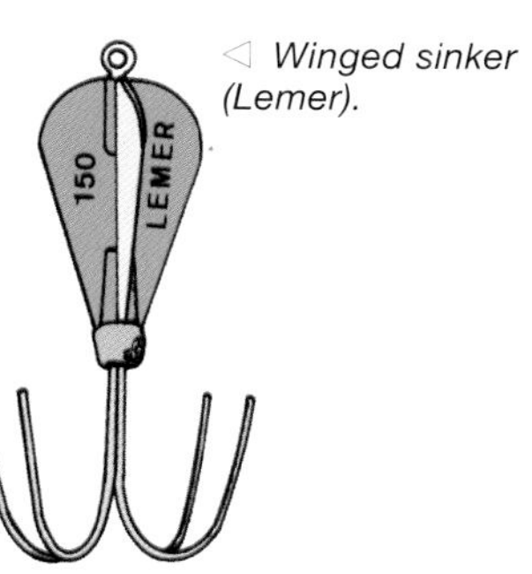

◁ Winged sinker (Lemer).

◁ Trilobe sinker.

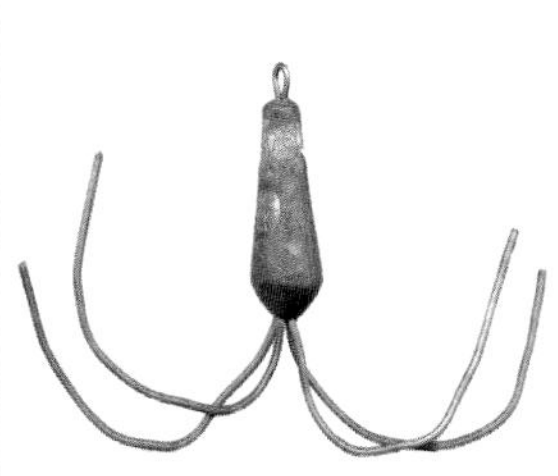

△ Traditional claw sinker.

Traditional three-paternoster rig

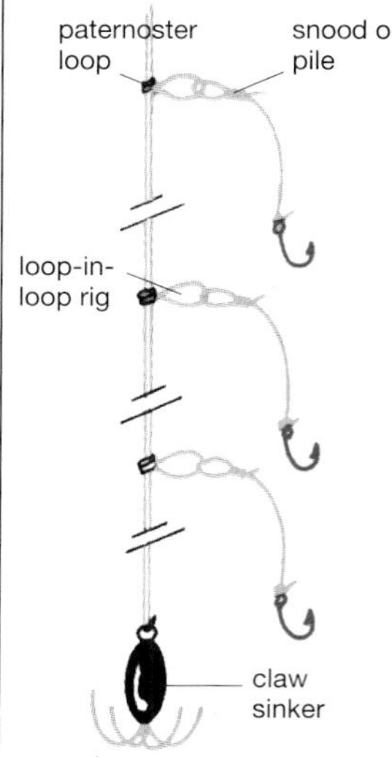

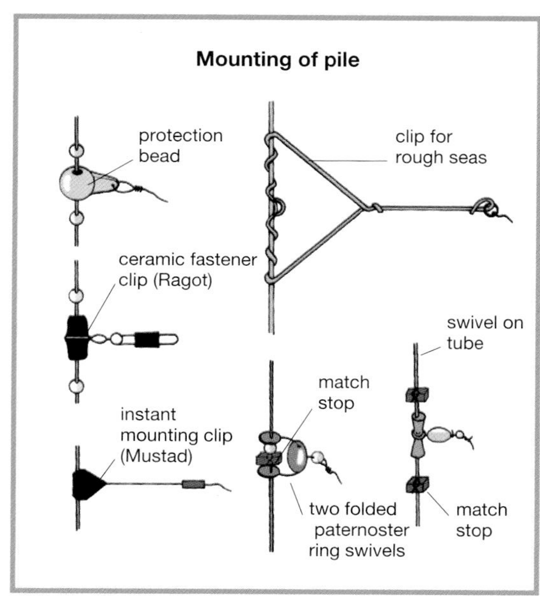

a single one in the rig illustrated. Instead of attaching the bottom line with a paternoster loop (which is a difficult task), a mounting using a barrel swivel is preferred, mounted between two beads.

This system lets the snood rotate around the line without spinning or getting tangled in it. For even greater freedom, four beads are used – with both ends fixed – glued with superglue or stopped using stop-knots, or again a small piece of match held in a capstan knot (which is very easy). The two movable beads will facilitate the rotation of the swivel. Another anti-tangle system, known as a "helicopter",

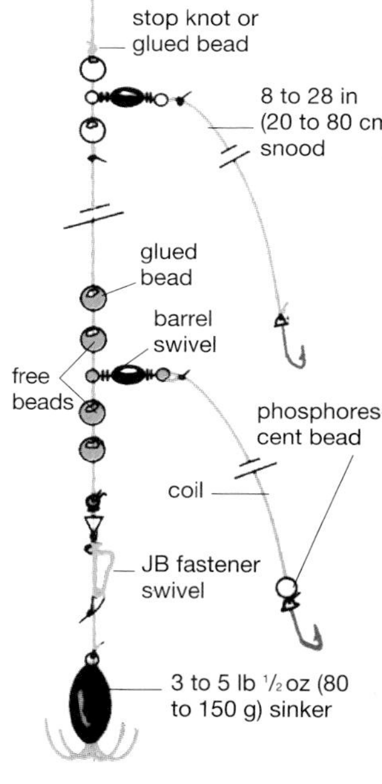

Modern paternoster rig

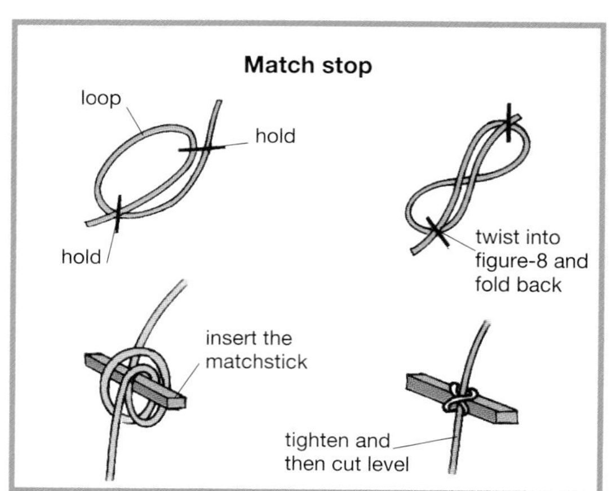

consists in inserting a small plastic tube (cut from a ballpoint pen) into one of the loops of a no. 8 barrel swivel. In this way, the barrel swivel is kept vertical to the bottom line, which is not the case when the swivel moves between the beads, when it lies flat.

Furthermore, at night, phosphorescent beads can stimulate attacks by fish, if they are placed just behind the hook. Longer 4 foot (1 m) snoods are suitable for a rough sea with a regular swell. The two snoods need to be sufficiently far apart for them not to hook each other, and the pre-prepared bottom lines are connected to the backing line by a fastener swivel.

– The variant of straggler rig is a compromise between a paternoster rig and a straggler; this rig consists of a long, 8 foot (2 m), coil fixed so that the hook is positioned almost level with the sinker upon casting. Once in the water, it can move above or near the bottom due to wave action, its main advantage. This rig allows livebait such as sand-eels, smelt, sardine, or squid to be presented in a natural way, so that even when dead, they bob about in the water, which is enough to excite many fish.

To give a natural look to the bait, the snood may be mounted on a bead or sliding tube supporting the sinker. This will make the bite even stronger, and clearly felt by the fisherman, provided he has left a little slack in his line.

◁ *A shielded bait-hook protects the bait and does not slow the cast down much.*

• Hooks

The primary function of a hook is to pierce and penetrate the mouth of the fish.

To ascertain that the hook is sharp, place the point on your thumbnail; the hook should not slide. If it does, it must be sharpened with a file or sharpening stone. Manufacturers are now making hooks made from a carbon alloy or ones which are sharpened chemically, and these are thinner and thus sharper and more penetrating.

– Size of the hook

This must be determined by the size of the bait presented and also the attachment line. Proportions must be respected. For example, a 30/100 line allows hooks no. 1 to no. 2/0 to be attached; a 40/100 line, hooks no. 2/0 to no. 4/0; and a 50/100 line, hooks no. 4/0 to no. 6/0. Since the main advantage of surf-casting is to make it possible to try and catch a great variety of fish, it is impossible to use a single hook for all types of fish. For medium-size fish (bass, sea bream, turbot, sole), a no. 2/0 is generally suitable. For larger fish (large bass, meagre, ray, skate, and conger), a no. 5/0 or no. 6/0 hook will be appropriate for both the size of the fish and the large bait presented (squid, cuttlefish, octopus, small mullet, or other live bait). However, it should be noted that manufacturers' measurements are not uniform, and that a no. 2/0 in one brand may be a no. 4/0 in another.

– The shape of the hook

Hooks come in various shapes. Long-shanked steel tips are suitable for lugworms but can also be used for baiting with knives or small dead fish (sand-eels or smelt), pierced through the mouth and exiting through the middle of the body. Still

Variant of drag rig

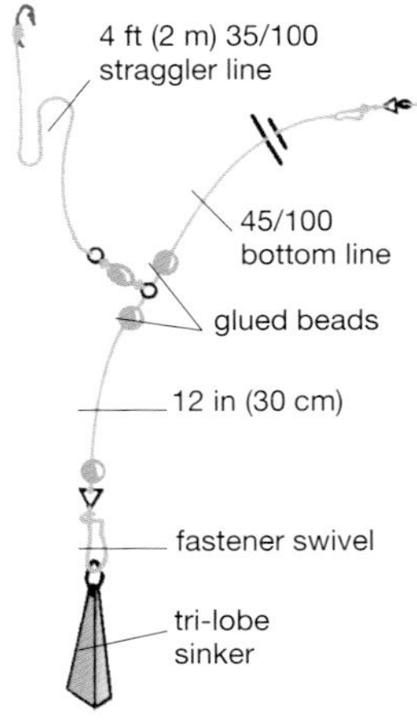

Helicopter slider

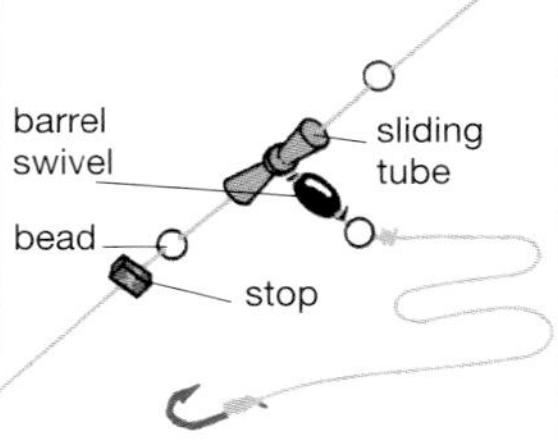

Long paternoster mixed rig

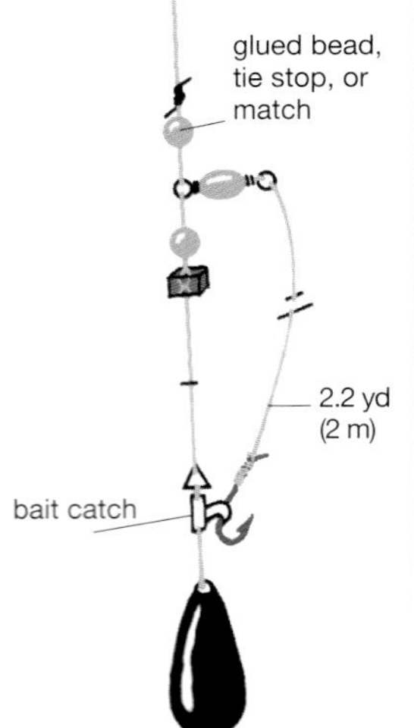

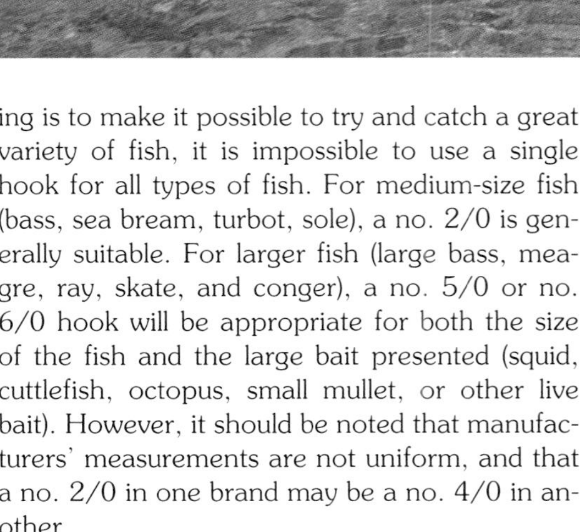

PERSONALIZE YOUR HOOKS

Some fishermen attach great importance to the look of the hook. Without going to the length of painting it to match the current bait, some people prefer their hooks to be dull, others brightly chromed and varnished with a liquid, inodorous varnish, such as is used as an insulator in the electronics industry or as a metal varnish.

◁ *Surf-casting in Corsica, the catch is a sea-bass.*

with rods, but with an inverted curve, hooks like VMC "surf" hooks also let you fish with worms or small shellfish.

Octopus strong-irons such as Mustads, VMCs or Gamakasus are more resistant (suitable for gilt-head bream) but need a sharp point. They are intended for fishing with squid, octopus, crab, and pieces of fish, and are intended for heavy catches (large bass, congers, meagre, and ray), using sizes no. 4/0 through no. 6/0.

– *Fixing the hook onto the coil*

The ring-hooks which are most frequently used because they are the most practical to fix, especially while fishing the position, are attached with three types of knot:

– the Palomar, which has already been mentioned in connection with multifilament lines, but which is simplified for nylon line, is easy to make, but rather thick for small, fragile bait such as worms and small oysters;

– the fastening, or half-barrel, knot,

– the hangman's, or universal, knot, which has the merit of being self-tightening while allowing the end used for stopping the worm, which always tends to bunch up, to extend. The Stewart rig is used to avoid this presentation fault. In this rig, the first hook is tied on, leaving a sufficiently long end to be tied to the second hook. This rig is often used for worms, cuttlefish strips, squid, or livebait. The only disadvantage is that the gap between the two hooks is not always the same as the size of the bait. This can be remedied by using an Octopus with an external eyelet as the first hook, which slides of its own accord on the line by using a suitable tie (a small copper or brass wire rolled into six to eight very tight coils). A stop-knot is not needed, and it is very simple to make.

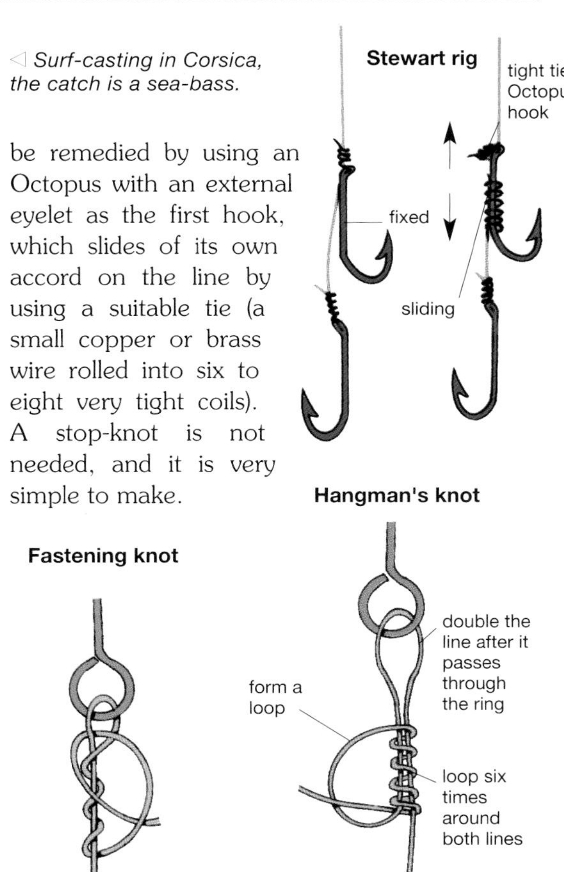

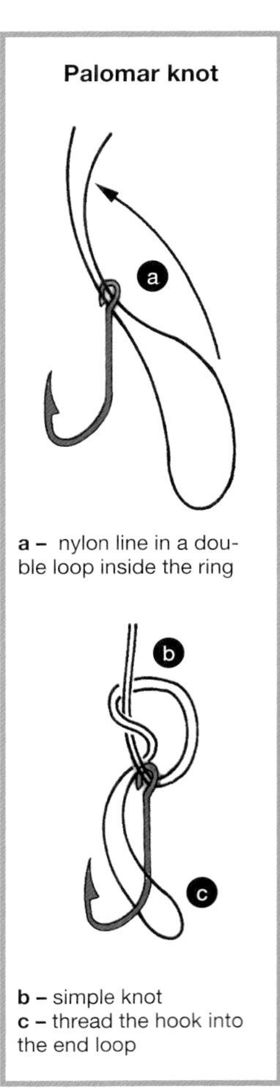

a – nylon line in a double loop inside the ring

b – simple knot
c – thread the hook into the end loop

Wishbone rig

A wishbone rig is also frequently used for fragile baits such as soft-shell crabs or for large livebaits, taking care in this case to tie both hooks with different lengths of line. It is made by forming a long loop using a "surgeon's" knot.

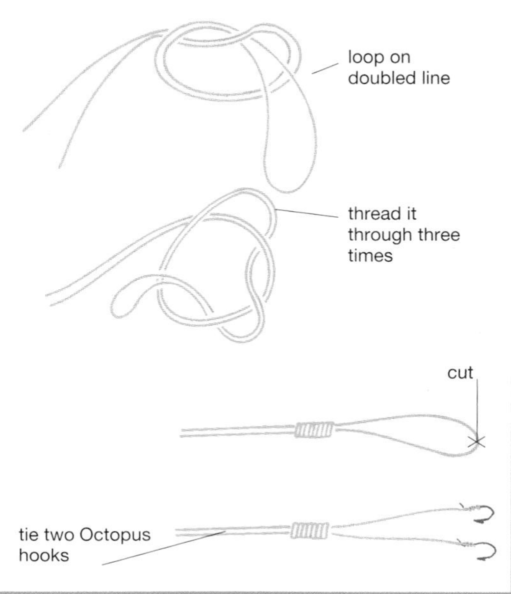

◁ *A bunch of lugworms, excellent bait for all fish.*

BAIT FOR SURF-CASTING

Four categories of bait are winners when it comes to surf-casting:
- worms, lugworms, clamworms, sea-mice, or imported worms are universally popular baits;
- octopus, cuttlefish or squid;
- clams, mussels, and oysters
- fish, dead or live, in sections or whole, the best baits being oily fish, such as mackerel, sardine, or herring;
- crustaceans, especially soft-shell (peeler) crab, shrimp being reserved for the finest fishing.

• Worms

— Lugworms

In coarse, muddy sands, lugworms burrow in a U-shaped tube, and give themselves away by their coiled casts left on the sand. You have to dig for them with a garden-fork, if possible working with someone else, so there is one person shoveling and the other picking up the worms and rejecting or putting aside any damaged worms. Almost all retailers supply lugworms to fishermen. The way to store them is to wash them well in seawater where you find them, then put them in small boxes or wooden crates, which absorb the mucus and casts. They can also be rolled up separately in newspaper, and placed in the vegetable compartment of a refrigerator, though they must never be mixed up with other worms such as ragworm. After a few days they must be emptied and salted. But nothing is ever as good as a fresh lugworm.

– Sand-eels

Sand-eels move about a lot, and their twists and turns in the water attract many fish. They are sometimes found with sandworms or in the muddy sands of ports and estuaries. Since it is impossible to detect their presence, you have to dig at a shallow level, at random, until you find a deposit (which will be known to locals): watch carefully where people with spades go at low tide. Sand-eels are kept in exactly the same way as sandworms, unless it is possible to keep them in recycled or oxygenated seawater (using a battery-powered aerator). Since its main attraction is its wriggling, a fine iron hook is essential, which will have on it three or four sand-eels attached to one end. Unfortunately, not all of them will reach their intended destination, unless a bait-safe capsule is used, which is a sort of hollow sinker which keeps the bait in place.

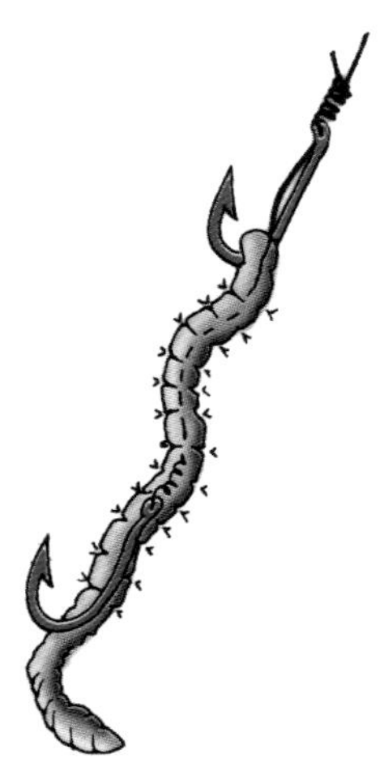

△ *Baiting a lugworm.*

– Sea-lice

These are not lice at all, but worms with flattened bodies. Look for them in soft, decomposing rocks, the crevices between crumbly rocks, veins of gravel and rotten wrack.

– Sea-slugs

These "miracle" worms, which are very long and thin, and a pinkish-orange color, work wonders. They live in the strata of soft rocks, in heaps of oyster shells or under stones, and on the edges of artificial rock structures. They are difficult to extract, but can sometimes be found in large numbers at the low watermarks of strong tides. Sea-slugs can be kept in sea water using the same method as for lugworms (removal of injured or dead slugs and renewal of water).

– Tube worms

These are greenish-brown and iridescent, and very attractive, notably at night, but quite fragile. Their presence is revealed by the end of a very long tube. They live in calm water and decomposing seaweed. They are harvested at low tide in the same way as razor-shells. Coarse salt is poured into the tube, a trick which makes part of the worm emerge, and you then quickly scoop it up in a shovel. Tubeworms are stored in the same way as sea-slugs.

RAGWORMS

These are found in the muddy sand of estuaries. They are excellent, although fragile for use in surf-casting. To stop the ragworm from falling off the hook, wrap the baited hook in a small bag of Solucit, which dissolves and rapidly disappears in water. A bait-fastener is required. Flatfish, such as sole, love ragworm.

— Imported worms
Worms are imported from North America or Korea and these are available from angling retailers and by mail order, but are quite expensive. They are a useful alternative for anyone who does not live close to the sea or does not have a whole weekend for fishing.
American worms are thick and about 6 inches (15 cm) long; they must be used whole and with care. If they are incorrectly hooked, these blood worms lose their attraction, hence the usefulness of a baiting-needle to thread them on to a straight, fine iron hook. Sea-bream love them.
Supercordelles are amazing worms, since they can be cut up as desired, starting at the tail, without affecting their ability to attract. As they are 4 to 8 feet (1 to 2 m) long, it is easy to understand their usefulness for fisherman. In addition, unlike other worms, they can be stored at quite high temperatures (77°F (25°C)), and consequently are very suitable for summer fishing.

• Mollusks
Cuttlefish and squid are the favorite baits of surf-casting fishermen. They have high resistance to casting, a good flavor while fresh, and a phosphorescent whiteness which is advantageous at night.
— Squid
"Gather squid in May, catch bass every day." This French proverb dates as far back as the 1960s! Baby squid are mounted whole on a hook, using the Stewart rig. Strips of squid cut from the mantle or the head will be ideal for many fish. They should preferably be harvested in the evening, using squid jigs jiggled at the foot of shoreline rocks, sea walls, pontoons, landing-stages, and piers. They can be acquired from fishing vessels returning to port, if they have not been kept too long in ice, which is their worst enemy. Failing this, they are available from fishmongers (make sure they are fresh). Squid can easily be stored in the freezer, wrapped in aluminum foil.
— Cuttlefish
Cuttlefish are very similar to squid and are used in the same way. The small ones are impaled whole on the hook, larger ones are cut into strips (cuttlefish white). When only the head and tentacles are used, they undulate in the water and are particularly attractive to all fish.
When using a strip of squid or a small squid, it is important to avoid twisting it on the hook (spinning) or even letting the end extend too far behind the ring.

△ *Ready-to-use cuttlefish strips.*

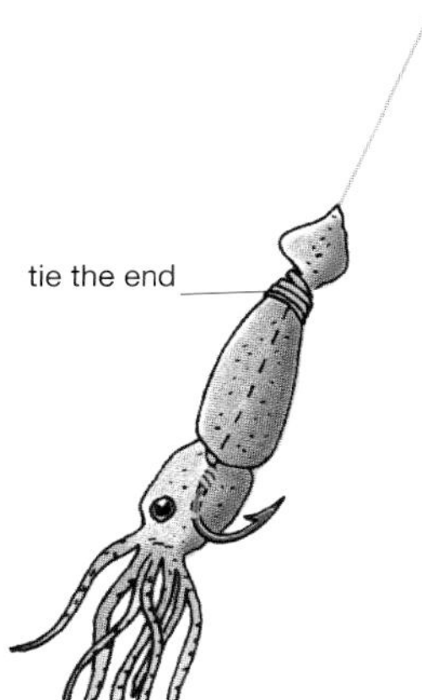

△ *Squid.*

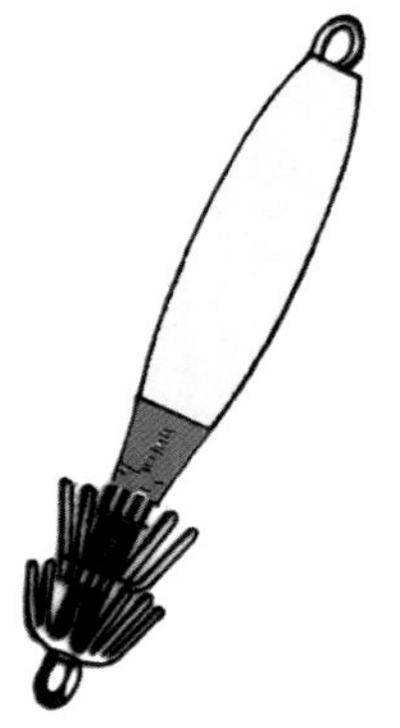

△ *Phosphorescent squid jig.*

If required, a rudimentary tie will prevent the bait from fluttering too much in the current.
— Octopus
These are fished and used in the same way as squid and cuttlefish. Their long tentacles grip remarkably well onto hooks, and become watered down more slowly.

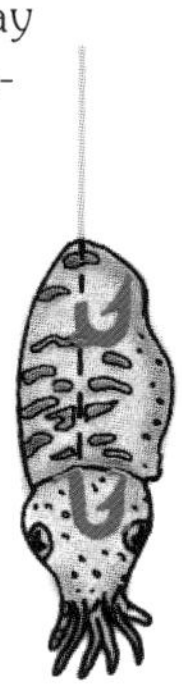

Cuttlefish. △

• Sea-snails, limpets, and bivalves
One of the first sources of wonder for children on beaches are shellfish, tiny cockles, the mother-of-pearl of ormers, and spiral whelks. When we have grown up, we are interested only in eating them and, where fishermen are concerned, in their fishing qualities.
— Razor-shells
These live at the lowest low-water marks, buried in 16 to 20 inches (40 to 50 cm) of sand, and their presence is revealed by their hole which has the shape of a figure eight. Razor-shells live in colonies, and are abundant on many sandy coasts. They can be extracted in various ways, including putting a pinch of salt down the hole, or using a long steel rod bent to form a hook, which is pushed in and turned through a quarter-turn to extract the razor-shell. The latter method often damages them.

Sections of octopus are particularly good for support fishing for conger. ▷

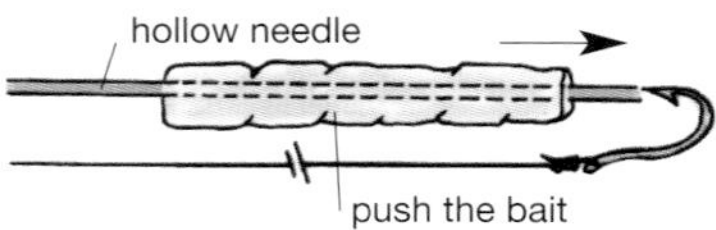

Baiting with razor-shell

– *Common piddock*
These constitute one of the best baits for bass and possible surf-casting fish. They have consistency, size, and phosphorescence, in other words everything needed for excellent fishing. When boring a well in soft rocks, common piddock squirt a powerful water jet which attracts the attention of hunters who know its favorite haunts. A crowbar or pick are indispensable. Using a long, bent iron rod, like a razor-shell hook, may be effective. Common piddock may be frozen.
– *Soft clams*
These are easier to extract from muddy sands, and also syphon when you approach them. Soft clams are a large bait item. They are fished through their hole, like razor-shells.
– *Other shellfish*
Other shellfish such as cockles, can be used. Cockles and small clams are easy to dig for, using a rake on beaches where they are present in large numbers, and to which sea-bream, pout, or even bass may be partial. There are also donax clams, or sea olives, with shiny shells which lie on the surface of moist sand.

△ Common piddock.

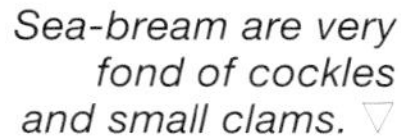
Sea-bream are very fond of cockles and small clams. ▽

• Fish
One fish gets eaten by another – this is a perfectly normal part of the food chain. The best example is the mackerel, a predator whose flesh excites the appetite of others. A fresh fish will always be better; however, a frozen mackerel may do the job for a fisherman in a hurry. The skin must be sewn meticulously on to the hook with a bit of flesh. A fillet lifted from a mackerel will hold it firm on a Stewart rig. A strip taken from the tail, which is the toughest part, the traditional "mackerel mouth", will tempt many fish.
Other small fish (small mullet, chinchard, pout, smelt, or goby) may be used, but the places in which they are caught are rarely those where they are of most use. The problem of how to preserve them and transport them then arises, and this is particularly critical with livebait as effective as sand-eels.

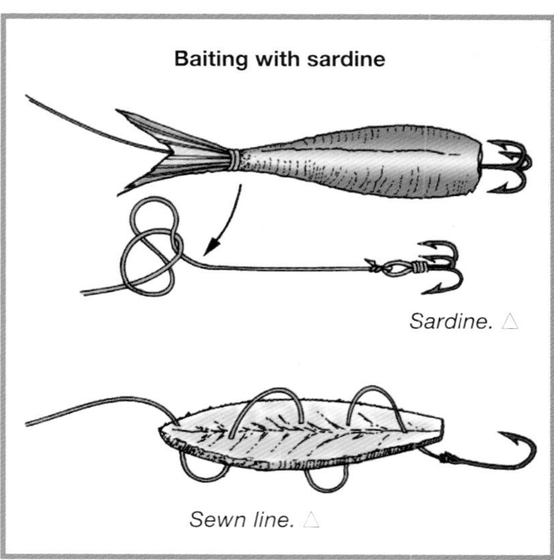

Sardine. △
Sewn line. △

The sand-eel is often confused with its cousin, the smooth sandlance (Mediterranean sand-eel, or talarek). The smooth sandlance, which is smaller, can open its protractile jaws very wide. These rangy fish shine with a great, silvery brilliance, which is bluish-green on their backs, and they wriggle as they undulate. They have color, odor, flavor, and vivacity: everything to drive bass and other predators wild with excitement.
Fishing with live sand-eels demands a lightness of touch, finesse, and flexibility in casting. Choose a fairly calm sea, which will let an 3 oz (80 g) sinker stay on the bottom. A bubble-rod will be more suitable than a strong surf-casting rod. A medium heavy reel containing 1000 feet (250 m) of 30/100 nylon line will help absorb the shock of the immersion better than multifilament line, thanks to its elasticity, by deceleration and light unwinding of the line at the end of the casting action, by placing a finger on the edge of the coil.
The rig described, which is a mixed one, seems well suited to this firm bottom-fishing. The sliding bottom line may be assembled on a hexagonal, flat, pierced sinker with spikes or a four-blade (A). If you are worried that the sand-eel might seek refuge in the sand, jam in a microporous ball (bait-float), impregnated with sardine oil, which will maintain the bottom line above the sea-bed. Nothing is simple with sand-eels, but then again everything is possible, and by taking the trouble you may even hook the best bass you have ever seen!

HOW TO WORK WITH SAND-EELS

When sand-eels linger in harbors, along wharves or eddies in front of sea walls, it is then possible to fish for them by bobbing strings of brilliant lures with faceted beads attached to golden hooks, wiggling them from side to side. At low tide, they burrow into wet, coarse-grained sand at the edge of pools, channels, or in ripple marks. This is the place to unearth them, using a shovel or rake. It is a good idea to get someone to help, since they jump about and bury themselves quickly. Jumpers should be gathered in a burlap bag, and buriers, which will be given away by the palpitation of the sand on the surface, should be lifted out as soon as they try to burrow underground. If permitted, they can be captured using a fine-mesh net, by capturing them in a large rock-pool, where they will take refuge at low tide. This is when the difficulties begin. As soon as they are caught, drop them into a large bucket of seawater with a perforated or mesh-covered lid, fitted with a battery-powered aerator to

△ *Digging for sand-eel is a tricky business, and you need a spade, rake or garden fork.*

Sand-eels are difficult to gather, but are wonderful bait for bass and pollack. ▽

protect the fragile health of these wriggly and often stressed creatures. Even then, you have to change the water often if they are not being used immediately. For short journeys, oyster keep-nets containing sand obtained at the location may be worth considering. You have to work hard with sand-eels!

A no. 1 hook, with a short, iron-tipped shank, may be fixed in three different ways:

– through the lips: a quite fragile mounting which prevents breathing;

– through the skin of the back, just behind the eyes, before the start of the dorsal fin. This is a good mounting, but one that requires you to cast very gently;

– through the caudal peduncle; this is stronger and more effective, since bass often chase sand-eels from behind.

• Crustaceans

– *Soft-shelled (peeler) crab*

When they molt, that is when they lose their shell and grow another one, all crabs go through a period when this protection is not solid. This makes them very vulnerable and arouses the appetite of most predators. They are then called soft-shell or peeler crabs. Fishermen generally use green crabs or swimmer crabs which are easy to gather at low tide. The best place to find soft-shelled crabs or crabs about to molt is mainly on sand-and-rock beaches, rocky beaches, or even sandy beaches, provided they are dotted with pools left by the sea on an

How to bait a smooth sandlance or sand-eel

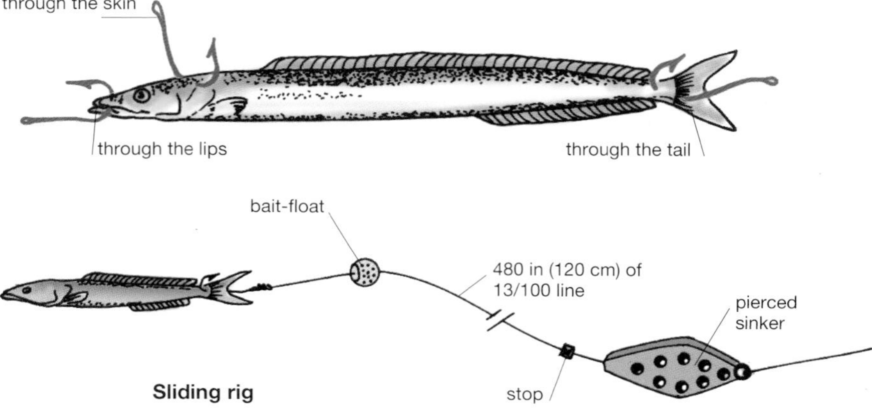

△ A green crab and its molt. A crustacean which has just rid itself of its shell is then called a soft-shell crab.

ebb-tide. The best time is on an incoming tide where crabs find refuge, at least while the tide is rising.
High-factor tides with fast-moving waters are better than stillwater tides, although this is not an absolute since, in summer, crabs are quite common along the coastline, because they like warm water which increases the speed at which they molt.
The ideal pools are shallow, and edged with bladder-wrack which must be lifted out with a hook without tearing it. Those nervous of being pinched by a crab pincer should wear gloves. If there is a stone in the center or corner of the pool, the crab will be underneath it; lift it without overturning it, so as not to cause ecological damage. If the bottom is sandy, a puffiness will betray the presence of the soft-shelled crab, which will have buried itself in the shallows. The smallest rocky crevice should be prospected, and the warmest locations are the best ones. Soft-shell crabs are also found in harbors which are silted up. They hide under debris or rotting seaweed, and also in the muddy channels which feed into salt marshes or communicate with brackish pools. At the low-tide mark, you may find a soft-shell velvet crab or, better still, a soft-shell edible crab. Soft-shell crabs, or crabs on the point of moulting, keep very well in wooden, lidded containers, filled with fresh seaweed which is changed often. To keep them longer (8 to 10 days), put them in a small children's shrimping net in a bucket, covered with seaweed, or in the vegetable compartment of the refrigerator. A short daily stay for 2 minutes in a saltwater pool will refresh them and allow you to pick out any dead crabs, which should be used immediately.

Mounting a soft-shell crab for bait

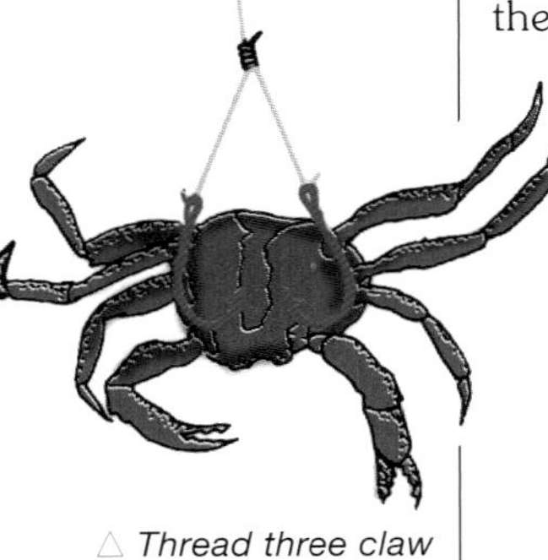

△ Thread three claw attachments and bring out the point on the back for each hook.

Simple bait-mount for a soft-shell crab

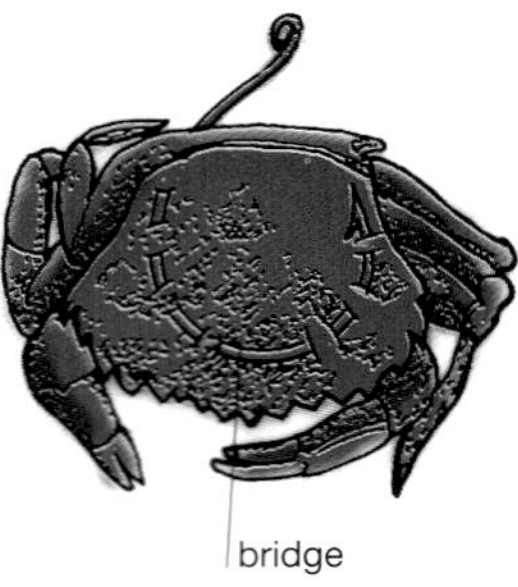

△ Thread four ligaments located on either side of the stomach.

While fishing, keep the crabs cool and shaded from the sun, in a small, moistened burlap sack.
How should a soft-shell crab be baited and impaled on a hook? First, choose a suitable hook, such as an Octopus with an external eyelet, a no. 3/0 for a small one the size of a clam, a no. 4/0 or no. 5/0 for a larger one. If the crab is really big it should be cut in two; this will work just as well. For a beginner, the best bait-mount is obtained by using a wishbone mounting with two no. 3/0 hooks. Each hook should be threaded through three or four claw joints, which will have been removed (see illustration below). These claw jointing cavities are the most robust. If necessary, the arrangement can be strengthened using a small rubber band or cotton darning thread, tied in the middle. An expert will thread a single no. 4/0 hook, firstly on one side, through the claw attachment ligaments; he will then bring the point out through the back and, turning the crab over, will once again thread two or three articulations on the opposite side, the curve of the hook acting as a bridge on the back of the crab. This is what the experts do; others can then cover it with a Solucit bag, or in a bait-safe capsule. When surf-casting, soft crabs can be used on a drag or mixed rig.

– *Other crustaceans*

Among the other crustaceans which fish love, there are live

shrimp, pierced through the penultimate segment of their carapace. However, they are hardly ever used for surf-casting, since they are too delicate to cast over a distance, even on a fine line. Use them for other fishing techniques.

Conversely, hermit crabs may be considered. This crab with a soft, highly exposed abdomen takes refuge in empty shells of the whelk or murex type, letting only its head and claws protrude. It is quite common, and can be attracted by baiting with crushed shells.

In order to extract it, you obviously have to break its shell with a gentle hammer blow, making sure not to crush it. The hermit crab is presented pierced at the end of the cephalo-thorax, threaded using a baiting-needle or, more simply, using only the abdomen, with two or three threadings on the hook. Hermit crabs may be kept in a moist environment, in wooden containers with plenty of seaweed.

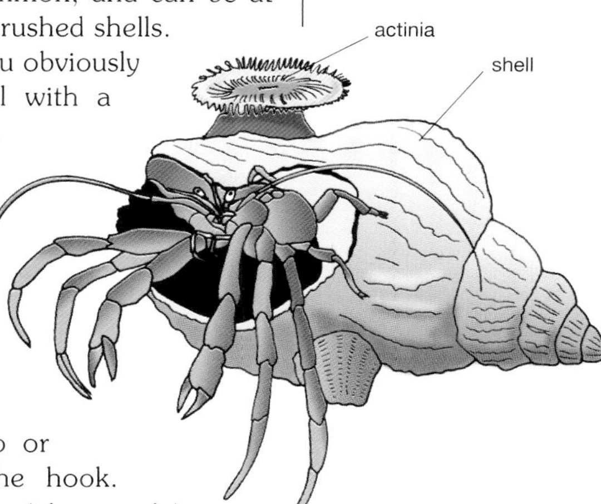

▽ Hermit crabs are often in commensal relations with sea anemones.

LONG-DISTANCE SURF-CASTING

Although a long distance is not absolutely necessary for surf-casting, there is no doubt that a fisherman, who often has two or three rods, will increase his chances of catching fish if one is 350 feet (100 m) and the rest 160 to 250 feet (50 to 70 m) from the shore. Particularly when the angler is facing into the wind, he will have difficulty in casting further than 200 feet (60 m), even if he has the appropriate equipment, including a fine line, a large sinker, a bait-fastener, and a single, short hook. The bait, which is often bulky, is a major slowing factor. It is estimated that 66 through 100 feet (20 to 30 m) is lost, in comparison with the same cast using only the sinker. How can these lost feet be regained without mutilating or losing the bait, and forcing the casts exaggeratedly and pointlessly?

• Cableway

All you have to do is use a system that is used for pike fishing in ponds, and which is called a cableway. The principle is simple: cast the bottom line without a bait, then slide the snood supporting the bait using an additional sinker.

The rig comprises a 35/100 nylon backing line or, better still, an 18/100 or 20/100 multi-filament line, which is put to good use here. At the end there is a 3 ½ oz to 5 ½ oz (100 to 150 g) claw sinker. Above the multi-filament line, a stop bead (or any other stop) is fixed approximately 20 to 60 in (50 to 150 cm) away, depending on whether a drag or mixed rig is envisaged, according to the

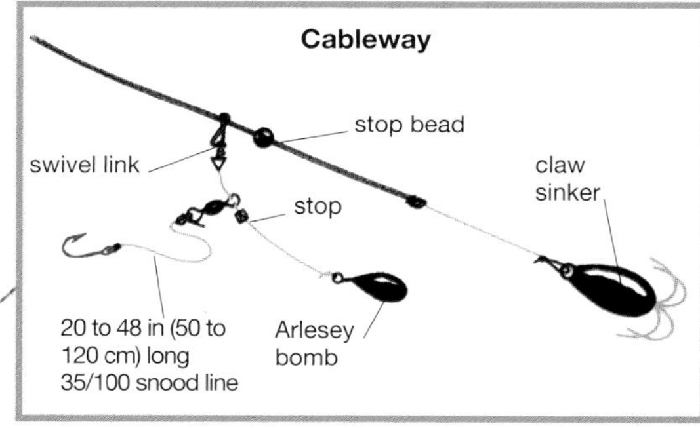

▽ Surf-casting on a sandy shore: waiting for the bite!

bait and the condition of the sea (use a shorter snood in rough seas). Once the rod has been stuck in and the line correctly tautened, the baited 35/100 bottom line is attached. The latter will slide along the backing line, dragged along by a secondary 16 to 20 inch (40 to 50 g) sinker. The snood may be mounted on a barrel swivel or paternostered to the 45/100 sinker line. This technique only works if the taut line is at a sufficiently inclined angle. On a beach with a shallow slope, when the line has been cast, you will have to try and find a vantage point, such as a sand-dune, rock, breakwater, or a cliff. Thanks to this overhang, there is a good 100 feet (30 m) between the end of the rod tip and the claw sinker, the bottom line may slide until it comes to rest against the stop, thus carrying bait in perfect condition, whether it is livebait, such as sand-eels, fragile bait, such as sardines, or simply crab, squid, or cuttlefish, which would not have been able to reach such a distance.

This may be a deepwater location where gulls swoop onto the bass's hunting-grounds, or a distant shallow where waves break.

NIGHT SURF-CASTING

Preparation for night fishing is made during the day. Choose a place where the crest of the waves curve round, where waves can break to the right or the left or, alternatively, places where rollers crash noisily onto the beach, if you are looking exclusively for bass.

A corridor between two raised flat sections of beach may also prove excellent.

Once this reconnaissance work has been done, the tackle must be prepared. At night, the most commonly used baits are ragworms, lugworms or imported worms, crab, squid, and cuttlefish with phosphorescent flesh. Fragile bait requiring delicate rigs should be avoided. Flatfish, such as sole, which are fished at night, are sensitive to shiny objects.

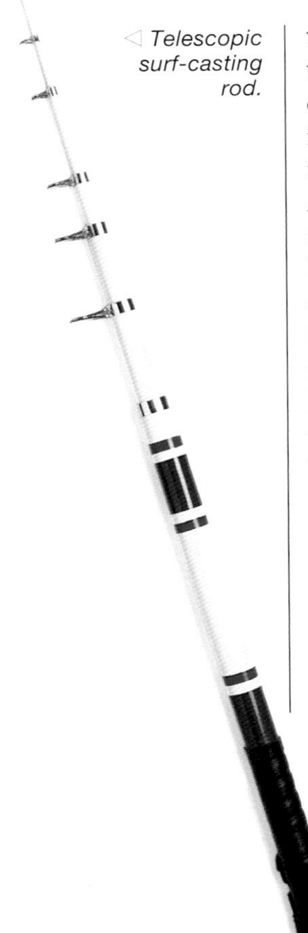

Telescopic surf-casting rod.

This is the favorite rod for dawn and dusk, when the biggest fish swim inshore.

main line, of 40/100 nylon
3/4 in (2 cm) 45/100 sliding bottom line
phosphorescent bead
sinker with or without claws for drifting
stop
no. 2/0 through no. 4/0 hook

A simple but sensitive rig

Since anything can happen at night, a rod to which bulky bait is attached and reinforced rigs will be ideal for corb, stingray, small sharks, dogfish, or large meagre. The rods should be grouped together to prevent bites from going unnoticed, despite the light signals. Illumination should be provided by a fluorescent rod tip or rings, and, even more effectively, a cyalume, a luminous stick which uses a chemical reaction to produce a powerful and lasting light and should be tied to the rod tip head.

There are also plenty of suitable bite indicators available. The oldest type, the bell, has the disadvantage of ringing in the slightest wind.

An electronic bite detector, which is much more sophisticated, is fixed above the reel and may be adjusted so as to avoid confusion between waves and fish. These bite detectors make a noise and light up, but they hate sea spray and mist.

Alternatively, a very rough and ready solution is a polystyrene cube which has been split and jammed on to the very loose line coming from the rod. This acts as a quite an effective bite indicator, and one which is very visible in the beam of the lantern.

A light bulb or a diode may be fixed to the point of the top-piece and powered by a lithium battery. It will not discharge when not in use, but it is sensitive to corrosion.

Yet another way of indicating bites is to use a small weight painted with fluorescent

or phosphorescent paint, which is fitted with a single hook to release it easily at the point at which it emerges from the reel.

SUPPORT FISHING

By definition, support fishing consists in supporting a line positioned at the base of a rod. It is thus practiced in quite deep waters, such as at the foot of shore rocks, piers, sea walls, breakwaters, and rocky structures. In principle, this rules out any casting. In fact, there are various types of support fishing, some of which are very similar to surf-casting. The classic rig is of the traditional surf-casting type, except that a claw sinker cannot be used, and the hand-held rod allows the bottom line to be wiggled up and down, attracting the fish. The baits are identical to those previously mentioned, with a preference for fragile baits, and livebaits, such as shrimp, sea-mice, and sand-eels, which are just as attractive if they are positioned rather than cast.

TACKLE

The rods are of average length: 4 to 5 feet (3 to 3.60 m), with the point action required for immediate striking. Reels with a capacity of less than that needed for surf-casting will do, which means they can be lighter.

The great advantage of support fishing lies in the possibility of baiting the position, and attracting fish with sardine bait, for example, or crushed crab-based baitballs, or oily fish, such as sardine, pilchard, or mackerel, ground in a blender and mixed with peanut flour and sand.

CASTING SUPPORT FISHING

This technique consists in casting the bottom line onto sand-and-rock beaches. This is almost surf-casting, with the fundamental difference that the rod is always supported in a fishing action – the line is controlled with the finger – and the fisherman targets very precise locations identified at low tide.

The best positions in rocky areas

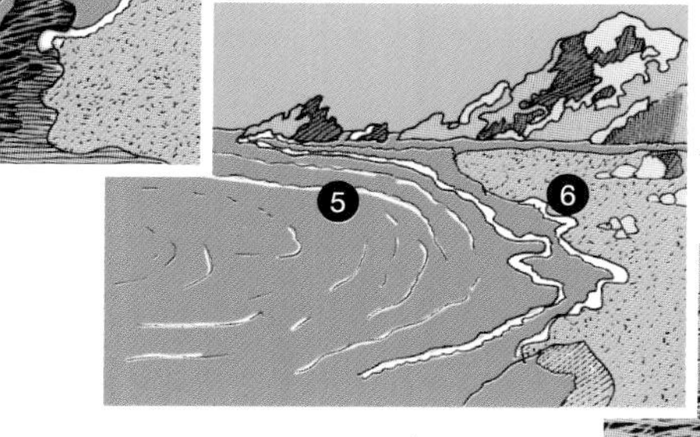

1 – rocky basin
2 – current
3 – rocky bank
4 – flat section
5 – shore of headland
6 – cleft
7 – channel
8 – inlet
9 – isolated rock at entrance to a channel

To support-fish without becoming excessively tired, you should choose a less powerful rod than for surf-casting, approximately 5 feet (3.60 m) in length, made of carbon fiber if possible, and a medium (1 lb 2 oz (500 g)) reel, with a high recovery speed (at least 300 feet (90 m)), so as to be able to recover the weighed bottom line at top speed, avoiding getting snagged as you do so. When fishing in a location with an uneven bottom, the bottom line should be very simple, meaning that no accessories may be used which might get trapped in the slightest crack in the rock.

There should be no swivels, notably paternosters, no fasteners, and no beads, nothing but a smooth, supple, sturdy line. In a typical bottom line, the coil bearing the hook is not added on, it comes directly from the backing line (for strength).

The line supporting the sinker is mounted as a paternoster. A flat-sided sinker, winged if possible, will make bringing up easier, and prevent it from rolling around on the bottom. The best place for practicing support fishing is on steeply sloping beaches, where there is no need to cast a long distance, and where there are plenty of flat overhanging rocks, deep channels, sandy corridors, or shallows at water level at low tide. The drawings on this page give an idea of the best locations in rocky areas.

It will be no surprise to learn that casts must be precise, but this is made easier by the short distances involved (160 to 200 feet (50 to 60 m)). This is by no means a lazy man's way of fishing. The fish that are targeted are sport fish, large bass and, possibly, gilt-head bream, or even wrasse.

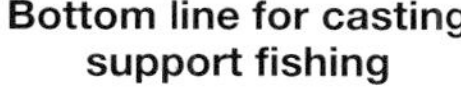

Bottom line for casting support fishing

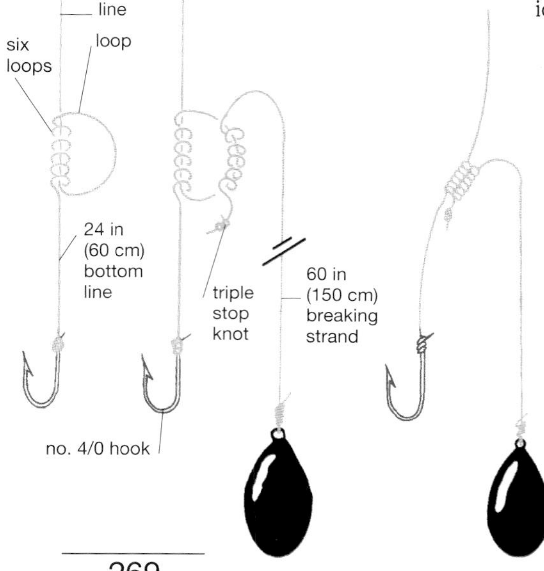

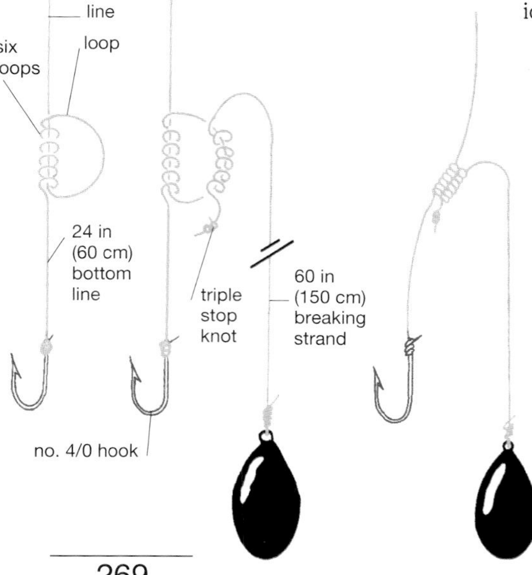

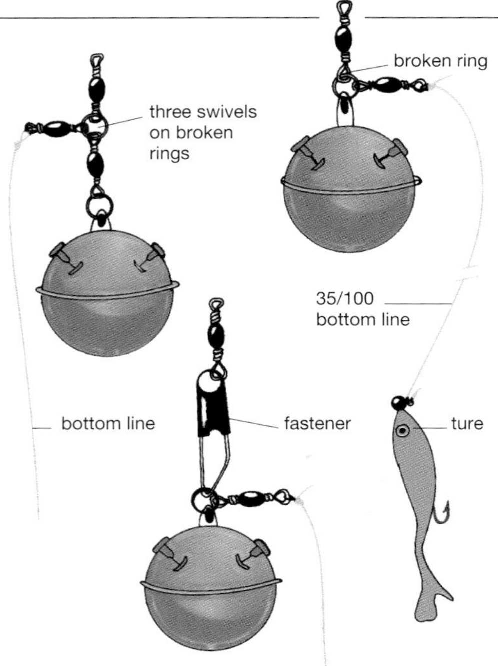

Various methods for fastening bubble-floats

The ideal bait is soft-shell crab, but squid, cuttlefish, razor-shell, large worm, or common piddock may also work. This is fishing with tact, observation, and by moving from one position to the next since, waves, breakers, and rollers are moving differently and changing their sequence as the tides ebb and flow.

CAST FISHING

Cast fishing is undoubtedly the most common method by the seashore, for two reasons:
— the ease and speed of implementation;
— the high performance of modern lures.
Be aware, though, that there is a huge variety of lures, perks, jigs, wagglers, and so on available. Every year, a new type is introduced, and fishermen may become so confused when the time comes to use them, that the fishing trip then becomes some sort of bench test. Do not forget that a crude lump of rubber, without head or tail, may work as well as the highly-sophisticated Rapaloup which emits distress signals. The old rubber lure will still catch fish, despite their increased wariness and scarcity.

BUBBLE FLOATS AND VARIOUS WAYS OF USING THEM

Everyone has a good word for the bubble-float, due to the ease with they can be used in order to place lures into the most tricky situations. Marine bubble floats were originally used in rivers by fly fishermen, and have become oval, for lengthier casting through the air; they are also now made of solid plastic to prevent them breaking on rocks and have become luminous for night-fishing, and even slightly submersible for semi-deep sea fishing. In short, this is the universal weighed float. Even though a good carp rod can be used for bubble-float fishing, there are more appropriate rods on the market. The rod should be a light (12 oz (350 g)) carbon rod, since it will be constantly moved and approximately 12 feet (3.9 m) in length, bearing in mind the long bottom line (8 to 10 feet (2.5 to 3 m)). Its nominal strength should be between 1 to 3½ oz (30 and 90 g), generally giving a semi-parabolic action. The reel should be light (preferably

WHICH FLOATS TO USE FOR WHICH TYPES OF FISHING

Compared to traditional balls and floats, modern, synthetic floats with closed cells are robust and satisfy most requirements.
The shape of the float depends on the weather and water. In calm and sheltered water – harbors, lagoons, and behind sea walls, spindle-shaped floats are good for moving through water. They are for fishing small catch, such as smelt or mullet. Floats used for coarse fishing for roach or bleak will be suitable for this type of fishing if they have a capacity of over 1/20 oz (2 g), with pole-fishing (using a very long rod without a reel). In the sea, additional weights may be needed at the base of the antenna.
In rougher seas, the float body used should be more rounded in shape, so that it does not sink under the slightest wave and, to facilitate distance casting, it should be sliding. At night, these floats may be equipped with a luminous stick or even a battery-power indicator light. Sliding floats which support heavy weights are the most effective for casting, and present baits (shrimp or worms) just above a bottom which cannot be reached with a fixed float, for example among the rock piles below a sea wall, where fish often gather in large numbers.

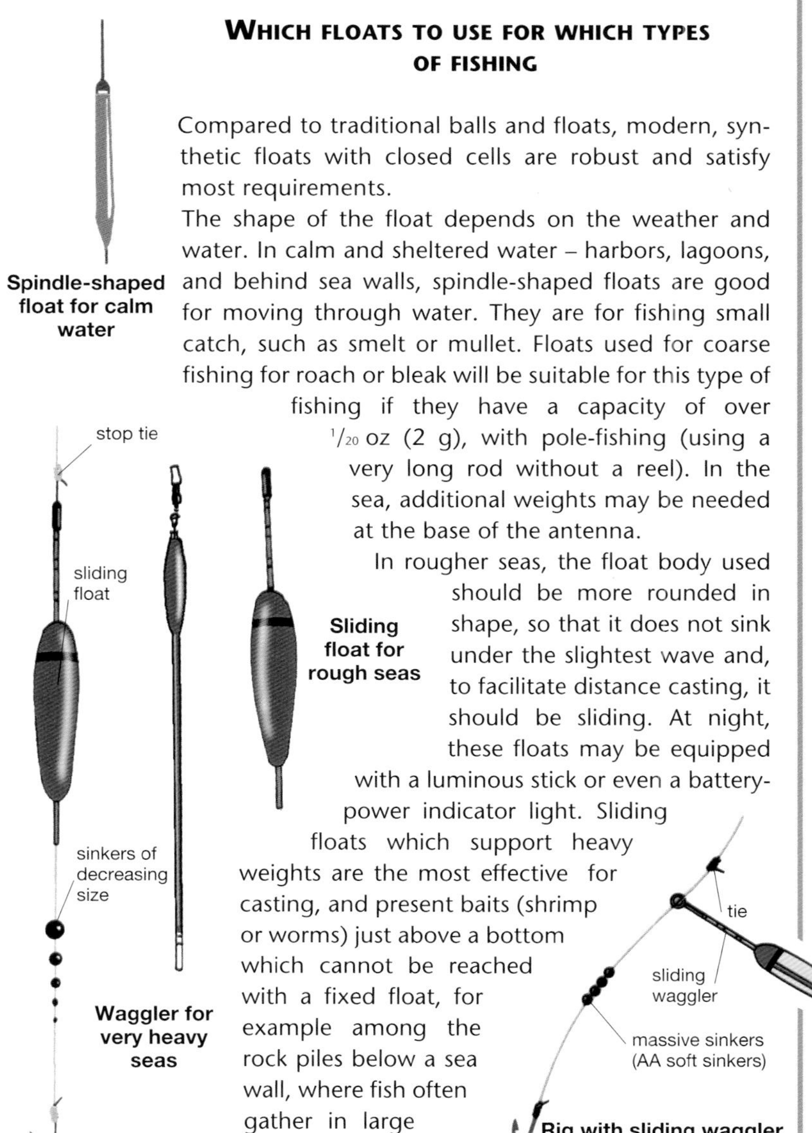

Spindle-shaped float for calm water

Sliding float for rough seas

Waggler for very heavy seas

Rig with sliding waggler

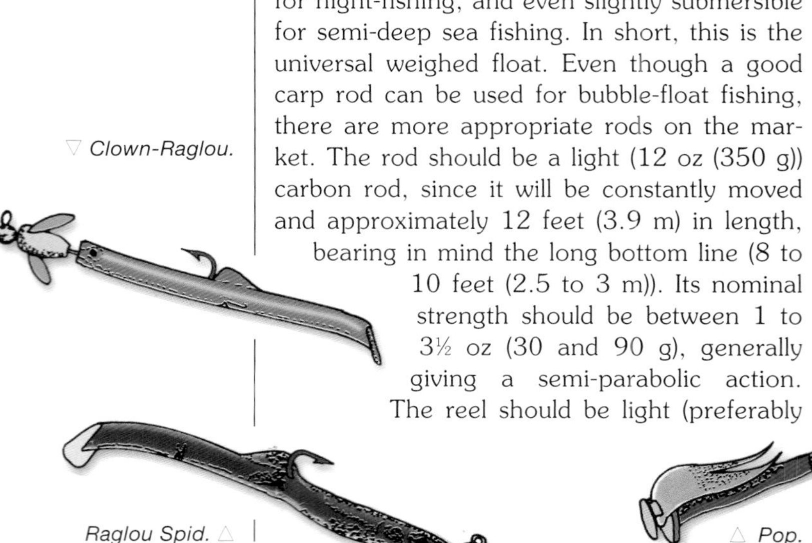

▽ Clown-Raglou.

Raglou Spid. △

△ Pop.

△ Unhooking a wrasse caught using support fishing on a rocky coast.

made of graphite) and appropriate for the rod; otherwise the entire tackle may become unbalanced.

The conical coil and crossed rolling will facilitate casting; if multifilament lines are used, a pick-up with a basket handle and micro-adjustable clutch should be added. Most of the time, nylon lines should be no shorter than 28/100 in calm water, and 30/100 and 35/100 are the most common. Recovery speeds of between 30 to 38 inches (75 and 95 cm) per crank turn, lets the lure be worked at different speeds. Bottom lines should be of a diameter 5/100 greater than that of the backing lines. So as to be able to best deal with this very exposed part they are connected to the bubble-float by strong swivels (Berkeley or MacMahon no. 5), using a broken ring or fastener. A second swivel, in the upper position, should be used to attach the nylon line wound onto the reel. This paternoster arrangement is preferable to a linear arrangement, since it gives the rig mobility and flexibility, whilst limiting tangling on casting. A third swivel is sometimes added, which reduces spinning still further, especially when fine nylon lines are used. The bubble-float is filled with fresh water, which is denser than salt water. Some people put silvery spangles or sequins in the float in a further attempt to attract the attention of those fish which are attracted by shiny objects.

▽ Angel Bar.

▽ Undulating Rapala.

◁ Shad Rap lure by Rapala.

Nessie. ▷

Rapala Magnum Silver, just the thing for bass! ▷

LURES

A lure is an inert object which dupes the fish by giving an impression of life, thanks to the water resistance and the way it moves through the water. The lure undulates and twirls, and causes vibrations which are clearly perceived by every fish, notably carnivorous ones. Hence the need for the fisherman to waggle the lure, using the rod and the reel.

FLEXIBLE LURES

Lures used in bubble-float fishing are of the surface type and are light and flexible. The veteran red or white rubber eel is still in use, although it tends to spin. The commonest bubble float lure is still an imitation sand-eel with a flexible tail which ends in a caudal fin acting as a deflector. Among the best known are the Raglou and its counterparts: Red Gill or Delta with a forked tail, the sizes of which range from 2½ in (6 cm) in calm water, to 5 in (13 cm) or more in rough seas. These lures should have an off-center Spid sinker in their heads, to stop them spinning and also prevent the lure from swimming on its side, which would make it ineffective. A variety of Raglou, the Rag Bar, has the inside of its head weighted. Apart from the above mentioned advantage, a lure that is weighted at the front and left alone for a moment will sink to the bottom whilst continuing to scull, and this will excite hunting fish tremendously. Another variant, half-spoon and half-Raglou, the Angel Bar, is greatly appreciated for its vibrations. A winged device called a Clown may also be combined successfully with a Raglou.

THE FLOWERET

A different type of lure, a floweret, consists of undulating strips of real or artificial skin. They include the Shad Rag and the Nessie by Ragot, or the Pop by Fisheur, and all have proven to be effective. One of the most recent types, the Vitala, has flexible

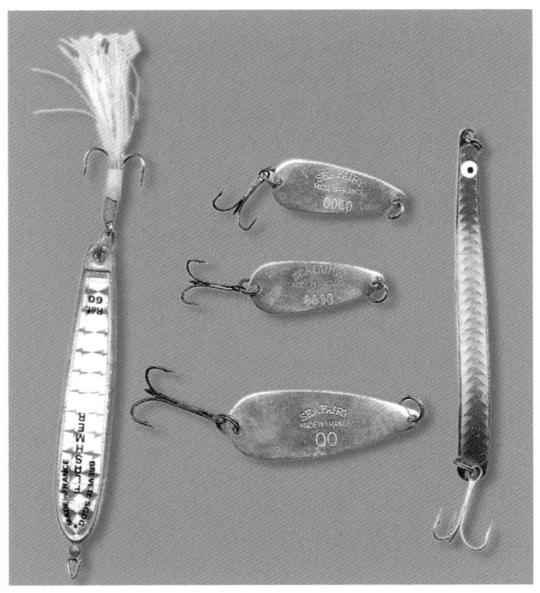

◁ *Undulating spoons for bass and pollack:*
- *Flashmer (left)*
- *JB (center)*
- *Norwegian Jensen Toby (right).*

strips of leather, and imitates a livebait in difficulty, whilst the Solette Ragot swims on shallow bottoms without catching. If strong nylon lines are used, the lure can be attached with a hangman's knot, as this will not affect the movement of the lure.

RIGID LURES

• Swimming fish

Bibbed swimming fish are a type of rigid lure which some anglers think are only useful for drag-fishing from boats, but they may also be used with a bubble-float. For example, an electric blue Shad Rap 8 GP, or a Countdown CD 11 will not descend much deeper than 4 feet (1 m) or a Rapala CD 9. If these lures are not recovered quickly enough they will pass through shallow, fish-filled waters, such as oyster-beds or shallows covered in razor-shells. We should also mention a half-spoon, half-fish lure, the undulating Rapala. With lures such as these, well-armed with treble hooks, there is a danger of looping on the line during casting. It is thus all the more important to slow down the bubble-float's descent before it splashes into the sea, in order to throw the bottom line forward. Placing the left-hand index finger on the edge of the coil is essential whenever you are casting with a bubble-float. There should be a distance of 24 in (60 cm) between the head-ring and the bubble-float at the start of the cast, and it is important to check that the lure has not become hooked into the bottom, and that the bottom line has not suffered excessively from repeated casting among rocks, or from stresses inflicted during the successive recoveries and strikes. It is important to check the reliability of the ring's fastening knot at the head of the lure (a double knot or a plastic sheath). Lastly, if you use multifilament 16/100 or 18/100 lines, which increase casting distances, you should protect your index finger with sticking plaster.

• Undulating spoons

Still on the subject of rigid lures, light undulating spoons of the Leman or Cybèle type have a snaky, sculling swim which greatly excites fish such as bass, notably when they hunt in shoals, on the surface. The size of these lures, their streamlined shape, and the flashes from their nickel-plated blades, are reminiscent of the silhouette and coloration of anchovy or sprat, fodder fish which are extremely popular with carnivores.

It is then a good idea to mount one or two flies with white feathering on a short paternoster line, 16 in (40 cm) above the spoon, in order to simulate a few lost alevins, chased by the small fish supposedly represented by the spoon.

By pulling back the spoon-bubble-float combination in short jerks at the edge of the shoal of targeted fish, and by alternating between acceleration in the troughs between waves, and slowdowns on their crests, this fishing method can be wonderfully effective.

Bubble-float fishing

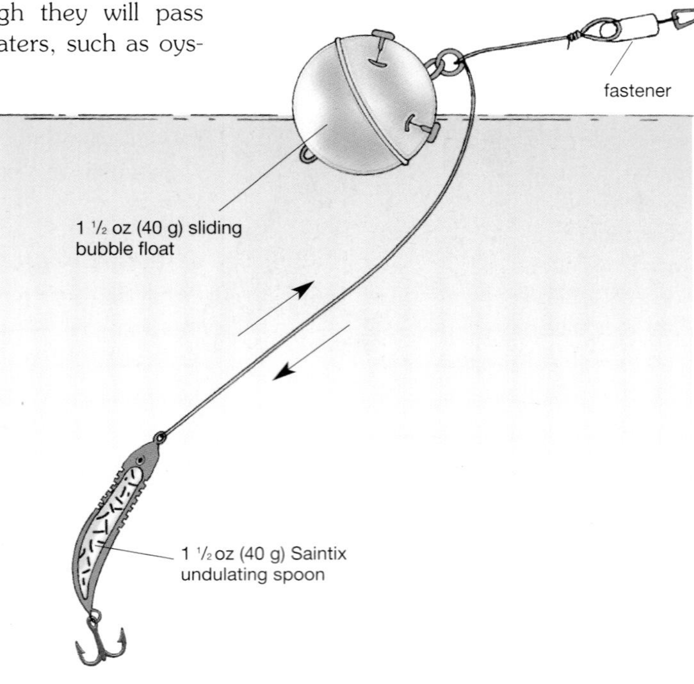

Treble lines are also common. When surface hunts dwindle, you should not stop, but try to fish at a deeper level using medium to heavy undulating spoons, such as Yann, Flashmer, Saintix, etc. If you are worried about using them alone (because they may snag), assemble them with a bubble-float as follows:

– thread an oval bubble float or Bulrag on the bottom line and then attach the spoon;

– approximately 10 feet (3 m) from the spoon, position the fastener which will act as the stop; by this means, the bubble float will slide along the bottom line, and the fisherman may, if he wishes, stop the recovery, allowing the spoon to go into freefall (a very attractive, dead-leaf-style glide) or, alternatively, he can lift it back up by raising his rod sharply. By this means, a sort of waggle is imparted to the lure, giving it an up-and-down movement which never fails to attract a bass, especially a large one. Lastly, a detail which should not be overlooked at the start of the cast is that since the bubble-float and spoon are used in conjunction with each other, this considerably increases the weight of $2\frac{1}{2}$ oz to 3 oz (60 to 80 g) ($1\frac{1}{8} + 1\frac{1}{8}$ oz or $1\frac{1}{4} + 1\frac{1}{4}$ oz (30 + 30 g or 40 + 40 g)), which will beat all distance records, even with a 40/100 line, a thickness which is necessary to prevent it wearing out prematurely in the bubble-float's fastening eyelet. If a multifilament line is being used, it is the eyelet which might wear out. Bubble-float fishing is a cast-and-return type of fishing, i.e. prospect fishing, something like support fishing with baits. It is practiced, moreover, on the same type of hilly sand-and-rock, or exclusively rocky, coasts, and using the vantage points which hunting fish (particularly bass) swim past.

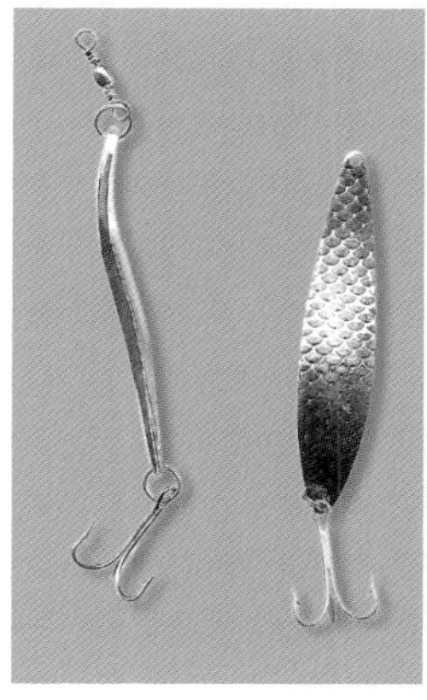

△ *Undulating spoons: for cod (left); for bass (right).*

A John Dory caught by casting. ▽

TRADITIONAL LURE CAST-FISHING

Lure cast-fishing can easily be practiced from a coast, without the assistance of a bubble-float. When the weight exceeds $\frac{3}{4}$ oz (20 g), using modern nylon lines, which are fine but resistant, and even more so with multifilament lines, it is possible to cast lures with metal bibs, of the Rapala type, over large distances (in calm weather conditions). If necessary, add a garden sinker in front of the lure; this sinker is fixed without a knot, using a distance/sinker ratio of 20 in (50 cm) per $\frac{1}{4}$ oz (10 g), which gives a depth of 16 feet (5 m) for a $3\frac{1}{2}$ oz (100 g) sinker, below the normal depth of the lure. However, the dangers of knotting and catching in the wind mean that, in rough seas, it is preferable to use a compact, heavy lure.

METAL LURES

A $1\frac{1}{2}$ oz to $2\frac{1}{4}$ oz (40 to 60 g) undulating spoon is best for such conditions: it can be cast far and precisely between the breakers, the spray of large waves or waves rolling onto sandy headlands at the entrances to trenches. Left to itself, an undulating spoon sinks in a gliding motion from side to side like a dead leaf, tipping up or down if the profile and mass have been designed correctly. This gives it the impression of being a small, dying fish. Bring it back up sharply using first the rod, then the reel, and it will do justice to its "undulating" epithet. In addition to the flutterings there will also be a few whirls.

If there is no bite, let it go down again freely, with the line released from the pick-up. A manual pick-up is recommended, and the ploy is continued near the bottom with little jerky movements. Any stoppage of the spoon during its descent, causing a slackening in the line, should be immediately followed by energetic striking. During the lift there will be no doubt, since the bite is so sudden. If gulls are wheeling

△ *An undulating spoon of the Flashmer type.*

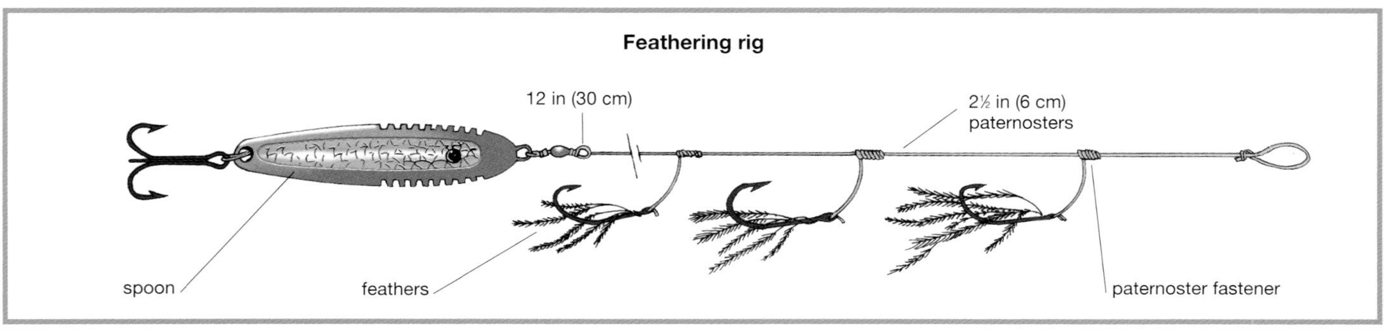

Feathering rig

overhead, indicating fish on the surface, cast at the limit of the area hunted by the gulls, letting the spoon sink down a few feet (it is often bitten at this moment), then recover using the reel, or knock down the rod to one side, whilst cutting upward. If nothing shows, it is essential to let the spoon redescend to the bottom, where the largest predators are lurking. When the gulls go away, continue fishing. The fact that the water is not disturbed does not mean that the predators have disappeared – quite the contrary. In a current which rounds a headland, cast upstream, across the current, in which position, turning the spoon over will add to its attractiveness.

Conversely, it is a good idea to precede the spoon with a string of miniature lures mounted on short paternosters, known as feathering.

White feathers, for example, emit subtle vibrations similar to those caused by small fodder fish, or again by small octopuses or eels, with a space of 12 to 16 in (30 to 40 cm) between them. These artificial alevins simulate a hunt, supposedly by the spoon, which has the effect of greatly exciting the real hunters. Any rig of this kind when waggled along the bottom, or cast across breaking waves, leads to many different kinds of bites.

Feathering and the rig knot

The equipment for use in this type of fishing is similar to that for bubble-float fishing. The rod should be long and light, with a preference for extra-sensitive rods, with a good tip action. A medium-to-heavy reel, containing 675 feet (200 m) of 40/100 or 45/100 nylon line, is also suitable. A multifilament line may be considered, although long casts are not necessary, but be aware that it may catch on the bottom.

As soon as you feel a tug which is much more sudden than the stopping motion of a bass, do not pull suddenly on the rod, that is quite the wrong reflex. What you should do is lower the rod in small jerky movements which often causes it to release itself from whatever was snagging it by tipping the spoon over. Another method takes advantage of the elastic properties of nylon.

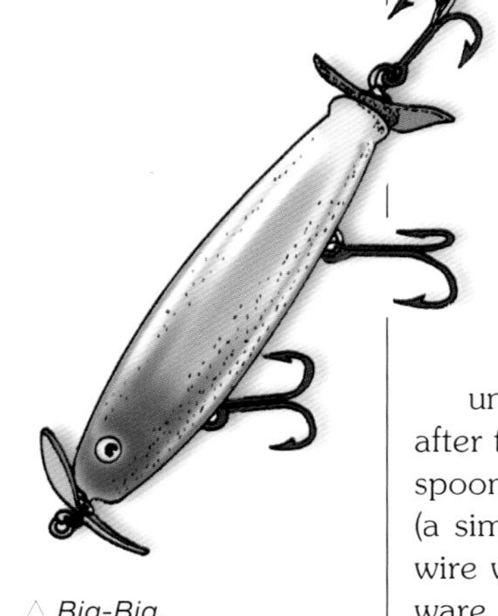
△ *Big-Big.*

Having stretched the line as far as possible with the rod, release the pick-up line. The sudden slackening causes the line to unhook itself from the obstruction when it snaps back. Moreover, using a double hook, or even a single one, a number 4/0, instead of a treble, limits the number of incidents of snagging substantially, provided the tips are directed to the bulbous side of the spoon. If the spoon is off-center, it will fall to the bottom, on its humped back.

Lastly, as the final attempt to release a snagged line, remove the broken ring, and replace it with a small loop of nylon, the resistance of which will be half that of the line. For example, 22/100 for a 45/100 line (using a glued surgeon's knot). Since this loop will probably be put under great strain, keep an eye on it, retie it after the smallest scratch, or have a set of spare spoons available. To prevent snagging, this loop (a simple knot) can also be made of fine brass wire which can be bought in spools from hardware stores. Try some experiments, snag the hook on the end of the spoon, and pull hard on the line nylon until the loop gives way. That is the cost, i.e. that of a single hook, of recovering the spoon.

If a fishermen's fears of the cost of snagging can be allayed in this manner, he can be encouraged to use undulating spoons, the technique for which is similar to that of fishing with a moving deadbait fish, which works wonders in rivers for zander, kissing cousin of the bass.

Among the other lures which can be cast alone, two have been fashionable in recent years, spinners and poppers.

Surface lures

• Spinners

The attraction of these lures lies in the way they churn up the surface water, giving the impression of a hunt which will stimulate predators such as bass. The two spinners, rotating in opposite directions, emit vibrations combined with the spluttering sounds of air bubbles, as though this were a fish jumping out of the water

△ *Helibar.*

to escape from its pursuer. Spinners weigh between $^3/_4$ to 3 oz (20 to 80 g), whether they are called Big-Big, Helibar or Mirolure, can thus be cast alone provided you use 24/100 to 30/100 nylon lines, which are very visible, or multifilament lines. They are cast using a rod of the bubble-float type, preferably with a fast tip action, allowing contact to be maintained with the lure. The fishing action consists in striking cleanly, with the rod raised, as soon as the lure hits the water, to make sure that it splashes around on the surface. Lastly, reel in by alternating quick and slow motion. You can even keep the line stationary, if you are fishing in a current. The bite often occurs at the start or end of reeling in, during the last "splash" of the Big-Big spinner. The best results are obtained in a calm or slightly choppy sea, provided the water depth does not exceed 13 to 16 feet (4 to 5 m).

In a rough sea, the largest lures ($4^1/_4$ to $5^1/_2$ in (11 to 14 cm)) must be used. These may be cast quite far out but, through their inertia, lead to fewer failures on striking. The latter will not occur when a hunting fish is identified following the lure on the surface. The fish is not seeking to devour it, but rather to oust the intruder by pushing it with its snout or body. This is the reason for the multiple bites outside the head or in the back skin. This sight fishing is very exciting over shallow bottoms in good weather.

△ *Bass popper: an excellent surface lure.*

• Poppers

These lures operate on the same principle as the spinner. They produce a lot of noise on the surface in order to bring up bass in shelter over shallows. Thanks to their strangely shaped, truncated heads, they create quite a commotion on the surface of the water, making the same popping noise as a champagne cork, hence the name.

Poppers are lighter than spinners and can only be used in calm weather. They bounce back on the water creating a very attractive wake. Sheltered coves, narrow gulfs, and rocky inlets are ideal for their jerky, provocative swim.

As with spinners, a premature strike will often lead to failure.

It is thus preferable to slow down, and even to stop, or to speed up the lure's swim when you detect a fish that is following it. This is a thrilling moment. Will it attack, won't it attack?

You may well wonder why a lure is attacked when it is just a caricature, and is normally odorless. Since sound waves propagate very far and very fast, the slightest vibration undoubtedly has some effect on the fish and they are thus attracted to spinners and poppers. So what makes it decide to bite? Hunger may be a factor. However, it would then be essential for the lure to look exactly like the prey in question, in terms of its shape, color, swim, and odor. Actually, the opposite seems to be the case. A perfect imitation would be most unlikely to be attacked, while an imperfect lure, swimming on its side, sculling and zigzagging, has a good chance of being bitten. Make your lures "suffer"; this reflects the cruel laws of natural selection – survival of the fittest and elimination of the weakest. Another common sight which is hard to explain is the way in which a small pollack leaps on a feather of a feathering rig. A large pollack, or a bass, however, will follow the rig and grab at the spoon, which it would perhaps have ignored if the "might is right" reflex and the urge to compete had not come into play. Hence the advantage of pairing two different types of lure. Territorial defense, which is so common in animals, can also play a role when, in a good fishing position occupied by an attractive fish, supposed competitors (spoons, spinners, or plugs) swim boldly past. This often leads to bites around the mouth of the "intruder". The same applies when, in the fall, hunting fish gather to protect their fry, and a spoon is tapped continuously on the bottom. This annoys them so they will attack it out of irritation and thus get caught. Lastly, it may be the case that under certain conditions predators succumb to a killer instinct, forgetting everything which enabled them to survive, because a genetic stimulus puts them into a sort of trance at the sight of this diabolical man-made invention, the lure.

FLOAT-LINE FISHING

The tackle consists of a fixed-reel rod approximately 17 feet (4 m long, fitted with many rings which spread the action throughout its length during a fight with a fish of substantial size, and a light reel with a very gradual clutch, containing 16/100 or 18/100 nylon line. The waggler may be mounted sliding, which facilitates casts, reduces risks of tangling, and permits fishing with livebait, in harbors (bass) where the water is calm, or with baits in open seas (garfish). Choosing your floats according to the type of sea is thus not as simple as it is in fresh water, but the right choice is likely to bring in a large catch.

THE CATCH

BASS

*The sea bass (*Morone labrax*), was well known in Antiquity and to the Romans, but its fame long remained confined to the Mediterranean. It is an attractive fish which is a great delicacy in southern France and the Mediterranean coast of Spain but ventures out into the Atlantic and is caught off the coasts of Britain and Norway. A closely-related species, the spotted sea bass (*Labrax lupus*), is found along the Atlantic coast of Europe, but only moves as far north as the southern Bay of Biscay. The name comes from the black spots on its sides.*

Bass are one of the most sought-after by inshore fishermen. Their spectacular defense and delicious flesh no doubt explain their popularity with anglers. ▽

A VORACIOUS EATER

Bass started to come into fashion in the 1960s. Some aspects of bass-fishing, such as its unpredictable behavior, or even its supposed exclusivity, have caused it to be compared to salmon-fishing.

Sea bass is a member of the Perciform family, the family to which groupers and tilefish also belong. As the name implies, it resembles a perch. The dorsal fins are tipped with prickly rays, the mouth is wide and membranous, though delicate, and the scales are large and silvery.

The sea bass is a voracious eater. It often hunts in large shoals, forcing its victims to the surface, where gulls lie in wait for them. The bass then return to the bottom, where they continue to lurk until the next hunt. They are thus particularly sensitive to anything with upward or downward movements. Casting with lures will thus prove very effective.

Furthermore, their voracity causes them to open their mouths to swallow any prey that may swim past, ranging from eel-pout as large as a human hand to the tiniest sand-flea, and including cuttlefish pulp. Fish, crustaceans, soft or hard worms, the bass will swallow them all. It is prepared to ingest the slimiest rockfish such as gobies, loach, and blennies, or the prickly species, such as bullheads and sticklebacks, and even the most aggressive crabs such as the velvet swimming crabs (*Macropipus puber*). Faced with such a wide choice of baits and lures, it is surprising that so few bass are actually landed!

WHERE DO THEY HIDE?

Frequently, fishermen are disappointed due to the sudden and prolonged disappearance of bass. In fact, a series of fishing trips, some incredibly successful, others a complete waste of time, show that the bass were around all along. They may have been right where you were fishing or just a few feet away. So, how come you had no luck? Bass fishermen must sometimes wait for better days, unless they use other methods by which to encourage the bass to bite at a time when they are not engaged in their famous feeding frenzy.

△ *Rocky coasts lashed by surf are the favorite locations of fishermen casting for bass.*

Unfortunately, the best fishing days are often those when the weather is at its worst. Biting winds coming in off the sea, overcast days, rain, massive breakers, spray, and surf are the secret delight of the bass fisherman, even though he will be unable to keep a bottom line in place at the height of the storm. But, as soon as the storm has passed, the exhausted ocean will yield up its fish.

This is the time for bass fishermen to be persistent, but they need to take many precautions in order to catch a fine specimen in the inshore waters.

Bass are floodtide fish. This means that at low tide, and often a good half-hour before the sea starts to come in, the fish have gathered at their departure points, and are within casting distance. As soon as the first floodtide wave edges the beach with a fringe of foam, the bass will move in on the floodtide current that is more or less parallel to the coast. As the tide rises, the bass will move further inshore. At first they will swim close to submerged or semi-submerged obstacles and headlands; then isolated rocks or, failing this, sandy bars; lastly, hidden hollows of the coast, inlets, coves, and crevices.

When bass are on the hunt they follow an almost identical route each time, and these will be modeled on the marine topography, even though it may not be self-evident if the beaches are sandy and devoid of rocks.

On each stage in their journey inshore the bass adopt an ambush position. Another remarkable characteristic of bass is that the incoming route passes over narrow trenches on the sea bed over which waves break and expand into stretches of white water. They also like sandbars and flat stretches, rocky ridges, and plateaux.

Bass are very regular in their habits. In a given position, they will appear each day at the same point in the tide, measured in terms of water depth. They use the sea level like a clock.

Although it is true that sea bass are not always easy to fish, once their interest is aroused they are surprisingly easy to hook.

The Sea Bass and Speckled Bass

Two main types of sea-bass are found along the coasts of Europe.

• Sea bass

Sea bass (*Morone labrax*) are called *loup* or *bar* throughout most of France, *loubine* in southwestern France, *drenec* in Brittany, and *Seebarsch* in Germany. Along the Atlantic coast, sea bass are found close to sandy beaches and in estuaries when they

TO LURE OR NOT TO LURE?

The increasing scarcity of fish, particularly the so-called noble fish, is beyond a doubt. With every passing year, more restrictions are placed on fishing, taking account of their behavior, the landmarks they use in their passage underwater, and the times at which they are most active. It has been noticed for some time now that night fishing produces a much greater catch than daytime fishing, which was clearly not the case in the past. Another observation is that lure fishing is becoming slightly less rewarding than in the 1970s and 1980s, when it was at its height. This is something that is particularly noticeable when fishing inshore from a boat where, in places previously known to be good fishing-grounds, drag-fishing no longer produces the desired results. If unlucky drag-fishermen are questioned, they assure you that there is nothing left, and that the sea is empty. If you manage to persuade them to stop their toing-and-froing, to weigh anchor, and try a surf-casting bottom line baited with a soft-shell crab (which you will have given them), to their great astonishment they catch a bass!

This is not to say that lures are ineffectual, far from it. Among two most recent world records, one was set by a fisherman using a lure and another by one using baits. Two outstanding bass, two different techniques, both equally effective... in the meantime.

are young and growing fast. The age-size relationship is significant. A four-year-old bass is 14 in (36 cm) long – below this size it is illegal to land them. A record weight of 29 lb (13 kg) has been recorded, which would mean that the bass would have been around 25 years old. Between these two extremes, a handsome specimen weighing 7 lb (3.5 kg) is about 13 years old, and an average bass weighing 4 lb 8 oz (2 kg) is around 10 years old. The age is determined precisely by studying the striations on the scales (a science known as scalometry), or by observing the otoliths, the loose piece of calcium carbonate inside the inner ear which grows with the fish.

• Spotted and other bass

Spotted bass (*Labrax lupus*) is smaller than the sea bass (2lb 4 oz – 4 lb 8 oz (1–2 kg)), has a more streamlined shape, a broad tail, a pointed head, and black spots on the back, sides, and fins. The markedly gregarious instinct of speckled bass makes them travel in tight, mobile shoals, which hunt small surface fish together. Fishing them will thus be above all a fast form of fishing, in series, using lures spaced out along the line.

American varieties of bass are the striped bass (*Labrax saxatilis*) found from the Gulf of St. Lawrence to the Gulf of Mexico, the black sea-bass (*Centropristes striatus*) which is found from Florida to Cape Cod, and the wreckfish or stone bass (*Polyprion americanus*), which despite its Latin name, is not limited to the western Atlantic but is also found as far south as the Mediterranean and as far north as Norway. All these varieties of bass make excellent eating.

A BIG MOUTH

When you open the mouth of a bass, the gape seems to be shaped like a disproportionately large funnel. There are small rough patches around the edges of the jaws, which do not contain carnivorous teeth. The only teeth are broad, flattened pharyngeal teeth, which manage prey in the stomach. The lower jaw is jointed by means of cartilaginous arcs linked to one another by membranes which yield when pressed with the finger.

From these observations, the obvious deduction is that since the mouth is so large, a large mouthful is required, attached to the appropriate hook. Such a hook will very rarely pierce the soft palate, though it may lodge in the tongue, but is most likely to embed itself in the membranous lateral walls, which are fragile and tear easily.

On the other hand, there is no problem about nylon coming into contact with the jaws, since they lack teeth. Quite thin lines can be used. If the flap of the sharp, spiky operculum (please mind your fingers!) is raised, wide tiers of gills with impressive branchiae are revealed, all full of scarlet oxygenated blood.

A VARIED DIET

Bass use seaweed for the cover they need when they lie in wait for their rich and varied diet which includes shrimp, fish, crab, etc. This is a fish that likes shallow, inshore waters, where vegetation is often rich.

Bass will be sensitive to lures which, handled well, will trigger an attack which is not motivated by hunger. In the past, bass were almost tame, curious rather than cautious. They could be fished 100 feet out to sea, and the first underwater fishermen were astonished to see the fish observing them. But bass are particularly sensitive to changes in shape and to movement. This is where the danger lies, a difficulty which is increased if they are being fished in limpid summer waters. At this time of year, dawn or night-time fishing is the preferred option.

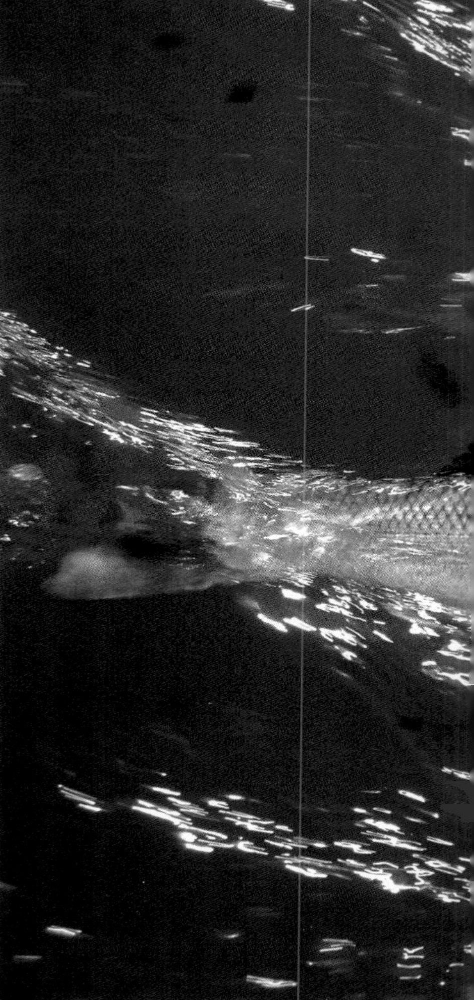

Bass caught by surf-casting, using a flexible lure. ▷

An examination of the stomach contents of the bass often yields astonishing results, both in relation to the variety of prey – fish, crustaceans, mollusks, shellfish – and for the size, quantity, and resistance of the prey. Hard-shelled crabs, a gruel of black cuttlefish ink, and lots of fishbones. These are clearly the results of a feeding frenzy, and are not something that happens every day. Apart from the fact that they are soon snapped up by fishermen, there are other negative consequences of their excessive gluttony for the bass.

When the fish retreats to its lair, what can it do if its stomach cavity is full to bursting? The ingestion of voluminous prey means that digestion is long and laborious. Having crammed itself "to the gills" for several days, it is likely that the bass will remain hidden in a crevice for quite a while. Prolonged inactivity will restore its body's physiological balance.

Live shrimp make excellent bass bait. ▷

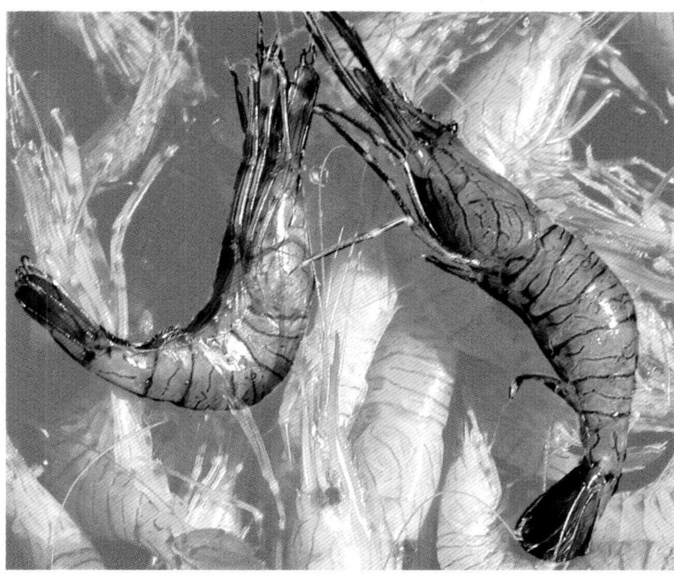

It is still possible to fish for bass inshore. There is night fishing, which is rarely disappointing when low tide coincides with dusk, or, alternatively, a young bass may be captured at dawn, since bass are always active on the first floodtide. The younger fish need their staple ration of food on a daily basis.

Research by the French National Natural History Museum indicates that 80% of the food of fully-grown bass consists of crustaceans, and, of these, three-quarters are crab. Shrimp of all sizes are as well-liked as crab. When used as bait in the Mediterranean when fishing for wary fish, bass is the proof of this. However, in the English Channel and the Atlantic, shrimp are too fragile for the rough seas, and they are not suitable for casting either. Worms, whether large and soft like lugworms, or small and wriggly like lobworms, will also be effective. In this case, quality replaces quantity, and a good size bass may well snap up a passing clam or oyster, but the same bait will look like a miserly morsel on the end of a hook.

Small, whole squid, tentacles, or strips of tentacles, are the ideal baits for surf-casting by skilled fishermen, who

A CARNIVORE'S SENSE OF SMELL

It is not known how close a fish has to come to its prey in order to be able to "sense" its presence. The organs of taste and smell are numerous and complex, and are distributed throughout the body, although there is a cluster around the mouth. These enable the bass to taste at a distance, and to "smell" exhalations. However, what excites the carnivorous instincts of a bass to fever pitch is when it senses prey that is in difficulty.

Razor-shells (razor clams) are the universally popular bait par excellence. ▷

are able to walk out beyond the rollers on large, flat beaches and reach the distant currents and trenches. Other excellent baits such as razor-shells (razor-clams) can only be used at specific spots on certain coasts. Sand-eels or small fish such as eelpout or sardines are even trickier to use.

BASS BITES AND DEFENSE

Normally, a bass's bite is characterized by two quick snaps in succession, which can be clearly felt as tugs on the line. The first is when the fish grabs the prey, the other when it makes sure it has its prey and paralyzes it in its mouth in order to swallow it. Unless it senses the presence of the hook and line, and moves its head sharply in order to try to rid itself of these foreign bodies, this type of bite usually ends in a "self-strike", without the fisherman having to intervene. A sudden departure then ensues. Young bass are inclined to act in this way, and their sudden bite often gives the impression that a huge catch is at the end of the line. If they were to escape, the reason would probably be because the bait and hook were too large. A no. 1/0 or no. 2/0 hook is quite sufficient for small bass. Mature bass will have lost this juvenile enthusiasm and will often make only a single grab for the bait, sometimes even a half-hearted one. A fisherman who monitors this attack, with the line on his index finger, will feel a sort of hesitation, a slackness on the line, which will start to sag. If you do not strike energetically at this moment, half the time it means that you lose the bass. Another favorite trick of bass consists in leaping on the bait head first toward the fisherman. This rush causes the bottom line to skid several feet, and there will be a lot of play in it. You must strike very quickly. If the rod is sitting on a rod-rest, rather than in your hand, grab it quickly. Naturally, bass bites vary considerably. The condition of the sea is important. If the water is turbulent or rough, bites will consist of a sudden gulp, for fear that a barely glimpsed prey will manage to escape.

The opposite is also true. If the water is calm, bites will be gentle. Similarly, a current will stimulate the bass to grab prey.

Bass loves to swim in the breakers, from which it can easily be fished by casting. ▽

Bass can also be caught very effectively using flies, which should be multicolored flies embellished with tinsel. The large streamers designed to resemble alevins, sand-eels, and squid are all suitable. ▷

Striking a bass is not the end of the story – you need to be able to hang on to it. The most basic mistake consists in pulling harder than the fish and making things worse by reeling in frantically. The second mistake is generally made only at the end of the struggle. It consists in losing contact with a fish which has been pulled back too rapidly on the surface. Its leaps and somersaults catch the fisherman unawares. In the first case, there is every chance that the hook will tear the mouth of the bass, and in the second, this same hook will be dislodged from the "eyelet" it will have made in the mouth cavity.

The way a bass defends itself has two distinguishing features. The first is that it rises rapidly to the surface. This fish does not obstinately try to hug the bottom like a sea-bream, or to shelter down there craftily like a conger. As soon as it is a few feet from the surface, it will suddenly dart to the right or left of the fisherman, forcing him to point the rod in the opposite direction. It will then head off in the direction of an obstacle, often a rock level with the surface, as if it were trying to hurl itself against it. It does not do so, but this possibility sometimes induces fishermen to use unsuitable maneuvers, such as pulling back as hard as possible. The second defense takes place on the surface, where it is always a bad idea to bring in a bass. Since bass are very good at acrobatics, it will not fail to demonstrate its gymnastic prowess by leaping, pirouetting, swerving, jerking its head in a rage, diving, and swimming up to the surface. All this often ends badly for the angler as the displays often take place near the shore and obstructions. When the fish is fighting on the surface, the jerks on the line can be felt much more keenly since they are not deadened by a great length of nylon in between, nor by the water pressure on the line. The risks of breakage around the hook fastening are increased, as is that of the mouth tearing, and the ease with which the fish may become unhooked. Every bass fisherman has seen a hook which appears to have held by a miracle inside the mouth of the fish he has just landed.

In a nutshell, the right way to land a bass consists in correctly gauging the pressure of the rod on the mouth of the fish, without slackening or exaggerating the tension.

BASS FISHING TECHNIQUES

The equipment for bass fishing consists essentially of two rods, one for casting, the other for surf-casting and support fishing, with their corresponding reels (see pp. 248, 250, 264, and 265).

• Best positions

These could be summarized as : "fish the surf". Here is a list of other fishing positions, once the beach has been closely surveyed at low tide:

– High rocky outcrops dipping down suddenly into the water
These are good for lure-casting or bait fishing techniques.

– Low headlands
These also take the form of distant, individual rocks or barely covered shallows. Bubble-float fishing is the best approach here.

– Rocky or sandy plateaux
These form shallows which are regularly exposed at low tide. As soon as the floodtide starts, when the waves break, fish here using a bubble float, a helix fish, or poppers.

– Channels between these plateaux
Support bait fishing by using a spoon or bubble float and flexible lures.

– Landslides consisting of large chunks of rock which have become detached from overhanging cliffs
These are places in which lures can get caught, but they are also rich in bass, precisely because they seem so perfect. Support fishing by using baits. When the rock slide descends to great depths: waggle-fish using a spoon, from the shore.

THE POPPER

Even large bass can be caught this way, victims of their own curiosity, if this unusual lure is threaded through and near obstacles which are being used as ambush points by a lone fish, or in beds where no-one would dare use any other lure. It must be drawn back in realistically. A Big Bomb, the best known popper, should zigzag, move forward in little spurts and leap up noisily, in order to alert a fish hunting in the vicinity. The attack is often sudden, though sometimes it is preceded by eddies behind the lure, indicating pursuit by the carnivore.

Fishing for bass by surf-casting on a Corsican beach. Note the excellent position provided by the small estuary, which attracts many fish.

– Near isolated rocks on a beach
All types of fishing are possible.
– Trenches
These are crisscrossed by currents, and can be identified by their smooth waters and darker blue color. Surf-cast or lure-fish around the trenches.
– Coves and small, steep-sided inlets with sandy or pebbly bottoms
By carefully fishing these beaches at low tide in strong seas, large bass can often be caught using baits.

• The best times of year

In January, February, and March, when the water temperature drops below 45°F (7°C), bass swim away from the shore and gather in deep water, over pebble bottoms, where they can be detected with an echo-sounder and are often fished by trawlers. For conservation reasons, it may eventually be decided that fishing should be banned at this time of year.

The best months for inshore fishing are May and June, during which bass are very active and are regaining their strength, particularly at the expense of crabs, which are sloughing off their hard shells during the same period.

In July, the influx of summer visitors will modify the bass's behavior, except on very rocky coasts. The bass now tends to become active only at night, to the delight of surf-casting fishermen. September, which marks the decline of vacationers, is when the coastal fishermen arrive in large numbers. October and especially November are good months for the largest bass.

THE GREATEST OF ALL BASS

When one young bass in a shoal gets into difficulty and emits chemical substances and probably vibrations as distress signals, the entire group reacts by fleeing, and may already be aware of the danger. This behavior persists even when the bass are larger and live in smaller groups. It is thus important not to keep using the same lure in the same way (such as in traditional drag-fishing, with the sinker hitting the bottom). After such an incident, the bass will often swim around in pairs.

Mistrust increases with age. When older, large bass withdraw into cautious solitude, causing them seek out the best hunting positions, those affording the best shelter (seaweed, rocky scree, crevices), and those with the best food supply. Vigorous and fast-moving prey will be ignored in favor of other, smaller or damaged food. Think about using bass feathers, soft-shell crabs, and lures which they can get their teeth around (undulating spoons), or poppers, which give the appearance of being in great difficulty. Of course, an attractive well-positioned livebait, or a large piece of cuttlefish will always be welcome.

When a shoal of alevins (sprats, anchovies, mullet, or sand-eels) happens to swim by, a bass will be the first to take advantage of the opportunity. Large bass often lie in wait on the bottom, close to the hunt, hoping for just such an event. This is where you should look for them, even when the feeding frenzy of the young bass is over for the time being.

LIFESIZE LURES

Rather than paint an eye on a lure, we think it is more important to make the size of the lure match that of the prey currently being targeted by the fish, especially during hunts. We have often noticed even large bass preferring to snatch at small feathers rather than jump on the spoon which followed, which was more bulky and, apparently, more appetizing. This is because the predators were hunting alevins. Conversely, the spoon was targeted first when sprats or sardines were the prey being hunted.

Rapala and Big-Big are two of the most commonly used lures for bass-fishing.

POLLACK

*The pollack (*Pollachius pollachius*), is a member of the large Gadidae family. It is an attractive fish with a streamlined shape, whose head is covered with small, bronze scales. It is able to camouflage itself to match its surroundings, so the color of the body may vary from bronze to copper, through orange, depending on the surroundings in which it finds itself. Pollack are superb game fish which take lures very well. In addition, their flesh is delicious, which makes them even more attractive a catch.*

Pollack, like bass, are fearsome predators which will take a bite at both natural baits and lures. ▽

"THE POOR MAN'S SEA-BASS"

At first sight, pollack give the impression of quiet strength, in contrast to their relative, the pugnacious bass (see p. 276). These two fish can cohabit in the same waters, although with a warlike bass around, the smaller pollack are at risk of being swallowed as a whole. They frequent the same weedy or rocky bottoms and feed on the same prey, and you may sometimes catch a pollack when you were looking for bass. However, pollack keep to the bottom rather more than bass, although they are not above tracking shoals of alevins on the surface.

A CAPRICIOUS AND GREGARIOUS FISH

Pollack are quite gregarious, and appear early near the coasts, as soon as the weather starts to become warmer. Specimens weighing 4 lb 8 oz – 10 lb (2–4 kg) always lead the shoal, followed by smaller individuals. In the height of summer, you may catch small, orange-speckled pollack which must be thrown back in the sea, for two reasons. Firstly because as anglers we respect the environment and rules of nature conservation and secondly because these fish are probably below the legal size for pollack which is 12 in (30 cm). A mature pollack can grow 40 inches (1 m) long and weigh 22 lb (10 kg), so it is a good idea to give the fish time to mature. The closely related fish known as saithe or coley in the United Kingdom and as pollack (*Pollachius virens*) in the United States has a darker back, and the inside of the mouth is also black. It grows much larger than its inshore relative but can rarely be caught from the shore.

WHERE YOU SHOULD FISH FOR POLLACK

Pollack are predatory fish which like powerful currents, so they will most likely be found lurking behind rocks on the sea-bed, lying in wait for their prey. Large, steep granite headlands, tumbling into a deep sea and extended by reefs, will be the most likely locations. There should be at least 16 feet (5 m) of water for pollack to feel at home. When they hunt smooth

Pollack are very easy to fly-fish, notably when they come to hunt for small fry in inlets (here in Ireland). ▽

sandlances they may venture into water as shallow as 4 feet (1 m). However, the general rule is, the deeper the water the larger the pollack.

Rocky coasts are thus good locations where the rock formations slope down to the sea and where there are promontories jutting out into fast-flowing, deep waters, blocking strong currents. There should be steep escarpments near trenches with a succession of steps, crevices and rock slides. This is a promise of good sport for fishermen.

Another feature of the pollack is that this fish is a sensitive creature which prefers clean, deep, fairly calm water. Gently lapping waves suit it fine. In a rougher sea, it will take refuge in the deepest stretches, and in very clear weather it prefers to hunt at dawn or dusk. Since it likes currents, it will naturally be active in an incoming tide, with increasing tidal factors, during the incoming and for half of the outgoing tide. Fortunately, the pollack does not necessarily hide on the bottom. It can be seen hunting near low outcrops rounded by a current, if there are underwater caves nearby, or close to islands that break up currents. Where the depth is average, it is best to fish in a choppy sea, with a moderate wind and an overcast sky. In bright sunshine, return to deeper water, where the pollack will happily hunt all day long. The high, rocky coasts of Brittany, Cornwall, and the west coast of Ireland are ideal for pollack fishing, provided you do not suffer from vertigo, are a good rock-climber, and you make sure you dangle your lures in water that is as deep as possible.

Rigs which have proved their worth

• Weighted rig

Pollack are very aware of even quite small eels, so rubber eels are a good

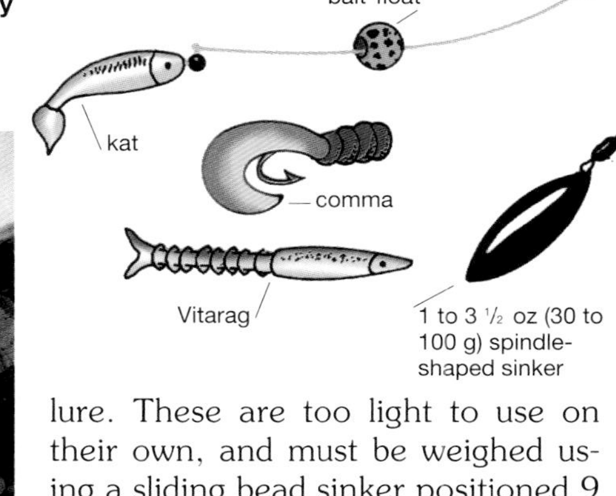

lure. These are too light to use on their own, and must be weighed using a sliding bead sinker positioned 9 to 12 feet (2.5 to 3 m) down the line or, better still, a Wye lead with a swivel, to stop the spinning typical of this type of lure. As for the colors, in clear water of average depth use white, gold, or red; in deeper, murkier water, choose darker tones, blue, gray, or black, or greenish- yellow, which is highly visible. Entice the pollack by using waggling movements, letting the eel be dragged by the sinker, and do not bring it back up too quickly, as you might do with a bass.

Instead of an eel, you could try Raglous, Red Gills, or Deltas with off-center weighted heads. Small kats or commas will also prove effective. Using this little up-and-down trick, you can also add a few of the feathers, since if there is a lure which excites pollack immensely, it is white or yellow feathers, which they associate with the alevins they love.

• Paternoster rig

To prevent too much line breakage, a paternoster rig will enable the sinker to touch the bottom before the lures. This will involve pole-fishing,

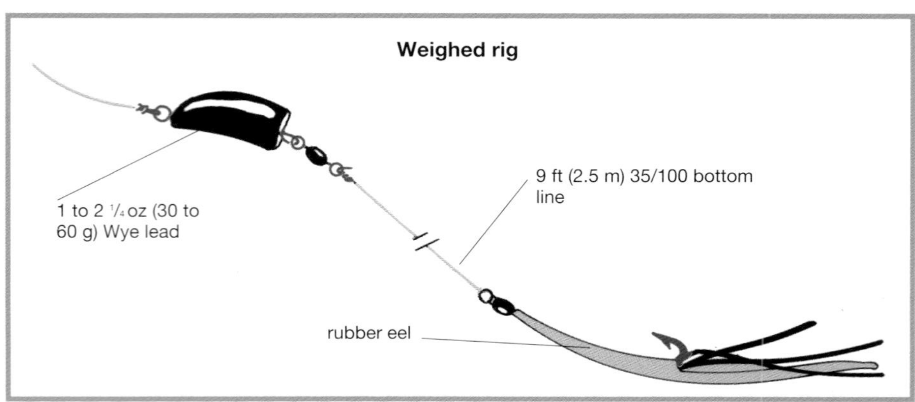

◁ *A lovely Irish pollack caught using a pirk.*

torments them as much as bass. The major problem is when you feel a jerk which stops the bottom line in its upward movement for a moment. This indicates that a large pollack has thrown itself on the pirk, but has not been caught. If that happens, and if there are attractive fish around, rearming the pirk means taking a minor risk, with a promise of superb fishing.

BAIT FISHING

The baits are the same for all fish that inhabit rocky sea-beds.

• Suitable rigs and baiting

Using a rod of the bubble-float type, you can fish either on the bottom, or using a float. On the bottom, use a sliding rig with a pierced, hexagonal sinker, stopped by a swivel link on the bottom line, which can be fitted with two hooks.

Explore the depths as accurately as possible, using different settings of the upper stop. You can also use a sliding float on the bottom line, weighted by bead sinkers, to find pollack from jetties or promontories. In either case, it is a good idea to use lots of bait to attract and hold the pollack, for example downstream of a current hitting a sea wall or headland. Sardines mixed with sand is the simplest bait. You can also mix mussels and chopped crab or mackerel pulp with peanut flour, and cast these baitballs, weighted with sand, at regular intervals, as close as possible to the position.

• The pollack's bite

Pollack have a sharp bite. A clean tug means that you should strike decisively. Its defense consists in diving to the bottom quite suddenly. After this, pollack come up quite smoothly, and appear politely at the surface.

A feathering rig

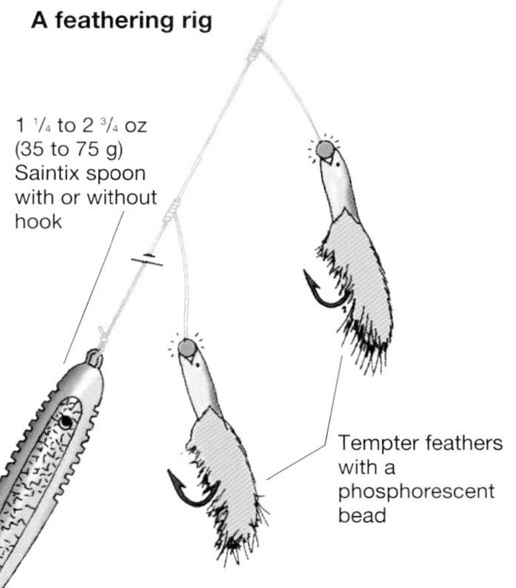

PIRKS AND JIGS

Spoons have been modernized and are now known as pirks and jigs. Pirks for deepwater fishing are brightly fluorescent or covered in shimmering silver holograms, which resemble scales. Some pirks are topped with a tuft of iridescent hairs, dyed feathers, tentacle-like strips, or a small rubber eel. However, it is just as much fun for the angler to devise his own pirks and jigs, using shiny plastic and other materials likely to catch the eye of a passing pollack.

provided you can feel the impact of the sinker using quite a sensitive rod of the bubble-float type. A bait-float bead, impregnated with oily attractants, takes the strain off the bottom line, preventing it from rubbing too hard against obstructions, and increases the attraction of the lure, since pollack have a highly developed sense of smell. The ideal fishing conditions are found during surface hunts, when traditional bubble-float fishing comes into its own again. Unfortunately, since such conditions are quite rare, you have to make do with fishing for pollack wherever you can find them, using heavy lures. Pirks are very effective here since, like the pollack, they can lurk on the bottom. You can also do without one by replacing it with a sinker of the multiple hook leger or spindle-shaped type, preceded by a string of four or five feathers. This works quite well with small and medium-sized pollack.

• Feathering for Pollack

Another solution consists in removing the hook from the pirk, which then acts as a teaser for the pollack, whose jealous instinct

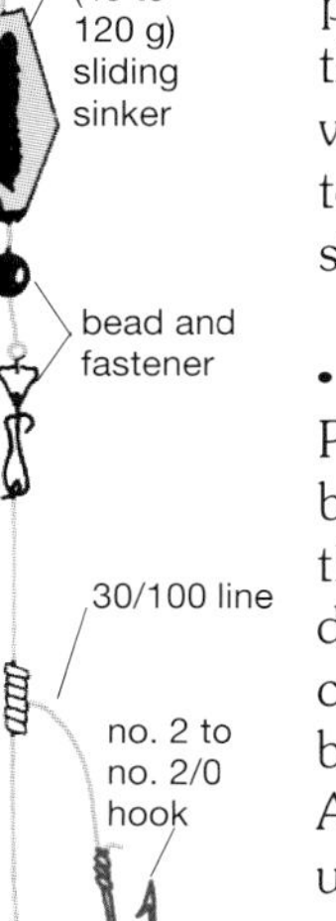

Rig for bottom-fishing for pollack

CONGER

Conger (Conger conger) and its North American relative the ocean conger (Conger oceanus) are undoubtedly one of the largest fish which can be caught on the end of a rod. The most handsome specimens weigh 90 to 135 lb (40 to 60 kg) and are fished from boats over wrecks but even inshore, you can expect catches of 36 through 45 lb (16 through 20 kg). When you become aware of the extreme combativeness of the conger, it is easy to understand why some fishermen want to fish for nothing else, despite the fact that the conger is not a great delicacy and has no commercial value. The best times of day for catching a conger, if you are fishing from the shore, are at dusk or at night.

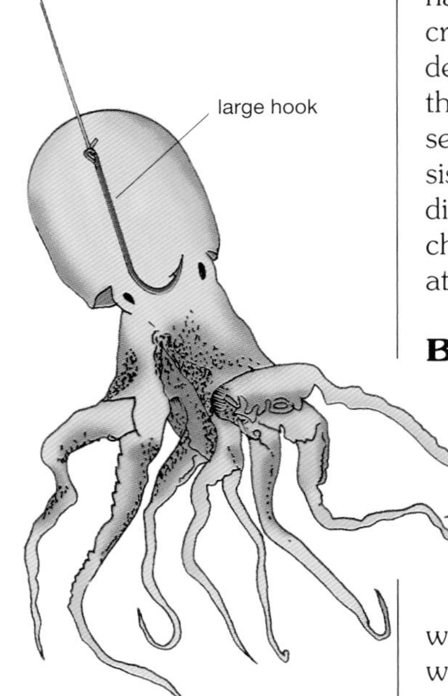

Head of a squid

The conger is a typical inhabitant of rocky coasts, where it hides among crevices, with a preference for wrecks. It is a ferocious predator, and may be fished equally well from the shore or from a boat. ▽

A TOUGH ADVERSARY

Congers are stay-at-home, rather lazy fish which do not stray far from their narrow lairs, which are deep clefts, crevices, or lobster caves. Their highly developed olfactory sense will cause them to emerge from their hole in search of their favorite prey. This consists of pout, mackerel, octopus, sardine, squid or cuttlefish. So you have a choice of baits, but there is one imperative: they must be completely fresh.

BAITS

The bait should be well presented. The best way is to use a Stewart rig. Fit it with a large no. 6/0 or no. 9/0 Octopus or O'Shaughnessy hook, with a long shank, followed by a smaller no. 4/0 Octopus with eyelet, which will slide if the brass or copper wire is twisted tightly. The small hook will act to keep the bait in position, preventing it from collapsing, which would cause it to look neither natural nor tempting.

• Octopus, squid, cuttlefish

The flesh of these baits is quite fragile, and is often damaged by pout, except when congers are swimming in the area. The largest hook should be inserted under the head, to re-emerge with the tip between the eyes. The small hook should be sunk into the back of the squid or cuttlefish, at a good distance, thanks to its self-blocking tightened tie. To economize on bait, fishermen often use just the head part of a squid. In this case, the large long-shanked hook is sunk under the head, re-emerging between the eyes, while the smaller one is stuck into one or two tentacles. The more firmly the bait is attached to the hooks, the less easily the conger will be able to grab it without being caught.

• Mackerel

Mackerel, with their fatty, firm, blood-rich flesh, are one of the best baits for conger. The largest hook (no. 6/0), stuck into the flank near the head, should emerge through the skull, with the shank on its side and held in place with trussing or Dacron thread, which are easy to tie. The second hook

(no. 3/0) should be inserted close to the caudal fin and, if required, two or three reverse half-keys (capstan knots used to form stops with a piece of matchstick) can be made around it. The fish will then be wound in several turns of the string; this will prevent the conger tugging at it, and will force it to swallow the bait whole.
You can also fillet a mackerel, but this makes the bait more fragile. It is better to cut a mackerel or cuttlefish lengthwise, including the head, and hook the half-fish in the same way.

△ *Conger fishing using support fishing on a rocky coast in Brittany.*

Where and how to fish for conger

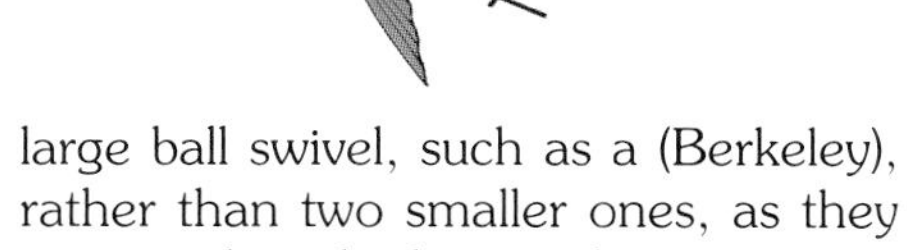

A tied mackerel

• Natural positions
The best natural positions are at the foot of shore cliffs where congers have at least 4 feet (3 m) of water over them, or in a nearby deep trench. These locations, which are found along rocky coasts, are quite common in the Atlantic and Mediterranean.

• Artificial positions
Artificial positions make use of jetties, piers, and the sea walls protecting deep water habors, which are anchored by heaps of large blocks of stone. Congers have worked out how to use these stone structures, which are rich in crustaceans and mollusks, to their advantage. Congers will usually emerge in the evening and at night in calm and quite warm water, since this predator does not like strong tidal currents.

• A suitable rig
Since the base of these rocky structures is broader, 12 to 15-foot (4 or 5 m) bottom lines must not be used; instead try support fishing, casting a simple rig. Use a flat-sided sinker mounted on a breaking strand, a slide, and a bottom line made from a steel braid sheathed in nylon, of the most flexible you can find (of the Steelon or Scale Mer type), with a 40-lb resistance. When making a rig for conger, it is a good idea to insert one large ball swivel, such as a (Berkeley), rather than two smaller ones, as they may weaken the bottom line.
A solid fiberglass boat rod measuring approximately 7 feet (2 m) will usually be used. The pulley in the top of the rod tip should have a strength of 30 to 40 lb, and there should be a rotating drum reel of the same power. A large fixed-drum surf reel may also be used if the nylon for the line is no thicker than 70/100. The rig for vertical support fishing over the position from the shore is based on the trolling rig. It sometimes uses an anti-spin mini-slide sinker-holder of the Sea Boom type, and an identical sliding bottom line. The stronger the current and the more congested the sea-bed, the more you should shorten the steel bottom line (to about 20 in (50 cm)) and, conversely, where there is no current and clear bottom, the bottom line should measure 80 in (1.5 m).

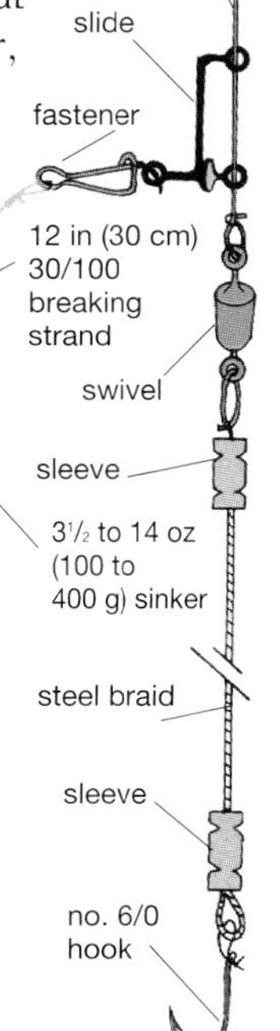

A simple rig

• Biting, striking, ascending
Congers are both finicky and impulsive. Their presence is first revealed by tuggings at the bait – hence the advantage of the slide and the need to give it 40 to 80 inches (1 to 2 m) of line when this happens. There is often a second pull, which should not be countered by striking. On the contrary, reel out a little more line. Only at the third tug should you strike vigorously and lift forcefully.
Congers sometimes appear to give in and allow themselves to be brought up without too much fuss. However, once they reach the surface, somersaults, spins, and bottom plunges follow each other in quick succession. Even when they are gaffed (using a two-hook gaff), the end is often a terrible struggle for both conger and angler.

A guarantee of freshness

The attractiveness of the bait depends on its freshness. "Fished and baited in the tide" remains the fisherman's dictum. There is nothing better than livebait. The flesh and blood contain juices which, even when diluted in seawater, will attract fish from greater distances than one might suppose. It will take about 15 minutes for livebait to die. Its watered-down flesh is now just a mass of empty cells and of no interest to the conger.

SEA-BREAM

*There are many varieties of sea bream which are known as porgy in the United States. Two of the commonest in European waters are the gilt-head bream (*Sparus auratus*), which has golden brows, and the other is the black sea-bream or old wife (*Spondyliosoma cantharus*), which is generally more abundant, but subject to temporary disappearances owing to its rather mysterious migrations. These and other varieties of sea-bream or porgy may be fished by support fishing or using a float line.*

Two black sea-bream caught using support fishing off Finistère, Brittany. These fish of average size are less sought-after than gilt-head bream and red porgy, but are nonetheless very interesting to fish and they make very good eating. ▽

Making a paternoster loop

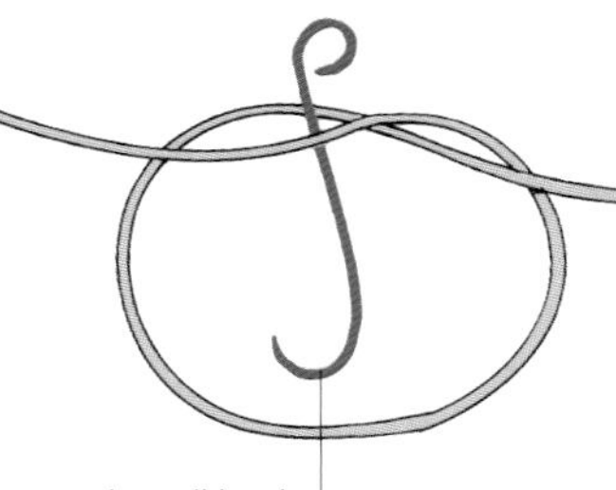

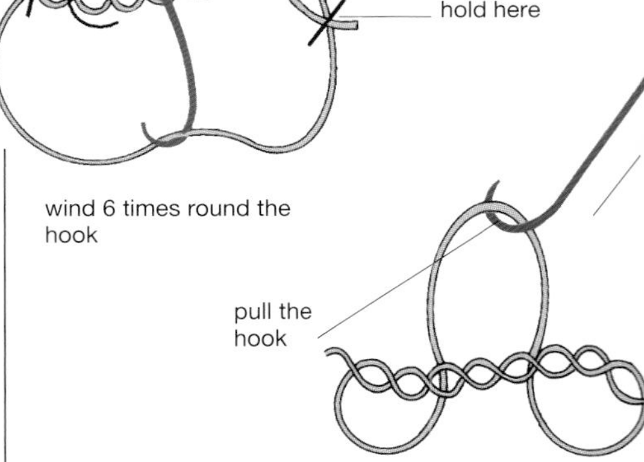

BLACK SEA-BREAM

The black sea bream or old wife is a gregarious fish; it lives in large shoals; it is sporty and hot-tempered, and may be fished by most methods.

• Typical positions

It is quite specific in the places in which it chooses to lurk. These include seaweed-covered rocks tumbling into the sea, rocky headlands, rock-strewn inshore waters, such as beneath jetties, sandy crevices in offshore rock-pools, and the outlets of deep channels. Sea-bream will also occupy various levels of shelving bottoms. Generally speaking, these typical positions will not be subject to excessively violent waves or currents. At the very least they will provide an opportunity of sheltering on the bottom. Sea-bream like to nuzzle up to rocks. Average tides (factor 60–75) are good. Lastly, do not forget that black sea-bream have small mouths, so use the appropriate lines, hooks, and baits.

• Suitable rigs

– Support bottom lines

This is the traditional bottom line with two or three short (6 in (15 cm)) paternosters, tiered and fixed loop-in-loop to paternoster loops, which are fiddly to make, unless you use the little hook trick. These nylon bottom lines must be made from nylon which is much finer than for surf-fishing, and the ideal backing line will be a 16/100 multifilament line, which is not affected by the current – disliked by gray sea bream – whilst permitting an immediate response (striking on a bite) due to lack of flexibility and elasticity.

– Sliding bottom line

This makes it possible to pass baits over submerged obstructions, such as rocky structures of deepwater harbor walls, groins, or the bases of tiered cliffs, all of which are favorite haunts of the sea-bream. This is a very sensitive rig which includes a small tube-slide which maintains the bead sinker in position. The latter, which is just sufficient to stay on the bottom, will be twice the weight of what a sliding spindle-shaped float can support, and is stopped at the top by a tie or line-stop. This stop must be located approximately 4 feet (1 m) above the bottom. It works like this: once the sinker is on the bottom, the line is pulled taut until the float is raised obliquely in the water.

– A semi-drag bottom line, known as a "helicopter" (see p. 253)

stop
1 oz (30 g) sliding float
stop bead
tube slide
swivel
stop bead
swivel link
$2^1/_4$ oz (60 g) Arlesey bomb
snood

Sliding assembly

This is probably the bottom line best suited for fishing black sea-bream, or porgy, which is truly fast fishing since this tricky fish can lick the hook clean in an instant, forcing the angler to react immediately. The other difficulty is to find the level on which sea-bream are lurking, since they change level during fishing. Hence the need for spare bottom lines on which the paternosters are arranged at different heights. Lastly, sea bream can be kept within reach of a line only by baiting. The simplest and most effective of bait consists of sardines mashed in a gloved hand and mixed with sand in a bucket. The sea-bream's defense is honorable. It consists mainly of using its wide flank to hinder its ascent, a few jerks of the head, a series of rushes, and a flattening on the surface of which you should be aware, since this is a prelude to a final headfirst dive toward the bottom, with the attendant danger of unhooking. Fishing with a fine line, black sea-bream will make for exciting fishing.

GILT-HEAD BREAM

This is a very attractive fish weighing around 10 lb (5 kg). In French it is sometimes called *sourcil d'or* ("golden eyebrow") a clearly appropriate name, since it wears "eyebrows" on a bumpy forehead, which slopes down over an obtuse-angled snout and thick lips. The jaw is powerful, capable of grinding up any shellfish. To complete the portrait of the sea-bream, we must not forget to mention the black and orange spots on the operculum, and the gold of the iris and silver of the robe. The gilt-head bream wears the jewels of a duchess on the shoulders of a wrestler.

• Typical fishing positions

Essentially on sand-and-rock coasts, and particularly flat sections where mussels grow and there are oyster-beds. Try searching around low headlands, wide-mouthed channels, inlets, and estuaries, open basins, and sandy flows snaking through rock, in which there are plenty of lugworms, crabs, cockles, and clams. Stop when you come to a place where the bottom is less exposed to the action of the water and consists of gravel, smooth pebbles, or large, rounded, seaweed-covered stones. Provided there is a rocky reef nearby, this is a typical sea-bream haunt.

Such specific advice often provokes the incredulity of amateur fishermen, but they are wrong. Sea-bream and porgy are very timid fish and tend to lurk close to the protection of rocks which are at the edge of a channel or current. Sea-bream and porgy will no doubt also be found on less rocky sea-beds, and anywhere they can find shellfish in abundance are favorite haunts. Clearly they are a pest in oyster-beds and mussel-beds and those who farm shellfish hate these fish. The areas around the beds, especially the inlet channels in which escaped shellfish often land, are good positions, which sea-bream will explore

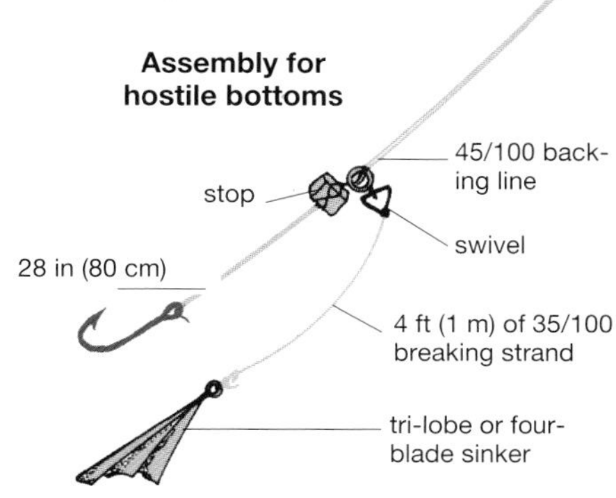

under the protection of a gray sky, when it is raining, or at dawn or dusk.

• Suitable rigs

The best rigs are similar to those used for bass, but they need to be strong (45/100 line in rocky locations. Lengthen the single snood (28 to 40 in (80 to 100 cm)), and use a sliding rig, so you can really feel the bite. The hook (a no. 2/0 or a no. 4/0) should be smooth steel with a well sharpened tip, and have as short a shank as possible.

– Rigs for difficult bottoms

This rig is suitable for the types of bottom frequented by the gilt-head bream, from which the fish must be removed as fast as possible.

This is a very simple and robust rig since no snood is added to the bottom line, which is an extension of the backing line. Nevertheless, it is a sensitive rig, since it is sliding.

USING RAZOR-SHELLS AS BAIT

The rubbery flesh of the razor-shell stays perfectly on the hook and resists supported casts. You can use the Stewart assembly with two hooks in tandem, or a hollow baiting-needle to pierce the razor-shell. Small pieces of razor-shell on fine hooks may interest black sea-bream. As for gilt-head bream and red porgy, they will not be put off by a whole razor-shell in its shell, quite the contrary. In this case, pull up the bottom line with a hook before fixing the fishhook into it. It holds perfectly, with the curve of the fishhook resting against the shell.

– Channel-fishing rig
This tends to be more appropriate for channels running between salt-water pools and the sea, since sea-bream, which love the warm water of lagoons, often frequent these areas. The rig can also be used for deepwater support fishing, at places where shellfish are piled up on the beaches, denoting an abundance of bivalves and suitable rocky hiding-places under water.

The principle governing sea-bream fishing is that there should be no resistance to taking the whole bait and it is reinforced here by a trick which consists in coiling the bottom line and holding it in place by a strip of Solucit. This frees up a greater length of the 7 feet (2 m) of coiled line as the bait dissolves in the water. Clearly, the rod needs to be modified appropriately, using a 1 to 3½ oz (30 to 100 g) bubble-float or a 13-foot (4 m) light surf rod.

• Striking
The bite occurs in two movements. First there are light quivers on the line, but when there are tugs it means that the sea-bream is chewing up the bait. If you strike at this point the

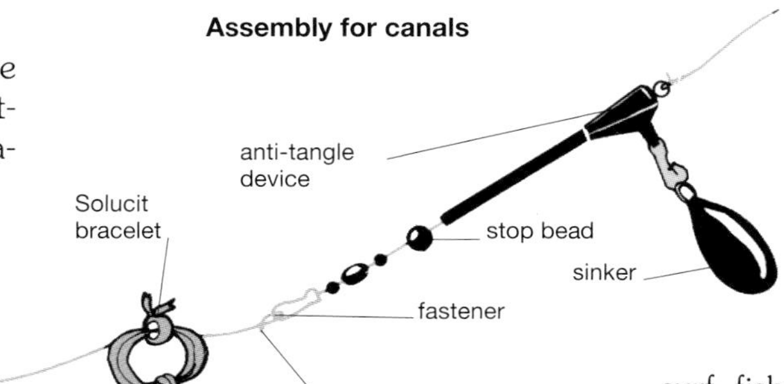

hook may be ground by the fish's powerful molars, which fear will cause to close in a vice-like grip. You have to wait for a clear start, and act as vigorously as the rod and nylon allow you to. It is no easy task to detach a sea-bream or porgy from the bottom. After this, there will be a succession of head jerks and side-to-side darts, though they will not give the impression that the fish is weakening. The back will break the water only at the last moment, when it starts a series of spins on the surface, often terminating in a masterly pirouette on the bottom line, the final liberating somersault.

• The best bait
The favorite bait is obviously shellfish, especially razor-shells, piddocks, mussels, cockles, and all types of clam; and then worms, large lugworms, and shrimp. Hard-shell crabs can be used without sea-bream finding them unattractive, provided you come across a shoal; otherwise, the best results are obtained with soft-shell crabs (see insert below). For surf fishing, you can use the razor-shell in its shell. You have to cast the bait crosswise to the current, and let it drift, then wait with the line held between thumb and index finger, which will slow down the unwinding of the reel coil, with the pick-up open. When your fingers feel a stopping movement, let go of the line and only begin to strike when you feel a tug. Sea-bream are usually hooked by their thick lips or in the gorge. After a premature strike and a few seconds of motionless struggle, the hook will return, straightened out, as straight as the exclamation mark which will punctuate your disappointment!

It is obvious from the above that when you fish for sea-bream or porgy, your equipment needs to be top quality and very robust. If it is, your fight with the sea-bream will be on an equal footing. The right attack merits a good defense.

LOOKING FOR SOFT-SHELL (PEELER) CRABS

If the crab is female, she will be protected by a male who will wait for her to have moulted before mating with her. If the crab is male, it has to fend for itself by camouflaging itself as best it can, but it will inevitably leave a trace of its presence. This may consist of the empty shell, abandoned, and often very visible. If you are not sure if the crab is male and it is still covered by its shell, pull on one of its smaller claws. This will yield, revealing the orangey skin, a sign you cannot miss. So a keen angler will watch out for two signs when seeking this precious bait, one is a crab being taken care of by another, and the other is a solitary crab with a shell lined with an orange skin. The soft-shelled crab, also known as a peeler crab when it has lost its shell, is an excellent bait for many sea fish, including sea-bream. It stays on the hook well and can be kept for a long time.

The moult takes place in two stages, one preparatory, the other operational. In the first, the shell becomes thinner, brittle, and turns purple or green; the crab is streaked with yellowish veins on the underside of its stomach. A yellow-orange skin develops underneath, the embryo of the future breastplate. At this point, the crab becomes weak and seems subdued, keeping its pincers and legs folded under its stomach.

In the second phase, when the moult is completed, the shell cracks, opening down the back like an oyster, and the animal painfully extricates itself from its increasingly tight clothing. The crab is now completely soft, in a very sorry state, and ripe for fishing.

Thanks to its very specific odor, and the hormones given off by the females, any predator, starting with bass, will recognize this succulent morsel from miles away. Furthermore, a soft-shell crab is so easy to swallow that hunting fish, which are not fanatical pursuers, will not be able to resist it.

Crabs have to replace their shell several times a year, once it becomes too tight. For a few days, while it remakes larger armor more appropriate for its size, this valiant fighter, having become naked and soft, will find itself highly exposed to predators and the hands of fishermen eager to use them as bait.

MULLET

*There are several species of mullet and they inhabit all the seas and oceans of the world. The most common European mullet is the thick-lipped mullet (*Chelon Labrosus*), which is recognizable by its fleshy mouth, of which the upper lip is covered with several rows of tubercles. The golden mullet (*Liza aurata*), has a bright yellow spot on the operculum. The mullet is an omnivorous predator, and may be fished using any of the sea-angling techniques. Its voracity causes it to snatch at both plant and animal baits, and it may even bite lures. It combines superb eating qualities with a spirited defense.*

Mullet look something like chub, with their thick, sturdy bodies covered in large, silvery scales. ▽

A CLEVER FISH

The silvery gray color and the presence of a very spiky first dorsal fin can cause the mullet to be confused with sea-bass. However, the two species frequent very different waters. Mullet prefer calm and even slightly polluted waters, such as silted tide-waters (estuaries), in which they will swim far upstream, sewerage outlets, and muddy harbors.

The strong, swift defense of the mullet, a very suspicious and finicky fish, is a boon to anglers who love sport fishing, and who often find themselves having to apply some of the tricks of freshwater fishing, such as are used on chub, loach, and carp. Even though the gray mullet does not reach record sizes (9–10 lb (4 to 5 kg) are record weights), a gray mullet weighing only 2 lb 2 oz (1 kg) can give a fisherman quite a run for his money, particularly if the line is fine (16/100 to 24/100).

Although mullet is a powerful fish, it prefers not to battle against strong currents, and likes to laze around in calm water; hence the attraction of harbors and sheltered coves.

If you see mullet swimming past in shoals, or circling round in the water, your chance of catching them from the shore will be slight. However, keeping a close watch on the areas in which this behavior is observed may prove valuable when there are 7 to 10 feet (2 to 3 m) of water over the heads of the inshore mullet. Remember, this is a very wary and prudent fish.

FISHING ON THE BOTTOM

Bottom-fishing for mullet can be performed in the traditional way. You can use a 1¾ oz (50 g) flat hexagonal sinker, sliding above a fastened bottom line, 28 in (80 cm) in length, and consisting of 24/100 line, and a reversed no. 6 hook. Alternatively, you could try using a paternoster rig, to which you have attached two or three short paternosters spread out above a Marie sinker. The latter rig has the advantage of being able to be changed without the need to have to undo lots of knots. Both techniques use the same nylon lines and hooks.

• Sardine gut assists fishermen

Bottom-fishing is more commonly practiced on a rocky coast than in a harbor. It is particularly effective in the eddies formed downstream of a current striking a headland or promontory. The bait should be generous and natural, which in any case is the rule with mullet. Sardine bait weighted with sand works well, especially if it is matched with the baits on the line. Sardine gut, which was a traditional favorite, has fallen into disuse, but it is ideal. Sardine gut contains two usable parts. The first is the tube which runs from the head and acts as an esophagus; it is cut out and wrapped around the hook like a worm. The second part is found at the end of the stomach cavity, and is prolonged by filaments of flesh. This fibrous part is used with the stomach cavity still attached to it, as this "pocket" keeps the bait in place on the tip of the hook. When both the worm-like and filamentous gut are used together, they are extremely attractive to the mullet.

FLOAT-FISHING

This is harbor fishing par excellence, and is practiced using a long, 16 ft 6 in (5 m), fishing-pole as you would when river-fishing, or a fixed-spool reel feeder rod. Both rods need to have a very sensitive rod tip, with a fast action.

Mullet have a huge appetite, and bite both lures and natural baits. ▷

• Floats to match fishing conditions

The simplest rig consists of a fixed, spindle-shaped float, which is very well balanced and level with the antenna by adding a series of sinkers of decreasing weights (A). However, this only works in calm, warm and windless water. When the weather is not so good, use a waggler, again with sinkers of decreasing weight. To make the waggler slide, move the upper sinker to the bottom line, and stop the float sliding by means of a tie or line-stop (B). If you are fishing in an early floodtide current, in a harbor access channel (a good position), use an underwater float on the backing line as this will maintain the bottom line almost vertical.

To prevent drift, the bottom line should be weighed with a Marie sinker (C). This is a very sensitive assembly, which must be closely supervised, the line being stretched far enough to slightly bend the end of the rod tip.

As soon as the rod bends even further, or slackens, you must strike. Inevitably, there will be some near misses, so sensitive are the lips of mullet, but these will be no more frequent than when fishing for other catches.

Miscellaneous floats

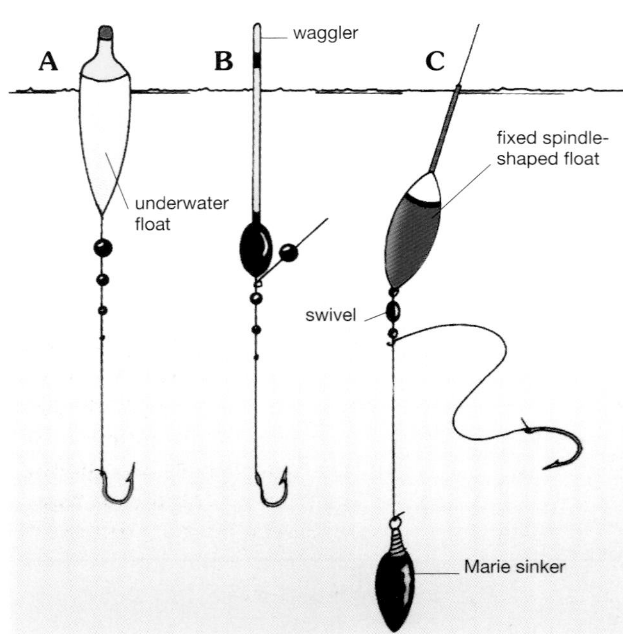

The mullet rig enables you to fish in locations which are not as heavily frequented as wharves, such as the deeps near rocks inshore, locations which can prove very productive.

WHICH SINKER TO USE

The way sinkers are arranged depends on the type of fish you are after. For wary fish, such as mullet, a set of sinkers in decreasing sizes will be effective and more sensitive, but will sink fast in rough water.

If the water is choppy, fish using a waggler. The technique consists in sinking the end or a part of the rod-tip, so as to protect the line from the action of the wind and waves. This technique allows you to fish quite a long way offshore using thin lines, so that you can feel the bites of a fish as cautious as the mullet.

FLEXIBILITY!

With the various casting techniques, even the simplest ones, if the fisherman uses his legs like a javelin-thrower or shot-putter, i.e. by bending his supporting leg when the fish starts, and releases it like a spring during the cast, the cast will be considerably improved. Too many fishermen cast whilst standing to attention, with their bodies straight and stiff. An angler needs to be as flexible as his rod-tip.

• Baiting and baits

As you might expect, preliminary baiting of the position, several days in advance, is recommended. For example, use bread dipped in a bucket, weighted with sand and flavored with sardine oil, ground, freeze-dried shrimp, or fish oil. The best bait consists of a ball of bread pulp kneaded on to the hook, or a piece of firm, whole-wheat bread – an old bait for river fishing – impregnated with sardine oil. However, mullet will eat anything, a piece of shrimp, a strip of tuna, or an oyster will do the trick.

BUBBLE-FLOAT FISHING

When angling on the coast or in or near tidewaters (estuaries), if you see shoals of mullet swimming past, it is very tempting to pursue them out to sea. If you do so, use a special mullet spoon, which is a small rotating spoon with a long shank, baited with an oyster or mussel, 7 feet (2 m) from a no. 3 bubble-float, using a 20/100 bottom line, and a 1 to 2 oz (30 to 50 g) casting rod. A light Sert with bubble-float (1 to 3 oz (30 to 80 g)) is effective. Mullet are sensitive to this spoon and when they stay off-shore, they bite more sharply. When the current is strong, weight the line with a sinker, bubble-float, and spoon. To prospect the various levels, partially fill a small no. 2 bubble-float. Reeling in should be slow, and may even be stopped if the current is strong enough to make the spoon rotate and stretch the bottom line. Releases may be decisive. You can even lay the rod down and wedge it while you deal with another one.

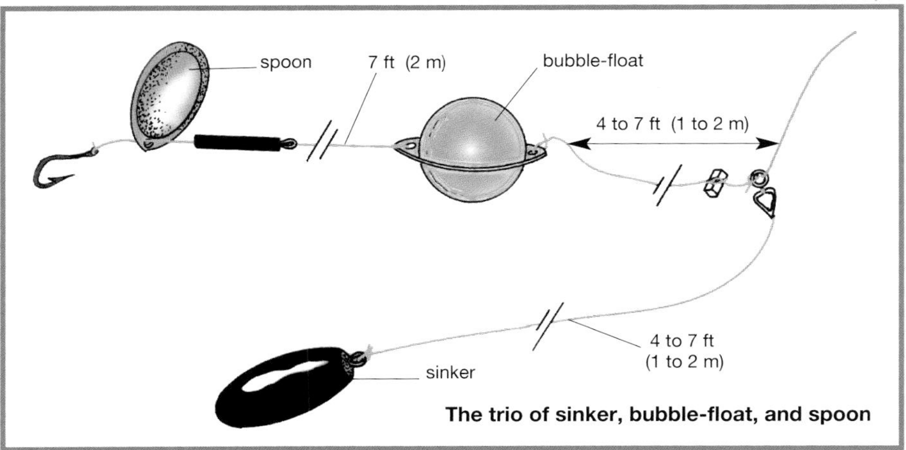

The trio of sinker, bubble-float, and spoon

RENÉ CLAIR'S "RAFT"

To conclude this detailed review of mullet fishing techniques here is an unusual one, which might even be a leg-pull given that it has been handed down by anglers from Provence. This unusual rig consists of a raft, known in Provençal as a *rusclet*, which is used in summer in warm water, with off-shore winds. It consists of cutting a block of cork or compact polystyrene, measuring approximately 4½ in (12 cm) by 2½ in (6 cm), ¾ in (2 cm) thick, which is sharpened to a point, and in which five or six narrow grooves are cut.

The raft is tied up with string like a package, and the end knot consists of a loop. The line, which contains five or six very short 30/100 nylon snoods, is held in the grooves and fastened to this loop, and some no. 6 or no. 8 hooks are baited with bread balls. A crust of stale bread the same size as the raft is attached to its underside with rubber bands and the raft is then pushed into the water. As soon as they spot this manna from heaven, the mullet go into a feeding frenzy and bite into the bread crust, thus impaling their mouths on the hooks. A rich harvest for the "raft" fisherman!

Duborgel, who taught us this amusing technique, told me that it was the French film director, René Clair, who had taught it to him. And he may well have learned it from the writer Marcel Pagnol. Michel was always inventive, and suggested that at the front of the raft you should stick a gull's feather for a sail. So that, he said in all seriousness, "you can fish for mullet as far as the coast of Africa or America..."

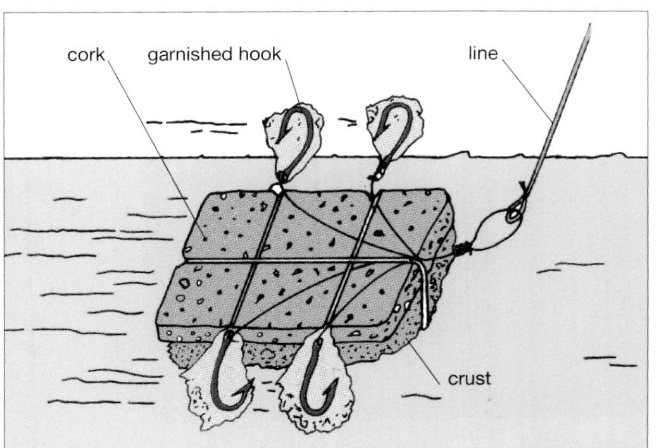

The little raft

FLATFISH

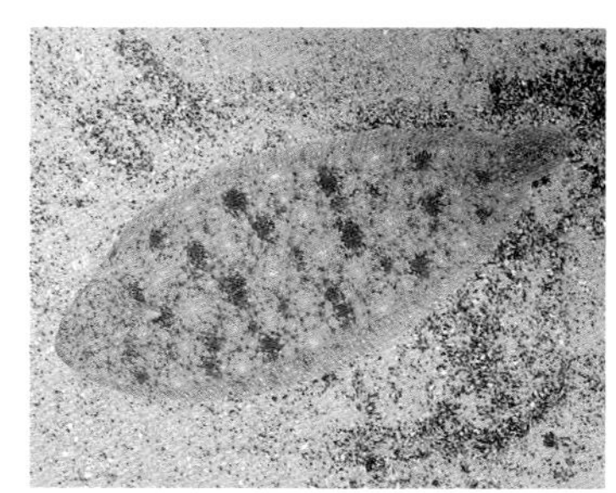

Members of the flatfish family, the Pleuronectidae, the fish are overcome by a great lassitude, caused by the fundamental change of shape that occurs as they grow. They lie on one side, and the upper flank, which contains both eyes, takes on the color of their surroundings. This sandy camouflage is the only defense these fish have against predators. They are confident in their sand covering, and generally swallow baits placidly. There are thus no complications with the gentle bite of a plaice, sole, or dab.

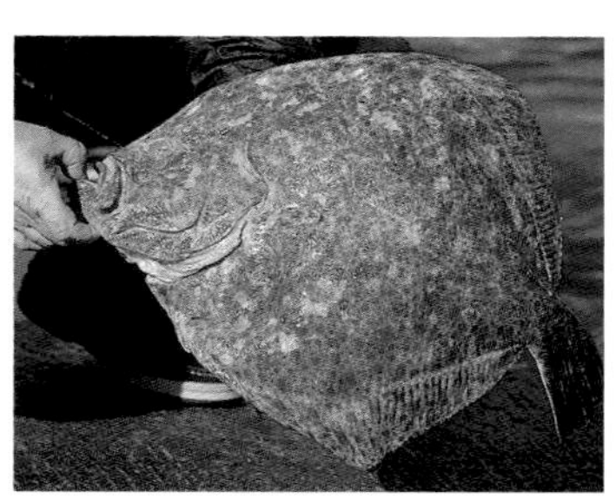

△ *Thanks to their clever camouflage, sole (top) escape most predators. Dab (middle) are above all deep-sea fish, and not of great interest to anglers. Conversely, turbot (bottom) are delicious, and very combative.*

A royal double for these deep-sea anglers fishing off southern Finistere, Brittany – a turbot and a gray sea-bream. ▽

SOLE

The sole or Dover sole (*Solea vulgaris*) is a fish with delicate flesh which was once so common along the Atlantic coast of Europe that the Latin name means "common". You could catch them by walking in the water and ramming a fish gig, a long fork, into the sand. Those days are long gone. Specimens weighing 1lb 2 oz through 2 lb 4 oz (0.5 to 1 kg), however, may still be caught by looking on flat sandy bottoms which are rich in lugworms, sometimes abutting on to rocks, in shallow water. The slow-moving sole clearly requires fishing conditions to be rather calm – a smooth sea and low tidal factors. So fish using a fine line, such as a 20/100 or a 30/100 nylon line, and a bubble-float or light surf line which can be cast at up to $4^{1}/_{2}$ oz (120 g). Suitable $2^{1}/_{4}$ oz (60 g) sinkers will be enough to maintain a bottom line in position. If it drifts slightly (use a watch sinker for this), the fishing will be better. A sliding hexagonal sinker with spikes will catch a sole in the evening, since they are less cautious than in daytime. The bottom line should be 80 in (2 m) of 22/100 nylon of the drag type, and could contain an additional, shorter snood, holding a different bait, shrimp for instance.

The commonest bait is lugworm and, curiously, the worm may be slightly rotten. Other worms may be used, such as blood-worms, ragworms, small oysters, lugworms, and jumbo, or American worms, and all of these may also be slightly "off". In southwestern France, the local bait is the so-called

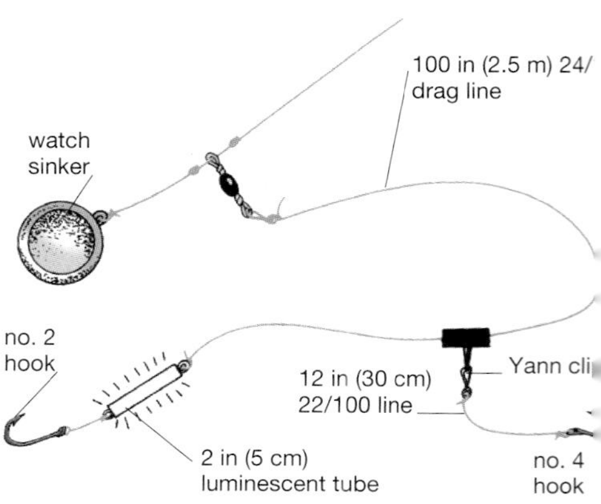

Assembly for sole

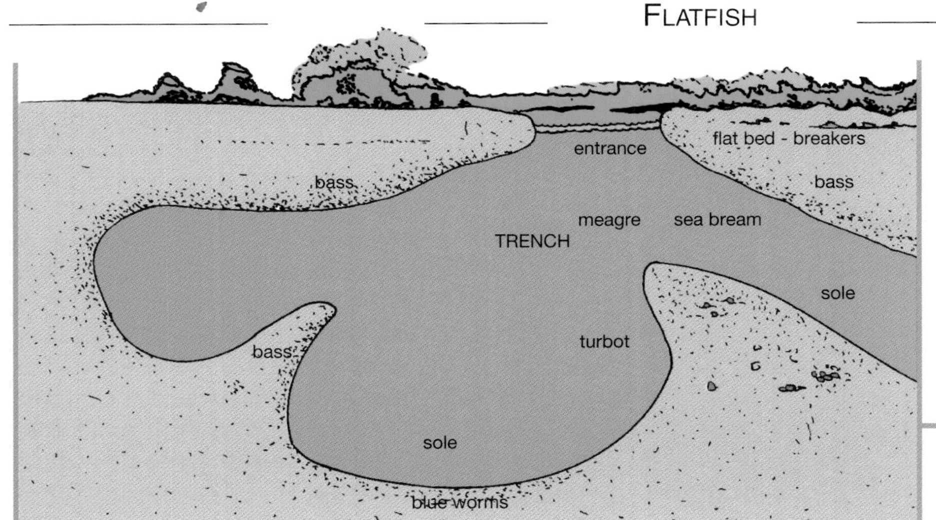

A wide trench of the type occurring in southwestern France

"blue worm", which may, in fact, be white, red, or yellow. These worms frequent the edges of the deep trenches in which the best fish, from bass through turbot, congregate, including the meagre, and, naturally, sole. Worms are tricky to attach to the hook as bait. Try an iron-tip no. 2 or no. 4 hook, and pierce worms through the tail, clustering them on the hook or gathering them into a bundle tied up by a strand of wool wound round the bend of the hook.

DAB

The streamlined, rough-skinned body, is bisected with a line starting from the right eye and arcing around the pectoral fin. The coloring of the dab (*Limanda limanda*) is quite variable, ranging from golden to yellow-brown. It is an Atlantic coastal species which is very common in the North Sea and the English Channel. It likes sandy bottoms where the pebbles end. Dab often stays in shallow water, preferably in eddies, where it looks for worms as the tide comes in.

To find a good-sized dab measuring 12–16 inches (30–40 cm), you have to cast far offshore from sandbanks swept by currents. Surf-casting will enable you to reach the dab. Offer it sandworms spread out above the claw sinker, using clips of the Clipobar type, tied in place with paternoster knots, and add swivels. This standard rig is suitable for most types of flatfish.

Draw fishing

PLAICE

Plaice (*Pleuronectes platessa*) are shaped like rounded diamonds. They have fine, brownish scales and typical orange spots with a very white underside. They weigh between $10\frac{1}{2}$ and 2 lb 4 oz (0.3 and 1 kg). Above this size they are becoming rare, although they are abundant on clean beaches rich in shoals of lugworms and sea-lice, the two main baits used to fish for them. However, they will not turn their noses up at a piece of razor-shell or a soft crab (peeler crab) claw.

Plaice are fished by surf-casting with exactly the same rigs used for sole or dab. Plaice are slightly more lively hunters than other flatfish, and can be caught using draw fishing where the terrain is suitable. This is an active type of fishing which uses a $1\frac{1}{2}$ to $2\frac{1}{4}$ oz (45 to 60 g) pirk, which replaces the sinker, and also acts as a teaser due to its brilliance and its jerky swimming movement. Fix a 16-inch (40 cm) 35/100 to 40/100 nylon bottom line behind the pirk, using a broken ring with a loop, and attach a worm hook. After casting, strike cleanly to make the pirk move forward jerkily, interspersed with pauses that are long enough for the fish to snatch the bait. The sand cloud raised by the pirk attracts the plaice, which should leap on the lugworm.

This attraction may be increased by using a pair of pliers to attach $2\frac{1}{2}$ or $3\frac{1}{4}$ in (6 or 8 cm) of 8/100 steel wire, folded back and twisted through the eyelet in the pirk. Store-bought scratch sinkers will also work. This pull-fishing, which is fun and effective, lets you cover more ground than static fishing, and thus gives you a better chance of encountering flatfish.

TURBOT

Turbot (*Psetta maxima*) is the climax to this review of flatfish. Turbot may grow as large as 34 lb (15 kg), and are the dream catch of the sea angler. They have become as rare as sole, whose habitat they share, especially in the sands of trenches. Their predatory nature incites turbot to go after various prey, lugworms as well as sand-eels on sandy bottoms, so that draw-casting may prove more productive than traditional surf-fishing. However, the latter can still be worthwhile if you use strips of squid, sand-eels, mackerel heads, shrimp, or soft-shell (peeler) crabs. However, local anglers may well be reluctant to reveal the secret of the best places to fish for turbot.

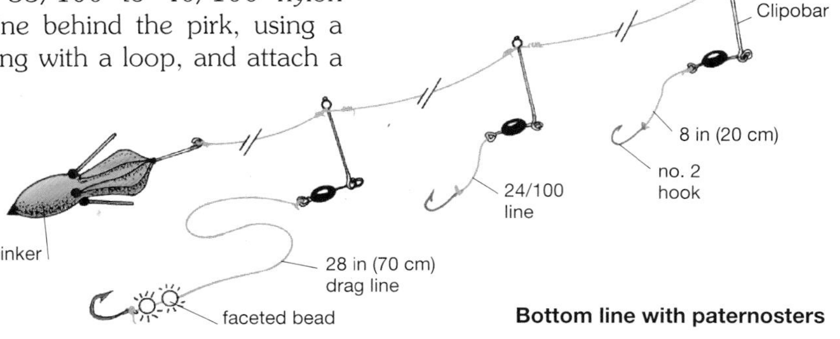

Bottom line with paternosters

Rockfish

The ballan wrasse (Labrus bergylta), which belongs to the Labridae family, lives in the shadow of underwater cliffs. Its flesh has an undeservedly poor reputation. ▽

Rockfish (wrasse and sea-bream) have the reputation of being of no culinary interest, except in soups. However, white bream have delicious flesh which belies this idea.

A typical scene in a rocky Mediterranean bottom, frequented by white bream, rainbow wrasse, and damselfish. ▽

White bream

White bream (*Diplodus sargus*) are members of the Sparidae family, and resemble silver sea-bream. They are striped vertically with nine dark rays, punctuated with a black spot on the caudal peduncle. White bream are the only members of the family which have small incisors and molars. White bream are coastal fish, swimming continuously, and they frequent the thickets of *Posidonia* and the rocky coasts of the Bay of Biscay in the Atlantic and the Mediterranean Sea. They are distrustful and combative, although small, weighing 7 oz to 2 lb 4 oz (0.2 to 1 kg), and are sought after for their fine flesh. You will have the best chance of approaching white bream without alarming them too much at dawn or dusk. You should fish for them using a floated line and a large fishing pole and small reel, a line reserve, and 22/100 nylon line; a very sensitive, phosphorescent spindle-shaped float should be balanced by a large bullet sinker followed by a short (6 in (15 cm)) 20/100 pile and a short stem no. 6 through no. 10 hook. As bait, use lugworms, shrimp tails, bread or cheese paste, or small cubes of razor-shell or cuttlefish flesh. Cuttlefish are good bait for withstanding the fierce onslaught of the white bream, which is similar to that of gray sea-bream. "Look for seaweed and you

The annular sea bream (Diplodus annularis) is very similar to the white bream, but has a more tapering body. ▷

△ The common white bream (Diplodus sargus).

The saddled bream (Oblada melanura), which like white bream belongs to the Sparidae family, lives in large shoals in the coastal waters of the Atlantic and Mediterranean. ▷

will find white bream" says an old French proverb. The seaweed in question has sometimes been torn from the sea-bed, and pushed by the currents towards inlets, where some of it is deposited, while the remainder flows back with the outgoing current. White bream accompany the carpets of floating seaweed, so cast a sliding line using a hexagonal flat sinker at the edge of a bed. The best bait is a small oyster or mussel on a reversed no. 8 hook. White bream are also very sensitive to baiting of the position, like most sea-bream.

SMALL ROCKFISH

Wherever there are rock-pools, even shallow ones, crevices, cracks, or large blocks of stone (sea walls, stones on gravel, or heaps of pebbles), there are famished little fish, ready to jump on the smallest prey – a piece of shrimp, a limpet, mussel, sand-flea or strip of worm.

• Goby

The goby (*Gobius* sp.) is a small fish which is excellent when deep-fried. It has a round, black body, with protruding eyes; the fused ventral fins form suckers.

With or without a rod, goby can sometimes be caught by sight, by immersing an 18/100 bottom line, with two or three round sinkers at the end, and one or two short (2 in (5 cm)) snoods, carrying a straight hook with a long no. 12 stem, the tongue of which has been folded back using a pair of pliers, to make it easier to extract from the goby's mouth.

• Rockling

This loach (*Gaidropsarus vulgaris*) with a blackish, smooth and barbelled skin, is bigger than the goby, being about 12 in (30 cm) long. It can be caught in quite deep pools, using a floated line and large baits. It sometimes takes bait from bass and wrasse lines.

• Blenny

The blenny (*Blennius* sp.) is a curious little brown fish which lives in families

△ Gobies live in the shallows, among outcrops of rock. They are frequently found in pools left behind by the receding tide.

Like goby, blenny live close to the surface, under stones. They can be used as live bait for bass fishing. ▷

under stones, and which is recognizable by the fleshy growths over its protruding eyes and the strong jaws with sharp little teeth.

It should be pole-fished as for the goby, in water-holes, and even dry, between two stones. If the bait is placed at the entrance to its cave, it will jump on it. However, if you need to wake up the blenny and attract its attention, tap the rock with the end of the rod-tip. The blenny is a fish full of vitality, perfectly

The chub is an inhabitant of the coastal zone, where it hides among the rocky crevices and seaweed. ▽

designed to act as a livebait for bass or conger fishing in a rocky location.

• Chub

The chub (*Enophrys bubalis*) has a very large, unattractive head. It is a sort of small-scale angler fish. It also acts as an excellent livebait. This lurking hunter is very voracious, and the perfect prey for coastal fishermen using floated lines.

• Rainbow wrasse

The rainbow wrasse (*Coris julis*), which is a close relation of the wrasse, merits the nickname "sea-parrot" due to its shimmering colors. It is a small wrasse, which savages the bait, and infuriates fishermen as it has a habit of stripping bait from a hook not intended for it, near jetties or in deep pools choked with seaweed.

Rainbow wrasse may be pole-fished, like other wrasse, or it can be caught quite easily with a small floated line. Fishing these rockfish is a very good initiation into fishing for children. The fish can be used as bait for larger fish if they are not caught for the table.

MACKEREL

*Although they are mainly fished by drag fishing from boats, large shoals of mackerel (*Scomber scombrus*) sometimes swim toward beaches or gather around harbor entrances, chasing schools of alevins. These invasions take place mainly during warm summers, when the sea is calm and smooth.*

△ Small mackerel are often caught by feathering.

FLOATED LINE

Mackerel, which are closely related to the much larger tuna, are vigorous fighters. If you want to have fun catching mackerel one by one on fine lines, fish with a 20/100 nylon floated line, baited with pieces of mackerel or sardine heads. However, since shoals of mackerel are constantly on the move, they must be kept at a rod's length by using a ground-bait to attract them. An excellent one consists of grinding sardines and mixing it with stale bread, soaked in water and squeezed dry, then adding peanut flour. Flavor the mixture with fish oil. Commercially available bait breads may be used effectively, and are less messy.

FEATHERING

A more efficient way of fishing for mackerel when they hunt near the shore consists in feathering. This involves sending an undulating spoon and sets of hooks into the shoal, preceded by three or four white or red feathers. The effect is immediate, and each time you will haul out a string of mackerel, pulling in all directions.

◁ Mackerel also takes natural baits very well.

Throughout the summer, mackerel swim close to the coast, where it is possible to catch them using lure casting. ▽

SMALL SHARKS

Small sharks, which swim within reach of lines along the coasts of Europe, are generally harmless to humans. Once you catch one, however, be careful when you handle them, both on account of their sharp teeth and the nasty sting possessed by some species such as the spur-dog. It is better to release sharks into the water, since most are endangered species. Ireland is a minor paradise for basking shark fishing, as they are very abundant in the coastal waters.

△ *The angelfish is very well camouflaged when they lurk on the bottom, pouncing on small passing prey.*

◁ *Some types of dogfish are so common that they are a nuisance for anglers, because they steal bait destined for more desirable catches.*

ANGELFISH

Angelfish (*Squatina squatina*), weigh around 45 lb (20 kg), and are a sort of missing link between a shark and a ray. The nostrils are on the side, and they have spiracles on their backs. Angelfish are brown or marbled gray in color and like most coastal sharks, they live on sandy and muddy bottoms, where they devour cephalopods, crabs, sand-eels, chinchard, and flatfish.

DOGFISH

Dogfish, both the lesser spotted (*Scyliorhinus canicula*), weighing 4 lb 8 oz (2 kg), and the larger spotted dogfish (*Scyliorhinus stellaris*), weighing 27 lb (12 kg), are members of the shark family which swim lazily and lie in wait for anything that falls to the sandy bottom, dead or alive. The fish have strong, round heads and eyes rimmed with mobile eyelids. They emit a sort of rattle, which explains the nickname of "sea-cow". Their skin, which is so rough that it may scratch a fisherman's forearm, around which it tends to wrap itself lovingly, while winking. The lesser dogfish also known as a nursehound, is a feeder on sandy and sometimes rocky bottoms. It often appears in open sea chewing baits, before swallowing them down.

Other types of dogfish encountered around European coasts include Tope sharks (*Galeorhinus galeus*), weighing 33 lb (15 kg) and colored slate gray, with a spiracle located behind the eyes and pointed teeth, and the smoothhound (*Mustelus mustelus*) which has blunt teeth, white spots on its body, and a very far forward dorsal fin. These are also called gray dogs. As for spur-dogs (*Squalus acanthias*), these are gray-blue in color, weigh 10 lb through 13 lb (5 to 6 kg), and have a strong odor. They swim about a lot and feed mainly on smaller fish.

Bottom lines for catching dogfish of all types should contain swivels, and drag on the bottom. They should be made of braided steel, although a strong nylon or multi-filament line may also work, since these sharks do not put up much of a fight.

Cod Whiting Pout Ray

Cod (top)
Whiting (middle)
Pout (bottom).▽

Cod

The skin of the cod (*Gadus morhua*) is brown and speckled, and may have green, yellow, or gray tints, the belly being pale. Cod favors waters as cold as 35.6 to 45°F (2 to 7°C), mainly in the North Sea and the English Channel, even if a few incursions into the Atlantic have been noted. Cod can grow to 22 lb (10 kg) on the coast, and are even larger further offshore.
Like pollack, cod prefer to dwell on the bottom. Good positions take account of this, and fishermen must reach cod holes located way offshore.

• Cast fishing

For this type of fishing, use heavy equipment, such as a very powerful 12 to 16 ft 6 in (4 to 5 m) rod able to cast up to 10 oz (300 g), such as the Surf Custom Shimano or the Télé-Caussel with large rings. The reel should be of the 498 Mitchell type, with finger pick-up. To cast similar sinkers, which are indispensable for holding onto the bottom at long range, use a 30 to 33 foot (9 to 10 m) snatch-rod with 60/100 nylon line, connected with a barrel knot. If it were not for the intense effort of casting, cod could be caught with 45/100 lines and 10/100 bottom lines, provided they had large clips to prevent entanglements. As for the hooks used with this voracious fish, there is no point in being too clever, particularly

Presentation of lug-worms

There are two ways to present lug-worms for angling. They can either be sewn on a hook with a long, straight stem, piercing everywhere as you turn the worm over, and bringing up a part of it above the hook ring, at which point you pierce another wriggly sandworm through the head; or you can thread a sandworm on the hook without piercing it, using a hollow loach-needle.
In the first case, you will need to have a bait-fastener attached to the bottom line.

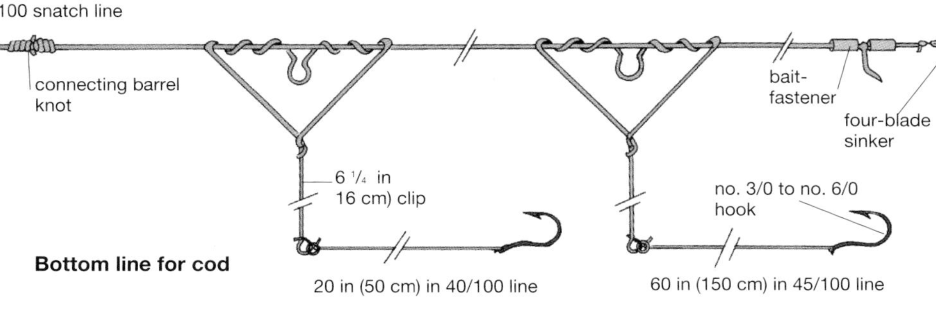

Bottom line for cod

since their shape is the same as the favorite bait of cod, large blackish lugworms with wrinkled skin. These should be threaded with a worm-needle to keep them more securely fixed on casting. A bait-fastener is not merely for cosmetic purposes, given the force of the cast.
The Boulogne fishermen, who operated from the Carnot sea wall, used to use a technique of rear-casting, with their backs turned to the sea. Thanks to the amazing properties of modern carbon rods, you can avoid the precarious structures of sea walls, and the strong currents which swirl around them, and cast without too much difficulty at their limit, in the fringe of cloudy water in which cod are to be found. Cod does not have a fierce bite nor does it put up a spectacular defense, since their mouths operate like vacuum cleaners, with a suction action. Striking prematurely, before the fish has started to feed, should be avoided at all costs.

Whiting

Whiting (*Merlangius merlangus*), are smaller than cod, but have many of the same features. They also need a good depth of water, and they are voracious feeders. On the other hand, unlike cod, they have quite a fast bite, which means that you will need to have a supple wrist enabling you to strike faster. Whiting live in shoals. In summer they come close inshore and hang around harbors although they tend to do so more frequently in the English Channel than in the Atlantic.

• The best rigs

Rigs should be identical to those used for cod. Two or three snoods on rotating clips (whiting are spinning fish), and a terminal snood, which should be longer, dragging on the bottom. Whiting like shiny objects, and will appreciate no. 1 through no. 1/0 hooks. The traditional bait, lugworms and nereids, suit them fine, as do small pieces of mackerel or squid tentacles. Apart from the strike, the fishing action presents no difficulties, since whiting are so greedy.

Pout

Pout (*Trisopterus luscus*), also known as poor cod, is a member of the Gadidae, the cod family. They tend to bite off more than they can chew and are similar in color and shape to yellow pollack. The flesh resembles that of whiting. They have barbels below the mouth like cod.
This is a fish which does not know the meaning of fear when it comes to exasperating a hapless angler; however, the pout is very wary of those who seek them in the rocky bottoms or at the tips of rocks, which are known as pout-holes.

• Varied fishing techniques

Any bait will work, especially if you waggle the sinker over the bottom a little. Sandworm, shrimp, clams, cockles, pieces of squid, pieces of mackerel and red sea-bream, etc. Use a support rig with 24/100 line, with three or four short snoods connected to swivels or rotating clips. The hooks should be no. 2 to no. 2/0 hooks to match the greediness of a large (2 lb 4 oz (1 kg)) pout. A pout will happily grab a hook intended for a conger if the conger eel did not leap on even more avidly! When you fish for pout at the edge of a shallow and the bites suddenly stop, this may mean there is a "bass under the rock".

Skate and Ray

These are cartilaginous fish with branchial slits and a mouth on the underside. The fins are triangular and flap like wings to propel the fish forward. The body is flat and diamond-shaped.
There are many varieties of skate and ray, and they are mainly fished from boats. The most commonly fished are the eagle ray (genus *Myliobatis*), weighing around 22 lb (10 kg), with a snout like that of a toad, and the stingray (*Dasyatis pastinaca*), weighing around 90 lb (40 kg), with a pointed snout. These two species are often confused; both have a tapering tail, with quite a dangerous barbed stinger. They frequent sandy or muddy coasts, and are especially fond of oyster-beds, where they are a nightmare for the oyster-farmer.
The skate and ray diet consists of shellfish, crustaceans, and cuttlefish. Fishing for skate and ray is practiced more or less at random during nighttime, surf-casting fishing. These fish are fond of carrion, and simply flatten themselves on their prey to smother it and swallow it. If you lift up a large stingray from the bottom, make sure it does not fall back on to your feet, as a ray's stinger is strong enough to penetrate a boot!

◁ *Surf-casting is a good way of catching skate and ray.*

The numbers in Roman script (10) refer to the running text; the numbers in *italics (10)* refer to captions for the illustrations; the numbers marked with an asterix* (10*) refer to the boxes; the numbers in **bold (10-12)** refer to in-depth treatments of the subject.

PHOTO CREDITS

P. Affre : 69 m, 94-95, 95 b; **Berthoule/NATURE:** 10 b, 18-19 u, 41, 52 b, 54 b, 148 u, 182 u, 194-195, 197 u, 205 b, 208 u, 210 b, 218-219 u, 220 u, 232-233 u, 235, 238, 241 u, 241 b, 245, 286 b; **U. Carmié:** 80; **Chaumeton/NATURE:** 16, 26 b, 46 u, 50 u, 58, 62, 75 b, 78 b, 85 b, 122, 136 u, 136 b, 156, 166, 208 b, 215 u, 215 b, 220 b, 224 u, 224 b, 226, 228, 234, 237, 240, 242 u, 242 b, 244 u, 244 b, 246 u, 246 b, 266 u, 276, 283, 291, 294 u, 296 u, 294 ur, 296 mr, 296 br, 297 u, 297 m, 299 u; **Corel:** 250, 251, 252-253; **L. Cortay:** 12, 15 b, 21 b, 26 u, 31, 33 m, 34 u, 34 b, 36, 38, 43, 46 b, 49 b, 50 b, 57, 63, 98 b, 112 bl, 113 m, 114, 115, 119 u, 120 u, 125, 126, 130 r, 139, 140, 147, 149, 150, 152, 154, 157, 158, 162 u, 162 bl, 163 u, 163 b, 164, 165, 170-171, 172, 173, 174 u, 174 b, 175 u, 175 b, 176, 177, 178, 179 u, 179 b, 181 u, 181 b, 182 b, 183 u, 183 b, 184, 185 u, 185 b, 186, 188, 190, 191, 192 l, 192 r, 204 b; **M. Courdot:** 70, 78 u, 83 b, 84, 89 u, 93 b, 99 u, 100 l, 104, 105, 109; **Dupraz:** 22 u, 32, 33 u, 35, 44-45, 48-49 u, 132-133 b, 248-249, 254 b, 255 u, 257, 258, 260-261, 271 u, 273 b, 277, 280 b, 281, 282, 287, 298 u, 298 br, 299 b, 301; **P. Durantel:** 7 b, 8-9, 15 u, 20 b, 22 bl, 24, 27 b, 28-29, 30, 37 u, 39, 40, 52 u, 54-55 u, 55 b, 56, 59, 60, 61, 64-65, 66 bl, 67 bl, 72-73, 74 b, 76-77 u, 77 b, 81, 88, 89 b, 90 b, 91, 92, 93 u, 101 ur, 102 u, 102 b, 110-111, 116, 121 bl, 123, 130, 134 ul, 134 bl, 135 u, 137, 138, 143, 145, 151, 161, 162 br, 167 ur, 169 u, 200 b, 202 u, 203 br, 205 ur, 210 u, 214 u, 221, 233 b, 262, 263 u, 264, 265 u, 265 b, 266-267 b, 268 b, 278-279 b, 279 u, 284, 285, 288, 292, 294 mu, 294 mb, 294 b, 298 bl; **Durantel/NATURE:** 68 u, 68 b, 96-97, 227; **Durantel-Pasquet:** 23 u, 25 u, 51, 53, 117 b, 148 b, 153; **Fiom/IFREMER (La Rochelle):** 300; **Huin/NATURE:** 247; **Lanceau/NATURE:** 216, 239, 263 b, 296 bl; **G. Lemaître:** 196 b, 199, 207, 212 b, 214 b, 217 b, 223; **Losange:** 5 u, 5 b, 6 u, 6 mu, 6mb, 6 b, 7 ur, 7 m, 10 u, 11, 18 b, 20 u, 21 u, 21 m, 22-23 b, 23 m, 25 m, 37 m, 66 u, 66 br, 67 ul, 67 ur, 67 m, 67 br, 68 ur, 68 m, 69 u, 69 b, 73 r, 74 ul, 75 u, 75 m, 76 l, 87 u, 87 m, 90 u, 98 u, 99 b, 100 b, 100-101 u, 101 bl, 101 br, 107, 112 u, 112 br, 113 u, 117 u, 118, 119 m, 120 m, 120 b, 121 u, 121 br, 134 ur, 134 br, 135 m, 135 br, 155, 167 m, 169 m, 169 b, 196 u, 198 l, 198 r, 200 u, 200 m, 201 u, 201 b, 202 m, 203 u, 203 bl, 204 ul, 204-205 u, 205 m, 206, 212 u, 213 b, 217 u, 254 u, 255 b, 268 u, 272 u, 273 u; **Sauer/NATURE:** 280 u, 297 b.

The numbers refer to the pages and the letters to the location of the illustrations: u = upper ; b = bottom ; m = middle ; l = left; r = right.

THE PRACTICAL GUIDE TO
FISHING